A GUIDE IN THE PREPARATION
OF MANUSCRIPTS; FOR WRITERS, EDITORS,
PROOFREADERS AND PRINTERS

WORDS
INTO
TYPE

NEW REVISED EDITION

BASED ON STUDIES BY MARJORIE E. SKILLIN,
ROBERT M. GAY, AND OTHER AUTHORITIES

APPLETON-CENTURY-CROFTS

Division of Meredith Publishing Company

NEW YORK

PRINTED IN THE UNITED STATES OF AMERICA
R–81130

PREFACE

In the half century just passed the manufacture of printed matter has changed from the simple routine of the old-time printer, who had a few cases of text type and two or three boldface fonts with which to work, to a complex process involving machines and scores of different type faces. A phenomenal growth in volume of printing began when the invention of typesetting machines accelerated the composing of type, at the same time decreasing the cost; and today an amazing number of persons are striving to write for publication, their output ranging from short articles in newspapers or periodicals to reports, essays, short stories, and book-length manuscripts.

In the manufacture of printed matter, certain rules must be followed if the work is to conform to a high standard of good printing. Footnotes, for instance, are to be used for specific purposes and set in a certain fashion. The use of punctuation and the manner of setting punctuation marks are more or less definitely prescribed; italics are for particular purposes, not to be used without reason. These rules of printing were formulated in the decades just preceding the widespread introduction of typesetting machines. Mechanization caused a general speeding up of all printing processes. Unless the author and the editor, who still have to a degree the time and opportunity to work moderately and thoughtfully, prepare their manuscripts to conform with standards of good printing, the sensibilities of trained readers may be offended and their attention to the message of the writer thereby lost.

Not all the rules of the old-time printer are worth retaining, and printing rules, like all others, are subject to change. But, it would be unfortunate indeed if the high standards once attained were lowered. Therefore, it is desirable to modernize and re-illustrate these rules for the guidance of authors and editors in preparing copy and for the convenience of all printing-office workers. For students and professionals this manual is a textbook of printing practice.

M. E. S.
R. M. G.

v

INTRODUCTION

The text has been divided into six Parts and an Appendix, but not to indicate thereby that Part I is solely for writers, Part III for editors, Part V for students, and so on, but to achieve an orderly grouping of content which will make it easy for the searcher to find quickly whatever he is looking for. In Part I are presented instructions about desirable physical form which the typist should observe, an explanation of the term "printing style," details relating to the acceptable forms for headings, quotations, footnotes, bibliographies, and tables, and as much information about illustrations as a writer needs. Following these general instructions for printing are sections describing the special responsibilities of a book writer and a brief summary of the copyright and libel laws. The aim is to show writers how to secure the best possible result without unnecessary expense.

The first time a writer receives proofs from a publisher he may quite naturally be somewhat uncertain about what is expected and required of him and what he is entitled to expect from the publisher and printer. Part II therefore seeks to remove all these uncertainties, instructing him at the same time how to do his work on proofs most efficiently. An incidental purpose of Part II is to present a picture of the work of editors, copyreaders, proofreaders, and copyholders that will reveal to the person unacquainted with these professions how intricate and exacting the work is.

Part III is the most technical part of the book, dealing exclusively with problems of typography and illustration. It has been written expressly for the person beginning a career in an editorial office, the student of editorial practice, and the writer who wishes to inform himself about the problems of the editor of a book.

Rules of present-day usage in all the details of printing style are presented in Part IV, with due recognition of the fact that rules are for guidance, not for slavish following, that they are continually changing, and that no rule can be universally applied to all kinds of printing.

Part V, Part VI, and the Appendix deal with usage, grammatical and verbal, as well as the aspects of grammar and the use of words that seem to be most troublesome to writers and editorial workers. What is given will suffice for those workers who are not concerned with complete discussions of disputed points. Several lists for further reference have been appended.

M. E. S.
R. M. G.

TABLE OF CONTENTS

A Bird's-Eye View of Book

PART I—MANUSCRIPT 1

PART II—TECHNIQUES FOR COPY AND PROOF 61

PART III—TYPOGRAPHY AND ILLUSTRATION 79

PART IV—PRINTING STYLE 180

CONTENTS

PART V—GRAMMAR 353

PART VI—USE OF WORDS 402

APPENDIX 523

INDEX 559

WORDS INTO TYPE

WORDS INTO TYPE

AN AUTHORITATIVE GUIDE FOR WRITERS, EDITORS, PROOFREADERS, AND PRINTERS

PART I—MANUSCRIPT

MAIN DIVISIONS

TECHNICALITIES OF FORM

Certain conventions of form and arrangement have become established by long usage as the clearest and most desirable manner in which to present various details in a manuscript. These standards need not be slavishly followed, but any radical departure from them is usually undesirable. Forms which are so unusual that they attract attention are likely to take the mind of the reader away from the thought of the text and lessen the effect of the author's words. Observance of the practice recommended in the pages following will lead to a satisfactory result with a saving of time and expense.

PHYSICAL FORM

Typewritten manuscript. Regardless of the nature of the matter to be printed, the manuscript copy that is sent to the printer should be in the best possible form. Since no handwriting can be read as rapidly and accurately as typewriting, most publishers refuse to accept handwritten copy. When a manuscript is typed, at least two copies should be made: the original, showing a distinct black impression of every letter, to be sent to the printer, and the duplicate to be retained by the writer. Paper should be uniform in size and of good quality, preferably white or cream colored; thin manifold or onionskin paper should never be used for printer's copy. Using cheap paper or paper wider than standard is being penny wise and pound foolish. Typesetters are usually well-paid skilled workers, and any condition which slows up their production or makes it less accurate costs more in the end than any saving in cost

1

of paper or typing. Paper too wide to go into the copy holder on the type-setting machine and copy that is hard to read because of thin paper or gray impression both affect the typesetter's work undesirably.

Margins. A liberal margin should be left on both sides to provide room for editorial instructions or slight corrections. For paper 8½ inches wide a satisfactory result can be secured by setting the typewriter for a 6-inch line centered on the page; in other words, 72 spaces in elite typing, 60 spaces in pica. The typist should try to have the lines as nearly as possible of the same length, but should not divide words contrary to good printing practice in order to gain this evenness. The instruction sometimes given not to divide words at all is ill-advised; such practice inevitably results in lines varying so much in length that an accurate estimate of the number of words in the manuscript is thereby made doubly hard. It is desirable also to have pages approximately uniform in length.

Spacing. Double spacing should be used for most of the text, including bibliographies and long footnotes. Single spacing may be used for long excerpts that are to be set in a size of type smaller than the rest of the text. (See p. 3.) Short footnotes may be single spaced. They are preferably typed immediately following the line in which reference is made to them, separated from the text by a rule above and below.

The spacing and arrangement recommended in the preceding paragraphs are illustrated in Figure 1.

Although double-spaced typing is usually more easily read and more rapidly set by the typesetter, there are times when single spacing can be used with discretion without forfeiting clearness or legibility. The page shown in Figure 2 would be considered good copy.

If the page shown in Figure 1 were a page of a thesis to be presented in typescript form or were being prepared for photo-offset reproduction,[1] desirable form would differ only slightly. Footnotes would then be typed, always with single spacing, at the foot of the page. More contrast between main text and quotations could be secured, if desired, by indenting the quotations on one or both sides. The page numbers could be typed at the foot. In short, the appearance of a printed page should be approximated more closely than is necessary for printer's copy. (Compare Figure 1 and Figure 3.) The page shown in Figure 2 is good for either printer's copy or photo-offset reproduction of the typescript.

---

[1] Photo-offset reproduction requires printing plates made by photographing the pages to be reproduced. Since the cost of editions of a few hundred copies produced by this method is low compared to having type set, texts intended for subsequent revision are often carefully typed and issued first by this method. The process can reproduce the same size, or enlarge, or reduce. It repeats exactly every detail of the copy.

- 169 -

PROBLEM 2

MAY LEARNING BE CORRECTLY DEFINED IN MORE THAN ONE WAY?

Thorndike defines learning in his earlier writings very simply as "changes produced in the learner." Freeman discusses it as "the modification of inherited responses and the acquisition of new responses." Colvin phrases it "the modification of the reaction of the organism through experience." Charters expresses it as "gaining appreciation and control over the values of life." The central thought in all these is the same as that developed in the opening pages of this unit

Learning as the acquisition of adaptations. A recent discussion by Morrison introduces a view of learning that differs in some points from that so far expressed. He says: 1/

1/ H. C. Morrison, The Practice of Teaching in the Secondary School (University of Chicago Press, 1926), pp. 19 ff.

.   . any actual learning is always expressed as a change in the attitude of the individual, or as the acquisition of a special ability, or as the attainment of some form of skill in manipulating instrumentalities or materials.

He goes on to say, "the new attitude inevitably modifies his whole social behavior." The other items in his definition, abilities and skills, are obviously modes of behavior. He refers 2/ to these learning results (excepting skills) as adapta-

---

2/Ibid., pp. 22 ff.

---

tions, using the term much as biologists use it, to mean an actual change in the organism itself. "The test of a real

FIG. I

Page of a Typewritten Manuscript Prepared for Printer's Copy.

GLOSSARY OF PRINTING TERMS

agate--an old name for a size of type slightly smaller than
five and one-half point, measuring fourteen lines to the
inch; for years the standard for measuring advertisements;
called ruby in England.

backbone, backstrip--the back of a book, connecting the front
and back covers. Type set lengthwise of the backstrip
commonly reads from the top down, but sometimes vice versa.
Also called shelfback and spine.

bearers--strips of metal, type high, placed around pages of
type when they are locked in a form from which electrotype
plates are to be cast. These show as a black border on
foundry proofs and proofs of molder plates.

bleed--illustrations which extend to the edge of the page
when printed are called bleed cuts. Printing is said to
bleed when the margins are overcut in trimming and the
printing mutilated.

break-line--the last line of a paragraph.

cancel--a leaf reprinted in order to correct an error in a
printed book, and inserted by the binder in place of the
incorrect page.

case--(1) a tray in which type is kept; (2) a cloth book cover
before it is placed on the book.

crop--to trim off a portion of foreground, background, or
sides of an illustration to secure desired proportions.

distribute--to return types to their proper location in the
cases after they have been used.

galley--a long and narrow metal pan, about half an inch deep
and open at one end, in which lines of type are placed
when they are first set, whether by hand or by machine.
The first proof of composed type is, hence, a "galley"
proof.

headband--a reinforcing band used at the head and tail of a
book in binding.

justify--to make a line of composed type equal in length to
all accompanying lines by inserting spaces between words;
to make different sizes of type used in one line all of
the same depth by inserting leads or spaces above or below the smaller types.

Fig. 2

Page of a Typewritten Manuscript Showing Acceptable Use of Double and
Single Spacing.

PROBLEM 2

MAY LEARNING BE CORRECTLY DEFINED IN MORE THAN ONE WAY?

Thorndike defines learning in his earlier writings very
simply as "changes produced in the learner." Freeman discusses it as "the modification of inherited responses and the
acquisition of new responses." Colvin phrases it, "the modification of the reaction of the organism through experience."
Charters expresses it as "gaining appreciation and control over
the values of life." The central thought in all these is the
same as that developed in the opening pages of this unit.

Learning as the acquisition of adaptations. A recent discussion by Morrison introduces a view of learning that differs
in some points from that so far expressed. He says: 1/

> . . . any actual learning is always expressed as a
> change in the attitude of the individual, or as the
> acquisition of a special ability, or as the attain-
> ment of some form of skill in manipulating instru-
> mentalities or materials.

He goes on to say, "the new attitude inevitably modifies
his whole social behavior." The other items in his definition,
abilities and skills, are obviously modes of behavior. He refers 2/ to these learning results (excepting skills) as adaptations, using the term much as biologists use it, to mean an

---

1/ H. C. Morrison, The Practice of Teaching in the Secondary
School (University of Chicago Press, 1926), pp. 19 ff.
2/ Ibid., pp. 22 ff.

-169-

Fig. 3

Page of a Typewritten Manuscript Prepared Especially for Photo-offset
Reproduction, but also Suitable for Printer's Copy, etc.

Reprint copy. Clippings from printed matter—called reprint copy by the printer—should be pasted on sheets of paper the size of the rest of the copy. If any part of the manuscript is in the form of leaves printed on both sides, the best plan is to use two copies of such matter and paste each page on a sheet of the copy paper. If the leaves are large, it may be equally satisfactory merely to cross out alternate pages of each leaf, so that combining the two leaves provides copy that is on only one side of each leaf. Sometimes, however, only one copy of printed matter is available. Then a satisfactory method is to paste each leaf to a sheet of paper along the left margin, with the instruction "over" at the bottom of each upward page. This extra work in preparation of copy is hardly necessary, however, if practically all of the manuscript is printed copy on leaves of a uniform size.

Numbering. Manuscript should be numbered consecutively throughout the text in the upper right-hand corner of pages. If additions are made later, after page 5, for instance, the new matter can be numbered 5a, 5b, and a note made on the bottom of page 5 that pages 5a, 5b, follow. If pages 5 and 6 are taken out after the manuscript has been numbered, the fourth page should be marked 4-6.

Additions. Nothing should ever be typed or written on the reverse of a page of copy, and insertions should never be written or typed on narrow strips and attached to the edge of the copy. These slips, called flyers or riders, are likely to be torn off and lost. The only safe and satisfactory way to make insertions is to type or paste them on a full-size sheet of paper, mark them "Insert A," etc., and indicate clearly the place of insertion. These pages should be numbered and inserted in the manuscript after, not preceding, the page on which they are to be inserted, in the manner noted in the paragraph above on Numbering.

Illustrations. See pages 36-38.

Shipping. Pages of manuscript should be separate—not fastened together in any way. They should be sent to the publisher flat—not rolled. They may be sent by express, insured; and all of the text should be sent at one time, together with the title page, the table of contents, and other preliminary pages, and all end matter except the index.

PRINTING STYLE

When publishers and printers speak of style, they mean printing style and have reference to the spelling of words, punctuation, capitalization, the use of abbreviations and italics, the expression of numbers, and the many details of typographical form and practice noted in the following pages. Printed matter should conform to recognized standards, because inconsistencies annoy the reader or arouse the suspicion that an author inaccurate in details may be inaccurate also in his thought.

Spelling. An author should make his spelling consistent with itself, at least. It is desirable to make it conform to some one dictionary—Century, Webster, Oxford, or some other. Publishers like to have the privilege of following their house style. Magazines, and technical publications issued periodically, usually have an office ruling about the dictionary spellings to be followed, and writers for such periodicals should conform to these rulings. For example, the writer on chemical subjects might well acquaint himself with the reports and rulings on nomenclature of the American Chemical Society. The author or the typist should verify the spelling of technical and unfamiliar words, especially proper names.

Punctuation. A writer should give careful regard to punctuation, for the clearness and force of his writing may be spoiled by misuse of punctuation or a failure to observe established conventions. Even if punctuation is used sparingly, good usage cannot be disregarded without inviting criticism. Rules for the use of punctuation marks are given on pages 242–297.

Capitalization. Having adopted one accepted rule, a writer should follow it throughout. When he uses capitals for emphasis or other special purposes, he should be strictly consistent in their use. A free use of capitals may give dignity to some kinds of printing, but an indiscriminate use of them without logical purpose is a serious defect. See the rules for capitalization on pages 215–242.

Abbreviations. Abbreviations should not be used with the expectation that the printer will spell them out. Whenever a form of abbreviation has been established by usage or authority, this form should be used in preference to any other. Each branch of writing has its list of commonly used abbreviations, and sometimes the same letters may stand for different words, according to the text. Therefore, if an abbreviation is circled in copy, thus indicating that it is to be spelled out, the word it stands for should be clearly indicated if there is any possibility of error. Rules and lists of abbreviations are given on pages 182–198.

HEADINGS

Uses. There are informational headings, headings used for mechanical purposes, and topical headings. Headings in newspapers are informational, designed to enable the hurried reader to grasp the gist of a news report by reading the heading and subheadings. The reporter sometimes composes these headings subject to the critical review of the desk man; sometimes the desk man supplies the headings.

Newspapers and magazines often insert headings in long articles more or less arbitrarily merely to break up the articles into sections for the sake of appearance. Such headings are not part of the writer's manuscript as submitted to the magazine or newspaper but are inserted by the editor or copyreader.

Topical headings are of quite different character and mark definite and well-thought-out divisions of the subject under consideration. They are the concern and the responsibility of the writer himself. If his work is intended for study or reference, a writer should give careful attention to this detail of form, for a logical and well-planned use of headings enhances the usefulness of any writing intended to instruct.

Construction. Topical headings should indicate concisely the subject discussed in the text that follows. They are usually nouns or phrases built about nouns:

Early Marriages   The Use of Fireplaces among
Freight Trains on Mules   the Indians

Phrases like *Description of, Discussion of,* and *Statement of* are superfluous.

Subheadings. Subheadings and sub-subheadings may be used, differentiated by different sizes or kinds of type. If further subordination is necessary it should ordinarily be represented by side headings, or by successive indentions in the form of an outline, using figures and italic letters, with either periods or parentheses but not both together. (See p. 114 for the correct form when more than two such subdivisions are needed.) Indication of the type in which headings are to be set is the responsibility of the copyreader; but the author should see that his copy shows clearly the comparative value of each heading. Three typescript forms are suggested in Figure 4. The third style, with all lines flush on the left, is most economical of the typist's time and could be edited as easily as the others.

Side headings. For adequate rhetorical form each side heading should contain a noun; and the words immediately following should preferably not be a mere repetition of the heading. Appearance, appropriateness, usefulness, and expense are considerations entering into the choice of form for side headings. Sometimes the decision as to style is made by the author, sometimes by the editor or the printer. In any case the manuscript should be typed in a consistent manner. The style of capitalization should be made clear: whether all important words are to be capitalized or only the first word and proper nouns. Side headings like the one used at the beginning of this paragraph are also called run-in headings. See Figure 5.

A side heading which precedes an indented paragraph is sometimes called

Chapter **V**

I S A I A H

JUDAH DURING THE EIGHTH CENTURY B.C.

The Political Situation. The political, social, moral,
and religious conditions in Judah during the activity of
Isaiah and his younger contemporary Micah were essentially

Chapter **V**

ISAIAH

JUDAH DURING THE EIGHTH CENTURY B.C.

The Political Situation. The political, social, moral,
and religious conditions in Judah during the activity of
Isaiah and his younger contemporary Micah were essentially

Chapter **V**

I S A I A H

JUDAH DURING THE EIGHTH CENTURY B.C.

The Political Situation. The political, social, moral,
and religious conditions in Judah during the activity of
Isaiah and his younger contemporary Micah were essentially

FIG. 4

Three Typewritten Forms Differentiating Weights of Headings.

a shoulder heading. This style of heading is indicated by the typescript form shown in Figure 6.

Development and Nutrition.--Ignoring the native differences in nervous systems through the influence of heredity,
the efficiency of the nervous system is largely dependent . . .
    Undeveloped Cells.--Professor Donaldson tells us on
this point that: . . .

_____

    Side headings. For adequate rhetorical form each side
heading should contain a noun; and the words immediately
following should preferably not be a repetition of the
heading. Appearance, appropriateness, usefulness, and
expense . . .

Fig. 5

Typewritten Forms for Run-in Side Headings.

Cut-in side headings are set in type smaller than the text and inserted by hand in a space left for them when the text type is set. They are in general **Cut-in side headings** falling into disuse because they necessitate so much extra work compared with the setting of ordinary side headings. In contrast to the two forms of paragraph heading shown in Figure 5 and Figure 6, in which there are no limitations on length, cut-in side headings must be short to look well, and the style is therefore limited in adaptability.

Section 170. Mention of Beneficial Rights under Covenants
        and Restrictions.
The benefit of any covenants running with the land conveyed will pass to the grantee, though not mentioned or referred to in the deed, but if a covenant does not run with . . .

Fig. 6

Typewritten Copy for a Shoulder Heading.

Marginal
notes

Very effective in some texts is a "running gloss," words or phrases placed in the margin, sometimes only at the beginning of a paragraph, but often opposite the line of text to which the word or phrase applies. Frequently such notes form an outline of the subject matter without in any way interrupting the flow of the text. The printer calls them marginal notes. Like cut-in headings they must be concise. They too are expensive by comparison with simple side headings.

OUTLINES

Topic outline

    A topic outline consists of headings which indicate the important ideas in a composition, and their relation to each other. . . .

Sentence outline

    A sentence outline is expressed in complete sentences punctuated as in ordinary discourse. . . .

Indention

    Indent and number all headings properly. . . .

Parallel form

    Express in parallel form all ideas that are parallel in thought.

FIG. 7

A Form of Typewritten Copy Easily Edited as a Simple Side Heading, a Shoulder Heading, a Cut-in Heading, or a Marginal Note.

The typescript form in Figure 7 could be edited easily as a simple side heading, a shoulder heading, a cut-in side heading, or a marginal note.

For notes on the typography of the foregoing, see pages 113–118.

EXCERPTS

When a writer quotes directly from the writing of another, he should indicate clearly what is quoted.

Excerpts denoted by quotation marks. The most common method of denoting excerpts is by enclosing them in quotation marks. For example:

> A recent discussion by Morrison introduces a view of learning that differs in some points from that so far expressed. He says: ". . . any actual learning is always expressed as a change in the attitude of the individual, or as the acquisition of a special ability, or as the attainment of some form of skill in manipulating instrumentalities or materials." He goes on to say . . .

A prose excerpt of more than one paragraph should have opening quotation marks before each paragraph and closing quotation marks at the end of the last paragraph. An excerpt of two or more stanzas of poetry should have opening quotation marks before each stanza and closing quotation marks at the end of the last stanza. If the excerpt is a letter, quotation marks may be placed before the first line and after the last; or opening quotation marks may be used before each line of the heading and salutation, before each paragraph of the letter, before the complimentary close and all following lines, with closing quotation marks at the end. (See also pp. 157, 158.)

Quotation marks within the excerpt should be changed—double marks to single marks—to conform to the rule that a quotation within a quotation should be enclosed in single quotation marks. (See p. 285.)

Reduced type. Instead of using quotation marks to indicate excerpts, the publisher and printer often use a smaller size of type for excerpts than for the rest of the text. Letters, poetry, extracts from plays, and the like are usually so set and are said to be reduced. The printer's term for such reduced quotations is "extracts." The appearance of brief quotations in reduced type is unpleasing; the method is therefore inappropriate for prose quotations less than five lines in length. Shorter ones may be reduced, however, if they occur close to longer extracts. Extracts may be further distinguished by indenting them slightly from the left margin, or from both margins. In the manuscript, typing with single spacing indicates that the excerpt is to be reduced. (See Figure 1.)

Since reducing the type indicates that the matter is a quotation, it is unnecessary to use quotation marks to enclose the entire quotation. Therefore quotation marks within the excerpt should remain as in the original.

Points of ellipsis. Three points, properly called points of ellipsis, are used to indicate an omission. They are, therefore, often used in excerpts. Their use within an excerpt is clear, but there is some confusion about whether to use them at the beginning of an excerpt.

If a prose quotation begins in the middle of a sentence, the fact is sufficiently indicated by writing the first word with a small, or lower-case, letter.

It contains a provision that "no bill shall become a law without the concurrence of a majority of the members elected to each house."

If the last portion of an excerpt is further reduced it should start with a small letter and be flush with the following lines of the excerpt.

> Mary began to think of all the other guests at the party who
>
> had taken advantage of the Queen's absence, and were resting in the shade; however, the moment they saw her, they hurried back to the game. . . .

Points of ellipsis at the beginning of an excerpt starting in mid-sentence merely emphasize a fact already marked by the small letter for the first word, but this emphasis is often desirable. If an excerpt is formally introduced, as in the example on page 3, the ellipsis points should be used to avoid the appearance of violating the rule that a quotation so introduced should begin with a capital.

Using points of ellipsis before an excerpt beginning with a complete sentence in the original, or at the end of an excerpt when the last sentence is complete, is equivalent to saying, "This is not all the writer of these words had to say on the subject." That fact would in most cases be understood by the reader without the ellipsis, but if it should be emphasized, the phrase "in part" in the sentence introducing the excerpt is often preferable to using the ellipsis points.

If an extract of poetry begins in the middle of a metrical line, which may or may not be the beginning of a sentence, the better practice is to use points of ellipsis at the beginning, even though deep indention and a small letter would make it clear that words at the beginning of the line have been omitted.

> It might have been the original of Poe's
>
> > . . . dank tarn of Auber
> > In the ghoul-haunted woodland of Weir.

Style within excerpts. In quotations from the Bible, records, manuscripts, archaic work, and standard editions of classics of all kinds, the original should be followed exactly. Editor and printer would not venture to depart from copy in such quotations, and the author may depend upon his copy being followed. Since responsibility for accuracy in copying is entirely his, the author should compare his copy of such excerpts with the original to catch any errors in typing.

However, it is often necessary to modernize archaic spelling and punctuation. Even modern British spellings like *honour, connexion, waggon, kerb,* should be Americanized sometimes, as, for instance, in a school text for elementary grades. The author should use judgment and discretion in these details. The proofreader should never presume to make any change.

If a quotation from less particular sources contains spelling or punctuation that is so contrary to ordinary usage that it might be thought a typist's error made in copying, the author would do well to indicate that the copy is correct by marking it *stet* or *sic* or *O.K.* in the margin. Otherwise the editor may be tempted to make a change in order to prevent a reflection upon the author's scholarship or accuracy.

Most printers instruct their typesetters and proofreaders to follow copy exactly in *all* excerpts. Therefore if the author wishes the style of excerpts to be consistent with that of his own text, he should check his manuscript carefully for details of style.

If the author italicizes for the sake of emphasis any words not so presented in the original, he should indicate the fact in a footnote or in brackets immediately following the italicized words. Any insertions of his own within the quoted matter should be enclosed in brackets; parentheses are not sufficient for this purpose.

> "It may be fairly said that this necessary act *fixed the future frame and form of their government* [Webster's italics]. The character of their political institutions was *determined* [our italics] by the fundamental laws respecting property."

Acknowledgments.[1] Whenever a writer uses excerpts from the work of another, he should acknowledge his indebtedness either by a footnote or by a "credit" line. The excerpt used to supplement the writer's own composition, like that shown in Figure 1, should be accompanied by a bibliographical footnote, explicitly noting the source. The content and arrangement of such footnotes are noted in detail in the sections immediately following. A short excerpt such as an epigraphical quotation at the head of a chapter or article should be followed by a credit line, which may be only the author's name, or include also the title of the work. (See also pp. 137, 138.)

—SIDNEY LANIER
—SIDNEY LANIER, "The Crystal"

The quotation of a poem, story, article, or the like complete or essentially so requires a footnote stating that the original publisher or copyright owner has permitted use of the quotation (see p. 17). The name of the author may be given under the heading or in a credit line at the end. The word *Adapted* should appear in the credit whenever the extract is simplified or condensed

---

[1] See also "Legal Responsibilities of the Author," especially the paragraphs on infringement of copyright, page 56.

in any way. Such might be the case of a French story reproduced in English in a form more suited for comprehension by young readers than a literal translation would be.

—Alphonse Daudet (*Adapted*)

FOOTNOTES

Uses. Footnotes are used (1) for the acknowledgment of borrowed material, (2) for notifying the reader of the source of statements or quotations, (3) for the presentation of explanatory material not appropriate to the text, and (4) for cross references to other parts of the work.

References to footnotes. Superior figures—small figures set above the line—are generally used as references to footnotes. Unless footnotes are few and do not occur close together, it is best to number them consecutively throughout a chapter or article. If notes are numerous and are numbered by pages of manuscript, with the intention that when the type is made up into pages the first note on each page will begin a new series of numbers, a great deal of expensive correcting will be required; for the first note on a manuscript page is seldom the first note on a page of type. Sometimes every line in which a superior figure is changed will have to be reset. For these reasons the modern system of numbering footnotes by articles or chapters is much to be preferred.

Reference marks may be used instead of superior figures. If several marks are used on a page the proper sequence is:

* asterisk or star
† dagger
‡ double dagger
§ section mark
‖ parallels
¶ paragraph mark

If more are needed, the same marks are used double: **, ††, etc.

Because their number is so limited, reference marks are unsatisfactory when notes are numerous. A new series of marks should begin on each new page; therefore all references have to be verified when the type is made up in pages. These marks are used, however, in any case where superior figures might be confusing, as in algebraic matter: $A = b^2 + c^2$.† They should be used for footnotes within quoted matter to avoid confusion with the author's numbered footnotes. Notes to tables may be referred to by the star and dagger, etc., or by superior letters. The notes are then properly placed directly under the table. (See also p. 155.)

Both superior figures and reference marks may be used in an article or book—superior figures referring to citations, which are all given in a group at the end of the article or chapter of a book; reference marks for explanatory footnotes placed at the bottom of each page.

Position of references.   Reference figures or marks should be set after any mark of punctuation except the dash or a closing parenthesis if reference relates to matter within the parentheses.[1] They should be placed *after,* not before, a word or paragraph which is explained or amplified.

Each formed a single type, or rather *logotype.** The symbols . . .

> * It must be recalled here that the Chinese language is not an alphabetic but an ideographic language.

Practice varies in the placing of references to footnotes citing the source of excerpts.   The United States Geological Survey [2] instructs its writers to place the reference after the name of the author if the wording of the text makes this possible.

The following extracts from an article written by a former Director of the Survey [1] are suggestive and highly significant:

> [1] G. O. Smith, "Plain Writing," *Science,* new ser., Vol. 42 (Nov. 5, 1915), pp. 630–632.

A reference should not be placed after a name in the possessive form.

In his analysis Dr. Mann[2] wrote:
In Dr. Mann's analysis[3] the following statement is made:

The *Handbook of Style for Yale University Press* states that the reference should stand at the end of the excerpt, not in the text which precedes the excerpt.[3]   Thus placed, the reference does not distract the attention of the reader as it would elsewhere.   A possible result of this placement of reference is, however, that a note may not be on the same page as the beginning of the extract, a separation considered undesirable by some editors.

> A scholarly critic writes:
>
> I do not say that "etc." is not to be used, but its use should be rare, and chiefly for the omission of parts of quotations and the like.   When used by the author to eke out his own matter or to save himself trouble the reader is disposed to exclaim, "If you have anything more to say pray say it; if not, finish your sentence properly; 'etc.' conveys no meaning at all." [1]
>
> [1] Clifford Allbutt, *Notes on the Composition of Scientific Papers,* 2d ed., pp. 158–159.

The author should select the style which seems to him the most appropriate for his particular work, and follow the chosen practice consistently.

[1] In German, punctuation follows references.

[2] *Suggestions to Authors of Papers Submitted for Publication by the United States Geological Survey,* 4th ed. (Washington, U. S. Government Printing Office, 1935), p. 16.

[3] *A Handbook of Style for Yale University Press,* Laura H. Moseley, compiler, Preliminary Edition (New Haven, 1934), p. 109.

When a selection—poetry or prose or a table—is given with its title, the reference to the note giving the source or noting the copyright owner's permission to use is placed after the caption.

REMEMBERED ODORS [1]
By Thomas Wolfe
[Selection follows]

[1] *Look Homeward, Angel*, Charles Scribner's Sons. By permission of the publishers.

CHILDHOOD MEMORIES [2]
[Selection follows]

[2] From Mark Twain's *Autobiography*, Harper and Brothers, 1924. By permission of the publishers.

Content and order. When a copyright owner gives permission to quote from his publication he may specify the form in which he desires the acknowledgment of indebtedness. Such specifications should of course be scrupulously followed. They always include the title of the book, the name of the author, and the name of the copyright owner. The phrase "by permission" is often used, and bibliographic data may also be required.

Footnotes notifying the reader of the source of statements or quotations that he might wish to look up should be in a form sufficiently detailed to enable the reader to find the reference as easily as possible. Such references to books that have been printed in innumerable editions, like the Bible, Shakespeare, Milton, or Blackstone, should specify the book, chapter, and verse; the act, scene, and, if possible, the line; the canto, stanza, and line; or the section and paragraph.

I Cor. 13:4–7.
1 Henry VI, iii. 2. 14.
The Lady of the Lake, canto V, stanza xxi.
Summa Theologica, II, ii, q. 9, a. 2, ad. 1, English translation (London, 1917), pp. 114–115.

References to manuscripts should give the location, title, and number.

When authorities are cited in books of law, the reference is made as definite and concise as possible. (See also p. 164.)

[1] See M. E. Cohen, *Censorship of Radical Materials by the Post Office*, 17 St. Louis Law Review 95 (1932).

[2] Public Acts 1895, Chap. 205, Sec. 2; Purdon's Digest, 13th ed., p. 989, Sec. 370.

[3] Burleson v. United States *ex rel.* Workingmen's Cooperative Publishing Association, 274 Fed. 749, 260 U. S. 757 (1921).

[4] 62d Cong., 8th sess., H. Doc. 341.

References to patents should give the patentee, country, number, and date.

[1] C. E. Maynard, U. S. Patent 1,795,875 filed March 10, 1931.
[2] R. W. Byerly, U. S. Patent 2,309,930 issued Feb. 2, 1943.

The first citation of a work not in the categories noted, especially if it has been published recently or is of limited circulation, should, if possible, contain the following information, given in the order here noted. A simple, clear style of punctuation is to separate the items by commas and enclose the publication data (4, 5, and 6 of the outline below) in parentheses.

(1) The author's name, not inverted
> (Give the full name if it is known, in preference to initials. A single initial is particularly undesirable.)

(2) The title of the book, including the subtitle if there is one
> (Underscore this in the manuscript. Titles of books and serial publications are more often in italics than in any other form. If the writing is being done for a publication known to follow a different practice, write the manuscript to accord with its style.)

(3) The edition, if other than the first
> (The title page or the copyright page shows the number of editions.)

(4) The place of publication
> (Give the home office when several place names appear on the title page. A list of home offices is shown on pages 548–552.)

(5) The publisher
> (If the name is shortened, use the form adopted by the American Library Association. See the list on pages 548–552.)

(6) The date of publication
> (Use the date given on the copyright page. The date on the title page is changed with every printing, or impression.)

(7) Volume and page numbers

When articles in periodicals are cited, the following should be given:
(1) The name of the author
(2) The title of the article (enclosed in quotation marks)
(3) The name of the periodical (underscored in manuscript)
(4) The volume or number
(5) The month and year of publication
(6) The page numbers

Note. Inversion of names is unnecessary. This device is used in alphabetized bibliographies for the convenience of users of the list, but it would serve no purpose in footnotes.

Poor form:
¹ Cook, D. E., and Rahbeck-Smith, E., compilers, *Educational Film Catalog* (New York, The H. W. Wilson Company).
Better:
¹ D. E. Cook and E. Rahbeck-Smith, compilers, *Educational Film Catalog* (New York, The H. W. Wilson Company).

Models for Bibliographical Footnotes

Note. These models follow the style just outlined. It should be understood that variant forms of punctuation, capitalization, and abbreviation may be preferred by some reputable publishers as a matter of house style.

Book—one author:
¹ F. L. Whitney, *Methods in Educational Research* (New York, D. Appleton and Company, 1932), p. 182.
² Mason Long, *The New College Grammar* (New York, The Ronald Press Company, 1935), pp. 389–405.

Book—two authors:
¹ R. W. and A. J. Carlyle, *History of Mediaeval Political Theory in the West* (Edinburgh and London, Blackwood, 1936), Vol. VI, Pt. III, Chap. 3.

Book—three authors:
¹ D. C. Kimber, C. E. Gray, and C. E. Stackpole, *Textbook of Anatomy and Physiology*, 9th ed. (New York, The Macmillan Company, 1934), Chaps. 17 and 21.

Book—more than three authors:
¹ John S. Allen and others, *Atoms, Rocks, and Galaxies; a Survey in Physical Science* (New York, Harper & Bros., 1938), p. 46.

Book—association the author:
¹ American Medical Association, Council on Pharmacy and Chemistry, *Useful Drugs,* 11th ed.
² League of Nations, Economic Intelligence Service, *Money and Banking, 1936–37* (New York, Columbia University Press, 1937), p. 88.

Book—no author named:
¹ *A Manual of Style,* 10th ed. (Chicago, The University of Chicago Press, 1937), p. 131.
² *Chemical Formulary,* Harry Bennett, ed. (New York, The Chemical Formulary Co., 1933).

Book—author and editor:
¹ Francis Thompson, *Selected Poems,* Paul Beard, ed. (Nelson Classics; New York, Thomas Nelson & Sons, 1938).

Book—translator:
¹ Thomas Mann, *The Coming Victory of Democracy,* trans. by Agnes E. Meyer (New York, Alfred A. Knopf, 1938), p. 00.

Book—one volume of a work of several volumes:

[1] Clement Wood, *History of the World,* Vol. I, *The United States,* rev. ed. (New York, World Syndicate Publishing Co., 1937), Chap. 11.

[2] Charles W. Eliot, ed., *The Harvard Classics,* Vol. II, *The Meditations of Marcus Aurelius,* trans. by G. Long (New York, P. F. Collier & Son, 1909-10).

Book—one of a series:

[1] Richard R. B. Powell, ed., *Cases on Future Interests,* 2d ed. (American Casebook Series; New York, West Publishing Company, 1937), p. 00.

Technical bulletin, government report, or similar publication:

[1] Waldemar Lundgren, *The Tertiary Gravels of the Sierra Nevada of California,* U. S. Geol. Survey, Prof. Paper 73, 1911, p. 44.

[2] Ward H. Sachs, *Effect of Cultivation on Moisture and Nitrate of Field Soils,* Ark. Agr. Exp. Sta. Bull. 205, 1926.

[3] Martha Thorne Wheeler, *Indexing—Principles, Rules and Examples,* 3d ed. rev. New York State Library, Library School Bulletin 50 (Albany, The University of the State of New York, 1923), p. 00.

[4] *Sources for Reproductions of Works of Art,* Bulletin of the American Library Association, Vol. 30, No. 4 (April, 1936), p. 289.

[5] Norman H. Baynes, *The Political Ideas of St. Augustine's De Civitate Dei.* Historical Association Pamphlet, No. 104 (London, 1936).

[6] R. H. Moore, *Cell Specialization in the Epidermis of Maize.* Unpublished M.S. thesis, University of Oklahoma, 1929.

Part of a book:

[1] A. J. Carlyle, "St. Augustine and the City of God," in F. J. C. Hearnshaw, ed., *The Social and Political Ideas of Some Great Mediaeval Thinkers* (London and New York, 1923), Chap. 2.

Part of a yearbook:

[1] Ernest Horn, "The 3009 Commonest Words Used in Adult Writing," Fourth Yearbook, Department of Superintendence (National Education Association, 1926), pp. 145-172.

Part of a report:

[1] B. R. Buckingham, "New Data on the Typography of Textbooks," *The Textbook in American Education,* Thirteenth Yearbook of the National Society for the Study of Education, Part II (Bloomington, Illinois, Public School Publishing Company, 1931).

Article in a periodical:

[1] E. J. Crane, "The Standardization of Chemical Nomenclature," *Journal of Chemical Education,* Vol. 8 (July, 1931), pp. 1338-40.

or

[1] E. J. Crane, "The Standardization of Chemical Nomenclature," *Journal of Chemical Education,* 8:1338-40 (July, 1931).

[2] B. H. Lane, "A Uniform Scheme for Citations," *Science,* new ser., Vol. 75 (April 10), pp. 390-392.

8 "Accuracy," *Journal of Educational Research,* VIII (June, 1923), 63–67.

4 "Living Costs Have Declined in Two Years," *San Francisco Chronicle,* Section J, Vol. CXXXIII, No. 127 (November 19, 1928), p. 18.

Shortened forms. A reference that has been given once in full may be given later in the same chapter in a shortened form. If the author's name is in the text, it is not necessary in the footnote:

1 *The Century Collegiate Handbook,* p. 186.

The authors' names may be shortened:

2 Greever and Jones, *The Century Collegiate Handbook,* pp. 186–190.

A long title may be shortened after it has been given once in full within the chapter:

3 Greever and Jones, *Collegiate Handbook.*

Repeated references to the same book—unless more than one book by the same author is being used—may be shortened to the author's surname and the page reference.

4 Neal, p. 60.

If the author and the book are well known, the possessive may be used:

5 Darwin's *Origin of Species.*   6 Adam Smith's *Wealth of Nations.*

Abbreviations. Abbreviations may be used freely in footnotes. *Volume, Part, Book, Chapter, Section, page, line,* and other words used like them are regularly abbreviated. (See the list on p. 193.) Besides these, used in locating the reference, the titles of books and periodicals may be abbreviated. Classical references listed once in complete bibliographical form may subsequently be shortened as much as they can be and still be understandable. (The proofreader may not understand them but he can see that the forms used are consistent.)

7 Jornandes, de Reb. Get. c. 30, p. 654 (p. 87, ed. Lugd. B. 1597).

Abbreviated forms of titles of periodicals are commonly used when citations of them are numerous and the abbreviations are unquestionably intelligible to the reader; as *J. A. M. A.* for *Journal of the American Medical Association; Pol. Sci. Rev.* for *Political Science Review; Acad. Sci.* for *Académie des Sciences, Belles-lettres et Arts.* Well-known works or publications may even be referred to by symbols, provided their meaning is explained somewhere in the publication. For instance: *HDB,* for *Hastings' Dictionary of the Bible;*

NED for *New English Dictionary; PMLA* for *Publications of the Modern Language Association.*

Uniformity in abbreviating is imperative, and writers should follow approved forms. Since there are alternative forms of many words, the technical worker in a particular field would naturally obtain an authoritative list of the publications in that field. For instance:

For medicine: *Alphabetical List of Abbreviations of Titles of Medical Periodicals Employed in the Index-Catalogue of the Library of the Surgeon General's Office, United States Army* (Washington, U. S. Government Printing Office, 1916).

For law: *Corpus Juris Secundum*—1 C. J. S. Table of Abbreviations, viii–xviii. (See also the list of general abbreviations used—1 C. J. S., p. 276, notes 3–18.)

For chemistry: *List of Periodicals* published by *Chemical Abstracts.*

For science: *Science Abstracts,* Index to Vol. XL, 1937.

Use of "op. cit.," "ibid.," etc. Much unnecessary repetition in footnotes can be avoided by using *op. cit., loc. cit., ibid.,* and *idem.* The first two—*op. cit.,* for *opere citato,* "in the work cited," and *loc. cit.,* for *loco citato,* "in the place cited"—may be used only when accompanied by an author's name, which may be either in the text with the reference mark after it or at the beginning of the footnote. When a book or a magazine article is cited, the full title should be given the first time it is referred to, and sometimes, for the convenience of readers, the first time it is referred to in each chapter. In later references *op. cit.* or *loc. cit.,* with or without a page reference, may replace the title.

First reference:

[1] Garland Greever and Easley S. Jones, *The Century Handbook of Writing,* 4th ed. (New York, D. Appleton-Century Company, 1942), pp. 148–159.

Later reference:

[2] Greever and Jones, *op. cit.,* pp. 151–158.

First reference:

[1] H. V. Kaltenborn, "Wanted: Economic Peace," *The Commentator,* Vol. 3, No. 4 (May, 1938), pp. 70–74.

Later reference:

[2] Kaltenborn, *loc. cit.*

Or, if reference is more specific:

[3] Kaltenborn, *loc. cit.,* p. 74.

Or, if Kaltenborn appears in the text preceding the reference index:

    [4] *Loc. cit.*

Note that *op. cit.* cannot be used if more than one book by the same author has been cited.

The abbreviation *ibid.*, for *ibidem*, "in the same place," may be used when reference is made to the same work referred to in the preceding footnote on the same or the opposite page. (Some editors modify the rule to the extent of using *ibid.* referring to the preceding note in the chapter.)

First reference:

    [1] Kenneth E. Olson, *Typography and Mechanics of the Newspaper* (New York, D. Appleton and Company, 1930), pp. 119–162.

Any later reference:

    [2] Olson, *op. cit.*, p. 4.

Immediately following either of the above:

    [3] *Ibid.*, p. 119.

Identical with the preceding note:

    [4] *Ibid.*

Ibid. is understood to replace all words that are identical in consecutive notes. For instance:

    [1] *British Documents,* Vol. IV, No. 257, p. 279.
    [2] *Ibid.*, No. 261, p. 283.
    [3] *Ibid.*, p. 287.

In the second note *Ibid.* stands for "British Documents, Vol. IV." In the third note *Ibid.* stands for "British Documents, Vol. IV, No. 261."

The Latin word *idem* is occasionally used in footnotes to refer to the same person or reference as the preceding one. It is, however, disappearing in printed texts, perhaps because its use is not a matter of common agreement.

Capitalization. Footnotes ordinarily begin with a capital, but occasionally, in a book in which capitals are used sparingly, footnotes may begin with a small, or "lower case," letter.

    [1] p. 63.   [2] *id est.*

The nature of the notes may make lower case more logical and appropriate, as in the following from *Nineteenth Century Spanish Plays:*

    [1] *por la posta,* "in all haste."
    [2] *ab intestato,* "intestate," "without having made a will."

The library style of capitalizing in book titles only the first word and proper nouns is not often used in footnotes, although it has been adopted by some technical journals.

¹ A. S. Hill, *The principles of rhetoric*, pp. 18–22, 1895.

In German titles all nouns should be capitalized. Latin and French titles may or may not follow English practice (see p. 340 and pp. 314–317; therefore a style must be chosen and followed consistently throughout a work.

The abbreviations for *page* (p.) and *line* (l.) are never capitalized, except at the beginning of a note (but see the first sentence in this section). Other abbreviations of parts of a book, like *Vol., Chap.* or *Ch.,* and *Sec.,* are more often capitalized than lower case, though both forms are common. The form of the roman numerals used after these abbreviations usually varies accordingly: Vol. X, Chap. V, *or* vol. x, chap. v., etc.

Page references. As a rule, numerals referring to front-matter pages should be in lower-case roman type, the rest arabic. Numbers in page references are sometimes elided: 189–90, 170–2 or 170–72. If elisions are used at all, they should be used consistently and throughout.

TABLES
(See also pages 120–132.)

The author should assume full responsibility for the construction of tables that form a part of his manuscript. The following paragraphs point out principles which he should keep in mind. The typographical details for which the publisher or printer will be responsible are presented in a later section.

Purpose. Tables are used to make it easier for the reader to grasp the significance of a mass of numerical facts or other data that lend themselves to tabulation. Items that can be held in the mind only with difficulty when they are contained in a series of statements can be comprehended and easily compared if they are presented in tabular form.

Credit. If the table is not original, due credit should be given. The source may be noted under the caption or in a footnote.

Construction. Short tables are clearer and more forceful than long ones. A large, unwieldy table, therefore, should be broken up into separate smaller tables if the data will allow. All data should be arranged compactly so as to occupy a minimum of space and at the same time be clear. Numbers in a column are more easily compared than numbers in a line. If possible, items that are to be compared should be in the same column and in descending or ascending order of their rank. Only as many significant digits should be used as the precision of the data justifies.

In a column of numbers all denoting even dollars, decimal point and ciphers to the right of the decimal point should be omitted.

Poor:	*Better:* [1]
Less than $1,000.00	Less than $1,000
$1,000.00 to $1,999.00	$1,000 to $1,999
$2,000.00 to $2,999.00	$2,000 to $2,999

A table in which every number ends in three ciphers can be made more compact and easy to grasp by omitting the three ciphers and noting the omission in the caption.

OPERATION OF MUNICIPAL WATER PLANTS
(ooo omitted)

WHEAT—RECEIPTS AT PRIMARY MARKETS
(All figures in thousands of bushels)

The note may be placed in the column headings instead of in the caption.

Product	Quantity (thousands of unit specified)	Value (thousands of dollars) [2]

Column headings. Classifications of the data presented are placed at the top and left of the data. Column headings indicate the classification of the figures or facts beneath; they should not be omitted unless the text immediately preceding the table clearly states what the table shows. The first column of a table may present the classification of figures or facts along the same horizontal line. Left-hand columns of this nature are called stubs. Words above the stub should be an accurate heading to the column. This principle is violated in the following:

GRADE	U. S. SPECIAL	U. S. EXTRA	U. S. STANDARD	U. S. TRADE
Shell				
Air cell				
Yolk				
White				
Germ				

---

[1] Commas may be omitted in numbers of four figures. (See p. 202.)
[2] Dollar signs would not be used before the numbers in this column.

The word "Grade" in the upper left-hand corner is a classification of the column heads, not, as it should be, of the entries below it. The classifications in the headings and in the stub should be rearranged as follows:

GRADE	SHELL	AIR CELL	YOLK	WHITE	GERM
U. S. Special					
U. S. Extra					
U. S. Standard					
U. S. Trade					

The following table shows the same errors in construction:

COLOR OF PIGMENT	GREEN	YELLOW AND ORANGE	RED	WHITE
Name of pigment				
Solubility in water				
Effect of acid				
Effect of alkali				
Effect of prolonged heating				

The column headings in the table above should be placed in the stub, and the entries in the stub used as headings for the columns.

COLOR OF PIGMENT	NAME OF PIGMENT	SOLUBILITY IN WATER	EFFECT OF ACID	EFFECT OF ALKALI	EFFECT OF PROLONGED HEATING
Green					
Yellow and orange					
Red					
White					

A ruled table without a heading in the box over the stub is defective.

Column headings should be concise, with no unnecessary words. For example:

Births per 100,000 Population   1912   1932

is better than:

Births per 100,000 Population   In 1912   In 1932

Conciseness is equally important in the stub.

Wordy: Better:
    From $1 to $5 $1–$5
    From 6 to 10   6–10
    From 11 to 25   11–25

When column headings are subdivided, the relative value of items should be observed and primary items placed in the primary position. The following illustrates poor choice and placing of headings.

FOOD VALUES AND MEASURES IN TERMS OF AVERAGE
SERVINGS OF FOOD

| GRAMS | FOOD | HOUSEHOLD MEASURE | GRAM | | | | | GRAM | |
			CARBOHYDRATES	PROTEIN	FATS	CALORIES	CALCIUM	PHOSPHORUS	IRON

The relation and value of the above headings are better shown below:

QUANTITY IN GRAMS	FOOD	HOUSEHOLD MEASURE	CARBOHYDRATES, GM.	PROTEIN, GM.	FATS, GM.	CALORIES	CALCIUM, GM.	PHOSPHORUS, GM.	IRON, GM.

A table recently observed revealed a failure to distinguish properly between the data and the subjects of the data. It was arranged like this:

MARSH HERBS

CAT-TAIL FAMILY		BUR REED FAMILY		WATER PLANTAIN FAMILY	
(Perennial herbs with stemless leaves)		(Flowers in separate spherical heads)		(Herbs with long-stemmed leaves)	
Typha latifolia (yellow-brown—June, July)	Typha an-gustifolia (yellow-brown—June, July)	Sparganium eurycarpum (brown-white—May–Aug.)	Sparganium simplex (brown-white—June–Aug.)	Alisma plantago (white or pale pink—July–Sept.)	Sagittaria variabilis (white—July–Sept.)

The subjects should always be in the headings or the first column; the facts in the body of the table.

Cat-tail Family (Perennial herbs with stemless leaves)		Bur Reed Family (Flowers in separate spherical heads)		Water Plantain Family (Herbs with long-stemmed leaves)	
Typha latifolia	*Typha angustifolia*	*Sparganium eurycarpum*	*Sparganium simplex*	*Alisma plantago*	*Sagittaria variabilis*
Yellow-brown, June, July	Yellow-brown, June, July	Brown-white, May–Aug.	Brown-white, June–Aug.	White or pale pink, July–Sept.	White, July–Sept.

The author should try to visualize his tables in type and foresee possible difficulties in setting. A table with six or eight columns of information expressed in words (not figures) could be set across a narrow page only if the type were small; while at the same time, if it were set lengthwise of the page, the columns would be wider and consequently less deep, and the table would occupy, perhaps, only part of the page, resulting in wasted space and poor appearance. Much handwork would be required in setting a table like that above. The columns would be either very ragged or very unevenly spaced. Such a table as this can often be arranged in another way without any loss of force or clearness. For instance:

MARSH HERBS

Cat-tail Family (Perennial herbs with stemless leaves)	*Typha latifolia:* Yellow-brown, June, July *Typha angustifolia:* Yellow-brown, June, July
Burr Reed Family (Flowers in separate spherical heads)	*Sparganium eurycarpum:* Brown-white, May–Aug. *Sparganium simplex:* Brown-white, June–Aug.
Water Plantain Family (Herbs with long-stemmed leaves)	*Alisma plantago:* White or pale pink, July–Sept. *Sagittaria variabilis:* White, July–Sept.

Arranged as above the table adjusts itself readily to any size of page. Another advantage is that there is only one intersection of rules. Since in type composition a rule must be cut whenever it crosses another, the fewer rules used, the easier and less expensive a table is to set.

Here is another table (Figure 8) which shows a failure to visualize the appearance in type.   This would have to be set in very small type to get it within the measure of an average page.

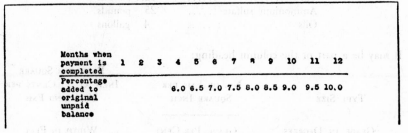

Months when payment is completed	1	2	3	4	5	6	7	8	9	10	11	12
Percentage added to original unpaid balance					6.0	6.5	7.0	7.5	8.0	8.5	9.0	9.5	10.0

Fig. 8

The same information can be presented much more clearly by a simple transposition (Figure 9).

Months When Payment Is Completed	Percentage Added to Original Unpaid Balance		Months When Payment Is Completed	Percentage Added to Original Unpaid Balance
1			9	8.5
2			10	9.0
3			11	9.5
4	6.0		12	10.0
5	6.5		13	10.5
6	7.0		14	11.0
7	7.5		15	11.5
8	8.0		16	12.0

Fig. 9

Units of measurement.   The unit of measurement may be in the stub:

	1919	1929
Dairy cows	620,000	619,000
Cow-testing associations	2	28
Sweet clover (1920) ...... (acres)	30,202	521,000
Sudan-grass (1921) .... (acres)	34,000	59,000

It may follow the figures in a number column:

Coke	1,500	pounds
Gas	11,360	cubic feet
Tar	12.4	pounds
Ammonium sulfate.......	25	pounds
Oils	4	gallons

It may be a part of the column heading:

		RATES PER SQUARE
	NO. OF EMS PER	INCH AT 40 CENTS PER
TYPE SIZE	SQUARE INCH	THOUSAND EMS
GRADE IN DEGREES	GRADE, PER CENT	WIDTH IN FEET

It may be a separate heading in italic immediately above the column:

DIET	ACID EQUIVALENT	NUMBER OF RATS	AVERAGE GAIN, 6 WEEKS	BERIBERI INCIDENCE	AVERAGE TIME TO ONSET
	%		gm.	%	days
G. caprylate	55	4	57	0	—

It may be in parentheses under the caption:

WORLD CONSUMPTION OF PURE NITROGEN

(In metric tons)

TABLE OF DENSITIES

(In grams per cubic centimeter)

If the unit of measurement is given in the column heading, it is not needed with the data in the column.

Captions. Tables are given a caption so that detailed description in the text will be unnecessary, reference to them will be easy, and the reader will have no difficulty in locating the desired data readily. The caption should be concise and not divided into two or more clauses or sentences. Unnecessary words should be omitted. For instance, *Table 1* is better than *Table No. 1;* such words as *showing* and *table showing* are superfluous.

Facts shown by the column headings need not be duplicated in the caption, especially if the table has already been described in the text. For example, the text description of a certain table is as follows:

Table VIII gives for the first, second, and third years of study the enrollments in all the modern foreign languages combined, as it occurs in the three grades of the junior high school. Table IX gives the same information for Latin.

This makes the caption below unnecessarily wordy.

TABLE VIII

ENROLLMENT IN MODERN FOREIGN LANGUAGES IN JUNIOR HIGH SCHOOL DISTRIBUTED AS IT OCCURRED IN THE FIRST, SECOND AND THIRD YEARS OF STUDY AND IN THE SEVERAL GRADES, IN THE SPRING OF 1925. ARRANGED BY REGIONS WITH NATIONAL SUMMARIES.

REGION	7TH GRADE	8TH GRADE		9TH GRADE		
	1st Yr.	*1st Yr.*	*2d Yr.*	*1st Yr.*	*2d Yr.*	*3d Yr.*
New England						
Middle Atlantic						

All that is needed for this caption is:

TABLE VIII

ENROLLMENT IN THE MODERN FOREIGN LANGUAGES, SPRING OF 1925

Numbering. When many tables are used in a work, they should be numbered, and for this purpose roman numerals are usually preferable, although arabic numerals are often the preferred style in statistical publications. Generally speaking, the numbering should be in consecutive order throughout a book, not beginning a new series of numbers with a new chapter. Much confusion often results if there are two or more tables numbered alike, and exact and accurate reference is difficult.

Footnotes. Uncommon abbreviations and qualifications or limitations of data should be explained in footnotes beneath tables. Reference marks (star, dagger, double dagger, etc.) or superior letters are generally used as references to footnotes so that there may be no confusion with the data of the table or with text footnotes. They should follow the item explained or amplified and be arranged in order reading across the columns.

Copy. Tables in typescript should approximate the appearance of printed tables. (See Fig. 9.) Examples of various kinds of tables are shown on pages 122–132. Copy for tables, especially for long ones, is best placed on sheets separate from the text, with the place of insertion in the text carefully marked. In the printing office the text will be given to one compositor and the tables to another; this separation of copy is made easy by having the tables separate from text, and thus composition of text and tables can proceed at the same time.

BIBLIOGRAPHIES

If bibliographical lists form a part of an article or book, the writer should give careful attention to their construction, and maintain consistency in their form. (See also pp. 132–135.)

Content. Bibliographies range from the simple list of references which is sufficiently complete when the only data given are the author's name, the title of the book, and the name of the publisher in a shortened form, to the book-list or catalogue type of bibliography which informs the reader about the number of volumes, the number of pages of front matter and text, the kind of binding, and the cost. Therefore the first thing to consider is the purpose of the list. The reader who will use the list must be kept in mind and the bibliography made as valuable to him as possible. For instance, a list for young readers to use in finding books at the library needs only a simple form:

> *The Peddler's Caravan* . . . . . William Brighty Rands
> *The Road to China* . . . . Olive B. Miller

Reading lists, which are often used at the ends of chapters in a serious work—history, biography, and the like—are frequently condensed to three items: surname of author, title of book, and page or chapter reference. All books so referred to are usually listed elsewhere in a bibliography in complete form. (In lists like the third below the period is often omitted at the end of each entry.)

READINGS

Breasted, *Ancient Times,* Chaps. IV–XVIII. Davis, *Readings,* I, Chap. VII; *A Day in Old Athens.* Seignobos, *History of Ancient Civilizations.* Van Loon, *Story of Mankind,* Chap. XVI. Wells, *The Outline of History,* Chap. XV.

FOR ADDITIONAL READING

H. L. Schoolcraft, *The Genesis of the Grand Remonstrance* (1902), an excellent study. John Forster, *The Debates on the Grand Remonstrance* (1860) and *The Arrest of the Five Members* (1860). J. A. Marriott, *Life and Times of Lucius Cary, Viscount Falkland* (1907). John Stoughton, *History of Religion in England* (6 vols., 1881), from the Nonconformist standpoint.

SHORT-STORY READING LISTS

Brewster, Dorothy, *A Book of Contemporary Short Stories,* The Macmillan Company.

Cody, Sherwin, *The World's Greatest Short Stories*, A. C. McClurg and Company.
Harte, Bret, *Selections from Poems and Stories*, ed. C. S. Thomas, Houghton Mifflin Company.

A bibliography listing the sources used in writing the text that precedes it, or one listing books that would supplement the information given in the text, should give all the details a mature reader would need in order to find a reference readily in a library or bookstore. A well-made bibliography of this kind presents the following information:

For a book:

(1) The name of the author in the form appearing on the title page, with the surname first
(2) The title of the book, and the subtitle, if any (underscored)
(3) The edition, if other than the first (shown on the title page or the copyright page)
(4) The place of publication (the home office) [1]
(5) The publisher [2]
(6) The date of publication (the date on the copyright page, not the one on the title page, which is changed with every printing)
(7) The number of volumes, if more than one

For an article:

(1) The name of the writer, surname first
(2) The title of the article (enclosed in quotation marks)
(3) The title of the periodical in which the article was published (underscored)
(4) The volume number
(5) The date of issue of the periodical (month, day, and year)
(6) The page number

Full bibliographies like this differ from bibliographical footnotes only in minor details of form. The authors' names are inverted for greater ease in alphabetical arrangement. The publication data are not enclosed in parentheses but are separated from the other items by a period. The models below show the desirable form.

Models for Bibliographies

Note. Variant forms of punctuation, capitalization, and abbreviation may be preferred by some reputable publishers as a matter of house style.

---

[1] A list of the home offices of certain publishers is given in the Appendix, page 548.
[2] It is recommended that if a shortened form of the publisher's name is used, it be the form shown in the list in the Appendix, page 548.

Book—one author:

Whitney, F. L., *Methods in Educational Research.* New York, D. Appleton and Company, 1932.

Long, Mason, *The New College Grammar.* New York, The Ronald Press Company, 1935.

Book—two authors:

Greever, Garland, and Jones, Easley S., *The Century Collegiate Handbook,* rev. ed. New York, D. Appleton-Century Company, 1939.

Carlyle, R. W. and A. J., *History of Mediaeval Political Theory in the West,* Vol. VI. Edinburgh and London, Blackwood, 1936.

Book—three authors:

Kimber, D. C., Gray, C. E., and Stackpole, C. E., *Textbook of Anatomy and Physiology,* 9th ed. New York, The Macmillan Company, 1934.

Book—more than three authors:

Allen, John S., and others, *Atoms, Rocks, and Galaxies; a Survey in Physical Science.* New York, Harper & Brothers, 1938.

Book—association the author:

American Medical Association, Council on Pharmacy and Chemistry, *Useful Drugs,* 11th ed.

League of Nations, Economic Intelligence Service, *Money and Banking, 1936–37.* New York, Columbia University Press, 1937.

Book—no author named:

A Manual of Style, 10th ed. Chicago, The University of Chicago Press, 1937.

Chemical Formulary, Harry Bennett, ed. New York, The Chemical Formulary Co., 1933.

Book—author and editor:

Thompson, Francis, *Selected Poems,* Paul Beard, ed. Nelson Classics. New York, Thomas Nelson & Sons, 1938.

Book—translator:

Mann, Thomas, *The Coming Victory of Democracy,* trans. by Agnes E. Meyer. New York, Alfred A. Knopf, 1938.

Book—one volume of a work of several volumes:

Wood, Clement, *History of the World,* Vol. I, *The United States,* rev. ed. New York, World Syndicate Publishing Co., 1937.

Eliot, Charles W., ed., *The Harvard Classics,* Vol. II, *The Meditations of Marcus Aurelius,* trans. by G. Long. New York, P. F. Collier & Sons, 1909–10.

Book—one of a series:

Powell, Richard R. B., ed., *Cases on Future Interests,* 2d ed. American Casebook Series. New York, West Publishing Company, 1937.

Technical bulletin, government report, or similar publication:

Lundgren, Waldemar, *The Tertiary Gravels of the Sierra Nevada of California.* U. S. Geol. Survey, Prof. Paper 73, 1911.

Sachs, Ward H., *Effect of Cultivation on Moisture and Nitrate of Field Soils.* Ark. Agr. Exp. Sta. Bull. 205, 1926.

Wheeler, Martha Thorne, *Indexing—Principles, Rules and Examples,* 3d ed. rev. New York State Library, Library School Bulletin 50. Albany, The University of the State of New York, 1923.

Sources for Reproductions of Works of Art. Bulletin of the American Library Association, Vol. 30, No. 4 (April, 1936).

Baynes, Norman H., *The Political Ideas of St. Augustine's De Civitate Dei.* Historical Association Pamphlet, No. 104, London, 1936.

Moore, R. H., *Cell Specialization in the Epidermis of Maize.* Unpublished M.S. thesis, University of Oklahoma, 1929.

Part of a book:

Carlyle, A. J., "St. Augustine and the City of God," in F. J. C. Hearnshaw, ed., *The Social and Political Ideas of Some Great Mediaeval Thinkers* (London and New York, 1923), Chap. 2.

Part of a yearbook:

Horn, Ernest, "The 3009 Commonest Words Used in Adult Writing." Fourth Yearbook, Department of Superintendence, National Education Association, 1926.

Part of a report:

Buckingham, B. R., "New Data on the Typography of Textbooks," *The Textbook in American Education.* Thirteenth Yearbook of the National Society for the Study of Education, Part II. Bloomington, Illinois, Public School Publishing Company, 1931.

Article in a periodical:

Crane, E. J., "The Standardization of Chemical Nomenclature." *Journal of Chemical Education,* Vol. 8 (July, 1931), pp. 1338–40.

or

Crane, E. J., "The Standardization of Chemical Nomenclature." *Journal of Chemical Education,* 8:1338–40 (July, 1931).

Lane, B. H., "A Uniform Scheme for Citations." *Science,* new ser., Vol. 75 (April 10, 1931), pp. 390–392.

"Accuracy." *Journal of Educational Research,* VIII (June, 1923), 63–7.

"Living Costs Have Declined in Two Years." *San Francisco Chronicle,* Section J, Vol. CXXXIII, No. 127 (November 19, 1928), p. 18.

Annotated bibliographies. Sometimes an annotated bibliography is desirable.

Russell, Charles, *Classroom Tests.* Boston, Ginn and Company, 1926. 246 pp. Part I outlines methods of constructing objective tests, while Part II deals with how to use such tests.

Hader, J. J., and Lindeman, E. C., *Dynamic Social Research.* New York, Harcourt, Brace & Co., 1934. 226 pp.

Detailed analysis of the conference committee in industry, and the psychological factors entering into conference methods and procedure.

———————

Hart, F. W., and Peterson, L. H., "The Present School District System in California." *California Quarterly of Secondary Education,* IX (October, 1933), 63–67.

A description and a criticism of the present system of school-district organization in California.

The book-list style. The bibliography may be in the style of a book list. Whenever shortened forms of publishers' names are used, it is advisable to use the forms adopted by the American Library Association, many of which are listed in the Appendix, pages 548–552.

Arrangement. The arrangement of bibliographies is usually alphabetical, but chronology or value may determine the order. The author should make his intention so clear in this matter that no question of it can arise.

ILLUSTRATIONS
(See also pages 171–177.)

Without illustrations of some kind a report, a magazine article, a book, or other printed production may be incomplete or lacking in force and vividness. The problem of illustrations ranges from "pictures" to the complicated diagrams and drawings of an engineering text. The author usually chooses the subjects for illustration and in some cases he provides the copy. Before he does anything at all about illustrations, however, he should consult the printer or editor and with him decide upon the kind (line, halftone, or color); whether figures in the text or plates printed separately; the size, especially the proportion.

The three basic reproduction processes are relief, planographic, and intaglio. Printing from type and from electrotype plates is relief printing, and the method of producing plates for relief printing is photoengraving.

Line engravings. The least expensive of photoengraved plates are line engravings. The printer speaks of these as line cuts, direct cuts, line blocks, or zinc etchings. The line cut is used for reproducing a piece of writing, a printed page, a sketch map or chart, a pen-and-ink drawing, a cartoon; in short, any picture consisting of black lines on a white background. There are no tones in a line cut. (See also p. 172.)

The author may make his own drawings for line cuts if he is sufficiently skilled, or he may submit sketches to the publisher, who will have finished drawings made by an expert. Maps, especially, should always be drawn by a professional. The drawings are commonly submitted to the author for approval before they are sent to the engraver for reproduction.

Blueprints are not suitable for reproduction, and photostats should not be used if any better form of copy is procurable.

Copy for line cuts should be made with black ink on white paper. Waterproof ink is preferable for this work and should be used on smooth or medium rough white paper of suitable weight that can be presented flat. Art work offered for reproduction should never be folded.

With few exceptions, line drawings should be reasonably bold and clean in execution. However, firm lines, even though finely drawn, will reproduce satisfactorily if work is done openly. Finely drawn subjects having cross-hatching or any type of shading with close, fine line work have a tendency to fill up, break away, or become ragged in appearance when reproduced.

If graph paper is used for drawings, a blue-lined paper must be chosen if the cross-lines are not to show, because blue does not photograph in this process. A graph or similar diagram in which the coördinate lines are desired in the cut should be drawn on brown-lined or black-lined paper.

Size. The proportions of the type page or column should be ascertained and the size and proportions of the drawing determined in accordance with them, allowance being made for a caption. Copy for illustrations should if possible be larger than the reproduction desired. Reduction in size results in sharper lines. Enlarging exaggerates all minor imperfections and tends to blur the lines. Coördinate lines should not be so close that they will run together and give a blurred appearance upon reduction, and all details should be large enough so that they will not become indistinct or disappear when the drawing is reduced in size. Reduction to one-half the original width produces an illustration one-fourth the area of the original. (See p. 174.)

Lettering. Lettering on drawings should be large enough to reproduce well when the drawing is reduced. Coördinate lettering should usually be incorporated in the drawing, and not left to be set in type. If large enough and if made in black ink on light areas and in white on dark areas, lettering will show up well on line cuts.

Halftones. The halftone is used for reproducing a photograph, wash-drawing, drawing in colors, crayon drawing, pencil sketch, etching, mezzotint, or any other picture that is made up of shading and tone. A halftone may also be secured by photographing an object directly. The process is practicable for such subjects as rugs, linens, cutlery, and jewelry. Direct halftones, so called, are faithful in detail and accurate in color. (The process of making halftones, including the use of screens, is described on page 173.)

The best copy for a halftone is a glossy photograph in black and whit with clearness and considerable contrast. A halftone made. from a print of a halftone is unsatisfactory.

Lettering on halftones is not often satisfactory.

Photographs that are to be used by an engraver as copy for halftones should always be kept flat, amply protected by corrugated board or Beaverboard, so that they will not become cracked or creased or torn at the edges. They should not be pasted on sheets or mounted except by an expert. Nothing should ever be fastened to a photograph by means of a metal clip, unless protected by a paper pad, for a clip impression which cannot be eradicated may thus be made in the surface of the photograph. It is best not to write on the back of an unmounted photograph, for even the slightest pressure may leave an impression that will show in the reproduction. A sheet of thin paper bearing necessary instructions can be lightly pasted on the edge of the back and folded over the front.

Regardless of size, the copy for each halftone illustration to be used in a printed work should be on a separate sheet of paper, and each sheet should bear a notation of the number and title the illustration will have when printed. A complete list of these titles, properly termed legends, but also often called captions, should be furnished separately.

Text illustrations for a book, both photographs and line drawings, should be numbered consecutively throughout the text in a single series, using arabic numerals, Fig. 1, Fig. 2. The preferred location for each illustration should be indicated by the author on the manuscript, by the use of the same numbers.

SPECIAL RESPONSIBILITIES OF THE BOOK WRITER

The author of a book also has certain other duties. In addition to the body of the book his manuscript should include front matter, and end matter if there is to be any.

The makeup of a book depends upon the nature of the subject matter and the simplicity or elaborateness of treatment. A simple book may contain only body matter preceded by a title page. Most books have also a copyright notice, preface, and table of contents, and often an introduction and list of illustrations. These parts constitute front matter, or "preliminaries," because they all precede the text. A serious work—historical, educational, scientific—may contain end matter ("back matter" or "subsidiaries"). In any such work the end matter should include an index, and in addition may include an appendix—notes, practice material, a glossary, or other supplementary information regarding the text.

Layout

The arrangement of the various parts of a book is called its layout. A book might contain the following, although few would have all these parts.

Front matter:
   Certificate of limited edition—an announcement of the number of copies printed in a limited edition (see also p. 139)
   Half-title (sometimes called the "bastard title")—the title of the book, standing alone on the page
   Imprimatur—the authorization to print (see below)
   Book card (or "face title")—a list of books by the same author or in the same series
   Frontispiece
   Title page
   Copyright
   Dedication
   Preface
   Acknowledgments
   Table of contents
   List of illustrations
   List of figures, maps, charts, or tables
   Introduction
   Epigraph
Text

Appendix:
   Notes
   Quotations
   Bibliography
   Glossary
Index
Colophon—a brief account of the book (see p. 152)

FRONT MATTER

The author should supply copy for any of the following parts of the front matter which he wishes to use in his book: imprimatur, frontispiece, title page, dedication, epigraph, preface, table of contents, list of illustrations, introduction.

Imprimatur. The imprimatur is the notice of license to print which appears in Roman Catholic publications immediately following the book half-title.

Title page. For the title page the author should supply copy showing the title of the book and the form in which he wishes his name to appear, together with his degrees and associations.

Epigraph. The epigraph is a short quotation appropriate to the content of the book.

CONTENTS

		page
Preface	. . . .	vii
chapter		
I.	The Desk Man's Duties	1
II.	News Origins	6
III.	The Copyreader's Symbols	11
IV.	Condensing Stories	27
V.	Removing Bias and Opinion	42
VI.	Making Stories Emphatic	61
VII.	Headlines	94
VIII.	The Need for Clarity	128
IX.	Suburban Copy	142
X.	City Copy	155
XI.	Display Headlines	175
XII.	Telegraph Copy	219
XIII.	Marking Copy; Sectional Stories .	248
XIV.	Spread Headlines	264
XV.	By-Lines and Color Stories	270
XVI.	Newspaper Law	289
XVII.	Crime and Suicide News	321
XVIII.	Propaganda	332
XIX.	Cuts	349
XX.	Make-up	358
Appendices:		
I.	A Headline System	385
II.	Proof Corrections	393
Index	. . . .	397

FIG. 10

Typewritten Copy for Table of Contents with Simple Chapter Titles.

Dedication. If the author wishes to have a dedication page, he should phrase the dedication as simply as possible.

Preface. Any remarks the author wishes to make to the reader should be placed in the preface. Usually these constitute a statement of the purpose of the book. Acknowledgments of indebtedness may also be included, or these may be under a separate heading. At the end the author should sign his initials and note the place and date of completion. If a preface is written by someone other than the author, it should be signed by the full name of the writer of it.

The terms *preface, foreword,* and *introduction* are often used interchangeably. It is, however, desirable to differentiate them. A preface or foreword deals with the genesis, purpose, limitations, and scope of the book and may include acknowledgments of indebtedness; an introduction deals with the subject of the book, supplementing the text, introducing the text, and in-

CONTENTS

OF KING ARTHUR

Chapter I

Of the Birth of King Arthur, and of his Nourishing,
and of the Death of King Utherpendragon, and
how Arthur was chosen King, and of Wonders and
Marvels of a Sword that was taken out of Stone
by the said Arthur   1

Chapter II

How King Arthur pulled out the Sword Divers Times   4

Chapter III

How Arthur was crowned King, and how he made
Officers   6

Chapter IV

How Griflet was made Knight, and how he jousted
with a Knight   7

FIG. 11

Another Typewritten Form for Table of Contents with Chapter Titles.

dicating a point of view to be adopted by the reader. The introduction usually forms a part of the text; the preface does not.

Table of contents. For the contents of a simple book containing no headings subordinate to the chapter titles, the chapter titles are listed with folios (the numbers) of the pages on which they begin. A preface or introduction should be listed. See Figure 10 and Figure 11.

If the chapters are subdivided and have subordinate centered headings, these also may appear in the table of contents, arranged so as to show their relation to one another. See Figure 12.

List of illustrations. Copy for the list of illustrations is easy to prepare. Brief titles of all the illustrations are listed. If there are both plates and text figures, they may or may not be listed separately.

CONTENTS

page
Chapter 1. Sensation and Perception 3
Sensation 4
Perception 13
Attributes 19
Nativism and Empiricism 28
Psychophysics 34
Notes 45

Chapter 2. Physiology of Sensation 53
Nerve Conduction 53
Sensory Conduction 62

CONTENTS

CHAPTER I. ECONOMIC CAUSES OF WAR 3
Economic factors neither exclusive nor final, 3
War as an end in itself, 4
Economic Objectives of War, 5
The quest for "living-space", 5
The quest for raw materials, 11
The quest for markets, 16
The quest for investment outlets, 19
Economic Interest in Warfare, 25
Economic Conditions Making for War, or, the Economics of Peace, 26
Summary, 29

CONTENTS

page
Preface ix
Introduction xxi

chapter
I. Pre-Typographic Writing Symbols, Materials and Books 1
The Cuneiform Characters. The Rosetta Stone. The Runis Writing Symbols. The Rök Stone. The Genealogy of Our Alphabet. Ancient Writing Materials for Manuscripts and Books. Papyrus Rolls. Parchment. Making books in Ancient Days.

II. Block-Prints and Block-Books 23
Early Block-Prints, Classification of Block-Books. The Zylographic Donatuses. Block-Printing After Typography. Wood-Engraving.

FIG. 12

Typewritten Copy for Three Tables of Contents with Chapters Having Subordinate Headings.

INDEXES [1]

Any book that is intended to be used for reference or for authority should have an index. This may be prepared by the author or by an experienced indexer. The author has the essential knowledge of the contents of the book, and he can make himself familiar with the principles and practice of indexing. The index should be made when page proof is received, and it should be done as promptly as possible so that completion of the book may not be delayed. (See also pp. 146–151.)

Procedure. First read over the pages and mark the entries. Underscore the key word of the entry with a wavy line, following words with a straight line; write in the margin any wording desired that is not in the text. When the entries have been so marked on the proof, write them on cards, one entry to a card. Filing cards three by five inches in size, or flexible slips of the same size, are very satisfactory. Arrange the cards in alphabetical order by the key word; then arrange each group of cards that have the same key word, either alphabetically or numerically, making sure that each subhead reads back properly to the key word. Finally read the cards carefully to catch any errors of form or wording, to eliminate any key words that are not to appear in print, and to indicate subentries by making the sign for an em space in front of them (□), sub-subentries, if any, by a double space (□□). If the handwriting is reasonably legible, send the cards to the publisher for copy; if it is not neat and clear, type the index from the cards and then read back against them before sending it to the publisher.

Kinds. Most books require only one index, the so-called dictionary type, listing names, titles, and subjects in one alphabetical sequence. In special cases, however, more than one index is desirable. For instance, a book containing selections from many different writers may have a useful index of authors; a book containing many citations of legal cases might well have a separate index of the cases, a "table of cases." An anthology would likely require an index of authors, another of titles, and a third of first lines.

Index of authors. The simplest of all indexes to compile is an index of authors, since it requires only the transcribing of the names with the surname written first, and then an arrangement of the names in strict alphabetical order. The most efficient way to arrange the cards is first to sort them into alpha-

---

[1] More detailed instruction in index making than can be included here may be found in *Indexing—Principles, Rules and Examples*, by Martha Thorne Wheeler (New York State Library, Library School Bulletin 50, 1923). Also in *Rules for a Dictionary Catalog*, by Charles A. Cutter (Washington, U. S. Government Printing Office, 1904). (A dictionary catalogue is defined as one in which author, title, subject, and form headings are arranged in alphabetical order.)

betical groups and then to arrange each group in order by the second **or** third letter as may be necessary, a, ab, aba, ac, and so on. (For the order in foreign alphabets see the sections on Composition of Foreign Languages.)

Questions occasionally arise concerning the arrangement of names with prefixes, Spanish names, pseudonyms. The accepted usage in these details is presented on pages 48–50.

Table of cases. Also dealing with names but involving more problems is a table of cases. Index simple citations, such as *Trevett v. Weeden,* under both names.

Trevett v. Weeden........ 49
Weeden, Trevett v. 49

Invert phrases like *In re, In the matter of,* and *Ex parte.*

Ashley v. Winkley—60
Ashman's Estate, *In re*—108
Ashurst's Appeal—76

Index of titles. A simple index of titles requires the listing of the titles, inverting an initial *A* or *The.* Such a list is usually alphabeted word by word, but see Alphabetical Order, pages 53, 54.

La Nouvelle Héloïse, 100	*I Come to Bury Caesar,* 40
Lady of Shalott, The, 405	*I Wandered Lonely as a Cloud,* 50
Lake Isle of Innisfree, The, 60	*Il Penseroso,* 106
L'Allegro, 76	*In Memoriam,* 109
Lamb, The, 86	*Indian Summer,* 58

(but *De Fust Banjo,* 92)

If an index of titles is to be arranged by subject, the indexer's work is far from simple. The word best expressing the subject must then be placed in the key position, inverting whenever necessary. If no word in the title expresses the subject accurately, one must be supplied, placed in the key position followed by a colon, the title following in regular order.

Alaska, A Guide to, 20
Electrical Engineering, Fundamentals of, 68
Home Decoration: *A House in the Country,* 31
Vocabulary, Twelve Ways to Build a, 55
Héloïse, La Nouvelle, 102
Niagara, Les Chutes de, 10

Index of authors and titles. An index of authors may be combined with an index of titles, using distinct type forms for each. For instance:

DALMON, CHARLES
David Copperfield (Charles Dickens)
DAVIDSON, JOHN
Dead, The (Rupert Brooke)
Definition of a Gentleman, The (John Henry Newman)
DE LA MARE, WALTER

Compiling an Index of the Dictionary Form

The ordinary book index, by contrast to the foregoing kinds, is often exceedingly hard to compile, for compilation involves not merely a transcription of names and titles, with an occasional inversion, and arrangement according to set rules; it also requires discretion and judgment in choosing what is to be included and in placing the best word in the key position. Intimate acquaintance with the text is required as well as familiarity with accepted practices in indexing.

The index maker's first problem is what to put on the index cards, then how to write the entry. Only after his cards are all written does the question of order arise. The sections immediately following, therefore, concern choice of entries and the form in which they should be written. The alphabetical arrangement of the cards is discussed on pages 52–55, and the typographical details that are more particularly the concern of the editor are presented on pages 146–151.

Entries. Make entries on the index cards to cover the following: proper names, titles of books referred to, events and periods, definitions, specific topics or subjects.

Choice of the key word. Choice of a key word depends mainly on the needs of the average reader. Think what he might look for. File "Marriage among the Navahos" under the two obvious words and also under *Customs* and *Indians*. File "Spanish Architecture in the Southwest" not only under the three obvious words but also under *Churches* and *Homes*.

When the subject has been determined, place the substantive which expresses it first, as the key word for the entry, inverting qualifying words if necessary. Give careful attention to punctuation, for it is understood that subentries read back to everything in the main entry up to the first comma. (If subsubentries are being used, see pp. 149, 150.)

Compound nouns. Distinguish compound nouns, properly indexed like simple nouns, from noun-and-adjective combinations, which should be inverted and indexed under the noun.

prize fighting	figurines, earthenware
Triple Entente	granaries, public
water supply	tablets, ancestral

If there is any question whether certain words form a compound, make entries in both ways, and if there are only a few references, give them with both entries. The references take less space than a cross reference, and the searcher is saved time. (This is called double entry.)

The following shows a failure to bring the significant words to key positions; an adjective should not be used as a key word.

Poor:

Divine, art, 000; art and the, 00; the, and earthly beauty, 00; the, as material, 00; origin of art, 00; purpose explains beauty, 00; purpose explains pleasures of imagination, 00

Better:

Art: divine, 00; divine origin of, 00
Divine, the: art and, 00; earthly beauty and, 00; as material, 00
Divine purpose: explains beauty, 00; explains pleasures of imagination, 00

Impure, art, 00; ideational style, 000; music, 000; sensate style, 00
Inner, aspect of culture, 00; character of architecture, 000; character of literature, 00; character of music, 00; experience, 00; culture of mentality, 00

Architecture, inner character of, 00
Art, impure, 00
Culture, inner aspect of, 00
Experience, inner, 00
Literature, inner character of, 00
Mentality, inner culture of, 00
Music: impure, 00; inner character of, 00
Style: impure ideational, 00; impure sensate, 00

Phrases. Arrange phrase headings logically, with the significant word in the key position.

dress, forms of
humor, sense of
Labor, Department of

Bill of Rights
Elixir of life
Society of Jesus

Do not use descriptive phrases as headings, but invert to bring to the key position the noun denoting the topic of the paragraph or article indexed.

Wrong:

Agriculture—
formation of prorate districts
regulating livestock grazing on U. S. public lands
relating to quarantine on date palms
relating to storage of eggs
salary of director of
transportation regulation of grapevines

Better:

Agriculture—
date palms, quarantine
director of, salary
eggs, storage
grapevines, transportation regulation
livestock grazing on U. S. public lands
prorate districts, formation

Highways—
  establishing an additional state highway
  making an appropriation for the construction of
  relating to the width of highways

Highways—
  additional state highway, establishing
  appropriation for construction of
  width of

Inversions. When the natural order of closely connected words is changed to bring the important word to the key position, place such words as closely together as possible.

Brown, James, Jr. [*not* Brown, Jr., James]
Homer, poetry of, popular theology in
James I, King, anecdote of [*not* James I, anecdote of King]

Apply the rule with discretion and avoid unnecessary inversion.

Poor:
Great Britain, isolation of, German policy of, 106
Hoare, Sir Samuel, Laval and, peace plan of, 28
Schuschnigg, Dr. Kurt von, Government of, overthrow of, 70

Better:
Great Britain, German policy of isolation of, 106
Hoare, Sir Samuel, peace plan of Laval and, 28
Schuschnigg, Dr. Kurt von, overthrow of government of, 70

Conciseness. Words and phrases like *concerning, regarding, relating to* have no place in an index. Omit prepositions, conjunctions, and articles that are not necessary to clearness. The articles *a* and *the* are seldom required in an inverted entry,[2] unless they are the first word of a capitalized title; even then they might sometimes be omitted. (See also p. 44.)

Not concise:
Hosea, 38; conditions of, 39; marriage of, 40; message of, 46; person and life of, 43; teaching of, 49

Macmillan Company, The, 168
See also Ascot; Derby, The; Grand National
Society of Jesus, the, 96

Better:
Hosea, 38; conditions, 39; marriage, 40; message, 46; person and life, 43; teaching, 49

Macmillan Company, 168
See also Ascot; Derby; Grand National
Society of Jesus, 96

Take care not to omit a preposition that is necessary to the meaning. For instance, *Acceptance, benefits* is ambiguous; a preposition is needed to make

---

2 An example of an article necessary to meaning is shown on page 46: divine, the: art and, 00; earthly beauty and, 00.

the meaning clear: *Acceptance, of benefits* or *Acceptance, benefits of.* So, also, in the following:

Exchange, 30; restrictions on, 32
Massachusetts, first settlement in, 20
  Puritan emigration to, 23

Geographic names. Index under the specific word unless the parts are inseparable.

Fundy, Bay of   Cape of Good Hope
Horn, Cape   Lake of the Woods
Olympus, Mount   Mount Vernon

Names of persons. Observe established usage in the indexing of proper names. Persons referred to in the text by the surname only should be identified in the index by forename or initials.

English compound names. Index under both parts.

Campbell-Bannerman, Sir Henry, 76
Bannerman, Sir Henry Campbell-, 76

Spanish compound names. Index under the first part.

Avila Camacho, Manuel
Cervantes Saavedra, Miguel de
Moreto y Cabaña, Agustín
Vega Carpio, Lope Félix de

Noblemen. Unless the family name or a lower title is much the better known, index under their highest title.

Buckingham, George Villiers, Duke of
Chesterfield, Philip Dormer Stanhope, Earl of
Disraeli, Benjamin, Earl of Beaconsfield
Pitt, William, Earl of Chatham

Sovereigns, princes, writers. Index under the first name if the person is generally so known.

Bonaparte. *See* Napoleon.
Napoleon, 106

Index under the full name if the person is habitually so spoken of.

Kemal Ataturk
Mark Antony
Omar Khayyam

Pseudonyms. Index under pseudonym if that is better known than the real name; otherwise under the real name with a cross reference from the pseudonym. Use double entry if desirable.

Henry, O., 42
Porter, Sidney. *See* Henry, O.
Clemens, Samuel L., 70
Twain, Mark. *See* Clemens, Samuel L.

Names with prefixes. For an Englishman or an American retain the prefix:

De Forest, Lee   La Follette, Robert
De Quincey, Thomas   Van Buren, Martin

For a Frenchman or a Belgian retain the prefix when an article is involved:

La Fayette, Comtesse de   La Bruyère, Jean de
L'Enfant, Pierre Charles   Du Guesclin, Bertrand

but invert a pure preposition:

Balzac, Honoré de   Sévigné, Madame de

For a Spaniard or a Dutchman retain the *de:*

de Sitter, Willem   De Soto, Hernando

For a German or a Dutchman invert *von, van*:

Beethoven, Ludwig van   Hoff, van't
Bernstorff, Johann, Graf von   Gogh, Vincent van

In doubtful cases (Van Eyck, Della Robbia) list under the specific name and the preposition also.

Arabic names. In Arabic names *abu* (father), *umm* (mother), *ibn, bin* (son), and *ahu* (brother) are considered to begin the surname and therefore determine the alphabetical position.

abu-Bekr   ibn-Saud, Abdul-Aziz

Articles—*al-, ad-, ar-, as-, at-, az-* —are disregarded in determining the alphabetical position but are not inverted.

al-Masudi—under M

Oriental names. In indexing names of Orientals take care not to mistake titles for names. The following are titles: *Babu, Bey, Emir, Pasha, Pundit, Sri.*

Ibrahim Pasha—under I

In Chinese names the surname always comes first; therefore there is no inverting when such names are indexed.

Chiang Kai-shek   Sun Yat-sen

Japanese names are written in the same order as English names.

Noguchi, Hideyo   Yamagata, Prince Aritomo

Alternative foreign names. Use the English form of foreign names unless the foreign form is better known.

William, Kaiser [*rather than* Wilhelm] Raphael [*not* Raffaelo]
Cologne [*not* Köln]   Antwerp [*not* Anvers]
Florence [*not* Firenze]   Brussels [*not* Bruxelles]
Nuremberg [*not* Nürnberg]

Many names of places have been changed in recent years or the local names have replaced previously used English forms. In indexing it should be remembered that the newer forms are unfamiliar to many, and for their convenience cross references should be used freely.

Angora. *See* Ankara.   Christiania. *See* Oslo.
Queenstown. *See* Cóbh.   Finland. *See* Suomi.

Words with more than one meaning. Make a separate entry for each subject. *Form,* for instance, can mean *a body, a social convention, physical and mental condition, a rank of students,* or *a printing frame.* Make a separate entry for each separate meaning. If headings spelled alike name persons and places as well as subjects, the correct order is person, place, subject, title.

Stage, best height for, 62   Lynn, John A., 78
Stage, celebrities, 96   Lynn, England, 80
Stage, Hartford to New Haven, 14   *Lynn, The Bells of,* 82
Stage, larval, 203

Words with different uses. The following paragraph incorrectly combines, under the heading *water,* seven other distinct topics besides *water.* The noun *water* is one subject. Where *water* is combined with another word to form a compound noun a new main heading is needed. (See also pp. 149–150.)

Wrong:

water, 00; beetles, 00; bodies of, 00; ducts, 00; evaporation of, 00; gradation agent, 00; horse (hippopotamus), 00; is everywhere, 00; meter, 00; properties of, 00; running, 00; supply, 00; tubes, 00; vapor, 00; vascular system, 00; as wonder worker, 00; work of, 00

Right:

water, 00; bodies of, 00; evaporation of, 00; gradation agent, 00; is everywhere, 00; properties of, 00; running, 00; supply, 00; as wonder worker, 00; work of, 00

water beetles, 00

water ducts, 00

water horse, 00

water meter, 00

water tubes, 00

water vapor, 00

water vascular system, 00

Singular and plural forms. In an ordinary index place all references to a given subject under one heading whenever possible, either the singular or the plural. Keep in mind the convenience of the person who uses the index. In alphabeting, the singular and plural forms of a word might be widely separated, and one group of references might be overlooked as a consequence. Except in indexing exact titles, it is usually possible to group all references under one entry.

Subheadings. Break up with subheadings a comprehensive heading followed by many page references, so that the searcher will be able to find quickly the material for which he is looking.

Jehovah: fatherhood, 00; glory, 00; holiness, 00; love, 00; majesty, 00; name, 00; nature and character, 00; righteousness, 00; sole deity, 00

Lighting: direct, 313; electric, 305–307; gas, 305, 306; indirect, 314; kerosene oil, 303, 304; methods of, 326; semi-direct, 314

The arrangement may be alphabetical, as in the preceding examples, or numerical; when a time sequence is important the numerical is preferred.

Rome:

beginning of, 137–138

growth of, 144–146

in conflict with Carthage, 145–147

laws of, 152

slaves in, 154

downfall of, 157

Architecture: Oriental, 46, 47, 83, 85; Aegean, 56; Greek, 195–196; Roman, 197–200; Byzantine, 242; Arab, 251; medieval, 293–361; Renaissance, 328, 329; modern, 658, 659

Place after the main heading all page references to which no subheading is attached.

Wrong:

Calhoun, John C.: Sectional Southern party plan, 74, 77; 189; James Murray Mason and, 244

Right:

Calhoun, John C., 189; Sectional Southern party plan, 74, 77; James Murray Mason and, 244

Cross references. Use a cross reference (*see*) from an entry for which a searcher *might* look to another with which references are given, especially if there are subheads or related topics that might otherwise be missed. (If the entry is not subdivided and page references are few, give the references with both.)

Coins and coinage. *See* Money.
Currency. *See* Money.
Money, 42–45, 60, 72
   [subheads follow]
Jesuits. *See* Society of Jesus.

Use a cross reference (*see also*) from an entry with references to another on a related subject.

Horse racing, by moving pictures and by radio, 49. *See also* Ascot; Derby; Grand National.
Alliances, 100 ... *See also* Coalitions.

In the paragraph form of index a *see also* reference is placed at the end of a paragraph. In the entry-a-line form it is generally but not always after the last subhead, beginning a new line, indented.

Class work, oral, 5, 13, 20–22
   written, 53, 380
   See also Recitations.

Alphabetical Order

Two systems of alphabeting are in use, one followed by dictionaries and similar works and one followed in book indexes. Usage tends strongly to adopt the dictionary practice, which is the simpler, for all index work.

The dictionary method. Dictionaries, cyclopedias, and atlases list entries alphabetically letter by letter, and this system should be followed whenever all the entries are simple or compound names or nouns.

prize	New Orleans
prize court	Newport
prize fight	New Rochelle
prizeman	Newton
prize money	New York
prizer	
prize ring	East Africa
	Eastbourne
Postmaster General	East Cape
Post Office Department	Easter Island
	East Indies

Vanadium	Lava
Van Briggle pottery	La Veta Pass
a.d.	*School for Scandal, The*
Adam's Peak	*Schoolmaster, The*
ad amussim	"School of Athens, The"
adaptable	

The book-index method. The system of alphabeting letter by letter is not generally followed in ordinary book indexes, in which entries may be one word or several. In this kind of work alphabeting is generally word by word, in accordance with the following principles.

Apply the rule "Nothing precedes something," or "Something follows nothing," whenever a simple noun and a heading containing the same word together with other words are to be indexed: place the simple heading first. as in the following:

index, price	Pasteur, Louis
index numbers	Pasteur Institute
police, state	Tennessee Valley, map of
police courts	Tennessee Valley Authority
Bethlehem, music of Moravians	citizens, influence
Bethlehem Library	citizenship

In book index style if the heading—the words preceding the comma—is a combination of adjective and noun, a phrase, or the like, consider the initial word first, next the alphabetical order of following words.

group phenomena	Indian snake dance
grouping	Indians
social work	slave trade
socialized medicine	slavery
Civil War Workers' Committee	New York
civilians and health insurance	Newark
	news
palm trees	
palmate leaf	sweet potatoes
	sweetbreads
air transportation	
airplane journey	book lists
	book plates
social security	book reviews
Socialist party	booklets

Compound words. In the book-index style, index compounds as one word unless they are temporary, or made up for the occasion.

Index as one word:
pre-school
Anglo-Saxon
passer-by

Index as two words:
All-Russian [congress]
crop-growing [season]
rainy-day [styles]

Index compound names of persons as if single solid words.

Vanadium
Van Dine

Lamont
La Rochefoucauld

Names with a prefix. In book-index style treat as one word.

Leavenworth
Le Bourget

Sanatoria
San Diego

Exact titles. In book-index style determine the order of exact titles first by the alphabetical position of the first word, then of following words; take into account every word except initial articles.[3]

Sea Horses
Sea-Wolf, The
Seasons, The

I never saw a purple cow
If I were a snake
If I were little as a bee

First lines. In indexing first lines, consider the initial article as the first word. Do not invert.

A bird came down the walk, 261
A wounded deer leaps highest, 120
Advance is life's condition, 1130
Alter! When the hills do, 557

Apostrophes. In either style of index an apostrophe does not affect the alphabetic position of an entry.

o'er the sea
of things
one's heart sings

Boy's King Arthur, The
Boys of Yesterday
Boys' Workshop

Abbreviations. An abbreviation takes the alphabetic position it would have if it were spelled out (except in a list of abbreviations). This rule includes *Dr., M., Mme., Mr., Mrs., MS., MSS., Mt., St., Ste., SS.,* and initials standing for organizations like *Y.M.C.A., C.C.C.*

Mirrors of Downing Street, The
Mr. Britling Sees It Through
Mrs. Wiggs of the Cabbage Patch
Moby-Dick

Y.W.C.A.
Youth movement

U.S. Army
United States Catalog

St. Clair
Saint-Cyr
Sainte-Beuve
Saint-Gaudens
St. John
Salisbury

alt., altitude
Alta., Alberta

[3] The *Rules for Filing Cards* of the Carnegie Library of Pittsburgh lists the articles in foreign languages, pp. 7–10.

Mc and M'. List *Mc* and *M'* as if *Mac.*

McClure, S. S.
MacDonald, Ramsay
Machado, Gerardo
Machinery
McKinley, William
MacLeish, Archibald
Magazines

Numerals. Alphabet numerals as if they were spelled out.

Insignificant words. Articles, conjunctions, and prepositions may or may not be disregarded in determining the order of subentries. Usage tends to follow letter-by-letter alphabeting in subentries, even though this obliges the user of the index to read all the subentries to be sure of not missing what he is looking for. Whenever clarity will allow it, omit insignificant words.

Small words disregarded:
Angle, of any magnitude
    to construct from a function
    cosecant of
    cotangent of
    elevation and depression
    how generated
    tangent of

Formulas, from facts by generalization
    for radius of inscribed circle
    reciprocal relation
    for solving triangles

Small words considered:
Angle, cosecant of
    cotangent of
    how generated
    of any magnitude
    of elevation and depression
    tangent of
    to construct from a function

Formulas, for radius of inscribed circle
    for solving triangles
    from facts by generalization
    reciprocal relation

LEGAL RESPONSIBILITIES OF THE AUTHOR

Two laws concern writers particularly—the copyright law and the libel law. A writer may be held responsible for violations of these laws; he should therefore be informed of their provisions.

THE COPYRIGHT LAW [1]

The common law protects the rights of an author in an unpublished manuscript. After publication this protection ceases, and the author must have

[1] For more detailed treatment of the law of copyright see *A Manual of Copyright Practice for Writers, Publishers, and Agents,* by Margaret Nicholson (Second Edition, New York, Oxford University Press, 1956); or *The Copyright Law,* by Herbert A. Howell (Third Edition, Washington, D.C., The Bureau of National Affairs, Inc., 1952).

his work copyrighted or else it becomes public property, "falls into the public domain." Copyright can be secured on books, pamphlets, periodicals, newspapers, gazetteers, addresses, lectures, sermons, dramatic or musical compositions, charts, maps, engravings, prints, photographs, paintings, drawings, plastic works. The protection lasts twenty-eight years and may be renewed for a like period. During that period copying, translation, adaptation, and abridgments are prohibited in the absence of specific permission by the holder of the copyright.

Infringement of copyright. There is no copyright in the title of a book, but if there occurs a clear case of dishonest imitation, legal action may be taken. Quotation is not always infringement. Long custom has recognized the right of reviewers to quote passages of sufficient length to illustrate their criticisms and indicate the quality of the book under review, though not to the extent of materially robbing it of its value as literary property.

A writer of a technical work, such as a medical or legal treatise, usually intends that it be cited and quoted for professional purposes in subsequent works on the same subject.

In interpreting the law the courts look to the nature, quantity, and value of the material used and determine whether its use was unfair to the quoted author. A quotation so large or significant as to injure the worth of the original and in a measure satisfy the market for it is beyond question an infringement. On the other hand, limited extracts in school books and reasonable extracts for reading would not generally be called unfair. However, consideration and courtesy require that if a writer wishes to make any excerpts whatever from a copyrighted work, he should secure permission from the copyright owner to do so.

There is no copyright in ideas or information, only in the form in which they are expressed, but a paraphrase or a condensation, though it may be more freely used than a literal quotation, should be acknowledged.

The author should have secured all necessary permissions before he sends his final copy to the publisher. For short excerpts there is usually no charge, but copyright owners usually require compensation for the use of a poem or story or an extended passage.

Acknowledgments. Usually the owner of a copyright permits the borrower to phrase the credit lines. The borrower can then approximate a uniform style, placing the acknowledgments on the verso of the title page or in a footnote thus:

[1] George Ellis Moore, *A Banner in the Hills* (New York, Appleton-Century-Crofts, 1963), pp. 29–32. Copyright © (year date) by (copyright proprietor).

When a publisher specifies the phrasing to be used in the credit line his instructions must be followed precisely. A chart or table often has a credit line in small type directly below it on the left, or the credit may be set within parentheses directly under the caption. Occasionally it follows the legend. A photograph sometimes has an acknowledgment in small type directly under it at the left, and beside it at the right the photographer's name. (See credits for tables, p. 24, and for cuts, p. 178.)

Securing permission to quote. Written permission must be secured from the owner of the copyright to use copyrighted material, including charts, tables, and illustrations. Some publishers who hold many copyrights have a form which they send to writers who wish to make requests for permission to use excerpts from books on which they hold copyright. One such form requires the following information:

Title of the book to be quoted from
Nature of the work for which the selection is desired
Name of the author or compiler
By whom the book is to be published
The intended time of publication
Selections desired. (These are to be specifically designated by giving the first
   word and the page on which it appears and the last word and the page on
   which it appears.)
Total pages or total lines

Securing a copyright. Copyright for a book, short story, article, or other similar work is secured by the act of publishing the work with the prescribed copyright notice on the copies. Copyright cannot be secured for manuscript book material, which is protected under the common law prior to publication. (Unpublished dramatic works, music, and certain other classes of works may, however, be copyrighted.)

No permission is needed to use the copyright notice; the author or someone authorized by him may place the notice on the work. Whether the author retains the copyright or transfers it to the publisher is a matter for agreement between them. In most cases the publisher attends to the registration of the claim. Promptly after publication two copies of the work, a completed application form, and a $4 fee should be sent to the Register of Copyrights, Library of Congress, Washington, D.C., 20540. "Publication" is generally regarded as the placing on sale, sale, or public distribution of the copies. It does not refer to the method of reproduction, which may be by printing or some other method.

There are a number of different application forms for the various classes of works. Form A is for books manufactured in the United States. There are other forms for books manufactured and published outside the United States. Form B is for periodicals, and Form BB for contributions to periodicals. Application forms may be obtained from the Copyright Office without charge, as well as information and special circulars on subjects such as renewal, the copyright notice, recording assignments, new versions, and the like.

A new copyright cannot be secured for reprints, but a registration may be made for each new version of a work containing substantial new copyrightable material, provided the requirements for the form of the copyright notice are met. Copyright secured for a new version does not extend the term of the original work.

The term of copyright is twenty-eight years, with the privilege of renewing for one more term of twenty-eight years if the renewal is made within the last (twenty-eighth) year of the first term.

Works of United States citizens may be protected in many foreign countries, but the methods for securing protection differ. Copyright is secured in the 46 countries currently parties to the Universal Copyright Convention if all published copies of a work bear the notice prescribed by the Convention, that is, the symbol ©, the name of the copyright owner, and the year date of publication. No registration abroad is necessary to secure copyright. Following publication, the claim to United States copyright should be registered in the Copyright Office in the usual way.

Great Britain and most continental countries are members of the International Union for the Protection of Literary and Artistic Works, better known as the Berne Union. Authors of a country which is not a member of the Union, such as the United States, can secure the rights granted by the Berne conventions, but only if they publish their works first or simultaneously in a country of the Union.

THE LIBEL LAW

What is libelous? "The law recognizes in every man the right to have his reputation unassailed by false and defamatory imputations. A defamatory imputation is one which tends to lower a man in the estimation of right-thinking men, or causes him to be shunned or avoided, or exposes him to hatred, contempt, or ridicule. Such imputation, if conveyed by writing or printed words or by picture or effigy, is called libel." [1]

Libel is a criminal offense for which author, publisher, and printer are liable and for which they may be sued for damages. All three need to be on the alert to avoid violating the law, since suit may be based on the publication of only one or two words that may be judged defamatory.

The general rule is that it is libelous *per se* to impute to a person in his official capacity, profession, trade, or business any kind of fraud, dishonesty,

[1] *International Encyclopedia.*

misconduct, incapacity, or unfitness. In his private capacity a person may not be called immoral, a blasphemer, a hypocrite, a ridiculous person, or by any term which would injure his reputation or social position.

Many derogatory terms are obviously libelous under this rule—*quack, ignoramus, cheat, swindler, smuggler, liar, rogue, perjurer, informer, drunkard, adulterer.* Incapacity, dishonesty, misconduct, and criminality imputed less outspokenly are equally actionable, such as charging infringement of a patent, characterizing a jury verdict as infamous, charging jurors with having done injustice to their oath, imputations on character in allegory or irony, stating in the criticism of a book that the motives of the author are dishonorable or disreputable. No names need be mentioned to make libelous words actionable if the person will be recognized by readers.

A news reporter not keenly aware of the possibilities of violating the libel law might by a careless use of words put his paper in danger of a libel suit. The word *murderer* is libelous until the slayer is convicted. The phrase *the Smith woman* has been judged libelous. A "questionable" check should not be called worthless unless it has been proved in court that it is worthless. A writer might unintentionally commit a libel by using a word without realizing its implications. Or his handwriting might be so poor that typist or compositor might misread a proper name and an innocent person be accused of conviction in a criminal case. A judgment has been given a white man for having been called a Negro, though libel was quite unintended. The reporter wrote of the gentleman as *cultured;* his writing was misread *colored;* a copyreader changed the word to *Negro* to accord with the paper's ruling that Negroes were not to be spoken of as colored people.[2]

It is impossible to include here an exposition of the libel law sufficiently detailed to satisfy the needs of newspaper workers. They are referred to *The Style Book* of the Detroit *News* (1924), pp. 86–94; *Newspaper Desk Work,* by Robert Miller Neal (D. Appleton-Century Company, 1933), pp. 289–307; and for a thoroughgoing study of the law, to *The Law of the Press,* by William G. Hale (West Publishing Company, St. Paul), and *The Law of Newspapers,* by William R. Arthur and Ralph L. Crosman (McGraw-Hill Book Company).

Libel of the dead. "No one may recover damages for a libel of a dead person, but it is a misdemeanor at common law, punishable with fine and imprisonment, to write and publish defamatory matter of any deceased person, provided it be published with a malevolent purpose to injure his family and posterity and to expose them to contempt and disgrace. The malicious intention of the publisher to injure the family and posterity of the deceased must be expressly averred and clearly proved.

[2] *Judge for Yourself!* Albert W. Fribourg and David Stein (New York, The Vanguard Press, Inc., 1934).

"The law attempts to discriminate between the intentional vilifier and the disinterested and accurate historian. Writers of general good repute whose books or articles have been published by reputable publishing houses have seldom been prosecuted even though the work itself may vilify a deceased person." [3]

Right of privacy. "Louis D. Brandeis and Samuel Warren in 1890 contributed an article to the Harvard Law Review in which was developed the legal theory of the right of privacy. The authors asserted the right of individuals, based on analogies drawn from the law of literary property, to protect themselves from unwarranted and objectionable publicity. The law already provided a remedy for defamatory publications, but further protection was felt to be necessary against the publication of articles, pictures, and advertisements which although not defamatory caused either embarrassment or pecuniary loss to the person concerned.

"Publication of pictures violating the right of privacy includes two categories: pictures the publication of which involves pecuniary damage (pictures used in advertising), and pictures which although causing no monetary loss result in embarrassment or notoriety for the subject (news pictures). In four states . . . the courts have recognized a common-law remedy against the unauthorized publication of a picture for advertising purposes." [4]

[3] Fredrick Seaton Siebert, *The Rights and Privileges of the Press* (New York, D. Appleton-Century Company, 1934), pp. 147, 148.

[4] Fredrick Seaton Siebert, *The Rights and Privileges of the Press* (New York, D. Appleton-Century Company, 1934), p. 110.

PART II—TECHNIQUES FOR COPY AND PROOF

MAIN DIVISIONS

TECHNIQUES OF PREPARING COPY

The author who wishes to secure for his work in print the best possible appearance for the least expenditure of time and money will not fail to read the final draft of his manuscript with as much care as if he were reading the proof. By so doing he will avoid the experience of finding in the proof flaws which he would like very much to change but cannot because of the expense involved, he will reduce materially the charge for author's corrections, and he will make his work on the proofs very much easier and less time-consuming. These desirable results are well worth the effort required to make the manuscript as nearly letter-perfect as possible. This does not mean that the typewritten sheets should be as flawless in appearance as the final copy for a typescript book to be printed by the offset process, with no changes whatever indicated. It does mean that when the manuscript is set in type in accordance with the editorial marks and corrections, the proof will be so nearly what the author wants that almost no changes will be needed.

FINAL READING OF THE MANUSCRIPT

Primarily this final reading is a check-up on details of form, rather than of the content, upon which the writer's attention has been centered in all previous reading. He should not expect that the typist will have observed consistency in all details, nor should he expect that the printer will correct "obvious errors." Therefore in this reading he should check the typist's accuracy and his own success in following the style he planned—in spelling, capitalization, abbreviation, and the other details to which his attention has been called in foregoing pages.

61

The spelling and punctuation in quotations should be carefully verified, for such excerpts are set by the printer strictly according to copy. (See pp. 13, 14.)

All formulas and equations should likewise be carefully checked for accuracy. The distinction between capital and small letters should be clear, and Greek letters should be designated as such in the margin. There is often confusion between the small letter l and the figure 1, also between zero and the letter o. The author should be sure that the distinction is clear in the manuscript and also that all subindexes ("subscripts") and exponents ("superscripts" or "superiors") are plainly so marked: B_1, A_2; C^3, C^4. If equations or formulas are to be displayed—that is, centered on a line by themselves—either type the line exactly as it is to appear or else pencil a marginal note of instructions to the printer. Mixed fractions should be clear, so that $1\frac{1}{2}$, for instance, could not be interpreted $11\frac{1}{2}$. (In typewriting the only difference between these is a space between the 1's.) The author should indicate whether fractions are acceptable with a slant or should be set with a horizontal separating line:

$$a/b \text{ or } \frac{a}{b}; \quad 12\frac{2}{7} \text{ or } \frac{12}{7}.$$

The spelling of all foreign words should be noted carefully and all necessary accents marked in.

All lists supposed to be in numerical or alphabetical order should be checked. In short, all necessary checking and verification should be done at this time in order that none will be required when the proofs are being read later.

AUTHOR'S CORRECTIONS

Most of the money spent for author's corrections is money thrown away, as far as the author is concerned, because the changes could have been avoided by reading the manuscript as carefully as proof.

The printer is responsible only for following copy and reproducing it accurately in the type format specified. He is not responsible for consistency in spelling, punctuation, and other details, and if he makes any changes from copy he does so at his own risk. He cannot be held responsible for errors resulting from illegible copy.

Any change from copy made by an author after the manuscript has been set in type is an author's correction and is charged for on a time basis. The cost of changing 10 per cent of the text type is far in excess of 10 per cent of the original cost of composition. Insertion of a comma or one letter in a galley or page of monotype requires respacing of at least one line; in linotype the whole line must be reset and substituted for the old line. The insertion of two or three words might require resetting several lines. Notice the following paragraph, for example. In order to insert five letters in the first line, that line and all following lines in the paragraph must be reset, as is shown.

will furnish future generations∧with a supply of lumber.   *of men* /
There is much land which is unsuited for farming be-
cause of the type of soil or the slope of the land. Usually
land of this type is suitable for reforesting. Trees should
be planted which will do well in each particular type of
soil. The trees should be set in rows to aid future lumbering. At frequent intervals, a firebreak should be made.
This is an open roadway which is kept plowed to prevent the growth of underbrush and weeds. If a fire does
start, it is unable to cross the plowed strip because of the
absence of combustible material.

will furnish future generations of men with a supply of
lumber. There is much land which is unsuited for farming because of the type of soil or the slope of the land.
Usually land of this type is suitable for reforesting. Trees
should be planted which will do well in each particular
type of soil. The trees should be set in rows to aid future
lumbering. At frequent intervals, a firebreak should be
made. This is an open roadway which is kept plowed to
prevent the growth of underbrush and weeds. If a fire
does start, it is unable to cross the plowed strip because of
the absence of combustible material.

A correction like this made in a galley of type is expensive. If such a correction were made in type that had already been made up in pages, the expense would be much greater, especially if more than one page had to be handled. The remedy in the above case is to re-write and re-word the first two lines—as is indicated.

will furnish future generations of men with a supply of
lumber. There is much land unsuited for farming, be-

Corrections in electrotype plates are very expensive. Even a slight change requires resetting part or all of the line, reading, casting, cutting the incorrect part out of the plate and inserting the new piece. A correction that causes a change of more than a line is correspondingly expensive, besides seriously weakening the plate.

A certain amount of changing is unavoidable in making a book, and the publisher makes provision for it in his contract with the author. A percentage (sometimes 10 per cent) of the original cost of composition is commonly allowed the author for corrections, and the publisher ordinarily assumes the cost of arranging type beside narrow cuts, of adding or deleting to make pages the right length, and of other special adjustments.

EDITORIAL MARKS

Editors and proofreaders use certain marks and abbreviations that are universally understood by printers. Everyone who prepares manuscript for printing or who marks proofs should conform to these established methods.

Capitals and small letters. To indicate that a small letter—always called lower-case[1] letter by printers—is to be capitalized, draw three lines under it. If a capital is to be set lower case, draw an oblique line through it.

Small capitals are the shape of capitals but only the height of lower-case letters. They are indicated by two-line underscoring.

The abbreviations for the forms noted above are *caps* (capitals), *l.c.* (lower case), *sm. c.* or *s.c.* (small capitals), *c. & l.c.* (capitals and lower case, "cap-and-lower"), *c. & sm.* or *c. & s.c.* (capitals and small capitals, "cap-and-small").

Italic and boldface. Italic is indicated by single underscoring, boldface by wavy underscoring.

Paragraphs. Paragraphs may be indicated by a paragraph mark (¶). The newspaper copyreader uses a downstroke with a right-angle turn.

If typewritten copy has a paragraph where none is necessary, a connecting run-in line may be used.

Insertions. If a letter or word is to be inserted in a line, make a caret ($_\wedge$) at the point of insertion and write the word above it if there is room, otherwise in the margin. If anything is written in the margin, write it horizontally across the margin as nearly opposite the caret as possible.

Avoid writing on copy lengthwise of the margin if possible, but if it must be done, always write upward from the line in which the correction is made. The reason for this is simple. On typesetting machines there is a copy holder that works somewhat like the paper holder on a typewriter. A sheet of copy is inserted and a little wheel at the end is turned until the first line just shows above the front edge of the holder. When the line has been set, the copy is turned up until the next line shows. If, then, a correction runs below the level of the line, the sheet of copy must be rolled up until all of the correction is revealed, then afterward rolled back to position. All these extra movements waste the typesetter's time. Never use staples on copy.

Circle instructions written in the margin if there is any possibility of their being mistaken as part of the copy.

Deletions. If anything in the copy is to be omitted, erase it or mark through it unmistakably; do not enclose it in brackets or parentheses.

If a hyphen is deleted, use close-up marks ($\bigcirc$) or a space mark ($\#$) to indicate whether the word is to be one word or two.

[1] For the origin of this term see page 547.

Restorations. If words have been crossed out by mistake, place dots under the words that should remain and write *stet* in the margin opposite. *Stet* is a Latin imperative meaning "Let it stand."

Indentions. Mark matter that is to be indented by using the sign for an em space ($\square$) before the line to be indented.

Alignment. Alignment is indicated by a line drawn downward beside the characters to be set in line. Horizontal alignment is indicated in a similar manner.

Spaces. A straight line down between letters indicates a space; and curves above and below a space mean to close up spaces incorrectly placed.

Transpositions. To transpose adjacent letters, words, or phrases draw a line over one and under the other.

Abbreviations. A circle around an abbreviation or number means that it should be spelled out. Such a ring is said to mean "Use the other style"; therefore a number spelled out may be circled to indicate that figures are to be used. This use of a ring, however, is not common, and the change can often be made more clearly by crossing out the incorrect form and writing the correct form above.

Superiors and inferiors. Figures, letters, or symbols that are to be set above or below the line—called superiors or superscripts, inferiors or subscripts—often require special indication in the manuscript. This need not be carried to the excess of marking asterisks, daggers, the symbols for degrees, minutes, seconds, and the like, which are always above the line.

Superior letters and figures are best indicated by typing a "shelf," but not all typists are acquainted with this device. The superior is underscored and followed by a stroke (see Figure 1).

Hyphens and dashes. When it seems advisable to mark a hyphen or a dash so that it will not be taken for some other mark, indicate a hyphen by two short lines—a double hyphen—and a dash by drawing a line down each side of the dash.

A 2-em dash is marked by a 2 above the dash and *m* under it.

Peculiar spellings. Spellings so unusual or peculiar that the editor or proofreader might question their accuracy should be verified and stet marks (a series of dots) placed under them.

WORKERS ON COPY AND PROOF

After the writer of a book has sent his manuscript to the publisher, he will be obliged to wait some time for the processes of manufacture to get under way. (It is assumed that the manuscript has been contracted for and there is no question of acceptance or refusal.) During this period the editor will read the manuscript critically and attend to the numerous details of manufacture that are his responsibility. Another reading will then be given the manuscript by a copyreader, with attention to typographical details and preparation for the printer. As soon as practicable the manuscript, now spoken of as "copy," will be sent to the printer, who will have it set in type and read before sending proofs to the publisher, who will in turn send a set to the author.

If the author has a clear picture of the responsibilities of those who work on his manuscript and proofs, he will understand why he has to wait so long for his first proofs. The following paragraphs are intended to give him that picture.

THE EDITOR [1]

The editor's first reading of a manuscript is critical of content, appraising its value, detecting its weaknesses and its strong points, judging its literary style and the skill, or lack of it, shown in the assembling of the subject matter. He will look at the book also from the standpoint of marketability. His acquaintance with the books of other publishers on the same or similar subjects may lead him to suggest changes in scope or emphasis. Expansion of some parts and simplification of others may seem to him desirable. He may, indeed, advise rewriting of large portions.

Should the editor find that the manuscript is substantially satisfactory, his next task may be to decide upon all the details of format—size and bulk of the book, paper, binding, dimensions of the printed page, and similar matters. (In some offices the production department or the designer decides upon details of format, sometimes in consultation with editorial, sales, and advertising departments.) If the book contains illustrations, all the questions relating to them must be answered. For the use of the copyreader the editor will then indicate the form of headings, quoted matter, tables, footnotes, and the like, and his preference in all the details of style.

With all format and type styles decided upon, the manuscript will be read again, with attention focused this time not on the larger aspects of content and arrangement, but on details, both of what the author has written and of how he has expressed it. In this critical reading the editor will make sure that no libelous remarks have been made and that there are no infringements of copyrights or trade-marks. He will see to it that the sensibilities of the readers of the book have been respected and not unnecessarily offended. Local prejudices will be kept in mind and respected whenever possible.

[1] An interesting book on the subject of the manuscript editor's work is *Editor at Work*, by Julie Eidesheim (New York: Farrar & Rinehart, Inc., 1929).

The editor considers thoughtfully all factual details, and is alert at all times to inaccuracies and conflicting statements. Geographical features must be carefully checked, an exacting task in some books. Classical, historical, and literary references may be inexact and must be scrutinized. Dates and all references or statements in which there is a time element must be examined with care

The application of familiar expressions must be checked for correctness since the exact meaning of such expressions is often not clearly understood by authors. For example, "the devil to pay," signifying a hopeless situation, a virtual impossibility, is often inaccurately used. A similar fault is often observed in the use of foreign phrases. *Vice versa* is a common term that needs watching because it is often used carelessly. The propriety of using non-English words is often questionable. Some writers in English like to use foreign words, and they do so with no apparent regard for the exasperation they cause many readers, whose education has not included enough foreign-language study to enable them to recognize the meaning of these words. Whenever an equally expressive English word can be substituted, it should be.

The whole matter of expression, indeed, is carefully considered by the editor in his critical reading. More quickly than the author himself, the editor will notice a habit of using clichés, and of repeating pet expressions. He will be quickly aware of an overabundance of elliptical phrases, of too frequent use of *but* at the beginning of sentences, of shifts from third person to second where parallel construction would be preferable. In short, the diction, grammar, and rhetoric of the writer are subject to critical inspection. The editor has learned from experience that the possibilities of error are limitless, and he does not expect the author to have detected his minor blunders.

At the same time that he is noting carefully what and how the author has written, the editor must keep printing conventions in mind. His experience with the work of many writers has shown him in general the sort of inaccuracies he may find. He knows that tables are often not constructed to the best advantage; that footnotes and bibliographical references are often incomplete; that cross references are not always in the most desirable form. It is better, for instance, to write, if possible, "in Figure 1" than "in the illustration above."

Last but not least he must examine the illustrations, since unusual and unexpected inconsistencies are often discovered in them. They must show exactly what text and legends say they show. For instance, if a character is described in text as wearing eyeglasses, he should not be shown in an illustration wearing spectacles; if he is described as short, he should not be pictured taller than a companion; if his face is scarred, he should not be shown without a blemish. Drawings sometimes show surprising inaccuracies, such as cows being milked from the left, or horses mounted from the right. The Western bad man shooting his single gun with his left hand, or the farmer driving with the reins in his right hand, whip in the left, might be left-handed, but so drawing them is questionable. Such minor matters as these must be detected.

No single book would bring all these problems to the editor, but in the course of his work he would meet them all more or less often. Many of them are specifically considered in following pages.

THE COPYREADER

To the person inexperienced with book manufacturing it would seem that after all the reading and preparation described in foregoing pages a manuscript should certainly be ready for the printer. The copyreader knows otherwise. Enough remains to require his concentrated attention and painstaking care to complete his work satisfactorily. He is probably the last one who will see the book as a whole until it is completed. From him it will go to the printer, who may give it to several different compositors to set in type, and to different proofreaders to read. Half a dozen typesetters and proofreaders cannot keep to one style; therefore it will not be satisfactory to write "Capitalize this throughout," "Italicize when so used"; the style must be carefully marked from beginning to end.

The copyreader will have received from the editor, along with the manuscript, a schedule of the types to be used for text, extracts, footnotes, tables, and headings, and instructions about any special forms called for. He will be held responsible for marking the copy throughout in accordance with this schedule. He will see that chapters, sections, numbered tables and illustrations, and other numerical sequences are in order; that footnotes and bibliographies follow a style consistently. He will note throughout the use of italics, abbreviations, figures, capitals, and other details and correct any inconsistencies.

At the same time he is expected to read the text with care. He will make sure that proper names are spelled correctly, that dates are accurate, that quotations from Scripture and from classical works have been copied correctly. Realizing the multiplicity of details the editor had on his mind, the copyreader does not expect that he will have noticed all errors, and will be alert himself to detect what the editor may have overlooked.

THE PROOFREADER

Not the least important of those workers who help to make a book is the proofreader in the printing office. It is next to impossible for the average worker to set type without making errors that need correction. No person not a printer could possibly imagine the numberless ways in which typographical composition is liable to error. The book printer therefore finds it necessary to employ trained proofreaders to detect such typographical errors and to mark them for correction.

Typographical errors. It has been said in a foregoing paragraph that the printer is responsible only for reproducing the copy accurately, whether the copy is correct or not. Of first importance, therefore, in the mind of the printer, is the detection of poor spacing, imperfect letters, crooked lines, protruding spaces, letters of wrong style or size ("wrong fonts"), transpositions, inverted letters, missing letters, "outs" (a word or words omitted), "doublets" (a word or words set twice), and wrong indentions. Next come the misspelled words, of which there are two classes: first, such spellings as *ecstacy, sieze, her's, childrens'*; second, such errors as *stationery* instead of *stationary, therefore* for *therefor*. To detect the first calls for spelling ability and a quick and accurate eye; to catch the second requires a mind alert to the meaning of what is being read.

Style. The extent to which the proofreader in the printing office may exercise the editorial functions involved in correcting punctuation, capitalization, and other details of style depends on the kind of work and the policy of the office. In some offices the pressure of the machine for more and faster production has deprived him of most of his editorial privileges; nothing is expected of him but typographical accuracy. In others the proofreader still retains the responsibilities common to him in the recent past, as outlined in following paragraphs.

The proofreader is usually cautioned not to quibble over punctuation, for that exasperates the printer, the publisher, and the author, which the reader ought never to do. He is told that if the use or non-use of a comma can be justified by any recognized rule of punctuation, no change should be made; and that particular care should be taken not to change the meaning of a sentence, as can so easily be done, oftentimes, by changing the punctuation.

The reader should correct or query improper capitalization, irregular compoundings, wrong paragraphing, and inconsistencies of spelling. As to inconsistencies of style he should exercise judgment and discretion. He should ask himself if the inconsistencies are sufficiently obvious to justify the expense of changing. It is generally understood that if spelling is inconsistent and the order specifies a particular dictionary to be followed, he must change all spellings not conforming; but if the order is to follow copy, all the reader can do is to call the inconsistencies to the attention of the author.

Grammar and rhetoric. The proofreader should catch errors in grammar: disagreement of verb with subject, failure of a pronoun to refer clearly to its antecedent, the fragmentary sentence, and so on. The incomplete sentence is often caused by changes in the original copy. All such errors as these should be called to the attention of the author, in other words, "queried." The proofreader may correct or query such common errors as the use of two *that*'s where only one should be used; and tautological expressions like *funeral obsequies, present incumbent, first beginning.*

THE COPYHOLDER

The printer's proofreader reads galley proofs with the help of a copyholder; the author will find it advisable to do likewise. The copyholder is the proof-reader's eyes as far as the copy is concerned, and the most important requirement is that he be accurate. He reads aloud from the copy as the reader follows on the proof, and it is essential that he read exactly what is in the copy. This requires painstaking care. It is, for instance, easy indeed to read *judicial* for *juridical,* or *alteration* for *alternation.* The typesetter may have made the same error, and the proofreader may not notice by the sense that the expression is imperfect.

The copyholder should read in a low but distinct voice, being attentive to the wishes of the proofreader and pausing momentarily to allow him to make corrections upon the proof. However, the reading should run along smoothly. Some copyholders are jerky readers. This jerkiness can be overcome by training the eyes to move one or two words ahead of the tongue; that is, as one starts to speak a word, the eyes should be on the next, telegraphing it to the brain so that one is ready to say it when the preceding word is done. The copyholder should not read in a deadly monotone, pausing for breath without any regard to punctuation, for such reading is difficult to follow. He should remember that the proofreader must grasp the sense of what he is reading, as well as the details of phrasing. Therefore, he should drop his voice at the end of a sentence, pause slightly at commas, and at all times read understandingly.

Reading practices. The copyholder's manner of reading is somewhat different from that of ordinary reading. Much more is required of him than simply reading words. Italics, boldface, and capitals must be clearly denoted, and most of the punctuation read. In order to read accurately, the copyholder must be able to interpret correctly the marks and abbreviations used in editing and proofreading. (These are described and explained on pages 64, 65, 74.) In order to read efficiently he must know the shortened forms familiar to all proofreaders and how and when to use them.

Reading type and punctuation. The shortened forms used in designating type and punctuation are listed alphabetically below. Boldface and italic words should be indicated, but not roman unless they appear in the midst of boldface or italic type. Paragraphing should be mentioned. Punctuation marks should be named with the exception of obvious uses of the period and the comma. For instance, *U.S.S.R.* should *not* be read "U point S point S point R point," nor should *New York, N. Y.* be read "New York com, N point Y point"; nor *John A. Doe* be read "John A point Doe"; nor *May 6, 1942* be read "May six com, nineteen forty-two." If commonly used punctuation is omitted, the fact should be mentioned; for example, the symbol *USSR* should be read "U S S R no points." The hyphen should not be read in words that are always spelled with a hyphen, like *twenty-five, sister-in-law.*

TERM	COPYHOLDER'S SHORT FORM
apostrophe	pos
boldface	bold
capital	cap
capitals and lower case	cap-and-lower
capitals and small capitals	cap-and-small
colon	colon
comma	com
diphthong	diph
ellipsis points	ellipsis, *or* three points
exclamation point	exclam
hyphen	hyph
italic	ital
paragraph	para
parenthesis	paren, close paren
period	point
question mark	query
quotation marks	quote, close quote
semicolon	sem
two-em dash	choke

Reading names. Any variation from the common form of spelling a name should be told the reader. For instance, *Laurence* should be read "Laurence with a u," because otherwise the reader will suppose it is spelled *Lawrence.* Similarly, "Elisabeth with an s." Many names can be so pronounced as to indicate their spelling: "Pī-erce," for *Pierce;* "Sawnders," for *Saunders,* "Sanders" for *Sanders;* "Wim" for *Wm.* Most readers have other shortcuts if they read a great many names.

Reading numbers. Numbers should be read as clearly and concisely as possible. "One sixty-five" is the proper way to read 165, not "one hundred and sixty-five"; "four o eight" for 408, not "four hundred and eight." A four-figure number in which no comma is used should be read in twos: "twenty-six forty-five" for 2645, but "two, six forty-five" for 2,645. A number of five or more figures should be broken at the comma: "three eighty-nine, one fifty-six" (389,156). If the figure preceding the comma is a cipher—as in 30,156—the number is better read "three o, one fifty-six," so that it cannot be mistaken for "thirty-one fifty-six (3156). Some proofreaders like the commas read in numbers of four or more figures, but this seems unnecessary. Fractions are read with the word *over* or *slant*: $\frac{4}{5}$ is "four over five," $\frac{4}{5}$ is "four slant five." An expression of proportion should be clear to anyone if it is read normally: 2:3::4:6 is "two is to three as four is to six." Roman numerals are read by the letters of which they are composed; that is, III is read "three i's" (not "three"); LXXIV is called "l, two x's, i, v (not "seventy-four"). Since the capitalized form is the common one, the lower-case form is the one specifically designated.

Reading accents and signs. Accents and signs must be recognized and accurately named.

Accent or Sign	Copyholder's Term
acute (´)	acute
grave (`)	grave
circumflex (^)	circum *or* flex
tilde (˜)	tilde *or* Spanish
cedilla (ˌ)	soft
macron (¯)	long
breve (˘)	short
dieresis (¨)	di
(¹)	mod
(°)	circle
asterisk	star (*not* sup asterisk)
superior figure	sup (2/ is sūp 2)
inferior figure	sub (₂ is sŭb 2)
foot or minute (')	prime
inch or second (")	double prime
multiplication sign	mul
division sign	div
per cent sign	per sign
cents (¢)	cut c
per, shilling (/)	slant
thousand (M̶)	canceled M
dollar sign ($)	dollar
pound sign (£)	pound

Application of methods. The foregoing instructions may be more clearly understood by comparing the two paragraphs below with the paragraphs as they should be read by a copyholder.

B.C. and A.D. (for *before Christ* and *anno Domini*).—Set in small capitals, with no space between the letters. Place date before the letters: 14 B.C., 28 A.D.

Company.—Abbreviate *company* in firm names when preceded by "short and" (ampersand), as: *Harris, Forbes & Co.* Spell out *company* in names of corporations, as: *Jordan Marsh Company* (unless, as rarely happens, the abbreviation *Co.* is the corporation's approved form of signature and imprint).

As the copyholder would read them: "B.C. and A.D., all bold, paren, for before Christ, two ital, and anno cap Domini, two ital, close paren, point dash. Set in small capitals, com, with no space between the letters. Place date before the letters, colon, fourteen B.C., small caps, com, twenty-eight A.D., small caps.

"Para company, one bold, point dash. Abbreviate company, one ital, in firm names when preceded by quote short and, close quote, paren, ampersand, close paren, com, as, colon, Harris, com, Forbes short and Co, four ital. Spell out company, one ital, in names of corporations, com, as, colon, Jordan Marsh Company, three ital, paren, unless, com, as rarely happens, com, the abbreviation cap Co, one ital, is the corporation pos s approved form of signature and imprint, close paren, point."

TECHNIQUES FOR READING PROOF

PROOFREADER'S MARKS

The proofreader uses many of the editorial marks mentioned on pages 64, 65 and several others applicable only to proofs. Every correction in a proof must be indicated in the margin; therefore each one requires two marks, one within the page and one in the margin. The one within the page is usually a caret or a line indicating where the correction is to be made. See Figure 13.

THE AUTHOR'S READING OF PROOF

Galley proofs. The first proofs to come to the author will ordinarily be in strips called galley proofs or galleys. (A simple text that has been well prepared may be made up into pages before proofs are sent to the author, an economical and time-saving procedure which could be adopted more generally if authors could be persuaded to prepare their copy for printing with painstaking care.) He will receive two sets, a marked set—sometimes spoken of as the master proof—and a duplicate set. He is expected to read the galley proofs with care, checking them against the copy just as the proofreader does. He will find his reading easier if he adopts the methods of reading used by

STANDARD PROOF MARKS

✗	Defective letter	⊙	Colon	no ¶	No paragraph
⊥	Push down space	;/	Semicolon	wf	Wrong font letter
9	Turn over	V	Apostrophe	stet.	Let it stand
ℛ	Take out	V̂	Quotation	tr.	Transpose
∧	Insert at this point	-/	Hyphen	Caps	Capitals
⩗	Space evenly	///	Straighten lines	S.C.	Small capitals
✳	Insert space	⊏	Move over	l.c.	Lower-case letter
⌣	Less space	▢	Em quad space	ital.	Italic
◠	Close up entirely	|—¹—|	One-em dash	Rom	Roman letter
⊙	Period	|—²—|	Two-em dash	(?)	Verify
,/	Comma	¶	Make paragraph	○	Spell out

EXAMPLE OF MARKED PROOF

Printing Educates

tr ⊥ — Even if none of thees boys should ever follow the craft — e/✗
⊥ — of the printer in years to come, the education that they — ,/
wf — get in this department will prove of real value in prac- —
ℛ — tical life, whatever life of occpation or profession they — n/u
9 — may later choose. The printing trade isa thoroughly prac- — #
— tical school of education in itself/ It provides practical — ⊙/Cap.
— lessons in the principles of language, composition, punc- —
— tuation, and other every day exercises, in addition to the — ◡
— vast fund of general knowledge which passes under the —
l.c. — Worker's observation.   ...An excerpt from an editorial
in the Portland Press Herald. ⊢—⊣ —ital.

Courtesy of American Type Founders

Fig. 13

the proofreader and copyholder in the printing office, as described in the foregoing sections.

Marking proofs. The marked set of proof should be used by the author when he reads. At the top of the galley may be words and numbers not a part of the text. These may be circled, but never should be obliterated. They have significance for the printer, and he will not fail to discard them when he makes up the pages.[1]

It is necessary to use ink of a different color from that of any markings already on the proofs so that the author's alterations will be clearly distinguishable from the printer's errors. Corrections should always be marked in the margin, because a correction written within the page with no mark in the margin is more than likely not to be noticed by the printer. If more than one error occurs in a certain line, the corrections in the margin should always read from left to right. That is, if two or more corrections are written in the left margin, the first one should be written far enough to the left so that the next one can be written to the right of it. The conventional proofreading marks shown on page 74 should be used.

New material and insertions of more than one line should be typed, and the place of insertion clearly indicated, so that the typesetter, the corrector, and the reviser will not lose time deciphering handwriting. Small slips bearing insertions should never be pinned to proofs because they are likely to get lost; they may be pasted *on* the margin but not *to* it.

Correction. Proofs are pulled on cheap paper on a hand press. They should be clear and good, but they are never so clear-cut as the final printing will be. It is therefore a waste of time for the author to bother about evenness of printing. Rows of crosses opposite a line in which the type looks broken are useless and really defeat their purpose.

The author's attention in reading should be directed to accuracy of the content, rather than to literals—that is, typographical errors. He should verify carefully all unusual or less well known names, all tables and numerical calculations and formulas, and the spelling and division of foreign words and phrases. He should not make any changes in style, form of abbreviations, or like details without consulting the publisher. He may make only changes that are necessary or that are of vital importance. If he makes an addition, he should try to make a compensating deletion, thus lessening the expense of the change.

General directions, such as to spell a word a specified way throughout, or

---

[1] Arranging type matter in pages, inserting illustrations, running heads, and folios, and placing footnotes in position is termed "makeup" in the printing office. The workman who "makes up" pages is a "makeup man."

"All instances like this should be arranged as here marked," should not be given by the author on the proof. The only way he can be sure of obtaining the form desired is to mark each instance himself. Blanket orders to the printers are commonly not carried out.

Queries. *Qy., Qu.,* or a circled question mark is the proofreader's way of calling the author's attention to a particular detail which it seems to him might be a slip. The author should read carefully the passage questioned and answer the queries. If the change suggested meets with approval and he wishes it made, he should cross off the question mark or *Qy.;* if the change is not to be made, he should cross out the entire query, so that there will be no doubt about what he wants. It is not enough to write simply *O.K.,* because it is not always clear what is O.K. For instance, suppose the query is *?/tr,* and the author simply writes *O.K.* The printer will not know whether he means "The phrase is O.K. as it is," or "All right, make the transposition."

The author should never erase any marks made in the margin by the printer or publisher. If they indicate a change that is not desired, they should be crossed through and the words "O.K. as set," or similar phrasing, written in the margin.

Under no circumstances whatever should any change be marked on the copy after it has been to the printer.

Illustrations. Illustrations that are numbered will be inserted by the printer as near the point of reference as the limitations of makeup will allow. If an illustration *must* be inserted in a given paragraph, however, the fact should be clearly indicated on the galley proof.

Some publishers submit to the author a "cut dummy"—proofs of all illustrations, pasted on sheets of uniform size, with the figure numbers in the lower corner. The author should transfer from the original drawings to the cut dummy the figure numbers and titles for the cuts; and should mark here also all corrections to be made in the illustrations. These cut dummies should be returned with the corresponding corrected galleys.

Return of proofs. The marked set of proof, together with the corresponding copy, should be returned as promptly as possible to the publisher. The duplicate set should be retained.

Page proofs.[2] Page proofs are sent to the author principally for the verification of cuts and captions, for the adjustment of long or short pages, for filling in of page numbers in cross references, table of contents, and list of illustrations, and for the making of an index. These proofs also are on cheap paper, pulled on a hand press. The author should not be disturbed because

---

[2] See pages 152–156 for rules governing makeup of pages.

the pages do not line up, are not square on the paper, or vary in heaviness of impression.

Revision. In printing terminology, revising is the process of comparing a proof with a previous proof of the same matter to see if all corrections marked on the earlier proof have been made accurately. Page proofs are always revised in the printing office, and the printer is responsible for accuracy in correcting, but the author will do well to revise his page proofs carefully, at the same time checking the headings at the top of each page ("running heads") and the folios (page numbers). (See p. 117.) It should be remembered that in linotype composition a whole line must be reset for a change of a single letter, and in correcting one mistake another is sometimes made elsewhere in the line.

Long and short pages. A new page should not begin with a short tag-end remnant of a paragraph; try instead to bring forward one or more full lines from the preceding page. The last page of a chapter should have at least four lines on it; a heading should always have at least two lines under it on the same page. It is not always possible to secure pages of the right length without changing the wording slightly. If the makeup man in the printing office finds it impossible to adjust the length by changing the spacing around headings, he may mark the page long or short; in a short page he may insert a turned slug at the end of a paragraph. This will show in the proof as a wide black line. If the author can conveniently add enough near the end of the paragraph to "gain a line," the correction of the short page will be simplified for the printer. Otherwise when the pages are returned to him he will have to space the words more widely as far back in the paragraph as will be necessary to force at least four letters into the next line. Similarly, a page marked long can sometimes be corrected by crowding back a word or two. The author will make the printer's work easier and save time and expense if he will make some change near the end of the paragraph which will "gain a line" or "lose a line" as needed.

Cuts, etc. The printer will have inserted the illustrations and the larger tables in the pages as near to the point designated by the author or editor as the type will allow. The author should verify their position and their titles and such phrases in the text referring to them as "in the figure above," "on the next page," "opposite," "below." When a narrow illustration is inserted in a type page it is desirable to have the type form an even frame around it. Sometimes a paragraph ends beside the illustration so that the even outline is broken. The author can then, often, add a word or two to fill the blank space and thus improve the appearance of the page. (For printing conventions relative to the placement of illustrations on the page, see p. 155.)

Front matter. When the page proofs are received, all folios can be filled in. Therefore the table of contents and the list of illustrations can be completed. For linotype books these are not generally set until the folios can be inserted. All front-matter pages should be read with particular care, especially the title page and the copyright page.

Return of proof. It is advisable to keep all the page proof until the index has been prepared, work which should be started as soon as the first page proofs are received. Inconsistencies of spelling or statement often come to light during the index work, and if all the page proofs are at hand, corrections can be indicated. As promptly as possible a complete set of page proofs should be returned to the publisher. Return of the page proofs indicates to him that the book is "O.K. for press." The author should not thereafter ask for any further changes.

PART III—TYPOGRAPHY AND ILLUSTRATION

MAIN DIVISIONS

THE MECHANICS OF PRINTING

Any person dealing with printers should have a sufficient knowledge of type and its use to be able to give intelligent directions. Editors should be well-informed in such matters, for their problems sometimes include kind of composition (linotype or monotype), style of face (old style or modern), size of page. Necessary for intelligent decisions is a knowledge of the working materials of printing, how they are used, how they are measured, and their adaptability.[1]

---

[1] For more detail on type and its uses, printing tools and methods, see a good text on printing like one of the following: *Practice of Printing,* by R. W. Polk (Peoria, Illinois: Manual Arts Press, 1926); *Printing for School and Shop,* by F. S. Henry (New York, John

TYPE

Movable types are now made of an alloy of lead, tin, and antimony. Lead is used in the greatest proportion, but would be too soft used alone. Tin is added to give toughness and to form a union of all the metals; antimony gives hardness and has the peculiar property of expanding, rather than contracting, upon solidification.

Type that is to be used more than once is made of a harder alloy than is used by the monotype or linotype machines, which cast type in the composing room. After machine-set type has been used for printing or casting, it is remelted and prepared for re-use.

Typesetting methods. Type may be set by hand or by machine. Two machine systems are in wide use, the monotype and the linotype. The monotype system requires two machines—one a keyboard by means of which a paper roll is perforated to correspond to type characters, the other a casting machine (commonly called a caster) which casts each character as a separate piece of type. The operation of the caster is automatic, guided by the perforated roll, casting each character in its proper order and each line to its proper measure (width), requiring only occasional attention from the machinist attendant. Corrections of monotype are made by hand, incorrect letters being replaced by letters taken from a type case containing the font, omitted words set by hand and inserted, and so forth.

The Linotype machine (and the Intertype which resembles it) composes type molds (brass matrices) of letters into lines from which solid slugs or lines of type are cast, the whole operation taking place in one machine. Corrections are made by resetting and recasting the entire line in which the error occurs. No matter how slight the correction, the whole line must be reset.

The monotype is especially adapted to tabular composition where it is necessary to use column rules and box headings. Involved formulas, equations, and the like are usually composed to better advantage by monotype. (Some very skilled linotype operators are able to set such matter quite well. A comparison of prices, with the factor of corrections taken into consideration, is often advisable before making a decision as to which method of composition is most advantageous.)

The linotype, largely by reason of its greater speed in turning out finished composition, is best adapted to newspaper and magazine work and any straight matter in which no great amount of resetting will be required. As a rule, foreign language matter is best composed by monotype, although there

Wiley & Sons, 1917); *Hand Composition,* by Hugo Jahn (New York, John Wiley & Sons, 1931); *Introduction to Typography,* by Philip Van Doren Stern (New York, Harper & Brothers, 1932).

are some linotype operators able to do excellent work of this nature and they will argue this point with some merit.

All composition, whether hand or machine, requires *justification,* which is the accurate, uniform spacing of lines of type. In hand composition this is accomplished by the insertion of spaces and quads. The linotype (and inter-type) perform this operation automatically through the use of space-bands, which are wedge-shaped, and are dropped between the matrices. Justification of monotype lines is provided for, also automatically, as it is being keyboarded and the proper spaces are cast with each line.

PARTS OF A PRINTING TYPE

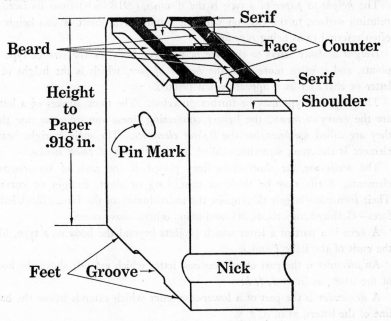

Courtesy of American Type Founders

FIG. 14

Parts of a type. (See Figure 14.) The *face* of a type is the printing surface, which stands in relief on the upper end of the type.

The *body,* or *shank,* is all that part below the raised portion.

The *feet* of a type are the parts (the base) on which it stands, and they are formed by the *groove,* which runs across the lower end of the type.

The *shoulder* is the space on the upper end of the body above or below the outline of the face.

The *neck,* or *beard,* is the slope between the face and shoulder.

The *counter* is the depression between the lines of the face.

The *pin mark* is a small round depression in the side of the body, sometimes enclosing figures denoting the size.

The *nick* is a notch across the body of a type on the side which is uppermost when type is set. There may be one to four, variously grouped, no two fonts of the same size being marked alike. The nick serves the compositor as a guide in setting and enables him to distinguish between the different fonts when he is returning used type to the type cases ("distributing").

The *height to paper* of a type is the distance (.918 inch) from its face, or printing surface, to the base on which it stands. An object of this height is often referred to as being *type-high.*

Height of body refers to the size of the type body, or the size of type in points, and is often more than the *height of face,* which is the height of a letter or character as it appears when printed.

The face of a type may be further dissected. The thick strokes of a letter are the *heavy elements;* the lighter connecting lines, sometimes so fine that they are called *hairlines,* are the *lighter elements.* The main upright heavy element is the *stem,* sometimes called the *body mark* or *thick stroke.*

The *serifs* are the short cross lines placed at the ends of unconnected elements. Serifs may be thick or thin, long or short, straight or curved. Their formation largely determines the individuality of the face. Block-letter faces—Gothic, Sans-serif, Kabel, and many others—have none.

A *kern* is a part of a letter which projects beyond the body of a type, like the ends of the italic *f* and *j.*

An *ascender* is the part of a lower-case letter which extends above the body of the letter, as in *b, d, f, h.*

A *descender* is the part of a lower-case letter which extends below the base line of the letters, as in *q, p, y.*

A type font. A font of type is an assortment of types of one body-size and one style of face. Fonts vary in size from a job font, containing the smallest practicable assortment, to a font for intricate composition requiring accented letters, signs, and symbols. For machine composition printers require fonts of matrices (type molds), and such fonts include the companion italic. The less frequently used types are called side sorts, or peculiars.

An ordinary font of roman type for book work contains the following:

Capitals: A to Z, Æ, Œ
Small capitals: A to z, Æ, Œ

Lower case: a to z, æ, œ, fi, ff, fl, ffi, ffl
Accented or specially marked letters: á, à, â, ä, é, è, ê, ë, í, ì, î, ï, ó, ò, ô, ö, ú, ù, û, ü, ç, ñ
Figures: 0 1 2 3 4 5 6 7 8 9
Solid fractions: ⅛, ¼, ⅜, ½, ⅝, ¾, ⅞
Superior figures: ⁰ ¹ ² ³ ⁴ ⁵ ⁶ ⁷ ⁸ ⁹
Punctuation marks: . , ; : ' ' " " ? ! ( ) [ ] - – —
Reference marks: * † ‡ § ‖ ¶
Signs: &, $, ¢, %, ♯, ℔, @, /
Spacing material: 5-em, 4-em (thin), 3-em [2] (thick), and en (nut) spaces; em, 2-em, 3-em, and 4-em quads.

Ligatures. Some fonts do not contain the ligatures fi, ff, fl, ffi, ffl, sometimes inaccurately called logotypes; others contain these and several others besides.

Spacing material. The quads are used to fill out a short line. The spaces are of five different thicknesses; alone or in combination, therefore, they are adequate to space any line to the required width. (See sections on spacing, pp. 109, 110. For spacing between lines see Leading, p. 109.)

Fractions. Fractions are of three kinds: solid, piece, and adaptable. A solid fraction is a single type, and fonts usually include the simple fractions listed above. A piece fraction, also called a split or built fraction, is in two parts:

1 2 3 4 5 6 7 8 9 0 ₁ ₂ ₃ ₄ ₅ for the horizontal form; or

¹⁄ ²⁄ ³⁄ ⁴⁄ ⁵⁄ ⁶⁄ ⁷⁄ ⁸⁄ ⁹⁄ ⁄₁ ⁄₂ ⁄₃ ⁄₄ ⁄₅ ⁄₆ ⁄₇ ⁄₈ ⁄₉ ⁄₀ for the diagonal form.

With these parts fractions of any size can be made: ½ ⁴⁹⁄₅₀ ⁴⁴⁹⁄₁₀₀₀ ⅘ (If a comma were inserted in the denominator of a horizontal fraction, the separating rule would be broken.) Large fractions can also be set with separate types for numerator, slant, and denominator: 25/53. Such fractions are the easiest to set because they require the least hand work.

Superior figures. Superior figures are used for various purposes, but principally as references to footnotes and as exponents. As references, except in German composition, they follow all marks of punctuation except the dash. In other uses they precede punctuation.

... per in.[2], or 49.
... in *Golden Bough* [5]. (In bibliographies, meaning the 5th edition.)
See *aery* [2]. (A dictionary reference to the second meaning given for *aery*.)

Reference marks. The star, dagger, double dagger, section mark, parallels, and paragraph mark, in the order given, are often used as references to foot-

---

[2] More accurate terms that printers find too cumbersome are 5-to-an-em, 4-to-an-em, 3-to-an-em.

notes, appearing both in the text and before the footnote. (See p. 15.) They should, in English, follow all marks of punctuation except the dash.

The asterisk is sometimes a convenient indicator of a particular trait or special circumstances. For example, in a list of items it may be placed before or after those most appropriate for a certain purpose, or those which are indispensable while others are merely desirable; in a list of books it may indicate those illustrated; in a list of names, those persons who have died (the dagger is often used for this purpose). The significance should always be explained.

The "slant." The solidus, usually called a slant, has a variety of uses:

It separates the numerator from the denominator in fractions: a/b
It is the sign for shilling: 6/
Between *and* and *or* it means "or":

   Books of Catholic and/or Irish interest.
   Lost or obliterated corners, and/or reference points.

In bibliographical matter it is a separatrix, indicating where one line ends and another begins:

   The Last Sheaf/Essay by/Edward Thomas/(device)/With a Foreword by/Thomas Seccombe-Jonathan Cape/Thirty Bedford Square/London

TYPE MEASUREMENT

The point system. Before 1878 type sizes were known by size names and varied from one another by irregular amounts. Since sizes cast by different foundries under the same names usually varied slightly and could not be used together, they caused printers much inconvenience and trouble. Standardization of type sizes was badly needed and was finally achieved about 1878 by the adoption of the point system devised by a French typographer named Pierre Simon Fournier. This is a system of measurement based on a unit called a point, practically 1/72 inch.[1]

   1 point = 1/72 inch
   6 points = 1 nonpareil
   12 points = 1 pica
   6 picas = 1 inch

All sizes of type and materials cast according to this system are exact multiples of some other types or materials. Sizes are designated by points measured by the type bodies (see Fig. 14). There is a regular gradation

[1] Actually .013837 inch.

of sizes differing from one another by half-points from 3-point to 7-point, by single points from 7-point to 12-point, by two points from 12-point to 24-point, and by even numbers of points beyond that size.

This line is set in 6-point
This line is set in 7-point
This line is set in 8-point
This line is set in 9-point
This line is set in 10-point
This line is set in 11-point
This line is set in 12-point
This line is set in 14-point
This line is set in 18-point

The em.   Another unit of measurement in printing is the em, which is the square of the body size of the type.   The name originated from the fact that the body of a letter M in a normal face is the same number of points wide that it is high.   The amount of type in a piece of composed matter is measured by ems of the size of type in which it is set; the work of compositors is measured by the number of ems they set.

Certain quite condensed faces, referred to as "lean" or "skinny" faces (Granjon and Caslon Old Face are examples) sometimes are measured and charged on the basis of a point size smaller in width (*i.e.,* 11 point as 10 point), or a variation of such a basis.

For the measurement of column and page widths, printing space, and printing materials the pica em is used.   This is twelve points high and twelve points wide and makes a convenient unit because it is approximately one-sixth of an inch.   *Picas* is the shortened term to use.   For example, a page (or a section) of type might be said to be set to a *measure* (width) of 21 picas, practically three and one-half inches.

The monotype system uses also *unit* and *set-em* as terms of measurement. An em, regardless of size, is eighteen units wide; therefore M is an 18-unit character and other letters are varying units in width.

The set is the width of the 18-unit characters of a face expressed in points. Some faces are lean, condensed; others are fat, or extended.   (See below.) Therefore the width of an M might be greater or less than its height.   The term *set-em* is used to designate an em which pointwise (in height) is the same as the point size of the face being measured and setwise is the width of the 18-unit characters of that face.   Thus, the set-em of 10-point, 10½ set, would be 10 points high and 10½ points wide.   For instance:

These lines are set in 12-point Cheltenham (No. 164), in which the M is 12 points high and 12 points wide.

These, for comparison, are set in 12-point Cheltenham, 10½ set, —a condensed face—in which the M is 12 points high but only 10½ wide.

Sizes of type faces. As explained above, the sizes of type are designated by the number of points measured by their bodies, not by the height of their faces. It is extremely difficult for any but the experienced to distinguish sizes of type by their faces. Compare, for instance:

10–POINT CASLON

The monotype system of setting type was invented by Tolbert Lanston in 1888. It consists of two machines, a perforating machine with keyboard and a casting machine. The keyboard consists of 276 keys and is controlled and operated by compressed air. The "lay" of the keys is similar

10–POINT BODONI BOOK

The monotype system of setting type was invented by Tolbert Lanston in 1888. It consists of two machines, a perforating machine with keyboard and a casting machine. The keyboard consists of 276 keys and is controlled and operated by compressed air. The "lay" of the keys

10–POINT JANSON

The monotype system of setting type was invented by Tolbert Lanston in 1888. It consists of two machines, a perforating machine with keyboard and a casting machine. The keyboard consists of 276 keys and is controlled and operated by compressed air. The

10–POINT GRANJON

The monotype system of setting type was invented by Tolbert Lanston in 1888. It consists of two machines, a perforating machine with keyboard and a casting machine. The keyboard consists of 276 keys and is controlled and operated by compressed air. The "lay" of the keys is similar

10–POINT BASKERVILLE

The monotype system of setting type was invented by Tolbert Lanston in 1888. It consists of two machines, a perforating machine with keyboard and a casting machine. The keyboard consists of 276 keys and is controlled and operated by compressed air. The

10–POINT CASLON OLD FACE

The monotype system of setting type was invented by Tolbert Lanston in 1888. It consists of two machines, a perforating machine with keyboard and a casting machine. The keyboard consists of 276 keys and is controlled and operated by compressed air. The "lay" of the keys is similar to that of

10–POINT SCOTCH

The monotype system of setting type was invented by Tolbert Lanston in 1888. It consists of two machines, a perforating machine with keyboard and a casting machine. The keyboard consists of 276 keys and is controlled and operated by compressed air. The

10–POINT ELECTRA

The monotype system of setting type was invented by Tolbert Lanston in 1888. It consists of two machines, a perforating machine with keyboard and a casting machine. The keyboard consists of 276 keys and is controlled and operated by compressed air. The

10–POINT O S #7

The monotype system of setting type was invented by Tolbert Lanston in 1888. It consists of two machines, a perforating machine with keyboard and a casting machine. The keyboard consists of 276 keys and is controlled and operated by compressed air. The "lay"

10–POINT CALEDONIA

The monotype system of setting type was invented by Tolbert Lanston in 1888. It consists of two machines, a perforating machine with keyboard and a casting machine. The keyboard consists of 276 keys and is controlled and operated by compressed air.

10–POINT ELZEVIR

The monotype system of setting type was invented by Tolbert Lanston in 1888. It consists of two machines, a perforating machine with keyboard and a casting machine. The keyboard consists of 276 keys and is controlled and operated by compressed air. The

10–POINT SANS-SERIF

The monotype system of setting type was invented by Tolbert Lanston in 1888. It consists of two machines, a perforating machine with keyboard and a casting machine. The keyboard consists of 276 keys and is controlled and operated by compressed air. The "lay" of the

In the foregoing illustrations the designations Caslon, Janson, Baskerville, Scotch, O S #7, Elzevir, Bodoni Book, Granjon, Caslon Old Face, Electra, Caledonia, and Sans-serif are the names given to the respective type faces, each of a different design. As they are all 10-point, the types are all of the same size (i.e., body size) from a printing standpoint. From "actual appearance" to the eye, however, their largeness or smallness varies—but the "size" (i.e., the face of the type) from this angle is not the point size.

CLASSIFICATION OF TYPE FACES

All type faces may be grouped in five general classes: roman, italic, script, gothic, and text. Roman, together with its companion italic, is the type used for books, magazines, newspapers, and all classes of ordinary reading matter. There are two styles of this face, differing from each other slightly in proportion, shape, and shading. The older form was cut in 1470 by Jenson at Venice, and is called Old Style (in England Old Face). The principal identifying features of Old Style letters are the sloping serifs. Note their form in the following line.

Caslon—an Old Style Face

Note the sloping serifs in these letters: T R t r y c e

This is Caslon italic, designed to be used with Caslon roman.

The figures for Old Style faces are termed *hanging figures* because the 3, 4, 5, 7, and 9 "hang" below the base line of the figures. The 6 and 8 extend above the other figures. Many Old Style fonts now have so-called modernized (referred to as *lining*) figures, which retain the characteristic features of the font but align at top and bottom.

Granjon hanging figures: 1 2 3 4 5 6 7 8 9 0
Granjon modernized figures: 1 2 3 4 5 6 7 8 9 0

The Old Style face was used until about 1800, when it was largely superseded by a new face called Modern, which was designed in 1783 by Bodoni. The serifs in this face are straight, the bottom of the t curves upward, y ends in a curve and a dot.

Bodoni—a Modern Face

Compare the letters T R t r y c e with the Old Style.

This is Bodoni italic.

The figures in Modern fonts are lining, or ranging, figures. All are the same height and none hang below the base line.

Bodoni figures: 1 2 3 4 5 6 7 8 9 0

Both Modern and Old Style faces are in common use now, and numberless faces have been cut based upon these two styles. Each has italic forms. Commonly used Old Style faces are the monotype Caslon, Baskerville, Century Old Style, and Garamont, and linotype Granjon, Garamond, Elzevir, and Franklin. Scotch, Bodoni, and De Vinne are Modern faces.

Antique and boldface are heavy forms of Old Style and Modern faces.

This face is Old Style, Monotype No. 25

This face is Linotype Antique No. 3.

This is a linotype face called Old Style Antique.

The older faces used before roman was designed are now used mainly in small jobs, as they are not suited for straight reading matter. The oldest style of type face imitated the hand lettering which prevailed before movable types were invented, and in appearance is black and ecclesiastical. This style of face is called Text or Black-letter.

Cloister Black   **Wedding Text**

Script types are imitations of handwritings; their use is limited, as they are employed chiefly in announcements, invitations, display lines of checks, and similar matter.

Bernhard Cursive   *Trafton Script*

The Gothic types, especially some of the newer faces, like Kabel, Spartan, and Futura, have come into rather wide use for headings and captions. Gothic type has a perfectly plain face with lines of uniform thickness and without serifs. It appearance, however, can be wholly changed by the addition of serifs, and each style of serif that is added to it seems to give it a new form. It is sometimes called Block-letter or Sans-serif. In England it is called Grotesque or Doric.

GOTHIC COPPERPLATE

Futura, the popular face

COMPUTATIONS OF COPY AND TYPE

Authors, editors, and printers often need to know how to estimate the length of copy and how to compute the space it will fill when it is set in type. The author's problem, often, is to know how much copy will be required to fill a given space, as when pages need adjustment, or an article or book must be of a certain length. The editor's problem may be how to get the copy within the space available for it, involving decisions of type size and face and amount of leading. The printer needs to have calculations of length of copy on which to base his cost estimates whenever he is required to submit a bid for printing. Methods of securing these necessary facts are described in the following paragraphs.

Estimates are secured by a count of words or of characters. A character count is the more accurate and is therefore preferable; it is likewise easier to make.

Character counts. Copy is generally typewritten, and the number of characters to the lineal inch is invariable: pica typewriting has 10 characters to the inch and elite typing has 12. Punctuation marks and spaces between words are counted as characters. The length of a line in inches, multiplied by 10 or 12, depending on the style of typewriting, yields the number of characters in the line. To make a count of a paragraph or a page, a line of average length should be measured and the count of that line multiplied by the number of lines. A short line, as at the end of a paragraph or in dialogue, should be counted as a full line. To illustrate, on a given page of pica typewriting the lines average 6 inches in length. The characters in the line therefore number 6 × 10, or 60. If the page has 26 lines, there are 26 × 60, or 1560, characters on the page.

If the count is to be made of a book-length manuscript, each chapter should be counted separately for greatest accuracy, and the number of headings also noted. If different sizes of type are to be used, each size must be counted separately.

The estimator can simplify his work by making and using a line gauge in the following way. Transparent paper is best but ordinary paper will do. Take a sheet about 8 by 10 inches in size. Starting at the upper *right*-hand corner, mark off the top edge in inches. If the gauge is for pica typing, divide each inch into tenths and number the inches 10, 20, 30, 40, etc. (thus indicating ten pica characters to each inch). If it is for elite typing, divide the inches into twelfths and number the inches 12, 24, 36, 48, etc. (12 characters to the inch). Place the gauge with the top edge at the base line of the first line of typing. Mark off on the right-hand edge at the base line of the fourth line of typing, single spaced, and at the base of every fifth line down the length of the page. Cut off the lower left-hand corner of the gauge. To make the count of a page place the gauge with the top edge at the base line of the first line of typing and the right edge at the end of what appears to be an average line in length. Suppose the gauge shows 50 lines. Subtract the blank lines. If there are no headings but the page is double spaced, the count of lines is 25. Multiply this by the number of characters in the lines, as shown at the top of the gauge, to get the count for the page.

Word counts. Some persons prefer to make a word count, but a word count cannot be so accurate as a character count. An actual count of words with the idea that long words and short words will balance each other might give a fairly accurate estimate in some manuscripts but in others it would be wide of the mark. A writer's vocabulary (whether predominantly Anglo-Saxon or consisting of words from the Latin), the subject of his writing, its nature (technical or nontechnical), and the age group to which it is addressed all affect the count of actual words. If the method followed is to count two short words as one word and a very long word as two, the result depends on the estimator's judgment or accuracy in guessing.

Rarely the estimator may have handwritten copy to count. Here a word count may be the only one possible, but the result in any case can be only approximate. Several lines should be counted to find the average number of words to a line, counting two short words as one word and a long word as two. Then the average number of words per line should be multiplied by the number of lines to get the full count. If a manuscript is partly type-written, partly handwritten, and partly printed ("reprint"), estimating length may require a combination of character-count and word-count methods.

Ways to simplify estimating. An author who wishes to make estimating as easy and accurate as possible should have his manuscript typed with the right-hand margin reasonably even and with the pages as nearly uniform in length as the nature of the text will allow. A special manuscript paper is made, ruled so that counts can be made rapidly.

COMPUTING THE LENGTH IN TYPE

Because of the many variables involved, as kind of type, size, style of face, and leading, computing the length in type is much more complicated than estimating copy length. But the printers' type books have simplified the editor's task by giving, along with their specimens of type, a notation of the number of words or characters to a given space. Some have tables showing the number of words or characters in each face and size of type for pages from 18 by 26 picas to 25 by 41 picas. If only one size page is given, a simple formula can be used to find the number in a different size.

Following are two tables that often prove useful in type computation. The data are for faces of normal width. From these two tables various computations can be made if it is remembered that 6 picas equal approximately 1 lineal inch. For instance, a square inch of 8-point solid type is the equivalent of a line 54 picas long (9 lines an inch long).

APPROXIMATE NUMBER OF CHARACTERS PER LINE

LENGTH OF LINE IN PICAS

Point Size of Type	6	8	10	12	14	16	18	20	22	24	26	28	30	32	34	36
6	22	29	37	45	54	62	70									
8	17	23	30	36	42	48	54	60	66	72	78					
10	15	20	25	30	35	40	45	50	55	60	65	70	75	80	85	90
12	13	18	23	27	32	36	41	45	50	54	59	64	68	73	77	82
14	10	13	17	20	23	27	30	34	37	41	44	47	50	53	57	60
18	8	11	14	17	20	23	26	29	32	35	38	41	44	47	50	53

It should be kept in mind that the figures given in these tables are average only. As has been explained type faces of the same point size often vary set-wise (width) and these variations will affect the figures in the tables.

There is more variation in width of letters in linotype faces than in foundry and monotype faces. A more nearly accurate approximation of linotype faces can therefore be secured by using *A Simple, Accurate Method of Copy-fitting,* eight pages of tables and instructions issued by the Mergenthaler Linotype Company.

The Linotype method of copy-fitting is simple and quite accurate. It is recommended that it be followed whenever possible. It can be adapted to use with Intertype faces and with Monotype. It is necessary only that the lower-case alphabet length (in points) of the face be known. These figures can be secured from the manufacturer or from the compositor.

Point Size of Type	Approximate Number of Words per Square Inch		Lines of Type per Inch	
	Solid	2-Point Leaded	Solid	2-Point Leaded
6	47	34	12	9
8	32	23	9	7 +
10	21	16	7 +	6
12	14	11	6	5 +
14	11	7	5 +	4 +
18	7	5	4	3 +

PROBLEMS OF FORMAT

THE TASKS OF THE EDITOR

In general, it may be said that the work of the editor is to see that the manuscript is editorially and factually correct. It falls within his province to "style" the manuscript: that is, to see that spelling, punctuation, and the like, are correct and consistent throughout. It is important that these matters be attended to before type is set; otherwise, the cost of making corrections may be considerable.

In most modern publishing offices the manuscript is then placed in the hands of the production department, which decides upon details of format and manufacture. In a few publishing offices some of these details may be left to the editor, but as a rule his preparatory task is completed when the manuscript is editorially and factually approved.

THE TASKS OF THE PRODUCTION MAN

While a general understanding of the methods and the materials concerned in book manufacture is often helpful to the editor, the actual design and manufacture is something that is usually directed and supervised by a trained production man. The production department visualizes the completed book and decides upon the details of format and manufacture. This is usually done in close coöperation with the sales and editorial departments.

The production department cannot have too thorough a knowledge of all the processes involved in the manufacture of a book, from estimating copy and type to presswork and binding. The same may be said of its knowledge of materials. Some of this essential information is set forth in the following pages.

In studying the pages which follow, in Part III of this book, the word "editor" should be interpreted loosely. It may mean either *editor* or *production man,* depending on the type of organization in the publisher's office, as well as on the size of the company.

THE SIZE OF THE BOOK

The length of the manuscript and the length of the book required are the details thought of first, for they must be adjusted to each other. Making the adjustment affects the determination of page size, the choice of size and face of type, and the type arrangement within the book. There are many ways of expanding a manuscript, such as using numerous center headings and shoulder headings instead of run-in side headings, and presenting data in columns rather than run in. To gain length the book may be set in a type face that has an alphabet length longer than average and looks best with wide leading. If the manuscript is long for a volume of the desired size, it may be edited for compactness; the size of the type page in proportion to the size of the paper may be larger than average, and a type may be chosen that requires only slight leading and sets more than the average number of words to a page. Valuable to the editor in making these adjustments is the table of alphabet lengths published in *Copyfitting* by the Mergenthaler Linotype Company.

The planning and production of commercial books has become increasingly difficult since the beginning of World War II, due to the relative scarcity of paper, printing facilities, and binding material, and the steady and substantial rise in the cost of paper, composition, plating, presswork, and binding.

This has made necessary a progressive increase in the prices of original editions and many reprints.

The effects of war-time publishing requirements still show in many phases of book-making, and many books are smaller than the public expects for the prices placed on them.

DETERMINATION OF PAGE DIMENSIONS

The figures which follow need not be observed too slavishly. Not all production men or all book designers agree on all problems of format. They sometimes differ markedly. Their differences of opinion on type faces, type page sizes, leading, margins, and other elements may tend to confuse the uninitiated. Some of these differences are born of personal likes and dislikes for certain types and their use.

If the beginner will keep in mind the purpose for which a book is to be used and who is to use it, and strive for readability and a proper functional design, avoiding "freakish" types and type treatment, he probably will not go far wrong.

The first thing to decide upon is the measure, or length of line, to be used. Much work has been done to discover the relationships of line length and type size that lead to accuracy and ease in reading. The conclusion of the foremost investigators is that line widths (for usual 10-point book type such as Baskerville) in the neighborhood of 19 picas are satisfactory, and that they should not be shorter than 14 nor longer than 28 picas. A line of 19 picas will set about 49 characters of 10-point linotype Baskerville.

The Mergenthaler Linotype Company experts state that the ideal length of line is about 40 characters of any size, and that lines of less than 30 or more than 50 characters should be avoided. The printer's adage has it that a line should not be less than one and a half times its alphabet length, and other experimenters have concluded that a line should not be less than three inches (18 picas) long.

Present-day practice in book work is to use a line ranging from 18 to 24 picas for 10-point, with the ideal width 22, slightly more than twice the alphabet length. Proportionately longer lines could be used for larger sizes of type.

When the width of the page has been decided upon, the length may be determined by some rule of good proportion. The skilled designer has no need of a formula or ratio of proportion. He has a feeling for balance and his good taste and experienced judgment may be depended upon to guide him correctly.

For those of less experience, some rules of mathematical proportion have

out of Mark's life and into his . . . then, coming back to this house, she'd left him completely behind her . . . "I don't know why I didn't," she said.

"I know!" His eyes blazed at her but he stood motionless, his hands still in his pockets. "You was—were—ashamed. You did have the decency to be ashamed. Stringing me along like that . . . letting me think you were waiting for me, letting me make a damned fool of myself—going to school, trying to get ahead, so we could be together!"

She closed her eyes against the storm of his words. "Laramie, I *didn't!*"

"Didn't what? Know I always meant to have you? Don't hand me that! You knew, all right. I didn't have to tell you. We didn't need to talk about it! We always belonged together . . . but you decided you'd rather have *that!*"

One hand came out of his pocket; he jerked contemptuously at her sleeve. She had been shaking her head blindly, dazedly, under the impact of his low, furious voice; at his touch she stumbled, dizzily and clung to him for a moment before his arms went around her. The confusion in her mind and in her body merged in the singing of her blood as he crushed her roughly against him and bent his head to take her lips. All her half-formed thoughts and formless longings, the vaguely yearning tenderness and romantic imaginings that had inspired her letters to Laramie, each mild "affair"— friendships spiced with the unconscious coquetry that was her heritage—with the boys she had gone to school with, her delight in Mark's homage and the mysterious thrill of her helpless response to the passion that blazed

FIG. 15

Publisher's Sample Left-hand Page for Margins.

out hesitation. He perceived now he had been mistaken.
Beth was not wearing the type of wrist watch to delight
Sally. He put the whole matter out of his mind, com-
pletely, and called the man to pay the check.

As they drove into San Buenavista, pennants waving
at the street corners, a holiday crowd jamming the road
to the festival grounds, Beth asked, "How long are you
going to speak?"

"About thirty minutes. Forty. I don't know."

"Why don't we meet after your speech? I'm all alone,
too. You might even like to listen to poor little me trying
to be a speaker."

"Why not?" said Barney. "We could have dinner
afterwards?"

"That would be fun," agreed Beth.

If he went to dinner with Beth, he ought to have a
chance to grab that poster and make certain some sort
of an accident happened to it. He supposed Beth would
blow up after he tripped and fell and, in falling, tore the
poster and ruined it. In a way, he was sorry for Beth.
He was sorry for himself. But his great concern was for
Saraphine. At least he could look forward to seeing
Saraphine Monday and hearing her cry of rapture and
relief when she learned that her poster had been returned
to its most irrefragable elements—and that her old man
had never let her down in a real crisis.

As they turned into the festival gates, Beth said she'd
meet Barney after his speech at the south corner of the
grandstand. She'd wait for him, there.

Twenty-three minutes after 3 P.M., from the platform
erected between the pitcher's box and the home plate,
Barney waited for the laughter to die down in the grandstand before completing his speech.

135

FIG. 16

Publisher's Sample Right-hand Page for Margins.

been laid down. These proportions vary and thus are apt to be a source of some confusion to the beginner. It may be said, however, that a type page of pleasing proportions is in approximately the ratio of 1 to $\sqrt{2}$, or 1 to 1.418. In other words, the length is 1.418 times the width. Variables of the proportion just set forth are 2:3 and the still longer page in the proportion 3:5. (In considering the page length, the running head is included.)

Margins. Type page dimensions must also be considered in relation to margins, that is, the position of the printed page on the leaf. Type area and white space should be about equal and the two facing pages of an open book should be treated as a unit in arranging the margins.

The margins around a *single* printed (book) page should of course not be equal on all sides. The ideas of the best individual designers may differ as to the exact position of the printed page on the leaf, but conform to one of the following plans:

(a) Perhaps the majority of book designers specify that the narrowest margin be on the inside or back, the next narrowest the head, the outside or front margin still wider, and the bottom or foot margin the widest.

(b) Some publishers, however (including the publishers of this book), prefer the practice of having the top or head margin the narrowest, then the inside or back margin a little wider. The front and bottom margins follow in the same order as in (a).

The desirable width of margins depends on the nature of the book and binding. The widest margins would be used in a de luxe edition of a formal, literary work. Biographies and books of travel and of history have liberal margins. In novels and in textbooks, wide margins seem out of place, yet they should not be narrowed to the extent that reading or study is discouraged. The wartime practice of narrower margins in general, conserving paper and printing, although departing from accepted standards, at least temporarily modified the generally accepted practices for margins. (See Figure 15 and Figure 16.)

Textbooks often require special consideration, especially those for students through the high school level, because schools are insistent on adequate back margins. The same may be said of reference books and the like for the reason that a greater inside margin, when margins are close all around, permits of easier reading.

CHOICE OF SIZE AND FACE

First of all to be considered in deciding upon the size of type to be used is the age of the reader. Experimental tests have determined that 14-point is the best size for children in the second and third grades, 12-point for fourth-graders. (As types of the same "point" size vary markedly in actual size, the types in mind in this paragraph are the usual ones used in book printing, as Baskerville, etc.) For adults 10-point is a usual minimum in a book designed for reading. The appearance of smaller types is repellent, and the reader is soon tired by the strain of reading. Eleven-point is most preferred by adult readers, but 9-point, 10-point, and 12-point are likewise quite readable providing optimum leading and line widths are employed for each type size.

Factors in choice of face. Factors to be considered in choosing a type face are legibility, adaptability, and appropriateness. Choice may be affected by the manner of printing, the kind of paper used, the availability of harmonious secondary types, and the length of the book.

Most type faces commonly used are about equally legible, but they vary widely in adaptability. Some faces can be used effectively for many different kinds of text, while others are more limited in their usefulness. Some are neat and businesslike, with an even and regular appearance; others have an irregular outline and variety in shapes of letters. Some are designed to convey ideas without making the reader conscious of type; others are designed to please the eye. Choosing a type for appropriateness to the text requires a judgment of the qualities of faces. Indispensable to the editor is the type book of the printer who is to manufacture for him. No printer can have every type font available, and his type book is made up to show the qualities of the faces he does have and the effect of a page composed in them. One of the best short analyses of several faces widely used at the present time is in Kenneth E. Olson's *Typography and Mechanics of the Newspaper,* pages 119–161.[1] For more comprehensive and detailed study of type faces, see Daniel Berkeley Updike's *Printing Types, Their History, Forms, and Use; a Study in Survivals,* 2 vols. (Cambridge, Harvard University Press, 1922).

Limitations on choice. If it should be necessary to print from type rather than from plates a work for which a long run is planned, the most satisfactory face will be one with little contrast between the heavy and the light elements. An Old Style face should therefore be chosen.

If a hard or coated paper is to be used, a face with delicate lines and strong contrasts will print most effectively. Modern faces have these qualities more than Old Style.

Since both monotype and linotype offer a wide choice of faces, cost is usually the determining factor in deciding which method of typesetting is to be used. Straight text matter, well prepared, with infrequent footnotes and no illustrations less than page width, can undoubtedly be done more speedily and economically on the linotype. The expense of linotype increases rapidly if

[1] New York, D. Appleton & Company, 1930.

much resetting is necessary in makeup. Any text which requires the use of
many characters not in a regular font, especially if they have to be inserted
by cutting the slugs, is not economical for linotype work. An experienced
linotype operator with the necessary matrices at hand can set any kind of text,
but in most cases intricate mathematical and chemical texts containing equations and diagrams should be set on the monotype.

Another consideration which may affect the choice of a type face is the
availability of harmonizing secondary types. Page after page of lightface
roman unrelieved by contrasting types is forbidding and tiring. Initials,
ornaments, rules, and other devices may be used in fiction. In books for study
and reference boldface relieves the dull appearance of a plain text. Sideheads
in boldface are valuable aids to the student, guiding his reading and helping
him to find references quickly. Any secondary types should harmonize with
the text; and occasionally an editor will find that none of the boldfaces available blend with his first choice of face for the text and a second choice must
be accepted.

METHOD OF PRINTING

Another decision which must be made is whether printing is to be from
the original type composition, from electrotype or other plates, or by the photo-
offset process. Printing direct from type is satisfactory only for a short run.
After a few thousand copies have been made, the type becomes worn and
the impression is no longer clear-cut. Moreover, type is so heavy and bulky
that it is hard to store for a later printing.

For printing a large edition or a small edition to be followed by others
later on, plates should be made. The order to cast plates should specify the
kind of plate—copper or steel (nickel); also the number—worker and molder [1]
or worker only. If the book contains halftones, instruction must be given
whether printing is to be done from the original cuts or from the electrotype
reproduction.

The photo-offset method is a planographic process requiring printing plates
made by photographing the illustration or the printed page that is to be reproduced. Until recently this method of printing was used largely for the
reproduction of pages previously printed in the usual manner and for line,
halftone, and color reproduction. For halftone color subjects it has the great
advantage of producing soft effects on rough or uncoated paper. Offset printing is splendidly adapted for school books, particularly primers and readers,

---

[1] A worker is a plate finished for use on the press. A molder is a duplicate plate kept
in reserve, from which a new worker can be cast at any time. A proof of a molder plate
looks like a foundry or "cast" proof, since the bearers have not been planed off and they
print as a wide black line around the page.

containing many illustrations in color and printed in large quantities. It is also well-suited for books with many illustrations which would otherwise be reproduced by halftones, requiring highly finished or possibly coated paper. Development of special papers and inks has led to an increasing use of this method of printing.

PAPER

Texture. Texture of paper depends upon the kind of pulp used, of which there are four general classes. When wood is ground up and the entire mass is used, including pitch, lignin, and other impurities, the pulp obtained when water is added is called mechanical wood pulp. The paper made from it is suitable for newsprint. Some pulps are made from old paper, the quality of paper obtained varying from poor to excellent. When wood is ground and then treated chemically to remove everything except actual cellulose fibers, the pulp is called chemical wood pulp. Most book papers are made of this kind of pulp. The finest papers are made of rag pulp.

Paper is either "laid" or "wove." Laid paper shows fine parallel lines watermarked in it, with other less frequent lines crossing them at right angles. These are produced by the pressure of a wire screen during manufacture. Wove paper is made on a screen in which the wires are woven together like the threads of cloth. The paper shows no wire marks but has a woven appearance on both sides.

Finish. The principal terms used in classifying paper according to finish are Antique, Offset, Machine Finish, English Finish, Super, and Coated. Antique paper has a somewhat rough surface, because manufacture is considered complete when the web of paper comes off the dry end of the paper machine. Machine Finish has a smoother surface produced by running the paper through a stack of smooth iron rolls. Coated paper is a Machine Finish type with a coating of clay or of some chemically produced product similar to clay. The purpose of coating is to create a surface better suited for the printing of fine-screen halftones.[1] Gloss, semi-gloss, and dull finishes are produced. English Finish paper is a smooth, firm sheet suited to the printing of halftones of moderately fine screen. The strength of English Finish may be varied by a change in pulp, to make one suitable for textbooks or one more mellow in quality with less strength to attain better printing results in halftones. Super is an English Finish paper that has been given a high finish by passing it through a stack of heavy rolls called supercalenders.

Weight. Papers are also classified by weight. The "substance weight" or merely "substance" is the weight of a ream (500 sheets) of book paper 25

---

[1] See p. 173

inches by 38 inches in size, which may vary from 30 to 100 pounds or more. The weight of other standard-size book sheets is reckoned from this unit or "basis."

The following table lists the weights of thirteen standard-size sheets in ten substances.

WEIGHTS OF PAPER PER REAM

SIZE OF SHEET	SUBSTANCE							
	30	35	40	45	50	60	70	80
25 × 38	30	35	40	45	50	60	70	80
28 × 42	37	43	50	56	62	74	87	99
28 × 44	39	45	52	58	65	78	91	104
30½× 41	39	46	53	59	66	79	92	105
33 × 44	46	53	61	69	76	92	107	122
35 × 45	50	58	66	75	83	99	116	133
36 × 48	55	64	73	82	91	110	128	146
38 × 50	60	70	80	90	100	120	140	160
41 × 61	79	92	106	118	132	158	184	211
42 × 56	74	87	99	112	124	148	174	198
43 × 63	86	100	114	128	143	171	200	228
44 × 64	89	104	119	134	148	178	208	238
46 × 69	100	117	133	151	167	201	234	267

To prove 25 × 38 50 lbs. equals 41 × 61 132 lbs. follow example:

Multiply 25 by 38 equalling 950.

Multiply 41 by 61 equalling 2501.

Multiply 2501 by the base weight 50 lbs. equalling 125050.

Divide 125050 by 950 giving you the answer of 132.

Grain. Paper has a grain, formed by its fibers. With papers heavier than 50-pound basis, for book work especially, it is important that the grain run up and down the page, that is, parallel to the backbone of the book. This will prevent wrinkling of the leaves and a wavy effect in the book as a whole. It also permits the book to open more freely and the leaves to fall more naturally against the covers.

An exception should be made with books to be printed by offset lithography, in more than one color, when close register of the colors is important. This is because of the water incident to this form of printing, which causes a perceptible expansion in the paper fibers. For that reason, grain should be considered in respect to its relation to this process of printing rather than in its relation to the book itself. In such cases, the grain of the paper should run the long way of the sheet. For ordinary one color offset printing, this is not necessary. The best advice, even to a person with some experience, is to confer with paper supplier, lithographer, and binder, and reach a mutually satisfactory understanding.

Bulk. The bulk of paper naturally varies with the substance and also with the finish. Substance 50 of English Finish bulks approximately 700 pages to an inch, substance 50 of Antique, only about 384; substance 70 of English Finish, about 500 pages, substance 70 of Antique, about 274. The paper manufacturers' sample books usually list the substance and the bulk of each kind and finish of paper they manufacture.

Computation of paper needed. When paper is ordered for a book, the size usually chosen is that which will print 32 or 64 pages on one side of a sheet (see table below). A sheet of this sort printed on both sides will contain 64 or 128 pages, which will be cut and folded in units of 16 or 32 pages, called

Standard Sizes of Book Papers, Inches	Pages to a Sheet	Size of Untrimmed Leaf, Inches
25 × 38	32	6¼ × 9½*
	64	4¾ × 6¼
28 × 42	32	7 × 10½
	64	5¼ × 7
28 × 44	32	7 × 11
	64	5½ × 7
30½ × 41	32	7⅝ × 10¼*
	64	5⅛ × 7⅝
33 × 44	64	5½ × 8¼*
35 × 45	64	5⅝ × 8¾*
36 × 48	64	6 × 9
38 × 50	64	6¼ × 9½*
41 × 61	64	7⅝ × 10¼
	128	5⅛ × 7⅝
42 × 56	64	7 × 10½
	128	5¼ × 7
43 × 63	64	7⅞ × 10¾
	128	5⅜ × 7⅞*
44 × 64	64	8 × 11
	128	5½ × 8
46 × 69	128	5¾ × 8⅜*

* The most common sizes for adult books at the present time.

signatures.[2] Suppose a book is to be printed containing 384 pages, on a sheet which will print 32 pages on each side, a total of 64. Dividing 384 by 64 gives us 6, which is the number of 64-page *sheets*[3] needed for one copy of the book. Hence for 5000 copies of the book, there would be needed 6 × 5000 sheets, *i.e.,* 30,000 sheets or 60 reams. It is always necessary to add a percentage for waste and spoilage, usually 5 per cent for 5000 copies. So 63 reams should be ordered for this book.

If double size paper is to be used, printing 64 pages on each side (a total of 128 pages on a sheet), half this quantity, or 31½ reams should be ordered.

The untrimmed size of 32-page signatures can be seen at a glance, because the page dimensions are always one-fourth of the sheet dimensions. If 64 pages are printed on the same size sheet (32 pages on each side), the page length is then one-fourth the width of the sheet and the page width is one-eighth of the sheet length.

BOOK SIZES

The common book-trade designations of sizes—quarto, octavo, twelvemo, and so on—were based on a sheet of paper measuring 19 by 24 inches. This sheet, folded once, formed a folio of two leaves (4 pages), 12 by 19 inches in size, untrimmed. Folded twice, it formed a quarto of four leaves (8 pages), 9½ by 12 inches. Folded three times, it gave an octavo, eight leaves (16

---

[2] The letter or numeral sometimes placed at the foot of the first page of a fold of sixteen pages, as an aid to the binder in collating, is also called a signature. Books are not always bound in units of 16. One variation is to inset a fold of 12 or 16 pages within another fold, making a unit of 28 or 32 pages, which to the bookbinder is one signature.

[3] If the sheet size is such as to accommodate 128 pages, 64 on each side, half the quantity mentioned will be required.

pages), 6 by 9½ inches. Twelve pages printed on a sheet this size would be 4¾ by 8 inches. As paper-making developed, many different sizes of paper were manufactured and were designated by name rather than by size in inches. Paper made by different manufacturers under the same name often varied slightly, so that we find "medium," for instance, varying from 18 by 23 to 19 by 25, "royal" from 19 by 28 to 20 by 25.

Name	Size of Sheet Inches	Octavo Fold Inches
Pott	12½ × 16	4 × 6¾
Foolscap	13½ × 17	4¼ × 6¾
Crown	15 × 20	5 × 7½
Post	16 × 20	5 × 8
Large Post	16½ × 21	5¼ × 8¼
Demy	17½ × 22½	5½ × 8¾
Medium	19 × 24	6 × 9½
Royal	20 × 25	6¼ × 10
Super Royal	22 × 28	7 × 11
Imperial	23 × 33	8¼ × 11½

It will readily be seen that to designate the size of a book accurately it would be necessary to give the name of the paper. An imperial octavo, for instance, indicates a book almost twice as long and wide as a pott octavo. These terms are in common use in England, but American paper manufacturers prefer to designate their book papers by size in inches, and most publishers use the size in inches of the trimmed page in describing their books.

If only approximate dimensions of book sizes are needed, the following designations of sizes, which were used prior to the general adoption of the book sizes given hereafter, may be of interest.

Name	Approximate Size of Page, Inches	Limit of Outside Height,[1] Inches
Atlas folio	16 × 25	15.74
Elephant folio	14 × 23	11.81
Folio	12 × 15	9.84
4to	9 × 12	7.87
8vo	6 × 9	9.84
12mo	5 × 7½	7.87
16mo	4¼ × 6¾	6.889
18mo	4 × 6¼	5.9
24mo	3½ × 6	4.9
32mo	3¼ × 5	
48mo	2½ × 4	
64mo	2 × 3	

[1] The American Library Association lists the outside heights of books to which the designations of book sizes may be applied. For example, a book more than 25 cm. high may not be called an octavo, one over 20 cm. may not be termed a 12mo. The measurements given are those of the A.L.A. changed to approximate inches.

TABLES FOR VISUALIZING A BOOK

16mo (4⅝ × 6¾ in.)	Text Words	Size of Type Page (picas)	Pages Text
10-pt. Baskerville			
10-pt. Caledonia (leaded 2)	50 M	20 × 32	182
11-pt. Baskerville (leaded 2)	50 M	20 × 32	206
11-pt. Caledonia (leaded 2)	50 M	20 × 32	206
10-pt. Janson (leaded 2)	50 M	20 × 32	182
11-pt. Janson (leaded 2)	50 M	20 × 32	206
11-pt. Granjon (leaded 2)	50 M	20 × 32	187
10-pt. Caslon (leaded 2)	50 M	20 × 32	168
11-pt. Caslon (leaded 2)	50 M	20 × 32	210

12mo (reg.) (5 × 7⅜ in.)	Text Words	Size of Type Page (picas)	Pages Text
10-pt. Baskerville			
10-pt. Caledonia (leaded 2)	65 M	21 × 35	205
11-pt. Baskerville (leaded 2)	65 M	21 × 35	230
11-pt. Caledonia (leaded 2)	65 M	21 × 35	230
10-pt. Janson (leaded 2)	65 M	21 × 35	205
11-pt. Janson (leaded 2)	65 M	21 × 35	230
11-pt. Granjon (leaded 2)	65 M	21 × 35	209
10-pt. Caslon (leaded 2)	65 M	21 × 35	189
11-pt. Caslon (leaded 2)	65 M	21 × 35	236

12mo (oversized) * (5¼ × 7⅝ in.)	Text Words	Size of Type Page (picas)	Pages Text
10-pt. Baskerville			
10-pt. Caledonia (leaded 2)	75 M	22 × 37	213
11-pt. Baskerville (leaded 2)	75 M	22 × 37	245
11-pt. Caledonia (leaded 2)	75 M	22 × 37	245
10-pt. Janson (leaded 2)	75 M	22 × 37	213
11-pt. Janson (leaded 2)	75 M	22 × 37	245
11-pt. Granjon (leaded 2)	75 M	22 × 37	223
10-pt. Caslon (leaded 2)	75 M	22 × 37	196
11-pt. Caslon (leaded 2)	75 M	22 × 37	245

8vo (reg.) (5⅝ × 8⅜ in.)	Text Words	Size of Type Page (picas)	Pages Text
10-pt. Baskerville			
10-pt. Caledonia (leaded 2)	85 M	25 × 42	185
11-pt. Baskerville (leaded 2)	85 M	25 × 42	212
11-pt. Caledonia (leaded 2)	85 M	25 × 42	212
10-pt. Janson (leaded 2)	85 M	25 × 42	185
11-pt. Janson (leaded 2)	85 M	25 × 42	212
11-pt. Granjon (leaded 2)	85 M	25 × 42	192
10-pt. Caslon (leaded 2)	85 M	25 × 42	172
11-pt. Caslon (leaded 2)	85 M	25 × 42	217

* The same table may be used for the 8vo (small), which measures 5¼ × 8 in.

8vo (oversized) (6⅛ × 9¼ in.)	Text Words	Size of Type Page (picas)	Pages Text
10-pt. Baskerville (leaded 2)	200 M	27 × 45	376
11-pt. Baskerville (leaded 2)	200 M	27 × 45	442
10-pt. Caledonia (leaded 2)	200 M	27 × 45	376
11-pt. Caledonia (leaded 2)	200 M	27 × 45	442
10-pt. Janson (leaded 2)	200 M	27 × 45	376
11-pt. Janson (leaded 2)	200 M	27 × 45	442
11-pt. Granjon (leaded 2)	200 M	27 × 45	419
10-pt. Caslon (leaded 2)	200 M	27 × 45	343
11-pt. Caslon (leaded 2)	200 M	27 × 45	446

The preceding tables will be of assistance in visualizing a book and selecting a format. The number of text pages given is approximate and allowance has been made for chapter breaks (the blank spaces at the beginnings and ends of chapters) and for page running heads. It should be kept in mind that the average length of words varies, to some extent dependent upon the nature of the text. For greater accuracy, use of the character count method is recommended. (To transpose the tables to a character count basis, figure six characters to an average length word, *e.g.,* 50,000 words equal about 300,000 characters.)

PROBLEMS OF TYPOGRAPHICAL STYLE

It has been noted in previous sections that the first task in starting a book manuscript on its way to manufacture is to decide questions of format, such matters as size, bulk, page dimensions, illustrations, and binding. Then must be considered such details as spacing, indention, the forms to be used for headings, extracts, synopses, quotations, initials, footnotes, bibliographies, tables, and any other special matter. Next to choice of face, leading, and margins, these factors are most important in determining the appearance of the finished work. They therefore require care and thought. The skillful editor visualizes the manuscript in type and produces as artistic a result as possible. The following sections deal with these matters of typographical style.

LEADING

Lines of type are separated by strips of metal 1, 2, or 3 points thick called leads. Matter spoken of as leaded is understood to have 2 points of space between lines. Double-leaded matter has 4 points of space between lines. When matter is to be leaded 1 point, the fact is especially noted, as: 10-point lead 1-point, or 10 on 11. Similar strips 6 points or more thick are called slugs. In composition by the linotype machine 1-point or 2-point leading is usually cast on the body of the type. For instance, 10-point leaded is usually a 10-point face cast on a 12-point body and is spoken of as 10 on 12. Matter set without any leading is "solid."

Extra leading is sometimes designated by the terms "white line," "blank line," or "quad line," signifying a space between lines the height of the type body—a line of em quads.

Two different sizes of type should always be separated by more space than is used between lines. The space should be approximately uniform throughout, but such spaces may be made wider or narrower in the makeup to adjust pages that need to be shortened or lengthened.

A heading within the text, either centered or flush at the left, should be closer to the type below, to which it belongs, than to the type above it.

SPACING

The spaces used to justify lines—that is, to spread out words to fill the line— are the following:

em quad	1 em
en quad (a "nut")	$\frac{1}{2}$ em
3-to-an-em (a "thick")	$\frac{1}{3}$ em
4-to-an-em ("thin space")	$\frac{1}{4}$ em
5-to-an-em ("thin space")	$\frac{1}{5}$ em
hair space	less than $\frac{1}{5}$ em

"Em" here, of course, means the square of whatever size type is being used, not a *pica* em. Thus a thick space of 12-point is 4 points thick, of 9-point it is only 3 points, and so on. A "pica thin space" is 3 points thick.

Text. The standards of good printing require that lines be spaced as evenly as possible and that spacing of a work be as nearly uniform as possible throughout. The space most used is the three-space, also called a thick or third space. Wider spacing is tolerable in leaded matter than would be acceptable in solid matter. An occasional 5-spaced line is permissible in solid matter but not in leaded text. Spacing between words in small capitals should be greater than between words in lower case. No less than an en space should be used between words set in even capitals.

A widely spaced line—an en quad between words
A normally spaced line—a thick space between words
A closely spaced line—a 4-space between words
A line spaced too tightly—a 5-space between words

The last line of a paragraph should be spaced about the same as lines above and below it, not widely spaced to fill the line or tightly spaced to secure open space at the end. However, it should not be allowed to stand with less than an em at the end but should be either full width or have an em, preferably more, at the end. The last word of a paragraph should never be divided if such a division can be avoided; and in no case except in very narrow measure should less than four letters be carried over to stand alone in the line, even if wide or tight spacing is required to avoid it.

Sentences. Until recently the space most used between sentences within a paragraph was the em quad, but many books published in recent years have been set with less space, sometimes the same as between words in the line—a justifier.[1] Sometimes a nut space or two thicks (in monotype this is a 12-unit space) plus a justifier is the spacing used between a period and a new sentence.

The tendency of some modern book designers to use only a justifier between sentences is not altogether commendable. While there may be some esthetic advantage to be gained from this close spacing, it leaves little chance for the reader to group words that belong together.[2] A little more open spacing between sentences in textbooks and books of reference is generally to be preferred. For instance, compare the following for readableness and quick comprehension.

The Basic Industries. 3. Products of the Soil. Many of the . . .
The Basic Industries. 3. Products of the Soil. Many of the . . .

Jeans, P. C., and Stearns, G.: Human requirement of vitamin D. J. A. M. A. 111: 703–711, 1938.
Jeans, P. C., and Stearns, G.: Human requirement of vitamin D. J. A. M. A. 111: 703–711, 1938.

---

[1] When type is composed on the monotype or linotype machines, spacing between words is adjusted automatically. In monotype the space is called a justifier, in linotype a spaceband.
[2] Educators voice the objection that this practice is helping to break down students' notion of the integrity of the sentence.

Appalachian Trail Club Bulletin, October, 1936, 12 pp. A descriptive account of the Trail features in southern Pennsylvania.

Appalachian Trail Club Bulletin, October, 1936, 12 pp. A descriptive account of the Trail features in southern Pennsylvania.

Guide Book of the Long Trail. The Green Mountain Club, Rutland, Vt. Contains generalized trail data. . . .

Guide Book of the Long Trail. The Green Mountain Club, Rutland, Vt. Contains generalized trail data. . . .

Punctuation. After a question mark or an exclamation point within a sentence the spacing should be less than that used after periods, usually an en if sentences are em spaced.

To arms! they come! the Greek! the Greek!
"Ha! There's some mischief afoot!" Raoul said to himself.

Following the period after a numeral that precedes a topic or a paragraph in a series an en space or two thick spaces may be used, in some cases an em quad. Consistency should be maintained.

1. How would you stimulate the imagination?
2. Explain the cause of such errors.
3. Classify the school subjects. [en space]

IX. Decisions
9. Decisions [2 thicks]

Unit IV. The Revolution [em quad]

Between double and single quotation marks a thin space should be inserted. Quotes and dashes are often separated from adjoining words by a thin space. References to footnotes look better thin-spaced away from the word preceding if no punctuation intervenes. In the footnote a thin space after the superior makes a better appearance than no space.

Some publishers use a thin space in contractions—except *don't, won't, can't,* and *shan't*—but this is not a general practice.

Letterspacing. Inserting thin spaces between the letters of a word is called letterspacing. Headings in caps or small caps are letterspaced sometimes to improve their appearance, or for the sake of a change from ordinary style. Space between words in a letterspaced heading should always be wide enough to separate them clearly: EDITOR'S PREFACE

Letterspacing in text is an expedient that should not be used if it can be avoided. In narrow measure, however, as in a column of a table or beside a text illustration, words may be letterspaced to fill the line. Whenever this is done, a short word should be spaced, not part of a long one.

In German, letterspacing represents italics. (See p. 329.)

INDENTION

The blank space left in setting a line in from the margin is called indention (never indentation), and everyone is familiar with indention as marking the beginning of a paragraph.

Paragraphs. The indention of paragraphs should be in proportion to the width of the page. An em space is enough for a page less than 27 picas— 4½ inches—wide. An em and a half looks better for widths from 28 to 35 picas; 2 ems for 36 picas or more. In books set in two or more sizes of type it is desirable to have the paragraph indentions as nearly alike as possible. However, a page containing paragraphs of 10-point, 9-point, and 8-point type will look very well if the paragraph indentions are respectively a 10-point em, a 9-point em, and an 8-point em. More exact measurements are not practical in linotype composition.

Outlines and similar matter. Indention is of greatest use in showing the relation of items to one another, in making clear the subordination or coordination of topics or statements.

Dairy Products: Meat Products:
  Milk   Beef
  Butter   Lamb
  Cheese   Pork

III. The legislative function

  1. Distribution of legislative powers between the House of Lords and the House of Commons

    a. Legislative powers of the House of Lords (see Chapter VIII, item VII, 2 and 3)

    b. Legislative powers of the House of Commons: the House of Commons possesses all powers of Parliament not belonging to the House of Lords, . . .

  2. Classification of bills

A. The problem and the assumptions

  1. Problem one of discovering how day-to-day prices result from the forces of supply and demand

  2. Approach by analysis of the actions of individual producers

    a. Assumptions: (1) Single homogeneous good, (2) aim to maximize revenue or minimize losses immediately or in the future, (3) full information, (4) freedom of access to market

The last two examples above illustrate different practices in regard to turned-over lines. The editor should clearly indicate his preference on the copy.

Explanation of terms. Indention is used in headings and display matter in several ways, which are denoted by the terms *paragraph, reverse, hanging, block, diagonal, drop-line, echelon, inverted pyramid, half-diamond,* and *lozenge.* Since paragraphs usually have the first line indented, *paragraph indention* means set with the first line indented and following lines flush. *Reverse indention* is the opposite: first line flush and following lines indented; the more common term is *hanging indention,* and paragraphs set with hanging indention are called flush-and-hang paragraphs. The block style uses no indention for any line except the last, which is centered. (A heading set in block style is shown at the top of page 115.)

Diagonal, or drop-line, indention, inverted pyramid indention, and lozenge indention are used for display. The drop-line indention (also called echelon when more than two lines are involved) is much used for newspaper headlines, the first line flush at the left, the second flush at the right.

Rare Antiques Lost
As Curio Shop Burns

Inverted pyramid indention, sometimes called half-diamond indention, is a common arrangement for headings taking less than three full lines. Each line is centered and shorter than the line preceding. In book work in earlier days the last several lines of chapters were frequently arranged in this form.

Rare Antiques Lost
As Curio Shop
Burns

HEADINGS

Type. Types are the clothes in which the writer's words are dressed. They may appear smart or dowdy, neat or untidy, attractive or repellent, too loud or too plain. The successful job printer is one who has enough artistic sense and skill to choose types and combine them in a way to secure a desired effect. Newspaper and magazine editors study the many job faces available for headings and choose those most suited to their purposes. The book editor, likewise, may if he chooses use for headings in a book faces or letters quite different from those used for the text. For example, Bodoni, Swash capitals with italics, and Gothic are adaptable for headings in conjunction with the commonly used Modern and Old Style faces. If, however, the same face must be used for headings as for the text, there are several combinations of types which can be used to distinguish main headings from subheadings. Five such are noted below.

1. MAIN CHAPTER HEADING IN CAPITALS

   a. FIRST SUBHEADING IN CAPITALS AND SMALL CAPITALS

     (1) SUBDIVISION UNDER THAT IN SMALL CAPITALS

       (*a*) *Next Subdivision Italic Capitals and Lower Case*

CHAPTER NUMBER IN SMALL CAPITALS

CHAPTER TITLE IN CAPITALS

SUBHEADINGS IN CAPITALS AND SMALL CAPITALS

CAPITALS OF TEXT TYPE

Boldface Capitals and Lower Case

Italic Capitals and Lower Case

CAPITALS OF TEXT TYPE, LETTERSPACED

BOLDFACE CAPITALS

Boldface Capitals and Lower Case

1. CAPITALS OF TEXT TYPE

   a. CAPITALS TWO SIZES SMALLER

     (1) SMALL CAPITALS OF THE LARGER FONT

       (*a*) SMALL CAPITALS OF THE SMALLER FONT

Coördinate divisions should have headings of the same size and style. Part headings, for instance, should be in one size and form throughout a work, and no other headings in the work should be of this size and form. The size and form used for chapter titles are generally used also for the headlines of the preface, contents, list of illustrations, introduction, appendix, notes, glossary, bibliography, vocabulary, and index.

Arrangement. In the body of a book a heading that can be set in less than three full lines should be arranged in inverted pyramid style, each line centered and shorter than the line above it.

STANDARDS FOR THE PRESENTATION OF OBJECTIVE DATA IN

REPORTS OF RESEARCH STUDIES

A longer heading, unless special directions are given by the editor to "pyramid," may be set in block style—that is, each line but the last flush left and right and the last line centered; or it may be set with the first line flush, following lines indented at least two ems, each line but the last occupying the full measure—a flush-and-hang paragraph. This form, which was much used in the recent past, is not now so up-to-date as the block style. It would not be good practice to use both forms in one book.

Block style:

Supervisory Guidance of Teachers in Expressing
School Work in Terms of the Purposeful Activi-
ties of Boys and Girls in Life Outside of the
School

Flush-and-hang:

Supervisory Guidance of Teachers in Expressing
School Work in Terms of the Purposeful
Activities of Boys and Girls in Life Outside
of the School

Punctuation. A centered heading should not be followed by a period. If the wording calls for an interrogation point or an exclamation point, however, this should not be omitted. In a heading set in capitals en dashes should be used for hyphens, and spacing between words should be not less than an en. The larger the type the greater should be the space between words.

ANGLO–SAXON GRAMMAR

Division. Dividing words and separating closely related terms or groups of words should be avoided whenever possible without marring the typographical appearance.

Figures. The typographical appearance of the regular Old Style hanging figures in a line of capitals is unpleasing. This should be borne in mind in planning the type format of a book containing many headings of this sort. Many Old Style fonts now have both the hanging and the lining figures (modernized figures).

TURKEY SINCE 1900
FROM 449 A.D. TO THE NORMAN CONQUEST, 1066

TURKEY SINCE 1900
FROM 449 A.D. TO THE NORMAN CONQUEST, 1066

Small capitals. No capitals should be used in a heading set in small capitals.[1]

1. NEW ENGLAND PSALMODY
THE REIGN OF ABDUL HAMID II

"Continued." If a heading contains the word *Continued*, the form of this word should be indicated. It is ordinarily italic cap-and-lower, preceded by an em dash or enclosed in parentheses.

[1] Rules for capitalization in headings set cap-and-lower and cap-and-small are given on pages 219–220.

STATE INSTITUTIONS—*Continued*

STATE INSTITUTIONS—*Continued*

STATE INSTITUTIONS—Continued

STATE INSTITUTIONS—*Continued*

State Institutions—*Continued*

A more pleasing form in some instances might be:

STATE INSTITUTIONS
(*Continued*)

Side headings. Side headings may be set flush at the left with space above and below; or they may have regular paragraph indention with the text running in after a period and a space or a dash. They are usually boldface or italic, occasionally caps-and-small, rarely small caps. Side headings may be capitalized like centered headings or only the first word and proper nouns may be capitalized. Three styles are shown below.

Side Headings.
Side headings may be set flush at the left with space above and below—a "shoulder head."

Side Headings. Side headings may be regular paragraph indention with the text running on after a period and a space or a dash; this is sometimes called a paragraph heading, or a run-in side heading.

Side headings. The capitalization in side headings may be the same as if it were a centered heading, or only the first word and proper nouns may be capitalized.

Cut-in side headings are set in type other than the text and inserted by hand in a space left for them when the text type is set. They are much less common in these days of machine composition than they used to be. In books they are generally placed under the first two lines of the paragraph. The space given them should be the same width throughout the book, but the depth may vary. The headings should be so placed in the space as to leave an even amount of white above and below, and horizontally should be at least 6 points from the text. They may be all on the left-hand side of pages or all on the outside, that is, on the left of left-hand pages and on the right of right-hand pages. In either position the lines of the heading should align on the left. (See p. 10.)

Marginal headings, or marginal notes,[2] are likewise set in other type and must be placed beside the text by hand. They are ordinarily set lower case except the first letter and proper nouns; they may be squared, or normal

[2] The term "side notes" is ambiguous.

spacing may be used and the notes lined up on one side only. They should be placed in the outside margin, not closer than an en space to the text page. If the notes are like headings in nature, they should be placed beside the first line of a paragraph. If they constitute a running gloss, they should be as nearly as possible beside the line to which they apply.

Running headings. Just as sinkage on the first page of chapters (more blank space at the top than on other pages) has become customary practice, so has the use of running headings on full-length pages. The headings may stand alone, centered in the line, the folio at the foot of the page:

NEWSPAPER HANDBOOK

BETTER NEWSPAPER ENGLISH

Or the folio may be in the line with the heading:

144   NEWSPAPER TYPOGRAPHY AND MECHANICS

TYPE FACES AND HOW TO USE THEM   145

The heading may be flush with the margin instead of being centered:

164   LIFE ON THE EARTH

THE LIVING COVER OF THE EARTH   165

Headings are most often made up in one of the following ways:

(*a*) *Left:* title of the book
     Right: title of the chapter

(*b*) *Left:* title of the part or unit
     Right: title of the chapter

(*c*) *Left:* title of the chapter
     Right: subject matter of the page

The running headings may also contain key words or numbers:

154   New Second Latin Book (IV, 29

IV, 32)   The Gallic War   155

Left: John 12:12—13:38   Lesson IX   First Quarter

Right: February 28   The New Commandment   John 12:12—13:38

The first arrangement noted (*a*) is of course the simplest. The only care required of the editor is to indicate on the galley proofs the wording to be used for any headings that are too long to set with at least an em space left between heading and folio. Headings following this cut-and-dried formula are, however, the least helpful to users of the book. For usefulness, (*c*) is a better choice, but this and other arrangements require careful checking, and the instructions to the makeup man should be so clear that they cannot possibly be misinterpreted.

If the running heading consists only of catchwords, the folio is then usually at the foot of the page, although if the page is wide and a catchword is placed at both left and right, the folio may be in the center.

EXCERPTS

(See also pages 12–15.)

The author is responsible for careful indication of all matter quoted from the work of another. For that reason, detailed instructions about how excerpts should be distinguished from an author's own text were given in Part I, pages 12 to 15. The editor should be thoroughly familiar with the rules and practices there set down, for he will need to check carefully the author's accuracy and good judgment in following those instructions. The editor must decide upon the typographical form and carefully mark each excerpt that is to be reduced; the printer will take no responsibility for consistency of treatment. In addition, the editor should observe the following typographical practices:

Prose. Letters, excerpts from plays, and prose excerpts five lines or more in length are usually reduced. Extra leading should always be used above and below an extract. If an editor wishes to have less space above than below, he should mark on the copy the spacing desired, unless, of course, the printer has standing instructions on this detail. Quotation marks are not necessary, but if type the size of the extracts is used to any extent for matter other than quotations, quotation marks may well be used to avoid any possibility of misunderstanding.

Poetry. Excerpts from poetry are generally reduced. Each citation, or each group without intervening text, should be centered as a unit, regardless of other extracts falling on the same page. Such extracts are usually not enclosed in quotation marks, but if these marks are used, the opening quotes should be set to the left to retain the alignment of the words.

> "Where the bee sucks, there suck I;
> In a cowslip's bell I lie;
> There I couch when owls do cry,
> On the bat's back I do fly
> After summer merrily."
>
> —SHAKESPEARE, *The Tempest*

When extracts are not enclosed, quotation marks within the poetry which is quoted should be set, as in the original, within the measure of the poetry, thus:

> "Why are you cross, Sammy Squirrel?"
> Questioned his mother one day.
> "You quite forgot your manners
> When Squeaky Mouse came to play."

When extracts are enclosed in quotation marks, double quotation marks in the original should be changed to single ones and arranged as follows:

> " 'Why are you cross, Sammy Squirrel?'
> Questioned his mother one day.
> 'You quite forgot your manners
> When Squeaky Mouse came to play.' "

If a poetical extract begins with part of a metrical line, this line should be set to indicate the fact clearly.

> "long and level lawn,
> On which a dark hill, steep and high,
> Holds and charms the wandering eye."

or

> "... long and level lawn,
> On which a dark hill, steep and high,
> Holds and charms the wandering eye."

If punctuation at the end of matter quoted is not appropriate in the text where the quotation is used, it may and should be changed.

> "Beauty is truth, truth beauty,—that is all
> Ye know on earth, and all ye need to know"

well illustrates how Keats . . .

[The original has a period after *know*.]

FOOTNOTES

(See also pages 15–24.)

If the author has read and followed accurately the instructions for the arrangement of footnotes given in Part I, the editor's work will be light. The editor must, of course, decide upon the typographical style, whether 6-point, 7-point, or 8-point, solid, or leaded. Footnotes amplifying the text or acknowledging indebtedness for excerpts give little trouble. The editor must make sure, however, that all necessary credits are given and that the form of the credit remains the same even if the rest of the note is in shortened form (see p. 17). Footnotes of the bibliographical sort are so full of details that only an experienced person can maintain consistency on all points. They will therefore require careful editing. Models for such footnotes are shown on pages 19–21. Publishers may, of course, decide upon a different style. In publications of the United States Geological Survey, for instance, italics and quotation marks are not used, only the first word and proper nouns in titles are capitalized, and the punctuation is different from that shown in this book.

Copy check-up. A check-up of the copy of footnotes can be made by answering the following questions:

Have references to footnotes been placed properly and in correct order?

Have all essential data been given?

Can the name be supplied for any initial that stands alone before a surname?

Have notes been given in shortened form whenever that is desirable?

Have the names of periodicals that are abbreviated been given once in full and the same abbreviation used for all others?

Have *ibid., op. cit.,* and *loc. cit.* been used as they should be?

Have the names of publishers been given in consistent form in all notes?

In the page references are numbers set in the same way, all in full or all double numbers elided?

Have *vol.* and *p.* been omitted when possible?

Are the punctuation and capitalization consistent?

TABLES
(See also pages 24–32.)

The following pages are concerned primarily with typographical aspects of tabular composition; matters of construction and arrangement of data were considered in Part I.

Type and spacing. Tabular matter should be set off from reading text by using a smaller type, with extra space above and below the table. For ruled tables a solid set or a body larger in point size than the face is usually chosen— for instance, an 8-point face on a 9-point body, as is common. The purpose of this is to avoid having to cut leads; if leads were used between the lines, each one would have to be cut whenever it intersected a vertical rule. When tables are ruled, the horizontal rules must be cut at each intersection with a vertical rule; therefore the fewer such intersections the easier the table is to set. Extra leading should be avoided whenever possible.

Lists in columns. The simplest kind of tabular matter is represented by lists in columns. If an uneven number of items is to be set in two columns, the first column may be one line longer than the second, or the last item may be centered under the two columns. If the number of items to be set in three columns lacks one of being a multiple of three, the first two columns should be one line longer than the third. If the number is one more than a multiple of three, the first or the second column should include one item more than the other two columns. This style cannot always be followed if there are turnover lines; in such cases as even an outline as possible should be secured.

A list in which most items are less than half the width of the page may be arranged in two ways:

              Bay of Fundy   Merrimack River
              Buzzards Bay   Mount Washington

Bay of Fundy   Merrimack River
Buzzards Bay   Mount Washington

When hand and monotype composition were the methods of typesetting most used, the first arrangement was common. Here the columns were set with a definite space between and the two columns centered as a whole in the width of the page. The second is more common nowadays and involves less work. The items are set in half measure, that is, in lines half as long as the width of the page, the lines being later arranged in two columns by hand.

When items in a list are numbered, alignment in the columns should be by the right-hand figures.

     1. New York   Part   I. General Administration
   10. London   Part II. Division of Animal Industry
 100. Paris   Part III. Division of Plant Industry

The example at the left below shows alignment of periods and of right-hand digits in a column of dates. In a list such as that at the right below the best practice is to align the opening parentheses and the list of names, which results in a slight variation in the space between the parentheses and the words.

  i. 311 A.D.   (*l*) William of Orange
  j. 476 A.D.   (*m*) Peter the Great
  k.   44 B.C.   (*n*) Magellan
  l.   4 B.C.   (*o*) Cortes
 m. 325 A.D.   (*p*) Xerxes
 n. 1066 A.D.   (*q*) Alexander the Great
 o. 1519 A.D.   (*r*) Marco Polo
 p. 1919 A.D.

Two-column tabulation. A simple two-column tabulation should be indented on both sides so that the columns are not too widely separated to be read easily.

1929	$5,471
1930–1932	5,500
1934	4,175
1935	3,500

Whenever possible a long narrow tabulation should be set in half measure and arranged in two columns.

SEEDS PRODUCED BY A SINGLE AVERAGE-SIZE WEED

Dandelion	1,700	Burdock	24,500
Cocklebur	9,700	Russian thistle	25,000
Oxeye daisy	9,750	Purslane	69,000
Prickly lettuce	10,000	Crab grass	89,600
Beggar ticks	10,500	Willow foxtail	113,600
Tumbleweed	14,000	Tumble mustard	1,500,000
Ragweed	23,000	Worm seed	26,000,000

Compactness. Tables are not always presented in as compact a form as their content would allow, and when space is limited, a slight rearrangement can often be made to reduce the space required. The table below is an example.

Section 1:
Massachusetts-Connecticut state line (Sage's
Ravine) to Jug End .... 9.8 miles
Section 2:
Highway at northern base of Taconic Range
to Swann Forest Headquarters .... 17.5 "
Section 3:
Swann Forest Headquarters to Jacob's Ladder Highway (U. S. Route No. 20).... 12.0 "

. . . . . .

Section 8:
Braytonville to Massachusetts-Vermont line. 5.1 "

Total .... 86.5 "

SECTIONS	MILES
1. Massachusetts-Connecticut state line (Sage's Ravine) to Jug End	9.8
2. Highway at northern base of Taconic Range to Swann Forest Headquarters	17.5
3. Swann Forest Headquarters to Jacob's Ladder Highway (U. S. Route No. 20)	12.0

. . . . . .

8. Braytonville to Massachusetts-Vermont
   line 5.1
                                    ———
   Total 86.5

The stub. When the first column of a table is a classification of the figures on the same horizontal line, it is called a stub. To emphasize this relationship to following columns, words in the stub are usually followed by dotted lines, "leaders," over to the second column. Leaders are variously spaced—one, two, or three points to an em. They should end at the same place in each line, at least an em space from the next column in an unruled table. The table below illustrates correct practice.

If it is impossible to get the table within the measure without turning over lines in the stub, the first line should be spaced to the full measure of the stub and the turned-over line should be indented one em or more under the preceding line. It is customary to indent the word *Total* more than any other line in the stub. The stub may have within it center headings, boldface or italic side headings, and several indentions. It may or may not have a heading above it; but in ruled tables omission of such a heading is poor form. (See also p. 26.) Capitalization in the stub should be consistent; the better style is to capitalize only the first word and proper nouns and proper adjectives. No punctuation is needed before leaders, but a colon or a dash should be used after lines that are in the nature of side headings.

YOUNG MEN GRADUATES

Number graduated	**76**	
Number employed:		
In business for self	4	
In business with father	2	
Working for others	56	62
	—	
Number in college	1	
Number sick	1	
Number out of work	2	
Number who did not reply	10	76
	—	

The word *Total*—always used in the singular—may be omitted when the footing is obviously a total.

Foregoing illustrations show leaders used correctly. The following shows an incorrect use of leaders, resulting in a table unnecessarily cumbersome, unduly separating the data to be compared.

Incorrect:

Costs in Commercial and Scholarly Publishing

	Commercial		Scholarly
Manufacturing	$ .36		$ .66
Editorial costs	.02		.03
Royalties	.17		.06
Selling and advertising	.19		.23
Shipping and mailing	.02		.02
Overhead	.18		.00
Bad debts, losses, profits	.06		.00
	$1.00		$1.00

Better:

	Commercial	Scholarly
Manufacturing	$ .36	$ .66
Editorial costs	.02	.03

Alignment. Columns of whole numbers are aligned on the right; decimals are aligned by the decimal points. Dollar signs, plus and minus signs, and the like are aligned.

					Grams per Day
Gold	Au	197.3	Protein		103
Hydrogen	H	1.008	Phosphorus		1.75
Indium	In	113.7	Calcium		.89
Iodine	I	125.85			

A column of dissimilar items may be aligned at the left or each item may be centered.

Tax Rate
11½ mills
?
$24.00
2.8%
?

525
25½
38.6
$50
25 oz.
A.—120

The dollar sign. If all the numbers in a column denote dollars, the dollar sign is used with the first number in the column and after every break such as ⊣ rule or a heading.

ASSETS

Cash	$ 80,000
Real estate	17,000
Furniture and fixtures	3,000
	$100,000

The dollar sign should be placed before the first number in the column, not at the top of the column.

12345	.....
3456	.....
4567	$1,456
5645	2,776

In double columns of figures in a single money column the dollar sign is used before both figures in the first line.

Shelter (rent, taxes, interest on mortgage, upkeep, etc.)	$576–$1,200
Food	480– 1,000
Clothing	408– 850

If the numbers in a column do not all denote dollars, the dollar sign should be used with every one that does.

Per cent literate	10
Colleges and normal schools	15
Students in public schools	100,000
Teachers in all schools	600
Property for higher education	$ 60,000
Annual expenditure for education	$700,000
Funds raised by Negroes	$ 80,000
Church property value	—

Ditto marks. Ditto marks may be used effectively in some kinds of tabular work, but it is better to avoid them in books and magazines, either by repeating the words or by changing the form of the heading. For example, note the following:

One pound of 10-point type will contain approximately 207 ems	
" " " 11-point " " " " 171 "	

EMS IN ONE POUND OF TYPE

Size	Approximate No. of Ems
10-point	207
11-point	171
12-point	144
14-point	108

Captions. The descriptive caption is most often set in caps and small caps. The table number, if there is one, is usually set in caps if it is on a separate line, the same as the caption if it is run in. If the tables in a book are set in two or three different sizes, because some are too wide to get within the measure unless they are set in smaller type, the captions should be all in one size. The heading over a narrow table is usually the width of the table.

TABLE I

EDUCATIONAL PROGRESS OF THE NEGRO

TABLE I. IMMIGRANT ALIENS ADMITTED TO
THE UNITED STATES

Fiscal Year Ended June 30, 1932

By Sex

SEX	NUMBER ADMITTED

Braces. A table may be constructed with braces and leaders instead of headings and rules.

Bones . . . . . {
  Function . . . {
1. Organs of support
2. Instruments of locomotion
3. Framework of hard material
4. Attachments for soft parts
5. Means for controlling internal pressures
6. Means for shaping whole body
}
  Classification . {
1. Long
2. Short
3. Flat
4. Irregular
}
}

Parts of braces are used sometimes as in the table below, in place of rules.

PER CENT CHANGE FROM PREVIOUS YEAR

Region	Week ended		
	May 2	Apr. 25	Apr. 18
New England	9.7	1.6	13.9
Middle Atlantic	9.7	5.5	10.0
Central Industrial	14.4	17.4	12.3

Column headings. There are no fixed rules about the size and face of column headings in an unruled table. They may be caps and small, caps and lower case, or italic caps and lower case, in the same size as the table or smaller. In an unruled table headings are preferably set so that they align across the bottom, and are centered over the columns to which they refer.

STATE	WHEAT	OATS	BARLEY AND RYE	TOTAL ALL GRAINS
Colorado	0,000,000	0,000,000	000,000	00,000,000

In a ruled table all column headings are centered vertically and horizontally in the boxes allotted to them.

CROP	INCREASE IN VALUE OF CROP PRODUCED BY FERTILIZER	ESTIMATED COST OF FERTILIZER	INCREASE IN VALUE OF CROP FOR EACH DOLLAR SPENT FOR FERTILIZER

TOTAL INCOME	IF INCOME ALL "EARNED" INCOME		IF INCOME ALL "INVESTMENT" INCOME	
	Income Tax (Including Supertax, If Any)	Effective Rate	Income Tax (Including Supertax, If Any)	Effective Rate
00,000,000	00,000	00	00,000	00

If columns have primary and secondary headings, as in the table above, they may or may not all be set in the same type. In an unruled table, however, different type should be used for primary and secondary headings, or else braces should be used.

COMPOSITION OF DRY AIR		
COMPONENT	PERCENTAGE	
	By Volume	By Weight
Nitrogen	78.0	75.52

It is sometimes necessary to set column headings sidewise in order to get them into the measure. Such run-up or vertical headings should read up from the columns, as in the table below. Normal spacing is used, no attempt being made to keep the right-hand side of headings even. Runover lines may be set without indention. The heading over a stub is set horizontally if possible, even if other headings are vertical.

Cumulative total of words arranged in an order of decreasing common usage	Number of words actually found in contest copy	ERRORS		AVERAGE ERRORS		Average decrease in number of errors made by second-year students
		By 79 first-year students	By 84 second-year students	Per first-year student	Per second-year student	
5	5	149	165	1.8	1.9	− .08
10	10	201	235	2.5	2.8	− .25
25	23	292	326	3.6	3.8	− .20
50	47	438	453	5.5	5.3	+ .15
100	84	549	573	6.9	6.8	+ .12

When tables are set broadside of the page—that is, reading across the length of the page, the stub of the table being at the bottom of the page—vertical column headings will be upside down when the book is in its normal position. Broadside tables should always face right.

Number columns. In unruled tables and those using braces to show the relation of headings to each other, the columns of numbers must always be centered under the headings, as shown in foregoing tables. In book and magazine work, where tabular matter is used to amplify the text, columns of figures in ruled tables are centered in the width of the column by the longest number. In books of statistics like the *Statistical Abstract* or the Census reports, columns of numbers are set an en space (less if the table is crowded) from the rule at the right.

A blank should be represented by an em dash—usually centered in the column—or by close leaders the full width of the column, never by a cipher. The dash is used in both ruled and unruled tables; leaders are seldom used in unruled tables but are often used in ruled statistical tables.

It is desirable to secure as even an outline as possible in a column of figures, but addition of decimal ciphers to chemical or mathematical data should be made warily, and only with sure knowledge that the significance of the number is not affected by the addition.

Rules. Totaling rules in an open table should be the length of the total, including the dollar mark if there is one.

$$\begin{array}{r} \$ \ .56 \\ 1.29 \\ 62.50 \\ \underline{.72} \end{array}$$

A double rule marks the end of a particular part.   A total that is to appear in the column that follows the sums added, and used in a second addition, may be set on the line with the rule or on the line with the last figure.

	675			675		
500		or	500			
10,650			10,650	11,150	11,825	
――	11,150					
	――	11,825				

Even if tables contain several columns and rather lengthy headings they may be set without rules, but the ruled style is preferable for all except simple tables. A double horizontal rule should follow the table caption. Single horizontal and vertical rules separate the column headings so that they are perfectly clear, and a single horizontal rule separates the headings from the data beneath. The end of the table may be marked by either a single or a double rule.

A double vertical rule should be used to separate the parts of a table that is doubled up.

VAPOR PRESSURES AT VARIOUS TEMPERATURES

TEMPERATURE (Boiling Points)	VAPOR PRESSURE (Mm. of Mercury)	TEMPERATURE (Boiling Points)	VAPOR PRESSURE (Mm. of Mercury)
0 C.	4.6	60 C.	149.2
10	0.0	70	000.0
20	00.0	80	000.0
30	00.0	90	000.0
40	00.0	100	000.0
50	00.0	110	000.0

A centered heading within a table should be preceded and followed by a single rule.

TABLE 11.   APPROXIMATE FEED REQUIREMENTS FOR
DAIRY COWS—QUANTITIES PER ANIMAL PER YEAR

PRODUCTION OF MILK PER COW, POUNDS	PASTURE, DAYS	CORN, BUSHELS	OATS, BUSHELS	CONCENTRATE, PROTEIN, POUNDS	SILAGE, TONS
I. FARMS WITH SILAGE					
Under 7000	175	14	14	265	3½
7000–8000					
8000–9000					
9000–10,000					
Over 10,000					

II. FARMS WITH NO SILAGE

Under 7000	175	18	13	260	—
7000–8000					
8000–9000					
9000–10,000					
Over 10,000					

A style of ruling frequently used in technical magazines of late years omits vertical rules entirely, using only horizontal rules as in the following table.

TABLE 1—SECTION AND BRANCH STATISTICS

	For Fiscal Year Ending			
	April 30, 1929	April 30, 1931	April 30, 1933	April 30, 1935
Sections				
Number of sections	54	59	60	61
Number of section meetings held	460	491	498	521
Total attendance	73,254	108,523	73,806	73,381
Branches				
Number of branches	100	109	111	117
Number of branch meetings held	940	1,137	1,036	986
Total attendance	47,408	51,807	59,439	36,629

Tables may likewise be "boxed"—that is, closed in on all four sides by a single rule.

Age	6	7	8	9	10	11	12
Weight (in lb.)	50	53	57	62	67	72	78

For another example of this style see page 92.

"Continued" tables. If a table is more than one page in length, the table number—the table caption if there is no number—should be repeated at the top of each page, followed by the word *Continued* or *Concluded*. It is not necessary to repeat both number and caption. The column headings should be repeated, separated from the caption by a single rule. Double rules, if used, should be placed only at the beginning and at the end of the table, single rules at the bottom of pages.

The table number and the column headings of a wide table set broadside of the page need be repeated only on left-hand pages.

Whenever a page begins with an indented line, a catchline should be inserted, made up of the preceding flush line, followed by "—*continued,*" condensed into one line. Whenever in any column there is an addition continuing from the preceding page, there should be inserted a line at the top: *Brought forward*..., corresponding to a line at the bottom of the preceding page, *Carried forward*...

Tables without figures. The tabular form may be used for the presentation of data expressed in words, not figures. Such tables are often difficult to set with a pleasing appearance. A choice must be made between even spacing of words with a ragged outline on the right and uneven spacing with occasional letterspacing to secure an even outline. Vertical rules should not appear crowded, but should have at least two points of space on each side.

PUPIL	ENGLISH	CIVICS	GENERAL SCIENCE
No. 1, Boy	*A* Father a busy librarian. Encouraged to read much and accustomed to hear correct English spoken.	*D* Family discusses literary curiosities rather than current events. No interest.	*B* Reads *Popular Mechanics* and has considerable knowledge about science, but no direct contacts.
No. 3, Girl	*B* Father a lawyer. Mother used to teach. Girl has read much but very superficially. "Flighty" in her class work.	*B* Hears current events intelligently discussed at home and reads the papers regularly.	*E* Has never helped with the housework; takes all scientific data for granted. Is bored with class work.

Sometimes the nature of the data makes it impossible to fill out lines as above.

	COTTON	LINEN	WOOL	SILK
Practicability	Rather strong. May collect chalk and dust. Easily laundered.	Strong. Needs frequent pressing. Easily laundered. Sheds dust, chalk, lint.	Rather strong. Holds lint and ravelings, chalk, and dust. Usually needs dry cleaning. Soils easily but cleans easily.	Strongest. Wrinkles little. Sheds dust, chalk, lint, and ravelings.

The editor who finds a table like this in a manuscript should consider the possibility of improving it by turning it. (See also p. 29.) The following arrangement of this table, for instance, would be much easier to set and be just as clear.

Material	Practicability
Cotton	Rather strong.
	May collect chalk and dust.
	Easily laundered.
Linen	Strong.
	Needs frequent pressing.
	Easily laundered.
	Sheds dust, chalk, lint.

Footnotes. Reference marks are better than superior figures for references to footnotes whenever tables are used in a text which has footnote material. Superior letters may also be used. The reference should, if possible, be placed after the heading or number explained in the footnote. If the reference cannot be inserted without breaking the alignment, it may be placed before the number. (See p. 31.) If a reference stands alone, it should be enclosed in parentheses and centered in the column.

The notes are best placed immediately below the table; they may be further distinguished from footnotes to text by setting them in a smaller size of type. If a table more than a page in length has a footnote reference on the table caption, the note should appear on the first page only. Footnote references on column headings and the notes to which they refer should appear on the first page and need not be repeated, though in some instances repetition on left-hand pages may be advisable.

Credits. The source of a table may be noted under the caption or below the table:

Source: Bureau of the Census, Department of Commerce.

BIBLIOGRAPHIES
(See also pages 32–36.)

Bibliographies require careful editing. The first decision to be made by the editor is whether the bibliography is in the form most appropriate for the text. If bibliographical lists occur at intervals throughout a work, he should note whether the same kind of information is given in each list. For instance, if an annotated list is given for some chapters, all the lists should be annotated; if the book-list form is chosen for some, all others should have manufacturing and price data.

Authors have been instructed in Part I in the makeup and typing of bibliographies. As there presented the examples of bibliographical form do not show the possible type variations. These variations will be considered here.

Names of authors. Names are usually inverted and are most commonly set in cap-and-small. A comma follows the name.

WHIPPLE, G. M.,
FLINN, A. D., editor
CHARTERS, W. W., and WAPLE, DOUGLAS,
BUERMEYER, LAURENCE, and others,[1]
BEARD, CHARLES AUSTIN, and BEARD, MARY,

If two or more books by the same author are listed, a 3-em dash is usually substituted for the name in the second and following entries.

BOBBITT, FRANKLIN, *How to Make a Curriculum.* Boston, Houghton Mifflin Company, 1924.
——— "The Technique of Curriculum Making in Arithmetic." *Elementary School Journal,* XXV, 127–143.

The dash in such cases is understood to replace the names, one or more, given in the preceding entry.

GROVES, E. M.
——— and Blanchard, P.
——— [*i.e.,* Groves and Blanchard, because all books by Groves alone would precede those by Groves and Blanchard].

Another practice is to use the Latin *idem,* "the same person," instead of repeating the name. Whichever method is adopted should be followed consistently.

33. LEWIS, T., The pathological changes in the arteries supplying the fingers in warm-handed people and in cases of so-called Raynaud's disease. Clin. Sc. 3:287–319, 1938.
34. *Idem,* Raynaud's disease and preganglionic sympathectomy. Clin. Sc. 3:320–336, 1938.

Titles. Book titles and titles of periodicals are usually italicized and titles of articles roman quoted. Subtitles should be retained and set like the rest of the title.

Units in World History: Developments of Modern Europe
Interesting Letters: How to Write Them
Hand Composition. A Treatise on the Trade and Practice of the Compositor and Printer

---

[1] This form—"and others"—is better than *et al.,* which is more appropriate in titles of legal cases.

Titles of bulletins, reports, and similar works may be roman capitals and lower case without quotation marks. Occasionally all book titles are so listed.

Curriculum Laboratory Publications, No. 35
Educational Monographs, No. 4
University of Iowa Studies in Education, Vol. IX, No. 3
Department of Education Bulletin No. 11
Farmers' Bulletin No. 534

If book titles are set in roman, a foreign book title should not be italicized.

GEDDES, A. E. M., "Meteorology. An Elementary Treatise."
SURING, REINHARD, "Leitfaden der Meteorologie."

Book lists frequently follow the style of capitalizing only the first word and proper nouns and proper adjectives in titles, but this is seldom followed in book or periodical lists of references.

HUEY, E. B., *The psychology and pedagogy of reading.* New York, Macmillan, 1909.

Publication data. The place of publication, the name of the publisher, and the date should always be grouped together. Separation by commas seems most logical, but other punctuation may be used. Enclosing these items in parentheses seems unnecessary unless a page reference follows.

Annotations. A variety of styles for annotations are in use. They may be run in after the entry, or set as a separate paragraph in the same type, full measure or indented, or set in smaller type, full measure or indented.

RUSSELL, CHARLES, *Classroom Tests* (Boston, Ginn and Company, 1926), 346 pp. Part I outlines methods of constructing objective tests, while Part II deals with how to use such tests.

HADER, J. J., and LINDEMAN, E. C., *Dynamic Social Research.* New York, Harcourt, Brace & Co., 1934, 226 pp. Detailed analysis of the conference committee in industry, and the psychological factors entering into conference methods and procedure.

HART, F. W., and PETERSON, L. H., "The Present School-District System in California." *California Quarterly of Secondary Education,* IX (October, 1933), 63–67. A description and a criticism of the present system of school-district organization in California.

Book lists. Here, also, the same material can be presented in many forms. Some are businesslike, some like a catalogue; others are made more attractive by a more imaginative selection of types and arrangement.

SAINTSBURY, George, *A History of Criticism,* 2d edition. London: Blackwood, 1906. 3 vols., pp. xxxiv, 372, 428, 462. Cloth. $10.00.

Quigley, Margery Closey, and Marcus, William Elder. Portrait of a Library. Appleton-Century, 1936. 190 pp. illus. $2.

RILEY, JAMES WHITCOMB
  A HOST OF CHILDREN   Bobbs $3.00
  Illustrated by Ethel F. Betts. Contains the old favorites: "The Circus-Day Parade"; "The Runaway Boy"; "The Nine Little Goblins"; "Little Orphant Annie," and others.
  THE RAGGEDY MAN, AND OTHER WELL-KNOWN VERSES   Bobbs $2.50

INITIALS

THE first word of a chapter is often made prominent by setting it in capitals or cap-and-small—sometimes flush and sometimes paragraph indention or more—or by using an "initial"—a letter much larger than the text, occupying the space of two or more lines. If the chapter begins with a synopsis, a quotation, or a stanza of verse indicating the theme of the chapter, the initial would appear at the beginning of the text proper.

A DESCENDING initial should align at the top with the first line of the paragraph. An ascending initial projects above the first line, aligning with it at the bottom.

Form and position of the initial word. The rest of the word of which the initial is the first letter should be set in capitals, rarely small capitals. If the initial is itself a word, as *A* or *I*, the word following it should be set in capitals. Some offices rule that if the first word has only two letters, the second word also should be set in capitals. If the first word is part of a proper name, the rest of the name should be set in capitals. This rule for capitalizing after an initial is similarly applied to chapters beginning with cap-and-small.

MOUNT WASHINGTON is in the state of New Hampshire.
THE NEWSPAPER GUILD has won another strike.
DEMENTIA PRAECOX is the most curious of all mental diseases.

In newspaper work, where the measure is narrow, the capitals following an initial should not extend over one line.

> MR. AND MRS. JAMES EDWARD
> Montgomery were host and . . .

UNLESS the initial is the article *A*, the pronoun *I*, or the vocative *O*, the capitalized word should be set close up to the initial. (The styles are shown in this paragraph and in the second paragraph below this.) If type initials of a large size are used, the letters *A* and *L* are usually mortised to allow the rest of the word to approach the face of the initial and thus avoid the white hole which there would be otherwise. Even *B, C, D, O,* and *Q* may be slightly mortised at the upper corner if they are of a comparatively large size.

Abutting lines. The second and following lines which abut on a descending initial should be spaced away from it the width of the space below it, which should not be more than an en unless the initial is very large. Many printers except the letters *F, P, T, V, W,* and *Y,* which have considerable white space at the bottom. With these letters they set abutting lines flush to the initial. (See the next paragraph.) If the initial is a square blocked one, it is especially important to see that the space at the side is equal to that at the bottom.

WHEN the paragraph beginning with an initial is so short that it ends before the initial is completely surrounded by type, the evenness of the white frame is broken. This is a matter the author can remedy by adding a few words to avoid beginning a paragraph at that point. The same difficulty of an even frame also arises when the initial is used to begin a poem that has alternate lines indented. An even frame for the initial is more important here than the indention of the lines.

Quotation marks. If quotation marks are used with initials, they should be of the text type, not of the type of the initial, and they should be set in the margin. Most printers nowadays omit them before initials.

SYNOPSES

The chapter heading may be followed by a synopsis set in some manner distinct from the text. A synopsis may be a flush-and-hang paragraph in italic; or a regular paragraph in type smaller than text; or a small-type paragraph with the first line flush and the last line centered, the whole indented on both sides. It may be a list of the subheadings, each on a separate line and the list centered as a whole.

CHAPTER IV

CONFIDENCE AND COLLAPSE—THE WORLD'S FINANCIAL CRISIS

The crash in June, 1931. The political causes. The Credit Anstalt. The German short-term debts. The Hoover Moratorium. The fall of the pound. The effect of the financial crisis upon the economic depression. The essence of the crisis; a "gap in the balance of payments unbridged by new credit." Its underlying causes: dead-weight debts, reckless lending, and high tariffs.

CHAPTER XIX   ..   THE ROLE OF THE MODERN HOME

I THE FUNCTION OF THE HOME

II THE ECONOMIC ASPECTS OF THE HOME

1. Formerly the Center of Production
2. Today an Agency of Consumption

III THE SOCIAL ASPECTS OF THE HOME

1. The Home and the Community
2. Vital Importance of Early Training
   (*a*) The Need for Durable Standards
3. The Character of the Home Itself
   (*a*) Abnormal Home Life
   (*b*) The Rule of the Impersonal
   (*c*) Social Mobility

IV CONCLUSIONS

CHAPTER I

OF THE DEFINITION OF CRIME, AND OF CERTAIN GENERAL PRINCIPLES
APPLICABLE THERETO

§ 1. Crime Defined   § 35. Criminal Capacity
   6. The Criminal Act   53. Intent in Statutory Crimes
 26. The Criminal Intent   58. Justification for Crime

EPIGRAPHICAL QUOTATIONS AND CREDITS

A quotation appropriate to the theme of an article or chapter is often inserted between the heading and the text. This is always set in type smaller than the text itself. An initial, if used, should be at the beginning of the text type, not in the quotation.

CHAPTER VI

THE OVATION

His life was gentle, and the elements
So mixed in him, that Nature might stand up
And say to all the world, This was a man.
—SHAKESPEARE

EVENING in the woods, on a still September night. In front, a river, which sends its current deep and dark, with steady pressure, against the base of a hill, as if it would undermine its broad foundation and float it off....

Poetry should be centered. A prose quotation may be set as a regular paragraph or a flush-and-hang paragraph, full measure or indented on both sides. Quotation marks are not necessary, but the source should be given. This "credit" may be the writer's name, the name of the literary work, or both. The type of the credit, whether cap-and-small or italic, the punctuation before and after, and the position in relation to the quotation or to the right-hand margin are all matters of style requiring the editor's attention.

> "If your will want not, time and place will
> be fruitfully added."   *King Lear*

> He that hath never done foolish things never
> will be wise.—CONFUCIUS

Note. If there is not room enough for the credit on the last line of the quotation, the credit should be dropped to the next line and aligned at the right, not divided.

FRONT MATTER

Arrangement. The copyright law specifies that the copyright notice must be printed either on the title page or on the reverse of that leaf. With this exception the arrangement of the various parts of the front matter has been established by custom rather than by rule, and an editor may, if he wishes, vary from the arrangement in any way that his copy seems to make desirable. Generally speaking, however, it is wise to follow an order such as the one below, to which readers have become accustomed.

Certificate of limited edition ("limit page")—unnumbered right-hand page
i—Bastard title, or book half-title
ii—Book card, imprimatur, monogram, or blank
Frontispiece (usually an unnumbered insert facing title, but occasionally facing the first page of text)
iii—Title page
iv—Copyright (and printer's imprint)
v—Dedication
vi—Blank
vii—Editor's preface, introduction, or foreword
viii—Editor's preface continued or blank
ix—Preface or foreword or special introduction
x—Preface continued or blank
xi—Acknowledgments
xii—Acknowledgments continued or blank
xiii—Table of contents
xiv—Contents continued or blank
xv—List of illustrations
xvi—Illustrations continued or blank
xvii—List of figures, maps, charts, or tables
xviii—List of figures continued or blank

xix—Introduction
 xx—Introduction continued or blank
 xxi—Half-title
xxii—Epigraph

The book card, the frontispiece, and the copyright notice are always printed on left-hand pages. An epigraph sometimes appears on the title page, sometimes on the back of the dedication; it may replace the second half-title or be on the back of it, facing the first page of text. Other sections of the front matter are, or begin on, right-hand pages. An errata list, if required, is often placed after the contents, but sometimes at other points in the front matter or even at the end of the book. A Preface to the Second Edition should precede a Preface to the First Edition.

Certificate of limited edition. This page, called limit page or limit notice, is an announcement of the number of copies printed, worded somewhat like this: "This edition is limited to 1000 copies of which this is No. ——." (The number is to be written in, and usually, also, the signature of the author or the publisher.)

Bastard title. The bastard title, also called false title, is ordinarily exactly like the half-title that precedes the text. If, however, the volume is divided into "Books," "Parts," or "Units," each preceded by a half-title, the bastard title should bear the title of the book, not the part title used on the first half-title.

Card page. The book card, also called card page or face title, is a list of books by the same author or a list of books in the same series. Card pages are variously arranged; sometimes the card is placed in one of the upper corners of the page, sometimes the card is centered as a whole, and sometimes each line is centered. In type and arrangement the card should be in harmony with the book.

Title page. The present fashion requires that the title page be simple and dignified, with plenty of white space so that the three principal facts it has to tell will stand out with distinctness. A concise title should be the most prominent line on the page, followed by the name of the author and notation of his position. At the foot of the page should appear the publisher's imprint. Other items may appear if the editor so chooses, but before adding anything he should consider carefully whether the title page is the proper place for the addition. For instance, if the book is one of a series, that information can be given on the title page but often would better head an advertising card on the preceding page or be placed on the bastard title. Lines under the author's name, *Author of* . . . are also more appropriately presented on the card page.

Copyright. The editor usually supplies the copy for the copyright notice, since he is familiar with the legal requirements and the forms adopted by the publisher.

The law specifies that the copyright notice use the word *Copyright,* accompanied by the name of the copyright proprietor and the date.

COPYRIGHT, 1940, BY

D. APPLETON-CENTURY COMPANY, INC.

Each revision must be copyrighted and the new copyright added to all former notices. If the copyright owner is the same, it is necessary only to add the new date.

COPYRIGHT, 1940, 1945, BY

D. APPLETON-CENTURY COMPANY, INC.

Since one requirement for securing copyright on a book in the English language is that it shall have been manufactured in the United States, there should also appear on the copyright page the printer's imprint or the words: "Printed in the United States of America."

If a book is published under a substantially different name or title from that under which it has been previously published in a periodical or newspaper, or in other form, the previously used title must appear on the copyright page. (The former title must also appear on the front flap of the jacket and be mentioned also in catalogues and circulars.) This is to comply with a ruling of the Federal Trade Commission.

The foregoing items of information are required. In addition, copyright pages usually carry the words *All rights reserved,* sometimes with a paragraph warning against infringement.

The copyright page in dramatic works often has a special warning against infringement, like the following, for example:

COPYRIGHT, 1914, BY LEWIS BEACH.
COPYRIGHT, 1921, BY BRENTANO.
COPYRIGHT, 1935, BY LEWIS BEACH.

All rights reserved.

CAUTION. Professionals and amateurs are hereby warned that "The Clod," being fully protected under the copyright law of the United States of America, the British Empire, including the Dominion of Canada, and the other countries of the copyright union, is subject to a royalty; and anyone presenting the play without the consent of the author, or his authorized agent, will be liable to the penalties by law provided. All applications for the right of amateur production must be made to Samuel French at 25 West 45th Street, New York, N. Y., or 811 West 7th Street, Los Angeles, California, or Samuel French (Canada) Ltd., 840 University Ave., Toronto, Ont., Canada. All applications for the professional rights must be made to the author, in care of Samuel French.

The number of the edition and of the printing is often specifically noted on the copyright page. A reprinting of a work without change from the preceding issue is termed an "impression" or a "printing." If changes have been made in the text, the printing is a new edition.

Copyright, 1925 and 1930
By Thomas Y. Crowell Company

Seventh Printing
(First Printing of Revised Edition)

COPYRIGHT, 1906, 1910, 1911, 1914, 1917, 1919, 1920, 1925, AND 1927
BY THE UNIVERSITY OF CHICAGO. ALL RIGHTS RESERVED
PUBLISHED NOVEMBER, 1906
Ninth Edition issued November, 1927
Fourth Impression June, 1930

COMPOSED AND PRINTED BY THE UNIVERSITY OF CHICAGO PRESS
CHICAGO, ILLINOIS, U.S.A.

Dedication. The style of the dedication page should always be formal and as simple as possible.

Preface. The preface is usually set in the same size and face of type as the body of the book. The heading is usually the same size as chapter headings, and the style of the first line is uniform with the chapters, whether beginning with a regular paragraph, flush, or initial.

Table of contents. A writer should send a correct Table of Contents (see page 40) with his copy. The editor can secure various effects in the appearance of the printed page by different combinations of types, so that the contents will be in harmony with the character of the book. Note how different the following pages look.

CONTENTS

CHAPTER I

SENSATION AND PERCEPTION

CHAPTER II

PHYSIOLOGY OF SENSATION

CONTENTS

CONTENTS

CONTENTS

CONTENTS

A contents with page references within a paragraph as above should not be
set in type until the book is in pages and correct page numbers can be filled in.
  List of illustrations. This page also can be variously set to accord with the
rest of the typography. It is usually similar to the contents in style, except
that caps and lower case or lower case is used rather than caps and small, the
predominant style for the contents.

ILLUSTRATIONS

PLATES

ILLUSTRATIONS IN THE TEXT

Errata. When constructing copy for this page the place where the error occurs must first be given and then the words *for* and *read* used in this manner:

Page 177, line 8: *For* Charleston represented *read* Charleston, favoring manu-
  factures as a relief to poor whites, represented
Page 202, footnote 100: *For* Sherill *read* Sherrill
Page 214, line 25: *For* adjured *read* abjured

No punctuation should be used at the end of corrections unless it is part of the correction.

END MATTER—APPENDIX

The appendix of a book should be set in the same face as the text, but in a smaller size. It should begin on a right-hand page, and sometimes may be preceded by a half-title. The following constitute end matter:

Notes
Quotations
Bibliography
Glossary
Index
Colophon
Advertisements

Bibliography. A bibliography in the appendix of a book should be in complete form. All the rules for content and order presented on pages 32, 33 and shown in the models on pages 34, 35 should be observed.

Glossary. A glossary is always set in type smaller than the text. If many of the entries are short, a two-column arrangement may save space. If economy of cost needs to be considered, the typography should be kept as simple as possible. For instance, lightface roman, italic, and cap-and-small would be more economical to set than these three faces with boldface in addition.

> **adobe** (a-do′bi), sun-dried brick used in the southwestern
> part of North America for building houses

DISPLAY ELEMENTS—The elements of advertising display are the illustrations, display type, body type, border and white space.

Imprint. The name of a publisher as printed on the title page of a book, or on the spine of the binding case.
Inferior characters. Letters or figures so cast on the body of type that they print below the alignment of normal letters.

SADDLE STITCH—A thread or wire stitched through the folded back of a pamphlet from the inside to the outside or vice versa.
S. & S. C.—The name of a smooth glossy finish on paper, meaning *sized and super-calendered.* Now generally called *super.*
SECTIONAL BLOCK—See *Patent Blocks.*

CAST PROOF.—*See* Foundry proof.
CHASE.—The rectangular iron frame in which pages of type are locked to secure them while being printed or plated.
COATED PAPER.—A printing paper with a fine, hard, smooth finish, suitable for printing halftone engravings.

INDEXES

(See also pages 43–55.)

Indexes are made sometimes by the author, sometimes by a professional indexer. Since some publishers feel that the author can often produce the better index because of his more intimate knowledge of the text, there was included in Part I instruction in the principles of indexing, together with rules relating to order of subentries and of identical headings and to alphabetical arrangement. The following sections deal with those matters of typographical form which are distinctly the concern of the editor.

Forms. Indexes occasionally resemble a table of contents in form, being set the full width of the page, in type smaller than the text but not so small as is generally used for indexes. This form is usual for legal cases.

Table of Cases

Rail v. National Newspaper Association 199, 201–7
Reade v. Sweetzer 321

No special difficulty arises with such indexes, except, perhaps, in one particular—the use of leaders. The purpose of leaders is to bridge a space between words or figures that belong together, and they should not be used where there is no space to bridge.

Wrong:
Little Father of the Wilderness, The...................
....................Lloyd Osbourne and Austin Strong 157
Right:
Little Father of the Wilderness, The
                          Lloyd Osbourne and Austin Strong 157
Ulysses ....Tennyson 284

When leaders connect entries on the left of a page with page numbers on the right, they should not be set closer than an em to the number. An entry which cannot be set in one line should be turned over at least two ems from the margin and all lines that turn over should be spaced to align at this point.

American Taxation, Speech on 330
Amorists, poetry of the 114
Anatomy of Frustration 648
Ancient Mariner, The 359, 390
                    401, 402, 449, 484
Andreas 37
Androcles and the Lion 578, 579
Anglo-Norman period and the Age of
    Chaucer 53–98
    characteristics of the Normans....... 54
    history 53
    language 57–63

The index of the *Handbook of Style for Yale University Press* illustrates another form of full-measure index. The editor will readily see that this is not a form that would save space if most of the entries were short. Nor is it one that the user will find so easy to use as the narrow form. Short lines that can be grasped in one or two eye-movements make it easy to find an entry quickly.

Reduced type, for *"Continued"* and *"To be continued,"* 92, 221; for quotations, 94, 104; quotes not used with, 105
Reference indexes, placing of, 267, 268
Reference marks, for footnotes to tabular material, 3, 268; for notes that are commentary on text, 3, 266; placing of, 268, 271; sequence of, 268
References, literary, abbreviation of parenthetical, 132; capitalization in, 51; italic and roman phrases in, 76; punctuation in, 193, 194; spelled out, 114
  See also Cross references.

Indexes in this form are comparatively infrequent, however, and most indexes are set in smaller type than text, half the width of the page, the columns separated by a rule or extra space.

Before the copy can be edited at all it will be necessary to decide whether it is to be set in the paragraph form (*a* and *b* below), or the entry-a-line form (*c* and *d* below). Most indexes that come to the editor could be edited for either form with equal ease. Often the determining consideration is the amount of space available, for the entry-a-line requires more space than the paragraph form. Wordy entries with multiple subdivisions require setting in the entry-a-line form in order to be clear.

(*a*)   INDEX

(Figures in italics indicate pages upon which illustrations occur.)

Abies, *165*
Absciss layer, *98*
Absinthin, 141
Absorption, epiphytes, 128, *129*, *130*; external factors, 9; foods, 131, 267 ff., 450; hairs, 128, *130*, *131*; land plants, 124; leaves, 123, 127, 130; rhizoids, *33*, *34*; roots, *7*, *9*, *26*, *27*; transpiration, 79; water and salts, 7, 9, 33, 35, 80, 123, *128*, *129*; water plants, 123, *124*
Abutilon, albescence, 40, *41*, 52

Bryophytes (see also Liverworts, Mosses), 69, 82

(*b*)

Haarlem, 19, 20
Hair spaces, 66
Halftone, 389, 391; highlight, 389; how to order, 394; newspaper, 392; process, 387, 391, 392; screen, 387, 391, 393
Handtooled faces, 146, 200, 342
Hanging indention, 210, 218, 237
Harmony in types, 200
Harvard Academy press, 41
Hawks, Nelson C., point system, 60
Headline, action, 210; banner, 214, 216, 226, 231, 232; Benedictine, 200; blanket, 227; Bodoni, 178, 180, 224; boxed, 276, 278, 341; Caslon, 184, 185

(*c*)

INDEX

The numbers refer to articles.

Abbreviations, 83, 90c
Absolute expressions
    defined, 58
    punctuation of, 91
Accept and *except,* 67
Ad, 68
Addresses, 87b, 87e

Adjectives
    classes of, 57
    comparison of, 57
    distinguished from adverbs, 56
    in a series, 91c, 91j
Adverbs
    classes of, 57

(*d*)

INDEX

References are to pages.

Diet
    light 484, 487
    liquid 482, 487
    soft 483, 484
Digestibility of meal 344
Dining room 105, 203, 205
Dinner
    plan 449

Diet, light 484, 487
    liquid 482, 487
    soft 483, 484
Digestibility of meal 344
Dining room 105, 203, 205
Dinner, plan 449

Indention. The paragraph form of index is compact, using only one indention—for the turnover lines. It is therefore easy to set and easy to use if it is properly compiled. The error to be watchful for is the combining of several subjects in one paragraph. (See pp. 46, 51.)

In the entry-a-line form the main entries, the headings, are set flush and each subentry begins a new line, the relation to the main heading being shown by indention.

    Abstract nouns, 62, 63
      contrasted with concrete
        nouns, 63
      definition of, 62
      formation of, 62

If no page reference follows the heading, the first subheading is usually run in. (Compare the two columns of example *d* above.)

    Clauses, definition, 23–24
      dependent, 24, 106, 298
        use of, as adjectives, 108–109
          as adverbs, 110–112
          as nouns, 113–114
      independent, 23, 24

An index in this form may become confusing, however, if more than two indentions besides that for the runovers are used. Preparation of copy becomes difficult, and the time consumed by the typesetter and the proofreader is more than doubled.

```
Amplifiers, suitable values of repeating
            inductance for, 000
    resistance repeating, 00
    transformer repeating, 00
        radio-frequency, 00
            tuned, 00
                difficulties with, 00
                effect of input circuit upon
                    amplification, 00
        tube, characteristics  for   different
                stages, 00
        noises in operation of, 00
Amplifying power of a tube, 00
```

Since a subheading is understood to read back to everything in the heading up to the comma, one em of indention may represent one or several words.

```
Computation of space, 48, 49
    leaded matter, 49
    solid matter, 48
```

Wrong: *Right:*

```
Autonomic nervous system, 68         Autonomic nervous system, 68
    and  cerebrospinal  nervous  system,    and cerebrospinal nervous system, harmony
        harmony of action between, 69          of action between, 69
```

(A further improvement could be made in phrasing the preceding entry, although the form shown above is common:

```
Autonomic nervous system, 68
    cerebrospinal nervous system and, harmony
        of action between, 69)
```

The principle should be carried through for sub-subheadings, the second em of indention representing all the words between the first and second commas.

```
Air, badness of, 92
    causes of, 93
    carbon dioxide in, 99
```

The following is poor form for three reasons: three subjects—air, air bacteria, and air currents—are indexed under one main heading; the adjective of an adjective-noun combination is used as a heading; under the main heading an em of indention is used for each word intended to be read before the sub-heading, whereas under the subheading an em indention stands for three words.

Poor:

Air bacteria, 87–89
   at different hours, 88
   carried by air currents, 89
  currents, 76–78
    velocity to carry bacteria, 77
     fungus spores, 78
   determining numbers of organisms,
    70

Better:

Air, determining numbers of organisms,
  70
Air bacteria, 87–89
  at different hours, 88
  carried by air currents, 89
Air currents, 76–78
  velocity to carry bacteria, 77
  velocity to carry fungus spores, 78

Dashes may be used instead of indentions if a heading is divided and sub divided, especially where subheads must be wordy and where everything is alphabetized by the key words the reader would expect to find. It is understood that a dash represents a word or a group of words set off by commas in the heading and subheading.

Acidosis, metabolic, 00
— — treatment of, 00
— respiratory, diagnosis of, 00
— — treatment of, 00

Punctuation. Periods are not necessary at the ends of lines in an index. A comma should be used after the heading, as it indicates what is to be read before subentries. In the paragraph form of index a colon may be preferable, particularly if no page reference is given between the heading and the first subheading.

Water, of crystallization, 47
  of hydration, 51

Levites: early status of, 124; distinction between sons of Zadok and other Levites, 128; status of, in Code of Deuteronomy, 130

A comma should be used between two prepositions to stand for the inverted subject of the first preposition.

Amylase, level of, in blood, 60
Amyl nitrite, use of, in angina
  pectoris, 75

Capitalization. Initial words of main entries are usually capitalized, though by no means always. Subentries usually begin with a lower-case letter, unless, of course, the initial word is a proper noun.

Costume, 139–213
  accessories for, 198
  armor, 206

Dances, 230–255
  country, 252–255
  Elizabethan, 234–235

Chapter and other topical headings in the book should not be capitalized if they appear in an index, but anything else capitalized in text should appear in the index in the same style.

Alphabetical divisions. Unless an index is very short and simple, the beginning of a new alphabetical group should be marked in some way, usually by inserting extra space, preferably two blank lines. (Use of A, B, C, etc., in the space is outmoded.) The first word of each group may be set in caps and small caps or boldface. When special types are so used, the whole heading up to the first comma should be set in this type, not a part only.

Dwight, L.   **Great Britain**
                                             [*not* **Great** Britain]
EAST, E. M., quoted

Special problems. Indexes are sometimes so complex that capitals and small capitals, italics, and boldface are needed. (See p. 45.) Boldface or italic figures are frequently used for the volume numbers when two or more volumes are being indexed at once; for section numbers; or for other special numbers when lightface figures are also used.

Checkup of copy. When the typographical form has been decided upon, the editor should check the work of the indexer. This may be done by looking over the cards with the following questions in mind.

Has a wise choice of headings been made? (See p. 45.)

Is the information given under headings the searcher would be most likely to look for first, and have cross references been made from other possible headings? (See pp. 44, 52.)

Are the headings nouns or substantive phrases, not adjectives or descriptive phrases? (see pp. 45, 46, 50, 51.)

Are phrase headings indexed logically, inverted if necessary to bring the significant word to the key position? (See p. 46.)

Have headings been sufficiently divided by subheadings to enable the searcher to find quickly the material for which he is looking? (See p. 51.)

Are the subheadings correct subdivisions of the key word? (See pp. 51, 52.)

Do the subheadings read back properly to the key word? (See pp. 47, 48.)

Are the subheadings arranged logically—chronologically or alphabetically? (See p. 51.)

Have all citations on a given subject been given under a single heading, not divided between singular and plural forms of the key word? (See p. 51.)

Are the entries concise, containing no such phrases as *concerning, relating to,* and no unnecessary articles and prepositions? (See p. 47.)

Have the rules for alphabetical order been accurately and consistently followed? (See pp. 52–55.)

A colophon is a form of appendix much used in earlier days. It gives a brief account of the book, the place of copying, the name of the scribe, the date, and other information. The following one occurs on the last printed page of *Portrait of a Library,* a book by Margery Closey Quigley and William Elder Marcus, published by D. Appleton-Century Company, Inc., 1936.

> The text of this book has been composed in 11 point Baskerville with other sizes for headings and notes. The initials and certain larger lines are in Linotype Granjon.
>
> John Baskerville, one of England's distinguished book printers of the eighteenth century, was a successful type founder. For nearly a century and a half his beautiful Roman was lost in obscurity. The matrices had been taken to France about the time of the French Revolution and had disappeared during that period. But in 1929 a complete set of the lost characters was rediscovered in Paris. They have been reproduced in facsimile for the types used in this book.
>
> H. L. G.

DETAILS OF PAGE MAKEUP

The revision of pages, sometimes called cut-off but more often makeup, requires careful attention to a great many details. Aside from verifying corrections, many things incidental to the changing of strips of type into pages are to be noticed. In the printing office this work is sometimes done by the proofreader, oftentimes by a "reviser." The editor should check carefully the accuracy of the reviser's work, but should direct his attention particularly to the position of the cuts and the addition or deletion of words to avoid short or long pages.

Folios. The pages of a book may be numbered in either of two ways:

(*a*) The first page of front matter may be counted as page 1, the paging to follow consecutively throughout the entire book with the use of arabic numerals.

(*b*) The more common method is to use *lower-case* roman numerals for the front matter. The text then begins with 1 in arabic numerals.

The folios may be placed in the running head or centered at the foot of the page. The latter are called drop-folios. In the front matter the numerals are printed only on the preface and following parts, which in most books means the table of contents, list of illustrations, and introduction. They may be omitted on the first page of each of these sections, but most publishers use drop-folios, set in smaller type. Drop-folios are also used on the first page of each chapter or other pages with sinkage. Under full-page tables or cuts that carry no running head they may or may not be used. They are almost never used on half-titles in the body of the book.

Front matter.[1] The half-title should be placed in the optical center of the page. This is about one-eighth of the page length above the actual center.

The frontispiece is usually an insert tipped in to face the title page; that is, a page printed separately because it requires a different kind of paper, and pasted in when the book is bound. If it is not an insert but is printed on the same kind of paper as the text, it is included in the pagination of the front matter.

The preface begins on the first right-hand page following the dedication, or if there is no dedication, on the page facing the copyright notice.

The table of contents follows the preface, starting on the next right-hand page. If *chapter* and *page* as small-cap headings are used on the first page, they should be repeated at the top of each following page of the contents, but not elsewhere, such as following a center heading.

An errata list, if required, is often placed over the title or at the end of the contents, but sometimes at other points in the front matter or even at the end of the book.

The card page or face title, the copyright, and the frontispiece are left-hand pages, and the epigraph may be. Otherwise each new subject in the front matter and in the Appendix must start on a right-hand page; if the section ends on a right-hand page, it must therefore be followed by a blank page.

Running heads. The form and wording of running heads, if they are used, should be a part of the instructions sent to the printer by the publisher. The commonest practice is to use the book title on left-hand pages and the chapter title on right-hand pages, but other arrangements are common. (See p. 117.) If, as occasionally happens, the title is run across two facing pages, the customary practice is to put the full line on one page whenever the facing page for any reason takes no running head.

The line carrying running head and folio does not ordinarily extend over marginal notes or line numbers.

"Widows." A page should not be broken before the last line of a paragraph, leaving less than a full line for the first line on the following page. Such a line is called a widow; it should be avoided wherever possible. Furthermore, a page should have at least five lines of text.

[1] See page 138 for the order of the parts.

Long and short pages. If the exigencies of the makeup require long or short pages, facing pages ought to be of the same length. When it is impossible to adjust a short page by the usual method of spacing out a line to make a word or two run over, thus gaining a line, a very thin extra lead, a "card," can usually be inserted between the lines to gain the desired length.

Headings. A heading should not be the last line on a page, but should have at least two lines below it or else be carried over. The page preceding a heading may run short. Cut-in headings often cause the makeup man much trouble, for they too should have a line—preferably two lines—between them and the bottom of the page.

Blank lines. If blank lines are used to indicate a lapse of time or a break in the continuity, a page should not break at this blank, for then the blank line is completely lost. The blank should be within the page with at least two lines of type between it and the top or the bottom. If asterisks are used for this purpose, they may stand at the bottom of a page, but not at the top.

Poetry. If poetry must be divided elsewhere than between stanzas, it should not be divided after the first line or before the last line of a stanza. It is best not to divide between rhymed lines if such a division can be avoided. If a page breaks within a group of poetical extracts centered by the longest line of the group, the position of each part should be carefully checked, for the part which does not contain the longest line may be off center. Ordinarily such a part should be centered.

Columns. If matter appearing on the galley in two or more columns has to be broken, the page should not be cut straight across the columns unless they are to be read across the page, not down each column separately. If a page breaks within matter set in columns with headings over the columns, the headings should be repeated at the top of a left-hand page but not necessarily on a right-hand page.

Ditto marks. When matter containing ditto marks is made into pages, the reviser must see that no ditto marks are allowed to stand in the first line of a column. Likewise in beginning to revise from a new galley the reviser should note whether a change to ditto marks is possible. (Errors in these details occur often when galleys are set from reprint page copy and the pages break differently in the new makeup.) The same caution applies to dashes used for the author's name in bibliographies.

"Continued." When an entry-a-line index or any similar matter consisting of short lines with one or more indentions is made up, an indented line should not be allowed to stand as the first line on a left-hand page. A "continued" line should be inserted, composed of the key word of the preceding flush line, followed by *continued*. For example: Education—*continued*. Such a line is often used to avoid beginning a second column with an indented line, but usually this is not considered necessary.

See also *Continued tables,* page 130.

Illustrations. Illustrations that are wider than the page and must therefore be placed sidewise should have the left-hand side of the cut at the bottom of the page; that is, the legend should be on the right-hand side of the page. Whenever possible, such illustrations should be on a left-hand page, because in this position they are easier to read when the book is turned sidewise. Running heads are usually omitted and drop-folios may or may not be used. Tipped-in cuts never carry either headings or folios.

Page-width cuts. Generally speaking, a single illustration on a page should be placed slightly above the center of the page; that is, there should be a few more lines of type below the cut than above it. Good appearance is the criterion. The relative number of lines is very often determined by the type matter, since a cut must not be followed by less than a full line. Halftone cuts as wide as the type page should not be placed below the center of the page, but a narrow (top to bottom) line cut might be so placed. The legend under a cut very nearly as wide as the page may be set the width of the cut or the width of the page.

Narrow and small cuts. Most printers, unless instructed otherwise, will center a cut narrower than the page in the width of the page, leaving the space on each side blank. Therefore, if the editor wishes the type run around narrow cuts, he should give the printer a specific notation to that effect. To determine the most desirable position for small cuts, facing pages should be considered as a whole and the cuts arranged with due regard to balance and symmetry. A single illustration narrower than the page with type down one side should be next to the outside margin. If two or more small cuts are used on a page, the first should be placed at the outside margin, the next at the inside, the third outside. The spacing on all three sides of an illustration should appear to be even. The legend should be set the width of the cut and not be allowed to jut beyond either side. When the type is reset to run around a cut, as even a frame as possible should be striven for. Letterspacing should be avoided if possible, but if it is used, a whole word should be spaced and not a part only.

Footnotes. Notes to tables are placed directly below the tables (see p. 132) unless they are numbered consecutively with text footnotes. The latter are placed at the bottom of the page, set apart from the text by a blank line, a short rule, or a rule the full width of the page. On a short page at the end of a chapter the note follows the text with the same space intervening; in other words, it is not dropped to the foot of the page.

Turnovers. It is sometimes necessary to break a page in such a way that part of a footnote has to be run over to the following page. If this happens, care should be taken, especially in running over to an even-numbered page, to see that the note is broken in the middle of a sentence, so that the reader will know that the footnote is not complete on that page. The runover must, of course, be more than one line.

Position in line. Short footnotes may be indented like longer notes or they may be centered; if they are very short and other short notes occur on the same page, they may all be set in one line. For instance:

[1] Hamilton's *History of the Republic,* Vol. IV, p. 25.
[2] See page 333.

or

[1] *History of the Republic.*

or

[1] See page 333.   [2] *The Federalist.*

A series of many short footnotes on one page may be run in or set in columns. Whichever style is indicated as the preference of the author or publisher should be followed consistently throughout a work.

For the meaning and use of *ibid., op. cit.,* and *loc. cit.* see pages 22–23.

Signatures. The system of marking signatures by numbers or letters in the lower corner of the first page of each signature has been largely superseded by the use of collating marks.

TYPOGRAPHY OF VARIOUS LITERARY FORMS

LETTERS

Heading. The heading of a letter is placed with the longest line or the last line one em from the margin on the right. On the left the lines may align or the second and third lines may be successively indented. The first or "block" style is the more up to date. The address is usually set cap-and-small, the date cap-and-lower. Punctuation at ends of lines may be omitted; in business and informal letters abbreviations may be used.

912 O STREET
SACRAMENTO, CALIFORNIA
November 23, 1931

2671 FIFTH AVENUE
SACRAMENTO, CALIFORNIA
November 23, 1931

Salutation. The salutation should follow the style of the heading, whether block or indented. The name is usually set cap-and-small. Titles and other words accompanying the name cap-and-lower. Punctuation should be consistent with that of the heading.

MR. NATHANIEL KEENE, President
Acme Metal Products Company
Talbot Building
Detroit, Michigan

MY DEAR MR. KEENE:
    It gives me great pleasure ...

An alternative style, somewhat less common:

MR. NATHANIEL KEENE,
    3460 Gray Avenue,
        Detroit, Michigan.
My dear Mr. Keene:

Complimentary close and signature. The position of the complimentary close and signature is governed by appearance on the page. A simple signature should be set one em from the right margin with the complimentary close beginning two or three ems to the left of the first word of the signature.

Yours sincerely,
(Mrs.) LENA M. GOODRIDGE

A notation of official position appearing after a signature is ordinarily set in italic.

Yours truly,
DRUE WHITTAKER, *Secretary*

Sometimes this italic is too long to set on the same line with the name. The arrangement might then be:

Very truly yours,
FRANKLIN P. MORGAN,
Vice President for the Third District

Use of quotation marks. Letters that are excerpts from another work are usually set in type smaller than the text (see p. 12). It is then unnecessary to enclose them in quotation marks. If they are presented complete with heading and signature in a book in which excerpts are enclosed in quotes, it is correct to use opening quotes before the first line of the heading and closing quotes at the end of the signature.

> "2671 Fifth Ave.
> Sacramento, Cal.
> Nov. 23, 1931

My dear Mr. Keene:

You have heard, no doubt, that the proposition advanced by our good friend Mr. Smith has . . .

> Yours sincerely,
> Charles M. Butler"

A less simple style is to set opening quotes before each line of the heading, each line of the salutation, each paragraph of the letter, and each line of the complimentary close and signature, with closing quotes at the end. This style is commonly used if the letter is not complete.

> "2671 Fifth Avenue
> "Sacramento, California
> "November 23, 1931

"My dear Mr. Keene:

"You have heard, no doubt, that the proposition advanced by our good friend Mr. Smith has . . .

> "Very sincerely yours,
> "Charles M. Butler"

The following example would seem at first glance to illustrate this style of quoting, but actually the quotation marks are used here not to mark an extract but to denote the spoken words of a person.

"Dear Billy [he read]:

"You have been so interested in the progress which was being made on the big job that I know . . .

> "Devotedly,
> "Marj

"P.S. Mother . . ."

POETRY

Position. Poetry is ordinarily centered on the printed page—that is, set with the same space on both sides. The amount of the left-hand indention is determined by setting the longest line and centering it. The indention of this line is then taken as the major indention for the stanza or stanzas. If, however, one or two lines of the poem are disproportionately long, the average longest line should be centered to obtain the centered appearance. Centering in this manner a long poem covering several pages might bring about a page with the type falling decidedly to the left of the center; but unless an author or editor specifically orders the page centered, no change in position will be made. A long poem in one of the newer metrical forms is sometimes arbitrarily indented two or three ems regardless of centering.

Indention. Poetry with rhyming lines is sometimes set with all lines aligned on the left, sometimes with rhyming lines indented alike. The indentions of the original must be scrupulously followed. The indention of runover lines should be different from any regular line if possible, usually one em more; but this is often impossible in forms that have some lines deeply indented.

Scansion. If the author has placed an accent over a vowel to indicate that a word should be pronounced with an extra syllable, the grave accent is the one to use.

> She saw the horseshoe's curvèd charm
> To guard against her mother's harm.

For details of typographical style concerning poetical excerpts, see pages 118–119.

PLAYS

Dramatis personae. The list of the characters in a play is ordinarily centered on the page facing the beginning of the play, under the caption *Dramatis Personae* or simply *Characters*. The names of the characters are usually set cap-and-small.

CHARACTERS

SILAS GREEN (*a store porter*)
LIZA (*his wife*)
EMMA (*their daughter*)
AUNT NANCY (*the chip woman*)
JIM (*her son*)
TWO OTHER MEN

CHARACTERS

JERROLD PAIGE, *an artist*
ANNE PAIGE, *his wife*
CLARABELLE BRENT, *completing the triangle*

Stage directions. It is important that the text of a play should stand out clearly from all other matter. For that reason italics and cap-and-small are used more freely than in most other kinds of type composition. Names of characters are usually set cap-and-small, occasionally in small caps or in italic. Settings and stage directions are always italic. Names of characters are frequently set cap-and-small when they appear within italic stage directions, but not always. Directions may be enclosed within either parentheses or brackets—parentheses are the more easily set. Capitalization and punctuation should be logical and consistent. For instance, a complete sentence or a virtual sentence like *Exit* should begin with a capital and may be followed by a period within the parenthesis, whereas a word or phrase following the speaker's name or within a sentence of a single speech requires neither capital nor period. A definite style of arrangement for stage directions should be chosen and followed consistently. Several arrangements are possible, some of which are shown below.

Scene: *A room in Joseph's home, Vienna*
Time: *The present*
A vast dining room with a high ceiling. Long curtains hang in ample fold over the two windows. Against the wall stands an old oak clock. There are three doors: one at the back, opening upon a corridor leading to the street; one at the left, to the garden; one at the right, to the bedrooms. At the center is a table, set for two. A fire is burning in the fireplace.
As the curtain rises, the faint tinkling of a near-by church bell is heard.

ACT I

Scene I

Night, in the garden of NAAMAN *at Damascus. At the left the palace, with softly gleaming lights and music coming from the open latticed windows.... Enter by the palace door, the lady* TSARPI, *robed in red and gold, and followed by her maids,* KHAMMA *and* NUBTA. *She remains on the terrace; they go down into the garden, looking about, and returning to her.*

Reënter THISBE

THIS. This is old Ninny's tomb. Where is my love?
LION (*roaring*). Oh— (THISBE *runs off.*
DEM. Well roared, Lion.
THE. Well run, Thisbe.
HIP. Well shone, Moon. Truly the moon shines with a good grace.
       (*The* LION *shakes* THISBE'S *mantle and exit.*
THE. Well moused, Lion.
LYS. And so the lion vanished.

Orl. I will no further offend you than becomes me for my good. [*Orlando goes R, and waits.*]
Oli. [*with a backhand gesture*]. Get you with him, you old dog.
Adam. Is "old dog" my reward? [*He crosses to Orlando, his back to*

Oliver.]   God be with my old master!   He would not have spoke such a word.
[*Orlando goes out R, followed by Adam.   Oliver paces back and forth
nervously.*]

BUNN.

You'll see tonight the kind of sport I am.   And mind you, Sally!   It'll always
be that way.   (*A final hug.*)

SALLY.

Oh, Alf!

BUNN (*crosses left*).

I'm not one of those birds that feeds a girl chicken à la king before he marries
her and chicken hash afterwards!   No, siree!

(*He exits.* SALLY *stands in the middle of the room staring after him.   The
telephone rings.   She starts, crosses right to the switchboard and puts the
receiver over head.*)

SALLY (*talking into the phone in a businesslike way*).

Reliable Automobile Company.   (*Changing her tone.*)   Oh, hello, Maizie!
That you?   Yea, dearie!   I'm a leap-year bride!...

SILAS (*returning*).   Ah don't know why ah done it, but ah told 'em to wait
a few minutes.

(*He sits.*)

AUNT NANCY.   Ah don't know, Jim might come.

(*There is another knock on the door.*)

SILAS (*rising*).   Ah wonder what they want now?

(*He goes out again.*)

AUNT NANCY.   That might be Jim.

LIZA.   Ah hope it is.

(*Silas returns, followed by* JIM.   *When* AUNT NANCY *sees who it is she
flies to him.* JIM *opens his arms and draws her to him.*)

AUNT NANCY (*holding him off and looking at him*).   Is it you sure enough,
Jim?

JIM (*smiling*).   Yes'm, it's me.

Metrical lines. Metrical lines are frequently broken in plays, two or more
characters each speaking part of a line. When the page is wide enough to
allow it, the second part should begin one em beyond the end of the first
part. If the page is too narrow to allow this, the second part may be set
flush to the right margin. If there would be no extra space at the left end
if the part were set in this manner, it should begin one em beyond the preceding line and the runover indented like other turned-over lines. The
following examples show the forms recommended.

GIRL. You must not talk of Death.
(*She comes hastily to him and holds
him tightly in her arms.*)
He is abroad this night. He rides on horses.
He walks the highways and he creeps through lanes
And knocks at many doors.
BOY.   He cannot break
The bolts upon our doors.
GIRL.   Poor fool, he breathes
With his thin icy breath out of the night
And our stout doors are thinner than thin mist.

FICTION

The typography of fiction presents few difficulties. More artistic and decorative faces can be chosen than would be appropriate for utilitarian texts written to instruct, and subsidiary types may give an opportunity to achieve varied effects in keeping with the subject. The editing of a work of fiction, on the contrary, often proves trying. Unless the writing has been carefully done by an experienced author, the editor is likely to find puzzling capitalization, faulty punctuation, and misused words. The story may be full of dialect or of localized words not to be found in the dictionary. It may contain slang which the author could not decide how to spell. Briticisms may be used inaccurately, or foreign words and phrases may be used to excess. Misquotations and the misspelling or misuse of common expressions are not uncommon; such expressions, for instance, as *lay* (not *lie*) *of the land, whited sepulcher, to the manner born, combat à outrance* are often misspelled. Anachronisms appear and likewise inconsistent statements: sometimes the girl who had blue eyes in the beginning of the story changes them for brown later on. In short, only by thoughtful concentration on details can fiction be satisfactorily edited.

Paragraphing. In dialogue a change of speaker is a signal for a new paragraph. Two remarks of the same speaker separated by text may be in one paragraph, but not the words of different speakers.

Nicknames. It is usually undesirable to enclose nicknames in quotation marks, though some offices follow the rule of quoting them the first time they are used. There are two reasons for this policy: (1) It avoids the spotty or bristling effect of a page sprinkled or thickly sown with quotes; (2) it assumes that the reader can guess that "Dusty" is a man without being nudged in the ribs by quotes. It is better to overrate than to underrate the intelligence of a reader. (See also pages 292, 293.)

Slang, cant, specialized words. Slang should not be enclosed in quotes. Words used in a localized setting should not be quoted merely because they may be new to the reader. For instance, in a Western cowboy story the single quotation marks are unnecessary in sentences like "He went out to 'bulldog' a steer"; "It's just a 'charco.'" War, aviation, nautical, racketeer, northern and other localized stories all use words or terms that might be quoted if used out of their setting but for which quotation marks are unnecessary when they are in their proper environment.

Abbreviations. No abbreviations should be used in dialogue except Mr. and Mrs. and abbreviations the speaker himself would use, such, perhaps, as R.A.F., O.K., A.W.O.L. Numbers, likewise, should be spelled out, for this is the way they would be spoken.

Dialect. No correction of grammar should be attempted in quoted speech. Such errors are usually intentional, to indicate the lack of education of the character speaking. No distortion of spelling should be used if the distortion would be pronounced exactly or approximately as the correct spelling is pronounced. Thus, "could uv" is a needless hardship because it is a common way of pronouncing "could of."

LEGAL WRITING: CITATIONS, ETC. [1]

Publishers of legal books have special style sheets of forms which are technical and largely inflexible. This present handbook attempts to cover only such problems as would normally confront a proofreader in a general printing office. Precedents could be found for styles other than those here shown, especially in the use of italics.

Names of cases. In a complete citation italics are unnecessary.

Davison v. Johonnot, 7 Met. (Mass.) 388

The name of a legal case appearing without citation numbers is usually set in italic.

McKeeman v. Goodridge   *Hogan v. French*

The phrases *in re, ex rel., ex parte,* etc., are generally italic in a roman title, roman in an italic one.

People ex rel. *Hogan v. French*
Ex parte Harold Elliston *et al.,* 36 Atl. 312

The first word in the name of a case, proper names, and words replacing proper names should be capitalized.

In the matter of Troutman
Hartwell, appellant, v. Carter, respondent
United States v. Nineteen Quarts of M-E Chlorine Solution

[1] A valuable little booklet called *A Uniform System of Citation* is published by The Harvard Law Review Association (Gannett House, Cambridge, Mass.), 6th ed. 1939.

References. The name of the case should be separated from the reference by a comma. Within the reference punctuation is reduced to a minimum, avoiding double punctuation.

Raher v. Raher, 150 Iowa 521, 35 L. R. A. (N.S.) 292
Rev. Stat. 1915 (Civ. Code) p. 1234

If the name of a state or of a reporter is given in full, no comma is needed between it and the page number or date.

140 Iowa 410   2 Black 635, 668

It is wise to be extremely cautious about making changes in the form of a citation for the sake of apparent consistency. For instance, in citations of Acts of Parliament, public Acts are cited thus:

3 & 4 Geo. V, c. 12, ss. 18, 19

Private Acts are cited:

3 & 4 Geo. V, c. xxii, ss. 18, 19

Again, parentheses and brackets are not interchangeable. In references to Law Reports published by the Incorporated Council of Law, dates up to 1890 are enclosed in parentheses; 1891 and later dates are in brackets. Note also the position of the comma: [2]

Cooper v. Whittingham (1880), 15 Ch. D. 501
Thompson v. City Glass Bottle Co., [1902] 1 K. B. 233

Abbreviations are used freely in references. Besides the usual abbreviations like bk., ed., pt., 2d, 3d, n. (note), and c. (chapter), names of persons, places, courts, books, and periodicals are all shortened whenever possible, not according to the whim of the writer but in accordance with established forms.[3]

Court reporters. Proofreaders sometimes fall into errors of punctuation with names of reporters, mistaking full names for abbreviations or vice versa. Some of these names are listed below.

Bail., Bailey	Ben., Benedict
Barb., Barber	Benn., Bennett
Barnard., Barnardiston	Bing., Bingham
Barr	Binn., Binney
Bay	Black

[2] See Horace Hart, *Rules for Compositors and Readers at the University Press, Oxford,* 29th ed. (London, Humphrey Milford, 1930), pp. 62, 63.

[3] For authoritative lists see Bouvier's *Law Dictionary,* Black's *Law Dictionary,* or *Corpus Juris Secundum* 1, viii–xviii and 276, notes 5–18.

Bland

Brock., Brockenbrough

Bull., Buller

Burn., Burnett

Burr., Burrows

Call

Car., Carrington

Cart., Carter

Cliff., Clifford

Cold., Coldwell

Colt., Coltman

Cranch

Curt., Curtis

Dall., Dallas

Daly

Day

Dears., Dearsley

Desauss., Desaussure

Dick., Dickens or Dickenson

Dill., Dillon

Dow

Drew., Drewry

Drink., Drinkwater

Gratt., Grattan

Heisk., Heiskell

Houst., Houston

Hun

Johns., Johnson

Kern., Kernan

Lea

Leigh

Leon., Leonard

Lush., Lushington

Man., Manning (Mich.)

Mann. & G., Manning and Granger

Marsh., Marshall

Mart., Martin

Pears., Pearson

Penne., Pennewill

Pet., Peters

Pick., Pickering

Port., Porter (Ala.)

Rand., Randolph (Va.)

Rich., Richardson

Rob., Robinson

Sim., Simmons

Strange

Vent., Ventris

Vern., Vernon

Wall., Wallace

Book titles. In citations the names of books, government publications, and periodicals are often set in caps and small caps.

ANN. CAS.: *American Annotated Cases*
L. R. A. (N.S.): *Lawyers Reports Annotated,* New Series
See 2 WIGMORE, EVIDENCE (2d ed. 1923) §856.
47 HARV. L. REV. at 618

WRITINGS ON RELIGION

References. The form in which references to Scripture are set is largely a matter of the personal preference of the author and the editor, but clearness is essential. Book names containing five or more letters are usually abbreviated. (Approved forms are listed on p. 183.) The use of numerals and punctuation shown in the following is the style preferred by many.

Luke 4:16*a*   II Cor. 1:16–20; 2:5
Matt. 2:5–13   Luke 3:6—5:2

(Some publishers use a space after the colon. The em dash, as in Luke 3:6—5:2 is used when the reference extends from one chapter into another.)

Another style frequently followed uses periods instead of colons, and lower-case or small-cap roman numerals for the chapter numbers.

1 Sam. xxv.23–31   Num. ii.10, x. 14
Job xxxii.32   Luke iii.6–v.2

Proper names. The spelling of some of the names of the books of the Bible in the Douay Version, the English version used by the Roman Catholic Church, is different from the King James spelling. Both spellings are shown on page 183. Some of the more familiar proper names that differ in spelling are listed below.

Douay	*King James*	*Douay*	*King James*
Agar	Hagar	Jezabel	Jezebel
Abiu	Abihu	Joas	Joash
Amorrhites	Amorites	Josaphat	Jehosaphat
Amalec	Amalek	Juda	Judah
Achab	Ahab	Lia	Leah
Aman	Naaman	Machabees	Maccabees
Assuerus	Ahasuerus	Madian	Midian
Barac	Barak	Menasses	Manasseh
Booz	Boaz	Mardochai	Mordecai
Bethania	Bethany	Mathusala	Methuselah
Caiphas	Caiaphas	Messias	Messiah
Dalila	Delilah	Nebuchodonosor	Nebuchadnezzar
Debbora	Deborah	Ninive	Nineveh
Elias	Elijah	Noe	Noah
Eliseus	Elisha	Noemi	Naomi
Eliu	Elihu	Pharao	Pharaoh
Gedeon	Gideon	Phinees	Phineas
Gethsemani	Gethsemane	Putiphar	Potiphar
Heli	Eli	Roboam	Rehoboam
Henoch	Enoch	Sara	Sarah
Ismael	Ishmael	Sisara	Sisera
Japhet	Japheth	Sem	Shem
Jephte	Jephtha		

Type. The words LORD and GOD are sometimes set cap-and-small in the Bible and hymnbooks, but this style is by no means universal.

The LORD will perfect *that which* concerneth me: thy mercy, O LORD, *endureth* for ever.—Ps. 138.

(The italic indicates that these words were supplied by the translator.)

Quotation marks are not used in the Bible.

Symbols. The following symbols may be used in religious work:

℞ Response—indicating the part repeated by the congregation in a responsive religious service.

℣ Versicle—indicating the part recited or sung by the priest.

✠ or + A sign of the cross used by the Pope, and by the Roman Catholic bishops and archbishops, immediately before the subscription of their names. In some service books it is used in those places where the sign of the cross is to be made.

SCIENTIFIC WRITING: EQUATIONS, FORMULAS, ETC.

Type. Letters in mathematical equations should be set in italics; likewise letters referring to geometrical figures.

$$x + y = 10$$
$$\angle\ ABC = \angle\ ABD$$

These letters should not be changed to roman when they are used in an italic context.

It appears from (2) that *lines parallel to the x-axis* (including the x-axis itself) *have the slope O.* For in that case $y_2 = y_1$.

In scientific writing many shortened forms are written without an abbreviating point. For example:

Chemical symbols are always roman and without a point.

| Na | O | NaCl | HNO$_3$ | P | CO$_2$ |

Likewise trigonometrical terms.

| cos | cosec | cot | log | mod | sin | tan |
| cosine | cosecant | cotangent | logarithm | modulus | sine | tangent |

Opening and closing parentheses, brackets, and braces used in mathematical equations should be of the same size and should be as wide as the widest quantity within them.

$$b\left[7a + b\left(6 - \tfrac{b}{a}\right)\right]$$

Superior figures. When both inferior and superior figures follow a number, the inferior should be set first: $5_2{}^2$. A prime is always set close to the figure or letter. Exponents precede all punctuation except the period of an abbreviation.

$$A' > B', a^2 > b^2$$

cm.^{2}, square centimeter, in.^{3}, cubic inch

Spacing. Signs—plus, minus, equality, arrow, etc.—are usually hair-spaced or thin-spaced. (An em dash should not be used for a minus sign.) (The editor would do well to send the printer a sample showing the amount of spacing he prefers, because some compositors tend to use an excessive amount.)

$$x + 3y - z = 0$$
Find the sum of 8 terms of the series 1, 2, 4, $\cdots$.
Use $x = -3, -2, \cdots, 6$.

(If the three points are set on the line instead of being centered as above, a justifier or spaceband should precede them: the notation B_1, B_2, B_3, ... is)

A hair space or a thin space is often used between figures and letters in formulas and equations.

$$2KClO_3 \rightarrow 2KCl + 3O_2$$

A thin space should be used before N and M in expressing normality or molarity.

$$2.5\,N \qquad\qquad 5\,M \qquad\qquad 0.1\,M$$

Position. A series of equations should be aligned by the equality signs and should be so set as to give the appearance of being centered as a whole.

$$x + y + z = 21{,}000$$
$$x = 2z$$
$$.05y = .06z$$

Thus, $(42)^3 = (40 + 2)^3 = 40^3 + 3 \times 40^2 \times 2 + 3 \times 40 \times 2^2 + 2^3$
$$= 64{,}000 + 9600 + 480 + 8$$
$$= 74{,}088$$

$$SO_2 + Cl = SO_2Cl$$
$$SO_2Cl_2 + 2H_2O = H_2SO_4 + 2HCl$$

Short equations and formulas can often be run in the text to save space, but important equations and formulas should be placed on separate lines ("displayed"). The printer will not presume to center equations if they do not appear so in the copy; therefore careful preparation of copy by author and editor in this detail is necessary.

Division. If an algebraic expression must be divided, it is best to break it after a sign rather than before it.

$$\left| \begin{array}{l} 15r + 6s - 11t + r - 9s + t - 2s + \\ 5r - 2t - 10r \end{array} \right.$$

An equation may be divided, but it is much better to set it on a line by itself, centered, in preference to breaking it. An equation that is longer than a full line should be broken at the equality sign or the arrow. Usually the first part should be set flush at the left and the second part flush at the right.

$$\sqrt{a^2 + ab + b^2} : \sqrt{c^2 + cd + d^2}$$
$$= \sqrt{a^2 - ab + b^2} : \sqrt{a^2 - cd + d^2}$$

$$CH_3 \cdot CH(NH_2) \cdot COOH + H_2O \rightarrow$$
$$NH_3 + CH_3 \cdot CHOH \cdot COOH$$

Note: The vertical lines show width of page.

An equation like the following that is too wide to set in one line is best set with the turnover indented to clear the equality sign.

$$S_1 = \text{the stress resulting from the direct tension in the cable.}$$

A formula written without plus or minus signs is indivisible.

Ferric ammonium alum,
$$[(NH_4)_2SO_4]\ [Fe_2(SO_4)_3]\ [H_2O]_{24}$$

Capitalization.   Equations are essentially sentences; therefore capitalization in the first half of an equation (the subject) is unnecessary for all except the first word:

$$\text{Life in hours} = 1,500 \div (P.F.)^2$$
$$\text{Radiant efficiency} = \frac{2 \times 25.1}{A \times G \times H}$$

Capitalization following the equality sign is largely a matter of the author's preference.   Practice varies widely, but consistency of form should be observed throughout a work.

$$\text{Power} = \text{force} \times \text{velocity}$$
$$\text{Per cent of error} = \frac{\text{Possible error}}{\text{Measurement}} \times 100\%$$
$$\frac{\text{Length of the arc}}{\text{Circumference}} = \frac{\angle \text{ of sector}}{360°}$$

Punctuation.   No punctuation is necessary after centered equations.

The equation for the above reaction is
$$2HCl + Zn \rightarrow H_2 + ZnCl_2$$
It gives us much more information ...

Notes on the use of mathematical signs.[1] The signs $<$ and $>$ mean "is less than" and "is greater than," respectively. It is therefore unnecessary to use a verb with them, or with similar signs.

Wrong: ...where A is $< B$. $C \parallel$ to AB
Right: ...where $A < B$. $C \parallel AB$

In etymological text $<$ is used to mean "derived from." It is much employed in this manner in dictionaries.

The verb used with the sign for equality should be consistent throughout a work. In the following *is* is preferable.

Possible: Does $\angle C = \angle Z$?
Preferable: Is $\angle C = \angle Z$?

The word following the sign $\therefore$, "hence," or $\because$, "because," is usually lower case:

$\therefore$ the distance is greater than 230 kilometers.

In text the form $a \div b$ or a/b is preferable to $\frac{a}{b}$ because this last form is hard to set, and the greater depth of the vertical fraction causes uneven leading of lines.

The American Standards Committee favors $a/b = c/d$ for proportion, rather than $a:b :: c:d$. The Committee also discourages the use of the sign $\doteqdot$, "approaches," preferring arrows: $\rightarrow$

If in consecutive lines $=$ and $::$ are used, they should align in the same way as a series of equations all containing $=$.

Mathematical signs in a reading text. The per cent sign should be used only when the nature of the text makes the use of signs appropriate. If a phrase like "44 to 50 per cent" is expressed with the sign, both numbers should be followed by the sign:

This contains 44% to 50% of ethyl alcohol by weight, and about 50% to 56% by volume.

There is no justification for the use in straight reading matter of such forms as: $+$ sign, "$+$" sign, "plus" sign. If the sign itself is used, the word *sign* is redundant. If the word *sign* must be used the preferable form is *plus sign*. Similarly incorrect are the terms "caret sign," "a dagger sign," "a $ mark." These should be written "a caret," "a dagger," "a dollar mark."

[1] Most dictionaries have comprehensive lists of mathematical signs, as well as others.

A superior plus sign following a letter symbol signifies a unit charge of positive electricity, a superior minus indicates a negative charge.[2] If two or more of these superiors follow a symbol, they are best placed side by side. Setting them one below another is difficult and expensive. Ca^{++} signifies a calcium ion carrying two positive charges.

A plus sign placed above the initial letter of a substance indicates that it is a base or alkaloid: $\overset{+}{M}$, morphine; $\overset{+}{Q}$, quinine. A minus sign over a letter indicates an acid.

The sign of multiplication (not an x) should be used to indicate magnification: $\times 1000$ indicates magnification of 1000 diameters. Less than life size would be indicated: $\times \frac{1}{2}$.

For the expression of dimensions, see p. 200.

ILLUSTRATIONS

On pages 36–38, under the heading Illustrations, only so much instruction was given as seemed essential for authors whose work required illustration. More technical treatment of the subject is included here to familiarize the inexperienced editor with terminology and methods, thus providing the groundwork upon which he can build by studying more comprehensive treatments of this very technical subject.

PHOTOENGRAVING

Wax engravings. A polished plate of copper or brass is covered with a thin film of specially prepared wax, and the engraving of this surface is done with a sharp-pointed tool. Straight lines are cut by machine, curved lines by hand, lettering by pressing ordinary types into the warm wax, one letter or one word at a time. Drawings may be transferred to the wax plate by tracing or by photography. The wax-covered plate thus becomes a mold, and a printing plate is made from it by the usual electrotyping process.

The wax method is the best for making printing plates for maps, charts, and diagrams. Ruled forms printed from wax-rule electrotypes show all joints perfect and corners square. Drawings supplied for wax engravings should be accurate, but they may be made with either pencil or ink. Any drawing

---

[2] A plus or a minus sign placed above the letter symbol may be used for these expressions, but the form noted above is preferable from a typographical standpoint because the superiors are far more easily set and do not cause any uneven leading between lines. Signs above the symbols must be placed in position by hand and the rest of the line filled with quads. The space between a line with a symbol and the line above will thus be greater than between other lines.

which will require photographing should be carefully executed in ink.

Line engravings. Line engravings are used for any picture consisting of black lines on a white ground. By photoengraving processes the chart, map, drawing, or similar subject is reproduced on sheet zinc or copper.

Ben Day cuts. The effect of shading can be procured in line cuts by a process called Ben Day. Blank areas of the design can be broken up into a printing surface of fine dots by using a Ben Day film or "screen." Such films are available in several hundred designs, ranging from fine dots to coarse rules and lace-curtain designs.

Line color plates. Line cuts can be made for reproduction with colored areas. A separate plate must be furnished the printer for each color used; *i.e.,* two-color work, two plates; three-color work, three plates, etc. Line drawings that are to be reproduced in color may be drawn complete in black ink as one copy. If, however, two solid or filled-in areas of the design are to appear line to line in different colors, a ragged edge should be drawn at the line edge of one represented color for separation.

When a lighter tone is desired in the reproduction of one or more solid colors, the Ben Day process is used. The strength of color tone is determined by the fineness of the screen, but a finer one than number 85 is impractical because most line color plates are etched on zinc.

When copy for color line cuts is prepared for the engraver, colors should be indicated in the following manner: A good tracing paper, the same size as the art work, should be pasted at the top of the drawing and laid smoothly over the design; then with wax crayon or water color the areas that are to appear in color should be traced and filled in. When Ben Day cuts are ordered, the film pattern desired should be ordered by number from the engraver's card.

Tint blocks. When a large area of solid color is desired, as for a background for a picture in another color, it is often most easily obtained by using a tint block, a metal plate made without a screen, which lays ink evenly on the paper.

Halftone process. Reproduction of photographs, wash drawings, oil or water-color paintings, and the like, for one-color printing is done by the halftone plate method. Halftones are produced on sheet copper in the same manner as line plates, except that when the negative is made, a mechanically perfect screen is inserted into the camera between the photographic lens and the sensitized plate. The screen is a piece of plate glass etched with black, opaque lines from top to bottom and from side to side, 65 to 150 lines or more to the inch, creating small square dots of transparency through which the light is filtered on to the sensitized camera plate. Thus the image or art work is automatically broken up into tiny dots, which are ultimately the printing surface of the plate; i.e., a halftone plate becomes a series of dots standing in relief.

Halftone color plates. The halftone color process is based on the fact that by combining red, yellow, blue, and black in correct proportion all desired colors and shades can be secured. To use this fact in printing it is necessary to have a separate plate for each of these colors, and to run the printing sheet through the press for each color. When a color prints over one or two or three others, the tints and shades of the copy will be reproduced.

The plates are secured by photographing the copy through filters made of celluloid stained with aniline in the complementary colors. That is, when the copy is photographed through an orange filter, all the blue in the picture will photograph, but no red or yellow. For the red plate a green filter is used; for the yellow, a violet filter; and for the black, a yellow filter. Proved with black ink, the plates made from these negatives will show in the proof as clear black for the pure color, and varying shades of gray for the portions that are mixed with other colors.

The usual order of printing a four-color-process illustration is yellow first, then red, blue, and black; but it may be printed in a different order. With all color process cuts the engraver will supply a set of proofs indicating the order of printing the colors and the mixture and make of inks. These proofs, called progressives, show the successive stages of printing, first the yellow, then the red on the yellow, then the blue on the yellow and red, and last, the black.

All types of cuts such as line engravings, Ben Day'd engravings, line color plates, halftone engravings, either black only or in color can be used by mounting on type high wood blocks, to be run with type or locked up with type for molding of electrotypes.

DETERMINATION OF SIZE

A drawing or picture of any size can be reproduced by the photoengraving process in any desired smaller size, in the same size, or—within limits—in a larger size. Reduction usually produces the most satisfactory result. When the order is given to the engraver, only one dimension need be given him, for the proportions always remain the same, whether the copy is reduced or enlarged. Since this is so, the dimensions of a reproduction can be quickly found by proportion:

New width is to new length as copy width is to copy length

Suppose a reproduction 3 inches wide is desired of a picture 5 inches wide by 7 inches tall.

$$3 / x = 5 / 7$$
$$5x = 21$$
$$x = 4\tfrac{1}{5}$$

Or the following simple formula can be used:

$$\frac{\text{new width}}{\text{copy width}} \times \text{copy length} = \text{new length}$$

$$\frac{3}{5} \times 7 = \frac{21}{5} = 4\tfrac{1}{5}$$

Or the reduced size can be determined in this manner: On a piece of paper the size of the copy draw a diagonal from the upper left-hand corner to the lower right-hand corner. Measure along the top edge the desired width of the cut and from this point drop a perpendicular. The length of this line to the point where it intersects the diagonal is the length of the reduced cut.

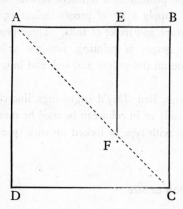

ABCD is the size of the copy

A to *E* is the desired width of the reduced cut

E to *F* is the length of the reduced cut

PREPARING COPY AND ORDERING CUTS

Indication of size. The width of the reproduction desired should be indicated in the margin of the copy by arrow points and numerals on one side only: ←3→. Photographs sometimes have an unnecessary amount of sky or foreground, some of which can be cut off, or "cropped," so that only the essential part of the photograph is reproduced. If only part of an illustration is to be reproduced, the part to be used may be indicated by means of small black lines in the margin. If lines are drawn across the face of the photograph, they may not be geometrically true and further cropping may be required to make the reproduction square; besides that, the photograph is spoiled for any later use.

Retouching. Engravers can increase the contrast in a photograph or bring out various details; or obliterate blemishes or unwanted material in copy. This work is not done unless ordered, and a special charge is made for it. Sometimes retouching of the plate is done to increase the clearness of it. This is called tooling for lighter tones and burnishing for blacks.

Finish of halftones. The edges of halftone cuts can be finished with or without a fine line border. If the border is desired, the order should specify "with line." A *vignette* is a picture that fades away toward the edges with no perceptible edge. A *hard vignette* edge is one that breaks abruptly with a very uneven outline. A *silhouette* is a cut showing the picture with no background. A *highlight* halftone is one in which the dots of the lighter shade have been cut away.

Screens. When halftones are ordered, the size of screen to be used should be specified.

    50-line—for stereotypes and general newspaper work

    65-line—for better quality newspapers

    85-line—for high-grade newspapers, blotters, colored bond paper

    100-line—for machine-finished papers, super, and the cheaper bonds

    120-line—for dull-coated stocks and high-grade bonds

    133-line—for coated stock

    150-line—for high-grade coated stock—fine book and catalogue work

    175-line—for the highest grade of coated stock—subjects having very fine detail

When there is any doubt about the best size of screen to use, the coarser screen should be chosen. The right screens for a given work should be selected by the photoengraver; and for good results he needs to see the material to be reproduced and to know at least (1) the paper to be used and (2) the method of printing. He should know whether printing is to be from original halftones or from flat or curved electrotypes; if a cylinder press or a multicolor press is to be used. If he knows what kind of stock and what kind of inks are to be used for color-process cuts, he can submit proof on the same stock and with the same inks.

PHOTOGRAVURE

Photogravure is intaglio photoengraving; that is, the printing plate made by photographing the subject is etched so that the parts that print are incised in the plate instead of standing in relief. When a photogravure is printed, the ink lies in the hollows, while the raised surface is wiped clean. Photogravures are more expensive than plates for relief printing, and a plate will yield only a few thousand good impressions. They give very satisfactory reproductions of photographic subjects.

Rotogravure is a modification of this process frequently used in magazines and widely employed for the pictorial supplements of newspapers. The plates are curved for printing on a rotary press.

LITHOGRAPHY

Another technique for the reproduction of pictorial matter is lithography, or planography. The earliest plates were of lithographic stone, but zinc and aluminum plates are more generally used now; hence the older term lithography, "writing on stone," is less appropriate than the broader one, planography, "printing from a flat or plane surface." The method is based on the antipathy between grease and water. The ink adheres only to the design, which is laid on the stone or metal with a greasy ink, and is rejected by the dampened remainder of the treated plate.

Some of the best scientific color printing is still done by lithography. Godey's illustrations were so made. The copy may be a drawing or a sketch, a photograph or a model.

The mercury process is a photolithographic process in which mercury is substituted for water as an ink-repellent medium.

PHOTO-OFFSET

Photo-offset is the planographic process most often used today. The plates are photographic positives on a flexible plate of zinc or aluminum. These plates are fastened on one of the three cylinders of an offset press. The inked impression is offset on to the hard-rubber surface of a second cylinder, from which it is transferred to the sheet of paper, which runs over the third cylinder.

Much finer reproductions are possible by this process than by photoengraving methods; screens as fine as 175 can be used in photographing halftones. Offset has the great merit of producing soft effects even on rough or uncoated papers. It is, in fact, the only method by which halftone color illustrations can be printed satisfactorily on other than highly glazed or coated paper.

Any picture, drawing, or object which can be photographed can be reproduced by photo-offset.

PHOTOGELATIN, OR COLLOTYPE

The most nearly perfect method of color reproduction is by photogelatin, or collotype, plates. The process resembles both planography and intaglio because the printing surface is differentially receptive to ink and moisture but also has raised parts of the surface that reject ink and depressed parts that receive it. The subject is photographed without a screen and the negative printed on a gelatin film, which is chemically hardened and fastened to a plate. Only about a thousand copies can be made, but the process produces very fine results.

LEGENDS ("CAPTIONS") [1]

Only a few printing conventions relate to legends; beyond them the editor is free to follow his own ideas as to type and arrangement. The type used is almost always of a font smaller than the body of the text, but larger than the type used for footnotes.

BEYOND THE HIGHWAY
North Chatham, N. H.

CAMPING IN LAPLAND
The construction of an igloo

Quotations from the text may be used as legends:

A LESSON IN LIBERTY
"They began to think and talk and act."

The Captain was given an audience.

There are many possibilities in the combination and arrangement of types in legends. For instance:

A Little Ray. A minute bit of
protoplasm secretes this marvelously
intricate shell.

[1] The term *caption* means *headline* and is properly applied to the title above a table, chart, map, or the like. *Legend* can refer to only one thing, the line or lines below an illustration. It would be well if this distinction could be retained, but many workers prefer to ignore it and use *caption* exclusively.

A Little Ray   A Little Ray   a little ray   **A Little Ray**

A minute bit of protoplasm secretes this marvelously intricate shell.

A minute bit of protoplasm secretes this marvelously intricate shell.

A minute bit of protoplasm secretes this marvelously intricate shell.

A minute bit of protoplasm secretes this marvelously intricate shell.

Figure 8. A Little Ray   Fig. 8.—A Little Ray

Editors sometimes seek change and variety in the typography of legends and may secure it by an unorthodox combination of faces and an arbitrary capitalization quite outside the rules. Note the following, from Pahlow's *Man's Great Adventure,* a history published by Ginn and Company in 1934.

If You have Trouble *with* Dates,
Here *is where your* Troubles
Began

Pompeii *Coming to Life again,* and
Vesuvius, *which* Never Died

The legend should be no wider than the cut, except that under a cut slightly narrower than the width of the page the legend may be the width of the page.

It is customary to use a period after a complete sentence used as a legend, but when the legend is topical no period is necessary.

Credits. Acknowledgment should always be made for illustrations reproduced by permission of copyright owners. The simplest credit is a line in 5-point or 6-point italic close under the cut, flush left or right. For example:

Courtesy U. S. Geological Survey   *W. H. Jackson*
Fremont Peak from Seneca Lake

© *Field Museum of Natural History*

Ewing Galloway

Certain copyright owners may require the inclusion of specified credit lines in the legend:

Figure 5
The Development of the Roman Alphabet
By permission of the
Norman T. A. Munder Company

Fig. 371. Ichthyosaur—Fish Lizard. (From
specimen at College of the City of New
York. Photo by Stratford.)

FIG. 104. *A*, diagrammatic representation of staminate inflorescence; *B*, diagram
of branch of staminate inflorescence showing three flowers; . . . *stp*, stipule. (Redrawn and adapted from Briosi and Tognini, *Istituto Botanico di Pavia*.)

FIG. 103. Habit of carpellate flowers of hemp.
(Reproduced from *Yearbook of U. S. Dept. of
Agriculture*, 1913.)

Fig. 290.—Schultze.
From Lacy, *Biology and Its
Makers*. Courtesy of Henry
Holt & Co.

PART IV—PRINTING STYLE

MAIN DIVISIONS

A person unfamiliar with printing terminology would be likely to think that "printing style" would refer to the dress of a book—its type face, arrangement, makeup, and binding. The printer, however, uses the word *format* in referring to these aspects and *printing style* to indicate printing practice in the use of abbreviations, italics, capitals, punctuation marks, and the like. Any printed matter therefore has style of some sort. Newspaper style and book style differ widely in some respects, and styles commonly preferred by periodicals or technical publications may be unlike either.

Publishers differ. One may have a style sheet to which all publications must conform. Another may have a preferred style but may willingly permit an author to follow some other authorized style if he can follow it consistently and intelligently. Most publishers are of this latter sort.

The following is a list of useful handbooks on the printing arts, printing style, etc.

A Manual of Style. Chicago, The University of Chicago Press. 10th edition, 1937.
This is the most widely known and used manual of book style. Most book publishers consult it for authority on any points not covered by their own house style sheet.

A Handbook of Style for Yale University Press. Laura Hadley Moseley, Compiler. Preliminary Edition, 1934.
Large portions of this handbook were taken from the Chicago *Manual,* but it does not follow the Chicago style in all matters.

Horace Hart, *Rules for Compositors and Readers at the University Press, Oxford.* London, Humphrey Milford. 29th ed., 1930.
This small volume is full of useful information for one who is trying to follow British usage.

F. Howard Collins, *Authors' and Printers' Dictionary,* 7th ed. Oxford University Press, 1933.
Although this is not a publishers' manual in the same sense that the books above mentioned are, it has a store of useful information on printing forms and is a most useful book of reference.

John Benbow, *Manuscript and Proof.* New York, Oxford University Press, 1937.

Porter G. Perrin, *An Index to English.* Scott, Foresman and Company, 1939.

C. O. Sylvester Mawson and John William Robson, *The Complete Desk Book.* New York, Thomas Y. Crowell Company, 1939.

G. B. Ives, *Text, Type and Style.* Boston, Little, Brown & Co., 1922.

Proofroom Manual, Kingsport Press. Kingsport, Tennessee, 1929.

Reference Handbook for the Preparation of Manuscript with an Order Form and a Manual of Style. Adopted by Composition Group, National Book Manufacturers Association, 1931.

United States Government Printing Office, *Style Manual.* Washington, 1935.
The rules in this style manual were compiled for use on work that is nonliterary and businesslike rather than artistic, and they represent good usage to follow in a vast bulk of printing that could not be classed as either book or newspaper work. This is a valuable reference book for anyone not concerned exclusively with books.

United States Department of the Interior, *Suggestions to Authors of Papers Submitted for Publication by the United States Geological Survey,* 4th ed. Washington, 1935.

Grant Milnor Hyde, *Handbook for Newspaper Workers.* New York, D. Appleton-Century Company, 1926.

The New York Times Style Book.

The Style Book of the Detroit News.

The Milwaukee Journal Style Book.

Chicago Tribune, Rules of Composition, 1934.

The Chicago Daily News Stylebook, 1930.

Style Book, Springfield Republican and Daily News.

Deskbook of the School of Journalism, 12th ed., 1935. The University of Missouri Bulletin, Vol. 16, No. 19, Journalism Series No. 72.

Iowa Newspaper Desk Book, University of Iowa Extension Bulletin No. 326, Oct. 15, 1933. School of Journalism Series No. 5.

ABBREVIATIONS

Use. The number of abbreviations which may properly be used depends upon the nature of the text. Very few are allowable in formal or literary compositions, but many may be used with propriety in nonliterary texts. In footnotes and citations abbreviations may be used freely.

Every branch of writing has a greater or less number of abbreviations commonly used to save time and space and to avoid repetition of cumbersome expressions. For instance, in arithmetic, L.C.M., G.C.D.; in algebra, Q.E.D.; in geometry, s.a.s., s.s.s.; in letters, inst., P.S., R.S.V.P.; in philology, OFr., MHG.; in education, I.Q. The number of abbreviations that can be used in their proper context is almost infinite. Nevertheless, an abbreviation that could be used with absolute correctness under certain circumstances might be extremely poor form under others. For example, it is proper in any text to speak of the Ratisbon MS. rather than *manuscript.* It is not at all good form to use the abbreviation as in the following sentence, taken from the acknowledgment page of a recently published schoolbook: "Sincere appreciation is expressed for permission to use the reader in MS. form in various classrooms, and for the service rendered by the teachers who used the MS." Again, *versus* should be abbreviated in citations of legal cases, but abbreviation would be inappropriate in such an expression as "Buymanship versus Salesmanship."

The following sections present general rules governing the use of certain abbreviations, and various lists for reference. Most dictionaries contain a list of abbreviations more comprehensive than can be included in this book, and such a list should be consulted for form and meaning of abbreviations not given in the following pages. The section on Composition of Foreign Languages contains lists of abbreviations in French, German, Italian, and Spanish.

Beginning a sentence. No sentence, except a footnote or a parenthesis, should begin with a symbol or an abbreviation (except M., Mr., Mrs., etc.).

The Greek letter μ is the symbol for micron. (*Not:* μ is . . .)
Number 3 mound was the next excavated. (*Not:* No. 3 mound . . .)

The Bible. In references to passages of Scripture the names of the books of the Bible may be abbreviated when they are used with numerals designating chapter and verse.

I Cor. 1:16–20

When reference is made to an entire chapter, it is better in text to spell out the name of the book.

In the thirteenth chapter of First Corinthians . . .
In the First Epistle to the Corinthians, chapter 13, . . .
In the Second Book of Kings, the second chapter, . . .
The first chapter of the Gospel according to John . . .

The following lists present accepted forms of abbreviation; many writers prefer to spell all names containing six letters or less. Arabic numerals are often used for the number of the book, but roman numerals are the preferred style. (See p. 165.)

OLD TESTAMENT

KING JAMES BIBLE		DOUAY BIBLE	
Books	*Abbreviations*	*Books*	*Abbreviations*
Genesis	Gen.	Genesis	Gen.
Exodus	Ex. or Exod.	Exodus	Ex. or Exod.
Leviticus	Lev.	Leviticus	Lev.
Numbers	Num.	Numbers	Num.
Deuteronomy	Deut.	Deuteronomy	Deut.
Joshua	Josh.	Josue	Josue
Judges	Judg.	Judges	Judges
Ruth	Ruth	Ruth	Ruth
I Samuel	I Sam.	I Kings	I Kings
II Samuel	II Sam.	II Kings	II Kings
I Kings	I Kings	III Kings	III Kings
II Kings	II Kings	IV Kings	IV Kings
I Chronicles	I Chron.	I Paralipomenon	I Par.
II Chronicles	II Chron.	II Paralipomenon	II Par.
Ezra	Ezra	I Esdras	I Esdras
Nehemiah	Neh.	II Esdras	II Esdras
		Tobias	Tob.
		Judith	Judith *or* Jth.
Esther	Esther	Esther	Esther
Job	Job	Job	Job
Psalms	Ps. (*plur.* Pss.)	Psalms	Ps.
Proverbs	Prov.	Proverbs	Prov.
Ecclesiastes	Eccles.	Ecclesiastes	Eccles.
Song of Solomon	Song of Sol.	Canticle of Canticles	Cant.
		Wisdom	Wis. or Wisd.
		Ecclesiasticus	Ecclus.
Isaiah	Isa.	Isaias	Isa.
Jeremiah	Jer.	Jeremias	Jer.
Lamentations	Lam.	Lamentations	Lam.
		Baruch	Bar.
Ezekiel	Ezek.	Ezechiel	Ezech.
Daniel	Dan.	Daniel	Dan.

OLD TESTAMENT

KING JAMES BIBLE		DOUAY BIBLE	
Books	*Abbreviations*	*Books*	*Abbreviations*
Hosea	Hos.	Osee	Osee
Joel	Joel	Joel	Joel
Amos	Amos	Amos	Amos
Obadiah	Obad.	Abdias	Abdias
Jonah	Jon.	Jonas	Jon.
Micah	Mic.	Micheas	Mich.
Nahum	Nah.	Nahum	Nah.
Habakkuk	Hab.	Habacuc	Hab.
Zephaniah	Zeph.	Sophonias	Soph.
Haggai	Hag.	Aggeus	Aggeus
Zechariah	Zech.	Zacharias	Zach.
Malachi	Mal.	Malachias	Mal.
		I Machabees	I Mach.
		II Machabees	II Mach.

The abbreviations for the names of the New Testament books, except the last, are the same in both Bibles. The Revelation of St. John of the King James Bible is called the Apocalypse of St. John in the Douay Bible.

NEW TESTAMENT

Matthew	Matt.	Thessalonians	I and II Thess.
Mark	Mark	Timothy	I and II Tim.
Luke	Luke	Titus	Titus
John	John	Philemon	Philem.
The Acts of the Apostles	Acts	Hebrews	Heb.
Romans	Rom.	James	James
Corinthians	I and II Cor.	Peter	I and II Pet.
Galatians	Gal.	John	I, II, and III John
Ephesians	Eph.	Jude	Jude
Philippians	Phil.	Revelation	Rev.
Colossians	Col.	(Apocalypse	Apoc.)

Books of the Old Testament Apocrypha are abbreviated as follows:

APOCRYPHA

Esdras	I and II Esd.
Tobit	Tob.
Judith	Jth.
The parts of Esther not in the Hebrew or Aramaic	Rest of Esther
The Wisdom of Solomon	Wisd. of Sol.
The Wisdom of Jesus, son of Sirach, or Ecclesiasticus	Ecclus.
Baruch	Bar.
The Song of the Three Holy Children	Song of Three Childr.
The History of Susanna	Sus.
The History of the Destruction of Bel and the Dragon	Bel and Dragon
The Prayer of Manasses, king of Judah	Pr. of Man.
Maccabees	I, II, III, and IV Macc.

APOCALYPTIC BOOKS

Book of Enoch	En.	Testaments of the Twelve	
Sibylline Oracles	Sib. Or.	Patriarchs	XII P.
Psalms of Solomon	Ps. Sol.	Assumption of Moses	Asmp. M.
Book of Jubilees	Bk. Jub.	Apocalypse of Baruch	Apoc. Bar.

Wherever abbreviations are appropriate the following forms may be used for the names of Bible versions.

MT	Masoretic text
LXX	Septuagint
Vulg.	Vulgate
A.V.	Authorized Version
E.V.	English Version(s) of the Bible
E.R.V.	English Revised Version
E.R.V.m.	English Revised Version, margin
R.V.	Revised Version
R.V.m.	Revised Version, margin
A.R.V.	American Revised Version
A.R.V.m.	American Revised Version, margin

Compass directions. In certain kinds of printed matter compass directions are regularly abbreviated, using capital letters, ordinarily without space between. Usage varies in the matter of abbreviating periods, some editors using the point only at the end, others using it after each letter, others using no period.

N.   E.   S.   W.   SE.   N.N.W.   SSW

Dates. See pages 206–208.

Dialogue. In dialogue and colloquial narrative, abbreviations may be used which are to be read as they stand, not amplified into the words they represent. Technical terms in their proper setting may also be so presented.

D.T.'s	W.P.A.	B.t.u.'s	
K.O.'s	a.w.o.l.	amps	
on the q.t.	B.V.D.'s	caps	
G.H.Q.	O.K.'d [1]	photos	

He is working for his Ph.D.
Cheers rang through the U.S.O. canteen.

Firm names. The abbreviations Bro., Bros., Co., Inc., Ltd., and & are frequently used in the names of firms and corporations; each firm name should be printed as the name stands on letterheads and other official docu-

---

[1] The Century and Webster dictionaries sanction the forms *O.K.'d, O.K.'ing.*

ments. It is not considered necessary, however, to preserve this form in all cases.[2] In text matter of books or in formal display these abbreviations are out of place and the words should be spelled in full. In notes, bibliographies, and general business printing, abbreviations are the better form. The *and* is usually spelled out if the name of the concern does not consist of proper nouns. To this practice, however, there are many exceptions, as Goodyear Tire & Rubber Company, American Car & Foundry Company. *Limited* is never abbreviated in the names of companies incorporated under the Companies Act by the Parliament of Canada. The word *Company* should never be abbreviated in the names of theatrical organizations: Chicago Civic Opera Company, Times Square Stock Company.

Forenames. It is not considered good form to abbreviate personal forenames in straight reading matter, even if the person himself does, or did, sometimes use that form. George Blank may sign his name *Geo. Blank,* and Charles Smith may habitually write *Chas. Smith,* but the full forms *George* and *Charles* should always be used in writing about them. Care must always be taken not to spell out a name which looks like an abbreviation but is in reality the full name. For instance, *Edw.* is plainly an abbreviation, but *Fred* might or might not be.

The use of initials for the first and middle names is allowable whenever brevity is in keeping with the nature of the text, as in lists of names, catalogue entries, and the like.

In this connection should be mentioned the abbreviations adopted by the American Library Association.[3] These include single letters followed by a colon or two points, arbitrarily selected to stand for certain names, as, for instance:

A.. Anna	B: Benjamin
A: August or Augustus	C.. Charlotte
B.. Beatrice	C: Carl, Carlo, or Charles

Geographical terms. In tabular matter and lists of addresses the abbreviations Ave., Bldg., Blk., Blvd., Pl., Sq., St., etc., are used freely; they are allowable in the heading of a business or informal letter. Abbreviations of the names of the states may be used likewise, but names having five letters or less are better spelled in full. None of these abbreviations should ever be used alone without a proper name preceding. The Government Printing Office rules that the names of the states may be abbreviated after geographical terms such

---

[2] See Yale *Handbook of Style* and the *Style Manual* of the Government Printing Office.
[3] A complete list is given in *Rules for a Dictionary Catalog,* by Charles A. Cutter, 4th ed. (Washington, U. S. Government Printing Office, 1904), pp. 157–161.

as names of counties, mountains, national forests, national parks, navy yards, reservations, and the like, but this is not good style for book work nor for periodicals that make any claim to literary merit. In such context it is better to spell the state name in full or, in some cases, to omit it.

References to any of the following cities is sufficiently clear, in most instances, without accompanying designation of the state.

Albany	Fort Wayne	Richmond
Atlanta	Grand Rapids	St. Augustine
Atlantic City	Hartford	St. Louis
Baltimore	Indianapolis	St. Paul
Boston	Jersey City	Salt Lake City
Brooklyn	Los Angeles	San Antonio
Buffalo	Memphis	San Francisco
Chattanooga	Milwaukee	Savannah
Chicago	Minneapolis	Scranton
Cincinnati	Nashville	Seattle
Cleveland	New Orleans	Spokane
Colorado Springs	New York	Tacoma
Dallas	Oklahoma City	Toledo
Denver	Omaha	Toronto
Des Moines	Philadelphia	Trenton
Detroit	Pittsburgh	Wheeling
Duluth	Providence	

In geographical names *Saint* is ordinarily abbreviated. *Fort* and *Mount* are usually preferable to *Ft.* and *Mt.* *Port* and *Point* are always spelled out.

The following are the official abbreviations of the United States *Postal Guide* for states, territories, and possessions of the United States. The abbreviations in parentheses are forms not sanctioned by the Postal authorities but favored by many printers and generally used in legal citations. *Alaska, Hawaii,*[4] *Guam, Ohio, Samoa,* and *Utah* are not abbreviated.

Alabama	Ala.	Georgia	Ga.
Arizona	Ariz.	Idaho	(Ida.)
Arkansas	Ark.	Illinois	Ill.
California	Calif. (Cal.)	Indiana	Ind.
Canal Zone	C. Z.	Iowa	(Ia.)
Colorado	Colo.	Kansas	Kans. (Kan.)
Connecticut	Conn.	Kentucky	Ky.
Delaware	Del.	Louisiana	La.
District of		Maine	(Me.)
Columbia	D. C.	Maryland	Md.
Florida	Fla.	Massachusetts	Mass.

[4] If abbreviation is necessary, T. H. (Territory of Hawaii).

Michigan	Mich.	Pennsylvania	Pa.
Minnesota	Minn.	Philippine Islands	P. I.
Mississippi	Miss.	Puerto Rico	P. R.
Missouri	Mo.	Rhode Island	R. I.
Montana	Mont.	South Carolina	S. C.
Nebraska	Nebr. (Neb.)	South Dakota	S. Dak. (S. D.)
Nevada	Nev.	Tennessee	Tenn.
New Hampshire	N. H.	Texas	Tex.
New Jersey	N. J.	Vermont	Vt.
New Mexico	N. Mex. (N. M.)	Virginia	Va.
New York	N. Y.	Virgin Islands	V. I.
North Carolina	N. C.	Washington	Wash.
North Dakota	N. Dak. (N. D.)	West Virginia	W. Va.
Oklahoma	Okla.	Wisconsin	Wis.
Oregon	Oreg. (Ore.)	Wyoming	Wyo.

The names of the Canadian provinces are commonly abbreviated as follows:

Alberta	Alta.	Northwest Territories	N. W. T.
British Columbia	B. C.	Ontario	Ont.
Cape Breton	C. B.	Prince Edward Island	P. E. I.
Manitoba	Man.	Quebec	Que. *or* P. Q.
New Brunswick	N. B.	Saskatchewan	Sask.
Nova Scotia	N. S.		

The initial abbreviations used in addresses to London designate the postal districts. They are usually printed with abbreviating periods but without space, though the periods are sometimes omitted.

Eastern	E.	South-Western	S.W.
Eastern-Central	E.C.	Western	W.
Northern	N.	Western-Central	W.C.
North-Western	N.W.		

Government agencies. Government agencies are frequently designated by the initials of the name. Abbreviations (with periods) and symbols (without periods) are almost equally favored, but in book work abbreviations are to be preferred.

A.A.A., Agricultural Adjustment Administration
T.V.A., Tennessee Valley Authority
HOLC, Home Owners' Loan Corporation

Latin words and phrases. The following abbreviations may be used in all except literary and formal texts, although each of them has a reasonably short and simple English equivalent which would in many instances be preferable.

i.e. (*id est*), that is
e.g. (*exempli gratia*), for example

etc. (*et cetera*), and others, and so forth

c., ca., or *circ.* (*circa, circiter,* or *circum*), about (used with dates denoting approximate time)

q.v. (*quod vide*), which see (plural, *qq.v., quae vide*)

viz. (*videlicet*), namely

It is not allowable at any time to use *e.g.* as it is used in the following sentence:

Wrong: Generalization, e.g., was developed through making the same response to different stimuli.

Right: Generalization, for example, was developed . . .

The abbreviation *etc.* should be used as little as possible, and it should never be preceded by *and* (*and etc.*). Neither *etc.* nor its equivalent *and so forth* should be used after examples preceded by the words *such as.*

Wrong: Many animals, such as rabbits, horses, etc., shed their heavy winter coat at the approach of warm weather.

Right: Many animals, such as rabbits and horses, shed their winter coat . . .

Not often appropriate to text except parenthetically but useful in footnote material are the following Latin abbreviations.

ad fin. (*ad finem*), at the end
ad inf. (*ad infinitum*), to infinity
ad init. (*ad initium*), at the beginning
ad int. (*ad interim*), meanwhile
ad loc. (*ad hunc locum*), on this passage
aet. (*aetatis*), aged
cf. (*confer*), compare
et al. (*et alibi*), and elsewhere; (*et alii*), and others
et seq. (*et sequens*), and the following (rarely used pl., *et sqq.*)
f. v. (*folio verso*), on the back of the page
ibid. (*ibidem*), the same [5]
id. (*idem*), the same
i. q. (*idem quod*), the same as
loc. cit. (*loco citato*), in the place cited
N. B. (*nota bene*), mark well
op. cit. (*opere citato*), in the work cited
sc. or *ss.* (*scilicet*), namely (in law)
s. v. (*sub verbo*), under the word; (*sub voce*), under the title
u. s. (*ubi supra*), in the place above mentioned
v. (*vide*), see; *v.* (*versus*), against
v. s. (*vide supra*), see above
v. l. (*varia lectio*), a variant reading (pl., *vv. ll.*)

For abbreviations of Latin phrases used in expressing dates and time, see pages 206-208.

[5] For the use of *ibid., op. cit.,* and *loc. cit.,* see pages 22, 23.

Laws, constitutions, by-laws. In setting laws, by-laws, and similar subject matter divided into sections it is customary to spell out Section 1 and abbreviate Sec. 2 and following sections.

Measure and weight units and terms. Units of measure and weight may be abbreviated when they are accompanied by a numeral.

A., acre(s)
A., Å, or A. U., angstrom unit(s)
a. c., alternating current
amp., ampere(s)
atm., atmosphere(s)
at. wt., atomic weight
bbl., barrel (*pl.,* bbl. or bbls.)
bd. ft., board foot (feet)
bdl., bundle (*pl.,* bdl. or bdls.)
b.h.p., brake horsepower
bkt., basket (*pl.,* bkt. or bkts.)
b. m., board measure
B.t.u., British thermal unit(s) [6]
bu., bushel(s)
Cal., large calorie(s)
cal., small calorie(s)
car. or K, carat
C.G.S., Cgs, c.g.s., or cgs, centimeter, gram, and second (*system of units*)
c.m., circular mil
c.p., candlepower
cu., cubic [7]
cwt., hundredweight
da., day(s)
d. c., direct current
doz., dozen
dwt., pennyweight
e.m.f. or emf, electromotive force
ft., foot (feet)
ft.-lb., foot-pound(s)
F.P.S., f.p.s., or fps, foot, pound, second (*system of units*)
gal., gallon(s)
g. cal., gram calorie(s)

gr., grain(s); gross
gt. gr., great gross
hhd., hogshead (*pl.* hhd. or hhds.)
h.p., horsepower
hr., hour(s)
in., inch(es)
kc., kilocycle(s)
kv., kilovolt(s)
kw., kilowatt(s)
kw. hr. or kw-hr, kilowatt hour(s)
lb., pound(s)
mc., megacycle(s)
mi., mile(s)
min., minute(s)
mol. wt., molecular weight
mo., month(s)
m.p.h., miles per hour
oz., ounce(s)
pk., peck (*pl.,* pk or pks.)
ql., quintal(s)
qt., quart (*pl.,* qt. or qts.)
r.p.m., revolutions per minute
S.A.E., Society of Automotive Engineers [8]
sec., second(s)
sp. gr., specific gravity
sq., square
T., ton(s)
tc., tierce
tbsp. or T., tablespoonful
tsp. or t., teaspoonful
wk., week (*pl.,* wk. or wks.)
yd., yard (*pl.,* yd. or yds.)
yr., year (*pl.,* yr. or yrs.)

[6] Collins's *Authors' and Printers' Dictionary* (Oxford University Press, 1933) lists B.Th.U. for British thermal unit, the abbreviation B.T.U. meaning Board of Trade Unit, or kilowatt hour.

[7] Terms of cubic and square measurement are best abbreviated with *cu.* and *sq.*: cu. ft., cu. in., cu. yd., sq. ft., sq. in., etc. The forms ft.^{2}, ft.^{3}, and the like are not recommended except for tables or equations or where space is very limited; they are likely to be mistaken for footnote references.

[8] Viscosity of oil is denoted—S.A.E. 20 is winter oil.

Except in highly technical work *cycle, dyne, erg, farad, henry, joule, lambert, volt,* and *watt* are not abbreviated, but in such work the first letter of each may be used to represent the word. Units of measurement for which there is no abbreviation are *gauss, gilbert, lumen, maxwell, mho, mil, ohm,* and *phot.*

Metric measurements. The three principal units of measurement in the metric system are the meter, the gram, and the liter.

Length	*Weight*	*Capacity*
mm., millimeter	mg., milligram	ml., milliliter
cm., centimeter	cg., centigram	cl., centiliter
dm., decimeter	dg., decigram	dl., deciliter
m., meter	g. *or* gm., gram	l., liter
dcm., decameter [9]	dcg., decagram	dcl., decaliter
hm., hectometer	hg., hectogram	hl., hectoliter
km., kilometer	kg. *or* kilo, kilogram	kl., kiloliter
mym., myriameter	myg., myriagram	myl., myrialiter
μ, micron	q., quintal	
mμ, millimicron	t., tonneau	

Surface	*Volume*
sq. mm. *or* mm^2, square millimeter	cu. mm. *or* mm^3, cubic millimeter
sq. cm. *or* cm^2, square centimeter	cc. *or* c.c., cubic centimeter
sq. dm. *or* dm^2, square decimeter	cu. dm. *or* dm^3, cubic decimeter
sq. m. *or* m^2, square meter	cu. m. *or* m^3, cubic meter
ca., centiare	s., stere
a., are	ks., kilostere
ha., hectare	
mya., myriare	

Note. The International Committee on Weights and Measures favors the omission of the period after abbreviations of metric measurements. The American Standards Association endorses the movement, and the latest style manual of the Government Printing Office likewise follows the practice. Except in scientific work the more familiar form is still the more common usage.

It is always poor form to use such abbreviations as the above without a numeral.

Poor: In this test a c.c. of salt solution is injected.
Better: In this test a cubic centimeter of salt solution is injected.
Or: In this test 1 c.c. of salt solution is injected.

Prescriptions. Many abbreviations are used in writing prescriptions. The following are common.

aa (*ana*), of each alike
aq. (*aqua*), water
coch., cochl. (*cochleare*), spoonful

[9] In British practice, according to Hart, *deca, hecto, kilo,* and *myria* are capitalized: *Dm., Hm., Km., Mm.*

dr., drachma
ea., each
g., gram
gr., grain
gt. (*gutta*), drop (*pl.,* gtt.)
ol. (*oleum*), oil
p. ae. (*partes aequales*), equal parts
q. l. (*quantum libet*), as much as you please
q. pl. (*quantum placet*), as much as seems good
q. s. (*quantum sufficit*), a sufficient quantity
q. v. (*quantum vis*), as much as you will
S. (*signa*), mark. (Indicates directions to be written on the package)
sc., scruple
sol., solution
t. i. d., three times daily
ut dict. (*ut dictum*), as directed

℥ ounce		Ʒi	one scruple
℥i one ounce		Ʒss	half a scruple
℥ss half an ounce		f℥	fluid
℥iss an ounce and a half		fʒ	fluid dram
℥ij two ounces		ℳ or ℳ	minim, or drop
Ʒ dram		℔	pound
Ʒi one dram		ℳ	mix
Ʒ scruple		℞	(*recipe*) take

Organizations. Abbreviations of the names of organizations are not in good form in literary texts but they are frequently used in nonliterary texts because the names for which they stand are cumbersome. Three or more capital letters so used are best set without spaces or with thin spaces between the letters. Some publishers omit the periods for certain organizations.

U.S.M.C., United States Marine Corps
U.N. or UN, United Nations
A.I.E.E., American Institute of Electrical Engineers
NATO, North Atlantic Treaty Organization
C.I.O. or CIO, Congress of Industrial Organizations

Philological terms. The following abbreviations of philological terms are used by some publishers without any periods, although periods are preferable.

A.F., or AFr, Anglo-French
A.N., Anglo-Norman
A.S., Anglo-Saxon
E.E., Early English
I.E., Indo-European
L.G., Low German
M.E., Middle English
M.H.G., Middle High German

M.L., Medieval, or Middle, Latin
N.Gr., New Greek
N.L., New Latin
O.E., Old English
O.F., or O.Fr., Old French
O.Gael., Old Gaelic
O.H.G., Old High German
O.N., Old Norse

References. In footnotes, bibliographies, and similar material—but not in text except parenthetically—words designating a part of a work are abbreviated when accompanied by a numeral. Capitalization is usually as here shown. A common error is the use of singular abbreviations with numerals denoting more than one.

App., Appendix
Art., Article (*pl.,* Arts.)
Bk., Book
Bull., Bulletin
Ch. or Chap., Chapter; *in law,* c. (*pl.,* Chaps.)
col., column, (*pl.,* cols.)
Div., Division
Ex., Example
Fig., Figure (*pl.,* Figs.)
fol., folio
f., the following (*pl.,* ff.) [10]
l., line (*pl.,* ll.)
n., note (*pl.,* nn.)

No. (*numero*), number (*pl.,* Nos.)
N.S., New Series
O.S., Old Series
p., page (*pl.,* pp.)
par., paragraph
Pl., Plate
Pt., Part
sec., section; *in law,* s. (*pl.,* ss.)
ser., series
st., stanza (*pl.,* sts.)
Supp., Supplement
v. or vs., verse (*pl.,* vv. or vss.)
Vol., Volume (*pl.,* Vols.)

Scholastic, military, or civil honors. Designations of rank or position, membership in monastic or secular orders, academic degrees, military or civil honors, are commonly abbreviated when they are used after a proper name. Most of such abbreviations consist of capital letters, and the prevailing practice is to set them without spaces between the letters.

M.P., Member of Parliament
U.S.N., United States Navy
S.J., Society of Jesus
LL.D., Doctor of Laws

M.Sc., Master of Science
R.N., Registered Nurse
F.R.S., Fellow of the Royal Society
D.S.O., Distinguished Service Order

Note also two italicized abbreviations used following names:

Cantab. (*Cantabrigiensis*), of Cambridge
Oxon. (*Oxoniensis*), of Oxford

In an informal context the abbreviations of academic degrees are sometimes allowable without an accompanying name.

Originality is highly desirable in the M.A. thesis.
Six years later the university gave him a B.A. degree.

Temperature and gravity. When temperature and gravity are expressed in figures with the degree sign, the name of the thermometer is usually abbreviated: 68 degrees Fahrenheit, 68° F.

[10] Before numbers with f. or ff. use a plural noun: pp. 50 f., 50 ff.

F., Fahrenheit   R., Reaumur
C., centigrade [11]   Bé., Baumé
Cel., Celsius   Twad., Twaddell
K., Kelvin   A.P.I., American Petroleum Institute
Abs., absolute

Time. See page 208.

Titles. The abbreviated forms *Mr., Mrs., Messrs.,* and *Dr.* are always used when the titles occur before proper names; also *Esq., Sr.,*[12] and *Jr.*[13] following names. The adjectives *Reverend* and *Honorable,* either in full or abbreviated, should never be used with a surname alone.

Wrong: Rev. Black; Hon. White; Reverend Black

If the article *the* is used, *Reverend* and *Honorable* should be spelled in full.

Right: the Reverend A. B. Black; the Honorable H. A. White; the Reverend Mr. Black.

If the article is not used, the abbreviated forms *Rev.* and *Hon.* are correct form.

Right: Rev. Alfred Black, Rev. A. B. Black, Hon. Harold White, Hon. H. A. White

Two titles of the same significance should not be used, one preceding the name and the other following.

Frank Morton, professor of Latin, *not* Prof. Frank Morton, professor of Latin
Dr. Walter Franklin *or* Walter Franklin, M.D.
Mr. Frank Milton *or* Frank Milton, Esq.
the Reverend Dr. Black *or* the Reverend A. B. Black, D.D.

But titles of different significance can be so used.

Professor Theodore Howard, D.D.S.

The titles *Mr., Dr., Professor,* and the like may properly be omitted from the names of authors cited. If mention of a person is personal, as in acknowledgment of courtesies or services, such titles should be used.

In this connection Arnold has stated . . .
The method suggested by J. W. Butler . . .
Calculations made in collaboration with L. A. Kilgore show . . .
The committee elected Dr. A. E. Kennelly its honorary president. Dr. Kennelly has served . . .

---

[11] *Centigrade* may properly be set lower-case as a common noun, but when it is used in the same text with *Fahrenheit,* the term is generally capitalized. "The absolute temperature can be calculated by adding 253.15 to the temperature of the centigrade scale."
[12] The British use *Sen.* for *Senior.*
[13] *Senior* and *junior* used rather informally in narrative should be spelled out:
It was all right for Thomas senior to take part in an affair of this sort, but quite another matter when Thomas junior was involved.

The title *Mr.* is not used before a name unless it is coupled with *Mrs.* or the forename or initials are not used.

> Among the many notable printers today Daniel Berkeley Updike, Bruce Rogers, Norman T. A. Munder, John Henry Nash, and William Edwin Rudge have commanded attention for the artistic excellence of their printing.
> The author wishes to thank his colleagues, Ralph Kamenoff, Herbert Johnson, . . . and Professors Herbert Ruckes, Earl Martin . . .

The French titles *Monsieur, Messieurs, Madame,* and *Mademoiselle* are abbreviated before names when they are mentioned in the third person.

> M. Monie is . . .
> MM. —— and —— entered the room.
> Mme. Curie was a remarkable scientist.
> Mlle. Rose took the children away.

If these French titles are used with the name in the second person, they should be spelled out.

> "How are you today, Monsieur Monie?"
> "Madame Curie, will you accept this . . ."
> "Mademoiselle Rose, will you please take the children away."

Monsieur, Madame, and *Mademoiselle* should be spelled out and capitalized when they are used alone in the third person as a substitute for a name.

> Then I slid into a compliment on Madame's flowers.
> When this untoward event took place, Madame went with all haste to tell her husband; but Monsieur only shrugged his shoulders.

When *Monsieur, Madame,* and *Mademoiselle* are used without a name as substantives in direct address, they should be spelled out and not capitalized

> "Oui, madame."
> "It shall be done at once, monsieur."
> "Can we help you, mademoiselle?"

The Spanish *Señor, Señores, Señora,* and *Señorita* and the Italian *Signor, Signora,* and *Signorina* are seldom abbreviated, but Sr. (*Señor*), Sra. (*Señora*), and Srta. (*Señorita*) may be used like M., Mme., and Mlle.

Titles denoting position or rank may be abbreviated before names only when the full name is given, including forename or initials. When abbreviations are appropriate to the text, the following may be thus used. Whenever there is any doubt of the propriety of using abbreviated forms of titles, they should be spelled in full. Titles like *Secretary of State, Secretary* when it is the title of a Cabinet member, *Senator, Ambassador,* and *Princess* should never be abbreviated.

Atty., Attorney	Msgr., Monsignor, Monseigneur
Atty. Gen., Attorney General	Pres., President
Dist. Atty., District Attorney	Prof., Professor
Gov., Governor	Sec., Secretary
Gov. Gen., Governor General	Supt., Superintendent
Lt. Gov., Lieutenant Governor	Treas., Treasurer

Adjt.,[14] Adjutant	Lt. Comdr., Lieutenant Commander
Adjt. Gen., Adjutant General	Lt. Gen., Lieutenant General
Asst. Surg., Assistant Surgeon	Maj., Major
Brig. Gen., Brigadier General	Maj. Gen., Major General
Bvt., Brevet	Orderly Sgt., Orderly Sergeant
Capt., Captain	Ord. Sgt., Ordnance Sergeant
Col., Colonel	Passed Asst. Surg., Passed Assistant Surgeon
Comdr., Commander	
Comdt., Commandant	Pvt., Private
Corp., Corporal	Q. M. Gen., Quartermaster General
First Lt., First Lieutenant	Q. M. Sgt., Quartermaster Sergeant
Gen., General	Second Lt., Second Lieutenant
Hosp. Sgt., Hospital Sergeant	Sgt., Sergeant
Hosp. Steward, Hospital Steward	Sgt. Maj., Sergeant Major
Insp. Gen., Inspector General	Surg., Surgeon
Judge Adv. Gen., Judge Advocate General	Surg. Gen., Surgeon General
	Surgeon Maj., Surgeon Major
Lt. Col., Lieutenant Colonel	

"United States." In parentheses, footnotes, tables, and the like the abbreviated form *U. S.* may be used before the word *Government* or the name of a government organization. In bibliographical matter it may well be used before the name of a government department. Always abbreviate *United States* before the name of a government vessel.[15]

U. S. Department of Agriculture	U.S.S. *Saratoga*
U. S. Geological Survey	U. S. monitor *Nantucket*

If *U. S.* in copy is circled to be spelled out, thought should be given to the form, which should in most cases be *the United States.* One exception is *Bank of United States*

[14] The abbreviations in this group are the forms used by the U. S. Government Printing Office.

[15] Practice of the U. S. Government Printing Office, except that U.S.S. is spaced.

SYMBOLS

Chemical elements. A symbol indicating an element or a combination of elements is not followed by a period.[1] These symbols are used freely in text matter as well as in equations and formulas.

Actinium	Ac	Holmium	Ho	Radon	Rn
Alabamine	Ab	Hydrogen	H	Rhenium	Re
Aluminum	Al	Illinium	Il	Rhodium	Rh
Antimony	Sb	Indium	In	Rubidium	Rb
Argon	A	Iodine	I	Ruthenium	Ru
Arsenic	As	Iridium	Ir	Samarium	Sm
Barium	Ba	Iron	Fe	Scandium	Sc
Beryllium	Be	Krypton	Kr	Selenium	Se
Bismuth	Bi	Lanthanum	La	Silicon	Si
Boron	B	Lead	Pb	Silver	Ag
Bromine	Br	Lithium	Li	Sodium	Na
Cadmium	Cd	Lutecium	Lu	Strontium	Sr
Calcium	Ca	Magnesium	Mg	Sulfur	S
Carbon	C	Manganese	Mn	Tantalum	Ta
Cerium	Ce	Masurium	Ma	Tellurium	Te
Cesium	Cs	Mercury	Hg	Terbium	Tb
Chlorine	Cl	Molybdenum	Mo	Thallium	Tl
Chromium	Cr	Neodymium	Nd	Thorium	Th
Cobalt	Co	Neon	Ne	Thulium	Tm
Columbium	Cb	Nickel	Ni	Tin	Sn
Copper	Cu	Nitrogen	N	Titanium	Ti
Dysprosium	Dy	Osmium	Os	Tungsten	W
Erbium	Er	Oxygen	O	Uranium	U
Europium	Eu	Palladium	Pd	Vanadium	V
Fluorine	F	Phosphorus	P	Virginium	Vi
Gadolinium	Gd	Platinum	Pt	Xenon	Xe
Gallium	Ga	Polonium	Po	Ytterbium	Yb
Germanium	Ge	Potassium	K	Yttrium	Y
Gold	Au	Praseodymium	Pr	Zinc	Zn
Hafnium	Hf	Protoactinium	Pa	Zirconium	Zr
Helium	He	Radium	Ra		

Book sizes. A symbol indicating book size is not followed by a period.

f°, folio
4to or 4°, quarto
8vo or 8°, octavo
12mo, duodecimo

16mo, sextodecimo
18mo, octodecimo
32mo, thirty-twomo

[1] A period may be used after a chemical symbol to signify a unit positive charge of electricity; two periods unspaced, two units. A writer so using a period should make his intention unfailingly clear in every case, for few know of this use.

Chess. Terms used in chess are represented by the following symbols:

B, bishop	P, pawn
K, king	Q, queen
KB, king's bishop	QB, queen's bishop
KKt, king's knight	QKt, queen's knight
KP, king's pawn	QR, queen's rook
KR, king's rook	R, rook
Kt, knight	

Trigonometry. Abbreviations of trigonometrical terms are symbols.

cos, cosine	log, logarithm
cosec, or csc, cosecant	sin, sine
cot, cotangent	tan, tangent

SIGNS

A special kind of abbreviation is the sign, also called a symbol. Some signs have different meanings according to the text in which they are used; others have only one meaning. Everyone is familiar with the common mathematical signs, plus ($+$), minus ($-$), multiplication sign ($\times$), and many others. Astronomy uses symbols for the planets, as $\odot$ for the sun, $\male$ for Mars, $\female$ for Venus, $\oplus$ for the earth. These are used with different meaning in biology: $\odot$ means an annual plant, $\male$ means a biennial plant, $\female$ means female, $\male$ means male. Other symbols can be found in dictionaries and technical works for weights and measures, physical and chemical constants, and terms of medicine, music, commerce, etc.

NUMBERS

In deciding the manner in which numbers should be expressed the nature of the writing should be considered and the literary style distinguished from the technical and scientific style. At one extreme is the very formal style of the Bible, proclamations, and similar writings, in which all numbers, even of years, are spelled out; at the other extreme is the statistical style, in which all numbers are expressed in figures. The following rules indicate good style in writing that is neither formal nor statistical.

NUMBERS EXPRESSED IN FIGURES

Large numbers. Unless they begin a sentence (see p. 203), numbers over one hundred, cardinals or ordinals, are set in figures, except round numbers and, generally, isolated numbers. (See *Exceptions*, p. 203.)

There were only 1,240 people in the town.
There were only twelve hundred people in the town.

A hybrid form of expressing large numbers has come into use in recent years. Numbers ending in six or more ciphers are according to this practice set as below. The practice should never be followed with thousands or hundreds.

The annual average was 2,206 million dollars.

. . . in which 5 million dollars par of preferred stock controlled 1500 million dollars capitalization of subsidiary companies.

. . . 2.4 billion dollars was obtained by selling goods to foreigners.

Her population in 1930 was composed of only 2½ million whites out of nearly 17 million inhabitants. There were almost 5 million Indians.

Wrong: The speed of light is 186 thousand miles per second (300 thousand kilometers per second).

Right: The speed of light is 186,000 miles per second (300,000 kilometers per second).

Wrong: Few are capable of carrying more than 4 to 6 hundred pounds per square foot.

Right: Few are capable of carrying more than 400 to 600 pounds per square foot.

Small numbers. Small numbers are set in figures when they occur in a group with larger figures and refer to similar things.

One booklet contained 36 pages, one 72 pages, and the third 108 pages.

Of a total of 358 landholder members there were 4 Irish peers, 98 sons of peers, and 155 near relatives of peers.

In dealing with more than one series of quantities only comparable numbers are set in figures.

The number so employed in the Lynn district was 68, as compared with 110 in the twenty-eight other districts.

Besides 300 men and 275 women there were 48 children under twelve.

One New York bank represents the merger of 38 financial institutions. There are 534 fewer banks in the United States now than there were eight years ago. Some time ago it was discovered that 6 large banks controlled 785,499 workers. Twelve New York banks hold 267 directorates in 92 of the leading railroads.

Small numbers may be set in figures for distinction and emphasis.

Find two consecutive even integers such that 7 times the first exceeds 5 times the second by 54.

When not more than 10 units of insulin are required in twenty-four hours, the entire dose may be taken at once, before breakfast, or 5 before breakfast and 5 before the evening meal. If 15 units or more are required in twenty-four hours, it is best to divide the dose into two equal parts and inject one before breakfast and the other before supper.

A small number referred to as a number and not as a quantity is set in figures.

Put water into a graduated beaker until it just reaches the 40 mark.
Change sentences 3 to 8 as numbers 1 and 2 are changed.
Count by 2's to 20.
The thermometer stood at 45, a rise of five degrees.
I transmit herewith a tabulation covering Items 1 to 5 in said resolution. The Department of Finance is compiling information concerning Item 6.

Numbers with abbreviations. Regardless of size, numbers used with abbreviations are set in figures.

No. 5　　　6 bu.　　　.5 mm.　　　67th Cong., 1st sess.　　　No. 645872

Fractions. Large fractions are better expressed in figures. If they can be written as decimals, typesetting is easier and the appearance is better.

Normal outdoor air contains only about $\frac{4}{100}$ of 1 per cent of it (or .04 per cent of it).

It has only about $\frac{1}{10000}$ part of the power of the motor that operates electrically driven phonographs.

Ages. Newspaper style, almost without exception, sets ages of persons and animals in figures; but in book work ages are spelled.

Decimals. Figures are used for decimals. (See also Money, p. 205.)

0.24	0.6 gram	45.5 degrees	a Colt .45
$6.41	.30–30	0.66 cent per pound	.36 caliber revolver [1]

Degrees. Temperature readings and degrees of latitude and longitude are usually set in figures.

temperature of 52 degrees　　　　latitude 49 degrees N.
52° F.　　　　　　　　　　　　　longitude 24 degrees west
60°–75°　　　　　　　　　　　　lat. 40° 20′ N.

Dimensions. Dimensions are set in figures, with *by* rather than *x* in text. If *x* is used, it should be spaced. Depending on the nature of the text the following forms may be correct:

3 by 5 inches　　　　　5 feet 4 inches
3 x 5 inches　　　　　　5 ft. 4 in.
3″ x 5″　　　　　　　　5′ 4″

[1] Means 0.36 inch bore.

Note that when the sign for the unit of measurement is used in giving dimensions it should appear with both numerals: 19″ x 24″.

Divisions. Numbers of divisions (parts, chapters, paragraphs, sections, rules) are usually set in figures, either arabic or roman numerals; also numbers denoting lines, notes, verses, figures, and plates.

Psalm 23	Item 6	question 2	verses 6 to 8
Hymn 49	Figure 30	column 3	line 10

House and room numbers. Except in dialogue house and room numbers are set in figures.

He lived at 249 Western Avenue.   He was sent to Room 46.

Page numbers. Figures are always used for page numbers.

On page 5 he tells us . . .

Percentage. Percentage is expressed in figures, using the words *per cent* in preference to the sign in all except tabular matter.

10 per cent   one-half of 1 per cent
2.3 per cent
As a result 1 per cent of the banks of the country control nearly one-half of the
total bank resources, while twenty-four New York banks, about one-tenth of
1 per cent of the total, possess about 15 per cent.
Note. Some publishers prefer always to spell out *one.*

Proportion. Figures are used for proportion.

proportion of 2 to 5   2:5   50–50   odds of 3 to 1

Street numbers. Ordinals over *one hundredth* naming thoroughfares are generally set in figures. In informal printing those over *tenth* may be so set. Expressions like *in the Forties* are better spelled.

412 Fifth Avenue   584 West 123d Street
Note. A few writers have favored the forms *110 Street, 121 Street, 162 Street.*
This style may be adopted by stenographers for addresses on envelopes, but printers
will be slow to sanction the usage.

Votes, ballots, scores, etc. Figures are the form to use.

5 votes   majority of 15
50 ballots   vote of 74 to 3
300 voters   a 10 to 1 shot
yeas 67, nays 42   Chicago 3, Philadelphia 5
His birdie three on the par four sixth made him 2 up.
Seabury defeated Lamb [in tennis] 10–8, 6–2, 6–3.

Years. The number of the year is set in figures, except in formal documents and the like.

General use: in 1892, in the year 1892
Formal: eighteen hundred and ninety-two, or one thousand eight hundred and
   ninety-two

Decades may be expressed in figures or in words, in full or in shortened form. The spelled-out form is usually preferable. (See also Dates, p. 206.)

the 1890's   the early 60's
the eighteen-nineties   in the nineties

How Figures Should Be Set

Use of commas. Numbers of five or more figures, except serial numbers—house, telephone, page, year, and the like—should be pointed off by commas. Four-figure numbers are usually set with the comma, but some printers prefer to omit the comma when the number is used in straight reading matter. In logarithm tables, etc., the comma is omitted.

Division. A number of large size may be divided at the end of a line, using a hyphen as in a word. The division should always be made at a comma, and the comma should be retained before the hyphen.

Fractions. It is incorrect to use *th* and *ths* after fractions:

$$\frac{3}{100}, \textit{not}\ \frac{3}{100}\text{ths} \qquad\qquad \frac{1}{25}, \textit{not}\ \frac{1}{25}\text{th}$$

A fraction expressed in figures should not be followed by *of a, of an.*

⅜ inch, *not* ⅜ of an inch.

If the sentence seems to require *of a,* the fraction should be spelled out.

Wrong: Fractions are first introduced as expressions of part of a whole—half a
   pie, ¾ of an hour, and so on.
Right: . . . half a pie, three quarters [*or* three fourths] of an hour.

If the writer of the example above wished for special reasons to use the form ¾, he should, for the sake of consistency, have used ½ also.

NUMBERS EXPRESSED IN WORDS

General rule. Except as noted above, spell out all numbers of less than three digits, cardinals or ordinals, and all round numbers. In other words, spell out numbers that can be expressed in one or two words.

The ply may be any number from two to sixteen, but seven to twelve is the usual range and the twists per inch may range from three to twenty.

An act to add twenty-three new sections to the Political Code
Bills have been introduced into the legislatures of twenty states.
They have been gone four months and have traveled more than twenty-five
   hundred miles.
Twenty-first Assembly District
twentieth century
Sixty-sixth Congress, second session
Twenty-third Psalm
Fifty-seventh Regiment

Exception 1. A round number that would be more easily grasped if expressed in figures is so written, even though the number is only approximate.

A $50,000,000 Airport
More than $300,000,000 worth of furs was sold in the United States in 1920.

Exception 2. When several approximate round numbers are used in a
paragraph or section, they should be set in figures; also round numbers
coming in close connection with numbers not round.

. . . having over 600 missionaries at work in 1895. In 1893 there were about
   55,000 Chinese communicants in Protestant churches, most of them in the
   coast provinces, and in 1889 missionaries numbered nearly 1300, not quite
   half of them men, representing 41 different societies. These figures were an
   increase from about 5700 communicants in 1869 and from about 189 missionaries in 1864.

Numerical expressions. Such expressions as the following should be
spelled.

forty millions of people   two and a quarter millions
two or three hundred years ago   a million and a half
a thousand and one reasons   a hundred and odd
          in nine hundred and ninety-nine cases out of a thousand
Wrong: 400,000,000 of people
Right: four hundred millions of people *or* 400,000,000 people.

Fractions. Simple fractions may be expressed in words. (See also p. 200.)

an uninhabited border about one-fifth of a mile wide
vote of two-thirds of its members
one-half of 1 per cent

Form determined by position. A numeral should not stand at the beginning of a sentence. A number so placed should be spelled out or the
sentence reworded to bring the number elsewhere in the sentence.

Wrong: $36,000 was the amount of the debt.
Right: The amount of the debt was $36,000.
Wrong: 1941 saw our entry into the war.
Right: The year 1941 saw our entry into the war.

If a large number at the beginning of a sentence is spelled out, editors sometimes repeat the number in figures, enclosed in parentheses. A common error is the misplacing of the gloss. For instance, "six thousand ($6,000) dollars" should be either "six thousand (6,000) dollars" or "six thousand dollars ($6,000)." The latter form is preferable.

If two related numbers occur at the beginning of a sentence, both should be spelled.

Fifty or sixty steers, 20 cows, and 150 sheep.

In expressions like the following, in which two numbers occur together, the first should be spelled out.

four 10-inch guns   ten 12-room houses   two 700 h.p. motors

Numbers in dialogue. Numbers appearing in a quoted speech in direct discourse should be spelled out; year dates may be excepted.

"I paid two dollars and forty-nine cents for it."

How to Express Numbers in Words

Whole and mixed numbers. When numbers of three or more figures are spelled out, *and* may or may not be used before tens or units; usage is divided, conservative usage favoring retention of the *and*. The *and* is always used when large numbers are spelled out in formal matter like documents, and it should never be omitted before fractions. No comma is needed between thousands and hundreds.

six thousand and twenty
six hundred and two thousand six hundred and twenty
ten thousand four hundred and fifty
sixty-two and three-fourths

Numbers of four figures, like 1,200, 1,260, are usually spelled *twelve hundred, twelve hundred and sixty,* unless the context is formal.

Fractions. The fraction $\frac{1}{100}$ written in words is better made *one hundredth,* rather than *one one-hundredth,* $\frac{7}{100}$ as *seven hundredths,* rather than *seven one-hundredths,* just as the decimals .01 and .07 would be written in words.

Fractions used as nouns do not require a hyphen between numerator and denominator, although many writers and printers prefer to use one. Certainly none should be used if either the numerator or the denominator is hyphenated.

Fractions used as modifiers should always be hyphenated unless the numerator or the denominator contains a hyphen.

seven two-hundredths   one-fourth part
twenty-three hundredths   one twenty-fifth part

MONEY

An isolated mention of a sum less than a dollar should be expressed as cents and spelled out.

eighty cents, *not* $0.80
fifty cents per thousand cubic feet, *not* 50 cts. per thousand cubic feet

A sum less than a dollar that requires more than two figures to express it should be set with dollar sign and cipher; and in statistical matter a uniform style should be followed.

$0.7525 per ounce
The cost is not high (about $0.02 per ton) and is distributed as follows: depreciation (10 per cent), $0.003; power, $0.006; maintenance, $0.012.

A sum of dollars with no cents expressed is usually set without the decimal point and ciphers; but if there is in close proximity a sum of dollars and cents, the ciphers may be used with the sum of even dollars.

$3, $486 $5–$10 [note two signs]
One owed $5.00, the other $5.45.

An isolated mention of a sum of dollars which can be expressed in one or two words should be spelled out:

forty-five dollars   three thousand dollars
He subscribed $250 to the fund.

If several sums are mentioned in a short space, all should be in figures, even. if some are only dollars or cents.

In dialogue all expressions of money should be spelled out.

"I bet you a dollar ninety-eight I don't find a thing wrong, and two-ninety that I find it was a heart attack."

Foreign money.   Sums of money in terms of foreign currency are expressed in much the same way as money of the United States.   Names of monetary units usually have abbreviated forms and often symbols, just as in English we use *cts.* or ¢.   These terms are not italicized in an English text (see p. 214).

Symbols precede numerals except in expressing contos and escudos (see below). Fractional parts of the basic unit are expressed in a manner similar to our method of expressing dollars and cents. A comma or a space is used in some cases instead of a decimal point; the space should not be increased in a widely spaced line.

Great Britain:	£308 4s. 7d. 3 far.	308 pounds, 4 shillings, 7 pence, 3 farthings
France:	10 f. 50 c., or 10·50 fr.	10 francs, 50 centimes
Mexico:	P. 262,50	262 pesos and 50 centavos
Brazil:	1:000$000	1,000 milreis
	627.431:259$079	627,431 contos, 259 milreis, 79 reis
Portugal:	4:265$50	4 contos, 265 escudos, 50 centavos
India:	25,87,000	25 lacs, 87,000 rupees

DATES

The year. The number of the year in a date should never be spelled out except in dialogue or in very formal writing such as proclamations.

nineteen hundred forty-two, or nineteen hundred and forty-two
Very formal: one thousand nine hundred and forty-two

The month. The names of the months should be spelled out except in statistical matter or in long enumerations. Accepted forms of abbreviation are:

Jan.	Mar.	Aug.	Oct.	Dec.
Feb.	Apr.	Sept.	Nov.	

May, June, and *July* are never abbreviated except in very much shortened forms called Dewey dates, used when space is very limited.

Ja.	Mr.	My.	Ju.	S.	N.
F.	Apr.	Je.	Au.	O.	D.

The day. The day may be expressed by an ordinal numeral preceding the name of the month or by a cardinal numeral after the name of the month. (Ordinals after the month are less desirable.[1]) If month, day, and year are given, *d, st,* or *th* should not be used.

second of January	January 1
third of June	January 1, 1942

---

[1] Some writers on printing style feel that forms like 21st, 22d, and 25th, which they call hybrid or impure forms, are bungling, and that the letters following the numbers are superfluous and should not be used. They permit a writer to use "on the 12 of April" if he wants to. The practice has not met with general acceptance, although it appears occasionally in addresses—35 West 32 Street. Usage sanctions both *2d* and *2nd, 3d* and *3rd.*

Decades. When decades are referred to as "seventies," "eighties," etc., words are preferred to figures, and no apostrophe is necessary.

seventies   70's

Elision. If two year numbers are connected, the hundreds may be omitted from the second unless the first number ends in two ciphers, when the full number must be repeated. If the next to the last figure is a cipher, only one numeral is needed after the dash.

1775–79   1800–1801   1901–2

"A.D." and "B.C." The abbreviations A.D. and B.C. have practically become symbols that are used with year numbers without conscious thought of the words for which they stand, and are therefore commonly placed after the number. Nevertheless, careful writers still place the A.D. before the number, B.C. after the number.

in 31 B.C.   A.D. 1941

British usage, as presented in Hart's *Rules for Compositors and Readers at the University Press, Oxford,* sanctions the expression "fifth century A.D."

Occurring in lower-case roman text, A.D. and B.C. are commonly set in small capitals without space. In a line of capitals and lower case, such as a heading or a displayed line, A.D. would be preferable. With italic lower case, italic capitals should be used.

The rule of Augustus continued to A.D. 14.
The First Council of Nicaea, A.D. 325
Kalidasa, Fifth Century (?) A.D.

Less common abbreviations similarly set are:

A.C. (*ante Christum*), before Christ
A.H. (*anno hegirae*), in the year of the Hegira (A.D. 622, the Mohammedan era)
A.A.C. (*anno ante Christum*), in the year before Christ
A.H.S. (*anno humanae salutis*), in the year of human salvation
A.M. (*anno mundi*), in the year of the world
A.P.C.N. (*anno post Christum natum*), in the year after the birth of Christ
A.P.R.C. (*anno post Roman conditam*), in the year after the building of Rome, 754 B.C.
A.R. (*anno regni*), in the year of the reign
A.R.R. (*anno regni regis,* or *reginae*), in the year of the king's, or queen's, reign
A.S. (*anno salutis*), in the year of salvation
A.U.C. (*ab urbe condita*), from the founding of the city (of Rome)
C.E., common era

Numerical dates. If a date is written numerically in copy and ringed to be spelled out, care should be taken to do so correctly. In the United States the month is written first; therefore 2-12-34 means February 12, 1934. In Great Britain the first figure indicates the day; therefore 2-12-34 according to that practice means December 2, 1934.

When time of day is given in straight text matter it is usually better to express it in words whenever the expression is simple.

at four thirty	at twelve noon
at five o'clock	at half past three

Less simple expressions of hours and minutes may be expressed in figures:

Wednesday afternoon at 2.35	at 10:40 Saturday forenoon

Usage is about evenly divided, apparently, in the use of the colon and the period in such figures. Those who prefer the colon object to the period because, they say, it makes the expression look like a decimal.

If time is expressed in figures it is proper to use abbreviations, usually set in small capitals, without space.

A.M. (*ante meridiem*), before noon
P.M. (*post meridiem*), after noon
M. (*meridies*), noon (12 P.M., midnight)

The phrase "2 P.M. in the afternoon" is incorrect and should be either "2 P.M." or "two o'clock in the afternoon."

The letters used in Roman notation are I, V, X, L, C, D, and M. Repeating a letter repeats its value. A letter placed after one of greater value adds to it. A letter placed before one of greater value subtracts from it.

Any number of thousands is expressed by a line drawn over any numeral less than one thousand. Thus $\overline{V}$ denotes 5,000, $\overline{LX}$, 60,000. So likewise $\overline{M}$ is one million and $\overline{MM}$ two millions.

As a medieval roman numeral Y stands for 150, $\overline{Y}$ for 150,000.

On clock faces IIII is sometimes used instead of IV.

1	I	5	V
2	II	6	VI
3	III	7	VII
4	IV	8	VIII

9	IX	70	LXX
10	X	80	LXXX
11	XI	90	XC
12	XII	100	C
13	XIII	200	CC
14	XIV	300	CCC
15	XV	400	CD
16	XVI	500	D (or I⊃)
17	XVII	600	DC (or I⊃⊃)
18	XVIII	700	DCC (or I⊃⊃⊃)
19	XIX	800	DCCC
20	XX	900	CM
21	XXI	1,000	M
22	XXII	2,000	MM
23	XXIII	3,000	$\overline{\text{M}}$M
24	XXIV	4,000	$\overline{\text{MV}}$
25	XXV	5,000	$\overline{\text{V}}$
30	XXX	6,000	$\overline{\text{VM}}$
40	XL	10.000	$\overline{\text{X}}$
50	L	100.000	$\overline{\text{C}}$
60	LX	1,000,000	$\overline{\text{M}}$

ITALICS

USE

Italics are used to distinguish letters, words, or phrases from the rest of the
sentence so that the writer's thought or the meaning and use of the italicized
words will be quickly comprehended. In italic text roman is used for words
which would be italic in a roman text. If a word ordinarily in italic is used
in text set in small caps or caps and small caps, it is quoted, usually, instead
of italicized.

Those Who Passed the "Studentexamen" in 1921

Italics are little used in newspapers. When the meaning might be ambiguous without some differentiation from surrounding words, quotation
marks are used. The following rules, therefore, do not apply to newspaper
work.

GENERAL RULES

Emphasis. Italics may be used to emphasize a word or phrase. Writers
should guard against too free use of italics for this purpose, for when used
too freely they lose their force.

We are in danger of being satisfied with the *forms* of knowledge without its
substance.

We not only *know* the various objects about us through sensation and perception, but we also *feel* while we know.

Force lost: If the last letter of the *stem* of a weak verb is *t* or *d*, the letter *e* is *inserted* between the *final letter* of the stem and the *t* which precedes the personal endings of the *imperfect tense.*

Differentiation. When a word is used not to represent the thing or idea it usually represents, but merely as the word itself, it should be italicized unless it is directly quoted from a previous sentence and is repeated for the purpose of definition or explanation. (See also pp. 290, 291.) As a rule, quotation marks should not be used in connection with italics.

Inexperienced writers are likely to use too many *and*'s and *but*'s.

Bromine takes its name from its odor. *Iodine* comes from the Greek word for *violet.*

Lord is the general term which is used to describe a landowner, usually a nobleman, who had a group of persons dependent upon him. *Vassal* is the name given to all persons dependent upon a lord or person of higher rank.

Diathesis. The term "diathesis" refers to a condition which . . .

When they came to the word *schlaf,* "sleep," their eyes would pop wide open.

This rule should be kept clearly in mind when writing sentences like the following. Acts and words can be said to have meaning, but objects and things cannot.

Wrong: What is the meaning of a plebiscite? From what word in Roman history is it derived?

Right: What is the meaning of *plebiscite?* [Do not use an article before a word used in this way.]

Italics may be used instead of roman quoted, as in sentences like the following, where quotation marks would be unwieldy.

To how many of these questions can you answer *yes?* If you can say *yes* to all of them, you are doing all you can to keep yourself well.

Note that in the examples above question marks following italic words are italic and that the *s* in the plurals *and*'s, *but*'s, is roman. These forms are correct. (See also p. 512.)

Book titles. Titles of books (including plays, motion pictures, essays, cycles of poems, and long single poems usually printed separately) are generally set in italics when they appear in text matter.

A Tale of Two Cities	*Gone with the Wind*
Love's Labour's Lost	*Beowulf*
The Wealth of Nations	*Nibelungenlied*

Following a possessive an article beginning a title may be dropped. If a work is merely referred to as already mentioned or as familiar to the reader, or if the title is abridged, an initial article may be omitted or left outside the italics.

He read Dickens's *Tale of Two Cities.*
The statement is made by Adam Smith in his *Wealth of Nations.*
Gibbon published the *Decline and Fall* between 1776 and 1788.

The following are not italicized:

Bible	Corporation Manual
books of the Bible: Genesis, etc.	Revised Statutes
Koran, Talmud, Mishnah, etc.	Social Register
Prayer Book	Blue Book
Book of Common Prayer	Constitution (of U.S.A.)
ancient manuscripts: Codex Sinaiticus,	Declaration of Independence
etc.; Book of Kells, Ratisbon MS.	Gettysburg Address

The italic style for book titles is generally followed in footnotes and bibliographies, also, but in book lists and book reviews these titles may be differentiated in other ways, often by using capitals and small capitals.

Characters in books. When characters in books or plays are merely referred to, it is unnecessary to italicize or quote their names.

Latin abbreviations. Several Latin words and abbreviations are in common use in English writing, especially in footnotes and references. Of these, *etc., versus* or *v.,* and *viz.* are commonly roman, *i.e.* and *e.g.* often are, and the rest are usually italic. (See the lists on pp. 188, 189.)

Legal citations. The names of the parties in the titles of court cases may be roman or italic. Such phrases as *et al.* and *ex parte* are italic if the rest of the title is roman; roman if the rest of the title is italic. (See pp. 163–165 for a fuller presentation of legal styles.)

Pagano *et al.* v. Charles Beseler Co., 234 Fed. 963 (1916)
Burleson v. United States *ex rel.* Workingmen's Cooperative Publishing Association, 274 Fed. 749, 260 U. S. 757 (1921)
In re *Wight v. Baker* the court ruled . . .
In the matter of the petition of John Smith for a change of venue
Wright, appellant, v. Johnson, respondent

Letters. Single letters are italicized when they are particularly referred to.

the *i*'s and *o*'s   the *n*th power

In an italic context italic rather than roman is still the choice of most editors.

A curve whose equation is of the nth degree is called a curve of the nth degree.

When a letter is used to designate shape, elegance calls for the use of a gothic letter, but roman is more often used. Italic is not satisfactory for this purpose.

a U-shaped tube   a great V of foam   an S-shaped cross section

Exception: a T-square
Letters in algebraic equations are italicized. (See also p. 167.)

$$ab + bc - cd = 62$$

Also letters in legends or text referring to corresponding letters on geometrical figures or illustrations, whether italic in the illustration or not.

We reach any point P of the plane by going from O a certain distance $x = OM$ along OX.
If then two propellers A and B, absorbing a given power but A turning at a speed of rotation twice that of B, are compared, a little computation shows that the top speed of the geared propeller B is about 30 per cent less than that of A.

Chemical formulas, however, should be set roman: Fe_2O_3. Likewise sin, tan, log, etc., in trigonometrical equations.

Letters in parentheses to indicate subdivisions are usually italic, likewise *a, b, c,* after the number of verse or page to indicate a fractional part: Luke 4:31*a*.

The abbreviations for shillings and pence, *s.* and *d.,* are usually italicized.

Musical compositions. Titles of songs and short musical selections are usually set in roman quoted; operas and oratorios are italicized; selections named by number or key are sufficiently distinguished by roman caps and lower case without quotes.

"The Star-Spangled Banner"   *The Messiah*   Quartet in A minor
the "Marseillaise"   *Lohengrin*   Fifth Symphony
"Sonata Appassionata"   *Peer Gynt Suite*   Opus 147, in B

Newspapers and periodicals. The names of newspapers and periodicals are usually italicized.

The New York Times   the New York *Herald Tribune*
the London *Times*   the St. Louis *Post-Dispatch*

Strictly speaking, an initial article should be italicized if it is part of the official title; but the fact is often difficult to verify and if many titles appear *in* a work, some of which have *The* and some have not, an apparent consistency of treatment is gained by setting all with a lower-case roman *the*. Official titles of newspapers are especially difficult to verify.[1] Some have the article and the name of the place of publication, some have the place and not the article, some have neither. The better style, in general, is to italicize only the distinctive part of the name.

If the name of a publication is used within itself, it is usually set in cap-and-small.

Resolutions and legislative acts. *Resolved,* in resolutions, legislative acts, and the like, is always italicized. The word *provided* in the body of such matter is also usually set in italics.

Resolved, That capital punishment is a deterrent to crime.
Resolved, That the Secretary of the Senate be authorized to . . .
Resolved by the Senate of the State of California, That the Judicial . . .
. . . either on its title page or on the first page of music: *Provided,* That . . .

Salutations. The salutation of an address is ordinarily italicized, and the salutation of a letter may be (see p. 157).

Mr. President, Ladies and Gentlemen:

Scientific names. Scientific names of genera, species, and varieties are generally italicized. The name of the founder of the species and abbreviations such as *sp.* and *cf.* are set in roman.

It is found in the camphor tree, *Laurus camphora.*

Ficus sp.   *Fenestella* cf. *F. tenax Ulrich*
Ficus harrisiana   Sweet corn (*Zea Mays* var. *rugosa*)

This rule is not generally followed in medical texts.[2] It may well be disregarded when the profusion of such terms would result in an excessive amount of italics.

Bacillus typhosus   B. coli   Staphylococcus albus
Among these are Manila hemp, derived from the leaf stalks of Musa textilis Nee; Sisal hemp, secured from the leaves of species of Agave; Mauritius hemp, obtained from the green aloe, Furcraea gigantea (D. Dietr.) Vent.; and Sunn hemp, procured from Crotalaria juncea L.

---

[1] The official title is the name on the masthead, or the statement of ownership found usually in the upper corner of the editorial page. The title at the top of the first page may vary. *The Boston Globe,* for example, has *The Boston Daily Globe, The Boston Evening Globe,* and *The Boston Sunday Globe* at the top of the respective editions.
[2] British practice as set forth in Hart, *op. cit.,* is to italicize.

Sounds. A combination of letters used to represent a sound is usually set in italics. If an onomatopoetic word is used, italics are not necessary, though occasionally they are used.

. . . never heard the *shw-u-sh! shw-u-sh!* of the rain . . .
"*Urr-aw! Urr-aw!*" suddenly barked an automobile horn.
The *dit-dar* of the Morse was growing stronger.
Cruuunch.
a long *whooooo*
the thud, thud of the horses' hoofs
the steady drip, drip of the rain
"Boom, bo-o-om," roared the surf.
Suddenly the bell rang—ding, ding, ding-ding-ding.

Vessels, airships. The names of vessels, submarines, airships, airplanes are usually italicized.

The frigate *Constitution*   *Spirit of St. Louis*
U.S.S. *Saratoga*   the *Graf Zeppelin*
Eagle No. 14   the *ZR-5*
H.M.S. *Ajax*   the *R-101*

Foreign words. Foreign words or phrases appearing in English text should be italicized unless they can be considered as having been adopted into the English language. Italics should not be used for the names of foreign coins; the names of churches, hotels, educational institutions, streets; foreign titles preceding proper names; or the names of foreign institutions.

Piéta   lira   Hochschule
rapprochement   Hotel Chaminade   Gestapo
hors de combat   Mar Toma   Ogpu
Légion d'honneur   Unter den Linden   Archives Photographiques
Croix de guerre   Abbé ——   d'Art et d'Histoire

It is not necessary to italicize foreign-language names of art objects, titles of poems, articles, and so forth, that are enclosed in quotation marks.

Cicero's "De Senectute"
Kuenen, "Uber die Männer der grossen Synagoge," in his *Gesammelte Abhand-lungen.*

An unmistakably foreign word that occurs repeatedly in an article or a book may be italicized the first time it occurs, usually accompanied by a definition of its meaning and use, and thereafter set roman.

Care should be taken to distinguish between an English word and a foreign word that have the same spelling but different meaning, as, for instance, *exit,* "he or she goes out," which set in roman means "a way of egress"; or *item,* "also," "likewise," which means "a separate thing" when it is set in roman. A list of foreign words and phrases is given in the Appendix.

CAPITALIZATION

Although there are many uses of capitals about which no one requires instruction, the question of what to capitalize and the necessity of following a consistent style of capitalization often prove troublesome details of the writer's, the editor's, and the proofreader's work. The following rules are generally accepted.

USE OF CAPITALS TO MARK BEGINNINGS

Sentences. The first word of a sentence is ordinarily capitalized.

A sentence set in small capitals for emphasis should begin with a capital and should capitalize all proper nouns.

In American usage names like *du Pont, van Dyke,* and others that usually begin with a small letter are capitalized if they begin a sentence.

A sentence that is one item of a series should begin with a capital.

> Examples of easy colloquial speech are such words as *folks; a raise; he don't* or *it don't;* Stop the car, please, *I want out; wait on;* He comes *of a Sunday;* This is *all the farther* the road goes; . . .
> *Case* has plenty of legitimate uses, as in: I am only putting a case; Circumstances alter cases; In case of fire, give the alarm.

Exceptions. The two sentences below, taken from a foreign-language textbook, illustrate a kind of sentence which may legitimately be begun with a small letter.

rr is forcibly trilled in Spanish.
a, o, and **e** are strong vowels.

A sentence enclosed in parentheses inside another sentence need not begin with a capital.

> That overstocking does not occur is due to ruthless fishing (man is a severe enemy of fish), to pollution, and to the many other enemies that surround fish.
> These can be drawings, pictures, pressed flowers, sunflower seeds (have you ever eaten sunflower seeds?), Indian relics . . .
> *But:* If the number of hours required is *t,* then the distance traveled by A is 30 *t* (Why?), and the distance traveled by B is 40 *t.*

Partial sentences. The word following an exclamation point or a question mark is not always construed as beginning a new sentence requiring a capital. If the matter following is closely connected with what precedes, completing the thought or making the meaning clearer, no capital is necessary.

Progress where? or, even more fundamentally, progress whence?

What a piece of work is man! how noble in reason! how infinite in faculty!—
SHAKESPEARE.

How is the gold become dim! how is the most fine gold changed!

Lord, who shall abide in thy tabernacle? who shall dwell in thy holy hill?

In a series of questions not in complete sentence form, such as are often used in school textbooks at the end of chapters, the usual practice is to capitalize after the question mark, for here the part following the question mark does not form an integral part of what precedes but is a new question requiring a separate answer. Some writers, however, consider the capital unnecessary here, also.

What part did Philip I play in the history of Holland?   Of England?

What effect might that have upon the market price of trees?   Upon the desirability of going into the business?

Although lower case may be as good usage as capitals in instances like the foregoing, there is no justification for lower case in sentences like the following.

Wrong: Do you wear out a few words? which ones?

Right: Do you wear out a few words?   Which ones?

The use of (*a*), (*b*) before the questions does not make it necessary to capitalize the first one.

Capital unnecessary: Who stands the loss if the car burns and freight is destroyed (*a*) As the result of being struck by lightning? (*b*) Because a match is carelessly thrown inside the car?

Better: Who stands the loss if the car burns and freight is destroyed (*a*) as the result of being struck by lightning? (*b*) because a match is carelessly thrown inside the car?

If each part following a letter in parentheses begins a new line, capitals are still unnecessary, but some writers and editors object to the appearance of a small letter in this position.

1. What methods of travel
   (*a*) were used by your grandparents when they were your age?
   (*b*) have been added since the year 1900?

or

1. What methods of travel—
   (*a*) Were used by your grandparents when they were your age?
   (*b*) Have been added since the year 1900?

Whether to use capitals or lower case is a matter of choice also in such instances as the following, but a consistent style should be followed throughout.

Factors Influencing Creative Work
  I. *The teacher should*
   1. be creative herself.
   2. possess a rich cultural background.
   3. plan for many worthwhile experiences.

Poetry. With the exception of some modern poetry in the newer metrical forms, every line of poetry should begin with a capital.

If for any reason two or three lines of poetry quoted in a prose text are run in, each line of the original should be marked by a capital.

"Froggy would a-wooing go, Whether his mother would let him or no."
"Till the war-drum throbb'd no longer, and the battle-flags were furl'd In the parliament of man, the federation of the world." [1]

Direct discourse. A cited speech in direct discourse, or a direct thought, should begin with a capital.

At this moment John said, "It's seven o'clock."
I glanced at the clock and thought, "Can it be seven already?"

Direct questions. The first word of every direct question should be capitalized.

There is one question the reader should always ask himself, and that is, Is the meaning clear?
We may ask, How can it best be understood?
We understand this question to mean, What number divided by 5 gives 6 as a quotient?
To introduce this topic ask pupils, Who are the owners of the vast grazing lands shown on the map on pages 110–111?

In sentences like the following, capitalizing a single interrogative word and using a question mark after it is too cumbersome, and the meaning and use of the word are better conveyed by using italics.

Less desirable: The subject is the word that answers the question Who? or What?
Better: The subject is the word that answers the question *who* or *what.*

Direct quotations. A quotation complete in itself, formally introduced, and not grammatically joined to what precedes, should begin with a capital.

[1] Examples are from H. W. Fowler, *A Dictionary of Modern English Usage* (Oxford University Press, 1934).

However, a quotation may be so closely woven into a sentence that no capital is required. (See also Excerpts, p. 13.)

> Golden Rule Jones probably did as well as anyone could with the baffling problem of defining law when he said that "law in the United States is anything that the people will back up." Emerson also observed to the same effect, "The law is only a memorandum."
>
> "It was a major victory for the Administration," states the Boston *Transcript*, with the conclusion that "it will be a blow to the utility interests of the entire country."

Rules, slogans, mottoes. The first word, and only the first, of rules, slogans, and mottoes should be capitalized.

> Another rule is, Divide the volume in cubic inches by 2150.
> All for one, one for all.
> Write up cases and incidents from your own experience that illustrate the truth of these sayings: Haste makes waste; A stitch in time saves nine; Better late than never.

Following a colon. The first word after a colon should be capitalized when it begins a complete passage or a sentence.

> In conclusion I make this prophecy: The coming year will show greater advance on this line of research than have the past ten years.
> They can be summarized as follows: (1) All trade is essentially an exchange of goods and services. (2) Goods are given . . .
> The following were elected: President, William Jones; vice-president, Frank Smith.
> You need tools to carry on in a science course: not just work-bench tools and laboratory test tubes and beakers, but books, magazines, visits to shops and museums.
> . . . two kinds of information: (1) the results of work in research which have been completed; (2) the results of work in the same field as the problem chosen.

Letters. In the salutation of a letter the name of the person addressed or the noun used in place of the name is capitalized, but not *dear* or other words standing between *My* and the name. (See also p. 157.)

> My dear Mr. Smith: My dear Cousin:
> My dear Sir: My dear Captain:

Subjects for debate, legislative acts. The first word following *Resolved* or any words in italic which follow it should be capitalized. Likewise words following introductory italicized phrases in documents and the like.

> *Resolved,* That woman suffrage has been of benefit to the country.
> *Resolved by the Senate, the Assembly concurring,* That . . .
> *Know all men by these presents,* That . . .
> *To whom it may concern,* Greeting: Know that . . .

The word WHEREAS, if set in caps and small caps introducing a paragraph, should be followed by a comma and a capitalized word. If *whereas* is not so distinguished from the rest of the sentence, no comma should follow and the next word should be lower case.

> WHEREAS, Substantial benefits . . .; now, therefore, be it
> *Resolved, by the Senate of the State of California,* That . . .
> Whereas the Constitution provides . . .; and . . .

The vocative "O." The vocative *O* in English is always capitalized; but *oh* is capitalized only when it begins a sentence or stands alone.

> Thy ways, O Spirit, are unconfined.
> For if you should, oh! what would become of it?

In Latin sentences capitalize *O* only at the beginning of a sentence.

> Hoccine seclum! o scelera! o genera sacrilega! o hominem impium!
> —TERENCE, *Adelphi*, III, ii, 6.

TITLES, HEADINGS, LEGENDS

General rule. English titles of books, pamphlets, newspapers, magazines; of parts, chapters, sections, of a work; of poems, articles, lectures, should be distinguished by capitalization. In such titles, in headings, and in similar matter set cap-and-lower or cap-and-small the first and the last word should be capitalized, regardless of what part of speech they may be. *Per Cent* and *Etc.,* for instance, should not be excepted. Also capitalize all important words, no matter how short; that is, capitalize nouns, pronouns, verbs, adjectives, and adverbs. Articles, coördinate conjunctions, and prepositions are generally considered unimportant and are not capitalized.[1]

What Is a Law?	All about Books
What May Be Taken	The Captain Who Stood By
Inside, As It Is to the Worker	The Hand That Keeps the World Informed
Determining Per Capita Costs	Should a Pupil Add Up or Down a Column?
Per Cent of Urban Population	Procedure If Cash Does Not Prove

Prepositions. The longer prepositions are sometimes looked upon as re- quiring capitalization, especially in newspaper, magazine, and similar work, for which the rule generally followed is to capitalize prepositions containing four or more letters.

Days Before History	The Universe Around Us
All Through the Night	Shout All Over God's Heaven

[1] The library style of capitalizing only the first word and proper names of book titles is occasionally followed in bibliographies, but it is not generally favored by publishers.

Prepositions that are an inseparable part of a verb should be capitalized.

Exercises Stressing What Is Called For in the Problem
Making Up the Beds
Getting Down to Business
How to Lay Off a Line through a Given Point That Shall Be Parallel to a Given Line
Things to Do With and Find Out About a Book

The usual form for infinitives is *to Be, to Do, to Go.*

If office practice is to lower-case all prepositions, a problem sometimes arises when prepositions are accompanied by an intimately qualifying word, forming, in effect, a compound preposition. An exception may well be made of such instances and capitals used for the sake of appearance.

According to	Except for	Instead of
Apart from	from Among	Just Before

Articles. In longer titles it is sometimes desirable to capitalize an article, preposition, or conjunction that immediately follows a marked break indicated by a punctuation mark.

Woodrow Wilson: The Man, His Time, His Task
Business, Politics, Diplomacy—An Autobiographical Biography
Looking Them Over—A Glimpse of the New Machine at the Show
Our Changing Social Order: An Introduction to Sociology
The Psychopathic Employee, A Problem of Industry

Hyphenated compounds. Only the first part of hyphenated compound words need be capitalized, but in work favoring a liberal use of capitals, other parts may be.

Absent-mindedness	Cul-de-sac	Twenty-one
Aide-de-camp	Son-in-law	Merry-go-round

If words are connected by a hyphen to show their syntactic relation to other words, the second element of the compound should be capitalized whenever it would be capitalized if it stood alone. Usage varies much. Some publishers consistently lower-case after hyphen, as *High-vacuum Jet Condenser;* others capitalize only nouns or proper adjectives, *Middle-Class, Power-driven.* The style here favored may with justification, therefore, be modified downward in work favoring a down-style of capitalization.

Internal-Combustion Engine
Present-Day Styles
Hand-Decorated Manuscript

General rule. Capitalize proper nouns and proper adjectives and words used as proper nouns.

Boston	Tennessee	Shakespeare
Bostonian	Tennesseean	Shakespearean

Exceptions. Proper names or proper adjectives used to designate a particular kind or variety of the common classification tend to become lower case, as *panama hat, graham bread, turkish towel;* yet this process is slow and the capital is often retained long after its origin has been forgotten. Any one of the following adjectives, for instance, may be capitalized.

arabic numerals	diesel engine	prussian blue
bologna sausage	gothic style	roman numerals
brussels sprouts	manila rope	turkish bath
cashmere shawl	norfolk jacket	valenciennes lace
chantilly lace	paris green	venetian blinds
china silk	portland cement	virginia reel

Medical terms as a rule retain the capital longer than commoner nouns. For example:

Achilles' tendon	Graafian follicles
Fallopian tubes	Gasserian ganglion

Proper names adopted as the common name of something should not be capitalized.

ampere	davenport	joule
boycott	derringer	oxford
braille	henry	watt

Nouns and verbs derived from proper names are usually lower case.

anglicize	fletcherize	marconigram
daguerreotype	macadam	pasteurize

Words used as proper nouns. No one has any difficulty in recognizing a simple proper name but even experienced proofreaders often become confused in determining when a common noun is used as a proper noun or is part of a compound proper noun and should be capitalized. For instance, is the correct form *King of England* or *king of England, Book of Genesis* or *book of Genesis, the Goverment* or *the government, my Uncle Charles* or *my uncle Charles?* Few would hesitate on *Massachusetts General Court,* rather than *general court*, but many are confused when the term *legislature* is used: *the California Legislature.*

Just as some writers consider many marks of punctuation necessary to clearness where another would dispense with them, so some writers seem to believe that capitals are quite necessary when others find the meaning is clear with lower case. British writers use capitals much more freely than Americans do, and French writers much less. Most printing and publishing offices have established an office style for capitalization which they follow if the author has no objection. Some book publishers like a free use of capitals, an up-style so called, while others prefer few capitals; most magazines follow an up-style, while newspapers generally follow a down-style. An extreme down-style also in use is so at variance with common practice that a writer for a publication using it must learn it from the style sheet or manual of the publication. Such forms, for instance, as *American Red cross, the Red cross, Articles of confederation, British isles, Good book,* look strange to most persons.

The rules that follow tend to favor an up-style; modifications of down-style are noted here and there.

Geographical Terms

Divisions of the earth's surface. Capitalize the names of the great divisions of the earth's surface; also the names of distinct regions or districts.

Arctic Circle	Great Divide
North Pole, the Pole	Tropic of Cancer
Torrid Zone	North Temperate Zone

Antipodes (when specifically referring to Australia and New Zealand)
Lower case: antipodean, equatorial, polar regions, the arctics, the tropics, the temperate zone.

Divisions of the world or of a country. Capitalize names of the divisions of the world or of a country.

the Old World, the New World	Lower California (Mexico)
the Near East, the Far East	North Atlantic States [1]
the Far North, the Far West	New York State
the Orient, the Occident	Middle West, Midwest
the Continent (continental Europe)	the Pacific Coast
East Africa	the Ohio Valley

---

[1] The divisions of the United States used by the United States Census are: New England States, Middle Atlantic States, East North Central States, West North Central States, South Atlantic States, East South Central States, West South Central States, Mountain States, and Pacific States.

Lower case: state (used in a general sense without an accompanying proper name); the valley of the Mississippi; the Ohio River valley; Pacific coast (when the meaning is the shore line of the Pacific Ocean, rather than a somewhat definite area within the United States); southern California; upper Mississippi Valley.

Names of points of the compass and adjectives derived from them are capitalized when they are part of a name established by usage as the designation of a definite area, but not when they denote simply direction or compass points.

Southwest Africa	eastern Gulf states
West Florida (1763–1819)	southern California
the South, the East	northern Michigan
	western Europe

Nouns and adjectives derived from the names of the compass points are best set lower case when used alone or with common nouns.

an easterner	western canners
a southerner	northern manufacturers

Regions and localities. Capitalize popular appellations for regions and localities.

the Levant	the Deep South
the Promised Land	the Eastern Shore (Chesapeake Bay)
the Eternal City	the Upper Peninsula (Michigan)
the Dark Continent	the Golden State
the Spanish Main, the Main	the City of Churches
the Gold Coast	the Battery
the Great Plains	East Side, West Side
the Badlands	the City, West End (London)
the Corn Belt, the Black Belt	the Loop, the Stock Yards (Chicago)
Down East	the National Capital

Lower case: fatherland, ghetto, no-man's-land.

Rivers, lakes, mountains. Capitalize generic terms like *river, lake, mountain,* and many others when they are used with a proper name and form an organic part of it. Newspaper usage in this detail is divided, some papers preferring lower case for the common-noun portion of the name unless it comes first, as in *Mount Everest.* When these terms are used with two or more proper nouns and belong equally to all, they are usually lower case.

Penobscot River	Bay of Naples
Casco Bay	City of Mexico
the Coast Range [2]	Lake Michigan
Ohio and Missouri rivers	lakes Huron and Michigan

[2] Lower-case *range* when reference is to an iron or copper district, not to mountains.

Make a careful distinction between nouns that have become established by usage as parts of proper names, and nouns used casually before proper names:

City of Mexico	city of Chicago
Isthmus of Panama	island of Cuba

When such generic terms are used alone for the whole name, they should be lower case even if the meaning is specific, except in a few instances such as the following.

the Canal (the Panama Canal)
the Channel (the English Channel)
the Cape (Cape of Good Hope)
the City (the financial district of London)
the District (District of Columbia)
the Falls (Niagara Falls)
the Gulf (Gulf of Mexico)
the Horn (Cape Horn)
the Islands (Philippines, or Hawaiian Islands)
the Isthmus (Isthmus of Panama)
the Sound (Long Island Sound)
the Street (Wall Street)

Office style books often list other similar terms of a local application, as, for instance, *the Hills,* meaning the Black Hills, and *the Falls,* meaning the Menomonee Falls, given in the style book of the Milwaukee *Journal.*

Religious Terms

The Deity. Capitalize all names or appellations of any member of the Christian Trinity, and of the Virgin Mary.

the Supreme Being	the Son of Man
the All-Wise	the Word
divine Providence	the Holy Spirit
Heaven (personified)	the Intercessor
the Godhead	the Comforter
the Holy Family	the Blessed Virgin
the Child Jesus (the Christ Child)	Madonna (meaning the Virgin or a
the Saviour [3]	picture or statue of her)
Lord of lords	Mater Dolorosa
King of kings	

Lower case: fatherhood, sonship, messianic.

[3] This spelling is generally considered preferable when referring to Jesus Christ.

Except in extracts from the Bible or the Book of Common Prayer, capitalize pronouns referring to the above unless their antecedent closely precedes. The relative pronouns *who, whom,* and *whose* are ordinarily lower case.

For God was a loving Father to whom His people could always go for comfort in their troubles.
Christ chose his apostles.
When Christ saw the multitude, He went up into the mountains.
Live in the Spirit of One who says first of all, "Come unto Me," and then, "Go ye into all the world."

The Bible. Capitalize all names for the Bible and its books and divisions; likewise the names of versions and editions of it.

the Good Book	Acts of the Apostles, the Acts
Holy Writ	Sermon on the Mount
(Holy, Sacred) Scriptures	Golden Rule
Old Testament	Lord's Prayer
Pentateuch	Ten Commandments, the Decalogue
Exodus, or Book of Exodus	Apocalypse
First Book of Kings	parable of the Sower
Wisdom Literature	King James Version
Major and Minor Prophets	Revised Version
Priestly Code	American Translation
Apocrypha	Douay Version
Synoptic Gospels	Septuagint
Gospel of John	Vulgate
First Epistle of Paul to the Corinthians	Polychrome Bible

Lower case: biblical, scriptural, apocryphal; gospel (except when reference is directly to one of the four books so named); epistles.

Ancient manuscripts. Capitalize the titles of ancient manuscripts.

Codex Alexandrinus   Codex Canonicianus
Lower case: the Alexandrian codex.

Creeds. Capitalize the names of creeds and confessions of faith.

the Apostles' Creed   the Augsburg Confession
the Creed of Chalcedon   the Westminster Confession

Denominations, monastic orders. Capitalize the names of religious denominations, monastic orders, and their adherents. The word *church* is capitalized when it forms a part of such names or of names of particular edifices, but *church* should not be capitalized when it stands alone unless it is used to denote a religious organization of the whole world or of a particular country. This form is usually found in contradistinction to *State:* the Church and the State.

Protestantism	Nonconformist
Catholicism	the Society of Friends
Baptist	the Plymouth Brethren
Fundamentalist	the Doukhobors
Modernist	St. James's Church
Mormonism	Friends' Meeting House
Latter-Day Saints	the First Church of Christ, Scientist [4]
Protestant Episcopal Church	High Churchman
the Mother Church	Black Friars
the Established Church	Carmelites
the Church of Rome	Church Fathers
High Church, Low Church	Papist
the Oxford Movement	Agnosticism

Lower case: spiritualist, theosophist, agnostic (in common-noun sense).

Theological terms. Capitalize theological terms used with definite application.

Ark of the Covenant, the Ark	Ecce Homo
the Chosen People	Day of Judgment
Annunciation	the Disciples (meaning the Twelve)
Immaculate Conception	the Apostle Paul, Paul the Apostle
Nativity	Pharisees
Last Supper	Gentile (*noun*)
the Magi	Satan, Beelzebub, the Enemy
Crucifixion	Paradise (meaning the Garden of Eden)
Resurrection	Hades
Ascension	

Lower case: heaven (meaning a place), hell, purgatory, paradise, nirvana, happy hunting ground; devil (unless used as a specific name for Satan); gentile (*adj.*), scribes; for heaven's sake.

Ecclesiastical terms. Ecclesiastical terms like the following should be capitalized.

Eucharist	Holy of Holies
Lent, Lenten	Holy Orders
Epiphany	Holy See, See
Septuagesima	Holy Father (the Pope)
Advent	the Sovereign Pontiff
Ember Days	the Consistorial
Holy Grail	Sacred College of Cardinals

[4] Capitalize *The* only when reference is to the Mother Church.

Sacred Congregations	Papacy [5]
Sacred Heart	House of Bishops
Pontifical High Mass	General Synod
Nuncio, Papal Nuncio	General Conference

Lower case, in secular writing: father, friar, brother, sister (except when used with name); benediction, holy communion, mass, high mass, confessional; papal (when not part of a title).

Capitalized: Christian, non-Christian, Christianity, Christianize, Christendom, Christology; but: christological, unchristian.

Other religions. Capitalize the names of other religions, their heads, their followers, and their sacred writings.

Hinduism	Taoist	Talmud
Buddhism	Parsee	Veda
Lamaism	Koran	Upanishads
Dalai Lama	Mishna	Zend-Avesta
Shinto	Peshitto	Dhammapada

Lower case: Olympic gods, the sun god, the god Baal; koranic, talmudic, vedic.

Quaker dates. Capitalize Quaker dates.

First-day, Eighth Month.

Historical Terms

Historical epochs. Capitalize the generally accepted names of historical epochs and movements.

Middle Ages, Dark Ages	the Norman Conquest
the Flood, the Deluge	the Crusades
the Reformation	Christian Era
Paris Commune, the Commune	the Exile
the Industrial Revolution	Colonial days

Lower case: twentieth century; medieval, medievalism.

Periods in the history of language, art, literature. Capitalize the names of periods in the history of language, of art, and of literature.

Neo-classical period	Old English
Elizabethan Age	Middle High German
Age of Pericles	post-Exilic writings
Renaissance	Revival of Learning

[5] *Pope* and *papacy* are often lower case in secular writing.

Philosophical, literary, and artistic schools. Capitalize the names of philosophical, literary, and artistic schools and their adherents.

Cartesian system
the Schoolmen
the Symbolic school of painters

Platonism, Neoplatonism
Epicurean, Stoic (lower case in the common-noun sense)

Congresses, councils, expositions, fairs. Capitalize the names of congresses, councils, expositions, and similar proper names.

the First Congress of Races
the All-Russian Congress of Soviets
Olympic Games
Tournament of Roses
the Mardi Gras

Passion Play (of Oberammergau)
Illinois State Fair, the state fair
the Council of Trent
Louisiana Purchase Exposition

Important events. Capitalize the names of important events.

American Revolution, the Revolution
Civil War (American)
War of 1812
World War I, World War II [6]
Thirty Years' War

Battle of the Marne
Fall of Rome
Reign of Terror
Whisky Insurrection
Louisiana Purchase

Historic documents. Capitalize the names of historic documents.

Declaration of Independence
Constitution (of the U. S.)
Magna Charta
the Edict of 1807; the great reform edict of 1807

Bill of Rights
Petition of Right
Turkish Capitulations

Treaties. Capitalize the word *treaty* only when it is given as part of the exact title of a treaty of historical importance.

Treaty of Ghent
Versailles Treaty

the treaty at Versailles
the Franco-German treaty
the Cuban reciprocity treaty

Military and Naval Terms

Officers. Capitalize the titles of high-ranking officers of the Army and the Navy, before or after the name or standing alone. Titles of lower-ranking officers are lower case unless they are used with the name.

General Commanding the Army, the General
Admiral of the Navy, the Admiral
the Chief of Staff
The Adjutant General [7]

[6] *Lower case:* before the war, prewar, postwar.
[7] Capitalization of *The* prescribed by law.

the Inspector General
the Judge Advocate General
the Paymaster General
the Surgeon General

Organizations. Capitalize the names of organizations of the Army and the Navy. *Army* and *Navy,* used as noun or adjective, are usually capitalized when standing alone if they refer to the Army and the Navy of the United States.

General Staff	Corps of Engineers
General Board (of the Navy)	Second Coast Artillery
Headquarters of the Army	Coast Guard
First Corps Area	Tenth Cavalry
Battle Force	Third Division
Naval Reserve	B Company, Company B
Air Service	National Guard, the Guard
Signal Corps	Regular Army, a Regular

Lower case: national guardsman, artilleryman.

Combatants. Capitalize the names of the parties participating in wars.

Federals	the Triple Alliance
Confederates	the Central Powers
Allies	the United Nations
Insurrectos	the Axis

Lower case: Italian front, western front.

Decorations. Capitalize the names of war decorations.

Congressional Medal of Honor	Victoria Cross
Distinguished Service Medal	Iron Cross
Navy Cross	Légion d'honneur
Flying Service Cross	Croix de guerre

Governmental and Political Terms

Political divisions. Capitalize the names of political and administrative units and subdivisions.

Holy Roman Empire, the Empire	the Colonies, Colonial (when referring
United Kingdom	to Colonial times, etc., in the U. S.)
French Republic	West Riding
Irish Free State	Essex County
the Republic (the United States)	Evanston Township, the township
the Union (the United States or the	Ward 2
Union of South Africa)	Precinct 4
the Dominion, or Provinces (Canada)	Eleventh Congressional District

Lower case: the first ward, the second precinct.

Judicial bodies.   Capitalize the name of an international court or the word *Court* used alone referring to it; a national, district or state court of law whenever it is named in full.   Names of city and county courts are lower case.

the World Court, the Court
the International Court of Arbitration, the Court
the Court of Impeachment (the U. S. Senate), the Court
the United States Supreme Court, the Supreme Court
the Circuit Court of the United States for the Second Circuit, the circuit court,
    the court
United States Commerce Court, the court
Court of Appeals of the State of Wisconsin, the court of appeals
Court of Claims, the court
Court of Customs and Patent Appeals, the court
Court of Private Land Claims, the court
District Court of the United States for the Eastern District of Missouri, the
    district court, the court

Lower case: the Lynn municipal court, the Boston police court, in justice court, federal court, the juvenile court, the land court.

In England the names of all courts are capitalized:

His Majesty's High Court of Justice, the High Court
the Court of Chancery
the Court of Session

Legislative bodies.   Capitalize the names of legislative bodies.

Congress	the Oireachtas
the Senate	Bundestag
House of Representatives, the House	Rada
Parliament (British) [8a]	Cortes
House of Lords, the Lords	Diet
House of Commons, the Commons	Storting
Chamber of Deputies, the Chamber	Texas Legislature [8]
act of Dail Eireann (no *the*)	House of Delegates

Lower case: the lower house, the two houses, the state senate, parliamentary law; congressional, senatorial, parliamentary (unless work distinctly favors an up-style of capitalization, when these adjectives should be capitalized).

[8] Unless the exact designation is used, there is no reason for capitalizing: Massachusetts legislature, New York legislature.   Twenty-three states designate their legislative body a "legislature"; twenty call it the General Assembly; a few call it the Legislative Assembly; and in Massachusetts it is the General Court.

[8a] But "the British parliament," in which *parliament* is a common noun.

The President. Capitalize all appellations of the President of the United States.

the President
the Executive
Chief Magistrate

Commander-in-chief
His Excellency
Great Father

Also: ex-President,[9] President-elect; the Presidency.

Departments, bureaus, offices, services, etc. Capitalize the names of United States departments, bureaus, offices, services, etc. Lower-case *bureau, department, commission,* etc., used alone in place of the full name.

Department of the Interior
Bureau of Pensions
Census Bureau
General Land Office
the Cabinet

General Education Board
Marine Hospital Service
Interstate Commerce Commission
Tennessee Valley Authority [10]
Civil Service Commission

Capitalize *Administration, Constitution,* etc., when referring to the United States Government.

The word *government* should ordinarily be capitalized when it refers to the United States or some other country and means "the state, or body politic" or "the administration, or governing body of persons in a state." Do not capitalize *government* when used otherwise.[11] Distinguish similarly between *the Federal Government* and *a federal government.*

The Government of Mexico replied to the effect that . . .
The two Governments (United States and Mexico) clashed.
The only way the Government can help is to give us a money system that will easily convey wealth from producer to consumer.
A government of the people, for the people, and by the people
A South American government
The expenses of government have mounted rapidly.
No government can guarantee security.
Nothing has been done to secure either government or finance to its proper function.

Civil titles. Capitalize civil titles of high-ranking officials of a government when used with the name or in place of it.

the Secretary of State, the Acting Secretary, the Under Secretary
the Attorney General

[9] *Former President* is better form in most instances.
[10] When the word *authority* is used alone in place of the full name, it usually seems necessary to capitalize in order to prevent ambiguity.
[11] In Great Britain *government,* applied collectively to the cabinet and ministers holding office at any given time, is construed as plural: "His Majesty's Government are resolved to assist." In the United States, *the Government* is construed as singular.

the Chief Justice
the Minister to Turkey
the Ambassador to the Court of St. James's
the First Lord of the Admiralty
the President of the Board of Education
Secretary of State for Home Affairs
Lower case: ambassador, the British ambassador, the minister.

Laws. Capitalize *act, law, bill,* only in the formal titles of bills that have become laws.

Volstead Act   Aldrich-Payne Tariff Act
Sherman Antitrust Act   the Eighteenth Amendment

Lower case: the prohibition amendment, the tariff act, the revenue act of 1921, etc.; established by an act of Congress. *But:* an Act of Parliament, public Acts, private Acts.

Political parties. Capitalize the names of political parties and their adherents.

Democratic party   Republicans
British Labour party   Farm Bloc
Mugwumps   Communist
the Solid South   the Left Wing, the Left
Black Shirts   Opposition (the party out of power in
                                          a foreign country)

Lower case: anarchist, bolshevism, communism, fascism, nihilism, socialism, socialistic (when referring to ideology, doctrine, or philosophy in general).

Miscellaneous

Academic degrees. Capitalize names of academic degrees and scholastic and military honors and decorations when they are used following a proper name, whether they are written in full or abbreviated. In the expression "the degree of Doctor of Laws" either capitals or lower case may be used, the nature of the publication determining the preferable form.

Walter Blank, Bachelor of Science
Charles Black, LL.D.
Frank White, Fellow of the Royal Geographic Society
Frank White, F.R.G.S.

Buildings and organizations. Capitalize the names of buildings, organizations, institutions, etc. (Newspaper usage in this detail is divided, some papers preferring lower case for the common-noun portion of the name unless it comes first, as in *University of Chicago, Hotel Astor.*)

the White House	Independent Order of Odd Fellows, an
the Blue Room	Odd Fellow
the Mansion House (official residence	Boy Scouts, a Boy Scout
of the Lord Mayor of London)	Camp Fire Girls
the Vatican	Red Sox, Cardinals
Ferry Building (San Francisco)	New York Central Lines
The Plaza Hotel	Boston and Albany Railroad
Hull House	The Macmillan Company
the Sphinx	City Club
the Pyramids	Dartmouth College
Tomb of the Unknown Soldier	Grolier Society
Rose Bowl	Chicago Civic Opera Company
Masonic Order, a Mason, a Freemason	Little Theater
Shriners	Boston Symphony Orchestra
American Legion, the Legion	Royal Northwest Mounted Police

Lower case: ladies' aid society, parent-teacher association, chamber of commerce (unless they are accompanied by a proper name); legionnaires.

Common-noun elements of these proper names, such as *club, college, company, hotel, railroad,* and *society,* should not be capitalized when they are used in the plural with two or more proper names.

the Union Pacific and Southern Pacific railroads
Simmons and Radcliffe colleges
the Warner and Paramount theaters

If the common noun is used alone, it should not be capitalized, even if the reference is specific, unless a capital is necessary to avoid ambiguity. A few such nouns that *are* capitalized when used alone are the following (they should be lower case unless they have the meaning here specified):

the Bank (Bank of England)	the Legion (American Legion or French
the Garden (Madison Square Garden)	Foreign Legion)
the League (the League of Nations)	the Street (Wall Street)
the Yard (Scotland Yard)	

Epithets. Capitalize epithets used as parts of proper names or as substitutes therefor.

Charles the Bold	the Emancipator
Coeur de Lion	the Tiger of France
Billy the Kid	the Grand Monarch
Gyp the Blood	the First Lady

When epithets and names of groups of people, parties, or localities have lost their original identity and have taken on the nature of institutions with a well-defined significance, they should be capitalized.

Big Business	Four Hundred	Little Italy
Big Four	Old Guard	Great White Way

Estates. Capitalize the names of homes and estates.

The Croft	The Maples

Family appellations. *Father, Mother, Uncle,* etc., should be regarded as proper nouns and written with a capital letter when they are used without a possessive pronoun.

I have had a letter from Mother.
I have had a letter from my mother.
Yesterday Uncle John came.
Did you know my uncle had come?

Flags. Capitalize names of national flags, emblems, and college colors.

Star-Spangled Banner	Great Union
Old Glory	Union Jack
Stars and Stripes	Tricolor
the Lilies of France	the Crimson

Games. Names of games are not capitalized unless they are new or unusual or generally unfamiliar.

golf	hide and seek	Musical Chairs
dominoes	blindman's buff	Monopoly
	"Let's play The Farmer in the Dell."	

In the game of chess all terms, unless proper names, should be lower case. For example: Ruy Lopez opening, Philidor's defense, king's bishop's gambit, queen's gambit declined, giuoco piano opening. Never capitalize the pieces, king, queen, bishop, knight, rook (or castle), pawn; but when moves are given by initials, set thus: K—Kt3, Kt—K6, K—R sq. P(Kt2)xP, KxB, Q—Kt8 ch, etc.[12]

Geologic names. Capitalize the accepted names for eras, periods or systems, and epochs or series.

Cenozoic era	Quaternary period
Recent epoch	Acadian epoch

[12] Rule from the style book of the New York *Times.*

No difficulty will be experienced with those terms whose proper-noun character is obvious. The situation is different with *upper, middle,* and *lower,* which are properly capitalized only when they are part of an accepted name for a period. The following are all the instances in which they are correctly capitalized.

Upper Cretaceous	Upper Jurassic	Lower Ordovician
Lower Cretaceous	Middle Jurassic	Upper Triassic
Upper Devonian	Lower Jurassic	Middle Triassic
Middle Devonian	Upper Ordovician	Lower Triassic
Lower Devonian	Middle Ordovician	

In addition, these adjectives may be capitalized with "Carboniferous," "Quaternary," and "Tertiary" if the terms are enclosed in quotation marks.

The following may be used in a titular sense if they are enclosed in quotation marks:

"Calciferous"	"Juratrias"	"Permo-Carboniferous"
"Coal Measures"	"Lignitic"	"Red Beds"
"Corniferous"	"Magnesian"	

Coal measures, calciferous, lignitic, magnesian, and *redbeds* may also be used as common nouns or adjectives. The forms *glacial, preglacial,* and *postglacial, post-Pliocene, pre-Cambrian,* are correct.

Such nouns as *anticline, dome, formation, group, member, syncline, terrace,* and *uplift* should not be capitalized when preceded by a proper name.[13]

Age is capitalized when lower case would be ambiguous, as: the *Age of Fishes* but *Paleolithic age, the stone age;* and it is capitalized by some publishers when it designates a specific period, as: *Stone Age, Machine Age, Air Age*

The names of the twenty-four great soil groups are capitalized.

Alpine Meadow	Laterite	Sierozem (Gray)
Bog	Pedalfer	Solonchak
Brown	Pedocal	Solonetz
Chernozem	Podzol	Soloth
Chestnut	Prairie	Terra Rossa
Desert	Ramann's Brown	Tundra
Gray-Brown Podzolic	Red	Wiesenboden
Half-Bog	Rendzina	Yellow

[13] Rulings above are of the U. S. Government Printing Office. See its *Style Manual,* 1935, p. 145.

Heavenly bodies. Capitalize the names of the stars, planets, and constellations.

North Star, Polaris	Cassiopeia
Milky Way	Halley's Comet
the Dipper	Leonids
the Southern Cross	Great Nebula
the Great Bear	Charles's Wain

Holidays. Capitalize the names of holidays, holy days, and festivals.

New Year's Day	Passover
the Fourth of July, the Fourth	Shrove Tuesday
Patriots' Day	Holy Week, Passion Week
Commencement Day, Commencement	the Feast of St. John
Christmas Eve, Noël	Yom Kippur, Rosh Hashana

Lower case: noël, or nowell (meaning carol or song).

Nouns with numerals. Nouns or abbreviations used with a letter or numeral, particularly a capitalized roman numeral, to denote a place in a numbered series are usually capitalized. Such words are often lower case in parentheses, footnotes, references, and similar matter, and office style sheets often note certain words as exceptions. *Line* (l.) and *page* (p.) are always set lower case. (Do not abbreviate these words in straight text.)

Act I	Volume II	Chapter 2	Grade 5
Article IV	Part I	Division 4	Room 8
Book III	Plate II	Figure 48	Ward 4

When *No.* is used between the noun and the numeral, it is good style not to capitalize the noun.

mound No. 3	bench mark No. 6
schedule No. 4	station No. 11

Used in the plural such words are often lower case:

Refer to tables 20 and 21.
Illustrated in figures 1, 3, 4.
See chapters XV, XVII, XX.
Especially opera 127, 131, 132, 135.

If the reference is to unnumbered columns or sentences, and could be expressed equally well by the use of an ordinal, like *the second column, the fifth sentence,* lower case for the noun is correct form.

sentence 5	column 2	question 4	item 3

Personal names with "de," "le," "von," etc. Articles and prepositions in the names of Englishmen and North Americans are always capitalized unless a preference for the lower-case form has been shown by the families themselves.

Thomas De Quincey   Martin Van Buren
Theodore L. De Vinne   Robert La Follette

In French, Italian, Spanish, Portuguese, German, and Dutch names these secondary elements are not usually capitalized if a forename or title precedes.

Catherine de' Medici   Ludwig van Beethoven
M. de Tocqueville   Herr von Ribbentrop
Lucca della Robbia   Hendrik Willem van Loon
Leonardo da Vinci   René le Bossu
Eamon de Valera   Miguel de la Torre

Here again family preference may determine the form.

Maxime Du Camp   Edmondo De Amicis

In French names *le, l', la* are sometimes capitalized.

Comtesse de La Fayette   Philibert de L'Orme
Jean de La Fontaine   Charles Le Brun

When names like these are used without a forename or title, they may or may not be capitalized. The rule most often followed in American printing is to capitalize; British practice is not to capitalize. The logic of the latter practice is evident, since many of these prepositions are often dropped, as *Hindenburg, Maupassant, Beethoven, Leeuwenhoek.*

De' Medici   Van Beethoven
De Tocqueville   Von Ribbentrop
Della Robbia   Van Loon
Da Vinci   Le Bossu
De Valera   De la Torre
Similarly: Ibn Saud, Abu Bekr.

Names of this sort are usually capitalized at the beginning of a sentence regardless of the form used within a sentence.

Parts of books. Capitalize *Preface, Contents, Index,* and other names of parts of a book when they are specifically referred to.

The meanings of technical terms can be found in the Glossary.
See the Table of Food Values on page 87.
The interested student will find in Chapter XI, "The Press and Its Working," a complete exemplification of the subject.

Peoples, races, tribes. Capitalize names and epithets of peoples, races, and tribes, including *Negroes* whenever the word is used in the ethnic sense or along with other names of this class.

Aryans	Negro	Cliff Dwellers
Caucasian	Sioux	Oriental (*noun*)

Lower case: redskins, whites, quadroons.

Note. To oblige the National Association for the Advancement of Colored People some writers and publishers always capitalize *Negro.*

Personifications. Capitalize personifications of abstract ideas or objects. Always capitalize *Mother Nature,* but capitalize *Nature* only when the personification is as clear as in the first example below.

The great artist, Nature, had finished her masterpiece.
If Headquarters says so . . .
"Go, go, go," Reason told him.

Prefixes. Prefixes added to proper nouns or adjectives are usually lower case; but *anti, neo, post, pre,* and *semi* are sometimes capitalized.[14]

ante-Norman	non-Euclidean
ex-President	pro-German
mid-Atlantic	un-American
anti-English	pre-Raphaelite
Anti-Semite	Pre-Cambrian
neo-Catholicism	semi-American
Neo-Hebraic	Semi-Pelagian
post-Exilic	inter-American
Post-Tertiary	Pan-Slavic

Scientific names. In botany, paleontology, zoology, etc., capitalize the names of all divisions higher than species, that is, genera, families, orders, classes, and phyla; but not adjectives and English nouns derived from them. Names of species are usually lower case, but if they are derived from a proper name they may be capitalized.

Clupeidae, clupeid	the genus Hydra; a hydra
Chiroptera, chiropter	the tall buttercup (*Ranunculus acris*)
Coelenterata, coelenterate	the harp seal (*Phoca graenlandica*)

Parasitism is emphasized in the study of Sporozoa, Platyhelminthes, and Nemathelminthes.

[14] Certain pairs of words like *un-Platonic* and *unplatonic* have different meanings. Usage has established the forms *transatlantic* and *transpacific* as correct.

Seasons. The names of the seasons are not capitalized unless they are personified.

Hail, Autumn, with thy joyous harvests!

"The." Capitalize *The* when it is part of a name.

The Hague   The Weirs (N. H.)
The Dalles (Oregon)   The Buttes (Cal.)
              The Adjutant General (prescribed by law)
Lower case: the Netherlands, the Bronx, the Bad Lands.

It is not necessary to capitalize *the* because the name following is capitalized or capitalized and quoted. (Note the position of the quotation marks; see also p. 290.)

the Virgin Mary   called "the North Star State"
the Tiger of France   the Joneses (*not* The Joneses)

For usage regarding *the* in titles of books and newspapers see pp. 211, 212.
The word *the* used before the name of an Irish or Scots clan designates the chieftain of the clan. It is sometimes capitalized but more often not.

the McManus   the MacGregor

Thoroughfares, parks, squares, aviation fields, etc. Capitalize the names of streets, avenues, parks, squares, aviation fields, and the like. In newspapers the words *street, avenue, park, boulevard,* etc., are generally set lower case, but in all other kinds of work such words are considered an organic part of the name.

Boston Common   Unter den Linden   Harbour Grace Field
Prospect Park   Trafalgar Square   the Prado
Champs Elysées   Mitchel Field   the Malecon
Lower case in the plural: Union and Market streets.

Always capitalize *Wall Street, Fleet Street, Downing Street,* and *Main Street* when they are used with special significance beyond that of a street name. When the word *street* or *avenue* forms part of the name of a building or organization, it should be capitalized, even in a down-style newspaper.

Fifth Avenue Presbyterian Church
Fourth Street Boys' Club

Titles. Capitalize civil and religious titles when they precede a name. Capitalization of such titles used after the name is definitely governed by the nature of the publication. In straight text all except those denoting high rank may correctly be lower case. In books using few capitals even these may be lower case. Other kinds of printed matter might require capitalization of all titles denoting position or rank when used following a name.

Superintendent Wagner	—— ——, Governor of Massachusetts
Deacon White	—— ——, parole officer
General Manager Howard	E. P. Wagner, superintendent of schools

Distinguish a title from a substantive and an appositive:

the general manager, John Howard   the papal legate, Riorio

When titles are used alone referring to specific persons, they may be capitalized.

the Prince of Wales	the Duke of Cornwall
the Apostle to the Gentiles	the Bishop of London
the Crown (referring to the sovereign of a country)	

King, Queen, Dictator, Pope, etc., may be capitalized, especially when reference is to the incumbent of the office; but the trend is to lower case in secular writing.

the king of England   the sultan of Turkey

The Turkish titles *bey, pasha,* and *hakim* usually follow the personal name and should be capitalized.

Capitalize titles of honor, nobility, and respect. In a formal text the pronouns should be capitalized; in a less formal one, lower case is preferred.

His Holiness Pius XII	her Grace
His Grace the Duke of Devonshire	your Excellency
His Excellency	your Honor

Capitalize titles used in direct address as synonyms of proper names.

Mr. Mayor, Ladies and Gentlemen:	"Come this way, Doctor."
"I am, Captain, your . . ."	"How are you, Pop?"
"Well, General, what is the next step?"	"I'll be there, Mumsie."
But: "Yes, miss." "Oh, no, sir." "Yes, my lord."	

Any common noun used as part of or in place of a proper name may be capitalized in a publication of limited circulation if the noun is highly specific for the audience addressed.

the Dean, the Prex (in a school publication)

Trade names. Capitalize copyrighted trade names.

Frigidaire   Pyrex   Flying Fortress   Stratoliner

Continued wide use of a trade name often reduces it to a common noun, but it should be remembered that manufacturers may insist on the capitalization of a trade name.

kodak	eau de cologne	linotype
victrola	multigraph	photostat
carborundum	tabasco	corn flakes
dictaphone	polaroid	shredded wheat

In text matter, names that are descriptive of an article may capitalize only the distinguishing part of the name.

Eagle pencil   Gem safety razor
Ford station wagon   Beech-Nut gum
Campbell's soup

Trains. The names of trains are capitalized (no quotes).

the Twentieth Century Limited   the Sunset Limited
the Dixie Flyer   the Owl

USE OF CAPITALS FOR DISTINCTION AND EMPHASIS

Quasi-quotations. Words that would according to a more common practice be roman quoted or italicized are often considered sufficiently distinguished by capitalizing initial letters.

Until then it was the New Era.

This text employs the term School and Home Shopwork to signify the life values of school shopwork in their home shopwork applications. All the school Standard Jobs are paralleled with Supplementary Jobs related to the home.

For purposes of flexibility and adaptation to individual differences the words are grouped in three separate lists: a Basal List, an Enrichment List, and Supplementary Words.

The topic may well be some unit of work or special activity; such as The Westward Movement, National Parks, Irrigation, or Machines at Work.

Announcements, etc. Words are often capitalized in advertisements, announcements, and circular letters for distinction and emphasis.

Containing a special article on French Pronunciation; a list of French Nouns of Double Gender; a table of Irregular and Defective Verbs, and their Conjugations; a special Vocabulary of Proper Names; separate Vocabulary of Geographical Names, etc.

Checks, etc. In reproductions in print of formal statements, checks, promissory notes, drafts, and the like, sums of money written in words are often capitalized.

Foreign languages. Rules for capitalization in foreign languages are given on pages 312–349.

PUNCTUATION [1]

Some writers use punctuation skillfully and accurately, thereby giving their words the greatest possible clearness, emphasis, and value. Some disregard accepted usages to such an extent as to cast discredit upon their entire work. The great mass of printed matter, however, is written by persons of neither of these sorts. They use punctuation sometimes inaccurately, sometimes awkwardly, usually reasonably well, though seldom so well that a capable editor or proofreader could not find faults to correct.

Since violations of good usage cast discredit upon the author and are, besides, exceedingly annoying to many readers, editors must give careful attention to punctuation if they are to prevent unfavorable criticisms of their company's publications. Theirs is the obligation to correct any faulty punctuation that they may find in the manuscript.

The privileges of proofreaders in relation to punctuation have been much curtailed in recent years. Printers feel that the responsibility for proper use of punctuation marks is the editor's or the author's, and they give their compositors and proofreaders instructions to follow copy. Nevertheless, proof cannot be read intelligently without a thorough understanding of the principles of good punctuation. Thus, author, editor, and proofreader need to know how to punctuate in accordance with accepted usage.

Most presentations of the principles and rules of punctuation, adequate though they may be for the purpose intended, are not sufficiently comprehensive and do not go deep enough into usage and into the difficulties of applying the rules to another person's written work to meet the needs of editors and proofreaders. Both need to know not only the rules and the principles underlying them but also the modifications allowed by usage in different contexts, and the details subject to the dictation of the publisher. Proofreaders need also to know which rules can be safely followed and which rules must always be left to the judgment of the author or editor. The following pages on punctuation have been compiled especially for proofreaders, with their problems and difficulties uppermost in mind. The examples are

---

[1] If the meaning of grammatical terms used in this section is not clear, see the Glossary of Grammatical Terms in the Appendix.

not pattern sentences in the sense of being made up to fit the rule, but were taken from actual writing; most of them were incorrectly punctuated when they came to the proofreader's attention.

Sentences. Use a period after a complete declarative sentence or words standing for such a sentence—that is, a virtual sentence.

It is a pleasant day. Yes, indeed.

Sentences containing an imperative may be marked by a period or by an exclamation point. The author, not the printer, must decide which shall be used, since the choice depends upon the degree of emphasis.

Come at once. Be careful!

Do not use a period after a complete sentence enclosed in parentheses and interpolated within another sentence.

Make composition a class exercise by having students suggest a topic (the teacher writes it on the board) and then develop the theme in outline form.

Abbreviations. Use a period after the abbreviation of a word or a single or double letter representing a word. (See also pp. 182–198.)

etc.　　Mrs.　　Co.　　St.　　LL.D.　　pp.

Exceptions. The following abbreviations use no period and therefore are properly termed symbols.

Chemical symbols: O Fe H_2O
Trigonometrical terms: cos cosec cot log mod sin tan
Format signs of books: 4to 8vo 24mo
Chess terms: K B K Kt
Also: S O S I O U A B C's IHS LXX (Septuagint)

(The wireless call S O S should not be confused with the abbreviations S.O.S., meaning Service of Supply; nor A B C's with A.B.C. Powers, meaning Argentina, Brazil, Chile.)

The following proper names use no period after the initials.

AE
J Harlan Bretz
W J McGee

Maurice L Rothschild
Charles C Thomas
Daniel D Tompkins

Some abbreviations may be set either with or without periods. Generally speaking, symbols are the more informal and therefore the less appropriate in book work.

Linguistic epochs: O.E. or OE   M.H.G. or MHG
Government agencies: T.V.A. or TVA   O.P.A. or OPA
Manuscript: MS., MSS. or MS, MSS

The French use no period after an abbreviation ending with the last letter of the word for which it stands. The practice is seldom followed in this country in an English text. If a superior form is used, the period should be omitted.

Mlle., Mme., Cie. *or* Mlle, Mme, Cie Mlle Mme Cie

Contractions. Do not use a period after a contraction, an abridged form of a word using an apostrophe for omitted letters.

m'f'g   sec'y   Ass'n

Shortened forms. Use a period after abbreviations of names, like Thos., Chas., Benj., but not after shortened forms of names.

Alex   Ed   Nell   Pete   Will

Some shortened forms in common use or appearing in a localized setting are not considered abbreviations.

exam	kilo	photo	noncom
gym	pro	electro	pro tem
lab	prof	mat	consols
math	ad	auto	

Shortened forms of the names of English counties are not followed by an abbreviating period.

Berks (Berkshire)   Lincs (Lincolnshire)
Hants (Hampshire)   Salop (Shropshire)

Letters. Use no period after letters used in place of names unless they are the initials of the name.

A said to B   Mr. A. (for Mr. Abbot)
Mr. A told Mr. B   Mr. B. (for Mr. Baker)

Numerals. Do not use a period after the ordinals 1st, 2d, 3d, etc.; they are not considered abbreviations.

Do not use a period after roman numerals except in enumerating items. Some publishers omit the period here also.

Charles I   Louis XIV   Vol. II   IV. Protozoa

Headings, non-sentences, indexes. Never use periods after centered headings and running headings. They are not necessary after topical side headings set on a line by themselves; after captions or legends not in complete sentence form; after items in a column; at the end of entries in an index.

Use with other marks. The period may be used in conjunction with dashes, quotation marks, parentheses, and brackets, but not with other marks unless it points an abbreviation.

If an exclamation point or a question mark comes at the end of a declarative sentence, omit the period.

> Have you ever eaten in a big city hotel and thought to yourself, "When I am earning enough money of my own, this is where I shall live"?
> He was holding one end of the heavy shirt of mail which an Elliott had worn many a time when answering the call of his king and country, "To arms!" [*Not:* . . . country, "To arms!".]
> From Hamilton, "At last!" [*Not:* From Hamilton, "At last!."]

With quotation marks. When the period is used with closing quotation marks, place it inside; very few American printers now do otherwise. (See p. 275.)

> The other was "The Old Folks at Home."
> "The other was 'The Old Folks at Home.'" [*Not:* . . . Home'."]

Do not mistake an apostrophe for a single quotation mark in sentences like the following:

> "He'll never hurt ye at a'."
> "Thank you kindly, ma'am, for a second helpin'."

With parentheses. When the last words of a sentence are enclosed in parentheses, place the period marking the end of the sentence after the second curve (called the "close paren"). (The preceding sentence illustrates the correct form.) The period is properly placed inside a parenthesis only when the matter enclosed is not part of the preceding sentence but is an independent sentence beginning with a capital. Note that in such constructions there is regularly a period before the parenthesis.

> Sometimes the knee-chest position is used. (See Knee-chest position, p. 51.)

Do not use a period after (1), (a), marking divisions—the parentheses are sufficient.

(1) The development . . .
    (a) Seeds . . .

THE EXCLAMATION POINT AND THE INTERROGATION POINT

Exclamations. The exclamation point is used after any expression of an exclamatory nature; that is, an expression which indicates strong feeling or emotion. At the close of a sentence beginning with an interjection an exclamation point is used if the emotion is strong enough to justify it, a matter to be determined by the author.

Hurrah!
How beautiful on the mountains are the feet of him that bringeth good tidings!
Oh, Anna, please hurry!
Alas, they were too late!

In the following sentence the exclamation point was incorrectly placed. This sentence scarcely needs an exclamation point, but if it is used, it should be placed at the end of the sentence.

Wrong: Oh! yes, it will be hard for us to think of the school in terms of growing self-discipline.
Right: Oh, yes, it will be hard for us to think of the school in terms of growing self-discipline!

Emphasis or irony. An exclamation point is also used to point an emphatic or ironical comment.

I remember a statute passed in one of our Middle States, I believe, to the effect that two trains approaching an intersection must both come to a full stop, and neither may start again until the other has passed!

Direct questions. Use a question mark after every direct question.

Where is he now?
It is well to ask, Can this be done without harm to anyone?
In the sentence "How do beavers build dams?" which words name things?
Nor was it disclosed—why need it have been?—that John had taken the case.
These two boats (can you find them?) gave the world not only steel fighting ships but the turret.
How is the resistance of a wire affected by doubling its length? by doubling its diameter? by halving its length? by halving its diameter?

Some writers prefer to use only one question mark with a series of questions like the last example above, and this form is certainly preferable whenever the construction is like that of the following example.

What is meant by the terms (*a*) atom of an element, (*b*) molecule of an element, (*c*) molecule of a compound?

The following sentences illustrate a use of interrogative words, essentially questions yet so short that the capital and question mark would be cumbersome. Italics may well be used in such sentences.

He must take the verb and ask the question *who* or *what* to find the subject.
They are easily recognized by asking the questions *how, when, where*, or *why*.

Place the question mark at the end of the question, not elsewhere.

Wrong: Will she fight Victor's case, I wondered.
Right: Will she fight Victor's case? I wondered.
Wrong: "It's a mighty hard pull, though, isn't it? when people don't have confidence in you."
Right: "It's a mighty hard pull, though, isn't it, when people don't have confidence in you?"

Sometimes a sentence declarative in form is to be read as an exclamation or an interrogation and is punctuated accordingly.

Surely it cannot be that you are so utterly barren of manhood that you will deny me what you promised!
Suppose I introduce you to the Burleighs?

Indirect questions. Do not use a question mark after indirect questions.

Artemas had wondered why.
He asked how old John was.
How to live—that is the essential question for us.

The difference between a direct and an indirect question may be slight.

Direct: It is well to ask, What is the precedent in such and such a case?
Indirect: It is well to ask what the precedent is in such and such a case.

There is a form of interrogation in which the exact words of the speaker are not given, neither is the sentence worded like a statement, as in the indirect questions given above. In such sentences the question mark is necessary, but quotation marks are not used.

Could it be possible? he asked himself.
When was it to be? they wanted to know.

Requests. A period, not a question mark, may be used after a sentence which is interrogative in form but is in reality a request.

Will you please close the door.
Will you kindly return this as soon as possible.
As you read the following selection will you write down each word whose mean-
ing you do not already know.

However, such sentences may be intended as definitely interrogative and be punctuated as questions.

Will you, please, close the door?

Likewise a statement of fact may sometimes appear to be a question. It should be followed by a period, not by a question mark.

"Do you know," she said, "I am making up a story about Donald Kane."

Doubt. An interrogation point, usually in parentheses, may be used to express a doubt about what precedes.

Edmund Spenser (1552?–1599)
Nest(?) of Nighthawk. The eggs are laid on a bare hillside with no effort to
build a nest.
On March 2(?), 1542.

Use with other marks. The exclamation point and the question mark may be used in conjunction with quotation marks, dashes, parentheses, and brackets. Usage varies as to the need or correctness of using these marks with commas, periods, and each other.

With quotation marks and parentheses. When either the exclamation point or the question mark is used in conjunction with closing quotation marks or a closing parenthesis, it should precede the quotation marks or the parenthesis if it is a part of the quoted or parenthetical matter; otherwise it should follow. This rule is invariable.

He cried out, "Wake up!"
How absurd to call this stripling a "man"!
"Did you memorize 'The Chambered Nautilus'?"
Ask the pupils, What did Whittier mean by "It sank from sight before it set"?
Another familiar idiom is "How do you do?" For this the French idiom is
Comment vous portez-vous? (How do you carry yourself?) and the German
idiom, *Wie befinden Sie sich?* (How do you find yourself?).

With a period. If an exclamatory or an interrogative sentence and a declarative sentence end at the same time, retain the exclamation point or the question mark and omit the period.

> But does not one sometimes say, "I don't feel quite sure about the first important problem in percentage"?

With each other. If a question and an exclamation occur within a question, both ending at the same time, retain the stronger mark. It is often hard to say which is the stronger mark, but the following sentences illustrate acceptable forms.

> "Has it ever occurred to you that she might retort, 'Dangerous for whom'?"
> "How about 'Where Are You Now, Old Pal of Mine'?"
> Will it invite that all-important question, "Where did you buy it"?
> Did you hear somebody yelling "Fire! Fire!"
> How many of you have heard the question, "Which is the more important for a person, his heredity or his environment?"
> Haven't you noticed the appeal, "Ten dollars down and ten dollars a month"?
> What would he think if we should turn to him and say, "Old man, just think, you're responsible for all this!"

With a comma. If a question or an exclamation ends within a sentence and the construction calls for a comma at the same point, the comma should in most instances be omitted. Punctuation marks are used to make the meaning clear to the reader, preferably without his being conscious of them. A comma and an exclamation mark or a comma and a question mark used together are so unusual that they attract the attention of the reader without in any way clarifying the sentence.

> *Poor:* The curriculum problem is clarified when we consider that it raises the question, not so much, What has? or What is?, or even What will be?, but rather, What should be?

No confusion of meaning results when the commas are omitted.

> The curriculum problem is clarified when we consider that it raises the question, not so much What has? or What is? or even What will be? but rather, What should be?
> Voices rose in a tumult of shouting: "Free her! Free her!" "Hang the bloody captains!" "Hang the villains!" "They're the murderers!"
> "Are Languages Practical?" *F. R.,* Vol. 5 (Nov., 1931), pp. 141–145.

There are instances, however, in which it may seem better to use the double punctuation.

Constance Lambert, *Music Ho!,* London, 1932.
Stung!, 498 [Index entry]

Some persons prefer to drop the question mark instead of the comma:

One who asks, "What is money, anyway," would be quick to kick if short-changed.

With a semicolon. When the sentence construction calls for a semicolon where a question or an exclamation ends, the semicolon is usually retained, in spite of its obviousness.

> . . . cultivate an interest in the following topics: "How Old Is the Earth?"; "The Beginnings of Life"; and "Human Beings."
>
> . . . the mottoes of which are the same: "Enjoy life, for it is short!"; "Wine, women, and song"; or, as in the present-day advertising: "Unhappy?—Buy a Chevrolet!"; "Buy Swift's ham and be happy!"; . . .

Type. Most printers set an exclamation point or a question mark in the same font as the word preceding it. A single italic or boldface letter does not ordinarily require a following mark to be italic or boldface; and italic geometrical designations are followed by roman punctuation.

> **Wie viele?** how many?
> *But:* What was the correct length of *AC*?

This practice is not pleasing to all publishers, some feeling that an italic or boldface word at the end of a roman sentence should be followed by a roman exclamation point or question mark.

> What can you say about this use of *do*?
> *But:* "*Halt!*" came the command.

THE COLON

The colon is used after a word, phrase, or sentence to introduce something that follows, such as a formal question or quotation, an amplification, or an example. It may be said to replace the words *that is,* or *for example.*

> All ten pins seemed to drop simultaneously: it was a perfect strike.
>
> Bacteria are everywhere: in the air, in water, in milk, in dust, in soil, in the mouth, and on the hands.
>
> Of both centuries, meanwhile, two things are true: neither in itself presents much literary variety, and most of what was published in each has already been forgotten.
>
> Cooking has various purposes: (1) to make food more completely digestible; (2) to make food better flavored; (3) to make . . .
>
> In the *Dictionary of Graphic Arts Terms* we may read: "Imposition is the operation of . . ."

Caution: Never use a colon before a list unless the items are in apposition with an introductory word. Do not use a colon between a verb or preposition and its direct object.

Wrong: . . . produced in large quantities, such as: cacao beans, coffee, fruits, and Panama hats. [The colon should be omitted.]

Wrong: The principal criteria determining the selection were: the economic importance of the plant, its suitability as a representative of the family to which it belongs, and the intricacy of its anatomical and morphological detail. [The colon should be omitted.]

Before a direct quotation or question a comma is often sufficient.

The question may be raised, Is the reaction really a reaction between the molecule of barium nitrate and the molecule of sodium sulphate?

Use neither colon nor comma before an indirect question or quotation.

Wrong: The problem is: How to conserve it for plant use.

Right: The problem is how to conserve it for plant use.

Or: The problem is, How can it be conserved for plant use?

Side headings. The colon is often preferred to the period after a side heading.

Instruction: Stand squarely before the mirror, . . .

Salutations. Use a colon after the salutation of a letter—except informal notes—and of an address.

My dear Mr. Barr: Gentlemen:

Mr. President, Ladies and Gentlemen:

Scripture references. References to passages in the Bible may use the colon after the chapter number. (See also p. 165.)

I Corinthians 13:4–7

Time. In expressions of time the colon is often used in preference to the period.

at 10:20 A.M.

Use with other marks. Whenever a colon is used in conjunction with closing quotation marks, place it after the quotes. It should likewise follow a parenthesis.

The combination of a colon with a dash is not incorrect but is going out of use; a colon is sufficient.

Type. In a roman text set the colon in italic if the word immediately preceding it is italic, but not if roman quotation marks or parentheses intervene; a single italic letter does not ordinarily require a following colon to be italic, and geometrical designations are regularly followed by roman punctuation. The same principle applies to boldface.

> . . . from *Appalachia:*   Debate (*debating*):

THE SEMICOLON

The semicolon indicates a more definite break in thought or construction than a comma would mark, and calls for a longer pause in reading. It is used wherever a comma would not be sufficiently distinctive.

> There is no undergrowth, no clinging vines, no bloom, no color; only the dark, innumerable tree trunks, and the purplish brown, scented, and slippery earth.
> Preliminary practice was given as follows: in the formboard, by two trials with eyes open; in the star tracing, by fifteen minutes of practice.

Coördinate clauses without a conjunction. When the parts of a compound sentence are not connected by a coördinating conjunction, they are best separated by a semicolon, especially if the parts express a contrast or an antithesis.

> He went to the door; opened it.
> The intention is excellent; the method is self-destructive.
> "The B-29 part of this plane is downstairs," he said; "all this up here is added on!"
> An engineer may use this construction to lay out a large circle; a navigator may use it to avoid a dangerous reef or a submerged rock; a surveyor may utilize it in locating a new point on a tract that has been partly mapped.

Coördinate clauses with a conjunction. When the clauses of a compound sentence are long, involved, or internally punctuated, use a semicolon between them.

> The governments of Europe adopted the parliamentary type which was developed in England through many centuries; and even the countries with dictators have more or less held on to the parliamentary forms of government.
> We have seen how the people of this state work, how they earn their living; now let us see how they play, how they use their leisure.

If the clauses of a compound sentence are joined by one of the conjunctive adverbs, *so, therefore, hence, however, nevertheless, moreover, accordingly, besides, also, thus, then, still,* or *otherwise,* a semicolon between the clauses is usually better than a comma; but before *so, then,* and *yet* a comma is often sufficient.

I saw no reason for moving; therefore I stayed still.
The importer pays the tax and then sells the articles at an advanced price; so the consumer is really the man who pays the tax.

Series. If one or more items of a series contain commas, semicolons are often necessary between the parts to make the meaning clear.

These were located in Newbury, Cambridge, Saugus, Watertown, and Rowley, Massachusetts; Portsmouth, New Hampshire; and Lincoln, Rhode Island.
The children were drawn from three schools: the Hebrew Orphan Asylum, New York City; School 38; and the Normal Practice School, Buffalo, New York.
Clear with commas: Mr. W. A. Stauffer, Principal, Mr. Leonard McKaig, instructor, Mr. Stanley Hawthorne, instructor, Jay Bonnet, winner of the state oratorical contest, and the members of the civics class of the Ripon High School were extended the privilege of the floor of the Assembly for this day.
Semicolons too heavy: An ellipsis; a two-letter syllable; a two-letter word (unless quoted or carrying closing quotes), or a dash must never be used as the concluding line of a paragraph.

Resolutions. In a series of *whereas* clauses in a resolution each clause is usually followed by a semicolon.

Whereas in virtue of Article 3, paragraph 3, of the Covenant, the Assembly . . . ; and whereas, according to Part IV, section III, of the report . . . ; the assembly decides . . .

Use with other marks. Whenever the semicolon occurs in conjunction with closing quotation marks, place it outside. If it is used with parentheses, always place it after the closing parenthesis.

Pronouns referring to the Deity should not be capitalized except to avoid ambiguity, as "We owe all to Him who made us"; but in a case like "The Lord pitieth them that fear him," the capital is not necessary.
Dates of the current month are designated as "the 18th"; dates in other months in this style: January 18.
Don't use "at the corner of" (say Michigan Avenue and 22d Street); "put in an appearance"; apt, for likely.

Note. Some writers present the rule that semicolons should be placed inside quotation marks if the semicolon was in the original printing of the matter quoted Such an arrangement leaves the sentence in which the quotation appears without the punctuation called for by its construction. Even if the semicolon was used in the original it has no significance in the new sentence unless it is placed outside of the quotation marks.

Type. A semicolon should be set in the font of the word preceding it, but a single italic letter in roman text does not necessitate the semicolon being set in italic, and intervening roman punctuation makes a roman semicolon correct form. Italic geometrical designations are regularly followed by roman punctuation.

the title *Fräulein;*　　　　　　　　　"*. . . wherever possible*";
in Figure 6*a*;　　　　　　　　　　　(*civis Romanus sum*);
as in the rectangle *ABCD*;

THE COMMA

All punctuation is related to sentence flow (called sentence sense). A comma is seldom needed unless the forward sweep of thought is broken by (1) a broken series (*and* or *or* left out) or (2) a detour (a parenthetic element). Do not use a comma unless it makes the meaning clearer or enables the reader to grasp the relation of parts more quickly. Intruded commas are worse than omitted ones.

Open and close [1] **punctuation.** The terms "open punctuation" and "close punctuation" are used mostly with reference to commas and mean, respectively, using only as much punctuation as is absolutely necessary for clearness, and using as many marks as the grammatical construction will justify. Close punctuation often results in jerkiness without making the meaning clearer.

Closely punctuated: The soil which, in places, overlies the hard rock of this plateau, is, for the most part, thin and poor.
Better: The soil which in places overlies the hard rock of this plateau is for the most part thin and poor.

Compound sentences. Separate the coördinate clauses of a compound sentence, usually by a comma, though a semicolon may be called for by complexity of thought.

Every English grammar has a chapter on the subject of punctuation, and there are many books of authority that treat of punctuation exclusively.
Of the goods available for export a part was sold abroad, and a figure representative of this part is furnished by the value of exports.

The comma may be omitted if the clauses are short and closely connected in thought, especially if the connective is *and;* but take care not to omit a comma that is needed to prevent the subject of the second clause being read, at least momentarily, as a part of the object of the first clause.

Faulty: Zinc oxide is substituted for calcium oxide and selenium and charcoal are added.

[1] Klōs, tight; not klōz.

Clear: Zinc oxide is substituted for calcium oxide, and selenium and charcoal
are added.
Faulty: The bland flavor of the egg white does not call for the addition of lemon
juice and more delicate flavors are used.
Clear: The bland flavor of the egg white does not call for the addition of lemon
juice, and more delicate flavors are used.

Clauses joined by *but* regularly take a comma; a semicolon may be used
when the contrasted clauses are complex or when one clause is balanced against
two others.

Printers may try to make a sentence clear by punctuation, but they cannot so
clarify one that is badly worded.
We know what he did and what he said, and we know what interpretations
his friend put upon his words and actions; but we can only guess at his ulterior
motives.

A clause introduced by the conjunction *for* should be set off by punctuation
to prevent misreading of *for* as a preposition. Either a comma or a semicolon
may be correct.

He must have been in a great hurry, for his leaps had been from twenty to
thirty inches long.
Confusing: The last two have much promise for the future for those fields have
only recently come into prominence.
Clear: The last two have much promise for the future, for those fields have only
recently come into prominence.

A clause beginning with *so, then,* or *yet* should be separated from a preceding clause, and a comma is often sufficient for this purpose. (See p. 253.)
Compound predicate. Compound predicates are regularly not separated
by punctuation.

It begins with a discussion of different types of soil and goes on to explain the
care of various kinds of flowers.
These people have been dominated by foreigners for centuries but have still kept
their language, culture, and racial integrity.

A comma is sometimes needed to prevent misreading.

Faulty: He stifled the cry that rose to his lips and lay motionless.
Better: He stifled the cry that rose to his lips, and lay motionless.

Punctuation of sentences like the following seems to trouble many writers
and readers. It is best here to use commas in accord with the way sentences
like these are naturally read. The pause instinctively made *before* the con-

junction in reading these sentences should not be disregarded, even if a
compound predicate is thereby divided; neither should an awkward pause
and jerky reading be forced upon the reader by inserting a comma *after* the
conjunction.

> She clapped her hands, and after bowing once more to her father, ran to find
> her mother.
> He escaped from the guard having him in charge, and crossing the frontier of
> the Papal territory, embarked at Naples.

No rule is disregarded in punctuating the following; the comma before
the conjunction separates the parts of a compound sentence, the other comma
separates a dependent clause or phrase from the main clause following it.

> Riga is ice-bound for a shorter time, and except for a few days each winter, ice-
> breakers can keep its harbor open.
> His wealth is entirely in the service of employment and production, and if it
> were taken from his management, his only loss would be the opportunity to
> serve.

Series. Two parallel elements connected by a conjunction require no
comma between them. Letters or figures in parentheses make no difference
in the rule.

> *Commas unnecessary:* Through the courtesy of Mr. West, Miss June Hucke, and
> members of the eighth grade of the Pleasant Grove School, were extended the
> privilege of the floor of the Assembly.
> *Better:* Through the courtesy of Mr. West, Miss June Hucke and members of
> the eighth grade of the Pleasant Grove School were extended the privilege of
> the floor of the Assembly.
> *Wrong:* South America may be divided into two sharply contrasted regions;
> namely, (1) the Pacific, and (2) the Atlantic drainage basins.
> *Right:* South America may be divided into two sharply contrasted regions; namely,
> (1) the Pacific and (2) the Atlantic drainage basins.

In a series of the form *a, b, and c,* or *red, white, and blue,* use a comma before
the conjunction, whether the items of the series are words, phrases, or clauses.

> Motion pictures, the press, and the radio have tremendous influence.
> Errors in spelling, typesetting, punctuation, or sentence construction lead to
> humorous statements.

Practically all dictionaries, handbooks of composition, and book publishers'
style sheets present the rule as above. Newspaper and magazine writers and
publishers do not generally observe the rule in all cases but use the comma

only when clarity demands it. If this modified form of the rule is followed, note the following:

A series of personal names should have the comma before the conjunction to prevent the first name of the series being construed as a noun in direct address.

> "Anna, May and Walter are here." (Might be read as telling Anna that May and Walter are here.)
> "Anna, May, and Walter are here." (Can mean only that three persons are here.)

In a series of phrases the comma is necessary before the final phrase whenever the preceding phrase of the series contains a conjunction.

> . . . for punctuation, choice and spelling of words, and good diction.
> Modern "strike anywhere" matches are tipped with a mixture of phosphorus sulphide and some oxidizing material such as potassium chlorate, powdered glass or some other material to increase the friction, and glue to bind the ingredients to the match.

When the phrase preceding the conjunction contains a preposition, a comma is needed to prevent misreading the last phrase as part of the object of the preposition.

> The electrochemical industry, battery action and cell action, the smelting of ores, the corrosion of metals, and many other important types of chemical changes are examples of the transfer of electrons.
> *Obscure:* The green trees, the sight of the hills and fresh raw meat had quickly revived the beast.
> *Clear:* The green trees, the sight of the hills, and fresh raw meat had quickly revived the beast.

In a series of three or more clauses clarity almost invariably requires the comma before the conjunction.

> A pencil placed in a glass of water appears to be bent, the moon appears to be larger at the horizon than when it is overhead, and lake water appears to be green or blue depending on the depth, the position of the observer, and other factors.

If one or more members of the series contain commas, semicolons may be necessary between the parts to make the meaning clear. (See p. 253.)

Inserting a comma after the last member of the series, thus bringing a comma between subject and verb, is contrary to modern American style. (If the conjunction is omitted, this comma is used; see the following rule.)

> *Not American usage:* Camels, llamas, elephants, and carabaos, are as valuable in tropical countries as horses in America.

Not American usage: One of the most outstanding lessons to be learned from the radio, television, and other great advancements of man, is the tremendous possibility of the human mind.

Not American usage: A strong unreasonable prejudice, class or personal hatred, or insane fear, bears its frightful fruits of death, destruction, and persecutions.

In a series in the form *a, b, c* (no conjunction), preceding a verb or clause that stands in the same relation to each member of the series, use a comma after each member.

Poise, dignity, the peace of a man at one with his soul, shone from his face.

We noticed the misery, the suffering, the hardships, that lay hidden in the neighborhood. (See also p. 271.)

Note. Writers should avoid careless use of this construction, for in many instances a conjunction is preferable to the awkward comma.

Poor: Flies, insects, buzzed about.

Better: Flies and insects buzzed about.

Undesirable: Potatoes, rice, spaghetti, barley, may be added for bulk and thickening.

Better: Potatoes, rice, spaghetti, or barley may be added for bulk and thickening.

No comma is needed in a series in the form *a and b and c* (conjunction between each two).

The figures and postures and expressions of the Madonna, of the saints, of the prophets and sages, were less stern.

Coördinate adjectives. Two or more adjectives modifying the same noun should be separated by commas if they are coördinate in thought—that is, if *and* could be used between them without changing the meaning; but if one or more adjectives are included in thought with the noun modified, virtually forming a compound noun, an adjective modifying this compound should not be separated from it by a comma.

a rotund, cheery little man	a huge boxlike affair
fine tall, straight timber	a titanic flaming red torch
cool, humid climate	cold corned beef
broad, shallow rivers	big white plantation house

bold, glaciated, bare rock mountain heights

Snowflakes are beautiful complex six-sided figures.

Wrong: On a little, native, banana plantation

Right: On a little native banana plantation

Wrong: From the many, quaint, old fishing villages have come . . .

Right: From the many quaint old fishing villages have come . . .

Nonrestrictive and restrictive modifiers.[2] A nonrestrictive clause is one that could be omitted without changing the meaning of the principal clause; it should be set off by commas. A restrictive clause, on the contrary, so qualifies or limits the word it modifies that it could not be omitted without affecting the meaning of the sentence, and it should *not* be set off.

Nonrestrictive: Many animals, such as rabbits and horses, shed their heavy winter fur at the approach of warm weather.
Restrictive: Animals such as the beaver, seal, rabbit, fox, and cat are protected against cold by a soft silky covering called fur.
Nonrestrictive: Bobcats make their home in a hollow log or cave in the rocks, where they raise from two to four young.
Restrictive: Cheetahs live in various regions in Africa and Asia where they are able to find deer and antelope.
Nonrestrictive: It was improved very little until the middle of the nineteenth century, when matches were invented.
Restrictive: We should not use formal language when simpler expressions would serve.
Right: Observe a bird which is a poor flyer, such as a chicken or a goose, and some good flyer, such as a swallow.

A sentence containing a restrictive or nonrestrictive relative clause may be so worded that only by the punctuation can the reader tell the meaning. The writer should always check the punctuation of such sentences with special care. In scientific work, the terminology of which may be unfamiliar to the proofreader, this is particularly necessary. (The preceding sentence is itself one in which the relative clause might be construed either restrictive or nonrestrictive.)

Nonrestrictive: They passed on to the next victim, who seemed to be suffering greatly. (The clause here gives us the information that the next victim seemed to be suffering greatly.)
Restrictive: They passed on to the next victim who seemed to be suffering greatly. (Here we understand that the victims suffering greatly were attended before those suffering less severely.)

A restrictive relative clause often incorrectly set off is one in which the conjunction does not immediately follow the word it defines or limits.

Wrong: They spoke of old battles, in which they had fought together.
Right: They spoke of old battles in which they had fought together.
Wrong: It is this William, for whom the rock in Salem harbor called Bowditch's Ledge is named.

[2] Some writers on punctuation prefer the terms *nonessential* and *essential, nondefining* and *defining,* or *nonlimiting* and *limiting.*

Right: It is this William for whom the rock in Salem harbor called Bowditch's Ledge is named.

Wrong: Any tissue, the dry substance of which is composed largely of proteins, may be considered as protein tissue.

Right: Any tissue the dry substance of which is composed largely of proteins may be considered as protein tissue.

Wrong: Comment on any news of the week, in relation to which it would be appropriate to use any one of the words.

Right: Comment on any news of the week in relation to which it would be appropriate to use any one of the words.

Essential phrases, as well as clauses, should be recognized as restrictive and ᵔot be set off by commas.

Wrong: The learning and staging of operettas, dramatically insipid and musically void, may vitiate a year's work in music.

As the preceding sentence is punctuated it states that all operettas are dramatically insipid and musically void. The commas should be omitted, thereby making "dramatically insipid and musically void" a phrase limiting "operettas."

Right: The learning and staging of operettas dramatically insipid and musically void may vitiate a year's work in music.

Wrong: Katmai volcano was smoking lazily, like some old man, deep in reflection.

As punctuated, the preceding sentence states that Katmai volcano was deep in reflection.

Right: Katmai volcano was smoking lazily, like some old man deep in reflection.

Wrong: It was a peaceful migration, rather than a military conquest, such as that of the German invaders of the Roman Empire.

Right: It was a peaceful migration, rather than a military conquest such as that of the German invaders of the Roman Empire.

Wrong: An exercise, like C I, should be done orally in class.

Right: An exercise like C I should be done orally in class.

Wrong: Find the annual premium which a man, born December 2, 1908, must pay.

Right: Find the premium which a man born December 2, 1908, must pay.

Appositives. Set off words in apposition by commas.

He was replaced by a German leader, Odoacer, and thus a ruler from the barbaric tribes was recognized in Rome.

Kid leather, the skin of young goats or sheep, is one of the finest of leathers.

Simple appositives like the above examples are usually recognized and properly punctuated, but when the appositional phrase is longer, the second comma is often overlooked.

Wrong: Emporia, the prophet's own county with its 10,000 inhabitants bought more than 2500 copies.

Right: Emporia, the prophet's own county, with its 10,000 inhabitants, bought more than 2500 copies.

Use dashes to set off an appositive whenever they would make the meaning and construction more quickly comprehended.

They determined the stimulus—sound or an electric current—that would just suffice to waken an individual.

Appositional "or." Words or phrases in apposition are often introduced by *or.* Such words should always be set off when they explain or define a noun, but the commas may sometimes be omitted about a phrase that defines an adjective. Alternative *or* and appositional *or* should be carefully distinguished and no commas omitted that are necessary to clearness of meaning.

Flying Mammals, or Bats
Connotation, or the Suggestive Power of Words
Destruction of the Original, or Virgin, Forests
They are of the mixed, or teratomatous, variety.

Restrictive appositives. A restrictive appositive is one used to distinguish its principal from other persons or things of the same name, group, or class. Such an appositive, which could not be omitted without robbing the sentence of meaning, should not be set off.

the poet Longfellow   his brother Will
Mary Queen of Scots   the yacht *Sally Jane*

Explain how the poem "Louisiana Night" brings to mind a railroad train.
The expression "Where am I at?" is a provincialism.
The threefold division *antiquitas, media aetas, recens aetas* becomes common.
Based on *U. S. Census Reports on Population* covering the period 1790–1930.

The most frequent failure to recognize the restrictive nature of an appositive appears to be in sentences like the following.

Wrong: The Greek philosophers, Leucippus, Democritus, and Epicurus, advanced a doctrine . . . (There were other Greek philosophers.)

Right: The Greek philosophers Leucippus, Democritus, and Epicurus advanced a doctrine . . .

Wrong: The early nineteenth century American publisher, Robert Bonner, laid down a set of rules . . . (This conveys the impression that Robert Bonner was the one and only publisher of the early nineteenth century.)

Right: The early nineteenth century American publisher Robert Bonner laid down a set of rules . . .

Parenthetical expressions. Set off a parenthetical phrase or clause, which interrupts the even flow of a sentence and could be omitted without altering the meaning of the sentence. A parenthetical sentence requires dashes or parentheses—commas are not strong enough.

Even heavy-soled shoes, to say nothing of thin-soled ones, are not proof against continued wetting.

The great event in typography, so far as western civilization is concerned, occurred about 1450 in Germany.

From the Amarillo field, in a pipe line eleven miles long, are carried the natural gases from which helium is made.

Read *Captains Courageous,* by Rudyard Kipling, and report on deep-sea fishing as described by him.

One of the most frequent mistakes in punctuation is omission of one of the two marks required to enclose an interrupter. "One to separate, two to enclose" should be kept constantly in mind.

Absurd: Senators must have been citizens of the United States for at least seven years prior to their elections, and each must be living at the time of the election, in the state from which he or she is elected.

Right: . . . each must be living, at the time of the election, in the state from which he or she is elected.

In the following sentence there should be two commas or none.

Possible: Watch someone, unobtrusively but closely, for five minutes.

Better: Watch someone unobtrusively but closely for five minutes.

The parts of a compound subject consisting of two members only are often separated by a comma. The second part should then be treated as a parenthetical element requiring a comma after it also.

The prominence given these proposed changes in tariff policy, and the sharp division of opinion fostered by the activities of the Anti-Corn-Law League, inevitably dominated the campaign.

The subsequent arrest of the pope by Guillaume de Nogaret, and the compulsory removal of the popes to Avignon, marked clearly this turn.

Note. These examples illustrate the use of commas to indicate the manner in which the writer himself would read the sentence. Since the grammatical construction does not require any punctuation, the writer should assume full responsibility for its use.   On the other hand, the proofreader should recognize this use of commas to indicate emphasis and inflection and should not presume to delete commas in such cases.   It should of course be recognized that so punctuating a compound subject does not make the subject singular—subject and verb are both plural.   The construction should not be confused with the sentence in this pattern: The captain, as well as the sailors, is . . .

Interpolations and transition words.   Set off an expression like *I think, to tell the truth, to say the least, in short, besides,* unless it is so close as practically to limit the accompanying words.   A word and short expression that does not require a pause in reading need not be so set off.

He will come, I think, on the noon train.
To tell the truth, I'm rather tired.
This was not military work, anyway.
There were two, in fact.
Of couse I will.   Indeed she may.   I too must follow.
Whereupon the President adjourned the meeting.
Possible: Pitiful, indeed, is the person who perpetually apologizes for himself.
Also possible: Pitiful indeed is the person who perpetually apologizes for himself.

The word *therefore* is not necessarily a signal for punctuation.

Commas necessary: An easy answer would be, therefore, to say . . .
   They will understand, therefore, why . . .
Commas unnecessary: Therefore it is the history . . .
   It is not so noticeable and therefore not so objectionable.
   It is the logical method and it therefore appeals to the rational person.
Commas may or may not be used; the question is one of emphasis:
   They may therefore reasonably assume . . .
   It must therefore be less . . .

Use of the comma after *accordingly, consequently, yet,* and *hence* is a matter of choice.

Distinguish carefully between words used for transition and the same words used as adverbs.

It is very small, however.
However small it may be, it can be used.
Thus has the earth been peopled with a wealth of life forms.

"Do you think."   One of the commonest of errors comes about through failure to recognize *do you think* (*do you suppose*) as an interpolation.   We find such obviously incorrect questions as "Why do you think they are carrying a cross?" under a picture of men carrying a cross; or "Why do you think he is called Thrifty?" immediately following a statement that he *is* called

Thrifty. The primary error in such sentences is faulty word order. The questions should be: Why, do you think, are they carrying a cross? Why, do you think, is he called Thrifty? When the words are correctly arranged, the nature of *do you think* is immediately apparent.

> *Wrong:* For what do you think the woman in the picture has been using her rake?
> *Right:* For what, do you think, has the woman in the picture been using her rake?

The phrase *do you think* is not always an interpolation, however, but may be the main verb of the sentence. The difference in use is clear in the following:

> Why do you think he has gone? (What reasons have you for thinking he has gone?)
> Why, do you think, has he gone? (He has gone; what reasons do you think he had for going?)

In similar questions introduced by *what* no difficulty arises; the phrase *do you think* can often be construed either as a main clause or as an interpolation, and the sentence punctuated accordingly.

> What do you think is a fair way to have the radio used in political campaigns?
> What, do you think, is a fair way to have the radio used in political campaigns?

Introductory words. Use a comma after a word like *Yes, No, Well, Why,* introducing a sentence. Take care to distinguish between *well, why,* and similar words used as mere introductory words and the same words used as adverbs.

Yes, I'll go. No, he is not here. Oh, yes, to be sure, sir.	
Well, I may.	Well I may.
Why, can't you?	Why can't you?
Still, the flag is waving.	Still the flag is waving.
Now, there are three who . . .	Now there are three who . . .

Observe the same care when words of this sort are used at the end of a sentence.

There, now.	
What's to be done, then?	What's to be done then?

For example, that is, and similar phrases, introducing an illustration or an explanation, should usually be set off from the rest of the sentence. The comma is sometimes omitted after *thus* and *hence* and after the abbreviations *e.g.* and *i.e.* *For instance* or *for example* used after the illustrative phrase may require no comma before it. Clearness may require that the illustration or explanation, together with the introducing phrase, be set off by dashes or parentheses.

> These sepals serve as a protective covering for the rest of the flower in the early stages of its development, that is, when it is a bud.
>
> To obey the general will, says Rousseau, is to obey the enlightened self. Thus, when a policeman rightfully arrests a burglar, the latter is self-arrested and afterwards self-condemned.
>
> Soils may be put into three groups, namely clay, sand, and loam.
>
> Other birds, the great horned owl for instance, are considered beneficial in some sections and harmful in others.
>
> They are getting the best kind of exercise obtainable—namely, exercise which is enjoyed.
>
> The President may veto an act of Congress—that is, forbid it to go into effect— or the courts may set aside a law.
>
> . . . who would argue that if what was "real" (that is, what existed) was reasonable, then the opposition or contradiction called forth by that which existed was likewise reasonable.

Adverbial phrases. Do not use a comma after an adverbial phrase beginning a sentence when it immediately precedes the verb it modifies. The comma should be omitted in all these sentences:

> *Wrong:* Against all these evils, is the overwhelming benefit which comes from the American system of government.
>
> *Wrong:* To the west of No. 1, is another enclosure.
>
> *Wrong:* Among these lines, may be seen the refracted rays.
>
> *Wrong:* Between Mars and Jupiter, are a large number of small bodies called asteroids.

After an adverbial phrase that is not independent of the part of the sentence that follows, the comma is not necessary unless confusion of meaning would result from its omission (as it would in this sentence).

> On our way home we met the returning fisherman.
>
> In many parts of the world the wind has an important part in soil making.
>
> In the complicated business of communicating our ideas to others we need different varieties of speech.
>
> In the year 1900 our exports were . . .
>
> To the altitude flyer mere height . . .
>
> *Note.* So many writers insert a comma after such phrases that printers almost invariably follow copy.

Whenever such a phrase ends with a verb or a preposition, use a comma before a following noun to prevent misreading.

> At the parties at which the dances were given, the parents were invited guests.
>
> On the sandy shores beneath, fishermen spread their nets to dry.
>
> Soon after, their first settlement was started.

Writers often punctuate incorrectly when such phrases as the above stand at the beginning of the second part of a compound sentence. The coördinate parts of the sentence should be separated and then, if desired, a comma may be inserted after the phrase. Very seldom should there be a comma before the phrase, setting it off like a parenthetical element.

> *Wrong:* Stars are punctual and, by use of a transit telescope, their passage can be accurately noted.
> *Right:* Stars are punctual, and by use of a transit telescope, their passage can be accurately noted.
> *Wrong:* He had come alone, and, as he made his way through the crowd, he saw no one he knew.
> *Right:* He had come alone, and as he made his way through the crowd he saw no one he knew.

Adverbial clauses. As a rule, use a comma after an adverbial clause preceding its principal clause. There is a strong tendency to omit the comma if the clause is short and no misreading would result from the omission.

> When a sufficient supply of oxygen is provided, any further increase has little effect.
> Before the individual tries to write a question on the board, let the group offer questions.
> After some years had passed, the situation changed.
> Were there space in this book we could cite hundreds of instances.

In the following sentences a comma is necessary after the adverbial clause to insure correct reading.

> As soon as he went down, the elevator fell.
> As the pond fills, the plants are killed off.
> When the glaze is worn off, the inner surface becomes absorbent.
> When we shoot, our bowstrings give a twang that's heard but a little way off.

Always use a comma after an adverbial clause introduced by *as, since,* or *while* if it is intended to express any idea of cause or condition, for without the comma these conjunctions express time only.

> As we flew over the lake we could see the cottages bordering it.
> As the plane was flying low, we could see the cottages distinctly.
> As we read the stories of the westward movement we shall see . . .
> As we learned before, from the time of the explorer Coronado the Spaniards had tried to establish settlements north of the Rio Grande.

Do not use a comma before an adverbial clause within a sentence, preceding the main clause on which it depends, unless the clause is clearly nonrestrictive and can be read as a parenthetical element.

Wrong: Dark walls of rock rise steeply from the shores and, when it is calm, snow-capped peaks and blue glaciers are mirrored in the water of the strait.
Right: Dark walls of rock rise steeply from the shores, and when it is calm, snow-capped peaks . . .
Wrong: This means that, if the cylinder is full of gas when the piston is at the bottom, the gas will occupy only one fifth of the volume . . .
Right: This means that if the cylinder is full of gas when the piston is at the bottom, the gas will occupy only . . .

Punctuation of an adverbial clause following the main clause depends upon its nature: a nonrestrictive clause, which merely gives additional information, should be preceded by a comma; a restrictive clause, which limits the action of the main verb to a particular time, manner, or circumstance, should not be preceded by a comma.

Clauses introduced by *though* or *although* are always nonrestrictive.

Such forms are still living in the Australian region, although they have become extinct elsewhere.

Clauses introduced by *if* are restrictive.

Publication can be hastened if the paper is made as concise as possible.
If a certain state charges $8 for each auto license, how many registered cars were there in the state if the amount of the license fees was $4,757,204?

Clauses beginning with *because* are usually restrictive, but they may be nonrestrictive.

Millions of stars cannot be seen with the eye because they are too far away to supply the necessary light for vision.
The Austrian Government proposed a new statute prohibiting the breeding of carrier pigeons, because carrier pigeons might be used by unauthorized persons for the purpose of smuggling military or industrial information out of Austria.

Clauses introduced by *unless* and *except* are usually restrictive.

The tense and the voice of the verbs in a composition should not be changed unless the meaning demands it.
Do not give space to unimportant negative findings except when convinced that they add to the force of the argument.
Intention is of no avail unless stated at the time of the contract.

Do not use a comma before a clause beginning with *before, when, while, as,* or *since* restricting the time of the action of the principal verb.

You should make it a point to master each of these facts before you attempt to write the assignment.
The Indians became more and more alarmed as the white settlements appeared farther and farther westward.

When a clause introduced by *as, while,* or *since* does not so restrict the verb but expresses cause or condition, use a comma before it.

> The liquid should be added hot, since a low temperature would harden the fat.
> The number for a large maple has been estimated at 200,000, while an oak may develop as many as 700,000 leaves in a single season.

Use a comma before a clause of result introduced by *so that* but not before a clause of purpose so introduced.

> This alloy possesses the peculiar property of not shrinking when it cools, so that the case is a sharp and accurate reproduction in relief of the letter cut in the matrix.
> Can you construct a line *MN* through a given point *P* so that it is parallel to a given line *CD?*

Absolute phrases. Set off an absolute phrase.

> Not having a sufficient number of cases to fill a car, he found two other merchants who were willing to coöperate with him.
> That being so, there was no binding contract.
> Having for five years experimented with simplified spelling in its columns, the Chicago *Tribune* has announced abandonment of thirty-three of the seventy-seven words it emasculated.

Take care that no comma precedes the participle in absolute expressions like the following:

> The commission having been reduced to an innocuous statistical and research agency, the problem of effective regulatory procedure was returned to a perturbed and disconcerted Congress.
> The offer being to ship not later than May 15, the buyer had the right to fix the time of delivery at any time before that.

Infinitive phrases. Do not set off an infinitive phrase used as the subject of a sentence.

> *Wrong:* To think of our solar system as a part of the Milky Way, gives us a diminished conception of our importance.
> *Right:* To think of our solar system as a part of the Milky Way gives us a diminished conception of our importance.
> *Right:* To neglect the integrity of the family or the prosperity of any considerable social class will sooner or later injure society as a whole.

Participial phrases. Set off a participial phrase unless it is restrictive or is used in place of a noun.

> The temperature of plants changes rapidly, depending on the amount of external heat they receive.
> In 1888 Roux, working in Pasteur's laboratory, found that the diphtheria germ produces a toxin which causes symptoms of the disease.

Making use of the maps and tables answers the questions and supplies the missing words.

Valued at only $15,000 in 1822, it was estimated at $450,000 by 1845.

Nonrestrictive: Some atoms broke up spontaneously, forming atoms of other elements.

Restrictive: Associated with the two dominant trees are ash, elm, walnut, linden, and a wealth of smaller trees and shrubs forming a lower layer under the higher trees.

Restrictive: Refer to the graph showing the price of wheat.

Restrictive: Make a collection of pictures showing the great extremes of land surface in our country.

Wrong: Describe a scene trying to convey an impression of heat, cold, restfulness, confusion, fear, horror . . .

Right: Describe a scene, trying to convey an impression of heat . . .

Faulty: Write to the father of a close friend urging that he let your friend spend a month at the same camp.

Better: Write to the father of a close friend, urging that he let your friend spend a month at the same camp.

Direct questions or quotations. Usually set off by a comma a short quotation, maxim, or similar expression; before a long, formal quotation or question use a colon. (See p. 250.)

It has been well said, "The tongue is a little member and boasteth great things."
The question is, How shall we know what are good books?

Quotations as parts of speech. A quoted word or phrase that constitutes the subject or object of a sentence need not be set off by commas.

He had a habit of saying "Understand?" at frequent intervals.
"If he says 'No,' what then?"
Miss B—— spoke on "Adjustment Problems and the Visiting Teacher."
"A soldier is no better than his feet" is an old saying that is true for all of us.
I'm not sure that the mother bird said "Thank you."
One of the important rules of singing is "Sing as you speak."
If a slogan must be carried in mind, perhaps "No calories without vitamins" is as good a precept as any.

Note. The writer and the proofreader may find in trying to apply this and the preceding rule that they conflict. One often sees sentences in which one person would use a comma before a quotation and another would not. The writer should therefore punctuate thoughtfully, and the proofreader should be most circumspect about making changes.

A quotation immediately preceded by the conjunction *that* should not be separated from *that* by any punctuation.

Wrong: The law stipulated that, "Employees shall have a right to bargain collectively."

Right: The law stipulated that "Employees shall have a right to bargain collectively."

Better: The law stipulated, "Employees shall have a right to bargain collectively."

Or: The law stipulated that "employees shall have a right to bargain collectively." (See also p. 218.)

Phrases used with quoted conversation. Mistakes are often made in punctuating descriptive phrases following a quotation. A participle and an adverb should be distinguished; a participle should always be set off, an adverb generally is not.

"That will never do," he said, laughing.
"That will never do," he said laughingly.

Sometimes a quoted speech is followed by such an expression as *he smiled*. This should not be joined to the quotation as if it were a verb of speaking or saying—one does not "smile" words—but should be set as a separate sentence.

"You're a very attractive young lady." He smiled.

When the words interrupting a speech are not words of speaking or saying, it is better to use dashes to separate them from the quotation. (See also p. 276.)

"I can't help thinking"—he smiled at her suddenly—"that part of it is me."

Antithetical elements. Set off an antithetical clause following the main clause upon which it depends.

The function of the heading is to tell the facts, not to give the writer's comment on the facts.
Deeds, not words.

An antithetical phrase introduced by *not* and followed by *but* may be set off by commas if it could be omitted without destroying the grammatical completeness of the sentence or changing the meaning. Many such phrases are so short, however, that commas are not necessary; others are so constructed that only one comma is needed. (The proofreader should center his attention, not on whether commas are used, but on whether, if they *are* used, they are placed correctly.)

Most redrawn faces are inspired, not by one face, but by several older faces.
The way that is at once easiest and most honorable is not to be silencing the reproaches of others, but to be making yourselves as perfect as you can.
Hence the mind resolves itself, not into reality, but into a name.

It was his mental not his physical qualifications that worried me.
What he offered me was not hospitality but detention.
Not more machinery but more intelligence is needed.

Correlative phrases. Do not confuse a correlative phrase and an anti-thetical phrase. A correlative phrase is not usually set off by commas.

They listen for the voice of God not alone in the records of the past but in the stillness and silence of their own souls.
It has become the chief trading center not only for the northwest section of the state but also for parts of Montana and Canada.

The phrases in the following sentence are nonrestrictive and should be set off from the main clause, the meaning of which would remain unchanged were they omitted.

The landscape varies greatly, not only from place to place but from season to season.

Omission of a common verb. When two or more clauses of a sentence require the same verb, the omission of the verb in clauses following the first should usually be marked by a comma.

One aspect of the League might be entitled Co-operation in the Works of Peace; the other, Co-operation for the Prevention of War.
Within this area Mohammedans have occupied the desert of the northwest; Hindus, the Deccan plateau and the upper and middle Ganges valley; and Buddhists, the Burman and Ceylon areas.
Tories Become Conservatives, and Whigs Liberals.

Elements common to more than one phrase. Use a comma before an element which belongs equally to two or more phrases but which is expressed only after the last.

They can, ought to, and most assuredly will, win.
Just as none of us are physically, so few are mentally, fit all the time.
They may play a secondary role in reinforcing or weakening, accelerating or re-tarding, disturbances.

Note. Many sentences requiring the application of this rule could have been expressed more clearly and smoothly. The proofreader, of course, can do no more than punctuate accurately.

Commas are not needed when a conjunction is used between the modifiers or coördinate elements.

Diseases which have been partly or almost entirely conquered.

Repeated words. Separate repeated words in the same construction by commas. Repeated words in different constructions often need separation by a comma for the sake of clearness.

> The mere knowledge of what this substance is, is of great value.
> What money there was, was steadily drained away.
> A dosage was arrived at, at which each bird was found to maintain constant weight.

Residence, position, title. Set off by commas phrases indicating residence, position, or title, following a person's name.

> Mr. and Mrs. Peters, of Portland, Maine
> William Russell, Dean of the College of Liberal Arts
> Donald Brown, Jr.

> *Note.* There is an evident tendency, especially in newspaper work, to omit the comma before *of* phrases as in *John Smith of Chicago, Harold Jones of Northwestern University.* Likewise before *Jr.* and *Sr.*

If such a phrase has practically become a part of the person's name, do not separate it from the rest of the name.

> Lord Curzon of Kedleston   Timour the Tartar
> King George of England

Specifying phrases. Set off a phrase, a name, or a number which makes a preceding reference more specific. It is in effect a parenthetical element which cannot be read without a slight pause before and after it.

> The president declared the provisions of Section 15, Article IV, of the Constitution suspended.
> The president declared the provisions of Article IV, Section 15, of the Constitution suspended.
> line 20, page 43, to line 17, page 44.
> In Figure II, column 1, are given the square Hebrew characters.
> *Exploring Books, II,* presents a series of problems.

Geographical names.

> He set up his shop in Cambridge, Massachusetts, in 1638.
> *Wrong:* Mail and stagecoach lines were established, traveling from St. Joseph, Missouri and Atchison, Kansas over the Oregon Trail to California.
> *Right:* Mail and stagecoach lines were established, traveling from St. Joseph, Missouri, and Atchison, Kansas, over the Oregon Trail to California.

Dates.

His death on May 20, 1506, attracted little attention.

When only the month and year are given, the number is usually set off, but commas may be omitted in display lines, and a few publishers have adopted the style of always omitting commas in such phrases.

July, 1890, was the time.   Armistice Day, 1918, . . .

Addresses. Do not use a comma in addresses between the number of the house and the name of the street, except in British addresses, and even in these the comma is not always used.

412 Fifth Avenue, New York   12, Warwick Lane, London

Distinct proper nouns. Separate consecutive proper nouns referring to different individuals or places.

To Elsie, Robert seems perfect.
To Europe, America is the land of opportunity.

Numbers. Do not use a comma in page or date numbers or after a decimal point. Other numbers of four figures may or may not take a comma after the digit representing thousands. (See also p. 202.)

1500 B.C.   p. 3675   .65842   4560 or 4,560

For the sake of clearness separate two unrelated numbers coming together.

In 1931, 100,000 more were sold than in 1930.

Dimensions, weights, and measures. Practice varies in the punctuation of phrases denoting dimensions, weights, and measures. The University of Chicago Press, the Government Printing Office, and many others do not use the comma within the phrase.

five feet seven inches   4 lb. 3 oz.   5 hr. 10 min.
His age is 6 years 4 months 12 days.

Direct address. Set off proper names and substantives used in direct address.

How are you, Mother? Come again, Uncle. Yes, sir. No, miss.
I move, Mr. Chairman, that the meeting adjourn.
Wrong: Awake, my little ones and fill the cup . . .
Right: Awake, my little ones, and fill the cup . . .

"O" and "oh." Do not use a comma immediately after the vocative *O*, as from its very nature it requires another word or words to complete it. After *oh*, on the contrary, use a comma if other words follow.

O lovely goddess!
Oh, Robert, how could you!
Oh, yes.
Oh, for Pete's sake!

Interrogative phrases. An interrogative phrase that changes a statement into a question should be preceded by a comma.

He hasn't it, has he?   You will go, won't you?

Inflection or emphasis. The proofreader should not forget that a comma represents a slight pause in reading, and that a careful writer may often use it to indicate the way in which he would like his sentence read.

It would have been better for them if they had become good farmers rather than poor doctors, or skillful mechanics rather than blundering engineers.
Though the sailing vessel is still used to some extent, it is too much subject to the vagaries of the weather, and too slow, to meet man's general needs.
That is important, and interesting, too.
Most of the people in the past have been like that, too.

Constructions likely to be misread. Use a comma to separate any sentence elements which if not separated might, in reading, be improperly joined or be misunderstood. (See also pp. 265, 266.)

To the courageous, men turn with respect.
Wherever practicable, translations of unusual German phrases have been included in the vocabulary.
The princes who had scampered away before the French eagles, came back to show that they had learned nothing and forgotten nothing.
Two new university extension courses, Singing for Recreation, and Business Law, will be started in this city Tuesday night.
It is called the Armada, and ever since, the word has been used in connection with a big naval undertaking.

Unnecessary comma punctuation. Do not separate a subject from its verb unless it is so long and involved that a comma is required for the sake of clarity.

What we seem to see is one continuously changing picture.
Whether any particular expression is suitable depends upon the purpose . . .
Prunella up against it would be dangerous to whoever threatened her security.
Those which approach the earth head on in the same direction as the earth moves will appear to be much slower.

Do not separate a verb and its object in a simple sentence like the following:

Wrong: It is only a means to an end and has for its purpose, (1) wise expenditure and (2), an accumulation of savings.
Right: It is only a means to an end and has for its purpose (1) wise expenditure and (2) an accumulation of savings.

Do not use a comma before or after the conjunction *that* in sentences constructed like the following.

Wrong: But the author believes that, with average high school classes it will take three recitations.
Right: But the author believes that with average high school classes it will take three recitations.
Wrong: It can be easily seen that, when such amounts are fixed too high, owners of property can be crippled and ruined by such high taxation.
Right: It can be easily seen that when such amounts are fixed too high, owners of property can be ruined by such high taxation.

Do not set off a phrase separating the parts of a compound conjunction.

Wrong: There are grounds for believing that no earlier period exhibits *such* a long-continued decline in the actual price, *as* occurred in the nineteenth century.
Right: There are grounds for believing that no earlier period exhibits such a long-continued decline in the actual price as occurred in the nineteenth century.
Wrong: Such is the connection between words and things, *that* a thorough study . . .
Right: Such is the connection between words and things that a thorough study . . .

Use with other marks. The comma may be used in conjunction with quotation marks, parentheses, and dashes, but not ordinarily with other marks. (See p. 249.)

When a comma and closing quotation marks fall alongside, set the comma inside. This rule is not universally followed but it represents the preference of practically all the writers of books on grammar, rhetoric, and English composition, and the practice of most American publishers and printers. The Oxford Dictionary practice, which is preferred by some, is to set a comma inside closing quotation marks only if it is part of the quotation. Under this rule time is wasted making distinctions that do not count.

If a sentence containing parentheses would require a comma were the parenthetical matter omitted, place a comma *after* the closing parenthesis.

Excerpts from the works of other authors (when they are more than a phrase or a sentence), problems, examples, and test questions are generally set in smaller type than the body of the text itself.

In the following sentences no comma is needed after the parenthesis.

Two admonitions are usually needed in preparing tables: (1) always put the title of a table above it . . . ; and (2) never put more than one kind of data in a table.

In the years after the Civil War both Seward (who had remained Secretary of State under President Johnson) and President Grant tried to buy the islands.

A comma may precede an open parenthesis only if the word or words in parenthesis clearly limit a following word.

Cheese, (full) cream
Adventitious, (of roots) those that arise from any structure other than a root; (of buds) those that arise other than as terminal or axillary structures

The profuse punctuation in the following is not good form in American printing.

Not American usage: Bles, (Geoffrey,) Ltd., 2, Manchester Square, London, W.1
American usage: Bles, Geoffrey, Ltd., 2 Manchester Square
Or: Bles (Geoffrey), Ltd., 2 Manchester Square

The combination of a comma and a dash is going out of use; either one or the other alone will make the meaning clear.

Ultraviolet and other short rays—too short for the eye to perceive—are especially active.
Our everyday speech is full of them, often too full, but we must keep the worst of them out of our written work.

Type. Set a comma in the font of the letter preceding it.

Decline **puella parva,** "a little girl."

THE EM DASH

The em dash is properly used "to mark a suspension of the sense, a faltering in speech, a sudden change in the construction, or an unexpected turn of the thought." [1]

The following sentences are properly punctuated with dashes.

I—I think so.
No doubt he could see—as who could not—that . . .
But the jewels—if they are sold they cannot be replaced.
Instead of which—but let me quote his own words.
Sound, normal people—that should be the result at which to aim.

[1] Webster's Dictionary.

The school will be constantly dealing with the live questions and problems of today—social, economic, political, what you will.

How did Larry get hurt? Fall over a cliff—stampede, maybe?

A further safeguard is sometimes used—aeration.

She was looking for gold, if you please—pretty yellow gold.

A tree, a potato, a cabbage growing in the garden, a daisy—all are alive.

In the following sentences there is no reason for the use of the dash and other punctuation would be better.

Poor: "What is it?—please tell me."
Better: "What is it? Please tell me."
Poor: He glanced at his watch again—it was five minutes of one.
Better: He glanced at his watch again; it was five minutes of one.
Too heavy: No two sets of teeth alike—man's or cow's.
Better: No two sets of teeth alike, man's or cow's.
Wrong: The question is—will they make trouble for you?
Right: The question is, Will they make trouble for you?
Wrong: . . . all sorts of devices: filter papers, double perforations—one large and one small—, pots of china, enamel, glass.
Right: . . . all sorts of devices: filter papers; double perforations, one large and one small; pots of china, enamel, glass.

Appositives. Use dashes to set off an appositive whenever a comma might be misread as a series comma.

The frontier—upland and mountain regions to be settled later in the eighteenth century—offered much more uniform conditions.

If commas are used to mark minor divisions within an appositive, dashes are generally needed to set off the whole appositional phrase.

A crate full of Murano glass—iridescent goblets, lovely shells of spun glass, beautifully shaped chalices—a tremendous English-Latin lexicon, . . .

Bismarck immediately demanded of the rulers of the larger North German states—Hanover, Saxony, and Hesse-Cassel—that they stop their warlike preparations.

Beans—navy, kidney, and soy—have only vitamin B.

The solid structure of trees—that is, the dry matter in the roots, stalks, and branches—is about 95 per cent carbon and oxygen.

A comma is not strong enough to mark clearly the end of an appositive or a parenthetical expression that is preceded by a dash. Unless the expression ends the sentence, another dash or a semicolon is necessary for clearness.

Wrong: Hampton Roads, which actually embraces five cities—Norfolk, Portsmouth, Newport News, Hampton, and Suffolk, provides anchorage for giant vessels.

Right: Hampton Roads, which actually embraces five cities—Norfolk, Portsmouth, Newport News, Hampton, and Suffolk—provides anchorage for giant vessels.

Wrong: Paracelsus held that the three elements—earth, air, and water, were represented by salt, sulfur, and water, respectively.

Right: Paracelsus held that the three elements—earth, air, and water—were represented by salt, sulfur, and water, respectively.

Confusing: Waltz in A flat—Brahms, Skaters' Waltz—Waldteufel, Minuet—Mozart, Lullaby—Brahms, and Rock-a-bye Baby—Traditional.

Clearer: Waltz in A flat—Brahms; Skaters' Waltz—Waldteufel; Minuet—Mozart; Lullaby—Brahms; and Rock-a-bye Baby—Traditional.

The combination of a dash and a semicolon alongside is incorrect.

Wrong: Observe (*a*) kinds of food purchased—e.g., fresh fruits, baking goods, etc.—; (*b*) buying habits—e.g., use of list, businesslike attitude, etc.—; (*c*) shopping courtesies; (*d*) sales talk; (*e*) brands sold.

Right: Observe (*a*) kinds of food purchased—e.g., fresh fruits, baking goods, etc.; (*b*) buying habits—e.g., use of list, businesslike attitude; (*c*) shopping courtesies; (*d*) sales talk; (*e*) brands sold.

Parenthetical expressions. Use dashes to set off a parenthetical expression whenever commas are needed for minor divisions within the expression.

The face—thin, harsh, cold, and forceful—was deeply lined.

It is probable that not only was the fur trade of great importance in providing the settlers with much of their heavy clothing—a portion of the trade, it may be noted, which would not swell the export figures—but that it was also one of the many minor ways that the settlers had of eking out a living.

Commas are not strong enough to set off a complete sentence interpolated within another; dashes or parentheses are required.

Wrong: Ace, people who don't know him well call him "Goody," is aided by a natural sense of humor.

Right: Ace—people who don't know him well call him "Goody"—is aided by a natural sense of humor.

Put the dash in the right place.

Wrong: A sight—a sound may be supernatural,—that is from the romanticist's standpoint,—but not a cough.

Right: A sight, a sound, may be supernatural—that is, from the romanticist's standpoint—but not a cough.

Wrong: I cannot remember them all now, but two do stand out clearly from the rest,—Thenaud's, *Notes on the Detection of Hidden Spaces*—and Wilson's, *Studies of Ancient Architecture.*

Right: I cannot remember them all now, but two do stand out clearly from the rest—Thenaud's *Notes on the Detection of Hidden Spaces* and Wilson's *Studies of Ancient Architecture.*

Poorly punctuated: Robert Haven Schauffler, in a charming little book—"The Joyful Heart" maintains that a joyful heart comes only to those whose life, whether in business or in study, is so organized that a surplus of energy remains at the end of the day's work, energy to be expended in recreation and intercourse with others.

Better: Robert Haven Schauffler, in a charming little book, "The Joyful Heart," maintains that a joyful heart comes only to those whose life, whether in business or in study, is so organized that a surplus of energy remains at the end of the day's work—energy to be expended in recreation and intercourse with others.

Divided quotations. When a quoted sentence in direct discourse is interrupted by phrases that are not words of speaking or saying, use dashes before and after the interrupting phrase.

"My dear little girl"—his tone was all concern—"I'm so sorry."
"At nine o'clock I gave her ten grains of trional in hot milk"—the doctor flickered an eyelid at me. "Umpf," said he—"and she took it without any trouble."

Distinguish sentences like those above from those in which the dash is part of the quotation and would be used if the quotation were not interrupted at that point. The dash should then be placed within the quotation marks.

"Because—" reasoned Jo, "because nobody . . ."
"Perhaps I can guess what's on your mind," he ventured, "—that in some way you are . . ."

Unfinished sentences. The sudden breaking off of a sentence is marked by a dash. If other words follow in the same paragraph, an em dash is used. No period should be used after the dash. If the sentence is interrupted by another speaker, a 2-em dash may be preferred.

"But if we—" he began.
"Then how can—?" he asked.
"It'll never—" He stopped suddenly.
"I will go to the King of Poland and I will tell him——"
"The King of Poland has no need of such as you."
"Now, if I can get two mo——"
We heard no more. He had fallen dead.

Dash or colon? A dash or a colon may be used with equal correctness in several situations. In plays the names of the speakers are usually followed by a colon, but in court reports, interviews, proceedings of public bodies, and the like a dash is usually preferred to a colon after the names of the speakers. Similarly:

Q.—
A.—

A dash or a colon may be used after a phrase introducing a series displayed by paragraphing. A colon would be preferred if the series did not begin a new paragraph. Often no punctuation is needed, as in the example below.

In it the bookkeeper records (*a*) the account to be debited, with the amount; (*b*) the account to be credited, with the amount; (*c*) a complete explanation of the transaction.
In it the bookkeeper records—
(*a*) the account to be debited, with the amount
(*b*) the account to be credited, with the amount
(*c*) a complete explanation of the transaction

In indexes a dash or a colon may be used after the main entries when all the subentries begin new lines.

Between a word and its definition a comma, a colon, or a dash may be used: a comma when the definition is a simple appositive, a colon for a more involved construction. A dash is usually preferred in a glossary.

Drop-folio—a page number placed at the foot of a page instead of in a running heading at the top of the page.

Mechanical uses. Besides the foregoing uses as a punctuation mark with more or less definite significance, the dash is a convenient mark of separation. Following a side heading a dash is often used, particularly if the type used for the side heading does not differ much from the following text.

Function of the colon.—The colon is used after a word, phrase, or sentence to introduce something that follows, such as a question or quotation, an amplification, an enumeration, or an example. It can be said to replace the words *that is* or *for example.*

A similar purpose is served in using a dash before a credit. Here, too, the dash may be omitted if the credit is in a type style that differentiates it clearly from the quotation.

Science is, in its source, eternal; in its scope, unmeasurable; in its problem, endless; in its goal, unattainable.—VON BAER.

Likewise purely mechanical is the use of the dash in presenting golf scores and the like. (Tennis scores are usually set with hyphens: 5-4, 6-3.)

87—10—77

In a vague date an em dash is used in place of numerals.

in 18—

THE EN DASH

To represent *to* between figures or words an en dash is used. (Some publishers accept a hyphen but those who use the en dash feel that a hyphen is a poor substitute and should be reserved for its own distinct uses, as a connector in compound words and as a separator in showing syllabication.) An em dash is sometimes used with this meaning when an en dash might be confusing, as in Scripture references extending over more than one chapter.

the years 1930–32   I John 1:3–5
pages 5–15   I John 1:1—2:5
the New York–Chicago bus
Berlin–Bagdad Railway

The word *to,* not an en dash, must be used if the numbers are preceded by the word *from.*

Wrong: Completion of the transcontinental railroad from 1869–1885.
Right: Completion of the transcontinental railroad from 1869 to 1885.
Or: Completion of the transcontinental railroad, 1869–1885.
Wrong: Chief among these were the two governors, George Clinton (from 1777–95) and DeWitt Clinton (from 1817–22 and 1824–28).
Right: Chief among these were the two governors, George Clinton (1777–95) and DeWitt Clinton (1817–22 and 1824–28).

An en dash cannot be substituted for *and.*

Wrong: Between 1923–29 Mussolini had transformed this.
Right: Between 1923 and 1929 Mussolini had transformed this.

Use an en dash instead of a hyphen in a compound when one of the components contains a hyphen.

English–Scotch-Irish parentage
Cambrai–St-Quentin direction

In a hyphenated word set in capitals use an en dash instead of a hyphen.

ANGLO–SAXON GRAMMAR

THE 2-EM DASH

The 2-em dash is used to indicate the omission of part of a name. In this use the dash is set close to the letter preceding it, but takes after it the regular spacing of the rest of the line.

I saw Mr. D—— and Miss M——

The 2-em dash is sometimes used to mark a sudden breaking off of thought or speech.

> "While I was here to get my sword and dagger ——"
> "And I gave it to you. Willingly, willingly."
> "——my sword and dagger, he had arrived."

PARENTHESES [1]

Parentheses are used to enclose expressions which are of such a nature that they would not be sufficiently set off by commas or dashes. Many times dashes or parentheses are equally good style, but parentheses should preferably be reserved to enclose matter having no essential connection with the rest of the sentence in which it occurs. (See also p. 279.)

> Dry out each substance in an oven under slow heat (do not char).
> In 1732 Joist Hite (he spelled his name in a variety of ways) entered the valley with sixteen families.
> Most took a "newspaper" (thirty days), a few a "magazine" (sixty days), and one gangster had pleaded guilty to carrying concealed weapons and had taken a rap for a "book" (a year and a day), rather than be held for investigation on a major charge.
> *Clavulina alazanensis* Nuttall (See *Pseudoclavulina alazanensis* (Nuttall).)

If matter enclosed in parentheses is a complete declarative or imperative sentence, the period is omitted; but any other mark of punctuation called for by the construction may be used within a parenthesis.

> Being inferior in strength (for who could be equal to the strength of Atlas?), he cried: . . .
> Investigations in McCollum's laboratory (Orent and McCollum, 1931, 1932) and at the University of Wisconsin (Kemmerer, Elvehjem, and Hart, 1931; Skinner, Van Donk, and Steenbock, 1932; Van Donk, Steenbock, and Hart, 1933), while differing somewhat in detail . . .

When italic letters *a, b, c,* etc., marking divisions of an enumeration, are to be enclosed in parentheses, most publishers use both open and close parentheses—(*a*), (*b*), (*c*)—but occasionally, at the beginning of paragraphs, only the close parentheses are used. (Note that when letters or figures are enclosed in parentheses, no period is needed.)

Type. Italic or boldface parentheses are seldom used in a roman text; when an italic letter or word in roman text is to be enclosed in parentheses, roman

---

[1] The terms *curves, brackets,* and *round brackets* are never used in printing offices for parentheses. The term there used is *parens,* separately designated *open paren* and *close paren.*

parentheses should be used, not italic, and the punctuation following should be roman.

How Our Governments Are Financed (*Pages 306–332*)
Work (foot pounds) = force (pounds) ✕ distance (feet)

BRACKETS [1]

Brackets are used to enclose comments, explanations, queries, corrections of error, or directions inserted in a quotation by some person other than the original writer. The matter enclosed may be wholly independent of the text, or it may be words supplied to secure complete and understandable sentences, as in the last of the group of examples below.

"Let them [all the sons who have abandoned the paternal house] return."
". . . to write with the Pen then [*sic*] to work with my Needle."
Nay, the most honest among them would hardly take so much pains in a week as now [after Dale's changes] for themselves they will do in a day."
"On October 11 [12] Columbus discovered the New World."
"Of the lighter kind, we have no poem anterior to the time of Homer, though many such in all probability there were [possibly on the lower planes of literature] . . . . [The first of these forms, developed later into tragedy,] originated from the dithyrambic hymn, the other [comedy] from those phallic songs . . . . "

The stage directions in plays may be enclosed in either parentheses or brackets. Brackets used to be the more frequent choice of publishers, but with the increase of linotype composition the parentheses are being used more because they are more easily set.

Sal. [*to the Commons at the door*] Sirs, stand apart; the king shall know your mind.

[*He comes forward.*

In reprints of early manuscripts brackets are used to enclose passages whose authenticity is doubtful.

Parenthetical matter. Some publishers use brackets also to enclose parenthetical matter within matter already included in parentheses, others use parentheses; therefore two parentheses or a bracket and a parenthesis may appear together. If brackets are used, they should be within the parentheses, not outside except in algebra.

Grote, the great historian of Greece (see his History, I, 204 [2d ed.]) . . .
(See Engineering Study No. 55(k).)

[1] The word *bracket* signifies only one thing to a printer. Asking him to use a square bracket is as unnecessary as asking the baker for a round pie.

This Po River country was called Cisalpine Gaul (Gaul on this side [i.e., Italian side] of the Alps) because there was another Gaul on the other side of the Alps (Transalpine [trans·al′pin] Gaul).

Use with other marks. No punctuation is used with brackets except what is required by the matter bracketed. If bracketed matter is inserted in a quotation, it is unnecessary to use quotation marks before and after.

"I could perceive [writes Warwick] he was very apprehensive."

QUOTATION MARKS

The main function of quotation marks, as their name indicates, is to mark words as spoken in direct discourse or as written at some time previous to the text of which they now form a part. In addition, quotation marks are used, more or less interchangeably with italics, to differentiate words or phrases from surrounding text in order to make clearer their meaning or use.

Direct quotations. Direct quotations, which may be of any length, from a word to an extract running through several paragraphs, should be enclosed in quotation marks.

According to one recent writer, the "working principle" of punctuation is emphasis.

When Tansey said "ironclad," I knew he meant ironclad, and not rusty iron, either.

"That's it," he murmured. " 'Pro and con' were the champ's last words."

Some of the phosphorus now in our bodies may once have "formed part of huge reptiles, living millions upon millions of years ago."

"United States casualties, one officer killed, ten enlisted men wounded." Contained in the "one officer killed" statement was the grimmest part of it all to us.

The question has often been asked, "What does aviation offer to women?" or "Is there an opportunity for women in this new field?"

A short quotation in a foreign language, set in italics because it is foreign, may be considered sufficiently distinguished from the text by the italics, and quotation marks may be omitted. A distinction is usually made between spoken and written words.

Nomina si nescis perit cognitio rerum, said Coke, with the acumen of the legal mind.

Cato ended all his speeches to the Senate by saying, *"Carthago delenda est."*

A common error is misplacing of the quotation marks when the quotation is introduced by *that.*

Wrong: This is done as a courtesy to the applicant, who may be discouraged and disheartened by a direct statement "that the office cannot even consider him as an applicant."

Right: . . . a direct statement that "the office cannot even consider him as an applicant."

Wrong: He received such a shock "that" in his own words, "He would not take another for the kingdom of France."

Right: He received such a shock that, in his own words, he "would not take another for the kingdom of France."

Equally frequent is unnecessary use of *that.*

Undesirable: There is doubtless much truth in the dictum of Plato that, "Ruin comes when the trader, whose head is lifted up by wealth, becomes ruler."

Better: There is doubtless much truth in the dictum of Plato, "Ruin comes when the trader . . . becomes ruler."

Possible: There is doubtless much truth in the dictum of Plato that "ruin comes when the trader . . . becomes ruler."

Excerpts. All direct quotations from the work of another should be enclosed in quotation marks unless they are set in type smaller than the text or set solid within a leaded text. If the quotation includes more than one consecutive paragraph, opening quotes should be used at the beginning of each paragraph and closing quotes at the end of the last paragraph, except extracts from plays, which are quoted only at beginning and end. (See also pp. 12, 118.)

Note. An old practice, called side quoting, which was generally given up long ago, was to use opening quotation marks at the beginning of each line of quoted matter. Some newspapers follow this style in their editorials.

"Never," said the late Lord
Balfour, "is a very dangerous
"word in public life. It is
"used only by very young men."
Sometimes, however, . . .

A quotation within a quotation should be enclosed in single quotation marks. If this, in turn, contains a quotation, this last should be double quoted. One within this should be single quoted.

The student who answered the question, "Who said, 'See that thou fallest not by the way'?" with "Elisha to Elijah when the latter started up to heaven in the chariot," was evidently airminded.

"This he said many times. Then he walked away and stood and talked to himself, and I heard him say: '*He* said, "Unless you repent, you shall die on a dark

> night, in a lonely spot, with no one nigh." ' And he kept repeating, 'On a
> dark night, in a lonely spot, with no one nigh.' And then he would look
> around him at the trees and the mountains and the solitary shores. . . ."

The British practice is the reverse, the primary quotation being marked by
a single quote, a quotation within it enclosed in double quotes, and so on.

Direct discourse. In discourse the exact words of the speaker should be
enclosed in quotation marks.

> "Yes, wasn't it strange?" Jo said softly.

Do not punctuate sentences of a single speech as if they were separate
speeches; nor separate speeches as if they were a single speech.

> As the two gentlemen approached they could hear shouts of "Open the bank!"
> "Let us in!" "When does the bank open?" and a medley of a similar tenor.
> "Nothing doing!" and "We wouldn't take your own word against yourself!" the
> officers reassured her.

The use of dashes between the words of different speakers does not always
make it quite clear that several persons are speaking. (See also p. 319.)

> *Obscure:* "Oh, la, la, la!—Something of damage?—An accident, eh?—Has anyone
> been hurt?—Oh, la, la, la!"
> *Clearer:* "Oh, la, la, la!" "Something of damage?" "An accident, eh?" "Has
> anyone been hurt?" "Oh, la, la, la!"

No quotation marks are used with direct discourse in the Bible.

> Thine ear shall hear a word behind thee saying, This is the way, walk ye in it—
> when ye turn to the right, and when ye turn to the left.

No quotation marks are necessary in interviews and dialogues when the
name of the speaker is given first, or in reports of testimony when the words
Question and *Answer* (or Q. and A.) are used.

> Mayor James M. Gordon—I believe the ordinance should be revised.
> William Jones—I am not in favor of revision at this time.
> Q.—Did you see the defendant in the room?
> A.—I did.

A quoted speech is often interrupted or followed by a phrase like *he said* or
replied Janet. This phrase should not be included in the quotation and should
be separated from it by some kind of punctuation.

> *Wrong:* "I choose this man" he says "to be my friend."
> *Right:* "I choose this man," he says, "to be my friend."
> *Or, occasionally:* "I choose this man [he says] to be my friend."

Matter enclosed in quotation marks is presumed to be the exact words of the speaker.

Wrong: What historians do not use expressions like the following: "It was the epoch of the rise and triumph of materialism, nominalism, the Gothic style, or socialistic doctrine," and so on?

Wrong: Imagine a medieval "highbrow" saying that "only last season the Chants, or the Kyrie, or the Gloria was performed, and now it is again on the program!"

How to punctuate such sentences is the author's or editor's problem—not the proofreader's. Brackets might be used acceptably in some such sentences, but oftener a change of wording will secure clearness.

In replying to an introduction do not say "I am pleased [*or* glad] to meet you."

Direct thoughts. Usually direct thoughts are enclosed in quotation marks, particularly if accompanied by words like *he said to himself.* Some publishers, however, rule that quotes are unnecessary.

"I had a fortune almost in my fingers," he said to himself.
"So are we," he muttered to himself, "but we're still in the race."
"What I won't do when I get in there!" he must have thought to himself.

Direct and indirect discourse are sometimes confused as follows:

Wrong: "Carlyon would not harm a woman," Andrews thought. "It is only a trap to catch me." But then, was it likely that they would plan such a trap for me, a coward? They could not expect to do anything but repel him by danger.

In the foregoing sentence *was* indicates indirect discourse and *me* could be only direct discourse. The sentence should read thus:

But then, was it likely that they would plan such a trap for him, a coward?
Or: "But then, is it likely that they would plan such a trap for me, a coward?"

If an unexpressed thought and a spoken thought occur together, both enclosed in quotation marks, take care to use the marks about each in such a way as to avoid any confusion to the reader.

"Some quarryman out of work" was his unspoken thought. "What does he want with me?" "Well," he said sharply.

Indirect discourse. Do not enclose indirect discourse in quotation marks.

Wrong: She signed herself, "gratefully his, Edith Kilgallen."
Right: She signed herself gratefully his, Edith Kilgallen.
Right: She signed herself "Gratefully yours, Edith Kilgallen."

Wrong: He told them to "Charge it to the county."
Right: He told them to charge it to the county.
Right: He told them, "Charge it to the county."
Wrong: "How had that happened?" I finally wanted to know.
Right: How had that happened? I finally wanted to know.
Right: "How did that happen?" I finally wanted to know.
Wrong: "Had he bungled? Was he hit?" were his first thoughts.
Right: Had he bungled? Was he hit? were his first thoughts.
Right: "Have I bungled? Am I hit?" were his first thoughts.

Much uncertainty seems to exist about how to construe *yes* and *no* in such sentences as the following, whether as direct or indirect quotations. Often these words are capitalized but not quoted.

A single answer is given and that is, No.
He could not say No to him.
He crossly said No.
Frances had said Yes to Stanley's suggestion.
Tell him Yes.
Wrong: Answer "yes or no."
Right: Answer "Yes" or "No."
Sometimes preferred: Answer *yes* or *no.*

Direct questions. Do not enclose direct questions in quotation marks unless the words have been borrowed.

The question arises, What is this book about?
She will ask herself the question, Does the study make this clear?
The question will arise, What does *reconstructed* mean?

After "entitled," "signed." Use quotation marks to enclose words or phrases following *entitled, marked, endorsed, signed,* except, of course, where the words would regularly be set in italics, as in the fourth example below.

They were told to mark the case "Handle with care."
The note was signed "Chas. Arnold, Assessor."
The bill was entitled "An act to provide county library systems."
A novel entitled *For Whom the Bell Tolls.*

After "called," "known as." The meaning and use of words or phrases following *termed, called, so-called, known as* are usually clear without quotation marks.

The black soil we call humus.
Intensive sales effort, the efficiency manager calls it.
Another type of loss is called consequential loss.
A secretary, or clerk, as he is called, acts as chairman.

It is now known as an acceptance.
Their children went to what we should call elementary schools.
This Theban phalanx, as it was called, won a complete victory at Leuctra.
Other Greeks began to write about what men did and called what they wrote history.
The so-called Alabama Claims
There grew up in France what is called the Napoleonic legend.
It has also been given other names, as the North Star State, the Land of Ten Thousand Lakes, the Bread and Butter State, and the Playground of the Nation.

Quotes are frequently used, however, as a substitute for *so-called.*

These data provide illustrations of the "principle of limits."
Or: These data provide illustrations of the so-called principle of limits.
What is the difference between overhead cost and "fixed charges"?
It is believed that insects perceive moving objects quickly; they also appear to "remember" landmarks. Bees see colors familiar to us and probably others beyond the violet end of the "human" spectrum.

Differentiation. Quotation marks (or italics) are frequently required to make clear the meaning or use of words or phrases. For instance:

Wrong: The Duke of Windsor had not been used as a title since the Black Prince used it in the fourteenth century.
Right: "Duke of Windsor" had not been used as a title since the Black Prince used it in the fourteenth century.
Wrong: Northern Ireland is the name of a distinct political division.
Right: "Northern Ireland" is the name of a distinct political division.
Better: Northern Ireland is a distinct political division.

Technical words. An unusual or technical word presumably unfamiliar to the reader may be enclosed in quotation marks. In a book of a serious nature such an unusual word or expression is often quoted—or italicized—only the first time it is used.

A high leak resistance may cause the tube to "block."
There comes a time, if the wind is not too variable, when the kite "stands," neither rising nor falling.
Why does an orchestra "tune up" before playing?

A word or phrase, however, which has long been familiar in the meaning required by the context should not be quoted.

The coffee and raised biscuits melted away.
All the farmers hereabouts were haying.
I was having the creeps like an old woman.
The city's Four Hundred.

The spirit of flaming youth.
The three R's.
He has no bump of direction.
I was in the Little Lord Fauntleroy tradition.
One of the high spots of the meeting was the debate.
Having majored in Latin in college, he has never felt that Latin is a dead
language.

Technical terms need not be quoted in a text addressed to persons to whom
the terms are familiar.

Poor form: When "setting up" a "take" of *Republican* copy marked for an initial
letter, allow the following indention on the first line, and an extra "en" space
on the next three lines. This applies to "7-point" type only.
Better: When setting up a take of *Republican* copy marked for an initial letter,
allow the following indention on the first line, and an extra en space on the
next three lines. This applies to 7-point type only.

Explanations. Enclose in quotation marks a word or phrase to which attention is called for the purpose of definition or explanation. If the word or
phrase has not been previously used, italics are commonly preferred. (See also
p. 291.)

The word "airplane" as used in this chapter includes seaplane or any combination
of landplane, seaplane, or boat.
By "federal" is meant a government with a strong central power.
What do we mean by "air conditioning"?

If the article *the* forms a part of the phrase referred to, take care to include
it within the quotes.

What is meant by "the Settlement of 1815"?
The four phrases "the Cultural Heritage," "the Basic Dividend," "the Unearned
Increment," and "the Just Price" were the abracadabra of Mr. Aberhart's
necromancy.
Or: The four phrases "Cultural Heritage," "Basic Dividend," "Unearned Incre-
ment," and "Just Price" . . .

A profusion of quotation marks mars the appearance of a printed page. If
following the rule above results in such a profusion of marks, use italics.

Most languages have only six words for comparison: *small, smaller, smallest;* and
great, greater, greatest. Therefore verbal quantitative specifications like *great
and small, more or less, increase and decrease, rise and decline, growth and
decay,* are limited in meaning . . .
Wrong: Use such descriptive words as "considerate, coöperative, well-poised,
cheerful, assertive, diffident," and so on.

Undesirable: Use such descriptive words as "considerate," "coöperative," "well-poised," "cheerful," "assertive," "diffident," etc.

Better: Use such descriptive words as *considerate, coöperative, well-poised, cheerful, assertive, diffident,* etc.

Right: Such terms as *antecedent, auxiliary, correlative, coördinate, active, passive,* were so much gibberish to the average boy.

Problem: The expressions Irish linen, English, Belgian, or German linens are household terms.

Commas are not an acceptable substitute for italics or quotation marks following the word *term.*

Wrong: The term, materials for research, is here understood to refer to materials of three types.

Right: The term "materials for research" is here understood to refer to materials of three types.

Definitions. Words defining another word or words are often quoted, sometimes italicized; sometimes neither quotation marks nor italics may be considered necessary.

I use that word "static" in the sense of "unchanging."
It was an Indian name signifying *he who splits the sky.*
Our word *priest* comes from the Latin word *presbyter,* meaning elder.
Chrestus, the Greek word for Messiah
Corporation (from Latin *corporare,* to form into a body)

If quotes are used and synonyms are given defining a word, quote each separately.

Lace at first retained the meaning of its Latin original, "noose," "snare," or "net.'
The Latin *camera,* "vault," "arch," later "chamber," became *chambre* in French

Translations. The English translation of a foreign word or phrase is usually quoted.

Although the etymology of the word *Interlude* is clear (*ludus,* "a play," and *inter,* "between" or "among"), the application of the term is uncertain.
Zeitgeist, "spirit of the times."
He sent home the shortest of all famous dispatches: *Veni, vidi, vici,* "I came, I saw, I conquered."
Julius Caesar began his *Commentaries* with the well-known sentence, *Gallia est omnis divisa in partes tres* ("Gaul as a whole is divided into three parts").

Articles, essays. Titles of books are usually set in italics, but titles of parts of books, articles in magazines, essays, poems, sermons, and similar titles are roman quoted. Titles of series may be quoted, but usually cap-and-lower-case is sufficiently distinctive. In referring specifically to the Preface, the Glossary, etc., it is not necessary to quote; capitalization is sufficient.

Chapter I, "The Manufacture of a Book"　　　English Men of Letters Series

An essay may sometimes be referred to by its subject matter rather than by its title; quotes and caps are not then used.

essay on how to read
essay on the poet

Art objects. Names of paintings, sculptures, and other works of art are usually quoted.

Claude Monet's painting "Antibes"
two Gothic sculptures, the "Bull Fight," by Goya and . . .
What is the background of Da Vinci's "The Last Supper" and of Michelangelo's
"The Last Judgment"?

Musical compositions. Names of songs and of short musical selections are usually quoted. (See also p. 212.)

"Old Black Joe"
"Stars and Stripes Forever"

Buildings, thoroughfares. Names of public buildings, hotels, parks, streets, and the like do not need quotation marks.

Berlin's famous avenue Unter den Linden . . . the Brandenburg Gate at the
entrance of the Tiergarten, a large park.

Nicknames and sobriquets. Whether a nickname should be enclosed in quotation marks depends largely upon how and in what context it is used. It would, for instance, be quite unnecessary to use quotation marks in naming Lefty Grove or Babe Ruth, Teddy Roosevelt or F. D. R. In almost any context in which the use of nicknames would be appropriate, a nickname would be recognized as such without enclosing it in quotes, as Shorty Long, Ducklegs Morton, Skiggles Hull. If the nickname is given together with the real name, as a further identification of the person under discussion, quoting the nickname would be appropriate.

Babe Ruth　　　　　　　　　Herman "Babe" Ruth
Skiggles Hull　　　　　　　　Roy "Skiggles" Hull
Hanley, William ("Bill"), "sage of Harney County"; quoted, 65

Clearness is of course the criterion. *Nicknamed* is like *called* or *christened*, and its object is sufficiently set off by capitals; but if the word *nicknamed* does not appear, quotes may be required as a substitute, just as noted about *so-called*, page 289.

> He had been nicknamed Thomas the Sudden.
> Thomas "the Sudden" was there too.

Slang. Do not quote slang. The practice of using quotation marks around a slang word or phrase as a sort of apology for using the expression is not commendable.

> What is your pet peeve?

Horses, dogs; rifle matches, races, stakes, cups; estates, cottages. It is unnecessary to quote names of these, but they should be capitalized.

Sea Biscuit	the Derby	Davis Cup
Man o' War	Preakness	The Oaks

Unnecessary quoting. Do not use quotation marks without reason. In the following sentences, for instance, none are needed, though all were printed with quotes.

> A font contains . . . most c's and a's; fewest z's and q's.
> The ballots were marked in a special way: those with one hole meant Nay, and
>   those with two holes Yea.
> Mrs. Brown was her name.
> The letter N must precede the license symbol.
> Swinging his Sop Camel through a gigantic figure 8
> Shop now for the holiday over the Fourth.
> Old Faithful geyser
> As question 4 should have suggested . . .

Single quotation marks. Single quotes are properly used to enclose quoted matter within a quotation. (See p. 285.) Other uses are more or less arbitrary and unusual. They may be used to save space when quotations are numerous, or to differentiate certain terms from others similar.

> 29. dissilire: 'is split,' as we speak of "a splitting headache."

A rather common practice is to use double quotes only for extracts and dialogue and single quotes in all other cases where quotes are called for.

Use with other marks. Set quotation marks outside of periods and commas. (The British practice of setting periods and commas outside of quotation marks whenever they are not part of the quotation is not liked by most American printers. (See p. 275.)

Quotation marks in conjunction with colons and semicolons should be set inside because the colons and semicolons are sentence punctuation, not part of the quotation. (See pp. 251, 253.)

Set quotation marks outside of exclamation points and interrogation points that are part of the quotation, inside of points that are not. (See p. 248.)

When quotation marks are used in conjunction with points of ellipsis or with *etc.*, particular care should be taken to see that the quotation marks are placed so that they indicate clearly whether the omitted matter is part of the quotation or not.

For style of setting quotation marks in poetry, see page 119.

Type. In most fonts of type open quotation marks are inverted commas, but in some of the newer faces the open quotation marks are made like this: "

If a word or a few words in italic are enclosed in quotation marks, roman quotes are more often used than italic, although some printers do use italic.

> "But now," he said, "I *know*."
> "Go *buy* some *makan*," I told him.
> If we ask the question, "**How** *tall?*" the answer comes immediately: "**Extremely** *tall*."

THE APOSTROPHE

The apostrophe is used to indicate the possessive case of nouns and the plural of letters, figures, signs, etc. (See p. 512.) It is also used to denote the omission of a letter or letters. In this last usage mistakes often occur, sometimes in misplacing the apostrophe or omitting it, sometimes in misspelling the word in which it belongs: as, *its* for *it's, your* for *you're, where're* for *where'er*.

An apostrophe may also mark the omission of figures, as in *the class of '92.*

The apostrophe is usually omitted in such shortened forms as *bus, cello, phone, coon, squire,* and similar commonly used words. Do not use an apostrophe in *Frisco;* nor in the expression *play possum.* Never use an apostrophe before *round* and *till.*

Do not use the apostrophe in place of a single turned comma in Scotch names like M'Gregor.

THE HYPHEN

Division. The hyphen is used at the end of a line to show that part of the word or number has been carried over to the following line. (See the rules relating to division of words, pp. 310, 311.)

In manuscript a hyphen at the end of a line should be carefully marked by the author or editor if it is to be retained. For instance, if the word *never-ending* were divided in the manuscript, *never-* on one line and *ending* on the next, the hyphen should be marked as a double hyphen to prevent the printer from setting *neverending*.

Syllabication. The hyphen is used to indicate syllabication. It is not needed with an accent mark. The space dot—a period cast in the center of the type body—is often used instead of the hyphen for this purpose.

lab′o-ra-to-ry spec-tac′u-lar

Prefixes and suffixes. Used at the end of an etymological part of a word, the hyphen indicates a prefix; before an element it indicates a suffix.

The hyphen is omitted when *in-* and *un-* are prefixed to a word.
Names of metals and metallic radicals usually end in *-ium.*

Connection. The hyphen is used to join words to form compound words. For rules regarding this use, see the sections under "Compounding of Words," pages *297–309.*

Separation. A hyphen is sometimes required between a prefix and a root to make clear the formation of a word. For instance, *un-* is written solid with what follows unless what follows is a proper noun or proper adjective; or if Webster's Dictionary is being followed and *un-* is prefixed to words like *co-operative,* the hyphen should be retained to avoid so confusing a form as *unco-operative.*

un-American	anti-inflation
pro-Axis	semi-elliptical
pre-Hellenic	supra-auditory
mid-Atlantic	sub-subheading

The hyphen is used to separate the prefix *re-* from the root in the following words to convey a meaning different from the same combination written without a hyphen.

re-act	re-dress	re-presentation	re-sound
re-ally	re-form	re-press	re-store
re-collect	re-formation	re-probate	re-strain
re-cover	re-lease	re-search	re-tire
re-create	re-mark	re-serve	re-treat
re-creation	re-pose	re-sign	re-turn
re-creative	re-present	re-solve	

Function. Three points, spoken of as points of ellipsis, are properly used to indicate an omission, a lapse of time, or a pause too long to be indicated by a 1-em dash (if the omission occurs at the end of a sentence a fourth point is used—the period for that sentence).

"All persons born in the United States . . . are citizens of the United States. . . ."
It might have been the original of Poe's
". . . dank tarn of Auber
In the ghoul-haunted woodland of Weir."
"Hm-m! Yes, malaria . . . mosquito infection without a doubt . . . tricky thing, malaria."

In textbooks points of ellipsis may be used to indicate words to be filled in by the student.

Three metals with a valence of one are . . ., . . ., and . . . .
"One of the geysers I saw this afternoon was . . ."

In telephone conversations where only one side is given, it is customary to indicate the pauses for the other side of the conversation by points of ellipsis, using quotation marks only at the beginning and the end of the conversation.

An omission of whole paragraphs or stanzas of poetry, a change of subject, or the lapse of time is indicated by a line of points or a line of asterisks.[2] The points or asterisks are usually set about two ems apart, and three, five, or seven are used, depending on the width of the page. They should never extend beyond the longest type line.

"And so forth." Points of ellipsis may be used as a substitute for *etc.* or *and so forth,* to show that a series could be continued beyond the units named. (This is in effect the adoption for use in reading text of the mathematical symbol . . . , "and so on.")[3]

Interpolations (*in short, besides, I think,* . . .) should be set off by commas.
Two kinds of quantities occur in algebra: the *knowns,* usually represented by *a, b,* . . . , and the *unknowns,* represented by *x, y,* . . . .

[1] Ellipsis points are usually spaced with en quads but in a closely spaced line the spacing of ellipsis points should be reduced. See also "suspension points," page 320.

[2] The use of three asterisks for an ellipsis within a sentence or paragraph is now rare, though formerly common practice.

[3] A more common convention for attaining the same end is omitting the conjunction before the last member of a series.
Reading, 'riting, and 'rithmetic [no others]
Peas, beans, corn, tomatoes [four examples casually selected from many]

Use with other marks. Points of ellipsis at the beginning or end of a quotation should be inside the quotation marks.

> In the early part of the eighteenth century Hawkins in his *Pleas of the Crown* stated: ". . . there can be no doubt, but that all confederacies whatsover, wrongfully to prejudice a third person, are highly criminal at common law. . . ."

COMPOUNDING OF WORDS

The term *compound word* suggests to most persons a word made up of two simple words connected by a hyphen. The term is not, however, so restricted in meaning, but includes also two simple words, written separately or as one word, that together express a single idea.

Principles of compounding nouns. Many compound nouns have the same meaning whether written as one word or two, and good usage sometimes sanctions more than one form. The dictionary makers have not all followed the same general rules in deciding this question. The *Standard Dictionary* determines the form of some compounds on the principle that all words should be separate that are "used in regular grammatical relation and construction, unless they are jointly applied in some arbitrary way." The forms *fellow citizen, he bear,* and *man servant* are examples of the application of the rule.

In Volume I of the *Oxford Dictionary* Sir James Murray writes: "In many combinations the hyphen becomes an expression of unification of sense. When this unification and specialization has proceeded so far that we no longer analyze the combination into its elements, but take it as a whole, as in *blackberry, postman, newspaper,* pronouncing it in speech with a single accent, the hyphen is usually omitted, and the fully developed compound is written as a single word."

The *Century Dictionary* follows the principle that familiarity with compounds originally written as separate words leads first to their hyphenation and next to their being written as a solid word.

Generally speaking, *Webster's New International Dictionary* uses fewer hyphens than other authorities. Whenever the question is one of hyphenating or setting as two words, the two-word form is preferred, and the adoption of a solid-word form follows whenever usage appears to call for it.

Many proofreaders and compositors get unnecessarily concerned about the inconsistencies in the forms of compound nouns, and seem to be annoyed because they cannot apply some hard-and-fast rule to each compound they come upon. Yet it is doubtful if anyone outside the printing and publishing offices is conscious of the form of compound nouns as he reads unless he comes upon some unusual form that is momentarily confusing because of its unfamiliarity. Some present-day writers seem to be too ready to combine into a single word compounds that are clear and not ambiguous as two words, with the result that the reader has to accustom himself to new forms. Compounding should be natural and should not anticipate usage too much. For instance, *copyholder* and *copyreader* have been used so long in these forms that they are immediately clear to everyone; *copyeditor* is theoretically almost as good, but most writers still prefer *copy editor*.

The same proofreaders who rail against the inconsistencies of compounding nouns are often the very ones who overlook the hyphen needed to make the meaning or syntactical connection of words clear. This use of the hyphen is far more important than the form of compound nouns and is too often disregarded.

Temporary compounds. Two words connected by a hyphen to show their syntactical relation to another word may be termed a temporary compound, in contradistinction to the permanent compounds whose form is determined by usage and given in the dictionaries. Few persons have much difficulty with permanent compounds, for if they are in doubt there is always the office style book or the dictionary to consult for information. Compounds which change their form according to their position in the sentence present a quite different problem. Some proofreaders have a great deal of trouble with such temporary compounds because they do not really understand the parts of speech and the relation of words to each other. It was such a reader who changed the sentence "He rubbed his bald head nervously" to read, "He rubbed his baldhead nervously," because she found *baldhead* in the dictionary. True enough, it is there, as a compound noun. This reader lacked the wit to see that she needed a simple noun modified by a simple adjective; she could not distinguish between "He had a bald head" and "He was a baldhead." There are many other nouns of this sort. It was the same reader who had the sentence "He touched up the picture with a camel's hair brush." *Hairbrush* was one of the words given in the office style book as a solid compound, so she changed the sentence to read, "He touched up the picture with a camel's hairbrush." These examples show how easy it is to make absurd changes if one does not have a solid grammatical foundation.

Some persons have difficulty in deciding whether a sentence calls for the word *firsthand* or the phrase *at first hand; altogether* or *all together; awhile* or *a while,* not to mention the frequent misuse of prepositions—*into* where *in to* would be correct, *within* where the sentence calls for *with in.* Proofreaders who make mistakes like these need to study their grammars until they understand the parts of speech; only by doing so can they read intelligently.

On the following pages a few rules are given relating to permanent compounds, many more relating to temporary compounds.

Form dependent on meaning. Two words may be joined to form a single word or a hyphenated word whose meaning is different from the meaning of the same words used separately.

anyone	Did you see anyone?
any one	Any one of these will be satisfactory.
everyone	Everyone will be there.
every one	Every one of the children will be there
anyway	I'll come anyway.
any way	I'll go any way you like.
sometime	Sometime in May
some time	Some time ago
apiece	5 cents apiece
a piece	5 cents a piece
hothouse	They have a hothouse.
hot house	They have a hot house.
handwriting	The handwriting on the wall
hand writing	The hand writing on the wall
matter-of-fact	He is very matter-of-fact.
matter of fact	It is a matter of fact
great-grandfather	He is a great-grandfather.
great grandfather	The boy thought him a great grandfather.
claim-check	Claim-Check Paid (*newspaper heading*)
claim check	Claim Check Paid (*ambiguous*)

"Full" and "-ful." Distinguish phrases like *car full of people* and *carful of people.*

Wrong: The car full of people stood up.

This plainly says that the car stood up.

Right: The carful of people stood up.
Wrong: Then came oars, sails, and steam; and finally the great ships that take trainloads of freight and a city full of people from country to country.
Right: . . . and a cityful of people from country to country.

Names of kindred. The following are correct forms for the names of kindred.

godmother, goddaughter, etc.
grandfather, grandson, etc.
stepdaughter, stepsister, etc., except step-parent
great-aunt, great-uncle, great-grandfather
half-sister, half-brother
foster child, foster brother, etc.
second cousin

Two nouns of equal value. Use a hyphen between two nouns used together to indicate that the person or thing referred to partakes of the character of both nouns.

man-child	priest-ruler	German-American
wolf-lion	soldier-statesman	bridge-tea
city-state	secretary-treasurer	dinner-dance

But: French Canadian, Latin American; Spanish American *or* Spanish-American, according to meaning.

Noun and possessive. In most dictionaries the hyphen is used in those very numerous botanical names that are made up of a noun preceded by a possessive.

adder's-tongue [1]	elephant's-ear	St. John's-wort [1]
bird's-eye [1]	Job's-tears [1]	shepherd's-purse [1]

Nouns of like construction other than botanical names tend to become solid words without any apostrophe.

beeswax	ratsbane	townspeople	sheepshead (*a fish*)

"Like." Adjectives ending in -*like* may be one word except when the root word ends in two *l*'s or is a proper noun or an adjective. Some prefer the hyphenated form whenever the root ends in *l*, as *fossil-like, snail-like.*

childlike	businesslike	quiet-like
womanlike	American-like	ball-like

"Self." Use a hyphen in compounds with *self* when this word forms the first element of the compound.

self-assured	self-possessed	self-control

Exceptions: selfhood, selfsame.

Adjective and noun. When an adjective and a noun combined to form a compound noun have lost their separate meanings and equal stress and have become a combination with one accent and a single specialized meaning, they are usually written as a single word. Not infrequently the compound word written as a single word has a meaning different from that of the compound written with a space between the parts.

aircraft	headway	seaweed	taxpayer
oilcloth	cornflower	lawgiver	bookkeeper

[1] The American Joint Committee on Horticultural Nomenclature has adopted other forms for these: *adderstongue, birdseye, St.Johnswort, shepherds-purse, jobs-tears.*

Compounds of this nature are not inseparable in the sense that whenever they are used they must be written as a single word. For instance, *cornstarch* is often written as one word. *Wheat starch,* on the contrary, is two words. In a discussion comparing corn and wheat starches the following would be correct form. (Note that *corn* and *starch* are equally stressed in reading this sentence.)

> For corn starch the maximum is about 91° C., and for wheat starch it is about 95° C.

Modified compounds. If a compound noun ordinarily written solid is preceded by an adjective which modifies the first part of the compound, separate the compound.

schoolboy	high-school boy	aircraft	lighter-than-air craft
ironworker	structural-iron worker	glassware	cut-glass ware
housekeeper	lodging-house keeper	grapevines	wild-grape vines
stockholder	common-stock holder	gristmill	grist and saw mills
taxpayer	income-tax payer	sawmill	

Wrong: The strong silent public schoolboys from Winchester and Eton.
Right: The strong, silent public-school boys from Winchester and Eton.

If a modifier is used before a compound noun written as two words, the noun must be joined to prevent misreading.

color filter	red color-filter	line design	fine line-design
letter writers	public letter-writers	place names	foreign place-names

Similarly, a compound must be joined if a prefix or a suffix is added.

dessert spoon	dessert-spoonfuls	measuring cup measuring-cupfuls

In the following the hyphen is incorrectly placed.

Wrong: ultralong-wave length
Right: ultralong wave-length

Adjectives. A compound adjective made up of an adjective and a noun in combination should usually be hyphenated.

cold-storage vaults	short-term loan
hot-air heating	small-size edition
toy-repair shop	different-size prisms [2]
ten-cent-store toys	present-day matches

[2] See p. 306. Some prefer *different-sized.*

The purpose of the hyphen in these modifiers and in those noted in other rules later is to prevent a misplacing of the stress or a momentary impression that the first word of the phrase modifies the third word instead of the second. For instance, *toy repair shop* might easily be read as if it were *toy repair-shop,* whereas *toy-repair shop* shows the correct reading immediately.

Following this rule strictly would result in the use of a great many hyphens, to which most writers and printers object. The rule is therefore usually modified by an exception like this from the manual of the Chicago *News:* "Two or more words used together to form the name of a particular place, district, institution, body, etc., do not require the hyphen when used adjectively.

school board members	grand jury room
city hall news	north shore residences"

Compound chemical or scientific terms usually need no hyphen when they are used as modifiers.

a carbon dioxide extinguisher	hydrogen ion activity

The copyreader and proofreader are cautioned not to insert hyphens in technical terms without exact knowledge of their appropriateness. If they are unwary, they may fall into serious error. Note, for instance, the following rule from the style book of the U. S. Geological Survey: [3]

"The Survey has adopted a uniform scheme for the use of hyphens in petrographic terms, based on the single principle that like names are connected by a hyphen and unlike names are not. The names used in such terms are of four classes—(*a*) rock names, (*b*) mineral names, (*c*) textural names, and (*d*) names expressing the kind of clastic aggregation. Any two or more names of the same class are connected by a hyphen; others are not. For example, in 'hornblende-quartz andesite' the two mineral names are connected by a hyphen; in 'quartz monzonite porphyry,' consisting of a mineral name, a rock name, and a textural name, no hyphens are used. . . . To avoid confusion, a term that, according to this principle, is not hyphenated should remain without the hyphen when it becomes a unit modifier preceding some other word—for example, bostonite porphyry, bostonite porphyry dike."

A compound of adjective and noun need not be hyphened when used adjectively if both parts are capitalized.

a Class A member	a Machine Age laborer
Safety First rules	the Open Door policy
Old World countries	Left Wing variety of Marxism

[3] *Suggestions to Authors of Papers Submitted for Publication by the United States Geological Survey,* 4th ed. (Washington, U. S. Government Printing Office, 1935), pp. 8, 9.

Verb and preposition. Compound verbs ending in a preposition are written as two words. The same two words used as nouns should be written as a single word or hyphenated.

Verbs	*Nouns*
break down	breakdown
lay out	layout
set up	setup
cave in	cave-in
stand by	stand-by
black out	blackout

Adjectives similarly formed should be hyphenated when they precede the noun they modify.

Everything must be speeded up.	a speeding-up process
a log hollowed out by hand	a hollowed-out log

An adverb preceding such a compound adjective usually modifies the whole compound, not just the first part. Two hyphens should be used.

a solution much sought for	a much-sought-for solution
The dialogue was long drawn out.	a long-drawn-out dialogue

No hyphen should be used between the adjective and the noun.

Wrong: He used the trade-in-value of his old car for the first payment on a new one.
Right: He used the trade-in value of his old car for the first payment.

Numeral and noun. Always hyphenate a compound in which one component is a cardinal numeral and the other a noun or adjective.

eleven-inch stick	one-sided affair
ten-pound bag	seven-pointed star
a three-hundred-dollar clock	

Strict observance of the rule is particularly important when the noun modified is in the plural, for without the hyphen the phrase might be misleading or at the least ambiguous. It is unsafe to depend upon the context to make the meaning unmistakable. Note the difference in meaning.

ten acre farms	ten-acre farms
two dollar tickets	two-dollar tickets

Usage is not strictly consistent in the number of the noun in the compound. Note, for instance: sixty-day note, six-months note; four-week period, two-fifths share.

Use hyphens logically. In the following sentence neither hyphen is needed, as will readily appear if the numbers are spelled.

Wrong: A customer hands you a $2-bill for a 72¢-purchase.
Right: A customer hands you a $2 bill for a 72¢ purchase (a two-dollar bill for a seventy-two-cent purchase).

Similar compounds using ordinal numerals are hyphenated when they precede the word they modify.

second-story room	third-class coach
third-race entries	second-rate hotel

Compounds with *-fold* have become established as solid words.

tenfold	hundredfold

Observe, however, the following:

His office visits increased five to ten fold.

Compounds with *-score* are also one word if they are used as adjectives.

within twoscore years	within four score of years

Compounds of a numeral with *odd* are hyphenated.

forty-odd	180-odd

Fractions. Always hyphenate fractions used as modifiers unless the numerator or the denominator contains a hyphen. Do not further hyphenate a fraction whose numerator or denominator contains a hyphen.

a one-third interest	four twenty-fifths
one-half life size	twenty-nine fiftieths
three-fourths inch	sixty-two hundredths
two and one-eighth inches	
one-third lower	

The average is about one-half that of winter wheat.
It weighs one-half as much as cork.
Add three-fourths the amount of olives.

Fractions used as nouns do not require a hyphen,[4] but many writers and printers prefer to use one just as in adjectives. There is the advantage to this practice that it saves the mental effort required at times to determine whether the fraction is an adjective or a noun.

[4] Webster's Dictionary, Winston's Dictionary.

It is never correct to hyphenate when the fraction is used as in the following sentences. Here the expression is a simple noun preceded by a numeral adjective.

Whatever it deposits during one half of a cycle it removes the next half.
One half of the planet is perpetually frozen, while the other half has a temperature around 660° F.
Its composition was three fifths copper, two fifths zinc.

Colors. A compound adjective denoting color need not be hyphenated when it follows the noun it modifies if the first component is an adjective ending in *-ish*. When a noun is compounded with a color, or two colors are combined, they should always be hyphenated.

bluish-purple flowers
yellowish-green foliage
blue-green
orange-yellow
pink-lavender
sky-blue

The leaves are reddish brown.
emerald-green
snow-white
coal-black
iron-gray

Compounds with the present participle. Hyphenate compound adjectives made up of a noun, adjective, or adverb and a present participle when they precede the noun they modify. Many such compounds have become permanent compounds, taking the hyphen regardless of their position.

fur-bearing
egg-producing
iron-containing
nerve-racking

unusual-looking
sweet-smelling
deep-lying
far-reaching

If the compound is preceded by an adjective or the like modifying the first word in the compound, omit the hyphen, or if necessary for clearness, use two hyphens.

beet-raising area
rot-producing fungus

sugar beet raising area
moldy-rot-producing fungus

Compounds with noun plus "-d" or "-ed." Ordinarily hyphenate compound adjectives of which one component is an adjective and the other a noun to which *-d* or *-ed* has been added.

able-bodied
blue-eyed
middle-aged
acute-angled
ripple-edged

old-fashioned
strait-laced
dimple-cheeked
freckle-faced
large-fruited

If the adjective so combined ends in *d*, omit this *d:* a child with *dimpled cheeks* is *dimple-cheeked,* not *dimpled-cheeked;* a boy with a freckled face is *freckle-faced,* not *freckled-faced;* a paper with a rippled edge is *ripple-edged,* not *rippled-edged.*

If the first part of the compound is qualified by a preceding adverb, omit the hyphen.

fine-grained fudge   extra fine grained fudge

The hyphenated form of modifier noted in the above rule is the correct form to use in describing, for instance, a man with a pleasant face. He is a *pleasant-faced man,* not a *pleasantly faced man.*

Wrong: She had permanently waved blue-white hair.
Right: She had permanent-waved blue-white hair.
Right: Her hair was permanent-waved.

Compounds with the past participle. Always hyphenate compound adjectives made up of a past participle combined with a noun or adverb when they precede the noun they modify. Many such have become established as hyphenated compounds regardless of their position in the sentence.

deep-seated	gold-filled	worm-eaten	poverty-stricken
tongue-tied	high-flown	hard-boiled	

Adverb-and-adjective compounds. Hyphenate a compound adjective of which one component is an adverb and the other an adjective or participle when it precedes the noun it modifies if the adverb could be misread even momentarily as a modifier of the noun. When it follows the noun it may be set as two words unless it has been used so commonly that it has become established as a hyphenated compound.

more-open creek bottoms	creek bottoms that were more open
best-informed man	man who is best informed
shows much-improved growth	growth is much improved
the most-prized furs	furs that are most prized
a long-desired outlet	an outlet long desired
the above-mentioned facts	the facts above mentioned
his so-called friends	his friends, so called

If the adverb ends in *-ly* or could not be misread as a simple adjective modifying the noun, the hyphen is not necessary.

equally effective cures	too ardent fisherman
newly found treasures	less rigid climates
poorly equipped factory	carefully thought out scheme
well organized and effectively managed life	

Since some adjectives end in *-ly,* adjectives and adverbs in this construction must be carefully distinguished.

a finely built, scholarly-looking man

Compounds with *well* and *ill* need not be hyphenated when they follow the noun modified, although the hyphenated form is often seen.

Well-bred cows well fed may turn out from four hundred to six hundred pounds.

If the compound adjective is preceded by an adverb modifying only the first word of the compound, omit the hyphen.

a well-organized program   a reasonably well organized program

Suspended compounds. When successive compound adjectives have one component the same in all, this component is sometimes omitted in all except the last. The best method is to retain the hyphen in each one.

experiences which cut across all such school- and book-imposed subject lines
When during the Crimean War ships protected by iron or steel armor were first built in France, and almost immediately afterwards in England, a large number of adjectives, as the *Oxford Dictionary* tells us, were used to describe them: *iron-* or *steel-* or *armor-plated, -cased, -clothed, -sided,* and many others, and *iron-plated* was the official adjective until 1866.
He estimated that out of thirty tons hauled twenty tons would be third- and fourth-class commodities and ten tons first- and second-class.

This is a much overused construction which writers should avoid when possible. Of the two forms of the following phrase, for example, the second is preferable and not at all cumbersome.

3-, 4-, and 6-inch mortars
3-inch, 4-inch, and 6-inch mortars
Undesirable: You can play an important part in developing such a program by studying in- and out-of-school facilities in Colorado.
Better: . . . by studying in-school and out-of-school facilities.

Similarly, avoid expressions like the following.

given and surname   cattle and sheepmen

They should be written:

given name and surname   cattle men and sheep men

Before using hyphens to form a suspended compound make sure the hyphens are needed. The following is a possessive construction. (See p. 372.)

Wrong: Examine a series of cross sections of woody stems, of one-, two-, and three-years' growth.

Right: Examine a series of cross sections of woody stems, of one, two, and three years' growth.

Phrases. There are many compounds made up of phrases and of words or syllables similar in form or sound, which are quite familiar to everyone as hyphenated words, such as:

Nouns	*Adjectives*
aide-de-camp	happy-go-lucky
daughter-in-law	helter-skelter
hocus-pocus	higgledy-piggledy
hurdy-gurdy	namby-pamby
jack-o'-lantern	topsy-turvy
touch-me-not	wishy-washy

Do not hyphenate phrases used as nouns in regular grammatical construction.

Wrong: Courses in how-to-read-and-study . . . Knowing how-to-study also connotes having right attitudes toward study.

Right: Courses in how to read and study . . . Knowing how to study also connotes having right attitudes toward study.

Phrases used as attributive adjectives usually require hyphenation to make clear their relation to the noun they modify. (Many such have already been noted incidental to previous rules.)

the how-to-study area　　　　　　a life-and-death struggle

If such a phrase modifier is hyphenated at all it should be hyphenated throughout; but no hyphen should be used between the modifier and the noun.

Wrong: low milk-and-cream yielding dam
Right: low milk-and-cream-yielding dam
Wrong: pay-as-you-go-plan
Right: pay-as-you-go plan

If there is scarcely any possibility of misreading, hyphens need not be used.

half a dozen different shops	yellow pine timber belt
two and a half seconds	white crêpe de Chine dress
a story and a half house	a mahogany and leather chair
cream of corn soup	red leather pocketbook
chicken and tomato soup	two hundred and twenty horsepower
a thirty per cent increase	radial
seven and one-half million dollars	

Writers should avoid unnecessary use of this construction. It is hardly fair to expect a proofreader to solve such a problem as is presented by the following:

three quarters of a billion dollar business
twelve and one half year old girl

The thoughtful author would write:

a business worth three quarters of a billion dollars
a girl twelve and one-half years old

Hyphenating a phrase used as an adjective makes it a single adjective. The writer of the following failed to see that he had two adjectives connected by *and,* each modifying the noun. This construction should be carefully distinguished from the phrase requiring hyphens.

Wrong: Add more of the chilled-and-partly "set" broth.
Right: Add more of the chilled and partly set broth.

Long phrases like the following should be hyphenated.

never-to-be-forgotten friend
twenty-dollar-a-week clerk
sun-and-wind-browned cheeks
one of those God-help-me-why-am-I-here expressions
that chap's funny-at-all-costs type

A foreign phrase used as an adjective need not be hyphenated.

viva voce vote   a pro rata assessment

DIVISION OF WORDS

In order to secure that evenness of spacing which is essential to the good appearance of a printed page, it is often necessary to divide a word at the end of a line, carrying over one or more syllables to the beginning of the next line. Numerous authors and editors have tried to formulate rules to govern this subject, often with the result that they have given so many rules and so many exceptions and qualifications that the student is utterly confused and usually gives up in despair. A complicating factor is that American dictionaries syllabicate according to pronunciation, British dictionaries according to derivation. For instance:

American	*British*
cen-ti-me-ters	cent-i-me-ters
phi-lan-thropy	phil-an-thropy
grammat-ical	gramma-tical
femi-nine	femin-ine
democ-racy	demo-cracy
idio-matic	idiom-atic

However, there will be little trouble with divisions if the following simple rules are observed.

GENERAL RULES

A word may be divided, of course, only at the end of a syllable. If one is not sure of the syllabication, he must refer to the dictionary.

Words pronounced as one syllable should never be divided.

cracked   drowned   through   often

Words of two syllables of which one is a single vowel—or its equivalent—should not be divided.

around   aegis   even   over

A terminating syllable of only two letters should not be carried over unless the exigencies of very narrow measure make it necessary. Some printers assert that an initial syllable of two letters should not stand at the end of a line, but such a division is preferable to a line more widely spaced than adjoining lines.

A division before a single vowel which alone forms a syllable is considered poor form except in the case of the suffixes -*able* and -*ible,* and words in which the vowel is the first syllable of a root.

munici-pal	consider-able	dis-united
privi-lege	remedi-able	inter-oceanic
deroga-tory	reduc-ible	un-equal

There are many words ending in -*able* and -*ible,* however—in which the *a* or *i* does not by itself form a syllable—which may be divided after the *a* or *i,* as, for instance:

ame-na-ble	char-i-ta-ble	pos-si-ble
ca-pa-ble	gul-li-ble	ter-ri-ble

The terminations -*cial, -sial, -tial, -cion, -sion, -tion, -gion, -cious, -ceous, -tious,* and -*geous* should not be divided.

se-ba-ceous   con-sci-en-tious   coura-geous   ad-van-ta-geous

The letter *t* belongs with the following letters in words like:

ad-ven-ture   for-tune   pre-sump-tu-ous   lit-era-ture

When the final consonant of a verb is doubled in forming the past tense or the participle, the second consonant belongs with the letters following it. Single or double consonants in the root word should not be carried over.

occur-ring	di-vid-ing	fore-stall-ing
for-get-ting	forc-ing	buzz-ing
re-gret-ted	trav-el-ing	dis-till-ing

When there is a distinction made in the pronunciation of a word to denote its part of speech, the word should be divided according to pronunciation.

proj'ect (*noun*)   pro-ject' (*verb*)   prod'uce (*noun*)   pro-duce' (*verb*)

Abbreviations like A.M., Ph.D.; I.W.W., Y.M.C.A., and the like; A.M., P.M., A.D., and B.C.; or the letters I O U, A B C's, S O S, etc., should not be divided.

Do not put the initials of a name on different lines, and if possible avoid separating initials, titles (Mr., Rev.), and degrees (M.D.) from a name.

Avoid, if possible—

dividing at the ends of more than two successive lines;

dividing the last word of a paragraph. If it is divided, carry over at least four letters;

dividing the last word on a right-hand page;

dividing a hyphenated compound word except at the hyphen (that is, avoid two hyphens);

dividing numbers expressed in figures. If they must be divided, divide only at the comma and retain the comma (4,656,-);

dividing combinations like £6 4s. 6d., 14 B.C., 6.30 P.M.;

separating (*a*) or (1), etc., from the matter to which it pertains.

A dieresis is placed over a vowel to indicate pronunciation of a separate syllable from the preceding vowel, as in *reënter, coöperation*. If, then, the word is divided between the vowels, no dieresis is needed.

Rules for the division of words of foreign languages will be found in the sections dealing with the respective languages, immediately following. They should be studied for the guidance they give in the division of words and names of foreign origin, as, for instance:

sei-gneur	zem-stvo	Pa-gli-acci	To-ma-szow
lor-gnettes	seragl-io	Bu-czacz	Lasch-tschenko

COMPOSITION OF FOREIGN LANGUAGES

Editors and proofreaders find a knowledge of languages frequently useful in their work. They would, for instance, be seriously handicapped if they could not recognize and call by name the Greek letters so often used as signs and symbols in technical books of many kinds. Even a smattering of foreign languages helps them to read correctly an indistinctly written foreign word. They often have to answer questions of how to divide or to capitalize in citations of works in foreign languages. The following sections are not intended as preparation for reading foreign-language texts, but they should be helpful for reference when questions of form arise concerning foreign words, phrases, and titles used in an English text.

ALBANIAN

The alphabet. The Albanian language uses twenty-five letters of our alphabet, *w* being omitted.

Divisions. When a word is divided at the end of a line, at least three letters should be carried over unless the lines are very short. Compounds should be divided according to their construction, prefixes and suffixes being kept intact. A division may be made before a consonant standing between two vowels, and the following combinations should be treated as single consonants: *dh, gj, ll, nj, rr, sh, xh, zh.*

ANGLO-SAXON

The alphabet. The Anglo-Saxon alphabet had no *j, k, q, v,* or *z,* but it did have two letters that we have not—*edh* (ð, capital Ð), for *th* as in *thine,* and *thorn* (þ, capital Þ), for *th* as in *thin.* In alphabeting, *edh* and *thorn* follow *t.* Æ, æ, and Œ, œ, should always be set as ligatures.

References. The *Manual of Foreign Languages,* by George F. von Ostermann, 3d ed. (Washington, U. S. Government Printing Office, 1936), presents helpful instruction in the composition of Anglo-Saxon.

BOHEMIAN

The alphabet. The Bohemian language uses twenty-five letters of our alphabet, *w* being omitted. The letters *g, q,* and *x* are used only in foreign words. In addition the following accented letters are used: *á, é, í ó, ú, ý; č, ď, ě, ň, ř, š, ť, ž; ů.*

Divisions. When a word is divided at the end of a line, at least three letters should be carried over unless the lines are very short. Compounds should be divided according to their construction, prefixes and suffixes being kept intact. A Bohemian word may be divided before a consonant standing between two vowels. The letters *l*, *r*, and *v* frequently have the characteristics of a vowel, and a preceding consonant (except *n*) should not be separated from them. The combinations *sk̑*, *šk̑*, *st*, *št*, and *sd* should be considered as single consonants. Other combinations of consonants may be divided. Two vowels may be separated.

Punctuation. The general rules of the English language are followed in punctuating Bohemian.

DANISH

The alphabet. The Danish language uses twenty-nine letters, our alphabet with the addition of *æ*, *ø*, and *aa*. In arranging Danish words alphabetically, *æ*, *ø*, and *aa* usually follow *z*, although *aa*, which is a single letter (not a double *a*) may be placed before *a*. *å* is sometimes used for *aa*, and *ø* may be replaced by *ö*, but not by *œ*. The letters *c*, *q*, *w*, *x*, and *z* are used only in foreign words and proper names.

Capitalization. Danish nouns are capitalized.[1] The pronouns *De, Deres, Dem* are capitalized when they mean *you* (polite form), lower case when they mean *he, she,* or *it*.

Divisions. When a word is divided at the end of a line, at least three letters should be carried over unless the lines are very short. Compounds should be divided according to their construction, prefixes and suffixes being kept intact. A word may be divided before a consonant standing between vowels. The combinations *sk̑*, *sp*, *st*, and *str* should not be separated, and belong with a following vowel. Other combinations of consonants may be divided.

Punctuation. The clausal construction of the sentences is closely followed.[1]

DUTCH

The alphabet. The Dutch language uses the English alphabet, but the letters *q*, *x*, and *y* appear only in foreign words. The following accents may be used: *ā, ă, ē, ĕ, ī, ĭ, ō, ŏ*. The vowel *ij*, peculiar to this language, is equivalent to our *y*: Bilderdijk, Huijgens. Both letters are capitalized if they begin a sentence or a proper name: IJssel Lake, IJmuiden.

Capitalization. Capitals are used in Dutch much the same as in English, except that if a sentence begins with a one-letter word, the second word is capitalized and not the first.

The pronoun *ik̑*, *I*, is not capitalized, but *U*, *you*, and *Uw*, *your*, are.

In family names *ten* and *van* are lower case: van 't Hoff, van Leeuwenhoek. (See also p. 237.)

---

[1] "Some modern authors tend to follow the English usage."—Ostermann.

Divisions. When a word is divided at the end of a line, at least three letters should be carried over unless the lines are very short. The component parts of a compound word should be kept intact. A word may be divided before a consonant standing between vowels. The combination *ch* is inseparable and belongs with a following vowel. A division may usually be made between two consonants standing between vowels. A combination of three consonants is divided phonetically.

FINNISH

The alphabet. The Finnish language uses the English alphabet, but *b, c, d, f, g, q, x,* and *z,* and also *å,* occur only in foreign words. The dieresis may be used over *a* and *o*: *ä, ö.* In alphabeting, *å* follows *z.*

Divisions. When a word is divided at the end of a line, at least three letters should be carried over unless the lines are very short. Compound words should be divided according to their construction, prefixes and suffixes being kept intact.

The Finnish language uses sixteen diphthongs, which may not be divided: *ai, au, äi, äy, ei, eu, ie, iu, oi, ou, öi, öy, ui, uo, yi, yö.*

A Finnish word may be divided before a consonant which stands between vowels. Double consonants may always be divided. If two or three consonants stand between vowels, a division may be made before the last.

FRENCH

The alphabet. All the letters of our alphabet are used in French except the *w,* which appears only in words foreign to French. The following accented letters are used: *à, â, ç, é, è, ê, ë, ï, î, ô, ù, ü, û.* The cedilla is placed under *ç* preceding *a, o,* or *u* whenever *c* is soft and should be pronounced like *s* in *sin* (*façade*). The dieresis is placed over the second of two vowels to show that the vowels do not form a diphthong: *naïf.* Accents may be omitted on the capital *A,* but they are always used on small capitals.

La Société provençale à la fin du moyen âge
LA SOCIÉTÉ PROVENCALE À LA FIN DU MOYEN ÂGE
LA SOCIÉTÉ PROVENÇALE A LA FIN DU MOYEN AGE

Capitalization. Capitals are not used so freely in French as in English. The following practice should be observed.

(1) Proper names: In names of persons *La* or *Le* is usually capitalized, unless the name is taken from the Italian.

La Fayette
La Rochefoucauld

le Dante
le Tasse

In names of places an article is lower case; likewise common-noun elements like *golfe, mer, mont*.

les États-Unis   la mer Rouge   le mont Blanc

(2) Names of the Deity:

le Saint-Esprit   Notre-Seigneur

(3) Names of religious festivals and holidays:

la nuit de Noël   la semaine de la Passion

(4) Names of historical events and periods:

la Grande Guerre   les croisades
la guerre de Cent ans   le moyen âge
la Conférence de la paix

(5) Names of streets, squares, buildings, and the like:

la rue Saint-Jacques   le lycée Louis-le-Grand
la place de la Concorde   l'église de Saint-Étienne-du-Mont

(6) Names of institutions and orders and their members:

la Légion d'honneur   un jésuite
l'ordre des Templiers   un templier
l'État, l'Église (as institutions)   protestantisme

(7) Titles:

Sa Majesté   M. le Prince
Votre Majesté   le général Gamelin

(8) Nationals:

un Anglais   un Irlandais

(9) Roman numerals:

Louis XV   tome IX
le XIVᵉ arrondissement   l'acte V
l'an IV

Numerals denoting centuries are usually set in small capitals:

xivᵉ siècle

Capitals are not used for the following:

(1) Names of the months and the days of the week:

avril 1939   le samedi passé

(2) Nouns or adjectives derived from proper names:

la Guerre franco-allemande   l'Académie française
le calendrier julien   Parlez-vous français?

(3) The word *saint* in naming the saints themselves (but see (5) above):

saint Paul, saint Louis   l'histoire de sainte Geneviève
L'autre est consacré à saint Maur.

(4) The titles *monsieur, madame,* and the like, in direct address (see also page 195):

Oui, monsieur.

(5) Salutations of letters:

Mes chers parents:

Titles and captions. The nature of the work in which a French title is used should be considered in deciding upon the best form of capitalizing to use. In the text of a book or article in English the title of a French book, magazine, story, poem, or the like is best capitalized in the same manner as similar titles in English.

This was Jean Baptiste Lamarck, whose book *La Philosophie Zoologique* appeared in 1809.

In French texts, textbooks in the French language, catalogues of French books, footnotes in English texts when citations of French works are frequent, and similar context, French book titles, headings, captions, and the like should follow a style more in accord with French practice.
The first word and proper nouns should be capitalized.

Vue générale de la littérature française
En Champagne

Also capitalize the first substantive and a preceding adjective.

Les Mois et les saisons
Le Tour du monde en quatre-vingt jours
Des Hommes exceptionnels

Les Pauvres Gens
Les Deux Sourds
La Vieille Maison retrouvée

Note. The above rules are those most commonly followed by American printers, but the proofreader should not without specific instruction presume to change copy prepared in accordance with the practice indicated by the following:

Capitalize proper nouns and capitalize the first word unless it is *le, la, les,* in which case the next word should be capitalized.

Petite pluie   le Monde où l'on s'ennuie
Une ténébreuse affaire   les Fauts ménages

Divisions. When a word is divided at the end of a line, at least three letters should be carried over unless the lines are very short. Division of abbreviated words should be avoided. Compound words should be divided according to their construction, prefixes and suffixes being kept intact.

extra-ordinaire   pre-avertir

Compound words containing an apostrophe may be divided after the apostrophe.

grand'-mère   grand'-route

A division may usually be made before a consonant standing between vowels.

lé-ga-taire   ba-lan-cer
che-va-lier   jeu-nesse

No division should be made before x or y, or after x or y before a vowel or h.

roya-liste   soixan-tième   Alexan-dre

When hyphenated phrases like *viendra-t-il* must be divided, the t should be carried over.

The combinations *bl, br, ch, cl, cr, dr, fl, fr, gl, gr, gh, ph, pl, pr, th, tr,* and *vr* should not be separated.

per-dre	qua-drille	pro-phé-ti-ser
cé-lé-brer	dé-pê-cher	Vau-ghan
ré-pu-bli-que	ca-tho-li-que	ou-vrier
dé-peu-ple-ment	qua-tre	au-tre-ment
dé-cret	pa-thé-ti-que	li-vrai-son

The combination *gn* should not be divided when it has the sound of *ni* in *onion,* but where the *g* and *n* have separate sounds they may be divided.

com-pa-gnon   in-di-gni-té   diag-nos-ti-que

Any other two consonants may be divided, including doubled consonants.

par-tir ma-nus-crit mil-lion

As a rule, two vowels are not separated.

mi-nuit théâ-tre joue-rai étions fouet-ter

Mute syllables may be turned over to the next line, but such divisions should be avoided if possible.

élé-gan-ces mar-che mar-quent hom-mes

Punctuation. Commas are not used so much in French as in English. No comma is used before a conjunction linking the last two members of a series of coördinate words, phrases, or clauses. Nonrestrictive relative clauses are often not set off. In dates the month and year are not, as a rule, separated.

Quotation marks. English quotation marks are often used in French texts and ordinarily in a text of which any part is in English. The French have, however, quotation marks, called guillemets, of a different form—small angle marks resting on the line. They should be set with a thin space between them and the text.

« J'ai, nous a dit le général Gouraud, fait mon livre pour les jeunes. »

Note that fewer quotation marks are considered necessary than would be used in English, since none are used, for instance, after *J'ai* or before *fait* in the preceding example.

If a quotation is two or more paragraphs long, opening guillemets should be used before the first paragraph, closing guillemets before each following paragraph and at the end of the last paragraph. If a quotation occurs within a quotation, the beginning of this sub-quotation is marked by opening guillemets, and closing guillemets are used before each line of the sub-quotation and at the end.[1]

> Le reliquat d'*Actes et paroles* donne cette variante inédite:
> « Le moment est venu de jeter sur l'ocean qui nous sépare ce pont immense, la solidarité.
> » Les peuples se parlent par-dessus les gouvernements, les peuples sont de grandes âmes qui s'entendent à travers l'obstacle, et qui proclament les principes pendant que la politique cherche les expédients. En ce moment suprême, le cœur de la France parle au cœur de l'Amérique, et voici ce que la France vous dit:
> « Vous êtes l'admirable Amérique, aucune nation n'est plus vénérable que vous. » Vous êtes colonisateurs et civilisateurs. Vos grands hommes font votre terre

[1] Ruling of the *Code typographique* of 1928.

» illustre comme la Grèce et l'Italie.   L'exemple de la grande vie a été donné chez
» vous par Washington et de la grande mort par Lincoln; vous avez eu Franklin
» qui a dompté la foudre, vous avez eu Fulton qui a dompté la mer; vous avez
» eu John Brown et Peabody qui tous deux ont imité le Christ, l'un du côté
» libérateur, l'autre du côté secourable.   Peabody la main qui donne, John Brown,
» la main qui délivre. »   [One pair of guillemets dropped.]

Six mois avant sa mort, le 24 novembre 1884, la dernière visite officielle que
fit Victor Hugo fut d'aller voir la statue de la Liberté, par Bartholdi.

If guillemets and punctuation come together, the following combinations
are allowable.

Within a sentence: »,   ! »,   ? »,

At the end of a sentence: ».   »! »? .» !» ?» ?»! !»? !»! ?»?

A period at the end of a quotation is dropped before a comma, and before
an exclamation mark or a question mark; and a sentence period is dropped
after a period, an exclamation mark, or a question mark.

Il ajouta: « Oui, cette belle œuvre tend à ce que j'ai toujours aimé, appelé: la
paix. »   [The sentence period is dropped.]
Le deuxième jour, il dit: « Que la lumière électrique soit! »

If the quotation is a word or phrase, the sentence punctuation should be
outside the guillemets.

Vous envoyer « l'Illustration ».
Mais chacun ici sait que, si elle a lieu, les agresseurs seront la France, que l'on
estime tant, et l'Angleterre, « poussées toutes deux par la juiverie et la finance
internationale »!

The dash.   In direct discourse opening quotation marks are often replaced
by em dashes (always spaced at least a hair), no closing quotation marks being
used.

— Moi, dit la jeune fille.
— Et moi, s'écria l'homme âgé.

Le professeur, impatient, s'ecrie malencontreusement:
— Vous n'avez donc jamais vu la lune?
Dans le silence, la réponse tombe, inattendue:
— Non, monsieur!
N'en pouvant croire ses oreilles, il insiste:
— Comment! Vous n'avez jamais vu la lune?

The beginning and the end of such conversational matter is sometimes
marked by guillemets, with each intervening change of speaker indicated by
an em dash; but the two marks should be used together only when the dialogue
constitutes a quotation.

Usually a new paragraph marks every change of speaker, but sometimes the words of different speakers are run into one paragraph.

Un jeune Américain, qui visitait Paris pour la première fois, demanda à un de ses amis où se trouvait « Complet ». — Toutes les fois le même mot « Complet ». Dites-moi donc où est cet endroit. — Comment! dit l'autre, vous n'avez pas encore vu « Complet » ? Il vous faut voir « Complet ».

English quotation marks may be preferred, placed at the beginning and at the end of a quoted speech.

"Partage," dit le lion au loup. "Sire, répondit celui-ci, à vous le morceau de choux, le bœuf." "Tu crois!" s'écria le lion. "Allons à toi, dit-il au renard, partage, et sois juste."

Points of suspension. Points of suspension are three points, set close together (a single type in some fonts), without any space at the left and always followed by a space. They are used in French text much as dashes are used in English—to mark an interruption or a pause or an abrupt change in thought or construction.

— Pierre, François, Jean-Paul, prenez vos bicyclettes, on descend au jardin... Anne-Marie, Hélène, vous vous occuperez de Gérard.

Le grand-père fait l'appel des petits qui sortent en gai tumulte de la chambre des jeux. Trois garçonnets, deux fillettes, et une poupée... un poupon, Gérard, dans les bras de sa grand'mère.

Les céréales, les animaux domestiques, la maison, la cité, la vie sédentaire... « La plus grande revolution de l'histoire... » Cette parole d'un professeur me revient à l'esprit.

« L'enseigne fait la chalandise », disait L⌐ Fontaine... et l'on voit au xviie siècle. Dès maintenant vous pouvez le faire... et facilement.

Numbers. In numbers of five or more digits, groups of three digits may be separated by either 'a point or a thin space. A decimal comma is used instead of a decimal point.

45.600   45 600   45,7

Note the following forms of expressing sums of money or measures of length or weight:

60 francs	60 mètres	20 kilogrammes
60 fr. 25	60 m. 50	20 kg. 5
60^{fr},25	60^m,50	20^{kg},5
à 23 h. 15		

Per cent is represented by *0/0, pour 100, p. 100, pour 0/0,* or *pour cent.*

Abbreviations. Abbreviations are used freely in French. Some of them are listed below. Note that no period is used after an abbreviation when the last letter is the same as the last letter of the word for which it stands.

a., *acte*, Act
A. J. C., *avant Jésus-Christ* (used in dates: 41 A. J. C.)
à/l., *à livraison*, on delivery (of goods)
Alt., *Altesse*, Highness
art., *article*, article
a/s. de, *aux soins de*, c/o
av., *avec*, with; *avril*, April
av. J.-C., *avant Jésus-Christ*, before Christ
b. à p., *billets à payer*, bills payable
b. à r., *billets à recevoir*, bills receivable
B. ès L., *Bachelier ès lettres*, Bachelor of Letters
B. ès S., *Bachelier ès sciences*, Bachelor of Science
b. p. f., *bon pour francs*, value in francs
c., *centime(s)*, centime(s)
ch., *chapitre*, chapter
cie, *compagnie*, company
c.-à-d., *c'est-à-dire*, that is
Cte, *comte*, Count
déc., *décédé(e)*, deceased; *décembre*, December
Dr, *docteur*, Doctor
dzne, *douzaine*, dozen
e. o. o. e., *erreur ou omission exceptée*, errors or omissions excepted.
esc., *escompte*, discount
etc., *et cætera*, et cetera
fév., *février*, February
fig., *figure*, figure
fr., f., *franc(s)*, franc(s)
h., *heure*, hour
in-f., *in-folio*, folio
in-8°, *in-octavo*, octavo
in-4°, *in-quarto*, quarto
1er, *premier (m.)*, first
1ère, *première (f.)*, first
IIe, 2e, *deuxième*, second
j., *journal*, newspaper
janv., *janvier*, January
juil., *juillet*, July
l/a., *lettre d'avis*, letter of advice
l/cr., *lettre de crédit*, letter of credit
liv., *livre*, book
LL. MM.,[2] *Leurs Majestés*, Their Majesties

---

[2] LL. MM., S. M., etc., are used only before another title: S. M. l'Empéreur.

M.,[3] *Monsieur*, Mr. (*pl.* MM.)

m. à m., *mot à mot*, word for word

Me, *maître*, lawyer

Mgr, *monseigneur*, my lord

Mis, *marquis*, marquis

Mise, *marquise*, marchioness

Mlle, *mademoiselle*, Miss

Mme, *madame*, Mrs.

Mn, *maison*, house

MS. or ms., *manuscrit*, manuscript (*pl.* MSS.)

N.-D., *Notre-Dame*, Our Lady

No, *numero*, Number (*pl.* Nos)

nov., *novembre*, November

oct., *octobre*, October

p. d. a., *pour dire adieu*, to say good-by

p. ex., *par exemple*, for instance

p. f., *pour féliciter*, to congratulate

p. f. s. a., *pour faire ses adieux*, to say good-by

p. f. v., *pour faire visite*, to make a call

p. p., *publié par*, published by

p. p. c., *pour prendre congé*, to take leave

p. r. v., *pour rendre visite*, to return a call

P. S., *post-scriptum*, postcript

p. v. t., *par voie télégraphique*, by telegraph

R.S.V.P., *Répondez s'il vous plaît*, An answer is requested

s., *sur*, on; e.g., Boulogne s/M (= *sur mer*)

S., Ste, *Saint, Sainte* (for names of saints)

S. A. I., *Son Altesse Imperiale*, His (Her) Imperial Highness (*pl.* SS. AA. II.)

S. A. R., *Son Altesse Royale*, His Royal Highness

sc., *scène*, scene

S. E., *Son Éminence*, His Eminence

s.-ent., *sous-entendu*, understood

s. e. o. o., *sauf erreur ou omission*, errors or omissions excepted

sept., *septembre*, September

S. Exc., *Son Excellence*, His Excellency

s. g. d. g., *sans garantie du gouvernement*, without government guarantee

S. M., *Sa Majesté*, His (Her) Majesty

S. M. I., *Sa Majesté Imperiale*, His (Her) Imperial Majesty

S. S., *Sa Sainteté*, His Holiness

St-, Ste-, *Saint, Sainte* (for names of places)

s. v. p., *s'il vous plaît*, if you please

t., *tome*, volume

tit., *titre*, title

t. p., *timbre-poste*, postage stamp

t. s. v. p., *tournez s'il vous plaît*, please turn over

---

[3] The abbreviations M., Mlle, Mme, Mgr, are not used in reproducing direct discourse (see p. 195).

v., vol., *volume,* volume
voy., v., *voyez, voir,* see
vve, *veuve,* widow

Phonetics.   The following symbols are those commonly used in the phonetic
transcription of French.

Letter	English Equivalent	Symbol	Example	
Vowels				
a, â	f*a*ther	[ɑ]	bas	[bɑ]
a, à	*a*sk	[a]	la	[la]
e	sof*a*	[ə]	le	[lə]
e, é, ai	m*a*de	[e]	les	[le]
e, è, ê, ë, ai, ei	l*e*t	[ɛ]	très	[trɛ]
i, î, ï, ie, y	mach*i*ne	[i]	midi	[midi]
i = y		[j]	vieux	[vjø]
o, au *final or followed by*	cl*o*th	[ɔ]	mol	[mɔl]
a consonant				
o, ô, au, eau	g*o*	[o]	vos	[vo]
u, û	(None)	[y]	une	[yn]
eu, œu	(None)	[ø]	deux	[dø]
eu, œu, ue	(None)	[œ]	seul	[sœl]
oi	w*a*sh	[wɑ]	bois	[bwɑ]
oi	w*a*ft	[wa]	voici	[vwasi]
ou	s*ou*p	[u]	sous	[su]
ui	(None)	[ɥ]	suis	[sɥi]
Nasal Vowels				
an, am, en, em	(None)	[ɑ̃]	dans	[dɑ̃]
			encore	[ɑ̃kɔːr]
in, im, ain, aim, ein, eim,	(None)	[ɛ̃]	fin	[fɛ̃]
yn, ym			main	[mɛ̃]
			faim	[fɛ̃]
on, om	(None)	[ɔ̃]	bon	[bɔ̃]
un, um	(None)	[œ̃]	lundi	[lœ̃di]
Consonants				
b	*b*at	[b]	balle	[bal]
c (*before* a, o, u)	*c*oat	[k]	car	[kar]
c (*before* e, i, y)	*c*ent	[s]	ici	[isi]
ch	ma*ch*ine	[ʃ]	chaise	[ʃɛːz]
d	*d*are	[d]	des	[dɛ]
f	*f*eet	[f]	face	[fas]
g (*before* a, o, u)	*g*o	[g]	gare	[gaːr]
g (*before* e, i, y)	plea*s*ure	[ʒ]	geste	[ʒɛst]

LETTER	ENGLISH EQUIVALENT	SYMBOL	EXAMPLE	
Consonants				
gn	*oni*on	[ɲ]	digne	[diɲ]
h	(Silent)		homme	[ɔm]
j	plea*s*ure	[ʒ]	joli	[ʒɔli]
k	*k*ick	[k]	kepi	[kepi]
l	*l*ate	[l]	lait	[lɛ]
ll (*after* i)	*y*et	[j]	famille	[fami:j]
m	*m*an	[m]	midi	[midi]
n	*n*eed	[n]	net	[nɛt]
p	*p*age	[p]	paix	[pɛ]
q (qu)	*k*ick	[k]	qui	[ki]
r	*r*ay	[r]	race	[ras]
s	mi*ss*	[s]	salle	[sal]
s (*between vowels*)	ga*z*e	[z]	église	[egli:z]
t	*t*able	[t]	table	[tabl]
v	*v*ery	[v]	votre	[vɔtr]
w	*v*ery	[v]	wagon	[vagɔ̃]
x	bo*x*	[ks]	luxe	[lyks]
x	ba*gs*	[gz]	exemple	[ɛgzɑ̃:pl]
z	ga*z*e	[z]	douze	[du:z]

ː is a sign of length.

GERMAN

The alphabet. The German alphabet contains the following letters:

A	𝕬	a	𝖆	N	𝕹	n	𝖓
B	𝕭	b	𝖇	O	𝕺	o	𝖔
C	𝕮	c	𝖈	P	𝕻	p	𝖕
D	𝕯	d	𝖉	Q	𝕼	q	𝖖
E	𝕰	e	𝖊	R	𝕽	r	𝖗
F	𝕱	f	𝖋	S	𝕾	s	𝖘 ſ
G	𝕲	g	𝖌	T	𝕿	t	𝖙
H	𝕳	h	𝖍	U	𝖀	u	𝖚
I	𝕴	i	𝖎	V	𝖁	v	𝖛
J	𝕵	j	𝖏	W	𝖂	w	𝖜
K	𝕶	k	𝖐	X	𝖃	x	𝖝
L	𝕷	l	𝖑	Y	𝖄	y	𝖞
M	𝕸	m	𝖒	Z	𝖅	z	𝖟

Three umlauted letters are used: ä, ö, ü and the diphthong äu.

Fonts of German type, technically known as *Fraktur*, contain no small capitals or italic.

Several of the letters in *Fraktur* resemble other letters so closely that they are likely to be confused. Such letters are shown together and the difference is pointed out.

𝔅 (B) and 𝔙 (V). *V* is open in the middle; *B* is joined across.

ℭ (C) and 𝔈 (E). *E* has a little stroke in the middle, projecting to the right, which *C* has not.

𝔊 (G) and 𝔖 (S). *S* has an opening at the upper right; *G* is closed, and has, besides, a perpendicular stroke within.

𝔍 (I) and 𝔍 (J) have the same form—𝔍. If a consonant follows, the letter is *I;* if a vowel, it is *J*. (Sometimes the two capitals differ slightly in form.)

𝔎 (K), 𝔑 (N), 𝔑(R). *K* is rounded at the top, *N* is open in the middle, *R*, like *K*, is united about the middle.

𝔐 (M) and 𝔚 (W). *M* is open at the bottom; *W* is closed.

𝔟 (b) and 𝔥 (h). *b* is entirely closed below; *h* is somewhat open, and ends at the bottom, on one side, with a projecting hair-stroke.

𝔣 (f) and 𝔰 (s). *f* has a horizontal line *through* it; *s,* on the left side only.

𝔪 (m) and 𝔴 (w). *m* is entirely open at the bottom; *w* is partly closed.

𝔯 (r) and 𝔵 (x). *x* has a little hair-stroke below, on the left.

𝔳 (v) and 𝔶 (y). *v* is closed; *y* is somewhat open below, and ends with a hair-stroke.

Note also that the German *y* looks much like an English *n*.

Ligatures. Fonts of German type contain the following ligatures: ch, ck, ff, fi, fl, ll, ſi, ſſ, ſt, ß, tz. These letters are not united, however, if they are brought together by the combination of prefixes or suffixes with roots. For instance:

auffahren	vielleicht
Auflage	dasselbe
schlaflos	achtzig
Wasserstoffionen	entzweien
verwerflich	heutzutage

There are no triple letters corresponding to English *ffi* and *ffl*. These combinations are set ſtoffig, trefflich, etc.

When German is printed in roman type (called by the Germans *Lateinisch*), as much of it is nowadays, a special character, ß, is used for ß. But many prefer the simple roman *ss*. (The substitution of *sz* for this combination is erroneous, yet unfortunately it has been used.)

Use of ß and ſ . The letter ß is used at the end of words, prefixes, and roots; the long ſ, in all other positions except in some words of foreign origin.

Haus, Häuschen   bis, bisweilen   ſagen   leſen   Schickſal

The following prefixes end with an ß:

aus=   bis=   diß=   dys=   ins=   plus=   ſus=   trans=

The long ſ is used at the beginning of a root following the prefixes di=, ſu=, or tran=.

The round ß is used at the end of a root before the following suffixes:

=bar	=ſa	=ler	=los	=tum
=chen	=ſe	=lich	=ma	=ber
=haft	=ſer	=ling	=mus	=voll
=heit	=ſus			

Capitalization. German practices in capitalization vary widely from English. Capitals are used for the following:

(1) The first word of a sentence
(2) The first word of a line of poetry
(3) The first word of a formal quotation
(4) Proper names. The preposition von preceding a name is always set lower case in German, regardless of its position in the sentence or of whether a title or name precedes. A thin space between von and the name is sufficient.

Es war von Bismarck.

(5) Nouns and words used as nouns

der Mann   die Armen

Certain nouns are set lower case when used to form part of an adverbial phrase:

heute morgen   geſtern abend

Neuter adjectives used as nouns after etwas, viel, nichts, alles, and allerlei should be capitalized.

etwas Gutes für ſeine Arbeit

(6) The pronoun Sie, "you," and its possessive form Ihr, "yours"
(7) Adjectives and pronouns in titles

Eure Königliche Hoheit   Seine Majeſtät

In contrast to English usage, capitals are not used for the following:

(1) Proper adjectives, except those derived from the names of persons anᵈ those used in geographical proper names

die Grimmschen Märchen   in den deutschösterreichischen
der Kölner Dom   Provinzen

(2) Proper adjectives denoting nationality, unless they are used in titles

das deutsche Volk   das Deutsche Reich

Note auf deutsch, "in German," but Studieren Sie Deutsch? "Are you studying German?"

Capitalization in titles, headings, captions, and the like is the same as in text.

Division. When a word is divided at the end of a line, at least three letters should be carried over unless the lines are very short.

Compound words, as a rule, should be divided according to their elements— prefixes and suffixes should be kept intact.

dar=auf   hin=auf   Auf=lage
Haus=tür   dort=hin   aus=sehen

In simple words a division may be made before a single consonant between two vowels.

tra=gen   Lie=fe=rung   Ver=tei=lung
Träu=me=rei   Phy=sio=lo=gie   Li=te=ra=tur

The combinations ch, sch, st, ph, and th are never separated, unless they belong to different elements of a compound.

brau=chen   ger=ma=ni=schen   Fen=ster
wa=schen   Be=ste   Ko=sten

When two or more consonants other than the combinations just noted occur between vowels, usually only the last goes with the following vowel; but in words of foreign origin b, p, d, t, g, k, when followed by l or r, go with the next syllable.

Fort=bil=dung   kamp=fen   Re=pu=blic
Was=ser   Bi=bli=o=thek   Qua=drat
sel=ten   Fe=bru=ar

If a word is divided at ck the c should be changed to k.

schrecken, schrek=ken   Glocken, Glok=ken
Flicken, Flik=ken   rucken, ruk=ken

Three identical letters should not come together; therefore the form Schiffahrt is correct, not Schifffahrt. But if such a word as this is divided, the third letter should be restored:

    Schiffahrt, Schiff-fahrt   Schalloch, Schall-loch

Punctuation. Dependent clauses are always set off in German, no distinction being made between restrictive and nonrestrictive as in English. Therefore a comma is used before daß, der, die, das, welcher, womit, and other subordinate conjunctions, relative pronouns, and the like.

    Die Dame, die uns jetzt besucht, ist sehr reich.

A comma is used before ohne ... zu, um ... zu, and anstatt ... zu (all of which are followed by an infinitive).

    Er ging an mir vorbei, ohne etwas zu sagen.

A comma is ordinarily used before the coördinate conjunctions und and oder, provided the following clause contains both subject and verb.

    Die Luft ist blau, und die Felder sind grün.
    Er legte sich hin und schlief sogleich ein.

The word aber, meaning "however," is not set off by commas; no comma is used before und or oder in a series of words or phrases; or to separate month and year in dates.

    Der alte Mann aber verlor den Mut nicht.
    Karl, Fritz und Johann sind meine besten Freunde.
    6. August 1936.

No comma is used before usw.

Usually exclamation points are used after the salutations of letters and after commands.

    Lieber Vater!   Folgen Sie mir!

Quotation marks („   ") are used as in English, to enclose a direct quotation. A colon regularly precedes a quotation.

    Der Fuchs sprach: „Die Trauben sind mir zu sauer."

If a word or phrase is enclosed in quotation marks, the closing quotation marks should precede a period, a comma, or a semicolon that is required by the sentence at that point.

    Der „Gebirgspfarrer", der allerdings ähnlich wie „Germelshausen" ... das
    Trauerspiel „Eines Bürgers Recht"; das Volksdrama „Theophrastus
    Paracelsus".

A quotation within a quotation is marked by single quotation marks of the same font as the double quotes.

„Der ‚Gebirgspfarrer', der allerdings ähnlich wie ‚Germelshausen' ...

The apostrophe is used to denote the possessive only after proper names ending in s, ß, or z. In other cases s only is used.

Demosthenes' Reden   Schillers Gedichte
Horaz' Oden

The apostrophe is used to denote the elision of letters in ist's, geht's, hab' ich, and the like, but not when a preposition and das are merged or when the final e of the imperative singular of a verb is suppressed: ans, ins, durchs, fürs; komm! sag!

Italics. Italics are represented in German type by letterspacing. In spaced words the following letters should never be separated unless they belong to separate elements of a compound: ch, ck, st, ß, tz; but ff, fi, fl, ll, fi, and ss may be spaced. If the composition is in roman type, all but ß may be separated.

Denn a l l e , mit alleiniger Ausnahme der im deutschen und im öster= reichisch=hungarischen Heere noch heute vorgeschriebenen Schreibung K o m p a g n i e neben Kompanie, beseitigte n u r der „Buchdrucker= Duden".

Numbers. In numbers of four or more figures groups of three digits are set off from those on the left by either a thin space or a period. Instead of the English decimal point, German usage requires a comma.

200 000 or 200.000   2,50 rm.   76,5%

Superior figures referring to footnotes precede punctuation.

... eingegeben[1].

Ordinal numerals are indicated by using a period after the cardinal number.

1, ein, one   1., erste, first   2. Band, second volume

Dates. Several forms of writing dates are acceptable practice in German. For instance:

den 3. Mai 1930   d. 3. Mai 1930   3. M. 1930

Hyphen. In a series of compounds in which the common element is expressed only in the last of the series, the suppressed element is represented by a hyphen.

Käse=, Butter= und Milchvorräte, cheese, butter. and milk stores.

Accented letters. Roman accented letters are sometimes used with German type in such foreign words as *Café*.

Abbreviations. Abbreviations are used much more freely in German than in English. Following are some of the standard German abbreviations.

a., *akzeptiert*, accepted
A., *Acker*, acre
a. a. O., *am angeführten Orte*, in the place cited
Abh., *Abhandlungen*, transactions (of a society)
Abschn., *Abschnitt*, section
Abt., *Abteilung*, division
a. c., *anni currentis*, current year
A. G., *Aktiengesellschaft*, joint stock company
Anm., *Anmerkung*, note
Art., *Artikel*, article
A. T., *Altes Testament*, Old Testament
Aufl., *Auflage*, impression
Ausg., *Ausgabe*, edition
Bd., *Band*, volume; Bde., *Bände*, vols.
bearb., *bearbeitet*, edited, compiled, adapted
beif., beiflgd., *beifolgend*, (sent) herewith
beigeb., *beigebunden*, bound (in with something else)
bes., *besonders*, especially
bez., *bezüglich*, respecting
Bl., *Blatt*, newspaper
bzw., *beziehungsweise*, respectively
ca., *circa*, about
d. G., *durch Güte*, kindness of
dgl., *dergleichen*, such like, similar case
d. h., *das heiszt*, that is to say (i.e.)
d. i., *das ist*, that is
d. l. M., *des laufenden Monats*, of the current month
Dr., *Doktor*, Dr.
Dr. u. Vrl., *Druck und Verlag*, Publisher, printed and published by
D-Zug., *Durchgangs-Zug*, a through train
ebd., *ebenda* (ibid.)
E. M. K., *electromotorische Kraft*, electromotive force
eng., *englisch*, English
entspr., *entsprechend*, corresponding
Ew., *Euer*, your
Exz., *Excellenz*, Excellency
f., *folgende Seite*, next page
ff., *folgende*, following
F. f., *Fortsetzung folgt*, to be continued
Forts., *Fortsetzung*, continuation
fr., *franko*, postpaid; *frei*, free
Fr., *Frau*, Mrs.

Frhr., *Freiherr*, Baron
Frl., *Fräulein*, Miss
F. u. S. f., *Fortsetzung und Schluss folgen*, to be continued and concluded
geb., *geboren*, born; *gebunden*, bound
Geb., *Gebrüder*, brothers
ges., *gesammelte*, collected, compiled; *gesamt*, complete
Ges., *Gesellschaft*, company or society
Gesch., *Geschichte*, history
gest., *gestorben*, deceased
G. m. b. H., *Gesellschaft mit beschränkter Haftung*, corporation with limited
    liability
Gr. 8°, *Grossoktav*, large 8vo
g. u. v., *gerecht und vollkommen*, correct and complete
H., *Heft*, number or part (of a publication)
hl., *heilig*, holy
hrsg., *herausgegeben*, published
Hs., *Handschrift*, manuscript (*pl.* Hss.)
i. a., *im allgemeinen*, in general
i. A., *im Auftrage*, by order of
I. G., *Interessengemeinschaft*, amalgamation, trust
i. J., *im Jahre*, in the year
i. J. d. W., *im Jahre der Welt*, in the year of the world
I. K. H., *Ihre königliche Hoheit*, Her Royal Highness
Ing., *Ingenieur*, engineer
J., *Jahr*, year
Jahrg., *Jahrgang*, annual set
Kap., *Kapitel*, chapter
kgl., *königlich*, royal
Kl., *Klasse*, class
Lief., *Lieferung*, number
M., *Mark*, mark (coin)
m. E., *meines Erachtens*, in my opinion
M. E. Z., *Mitteleuropäische Zeit*, Middle European time
näml., *nämlich*, namely
n. Chr., *nach Christo*, anno Domini
n. F., *neue Folge*, new series
no., *netto*, net
Nr., *Nummer*, number
n. S., *nächste Seite*, next page
od., *oder*, or
o. W., *österreichische Wahrung*, Austrian currency
p. c., *pro centum*, per cent
Pf., *Pfennig*, penny
Pfd., *Pfund*, pound
Q., *Quadrat*, square
Rab., *Rabatt*, discount
resp., *respektiv*, respectively
Rm., *Reichsmark*, reichsmark (coin)

s., *siehe*, see

S., *Seite*, page

sämt., *sämtliche*, complete

sel., *selig*, deceased, late

Ser., *Serie*, series

S. M., *Seine Majestät*, His Majesty

s. o., *siehe oben*, see above

sog., *sogenannt*, so-called

Sp., *Spalte*, column

st., *statt*, instead of

St., *Stück*, each; *Sankt*, Saint

s. u., *siehe unten*, see below

Thlr., *Thaler*, dollar

u., *und*, and; *unter*, among

U., *Uhr*, clock, o'clock

u. a., *unter anderen*, among others; *und andere*, and others

u. a. m., *und andere mehr*, and others

u. A. w. g., *um Antwort wird gebeten*, an answer is requested

übers., *übersetzt*, translated

u. dgl., *und dergleichen*, and the like

unbest., *unbestimmt*, indefinite

usf., *und so fort*, and so on

usw., *und so weiter*, etc., and so forth

u. v. a., *und viele andere*, and many others

v. Chr., *vor Christus*, before Christ

v. d., *von der* (in names, as *J. v. d. Traum*, written in full *Julius von der Traum*)

verb., *verbessert*, improved, revised

verm., *vermehrt*, augmented

Ver. St., *Vereinigten Staaten*, U. S. A.

vgl., *vergleichen*, compare

v. H., *vom Hundert*, of the hundred

v. M., *vorigen Monats*, last month

v. o., *von oben*, from above

vorm., *vormittags*, in the forenoon, a.m.; *vormals*, formerly

v. u., *von unten*, from below

Wwe., *Witwe*, widow

Xr., *Kreuzer*, cruiser; *Kreutzer* (a coin)

z., *zur*, to the

Z., *Zeile*, line; *Zoll*, inch, toll

z. B., *zum Beispiel*, for example (e.g.)

Zf., *Zeitschrift*, periodical

z. T., *zum Teil*, partly, in part

Ztr., *Zentner*, hundredweight

zw., *zwischen*, between

z. Z., *zur Zeit*, at present, now

CLASSIC GREEK

The alphabet. The Greek language used twenty-four letters.

FORMS			NAMES	SOUNDS
	Italic	Roman		
A	α	α	alpha	a
B	ϐ β	β	beta	b
Γ	γ	γ	gamma	g
Δ	ϑ	δ	delta	d
E	ε	ε	epsilon	e short
Z	ζ	ζ	zeta	z
H	η	η	eta	e long
Θ	θ	θ	theta	th
I	ι	ι	iota	i
K	ϰ	κ	kappa	k, c
Λ	λ	λ	lambda	l
M	μ	μ	mu	m
N	ν	ν	nu	n
Ξ	ξ	ξ	xi	x
O	o	o	omicron	o short
Π	π	π	pi	p
P	ρ	ρ	rho	r
Σ	σ	σ ς	sigma	s
T	τ	τ	tau	t
Υ	υ	υ	upsilon	u
Φ	φ	φ	phi	ph
X	χ	χ	chi	ch
Ψ	ψ	ψ	psi	ps
Ω	ω	ω	omega	o long

The letters ϐ and ϑ are rare forms of the delta, and should not be used as symbols.

The letter σ is the sigma used at the beginning or in the middle of a word; ς is used at the end of a word.

Accents and aspirates. The accents and aspirates used in the Greek are as follows:

᾿ lenis (smooth breathing)	῎ lenis acute	῏ circumflex asper
῾ asper (rough breathing)	῍ lenis grave	¨ dieresis
´ acute	῞ asper acute	∴ dieresis acute
` grave	῝ asper grave	∵ dieresis grave
῀ circumflex	῟ circumflex lenis	

These are placed over small letters, in front of capitals. In diphthongs the breathing is placed over the second vowel. Care should be taken not to misread a lenis for an apostrophe, or vice versa.

The acute accent is used only upon one of the last three syllables of a word. An acute accent on the last syllable is changed to a grave accent when another accented word immediately follows it in the same clause. The circumflex accent may be used only on one of the last two syllables of a word. The grave accent may be used only on the last syllable. A dieresis is used over ι or υ to show that it is a separate letter, not part of a diphthong.

Subscript. The tiny *i* sometimes appearing under vowels is called the "subscript iota": καιρῷ

Diastole. The diastole, which looks like a comma, is placed between two letters, without spacing on either side. Its purpose is to distinguish certain words from other words of the same form: ὅ,τε, neuter of ὅστε, distinguished from ὅτε, conjunction.

Capitalization. The ancient Greeks used only capital letters; so when capitals and lower-case letters are used, the capitalization follows a practice established by modern editors, among whom there is some difference of opinion. Capitals are used for the following:

(1) The first word of a paragraph

(2) The first word of a stanza of poetry, but not for the first word of each line

(3) The first word of a sentence, as a rule

(4) The first word of a direct quotation

(5) Proper names

Punctuation. The sign of interrogation is a semicolon. The colon and semicolon are represented by an inverted period. The apostrophe is used to mark the omission of a vowel or diphthong; when this occurs at the end of a word, the ordinary spacing of the rest of the line is used before the word which immediately follows. As punctuation was not used by the ancient Greeks, modern editors generally follow English style (except for the interrogation mark, colon, and semicolon) when they insert it.

Divisions. When a word is divided at the end of a line, at least two letters should remain on the first line and no less than three letters should be carried over unless the lines are very short. Compounds should be divided according to their construction, prefixes and suffixes being kept intact. Great care must be used not to carry over a final consonant belonging to the first element, as, for example, the prefixes ἀμφ-, εἰσ-, κατ-, καθ-, προσ-, συγ-.

A Greek word has as many syllables as it has vowels or diphthongs. The following are the principal diphthongs in Greek:

αι	υι	ου
ει	αυ	ηυ
οι	ευ	

In a simple word a single consonant between vowels belongs with the vowel following it.

χαλε-πῶν   τού-τοις

A combination of consonants which can begin a word should not be separated. The following forty-one combinations should not be separated:

βδ,	θλ,	μν,	σμ,	φθ,
βλ,	θν,	πλ,	σπ,	φλ,
βρ,	θρ,	πν,	στ,	φν,
γλ,	κλ,	πρ,	σφ,	φρ,
γν,	κμ,	πτ,	σχ,	χθ,
γρ,	κν,	σβ,	τλ,	χλ,
δμ,	κρ,	σθ,	τμ,	χν,
δν,	κτ,	σκ,	τρ,	χρ,
δρ,				

Other combinations of consonants may be divided.

πολ-λάκις

Numbers. Numbers may be represented in Greek by the letters of the alphabet together with an accent mark placed after the letter or inverted before the letter. Three special characters are used; ς', called *stigma*, for 6; Ϙ', called *koppa*, for 90; and ϡ, called *sampi*, for 900. (Another symbol for 6 is the digamma F.)

CARDINAL NUMBERS

1 α'	9 θ'	17 ιζ'
2 β'	10 ι'	18 ιη'
3 γ'	11 ια'	19 ιθ'
4 δ'	12 ιβ'	20 κ'
5 ε'	13 ιγ'	21 κα'
6 ς'	14 ιδ'	22 κβ'
7 ζ'	15 ιε'	23 κγ'
8 η'	16 ις'	30 λ'

CARDINAL NUMBERS

40	μ′	500	φ′	4000	͵δ
50	ν′	600	χ′	5000	͵ε
60	ξ′	700	ψ′	6000	͵ς
70	ο′	800	ω′	7000	͵ζ
80	π′	900	ꙥ′	8000	͵η
90	ϛ′	1000	͵α	9000	͵θ
100	ρ′	1111	͵αρια′	10,000	͵ι
200	σ′	2000	͵β	20,000	͵κ
300	τ′	2222	͵βσκβ′	100,000	͵ρ
400	υ′	3000	͵γ		

HEBREW

The Hebrew alphabet and much useful information about Hebrew composition are presented in the *Manual of Foreign Languages,* by George F. von Ostermann. The third edition of this work was published by the Government Printing Office in Washington in 1936. *Printing,* by Charles T. Jacobi (London, George Bell & Sons, 1893), presents material on the subject. *The American Printer,* by Thomas MacKellar (MacKellar, Smiths & Jordan, 1882), might be found useful. Helpful likewise are the transliteration cards issued by the Library of Congress (obtainable from the Librarian for a very small fee).

HUNGARIAN

The alphabet. The Hungarian language uses twenty-three letters of the English alphabet, omitting *q, w,* and *x.* The following accented letters are used: *á, é, í, ó, ö, ő, ú, ü, ű.*

Capitalization. Capitals are used for proper nouns but not for adjectives derived from proper nouns; as, *budapesti, magyar.* In other details practice follows English usage.

Division. When a word is divided at the end of a line, at least three letters should be carried over unless the lines are very short. Compounds should be divided according to their construction, prefixes and suffixes being kept intact. A Hungarian word may be divided before a consonant standing between two vowels. The following combinations of consonants are inseparable and belong with a following vowel: *cs, cz, gy, ly, ny, sz, ty, zs.* Any other combination of two consonants may be separated.

If *sz* is doubled when a compound word is formed, the combination is abbreviated to *ssz*. A division of the compound at this point restores the original form: *hosszu, hosz-szu.*

Two vowels standing together may be separated.

The alphabet. The Italian alphabet is the same as the English, though *k, w,* and *x* are used only in words of foreign origin. The grave accent is used on monosyllabic words to distinguish them from similar words: è, *is;* e, *and;* nè, *nor;* ne, *thence.* The grave or the acute accent may be used to distinguish *-ío* and *-ía* from unstressed *-io* and *-ia* at the end of a word.

Capitalization. Capitals are not used so freely in Italian as in English. When in doubt, do not capitalize.

Proper names are capitalized, but not adjectives derived from proper names.

gli Stati Uniti mare Mediterraneo
nodo gordiano gotico

Names of the Deity are capitalized:

Nostro Signore Messia Spirito Santo

But note that the following are not capitalized as they would be in English:

papista religione cattolica
capo d'anno cristiano
giorno di Pasqua gesuita

Capitals are not used for the names of the months and the days of the week.

marzo, aprile sabato, domenica

(In the date line of letters the name of the month is sometimes capitalized: Napoli, 23 Ottobre, 1927.)

In the salutation of a letter only the first word and proper nouns are capitalized, in the complimentary close none are.

Nonna carissima dal tuo affezionatissimo nipote

Headings, titles, captions. In headings, book titles, and other matter set in capitals and lower case, ordinarily only the first word and proper names are capitalized.

Storia della letteratura italiana
Le più belle pagine di Giacomo Leopardi
Fondamenti di grafia fonetica secondo il sistema dell'Associazione fonetica internazionale

Names of periodicals may, however, be capitalized as in English.

Divisions. If it is necessary to divide a word, at least three letters should be carried over. A single consonant between two vowels belongs to the following vowel.

ta-vo-lino   pre-ci-pi-tare   pre-zi-o-sa-mente

Likewise *ch, gh, cl, fl, gl, pl, gn,* combinations of *s* plus consonant, and consonant plus *r.*

ca-sti-ghi   re-flet-tere   mi-gliore
in-chio-stro   bi-so-gno   re-pli-ca-zi-one

Exception: An *s* belonging to a prefix should not be separated from it.

dis-gra-zia   tras-porto

Double consonants may be divided.

frat-tanto   nar-rare   mag-gio
af-flitto   cac-cia   vec-chio
ac-qua   nac-que

If the first of two or more consonants in the middle of a word is *l, m, n,* or *r,* it belongs with the preceding vowel, and the other consonant or consonants go with the following.

tem-pra   ar-ti-gi-ano   esul-tanza

Two adjacent vowels should not be separated unless the second is accented.

geo-gra-fia   ma-e-stro

A division should not be made after an apostrophe.

al-l'aura   del-l'acqua

Punctuation. Italian punctuation usage resembles French more than English. The following may be noted.

Conversational matter is indicated by dashes (spaced); and in contrast to French practice, a dash follows a quoted speech if other matter follows in the same paragraph.

— Gelata. Il cavaliere non vorrebbe che bevessi acqua gelata, perchè mi disturba, ma non ci resisto! — e, ripresa la padronanza di sè stessa, con aria di lieve canzonatura:

— Ammira la mia fretta di tornare qua? Ebbene, sapevo che Lei domani ci lascia e non ho voluto mancare, mi perdona? al mio dovere.
— Quale?
— Quello di salutarla.
Aldo fece un gesto di sorpresa:
— Lo chiama dovere?
— Se non Le va, metta un altro vocabolo, per esempio . . . piacere.

Points of suspension are used to indicate a pause or interruption—three points if punctuation precedes, otherwise four points.

Abbreviations. Following are a few of the abbreviations commonly used in Italian.

a. C., *avanti Christo*, B.C.	magg., *maggiore*, major; *maggio*, May
a. D., *anno Domini*, A.D.	Med., *Medico*, Dr.
a. f., *anno futuro*, next year	Nº, *numero*, number
affmo, *affezionatissimo*, most affection-	nov., *novembre*, November
ately	N. S., *Nostro Signore*, Our Lord
a. p., *anno passato*, last year	On., *Onorevole*, Honorable
b. p., *buono per*, good for	ott., *ottobre*, October
cⁱᵃ, *compagnia*, company	p., *per*, for
cº, *compagno*, partner	pag., *pagina*, page
d. C., *dopo Cristo*, after Christ, A.D.	p. es., *per esempio*, e.g.
d. c., *da capo*, again	S. A., *Sua Altezza*, His (Her) Highness
dic., *dicembre*, December	scel., *scellino*, shilling
ecc., *eccetera*, etc.	S. E., *Sua Eccellenza*, His Excellency
ediz., *edizione*, edition	sett., *settembre*, September
es., *esempio*, example	sez., *sezione*, section
febb., *febbraio*, February	Sigg., *Signori*, Messrs.
ferr., *ferrovia*, railroad	Sign., *Signor*, Sir, Mr.
frat., *fratello*, brother	St., *San, Santo*, Saint
genn., *gennaio*, January	v/, *vostra*, your
jun., *juniore*, junior	v., *vedi*, see
L. it., *lire italiane*, Italian lire	V. S., *Vostra Signoria*, Your Honor

Ordinal numerals are represented by the cardinal numeral followed by a superior *o*: 1º, *primo*, first; 2º, *secondo*, second; etc.

LATIN

Capitalization. The Romans used only one style of letters; therefore when capitals and lower case are used in Latin, the capitalization follows a practice established by modern editors. Capitals are used for the following:

(1) The first word of a paragraph

(2) The first word of a stanza of poetry, but not for the first word of each line

(3) The first word of a sentence (usually)
(4) Proper nouns
(5) Proper adjectives

In headings and titles the usual practice is to capitalize the first word and proper nouns and proper adjectives.

Aristotle: *De generatione et corruptione*

Capitalization in the style of titles in English may sometimes be preferable.

Philosophiae Naturalis Principia Mathematica. Newton (London, 1686).

Divisions. When a word is divided at the end of a line, at least three letters should be carried over unless the lines are very short.

Compounds should be divided according to their construction, prefixes and suffixes being kept intact.

prod-est	con-ci-pio
ad-est	eius-modi

There are as many syllables in a Latin word as there are separate vowels and diphthongs. Diphthongs are *ae, au, oe, ei, eu, ui.*

In simple words a division may usually be made before a consonant standing between vowels.

vo-lat	pa-ter
ge-rit	di-li-gen-ter
me-ri-dies	tre-pi-da

Unless unavoidable, a division should not be made either before or after *x;* if necessary the *x* may be carried over to the next line.

dixe-rat	di-xe-rat	maxi-mus	ma-xi-mus

The combinations *qu* and *ch, ph,* and *th* are treated as single consonants. Doubled consonants like *tt* and *ss* may be divided.

mis-sus	ne-ces-sa-ri-is

A division may be made before the combinations *bl, br, ch, cl, cr, dl, dr, fl, fr, gh, gl, gr, pl, pr, th, tl, tr,* unless the second letter introduces the second part of a compound word.

vo-lu-cris	ab-rum-po
pa-tris	ad-la-tus

Usage varies when the following combinations of consonants are involved: *bd, ct, gn, mn, ps, pt, phth, st, str, thl, zm*. Some authorities divide before them; others separate them. The editor and proofreader should therefore be informed of the writer's preference.

Other combinations of two or more consonants may be separated after the first consonant.

mon-strum	quan-tum	ad-ven-tant
nar-cis-sus	re-fe-ren-dae	for-tu-na

NORWEGIAN

The alphabet. The Norwegian language—or languages, since Norway has two official languages, *riksmål* and *landsmål*—uses twenty-nine letters, the English alphabet with the addition of æ, ø or ö, and å or aa. In alphabeting, these letters usually follow *z*. The letters *c, q, w, x*, and *z* are used only in foreign words and proper nouns.

Capitalization. Proper nouns are capitalized, but not adjectives derived from them. The pronouns *De, Dem*, and *Deres* are capitalized. Names of the months and of the days of the week are not capitalized. In other respects English usage is followed.

Divisions. When a word is divided at the end of a line, at least three letters should be carried over unless the lines are very short. Compounds should be divided according to their construction, prefixes and suffixes being kept intact. A simple word may be divided before a consonant standing between vowels. Two or more consonants between vowels may be divided before the last consonant, except *sk, sp, st*, and *str*, which are inseparable and belong with a following vowel.

POLISH

The alphabet. The Polish language uses twenty-three letters of the English alphabet, *q, v*, and *x* being omitted. The following accented letters are used: ą, ć, ę, ł, ń, ó, ś, ź, ż.

There are six words of one letter each in Polish: *w*, in; *z*, with; *i*, and, also; *a*, and; *o*, about; *u*, by, at, among, with, near, in.

Divisions. When a word is divided at the end of a line, at least three letters should be carried over unless the lines are very short. Compounds should be divided according to their construction, prefixes and suffixes being kept intact. A word may be divided before a consonant standing between vowels. The following combinations of consonants are treated as single consonants: *ch, cz, dz, dź, dż, rz, sz*, and *szcz, zd, dg*. Other combinations of consonants may be divided. The following combinations of consonants and vowels may not be divided: *bi, fi, gi, gie, ki, kie, mi, ni, pi,* and *wi.*

Punctuation. Punctuation is practically the same as in English.

The alphabet. The Portuguese language uses the English alphabet, but *k* appears only in foreign words, and *w* and *y* are rarely used. The tilde or til in Portuguese represents a nasalized vowel and is written over the first vowel of a diphthong, as in São Paulo, pronounced *soun powlõo.*

Divisions. When a word is divided at the end of a line, at least three letters should be carried over unless the lines are very short. A word may be divided before a consonant standing between vowels. The following combinations of consonants standing between vowels belong with the following vowel: *bl, br, ch, cl, cr, ct, dl, dr, fl, fr, gl, gn, gr, gu, lh, nh, ph, pl, pr, ps, pt, qu, sc, sp, st, th, tl, tr, vl, vr.*

Following a consonant *st* may be separated.

de-mons-tra-ção   cons-ti-tui-ção

Other combinations than the above may be separated. No division should be made between two vowels. The triphthongs *eia, éia, eão, ião, oei* should not be divided.

Russian is ordinarily written and printed in the Cyrillic alphabet. The alphabet and much useful information regarding the language and its composition are presented in George F. von Ostermann's *Manual of Foreign Languages* (U. S. Government Printing Office, 1936) and in the *Manual of Style* of the United States Government Printing Office. Also helpful are the transliteration cards for Russian issued by the Library of Congress, obtainable from the Librarian for a small fee.

Russian book and magazine titles transliterated into English are usually capitalized like English titles: *Vestnik Psychologii, Kriminalnoi Antropologii i Pedologii.*

A word may be divided before a single consonant standing between vowels. The following combinations of consonants are indivisible: *bl, ml, pl, st, str, stv, tch, shch.* Other combinations of consonants may be divided after the first consonant. The components of compound words should be kept intact; the following prefixes should not be divided: *bez, chrez, do, no, ne, ot, pere, pre, raz, vie, voz, za.*

SPANISH

The alphabet. The Spanish language uses all the letters of the English alphabet. In addition it has the double letters *ch*, *ll*, and *rr*, and the *ñ*, which in alphabeting follow *c*, *l*, *r*, and *n* respectively.

Accents. The acute accent is used to indicate a stressed syllable and to distinguish words otherwise identical in form but of different meaning or use.

mas	*but*	más	*more*	solo	*alone*	sólo	*only*
este	*this*	éste	*this one*	se	*himself*	sé	*I know*
tu	*thy*	tú	*thou*	el	*the*	él	*he*
te	*thee*	té	*tea*	de	*of*	dé	*give*
mi	*my*	mí	*me*	si	*if*	sí	*yes*

The following are written with an acute accent whenever they are used in an exclamation or a question.

¡cómo!	¿cuándo?	¿dónde?	¡qué!
¡cuál!	¡cuánto!	¿por qué?	¿quién?

The dieresis is used over *u* in the syllables *gue* and *gui* when the *u* is not silent but pronounced.

Capitalization. Capitals are used somewhat less than in English. They are used for the following:

(1) Proper names

el Mar Cantábrico   el Océano Atlantico   el Nuevo Mundo

(2) Names of the Deity

(3) Sobriquets

el Gran Capitán   el Caballero de la Triste Figura

(4) Titles of honor

Vuestra Alteza

(5) The first word and proper names in salutations of letters

Muy señor mío: Muy distinguida señora:

Note that an abbreviation used here is capitalized:

Muy Sres. míos:

Capitals are not used for the following:

(1) Names of the months and of the days of the week

marzo, abril   25 de junio de 1924

(2) Titles, unless they are abbreviated or form part of a place name.

Sí, señor   el señor don Enrique Palava
Sr. Palava   la avenida del Conde de Peñalver

(3) Proper adjectives or nouns derived from proper names

el idioma castellana   los jóvenes americanos
Los chinos hablan y leen el chino.

Headings and captions.   In headings, captions, titles of books, and the like, only the first word and proper nouns are capitalized.

El caballo del moro   *Antología de poesía española*
Las novelas ejemplares   Vista general de la ciudad de Valparaiso

La Alhambra: Interior de la Torre de la Cautiva
Secure the phonograph records of "La golondrina" and "La paloma."

Names of periodicals are usually capitalized:

El señor Norton [1] escribe artículos para "La Revista de Filología Española."

Punctuation.   Punctuation marks are used in Spanish very much as in English, but the following practices should be noted.

A question in Spanish is enclosed in question marks, the first one inverted and placed before the interrogative word beginning the question.   Exclamations are punctuated similarly.

Si no escribe a su padre ¿ qué ocurre?
Pero, ¿cómo podremos entrar aquí?
El sereno canta: ¡ Las once en punto y sereno!

Note that quotation marks are considered unnecessary in the third example.

If a sentence is both exclamatory and interrogative, the inverted exclamation point should be used at the beginning and the question mark at the end.

¡Usted se atreve a hablarme así?   (Do you dare to speak to me in that way?)
Es engaño.
¡ El Rey procurar mi daño,
Solo, embozado y sin gente?

Spanish quotation marks differ from English quotes: « »   They are used to mark quotations but not to enclose dialogue.

« Cortesía » significa « urbanidad ».
. . . y le dió permiso « para explorar, conquistar, pacificar y colonizar » el oeste de la costa sudamericana . . .

[1] Note that the definite article is always used before titles except in direct address, unless the title is *don, doña, san, santo,* or *santa.*

Dialogue is indicated by dashes, not by quotation marks.

—¿Qué tienes tú ahora?—rugió el maestro.   —A ti no te toca todavía leer
¡ Silencio!

— Pero, profesor—gimoteó el nino; —mire Vd. ¡Aquí vienen en el párrafo que
tendré que leer esos mismos tres hombres terribles!

Note that the end of the spoken words is marked by a dash when other
words follow in the same paragraph. Each change of speaker should be
indicated by a new paragraph.

English quotation marks are sometimes used:

Comedias de cautivos: "El trato de Argel," "El gallardo español," "Los baños de
Argel," "La gran sultana."

Points of suspension. Points of suspension are three points, set close together (a single type in some fonts), without any space at the left. They are
used in Spanish text much as dashes are used in English—to mark an interruption or a pause or an abrupt change in thought or construction.

¿Qué espero?   ¡Oh, amor gigante!...   ¿En qué dudo?...   Honor ¿qué es
esto?...

Divisions. Whenever it is necessary to divide a Spanish word at the end
of a line, carrying over a part, the following principles should be observed.
No fewer than three letters should be carried over unless the measure is very
narrow.

In simple words a single consonant between two vowels belongs with the
following vowel. The double letters *ch, ll,* and *rr* are considered as simple
consonants. The letter *y* standing between vowels is treated as a consonant.

ho-nor	co-che	ca-lle
ate-rido	mu-cha-cho	ca-rro
ca-ñón	ga-llina	re-yes

Prefixes and suffixes form separate syllables.

des-ampara	sub-inspección	super-abundante

Likewise: es-otros, nos-otros, vos-otros.

The letters *l* and *r* preceded by a consonant, except *rl, sl, tl,* and *sr,* must
not be separated from it, except to preserve a prefix intact.

ta-bla	sa-cro	con-tra-po-ner
bi-blio-teca	pu-drir	sub-lu-nar
si-glo	pa-la-bra	sub-ra-yar

Other combinations of consonants may be divided, including *cc* and **nn**, the only two consonants besides *ll* and *rr* which are ever doubled.

ex-cepto	at-lán-tico	sig-ni-fi-ca-ción
ac-tual-mente	de-sig-nar	avan-zar

The letter *s* does not combine with a following consonant.

cons-pi-ra-dor	ins-pi-rar	trans-fi-gu-rar
es-ca-lera	cons-tante	abs-ti-nen-cia
es-tar	pers-pi-ca-cia	ads-cri-to
Exception: ist-mo		

Division between vowels should be avoided, though if necessary two strong vowels (*a, e, o*), or an accented vowel and a strong vowel, may be separated. Other combinations of vowels form inseparable diphthongs or triphthongs.

Abbreviations. Abbreviations are used very freely in Spanish composition. In addition to the usual abbreviations of English—such as those of months, days, titles, weights and measures, coins, street, avenue, chapter, article, page— abbreviations for phrases used often in letters are in common use. For instance, note the following used to conclude letters:

B.S.M., *beso sus manos,* with great respect
S.S.S., *su seguro servidor,* your faithful servant

Likewise:

S.A.S.S., *su atento y seguro servidor*
Su atto., afmo. y s. s., *su atento, afectísimo y seguro servidor*

Similarly, in the salutations of letters:

Muy Sres. n/s, *or* Muy Sres. nuestros, *Muy señores nuestros*

The custom has been to use a great many superior letters in abbreviations, just as English did in Colonial days and before. These, of course, are hard to set in type and are being used much less than formerly. Instead of *Ag^to* we now see *Agto.; afmo.* has replaced *af^mo,* and so on.

The following abbreviations are commonly used in Spanish:

@, *arroba;* @@, *arrobas* (Spanish weight—about 25 lb.; Spanish measure—about 4 gal.)
A., *autor,* author; *plural,* AA.
ab., *abad,* abbot

a/c., *a cuenta,* on account
A. C. *or* A. de C., *Año de Cristo,* a.d.
a/f., *a favor de,* in behalf of
afmo., *afectísimo,* most affectionate
ap., *aparte,* aside; *apóstol,* apostle
apda., *apreciada,* valued
art., *artículo,* article
Avda., *avenida,* avenue
B., *beato,* blessed
B.L.M., *beso la mano* (I kiss your hand), respectfully
B. p., *Bendicion papal,* papal benediction
B.S.M., *beso sus manos,* with great respect
Br. *or* br., *bachiller,* Bachelor
c. *or* cap., *capítulo,* chapter
c^a, c^{ia}, *or* compa., *companía,* company
C. A., *Centroamérica,* Central America
C. de J., *Companía de Jesus,* Society of Jesús (S.J.)
c/l., *curso legal,* legal procedure
cllo., *cuartillo* (a unit of measure)
C.M.B., *cuyas manos beso,* very respectfully
col., *columna,* column
C.P.B., *cuyos pies beso,* very respectfully
cps., *compañeros,* partners
cta., *cuenta,* account
ctmo., *céntimo,* centime; *centésimo,* hundredth
ctvo., *centavo,* cent
c/u., *cada uno,* every one, each
D., *don,* Mr.
DD., *doctores,* Drs.
D. F., *Distrito Federal,* Federal District
EE. UU., *or* E.U., *Estados Unidos,* United States
E.P.M., *en propia mano,* in his own hand
E.S.M., *estrecho su mano,* I press your hand
est., *estimada,* respected, esteemed
E.U.A., *Estados Unidos de América,* U.S.A.
F.C., *ferrocarril,* railroad; *plural,* FF. CC.
fha., *fecha,* enacted
fra., *factura,* invoice of merchandise
fvda., *favorecida,* esteemed
G., *gracia,* favor
Gral., *general,* general
hh., *hojas,* leaves
Hnos., *hermanos,* brothers
L., Lic., Lcdo., *licenciado,* licensed
l., *ley,* law; *libro,* book
lin., *línea,* line
L.S., *lugar del sello,* place of the seal
Mons., *Monseñor,* Monsignor

m/m., *más o menos,* more or less

m/n., *moneda nacional,* national currency

n., *noche,* night

n.a., *nota del autor,* author's note

No., *or* núm., *número,* number

P., *peso; padre,* Father

pág., *página,* page; *plural,* págs.

pár., *párrafo,* paragraph

p/cta., *por cuenta,* on account

P.D., *posdata,* postcript

pdo., *pasado,* past

p. ej., *por ejemplo,* for example

P. O., *por orden,* by order

p. pdo., *próximo pasado,* preceding

P. R., Puerto Rico

P.S.M., *por su mandato,* by his orders

pta., *peseta* (a Spanish coin); *plural,* ptas.

pte., *parte,* part

Q.E.G.E., *que en gloria esté,* deceased

Q.E.P.D., *que en paz descanse,* deceased

r., real (coin); *plural,* rs.

R. A., *República Argentina,* Argentine Republic

S. A., *Sudamérica,* South America; *Su Alteza,* His Highness; *Sociedad Anónima,* stock company

S. E., *Su Excelencia,* His Excellency

sec., *sección,* section

S.M., *Su Majestad,* His Majesty

Sr., *señor,* sir

Sra., *señora,* lady

Sres., *señores,* sirs

Srio., *secretario,* secretary

Srta., *señorita,* young lady

Sto., *Santo,* saint

tom., *tomo,* volume

tip., *tipografía,* printing office

tít., *título,* title

U. *or* Ud., *usted,* you; *plural,* UU. *or* Uds.

últ., *último,* last

v., *véase,* see

V., *usted,* you; *vale,* bond, promissory note, I O U

v. *or* verso., *versículo,* verse

V. A., *Vuestra Alteza,* Your Highness

V. B., *visto bueno.* (The preceding document has been examined and found to be correct; consequently it may signify: Pay the bearer; Let him *or* the merchandise pass.)

v/c, *vuelta de correo,* return mail

vda., *viuda,* widow

V.E., *Vuestra Excelencia,* Your Excellency

v.g. *or* v. gr., *verbi gracia*, for instance
V. M., *Vuestra Majestad*, Your Majesty
Vm. *or* Vmd., *Vuestra Merced*, Your Worship
VV., Vds., *ustedes*, you (*plural*)

Ordinal numerals are expressed by using a superior *o* following the cardinal numeral: 1°, *primero;* 2°, *segundo;* etc.

SWEDISH

The alphabet. The Swedish language uses twenty-nine letters, the English alphabet with the addition of *å, ä,* and *ö.* These three letters are usually alphabeted in this order following *z.*

Capitalization. Proper nouns are capitalized, but not adjectives derived from them. Names of the months and of the days of the week are not capitalized: söndag, måndag.

Divisions. When a word is divided at the end of a line, at least three letters should be carried over unless the lines are very short. Compounds should be divided according to their construction, prefixes and suffixes kept intact. A Swedish word may be divided before a consonant standing between two vowels. The combinations *sch* and *sk* used for the sound *sj* are never separated and belong with a following vowel; *ng* always belongs to a preceding vowel unless *n* and *g* belong to different parts of a compound word

mar-schera   manni-ska

When any other two or more consonants stand between vowels, a division may be made before the last.

PHONETICS

Our alphabet was taken from the Romans, who got it in turn from the Greeks. Of the six vowels used by the Greeks, however, the Romans took only five: *a* as in *bar, e* as in *obey, i* as in *machine, o* as in *note,* and *u* as in *rude.* As a result of growth and of changes in spoken English, each of these vowels came to represent many different sounds besides the original one. Note, for instance, the sound of *a* in the following words: *late, chaotic, bare, add, infant, was, talk, sofa.*

When a need arose for closer indication of sound, diacritical marks were adopted; and by means of them dictionary makers have for many years represented the various sounds of the vowels and of those consonants—like *c* and *g*—that have more than one pronunciation. (The various dictionaries have not chosen the same symbols to represent given sounds. Therefore, when pronunciation of a word is being looked up, it is advisable to refer to the key words at the foot of the dictionary page.)

To students of language, however, diacritical marks were not satisfactory as indicators of sound. They desired a new alphabet, internationally uniform, in which one sign or letter should represent only one sound, and each sound should be represented by only one symbol. In 1888 the International Phonetic Association devised and endorsed such an alphabet, the International Phonetic Alphabet, which is now in general use (with various modifications) for phonetic transcription of speech. Typical symbols used for English are as follows:

PHONETIC SYMBOLS

Vowels

Sound	Symbol	Example
a as in—		
father	[ɑ]	[fɑðə]
ask	[a]	[ask]
at	[æ]	[æt]
pale	[eɪ]	[peɪl]
air	[ɛə]	[ɛə]
sofa	[ə]	[sofə]
all, law	[ɔ]	[ɔl]
e as in—		
end	[ɛ]	[ɛnd]
eve	[i]	[iv]
fear	[ɪə]	[fɪə]
i as in—		
ice	[aɪ]	[aɪs]
it	[ɪ]	[ɪt]
o as in—		
own	[oʊ]	[oʊn]
obey	[o]	[obeɪ]
song	[ɒ]	[sɒŋ]
four	[ɔə]	[fɔə]
u as in—		
up	[ʌ]	[ʌp]
sure	[ʊə]	[ʃʊə]
pull	[ʊ]	[pʊl]
mute	[ɪu]	[mɪut]
use	[ju]	[juz] (*v.*)

Other Vowel Sounds

Sound	Symbol	Example
o as in *word* *i* as in *fir* *u* as in *burn*	[ɜ]	[fɜ]
ou as in *house* *ow* as in *owl*	[aʊ]	[aʊl]
oi as in *oil*	[ɔɪ]	[ɔɪl]
oo as in *look* *u* as in *pull*	[ʊ]	[lʊk]
oo as in *do, ooze*	[u]	[du] [uz]
oo as in *poor* *u* as in *sure*	[ʊə]	[ʃʊə]
ea as in *bear* *e* as in *there*	[ɛə]	[bɛə]

Consonants

b as in *be, rob*	[b]	[bi]
c as in *cost*	[k]	[kɒst]
c as in *cell*	[s]	[sɛl]
ch as in *church*	[tʃ]	[tʃɜtʃ]
d as in *do, nod*	[d]	[du]
f as in *fat, stuff*	[f]	[fæt]
g as in *girl*	[g]	[gɜl]
g as in *gem*	[dʒ]	[dʒɛm]
h as in *hue*	[h]	[hju]
j as in *judge*	[dʒ]	[dʒʌdʒ]
k as in *kit*	[k]	[kɪt]
l as in *lie*	[l]	[laɪ]
m as in *man*	[m]	[mæn]
n as in *net*	[n]	[nɛt]
ng as in *ring*	[ŋ]	[ɹɪŋ]
p as in *pair*	[p]	[pɛə]
r as in *red*	[ɹ]	[ɹɛd]
s as in *soil*	[s]	[sɔɪl]
sh as in *shawl*	[ʃ]	[ʃɔl]
t as in *tea*	[t]	[ti]
th as in *thin*	[θ]	[θɪn]
th as in *then*	[ð]	[ðɛn]

Consonants

Sound	Symbol	Example
v as in *vise*	[v]	[vaɪs]
w as in *wit*	[w]	[wɪt]
wh as in *what*	[ʍ]	[ʍɒt]
x as in *box*	[ks]	[bɒks]
y as in *yes*	[j]	[jɛs]
z as in *zebra*	[z]	[zibɹə]
z as in *azure*	[ʒ]	[æʒə]

In addition to the above letter symbols the following signs are used:

A colon, preferably ː, after a symbol indicates that its sound is lengthened as compared with that of the unmarked symbol.

One dot, ˑ, is the sign of partial lengthening.

Stress is indicated by ˈ, secondary stress by ˌ, each of these accents being placed before the stressed syllable: buccaneer, ˌbʌkəˈnɪə.

A breve above a symbol indicates that the sound is unstressed: ĭ

A dot or a short vertical line under an *l, m, n,* or *r* indicates that the sound forms a syllable: bætl̩

Modifiers are signs indicating slight shifts in the position of the tongue.

Low modifier, ⊤   Front modifier, ˧

High modifier, ⊥   Back modifier, ⊢

The following are used under letters

. breath   ͓ specially open vowel

ˇ voice   ⊓ dental articulation

. specially close vowel   ͝ labialization

Note the following:

High level pitch	ā	High falling	à
Low level pitch	a̲	Low falling	a̩
High rising	á	Rise-fall	á̂
Low rising	a̗	Fall-rise	a̰

PART V—GRAMMAR

MAIN DIVISIONS

Since questions of grammar are bound to arise at almost any point in the long journey of a work from manuscript to printed page, the following section has been added to enable one to detect many of the most common errors and some of the less usual ones. The rules given are those that seem to be most often misunderstood or violated. Since most of the examples actually came to the reader's desk in faulty form, they show the kind of errors writers are most likely to make. No author is immune to the danger of making mistakes, and problems of correctness rise in the day's work of even the most experienced literary worker.

(Some of the examples bear the labels "Wrong," "Right," etc., and others require no special designation, being sufficiently explained in the text. Italics are sometimes used to call attention to certain parts of the examples, but when not really needed they are omitted. Frequently italics are used in the first example of a series for the sake of clarity, but omitted in subsequent examples in the same group.)

VERBS

Verbs show five changes of form: voice, mood, tense, person, and number. Common errors in the use of each of these forms are the subject of the following sections.

VOICE

The active voice asserts that the person or thing represented by the subject does something; the passive asserts that the subject is acted upon. The passive voice is formed by adding the past participle of a verb to the proper form of the verb *to be:* for example, *is called, was called, has been called, may be called, will be called.* Although the passive has legitimate uses, it is a weak voice, more likely to be used effectively in exposition than in narration. The ordinary use of the passive is seen in the following:

> The number originally assigned should be kept. The final numbering is determined by the chief illustrator after the finished drawings have been made. If new illustrations are prepared, they will be designated temporarily by fractions.

Where directness and vigor are desired, try the active voice first (the passive *may* be required for parallelism or some other reason).

> *Weak:* His procrastination showed that will power was lacking in him.
> *Better:* His procrastination showed that he lacked will power.
> *Weak:* Everything that was done by us that day was a waste of time.
> *Better:* Everything we did that day was a waste of time.

The editor should note and correct awkward passive expressions. The proofreader would scarcely be permitted even to query them.

> *Weak:* Useful wild animals known to the Indians were made known to the early explorers, and the "salt licks" which buffalo and other animals had sought out were likewise told about by the Indians.
> *Better:* The Indians told the early explorers about useful wild animals and about the "salt licks" which buffalo and other animals had sought out.
> *Poor:* This was not suitable for many purposes as was the puddled iron, and the older methods have still continued to be used.
> *Better:* . . . the older methods are still in use.

Especially to be criticized is a sudden shift from active to passive.

> *Poor:* We visited the museum, where many famous statues were seen.
> *Better:* We visited the museum, where we saw many famous statues.
> *Poor:* Such a book costs so little, and so much is learned from it.
> *Better:* Such a book costs so little and teaches so much.
> *Poor:* Stand on a book with the toes extending over its front edge. The toes are then bent up and down as far as they will go.
> *Better:* . . . Then bend the toes up and down as far as they will go.

MOOD

Mood refers to the form of the verb indicating the manner of doing or being. The moods usually recognized are the indicative, the subjunctive, and the imperative. The infinitive is sometimes called a mood, as are certain verb phrases: those formed with *may, might, can, could* being called the potential; with *should, would* the conditional; with *must, ought* the obligative.

The subjunctive. The verbs in the subordinate clauses in the following sentences are correctly used subjunctive forms.

He gave orders that the bills *be* paid.
It is important that the air which he breathes *be* fresh.
It is thus the insistent admonition of the wise men and of the elders that man *learn* the limitations of his own powers.
How can one insure that the power of Science *be* used for the benefit of man?
Nor is it necessary that the side chain containing the hydroxyl *occupy* a specific position.

The subjunctive is preserved in certain traditional phrases and idioms.

Far be it from me.	Be that as it may.
So be it.	Come what may.

The subjunctive is used to express a wish, or a condition improbable or contrary to fact. A clause expressing contingency may have a subjunctive form, but here the indicative often seems more consistent with modern usage.

Janet wished bitterly that her brother *were* (not indicative *was*) near to comfort her.
If some such device as this *were* (not indicative *was*) not used, every time sex cells united, the number of chromosomes would be doubled.

Many clauses introduced by *if* express neither a contrary-to-fact condition nor contingency but merely a condition, and it is in such clauses that the subjunctive is most often used incorrectly.

Wrong: If he were found guilty, he was probably outlawed.

This is merely a statement of fact in the past, and an indicative verb should be used.

If he was found guilty, he was outlawed.
Better yet, use its English equivalent if there *is* one.   (Not subjunctive *be one.*)
Oceans and lakes, if there *are* such (not *be* such) on Mercury, are composed of molten metals.
Next I looked to see if the ground *was* clear.   (Not *were* clear.)
The inexperienced singer, if he *is* (not subjunctive *be*) a good reader of English, will learn.

Clauses introduced by *as if* or *as though* usually express an unreal or contrary-to-fact condition and require a past subjunctive verb.

Some patients feel as if they were falling.

Many locutions in which the subjunctive would once have been the better choice of form now seem stilted and old-fashioned. The following sentences, for instance, would now be expressed by indicative forms.

> More of the juices will be drawn out into the water if the meat *is* (not subjunctive *be*) cut in small pieces.
>
> Instructors mark a paper unsatisfactory for numerous errors in form, even though it *is* (not subjunctive *be*) good in substance and thought.

Infinitives. English idiom is often violated by using an infinitive instead of a participle or a gerund or some other construction.

> *Unidiomatic:* These foods seem to have the property to prevent and cure rickets.
> *Correct idiom:* property of preventing.
> *Unidiomatic:* They needed a simple method to keep their trading accounts.
> *Correct idiom:* method of keeping.
> *Unidiomatic:* Water transportation of heavy articles costs less than to send them by railroad or truck.
> *Correct idiom:* costs less than sending.

Errors of this sort seem often to arise from confusion of constructions of synonymous words. For instance, the verb *help* may be followed by an infinitive, but *aid* may not.[1]

> The discussions have helped to crystallize points of view.
> The discussions have aided in crystallizing points of view.
> *Similarly:* forbidden to do, prohibited from doing; right to deliver, privilege of delivering; eager to return, desirous of returning; obliges one to keep, necessitates one's keeping.

There are many more expressions similar to these.

Shift of mood. A common error in syntax is a shift in mood.

> *Imperative to indicative:* Map the territory carefully, and you are also to note its topographical peculiarities.
> *Better:* Map the territory carefully and also note its peculiarities.
> *Subjunctive to indicative:* Whether their experience be unusual, or is only thought so by them they are not excused from the ordinary sanctions of morality.
> *Better:* Whether their experience is unusual, or is only thought so by them, . . .
> *Subjunctive to indicative:* If the terms of the invoice were stated 2/10, n/30, it would mean that 2% discount off the amount of the invoice would be allowed by the seller if the invoice is paid within ten days of its date.
> *Better:* . . . if the invoice were paid within ten days.

[1] See also Fowler's *Modern English Usage,* article Analogy.

The present tense. The present tense is used to express action in the present, a state existing in the present, habitual or customary action, a general truth. Idiomatically, it is used to express future action.

He is working in the garden.
He travels by bus.
Winters in this part of the country are very cold.
The ship sails next Tuesday.

The present tense is sometimes used in relating an event that occurred in the past. Though this is legitimate and effective usage on occasion, writers in this form are often inconsistent. (In the following example all verbs after the first should be in the present tense.)

> *Inconsistent:* Did you ever sit in on a ball game in the last half of the ninth—the score tied? The home team is up to bat. Two outs, three balls and the bases full! Oh, boy! You held your breath as the pitcher wound up. Then a vicious crack—and no, it can't be possible! Wait! You're grabbing on to the seat—then you let loose with a roar and the crowd went crazy. Man, it was a home run—four men in and it was all over.

The simple form *is* is sometimes incorrectly used for the progressive form *is being*.

> *Poor:* Up to the period of depression in which this is written the balance has been favorable.
> *Better:* Up to the period in which this is being written . . .

The expressions *that is to say* and *the fact is* are idiomatically used with a sentence in the past tense. *Is reported, is said,* and the like are correct, rather than *was said*.

That is to say, he had now made up his mind.
The fact is that the Americans themselves had again and again supplied the corroborating information.
It was on this occasion that the General is reported to have said . . .
Beyond was an empty shop—empty, that is, except for hats of all sorts and sizes.

The future and future perfect tenses. The future tense indicates action in the future. It is often misused for the future perfect tense, which indicates an action completed before a time in the future.

Soon a large body of knowledge *will have been* built up. (Not *will be* built up.)
In March I *shall have been* out here five years. (Not *shall be*.)

[1] On this subject of tense, especially, the student should read one or more of the books listed in the bibliography; for instance, George O. Curme's *Syntax* (Boston, D. C. Heath & Co., 1931), pp. 354–372.

Past tenses. The simple past tense is used to express action begun and completed in the past.

> The modern fair had its origin back in those times.
> They represent forms that lived and died long ago. (Not *have lived.*)
> We got our money's worth long ago. (Not *have gotten.*)

The present perfect tense is used to express action beginning in the past and continuing to the present; or an action that has already come to pass at the time of speaking.

> *Wrong:* From the time of Palestrina to the present day, Italian composers did not use so many folk songs in their works as the French and Germans did.
> *Right:* . . . Italian composers have not used . . .
> *Wrong:* Since that time the Roman arts became imitative.
> *Right:* Since that time the Roman arts have become imitative.
> *Or:* After that time the Roman arts became imitative.

Sequence of tenses. Proper sequence of tenses requires that time relationships be accurately expressed.

The present participle represents action at the time expressed by the principal verb; the past participle, action prior to that of the principal verb.

> It is an heirloom, *having been* first owned by my great-grandfather. (Not *being* first owned.)
> Having completed this work, he began another. (Not *completing* this work.)

The present infinitive is used for a statement true at the time of the principal verb. Violations of this rule are frequent with the verb *like*.

> If Lincoln *had lived long enough to have* a part in the reconstruction of the South . . . (Not *lived long enough to have had.*)
> It *might have been* to the interest of the Americans *to be* a little more ready themselves to forget recent disagreements. (Not *might have been* to their interest *to have been.*)
> How Ray *would have liked to range* alongside and wave a greeting to his comrades! (Not *would liked to have ranged.*)

The general rule of sequence is to use a past tense form in a dependent clause when the governing proposition has a past tense form.

> The witness said his name was Tom Jones and that he lived at 60 Summer Street. (Not *lives,* even if he does now live there.)
> This led them to believe that the earth was a sphere.

This rule is often not observed in expressing a statement equally true in the past and in the present: [2]

We were told in school that water boils at 212 degrees.
The speaker said that oak makes the best flooring.
Columbus proved that the earth is round.

The writers who used *is* in the following sentences evidently had confusedly in mind this rule about universally true statements; but these are not examples of the rule. The verbs are not dependent and each sentence expresses a fact in the past.

Tell the story of the life of Captain John Smith. What was (not *is*) his chief literary work?
The printing press was (not *is*) perhaps the greatest invention of the latter part of the Middle Ages.
Little Palestine was (not *is*) the birthplace of Christianity.

Always consider the tense of a dependent verb form in relation to the time expressed in the verb upon which it depends.

Wrong: How would natural conditions be affected if water continued to contract until it freezes.
Right . . . until it froze.
Wrong: The affirmative would probably argue that wherever the flag goes it should carry with it citizenship and equal treatment, and that if people who have received United States citizenship should decide later that they preferred not to have it, that would be their lookout.
Right: . . . should decide that they prefer not to have it, that will be their lookout.
Wrong: Were it not for the silent seaplanes bobbing at their tethers, the liner would have borne the appearance of an ordinary transatlantic steamship.
Right: Had it not been for . . .

Sometimes the subordinate verb fixes the time and the principal verb requires correction.

Wrong: If the unexpired subscriptions had amounted to $80,000, instead of $20,000, the adjusting entry would take the following form.
Right: . . . the adjusting entry would have taken the following form.

AUXILIARIES

An auxiliary verb is one used with another verb to indicate voice, mood, and tense. The auxiliaries are *be, can, do, have, may, must, ought, shall, will,* and their conjugational forms. They are often misused.

[2] Since the correct form is not always easily perceived or beyond question, the proofreader should exercise care in suggesting a change of tense.

"Can," "could," etc. With a governing verb in the present use *can, shall, will, may;* with one in the past, use *could, should, would, might.*

> The witness further testified that it was his intention to continue to serve water to all consumers until such time as a mutual company *might be organized.* (Not *may be organized.*)
>
> If we looked the remainder of our lives we might never find two that were identical in every respect. (Not *are identical.*)

Would in the main clause should be followed by *could,* not *can; will* should be followed by *will,* not *would.*

> Plan how you would combine a wheel and axle, a pulley, and an inclined plane so that a man using a 150-pound force *could overcome* a resistance of 60,000 pounds. (Not *can overcome.*)
>
> He will be able to raise money only on his personal property and credit, which *will be limited.* (Not *would be limited.*)

Could in an *if*-clause should be followed by *would,* not *will.*

> Even if he could secure such men, the salaries he *would have to pay* would in many cases be so high as to eat up the profits. (Not *will have to pay.*)

Can, could, will, and *would* should never follow *in order that.*

> In order that the teacher *may be able to use* any textbook . . . (Not *can use.*)
>
> In order that she *may go,* he is hiring a substitute. (Not *can go.*)

"Do." *Do* is a general-utility auxiliary in English, having uses hardly paralleled in other languages. It is used with another verb to intensify the meaning, and it is often used as a substitute for another verb. The latter usage is carried very far.

> You do snore (even though you say you do not).
>
> She did do it.
>
> He lied, though he says he didn't.

The use of *do have, does have,* for *have, has,* is accepted by some authorities, considered dubious by others. Here the *do* is not emphatic and is really unnecessary. The usage is, however, found in very good writers.

> We do not have the key pages.
>
> Do any of you have an aquarium?

Misuse of *did* for *has, have* should not be allowed to pass in written English.

> *Has* he come yet? *Has* it rained yet? *Have* you got yours yet? (Not *Did* he come yet? etc.)

"Shall" and "will." The auxiliaries *shall, will, should,* and *would* are used with verbs to express simple futurity and determination. No doubt the distinctions formerly made between *shall* and *will* are breaking down and are little observed in popular speech. Nevertheless the distinctions are taught in schools and are observed by most careful writers.

(1) In a declarative sentence simple futurity or mere expectation is expressed by *shall* (or *should*) in the first person, *will* (or *would*) in the second and third persons.

I shall (he will, they will, etc.) go next week.
I was afraid that I should be unable to come.
The odds are that we shall never do it at all.
We should hardly expect a tropical region to have much industry.
The forests, as you would expect, are peopled sparsely.
He found out how to design new auditoriums so that they would have just the right reverberation.

The word *one* is considered a third-person pronoun and is followed by *will* (or *would*) to express simple futurity.

The winter temperatures are milder than one would expect.
One would like to arrange the theaters of the world in exhibition.

(2) In a declarative or an imperative sentence, determination, threat, command, willingness, and promise on the part of the speaker are expressed by *will* (or *would*) in the first person, *shall* (or *should*) in the second and third.

I will (you shall, he shall) go next week.
A final *vote shall* be taken to allocate power and choose *who shall* wield it.
He shall make restitution.
All *bills shall* be sent to the Committee on Revision and Printing.
It is for them to determine when the *conversations shall* stop.

(3) In a question *shall* (or *should*) is used with the first person except when anticipating a reply or repeating a question addressed to the speaker. With a subject in the second or third person the correct auxiliary in a question is that which will be used in the answer.

Where shall we go now?
When will I find Mr. Clarkson here?
Will I do it for you? Why, certainly.
Shall you be warm enough?
Will you finish this for me?
Will you come again? *or* Shall you come again?
What should you expect to find true of the commercial value?

(4) In an indirect quotation the auxiliary should be that which would properly be used if the quotation were direct.

> He sometimes said that he should be better off if he were to stop smoking entirely. ("I should be better off if . . .")
> He told us that we would be sorry if we failed to visit it. ("You will be sorry if you fail to visit it.")

Should is also used in the sense of obligation and *would* in the sense of habitual behavior.

> A child should not be asked before the meal what he would like to eat.
> He would run away whenever my back was turned.

AGREEMENT

(Except in a few instances only correct forms are given in the following examples, although many of these sentences were incorrectly written or printed.)

General rule.   The rule of agreement is that in a sentence every part should agree logically with every other related part.   A verb, therefore, should agree in number with its subject.

> *One* of the serious results that come from the experience through which this country has been passing *is* loss of faith.
> The *Stars and Stripes was* floating above us.
> There *has been many a* benevolent dictator.
> *More than one* book by this author *has* been cited.

The rule of course holds if the subject follows the verb.

> The Normans, under which general term *are* comprehended the *Danes, Norwegians,* and *Swedes,* were accustomed to rapine and slaughter.
> What *signify* good *opinions* unless they are attended by good conduct?
> What type of veining *have most* of the long grasses?
> Where *are* the *Khyber Pass* and *Mount Everest?*

The general rule is simple, but determining the number of the subject is sometimes much less simple, as study of the following sections will show.

Some mistakes occur through failure to recognize a subject as plural. (See also Collective nouns, p. 366; also p. 525 in the Appendix.)

> Existing *data prove* that . . .

The number of the subject is sometimes obscured by words coming between it and the verb.

> The *list* of broadcasters thus selected *is* arranged in alphabetical order.
> The *extent* to which motor-driven vehicles and tractor-drawn farm machinery are being used on American farms *is* apt to lead . . .

An appositive does not change the number of the subject.

Our side, the Tigers, is ahead.
In this study the assumptions, the measuring stick, are placed clearly before the reader.

The number of the subject and verb is not affected by intervening words introduced by *with, together with, including, as well as, no less than,* and similar expressions.

The farmer's happiness as well as his profits arises from being a part of a neighborhood instead of being merely a resident in it.
The load of ore, together with the consignment of pig iron, was delivered on time.
The rhyming no less than the meter of the poem is amateurish.
All living things, and therefore protoplasm, are composed of these substances. . . .
Broth does not ferment or decay if the air, and consequently germs in the air, is excluded.

Writers sometimes use these phrases where a simple *and* would be better because the thought is plural. Editors and proofreaders should think of this when they come upon one of them followed by a plural verb when the simple subject is singular.

Poor: Heart disease, together with cancer, kidney diseases, and apoplexy are almost entirely diseases of middle life and older periods.
Better: Heart disease, kidney diseases, and apoplexy are . . .
Poor: This zygote, with the hyphae which develop from it, probably represent the diploid stage.
Better: This zygote and the hyphae which develop from it represent . . .

The word *plus* seems usually to be considered like *with* rather than like *and.*

The *metal* plus the oxygen *weighs* more.
Erosion Plus Dust *Ruins* Area Size of Kansas [Hdg.]

Singular substantives joined by "and." A subject consisting of two or more substantives joined by *and* requires a plural verb.

The *casting* of the line *and distribution* of the matrices *are* done automatically and do not interfere with the operation of the keyboard.
To understand them and to enjoy them require a certain degree of talent.
Whether the Commission will set high standards and whether the courts will support the Commission remain to be seen.

Sometimes the *and* is not expressed.

His face, his eye, were hardening to the crisis.

The proofreader should not be misled by punctuation which makes a plural subject appear to be a singular subject and a parenthetical phrase.

> The great diversity of the risks covered, and the complex nature of the business, introduce production problems of an unusual character.
>
> How the minstrel and his people spy on the boy, and how the young fellow succeeds in finding a happy home after running away from them, are told in an interesting manner.

With two nouns connected by *and* a singular verb may be used if the thought is definitely singular, as in the expressions "end and aim," "sum and substance," "wish and hope," "hue and cry," "name and address." Many writers stretch the rule too far, as might be considered true of the last two examples below.

> Beating and counting the different kinds of measure is interesting and helpful practice for any chorus.
>
> As the hand and arm of the conductor pictures the singing of the phrase, . . .
>
> Accord and satisfaction was not allowed until modern times as a means of discharging a judgment debt. (*Law*.)
>
> The invention and development of the vacuum tube has revolutionized the transmission of radio waves.
>
> This awakening and stimulating of the imagination results in emotional reaction.

Singular substantives joined by "or" or "nor." A subject consisting of two or more singular substantives joined by *or* or *nor* requires a singular verb.

> One or the other of the boys has been here.
>
> When sickness, infirmity, or reverse of fortune affects us, the sincerity of friendship is proved.
>
> Biting threads or cracking nuts with the teeth is an injurious practice.
>
> Neither tomb nor monument is needed.
>
> Salt or baking soda or a mixture of both possesses all the cleansing qualities of most toothpastes.

When the proofreader comes upon a plural verb following *or* and a singular noun, he should consider whether the real error may not be in the use of *or* instead of *and,* rather than in the number of the verb. (*And* should be substituted for the italicized *or* in each of the following examples.)

> *Wrong:* Water, potato water, *or* milk are the liquids commonly used in making yeast breads.
>
> *Wrong:* Ether *or* acetone vaporize very readily, while mercury *or* glycerin, which boil at much higher temperatures, have . . .
>
> *Wrong:* When kerosene and a soap solution in water are violently shaken, the kerosene divides into colloidal-sized particles. The whipping of cream, beating of egg-whites, *or* mixing of mayonnaise are the same in principle.
>
> *Wrong:* Individuals *or* information opposed to time-honored beliefs were exceedingly unwelcome.

Plural and singular substantives joined by "or" or "nor." When a subject is composed of both plural and singular substantives joined by *or* or *nor,* the verb should agree with the nearer.

Neither money nor men were lacking.
Neither the national Constitution nor the national statutes undertake to prescribe any comprehensive regulations.
Squalls nor storms nor burning sun takes the pleasure out of sailing for me.
Others are due to the fear that their interests or their property is being threatened.

Likewise when the subject contains the correlatives *not only . . . but also,* the verb agrees with the nearer substantive.

Not only the children but the mother was ill.

Positive and negative subjects. When a negative subject is joined to a positive one, the verb should agree with the positive.

It is Mary, and not her brothers, who drives the car.
Not Mary but her brothers drive the car.
Accuracy and not speed is the more important.

"Each," "every," etc. *Each, every, either, neither, anyone, anybody, every one, everybody, someone, somebody, no one, nobody, one,* and *a person* call for a singular verb.

Each plant and animal has its peculiar character.
Is either of these candidates worthy of our support?
Every leaf, every twig, every drop of water, teems with life.
No one but schoolmaster and schoolboys knows . . .
The regions in which each of these is found in greatest abundance are shown on the map.

When a singular verb following *each* seems awkward, it may be that *each* is misplaced, as it is in the following.

Poor: Paul has divided his garden so that two plots each make .25 of the whole garden and five plots each makes .1 of the garden.
Better: Paul has divided his garden so that each of two plots makes .25 of the whole garden and each of five plots makes .1 of the garden.

When the subject is really plural, *each* before the verb often needs to be transposed to follow the verb.

Poor: John, Bob, and Harold each have 15 marbles.
Better: John, Bob, and Harold have 15 marbles each.
Poor: The upper and lower anteriors each has only one canal.
Better: The upper and lower anteriors have only one canal each.

In other cases the meaning would be more accurately conveyed by *both*.

Poor: Thorium and actinium each gives a series of similar disintegration products.
Better: Both thorium and actinium give a series of similar products.

Sometimes the error is in using *each* at all.

Poor: Each of the symbols C, H, and O stand for atoms of carbon, hydrogen, and oxygen.
Better: The symbols C, H, and O stand for atoms of carbon, hydrogen, and oxygen.

"None." *None* may be construed as either singular or plural, according to the thought to be conveyed: "no amount" (when the following noun is singular), or "no individuals" (when the following noun is plural).

None of the fruit was eaten.
None of the volcanoes in Chile are active.

When the meaning is "not one," it is better to use *not one* than *none* with a singular verb.

Not one of the guests has arrived.

Collective nouns. A collective noun takes a singular verb unless the individuals forming the group are to be emphasized.

His family has just moved in. Are your family well?
The committee adheres to its decision. The committee have signed their names to the report.
The American Government continues confident. His Majesty's Government are resolved to assist.
The Infantry was detraining.
Counsel are of the opinion . . .
This people has become a great nation. A conquered people rarely are efficient producers.
Practical cultivation of health is what the youth need in these critical years.
Black specks marked the spot where a herd of buffalo were lying.

Similarly, if the subject of a sentence is a group of words that conveys the idea of a number of individuals, the verb may or should be plural even though the governing noun is singular.

A racial majority of the population are . . .
Only a fraction of the total species of any given period are likely to leave recognizable fossil traces.
A whole galaxy of poets have celebrated the divine maiden snatched away to dwell in the underworld.
A wide range of bacterial phenomena are involved.
A considerable series of them are available.

Such groups of words are sometimes pitfalls for the proofreader who is not alert to meaning, for in groups that look like these the noun is not always used in a collective sense.

> What is the highest percentage? What percentage of speeches spread on the Congressional Record are actually made in Congress?
> An average of fifteen for the month is about as good as one can expect. An average of fifteen men have been employed during the month.
> A combination of numbers and letters at the left corresponds to the Dewey Decimal System. A combination of factors were responsible.
> Another group of substances has been discovered. The group of words introduced by a preposition always act together as a unit to modify some other part of the sentence.
> The number of relationships involved is enormous. An unreasonable number of boards have grown up in most states.

Subjects plural in form but singular in effect. The expression of a singular idea may look like a plural; a singular verb should follow.

> Penal Acts was the legal name, Intolerable Acts what the colonists called them.
> Caesar's *Commentaries on the Gallic War* is a model of historical writing.
> "Cedar mountains" refers to the cedars of Lebanon in northern Syria, and "silver mountains" suggests the Taurus range.
> Taps was blown.

The number of the verb in numerical statements depends upon the intention of the subject; that is, whether the number named is thought of as a whole or distributively.

> Seven times nine is sixty-three.
> Five sixths of Spain is highlands.
> Four years is too long a time to spend in college.
> There was six feet of water in the hold.
> Forty inches of air space filters out almost all the short waves.
> Four fifths of the words in common use are of Anglo-Saxon origin.
> Millions of dollars were lost by the citizens of America.

Gerunds. A gerund used as the subject of a sentence should be followed by a singular verb.

> Greasing pans aids cookies.
> Depressing prices brings depression.
> Changing attitudes is an essential part of it. But such changing of attitudes is merely an external manifestation.

Relative clauses. The verb in a relative clause agrees with the antecedent of the relative pronoun, which is the nearest noun or pronoun and often is the object of a preposition, as in the phrase *one of those who, one of the things which.*

> Recall here again one of the sayings that follow the title page of this book.
> He is one of those men who talk much and think little.
> An argument was one of the diversions which were always welcomed by a cowboy.

The following is not an example of the construction above.

> Ask one of your classmates who knows the correct forms to listen as you read.
> (Ask one who knows.)

Expletives. After introductory *here* and *there* a singular verb is usually preferred when the logical subject consists of substantives joined by *and,* the first one singular in number; to this there are frequent exceptions, such as the last two examples below.

> There is always one or more who is not stupid.
> There is an outgoing baggage window and an incoming baggage window.
> There was one Jute, three Saxon, and four Angle kingdoms.
> The sun had set three hours before, but there was no moon and no stars.
> Here come Williamson and Friedberg.
> There were, besides, the owner and his son.

"What." *What,* unless it clearly has a plural antecedent, as in the third example below, equals *that which* or *the thing that* and should be followed by a singular verb.

> They journeyed through what is now the Dakotas.
> What is perhaps of greater immediate interest to the chemist is variations of the thiazole structure.
> My people were what were known as "God-fearing folk."

Predicate nouns. A verb should agree with its subject, not with its predicate noun, or complement.

> *One* of the most important things in the North *is* the feet of dogs and men.
> The night *sounds* of strange swamp creatures *were* the only thing that broke the stillness.
> The *Assamese are* an agricultural people of mixed race.
> The *dagger* you lost *and* the missing *weapon are* one and the same.
> *All* you told me about *was* the dangers.

In sentences like the last example above the complement may be felt so strongly to be the real subject that a plural verb may be used.

> All you told me about were the dangers.

Sometimes grammatical correctness can be secured only by rewording the sentence.

Problem: The way a patient feels and looks are also important indications of illness.

Better: A patient's feelings and appearance are also important indications of illness.

Agreement in person. A verb must agree in person with its subject.

You have been with our dear friend.
Thou hast a wit of thine own.

The Quakers and some others use *thee* as a nominative in the second person with verb forms of the third person.

Is thee going? Does thee feel well today?

When the subject consists of pronouns of different persons joined by *or* or *nor,* the verb agrees in person with the nearer.

Neither you nor I am concerned.
I or you are the person who must undertake the business proposed.

Since a relative pronoun agrees in person with its antecedent, the verb in the clause introduced by the pronoun should be of the person of the antecedent.

I, who am older, know better.
You, who are stronger, should be the one to go.

In sentences beginning with the indefinite subject *it* and completed by a relative clause the verb in the relative clause should be of the same person as the noun or pronoun that follows the principal verb. Do not confuse such sentences with those beginning with a pronoun.

It is I that am going. It is I who am hurt.
I am the one who is going.

NOUNS

It is fortunate that nouns do not have special forms for the objective case. The difficulties connected with number of nouns and with the possessive forms are quite enough for one part of speech.

NUMBER

Accord. The number of nouns or pronouns should be in accord throughout a sentence.

On the backs of the hands. (Not *back of the hands*.)
Read the questions one at a time, find the answers, and write them out briefly.
The bars tapered to a sharp point at one end and bore on their heavier end the name of Arthur Firman.

The above rule does not apply to *wall* in the sentence below, which is a use of synecdoche, a common figure of speech.

Copies of these famous pictures hang upon the wall of almost every schoolroom.

Singular with a plural possessive. To avoid ambiguity a singular noun is often used with a plural possessive when only one of the things possessed could belong to each individual.

Manufacturing helps many people in the smaller cities to earn their living.
Forbes knew most of them by their first name.
Some of them could not pay their rent.
They eyed each other furtively and cursed beneath their breath.
Many concrete verbs really carry their own adverbs on their back, both naming and describing the action.
Four pilots crashed to their death.

Similarly:

Think of the last name of five pupils in the room.
The steam line ruptured, causing the death of seven stevedores.
They doubled their efforts to discover the identity of two men who struck a man with their automobile and then fled.

Care must be taken not to apply the rule to the wrong noun.

Wrong: It is pretty clear that the smile on the *face* of Stalin and Hitler, whenever they look at each other, is not a sincere one.
Right: . . . on the faces of Stalin and Hitler. (*Smile* is the noun the rule applies to.)

"Kind," "sort." *Kind, sort, type, class, quality, brand, breed, species, size, variety,* and similar words are singular nouns with plurals regularly formed and used. The singular forms should therefore be modified by *this* and *that*, not *these* and *those*.

The singular forms of these words may be followed by a plural verb if individuals, rather than a class, are in mind.

This variety is hardy.
That make is most popular.
This variety are everbearing.
That breed are good watchdogs.

Expressions using *kind of, sort of,* etc., should preferably be in the singular, unless the plural idea is strong.

What breed of dog would you select for a quiet girl?
What type of cat appeals most to you?
The variety of clam most used is called Little Neck.
The kind of variation on which Darwin depended was the minute modifications everywhere evident.
The variations employed in survival are a particular kind of variation that are of hereditary significance from the start.
What kind of transactions decrease the proprietorship?
What does the table show regarding concerns making very high profits? What kind of concerns are they?
This is the magma of which the cone type of volcanic mountains are generally made.

The common error is failure to stick to the number selected.

Inconsistent: The kind of apple we grow keeps well if they are separately wrapped.
Better: The kind of apple we grow keeps well if each apple is separately wrapped.
Inconsistent: This kind of cats are native to Egypt, but it is common in America.
Better: This kind of cats are native to Egypt, but they are common in America.

The following would be better expressed entirely in the singular.

Inconsistent: Waterless cookers are really a type of pressure cooker which depends . . .
Better: A waterless cooker is really a type of pressure cooker which depends . . .
Inconsistent: The owls are a sort of self-appointed night watchman who discover and eat great quantities of mice.
Better: The owl is a sort of self-appointed night watchman who discovers and eats great quantities of mice.

After the plural forms *kinds of, types of,* etc., a singular or a plural noun may be used.

What kinds of illustrations are used?
The types of geological formation which are likely to contain oil . . .
There are 80 different sizes of offset presses.

POSSESSIVE CASE [1]

Inanimate objects. It is usually awkward to attribute possession to inanimate objects; an *of* phrase is preferable.

The management of the farm. (Rather than *the farm's management.*)
Start treatment at the first sign of the presence of the malady. (Rather than *malady's presence.*)

[1] For Formation of the Possessive Case see p. 512.

There are many exceptions, however, particularly expressions designating time or measure.

two weeks' vacation	six weeks' patrol
ten hours' start	a stone's throw
three days' session	several pounds' weight
five minutes' walk	ten thousand dollars' worth

These are not true possessives and are sometimes expressed by using hyphenated adjectives.

a ten-hour start	a three-day session

In some expressions similar to these the idea of possession is so remote that the apostrophe seems unnecessary, and the tendency is to omit it, construing the phrase as a noun with a compound adjective.

A two weeks waiting period is found in the laws of Alabama.
Oregon demands sixty days notice.
They offer ten thousand dollars reward.
He had manufactured the myth of the six months verdict.
At 30 inches pressure the boiling point is slightly above 212° F.
They consider the requests made by their foreign customers for three months, six months, and nine months time as unreasonable.

State prison, state rights, state's attorney, state's evidence, teachers college, units' column, tens' column, are preferred forms.

The apostrophe is frequently omitted in the names of organizations, buildings, etc., where the idea of possession seems obvious. Whether the omission is intentional or occurs through carelessness, the proofreader can only follow copy unless he knows certainly that the omission is an error.

Farmers Loan and Trust Company	Peoples Savings Bank
St. Elizabeths Hospital	

Possessive with an appositive. An awkward construction which editors should change if possible is the use of an appositive with a noun in the possessive case. If the object possessed is named, the apostrophe should be used only after the appositive. If, however, the object is not mentioned and the appositive ends the sentence, being explanatory or emphatic in nature rather than restrictive, the sign of possession should be used on the first noun.

My teacher, Mr. Smith's, book.
Your estimable employer, Mr. Tawney's, private domain.
A voice spoke. It sounded like Mason's, the city editor.
He promised to have dinner at her aunt's, Mrs. Timothy Eldredge.

Double possessive. When the thing possessed is only one of a number belonging to the possessor, both the possessive case and *of* are used.

a friend of my brother's   a book of Ginn's
. . . who, as a devoted friend of Darwin's, employed . . .

Possessive with a gerund. In sentences like the following, in which a phrase containing a noun or pronoun and a participle is used as the object of a preposition, the participle may be construed as a noun (a gerund) and the preceding noun made a possessive, or it may be construed as a modifier of the noun. The idea of possession is much stronger in some sentences than in others, and sometimes failure to use a possessive might give the sentence a meaning different from that intended. The last example below is such a sentence: "the lady wearing pearls" would convey a different thought from "the lady's wearing pearls."

What do you think of my horse's running away today?
It does not follow from a word's being given as OF that it is obsolete.
An entire meal can be served without anyone's leaving the table.
I object to the lady's wearing pearls.

PRONOUNS

CASE

The personal pronouns and the relative *who* have declensional forms to indicate case, and these in some constructions cause difficulty.

The subject of a verb should be in the nominative case.

In all that big theater there was only he and she.
It is not fit for such as we (are) to sit with the rulers of the land.
Is he as capable as she (is)?
Americans are as courageous as they (are).

An expression like *he says, you believe, she supposed, we pretend, it was thought,* etc., between the relative pronoun *who* and its verb does not change the case of the pronoun. Such parenthetical phrases are usually set off by commas.

Give the vocation of a person who you believe attained success.
Listen carefully to those who you have reason to believe know how to express themselves in well-chosen terms.

Whom is often misused for *who* because of failure to realize that the relative pronoun is the subject of the following verb, not the object of the preceding preposition or verb; the whole relative clause is the object.

I will exchange snapshots with *whoever writes.*
They should punish *whoever is found* to be guilty.
He was questioned as to *who* on his committee *was* to be given the position.

The object of a verb should be in the objective case.

Whom shall you appoint?
He is the freeman whom the truth makes free.
I should consider him more capable than her. (. . . than I should consider her.)
As a result, the company is unable to know whom it may be insuring.
Gentle reader, let you and me, in like manner, endeavor . . .
Ganowi eyed contemptuously him who had once been a swift killer.

Substantives connected by any form of the verb *to be* should agree in case. It should be remembered that the subject of an infinitive is in the objective case. Any doubt about the correct form can usually be cleared up by transposing the sentence.

What is he? Is it they? It is I.[1]
If it had been we, how the tongues would have wagged!
Who did you think it was?
They declared the culprit to be him and no other. (They declared him to be the culprit.)
The man whom I thought to be my friend deceived me. (I thought him to be.)
Whom do you suppose him to be? (You suppose him to be whom?)

The object of a preposition should be in the objective case.

Between you and me . . .
Some of us fellows went fishing.
All went but me. None but me was able to come.
The man whom the committee agreed on was younger than any one of them.
Whom, by the way, do you think they have gone with?

An appositive should be in the same case as the noun with which it is in apposition.

All are going—she, he, and we two.
He spoke to some of us—namely, her and me.
We all met—she, the officer, they you mentioned, and I.

The dative is not often used. An example is the familiar expression "Woe is me," literally, "Woe is unto me."

[1] "It is me" may be accepted for colloquial use but should be avoided in formal writing.

Since a pronoun is a word used in place of a noun to avoid repeating the noun, the word it replaces, its "antecedent," must be expressed or clearly understood, and with this antecedent the pronoun should agree in person and number.

Doubtful reference. The following sentences violate the rule that the antecedent of a pronoun should never be in doubt.

> Dirt and bacteria will not cling to rayons, nor are *they* affected by mildews.
>
> The Phoenicians seized the treasure in the temple of Apollo and hired mercenaries to defend *themselves.*
>
> Heracles' tasks began while he was very young. Hera, the wife of Zeus, was jealous of *his* mother, so she sent two large serpents to destroy *him.*
>
> As discoverers and pioneers pressed on to found new settlements *they* were always made close to streams of pure water.
>
> "In all my years of experience with shoplifters," declares a certain well known individual, who has spent a dozen of *them* as chief detective . . .
>
> Walt Disney's new picture is about a baby elephant. He has never made a better *one.*

Double reference. The same pronoun should not be used to refer to different antecedents in the same sentence, nor in the same paragraph unless the context makes the antecedent quite clear. The following sentences are incorrect.

> When the baby is done drinking *it* must be unscrewed and laid under a faucet. If *it* does not thrive on fresh milk, *it* must be boiled.
>
> They became close friends and when Bigelow was released *he* asked for Ward's parole so that *he* might work in his company.

Relative pronouns. A relative pronoun refers to its nearest antecedent. The following sentences are examples of vague or faulty reference.

> Vitamins are substances contained in various foods which are essential for growth, development, and other physiologic processes.
>
> Occasionally he would recall the fact that Mrs. Durward was in reality a woman of over forty, mother of a grown-up son, who according to all the usages of custom should be settling down into the drab and placid backwater of middle age.

"It." More often than other pronouns, *it* is used without a clear antecedent. Faulty sentences like the following are common.

> How many people were living in South Dakota when *it* was organized as a state? How does *it* compare with the present population?

When the total number of government workers who should be classed as administrators are lumped together, *it* reaches staggering proportions.

It is well to mention in passing that the continuous creation of slang terms is part of the natural process of language making, that *it* is often forceful and picturesque, and that slang expressions frequently rise to be acceptable colloquialisms.

Use of *it* with indefinite reference as in the following sentence is not accepted in written English.

It says in the book that the incident took place in 1643.

Much too often writers omit the pronoun *it* in places where correct interpretation of the sentence requires it. The following sentences illustrate this fault.

Stir *it* until *it* is thick and then turn over. (. . . turn it over.)
If your new underwear pricks you, turn inside out. (. . . turn it inside out.)
If this test is not conclusive, add a few drops of saturated ammonium oxalate solution and stand aside to settle for a few minutes. (. . . stand it aside to settle for a few minutes.)

The use in one sentence of pronoun *it* and expletive *it* should be avoided.

When the sun was out *it* was warm, but when *it* disappeared *it* became chilly.

The writer of the following did not understand the expletive use of *it*.

Wrong: Through the blackness moved a woman. She was Hilda, the housekeeper.
Right: . . . *It* was Hilda.

"They." The use of *they* as an indefinite pronoun is established colloquially and is not uncommon in literary usage. However, if another locution is equally expressive, it should be used because it is less open to criticism.

In the polar regions they do not worry about the common cold.
Poor: Why do they add copper to both silver and gold when these metals are prepared for commercial use?
Better: Why is copper added to both silver and gold?
Poor: If the design is one which they call a simple pattern, an attachment can be added to the regular loom.
Better: If the design is one which is called a simple pattern . . .

"This," "these." The antecedent of *this* or *these* should always be grammatically clear.

Antecedent in doubt: A thousand industries need such basic data on which to build progress. *This* is one purpose of the Bureau of Standards.
Better: A thousand industries need such basic data on which to build progress. *Providing these data* is one purpose of the Bureau of Standards.

Number. A pronoun should agree with its antecedent in number.

How can a tree (or any other green plant for that matter) develop into the great bulk that *it has?* (Not *they have.*)

Each of the calculations is introduced in a real setting, so that the pupil may be aware of its importance. (Not *their importance.*)

One should watch his step. (Not *their step.*)

Everyone kept his ticket. (Not *their tickets.*)[1]

A singular subject may look like a plural.

Read *Kent's Commentaries. It* will furnish you with a clear statement of the doctrine.

A pronoun referring to singular antecedents connected by *or* or *nor* should be singular.

Mary or Jane has lost *her* book.

A pronoun referring to a plural and a singular antecedent connected by *or* or *nor* should be plural.

Neither the members of the team nor the coach will give an inkling of *their* plans.

A pronoun referring to a collective noun should be singular unless the individuals forming the group are to be emphasized.

The crowd surged aside. Then *it* gasped and held *its* breath.

. . . advise the public how to protect *itself* against pickpockets.

He pulled a tangle of rawhide thongs out of the tub where *they* had been soaking.

A wise teacher never does for a class what *they* can do for themselves.

The error most often seen in this connection is a shift in number, as illustrated by the following sentences. In each, *their* should be *its,* unless the verb is changed to plural.

The committee *adds* to *their* report.

The race still *keeps* some traits of *their* barbarian forefathers.

The School for Printers' Apprentices *is* giving *their* spring dance at the Hotel St. Regis.

Drake Hotel *pays their* bill of September 6. Robinson Mfg. Co. *pays their* invoice of September 9.

[1] The use of *everyone* . . . *they* is defended on historical grounds, for the expression was used by Samuel Johnson, Jane Austen, and various other famous authors. Its reputableness is in dispute, however, and it is avoided by careful writers.

Gender. The gender of successive pronouns referring to the same antecedent should be the same for all.

Wrong: After a time the butterfly comes out of *its* chrysalis shell. *It* clings to the shell, spreading and stretching *his* wings until they are dried and strengthened.

Right: The butterfly comes out of its chrysalis shell. It clings to the shell, spreading its wings . . .

It is conventional to use *his* when both sexes are referred to, though of course *his or her* is hardly open to objection except as laborious.

Each student must give me *his* book before tomorrow noon.

In reading lyric poetry, each boy and girl must chart *his* own course.

Many a man and woman has an absorbing interest in a subject that brings *him* no material profits.

Person. Consistency should be maintained.

Thou shalt be required to lie down in death, to go to the bar of God, and give up *thy* account. (Not *your account.*)

Wrong: If *the members* of the club will consult the legal department, *you* will be given complete legal advice on matters pertaining to ownership and operation of *your* car.

Right: If the members of the club will consult the legal department, they will be given complete legal advice on matters pertaining to ownership and operation of their car.

Reflexive pronouns. The reflexive pronouns *myself, yourself, himself,* etc., should not be used needlessly in written English for *I, me, you,* etc.

My wife and I will go. (Not *My wife and myself.*)

This is for you. (Not *for yourself.*)

You and your family must be on board by nine o'clock. (Not *yourself and . . .*)

The minister rebuked my brother and me. (Not *my brother and myself.*)

Reflexive pronouns should be so placed in the sentence that they refer to the proper noun.

Wrong: Each of these cities is an interesting study in geography itself.

Right: Each of these cities is itself an interesting study in geography.

Editorial forms. In speaking editorially, or in regal and formal style, the forms *we, our,* and *ourself* may be used for *I, my, myself.*

. . . who sends this to delight *our* heart and stimulate *our* mind.

We're old enough *ourself* to remember it.

Writers sometimes avoid the pronoun *I* by using *the writer* or *the author*. In so doing they need to be particularly careful that the reference is clearly to themselves and not to another writer. *I* and *the writer* should not be used interchangeably.

"Each other," "one another." School handbooks of style insist that *each other* is properly used only of two; *one another*, of more than two. *Each other* has, however, been used of more than two since Anglo-Saxon times. In current literary usage the distinction is nevertheless generally observed.

"Either," "any one." "You may choose either of the two or any one of the three." Authorities are not agreed about the distinction. For three hundred years *either* has been used of more than two and is still occasionally so used by good writers.

"Anyone," "everyone," "someone." These indefinite pronouns must be carefully distinguished in use from *any one, every one, some one;* they should never be set as single words unless they are equivalent to *anybody, everybody, somebody*.

She would not see anyone.
You may have any one of these books you choose.
You must decide upon some one course.
Every one of these items should interest everyone.

ADJECTIVES AND ADVERBS

Adjectives and adverbs are grouped together in this discussion because both are modifiers, because both have positive, comparative, and superlative forms, and because errors in their use often arise from a failure to perceive that a noun is being qualified, not a verb, adjective, or adverb.

Numerous words can be used as either adjectives or adverbs and can be distinguished only by their function in the sentence; for instance,

best	early	hourly	low	short
better	fair	ill	much	slow
cheap	fast	just	near	soft
clean	first	late	pretty	straight
close	friendly	likely	quick	very
daily	full	little	right	well
deep	hard	long	scholarly	wide
direct	high	loud	sharp	wrong

Predicate adjectives. Verbs pertaining to the senses (*be, become, feel, seem, smell, sound, taste*) are followed by an adjective unless they mean action.

That is easy, seems rough, feels soft, smells sweet, sounds harsh, tastes sour.
I feel bad, fine, happy, etc.

Other verbs may be followed by an adjective modifying the subject or by an adverb modifying the verb, depending upon the meaning.

He kept it *safe;* he kept it *safely.*
He held it *steady;* he held it *steadily.*
He appears *good;* he appears *well* in public.
Second-hand furniture sold *cheap.*
Millions of Americans listened *breathless* to hourly broadcasts from every European capital.
Those whose names are written so *bright* on the pages of history.
The factories are located *convenient* to the coal fields.

Comparison. The comparative form of an adjective is used in comparing two persons or things, or in comparing a person or thing with a class.

The lower but more powerful branch.
If Pluto and Mars moved with the same velocity, which would have the greater momentum?

The word *other* or *else* is required with a comparative when a person or thing is compared with a class.

Dante was greater than all *other* poets of his day.
I like *Beyond the Horizon* better than anything *else* by Eugene O'Neill.

Similarly:

Wrong: Of all the heroes of the Celtic race, none were so greatly renowned as King Arthur. (*None* excludes King Arthur from the Celtic race.)
Right: . . . no others were so greatly renowned as King Arthur.
Wrong: There is not a vessel crossing the ocean in as little time as ours.
Right: There is not another vessel . . .

The superlative is used to compare more than two persons or things. The word *all* (not *any*) is used with a superlative to include the subject of comparison within the class.

Shakespeare is considered the greatest of *all* English poets.
He is the most affectionate of *all* the puppies I have owned.

A more natural expression of the preceding sentence would be "most affectionate puppy I ever owned." Had the author written "most affectionate puppy of any I ever owned," the editor would simply have deleted "of any."
When the noun following a superlative denotes a thing in a general or absolute sense, it should be preceded by *of.*

A baby's velvety skin needs the tenderest *of* care.
The blackest *of* smoke rolled out of the chimney.

Only things of the same class should be compared.

Wrong: Tom Spenser's explanations are the most sensible of all the boys.
Right: . . . of all those given.
Wrong: Texas is larger than Sweden; and the Swedish population is less than New York City. (This sentence has a second fault. The subject under discussion was Sweden. Swedish population is ambiguous and might be interpreted the number of Swedish people in Texas.)
Right: Sweden is not so large as Texas, and its population is less than that of New York City.
Wrong: Why is the Secretary of State considered the most important position in the United States Cabinet?
Right: Why is the position of Secretary of State considered the most important one in the United States Cabinet?

Similarly, in comparisons expressed by use of *similar to* or *like:*

Wrong: The French government is a federal state with districts having similar power to our states.
Right: The French government is a federal state with districts having power similar to that of our states.
Wrong: Like Whittier, Longfellow's subjects are often drawn from New England legend.
Right: Like Whittier's (or those of Whittier), Longfellow's subjects are often drawn from New England legend.

Comparisons are also expressed by using *as . . . as* or *so . . . as.* Many careful writers use *so . . . as* in negative statements, *as . . . as* in positive ones, but the distinction is of doubtful authority.

He is as rich as Jenkins but not so rich as Murdock.

Adjectives misused for adverbs. To qualify an adjective an adverb must be used, since an adjective preceding another adjective automatically modifies the first following noun.

Wrong: It is amazing how helpless an ordinary capable man can feel.
Right: It is amazing how helpless an ordinarily capable man can feel.

The opposite error is sometimes made:

Wrong: The British have a definitely written constitution.
Right: The British have a definite written constitution.

Nouns as adjectives. One of the commonest errors made by inexperienced writers and overlooked by equally inexperienced proofreaders is the use of an adjectival form of a word where the sense calls for a noun form.

lead-colored	*not* leaden colored
tuberculosis death-**rate**	*not* tuberculous death-rate
economics class	*not* economic class
ballistics expert	*not* ballistic expert
body odors	*not* bodily odors
numeral adjectives	*not* numerical adjectives
north-bound train	*not* northern bound train
explosives warehouse	*not* explosive warehouse
experiment station	*not* experimental station

Wrong: They may be taken accidentally by children, who then develop **poisonous** symptoms . . .
Right: . . . develop symptoms of poisoning.

The correct form is not always so easily determined by the sense as in the examples above, and many contradictions in usage exist. For example, *music critic* and *dramatic critic* are both accepted forms. Grammarians have been unable to offer dependable rules for the use of nouns in this way. The writer and editor should be guided by logic, custom, sense of effectiveness, and good taste.

"Above." The use of *above* as an adjective is not in good repute.

The foregoing paragraph is not included in the original edition.
The paragraph above is not included. (Not *the above paragraph*.)

"Barely," "hardly," "scarcely." These words should be completed by *when*, not by *than*.

Barely had the captain appeared *when* the third mate fell unconscious.
Hardly had we arrived *when* the storm began.
Scarcely had the drawbridge been raised *when* Sir Bedevere came riding.

Barely, hardly, and *scarcely* should never be used with a negative.

I could hardly believe it.
I have scarcely any left.

"Different." The adjective *different* is usually followed by *from*, and some authorities consider any other phrasing improper. But *different to* and *different than* are common usage in England and have long literary usage to support them. *Different than* is being increasingly used in this country when the object is a clause, probably because the construction required by *from* is often wordy.

Conditions are now very different from what they were when the Constitution was drawn up and adopted.
Cotton and linen are known as vegetable fibers and have different reactions than the animal fibers known as silk and wool (have).

"Due to." The rule is that *due,* an adjective, should be attached only to a noun or pronoun, and should not be used in place of *owing to, because of, on account of,* which are compound prepositions. To most minds the distinction between *due to* (adjective plus simple preposition) and *owing to* (participle plus simple preposition) seems artificial or forced; and that is no doubt the reason why it is so generally ignored, except by careful writers. According to the rules of the rhetorician the following are preferred forms.

> His failure was due to insufficient study.
> He failed owing to insufficient study.
> The division of the forces was due to a misunderstanding.
> Owing to (because of, on account of) the flood the villagers have moved away.
> Owing to (because of, on account of) the weather the game was postponed.

"Very," "very much." A frequent question is whether to use *very* or *very much* before a participle used as an adjective—"I am very pleased" or "I am very much pleased." An absolute answer cannot be given. A simple adjective is modified by *very,* a participle that retains its verbal force strongly, by *very much.* There are, however, several adjectives that have lost their verbal force yet still require *very much,* like *very much aware, very much awake.* It should be observed that *much* alone is usually as expressive as *very much.* and it follows that if *much* can properly be used before a word then *very much* may be, but if *much* cannot be so used, then the correct modifier is *very.*

> very tired (not *much* tired)
> very dignified (not *much* dignified)
> very drunk (not *much* drunk)
> (very) much afraid (not *very* afraid)
> (very) much impressed (not *very* impressed)
> (very) much concerned (not *very* concerned)

Sometimes either *very* or *very much* could be used correctly, conveying different meanings, however.

> very worn (showing signs of long wear)
> very much worn (worn a great deal or by many persons)

Sometimes neither is as good as some other adverb, perhaps *most.*

> most uninspired (not *very uninspired* nor *much uninspired*)

ARTICLES

The indefinite articles *a* and *an,* and the definite article *the* (also classed as limiting adjectives) are often misused and often omitted without reason.

THE INDEFINITE ARTICLES

Use *an* before words beginning with a vowel sound; use *a* before words beginning with a consonant sound—including *e* as in *ewe, euphonic, o* as in *one, u* as in *union*. *An one, an unit, an historical, an hypothesis,* and the like are now out of fashion, though once accepted usage.

Abbreviations. The same principle of sound governs the choice of *a* or *an* before an abbreviation when the name of the first letter begins with a vowel sound, as MS., N.C.O., S-pole. The writer must decide whether the abbreviation is to be read as letters or as the words represented. If *MS.* is to be read "manuscript," then "a MS. version" is correct. If the writer expects *S-pole* to be read "south pole," he will use *a* before it—*a S-pole;* otherwise he will write "an S-pole." Similarly, "a $10,000,000 fire" (a ten-million-dollar fire), "an 11-ton truck" (an eleven-ton truck).

Series. When the article is used with two or more coördinate nouns, it should appear before each noun unless the things named comprise a single notion.

He bought a horse and a cow. He owns a horse and buggy.
A house and lot; a house and a barn.
There was a good and a bad side to this.
A man and a woman were sitting on the piazza.
In the group she saw a doctor, a lawyer, and a dentist.

Unnecessary articles. An object and its name should not be confused.

Wrong: Look up the definition of a metal.
Right: Look up the definition of *metal.*
Wrong: A "cover" is a word used to designate the space for each guest's silver, dishes, napkin, etc.
Right: Cover is a word used to designate the space . . .
Or: A "cover" is the space for . . .
Wrong: Probably a "one-scene" play would be a better term than a one-act play.
Right: Probably "one-scene play" would be a better term than "one-act play."

THE DEFINITE ARTICLE

Series. If the article *the* is used before two or more coördinate nouns denoting different objects, it should appear before each noun.

Prior to 1760 it was necessary to depend upon the sun and the pole star in reckoning direction.
The press, the motion picture, and the radio constitute the most important agencies which mold public opinion today.
The land between the Hudson and the Delaware . . .
These coupons must be used between the first and the fifteenth of the month.

But note the effect of a following plural noun:

> The land between the Hudson and Delaware rivers . . .
> In the 16th and 17th centuries; in the first and second grades
> The first and the third Friday; the first and third Fridays

Use determined by meaning. Omission of *the* sometimes alters the meaning:

> We stand in awe before this great cosmic spectacle, in awe not tinged *with fear* of the ancients, but filling us with an unconquerable curiosity.
> We stand in awe before this great cosmic spectacle, in awe not tinged *with the fear* of the ancients, but filling us . . .

Unnecessary articles. Writers to whom English is an acquired language often lapse into the practice of their native tongue and use an article where English does not, writing, for instance, *the truth* for *truth*. The italicized articles in the sentences following should be omitted.

> Sometimes it comes with the overwhelming force of *the* floods.
> Explain the importance of the office of *the* Comptroller General.
> It would be a strange thing if *the* general good should result from *the* selfish action on the part of everyone.

Elliptical style. Instructions are sometimes written in a sort of elliptical style, omitting articles. Consistency should be observed, omitting all or none.

> With left palm toward *the* player place point of knife against *the* thick of *the* hand near *the* little finger side, handle of knife toward *the* thumb side of hand. (Omit italicized *the's.*)
> *Idioms:* in place of *not* in the place of:
> out of the question *not* out of question
> by the thousand *or* by thousands

CONJUNCTIONS

Conjunctions are either coördinating (joining elements of equal rank: *and, but, or, nor, for, yet, so*) or subordinating (introducing a subordinate element: *when, where, since, though, so that,* etc.). Coördinating conjunctions used in pairs (*not only . . . but also*) are called correlative.

COÖRDINATING CONJUNCTIONS

Faulty use of "and" before a "which" clause. Do not use *and* or *but* before *which* (or *who, whose, where*) when no relative clause precedes.

Wrong: It was then proclaimed to the world in the solemn document known as the Declaration of Independence, and which has already been mentioned. (*And* should be deleted.)

Wrong: One man may do a job of road rolling without any further assistance by making use of a new roller six feet high, and which is propelled by a gasoline engine. (*And* should be deleted.)

Faulty omission of "and." Use a conjunction, not a comma, between the parts of a compound predicate.

Poor: The voter takes this ballot into a private booth, marks out the names of those running for Governor. (. . . booth and marks . . .)

Poor: It hears appeals from local committees, fixes dates for primaries and for holding conventions. (. . . committees and fixes . . .)

Permissible omissions. The conjunction may be omitted between coördinate clauses if they are separated by a semicolon.

Conrad has introduced us to the languors and the heats of the river mouths of the Malay Archipelago; Somerset Maugham has spun many a tale of cynical intrigue in the same steaming surroundings.

A tool is for some ulterior purpose; a language exists as a world in itself.

In a series of three or more items omission of *and* before the last may indicate that similar items could be added to those given. In other words, omission of *and* implies *etc.* or *and the like.*

Use it in general cleaning—for floors, linoleums, refrigerators, tiling, marble, rubber.

The expansible plywood home idea is merely an outgrowth of the trend toward multiple-purpose rooms, which converts studies into music rooms, dining rooms into studies, studies into guest rooms.

"Or," "nor." In negative statements *or* is generally accepted to connect words and phrases if the verb is negative, *nor* if the verb is positive.

I cannot read *or* write. (Negative verb.)

He has no money *nor* credit. (Positive verb.)

Read so that you do not spoil the poet's meaning *or* interrupt his thought.

The battle was not confined to that period *or* to China.

However, *nor* may be used instead of *or* after a negative verb if it connects long clauses, or would be more emphatic.

It is not our purpose here to bring into our survey the important work of other scholars who deal with the same problems from other points of view, *nor* yet to appraise current judgments.

The Asian Christians must be full of endurance and faith; they must not be cowards, *nor* idol worshipers, *nor* liars.

Do not confuse *not* (*neither*) . . . *nor* in a correlative construction with the forms under consideration above.

The price level is not merely nor primarily controlled.

"So." As a coördinating conjunction *so* is permissible but is overused.

Permissible: He arrived at last, *so* we sat down to dinner.
Permissible: The simple partnership is a legal device of great antiquity; *so* there was little need of any essentially new rules of law.

So is too often used as a substitute for more exact connectives, such as *therefore, accordingly, on that account.*

Permissible: The Southwest was a region of small farms, *so* the general features of agricultural exploitation were closely comparable with French practice.
Better: The Southwest was a region of small farms; therefore . . .

The sentence containing coördinate clauses connected by *so* would often be improved by subordinating one of the clauses.

Permissible: The mile was too small a unit for measuring astronomical distance, *so* the light year came into use.
Better: Since the mile was too small a unit for measuring astronomical distance, the light year came into use.

SUBORDINATING CONJUNCTIONS

"So that." *So that* means *in order that* or *with the result that.* Its use should be carefully distinguished from that of *so.*

I invested in bonds *so that* my money would be safe. (In order that it would be safe.)
I invested in bonds, *so* my money would be safe. (Consequently it would be safe.)

Amateurish writers often use *so* and *so that* when other forms of expression would be preferable. Sentences like the following are often seen.

Poor: The schedule is flexible enough so that an individual pupil can go to the shop for a longer period if his interest and need warrant it.
Better: The schedule is flexible enough to permit an individual to go.
Poor: It was early enough so that we could hear the concerto.
Better: It was early enough for us to hear the concerto.

"But that." A study of examples is perhaps the easiest way to clarify the use and meaning of *but that.* Note first that *but that* is not interchangeable with *that.* These pairs of sentences express similar thoughts:

He was so strong that he lifted it easily.
He was not so weak but that he lifted it easily.
I am not so ill that I can't do it.
I am not so ill but that I can do it.

The two sentences below are almost opposite in meaning.

I cannot see that his chances are very good (= they do not look good to me).
I cannot see but that his chances are very good (= they do look good to me).

With no change of wording except *but that* for *that* a different thought is conveyed:

We are not sure that Father would be able to do it (= that he would have skill or time).
We are not sure but that Father would be able to do it (= of those considered perhaps Father would do it).

A change from positive statement to negative statement changes the implication.

It is impossible but that taxes will be higher. (Sure to be.)
It is not impossible that taxes will be higher. (May be.)

Sentences like those above cause little trouble by comparison with sentences using *doubt,* verb or noun. The verb *doubt* requires an object—a noun, pronoun, or noun clause. Noun clauses are introduced by *that,* not *but that.*

I do not doubt—
    that he lifted it easily.
    that they will win.
    that his chances are good.
    that Father will do it.

When the noun *doubt* is used after an expletive, think of *doubt* and its restrictive modifying clause as one unit.

There is no—
    doubt that he lifted it easily.
    doubt that they will win.
    doubt that his chances are good.

But that is sometimes equivalent to *without.*

It never turns but that it squeaks. (It never turns without squeaking.)

But that may be used instead of *except that.*

We can arrive at no other conclusion but that organic evolution or changes in living things have taken place.

"But what." *But what* is used correctly when *except* could be substituted for *but*.

He did nothing but what he pleased.

Colloquially, *but what* is sometimes used for *but that*.

I am not so ill but what I can do it.
There is hardly a minute now but what our swift flight carries us over some interesting community.

"That." A common error is the use of two *that*'s to introduce a single clause. This is a mistake a proofreader should unfailingly correct or query. The italicized *that*'s in the following sentences should be omitted.

It is extremely important that when aiding with any test, or preparing patients for scientific tests, *that* directions be carefully followed.
Insist that in securing material from an encyclopedia *that* the pupils take only what they can fully understand when they meet it.

When successive clauses introduced by *that* are numbered, the number and the conjunction should be in the same relative position before the clauses. Errors in this detail should be corrected or queried by the proofreader.

Poor: How does this topic show that (1) scientific knowledge advances slowly and by gradual steps and (2) that no great discovery was ever completely made by one man alone.
Better: How does this show that (1) . . . that (2) . . .
Or: How does this show (1) that . . . (2) that . . .
Poor: We have observed that: (1) the systems of truth have been fluctuating; (2) that empirical . . . ; (3) that laws . . .
Better: We have observed that: (1) the systems . . . ; (2) empirical . . . ; (3) laws . . .

The conjunction *that* sometimes slips into a sentence incorrectly, as in the sentences below. The parenthetical phrases were evidently not recognized as such. A comma should be substituted for the italicized *that*.

Near there, legend says *that* Norsemen trapped beavers long, long ago.
This story was written by Homer, the blind poet, who begged for bread while he lived, but when he died, it is said *that* seven cities claimed the honor of being his birthplace.

"When," "where." Do not define a word by saying it "is when . . ." or "is where . . ."

Wrong: Insomnia is when you can't sleep.
Right: Insomnia is inability to sleep.
Wrong: Freezing is where water reaches 32° above zero.
Right: Freezing is the solidification of water at 32° above zero.

Idiom requires that the word *example* or its synonyms be followed by *of*, not *when* or *where*.

Wrong: Can you give an example from your own experience *when* your own mood colored your feeling toward a particular place?
Right: Can you give an example *of how* your mood colored your feeling?
Wrong: Discuss examples in recent history *where* Public Opinion played an important part.
Right: Discuss examples in recent history *of* Public Opinion playing . . .

"Until." *Until* means *up to the time that* or *from this time to that time* and should not be used in place of *before* or *when*.

I was out of work *until* June.
It was not long *before* he called.
Wrong: We had not been there long *until* the phone rang.
Right: . . . *when* the phone rang.

"While." *While* is not an acceptable substitute for *although, whereas, but,* or *and*. It is an adverb of time and should be reserved for its primary sense.

Poor: While the season was a very dry one, the victory gardens yielded abundantly.
Better: Although the season . . .
Poor: Mr. White planted bush beans, *while* his neighbor preferred pole beans.
Better: . . . *but* his neighbor preferred pole beans.

CORRELATIVE CONJUNCTIONS

Correlatives. Correlative conjunctions are coördinating conjunctions used in pairs.

both . . . and	not only . . . but (also)
either . . . or	whether . . . (or)
neither . . . nor	though . . . yet

The constructions following correlatives should be parallel in form.

Both in England and in Germany; or, In both England and Germany.
Progress depends not only upon the proper method but also upon the proper motive.

Violations of this rule are often caused by misplacing the first conjunction.

Conjunction misplaced: Switzerland neither assumes obligations to send troops abroad nor to admit foreign troops to her soil.
Better: Switzerland assumes obligations neither to send . . . nor to admit . . .
Or: Switzerland does not assume obligations either to send . . . or to admit . . .
Ambiguous: We come in contact with many individuals who have names that are both difficult to spell and pronounce.
Probable meaning: . . . difficult both to spell and to pronounce.

Correction of a faulty correlative sometimes requires a change in the verb in one clause.

Faulty construction. It occurs not only in the blood of all vertebrates but is widely spread throughout the animal kingdom.
Better: Not only does it occur . . . but it is spread . . .
Faulty: You would have guessed that not only had she lived in the country all her life, but you would have known which country.
Better: Not only would you have guessed . . . but you would have known . . .

PREPOSITIONS

All but a few prepositions can be used as other parts of speech, most often as adverbs or subordinating conjunctions, to which prepositions are closely related. The more familiar prepositions are:

about	before	excepting	outside	to
above	behind	for	over	toward
across	below	from	past	under
after	beneath	in	pending	underneath
against	beside	inside	regarding	until
along	between	into	respecting	unto
amid	beyond	of	round	up
among	by	off	since	upon
around	concerning	on	through	with
at	during	onto	throughout	within
athwart	except	out	till	without

Compound prepositions:

according to	as to	aside from	instead of
apart from	on account of	because of	out of
owing to			

Terminal prepositions. The terminal preposition, as in "This is the book he told us about," "He is the man I spoke of," is frowned upon by those who do not know the history of English idiom, but has been well established for centuries. The alternative—"This is the book about which he told us," "He is the man of whom I spoke"—usually sounds stiff and bookish.

Allowable omissions of prepositions. The *to* of an infinitive is often not expressed.

He doesn't dare tell his mother.
Use of it may help you understand the problems.

The *in* or *at* of an adverbial phrase may be dropped.

Bills of exchange are sold the same way.

Adjective phrases like the following need no preposition.

Low tides are about the same height.

Incorrect omissions. Do not omit a preposition needed to make clear the relation of a phrase to the rest of the sentence. The italicized *of* in the following sentence is needed.

His investigations are adding much to our accurate knowledge of the dawn of intelligence and *of* the ancestral sources of human behavior.

Series. The items of a series should be parallel in form. Omission of one needed preposition is a common error. (It is not to be assumed, of course, that every series introduced by a preposition should have a preposition in each part also, for most of them do not.)

Wrong: Who were the first leaders in chemistry, physics, and in biology?
Right: . . . in chemistry, in physics, and in biology?
Wrong: They are equally disastrous to the farmer, to the consumer, and, in the final analysis, the railway engineer.
Right: . . . to the farmer, to the consumer, and to the railway engineer.

Part of a verb. Do not omit a preposition that is an inseparable part of a verb.

Wrong: The relationships between them are respectively orderly and peaceful without regard to what this order, peace, or equilibrium *is due.*
Right: . . . *is due to.*
Wrong: They quarreled long as to whom the bird rightly *belonged.*
Right: . . . whom the bird *belonged to.*
Poor: We never *tired watching* the tall mountaineers.
Better: We never *tired of watching* the tall mountaineers.

Faulty use of prepositions. Do not use a preposition before a noun clause used as an appositive.

Unnecessary preposition: It has the advantage over other alkalies *in that* its unused excess breaks up into water and ammonia gas. (. . . the advantage . . . that . . .)

Do not use a preposition before a restrictive appositive.

Unnecessary preposition: The name *of* artificial silk, first applied to them and later dropped, was incorrect. (The name artificial silk . . .)

Be watchful for the preposition that inadvertently slips into a sentence between a verb and its object.

Unnecessary preposition: The undermining of morals as a result of the war has been considered by some authorities *as* a greater loss than life and property. (. . . has been considered a greater loss.)

Unnecessary preposition: He was nicknamed *as* Thomas the Sudden. (He was nicknamed Thomas the Sudden.)

Unnecessary preposition: His term of office is *for* ten years. (. . . is ten years.)

Do not use two prepositions when one will convey the meaning: *for from, of between, for between, in behind, in between, to within,* are usually poor form.

Too many prepositions: Pasturage for a cow and a calf *for from* 42 to 68 days. (. . . for 42 to 68 days.)

Too many prepositions: Rights are selling *for between* $11 and $29. (. . . for $11 to $29.)

Do not use a preposition where the construction calls for a conjunction.

Faulty use of "to" after "between": The ratio *between* the width of the head *to* the length. (The ratio *between* the width *and* the length.)

Faulty use of "with" after "between": Comparisons drawn *between* the various tissues and the organs of this specimen *with* those of higher animals. (. . . between the tissues of this specimen and those . . .)

"Among," "between." As a general rule *among* refers to more than two and *between* to two; but *between* may be used of three or more items if each item is considered severally and individually.

We divided the money *between* the two.
We divided the money *among* the six.
Between morning, noon, and night.
Diplomatic talks *between* Italy, Germany, and Japan.
Between the rows of beans plant lettuce.

The word or phrase used after *among* or *between* should be logical and not ambiguous.

Faulty: They divided the booty among one another.
Better: . . . among themselves.
Faulty: Place dunnage wood between each two layers.
Better: . . . between layers.

"In," "into," "in to." *In* denotes position; *into* implies motion from without to within. *Into* cannot be substituted for *in to* (adverb and preposition) without marring the sense of the sentence.

He was *in* the room.
He went *into* the room.
He went *in to* his family, who were already in the room.

"On," "onto," "on to." The distinctions between *on, onto,* and *on to* are similar to those between *in, into,* and *in to.* *On* denotes position upon something; *onto* indicates motion toward the upper surface of something. *On to* should be used when *on* belongs to the verb.

> The children played *on* the haymow.
> They slid down *onto* the hay below.
> The perpendicular line *onto* which we project the motion is . . .
> It can be done by sticking the butts *onto* wire hooks.
> They marched *on to* Concord.
> Go right *on to* the next page.
> Hang *on to* the banister.

SENTENCE STRUCTURE

Many errors in the construction of sentences result from haste or from changes in wording made without sufficient attention to the structural pattern of the rest of the sentence. The omission of a word necessary to grammatical or rhetorical accuracy may be a typist's error. Writers should not, therefore, take offense if a proofreader calls their attention to such errors. The examples in the following sections were incorrect in proofs coming to the reader's desk, and therefore show the kinds of errors that writers, editors, and proofreaders must look out for.

Mixed constructions. Sentence constructions should be completed grammatically and logically.

> *Faulty:* Much of the direction of this new women's institution is to be committed to a special board, a majority of which should be composed of women.
> *Better:* . . . a majority of which should be women.
> *Faulty:* I had no illusions about the effects of books such as mine would have been on public opinion.
> *Better:* I had no illusions about the effects of books such as mine on public opinion.

Violations of parallelism. Parallelism is the principle that parts of a sentence that are parallel in meaning should be made parallel in structure. Two or more sentence elements in the same relation to another element should be in the same form. For example, "Seeing is believing," or "To see is to believe." The following are examples of violations of the rule.

> *Noun and infinitive not parallel:* The duties assigned to the Corps were the *operation* of tanks and *to recruit* and *train* the personnel. (. . . the operation of tanks and the recruiting and training . . .)
> *Noun and gerund not parallel:* The solution lies not in *prohibition* or *censorship* but in *developing* self-control. (. . . but in development of self-control.)

Gerund and noun not parallel: The simplest treatment consists in *keeping* the skin dry, the *avoidance* of overheating, and the *application* of talcum or cornstarch. (. . . keeping . . . avoiding . . . applying.)

Noun and clause not parallel: All the grower was responsible for was attractive packing and that he should ship his goods promptly. (. . . attractive packing and prompt shipment of his goods.)

Gerund and infinitive not parallel: Our life in camp was more concerned with *cooking* and *washing up* than *to study* nature. (. . . cooking . . . washing up . . . studying nature.

Infinitive and clause not parallel: Do you advise me *to go* to college now *or that* I wait till I am eighteen? (. . . to go now or to wait . . .)

Complete sentence and phrases not parallel: Some of the causes of failure are the following: Some important feature has been overlooked, lack of careful analysis before launching the enterprise, incorrect conclusions drawn from the analysis. (Some important feature has been overlooked, a careful analysis has not been made, incorrect conclusions have been drawn.)

Complete sentence and clause not parallel: The main pleas are, "You can't understand a people if you don't know their language" and that it "will promote the Good Neighbor policy." (. . . language" and "It will promote . . .")

Fraction and percentage not parallel: Poultry loses about *one third* of the live weight in dressing and drawing and another *12 per cent* in bone and other inedible parts. (. . . about 33 per cent . . . and another 12 per cent . . .)

Two questions, one parenthetical. A question that contains within itself a parenthetical question is often misconstructed, the parenthetical verb being construed as the main verb. So common is this error that every sentence containing the phrase *do you think* or *do you suppose* should be tested for correct form by reading a *that* after *think* to see if the sentence then conveys the meaning intended. Pattern sentences for correct construction:

"Why do you think he did it?" (It is not certain that he did it.)

"Why, do you think, did he do it?" (He did do it; what do you think were his reasons for doing it?)

Wrong: Why do you think each developed as it did?
Right: Why, do you think, did each develop as it did?
Wrong: Why do you think England withdrew from the Quadruple Alliance?
Right: Why, do you think, did England withdraw from the Quadruple Alliance?
Wrong: Why do you suppose that so many of us do these things for nothing?
Right: Why, do you suppose, do so many of us do these things for nothing?
Wrong: Why do you suppose it prints such a booklet?
Right: Why, do you suppose, does it print such a booklet?

POSITION OF MODIFIERS

The meaning of a sentence often depends upon the position of a modifier. Compare the sentences in the following groups.

You also are guilty of this crime.
You are also guilty of this crime.
You are guilty of this crime also.

Even he is not frightened by your news.
He is not even frightened by your news.
He is not frightened even by your news.

Do not place a modifier where it can appear to modify the wrong word.

Wrong: He almost swam two hundred yards.
Right: He swam almost two hundred yards.
Wrong: All the men didn't go.
Right: Not all the men went.
Wrong: When he was a small boy he asked . . . When he was still a little older . . .
Right: When he was a little older still.
Wrong: It scores the number of yards of the nearest line to which it strikes.
Right: . . . of the line nearest to which it strikes.

Adjectives. An adjectival modifier must be near its noun because a normal sentence contains several nouns; the opportunities for ambiguity are many.

Wrong: The people have a tendency to blame the party in power for panics and depressions, guilty or not guilty.
Right: . . . party in power, guilty or not guilty . . .
Faulty: At the age of eighty Aunt Sarah was a good hand with an ax. I have watched her, as a little boy, go into the woodshed . . .
Better: . . . As a little boy, I have watched her go into the woodshed.
Faulty: There is nothing more deadly than ridicule, and it is never deadlier than at the beginning of these movements. Scorched with laughter, now we can almost surely be confident that these "plots" will come to nothing.
Better: . . . We can be confident that these "plots," scorched with laughter, will almost surely come to nothing.

Adverbs within verbs. When an adverb is placed within a verb it should regularly follow the first auxiliary, not precede it—*may safely be used, will surely come.*

Faulty: The short *a,* for example, always must be modified.
Better: . . . must always be modified.
Faulty: There always have been circumstances . . .
Better: There have always been circumstances . . .

Split infinitives. An infinitive is split when an adverb is placed between *to* and the rest of the infinitive. Although in general the usage is inelegant, it is permissible if clearness, smoothness, or force would be lost in avoiding the split.

Poor: Reptiles too big to quickly adapt themselves to new conditions.
Better: Reptiles too big to adapt themselves quickly to new conditions.

The infinitive may have to be split in order to prevent the adverb modifying it from being read as the modifier of some other word in the sentence.

Split necessary: To study current issues so that one may pass sound judgment on the problems and values of today is to equip oneself *to best serve* society.
Ambiguous: To lose one's temper often signifies lack of self-control.
Clear: To *often lose* one's temper signifies lack of self-control.

Do not place an adverb modifying an infinitive before the infinitive if in that position it might seem to modify a preceding verb.

Faulty: It enables us better to understand ourselves.
Better: It enables us to understand ourselves better.
Faulty: Economic institutions enable mankind more efficiently to carry on the work of getting a living.
Better: Economic institutions enable mankind to carry on more efficiently . . .
Faulty: Teachers using these notes are urged carefully to study the many references to specific articles.
Better: . . . urged to study carefully . . .

There is no rule that a modifier of an infinitive must immediately follow the infinitive.

Faulty: It is ordinarily not the best practice to invent deliberately a figure of speech.
Better: . . . to invent a figure of speech deliberately.

Squinting construction. When a modifier is so placed that it might modify either of two words, the construction is called squinting.

Faulty: Careful attention must be given them *both* in writing and in revising. (Does *both* look forward or back?)
Faulty: The committee was charged with the duty of establishing the precise amount of reparations to be paid the various countries, *on or before* May 1, 1921. (Paid before May 1 or establishing the amount before May 1?)

Phrases of time, place, or manner. A phrase of time, place, or manner that modifies the verb of a main clause may well stand first in the main clause; it might sometimes be ambiguous or awkward in any other position.

Faulty: This may be done effectively with the hands *in loose soil.*
Better: In loose soil this may be done . . .
Faulty: The sea was up where this fossil was found *at one time.*
Better: At one time the sea was up where this fossil was found.
Faulty: The eggplant is very susceptible to serious injury *in all stages of growth* by a number of diseases.
Better: In all stages of growth the eggplant is . . .

Do not place such a phrase first in the main clause if it does not modify the main verb. Test the correctness of arrangement by reading the phrase after the main verb.

Faulty: In very early times it is probable that a baited line was used without a hook.
Better: It is probable that in very early times a baited line was used.

The proofreader can sometimes correct sentences of this sort by making a parenthetical element of the subject and verb of the main clause.

Faulty: In the liquid state we think these molecules have a good deal of freedom.
Better: In the liquid state, we think, the molecules . . .
Faulty: During the early part of the twentieth century it is said that some 40,000 artists were at work in Paris.
Better: During the early part of the twentieth century, it is said, some 40,000 artists were at work in Paris.

Dangling modifiers. A phrase or clause that because of its position in a sentence seems to modify a word that it does not logically modify is called a dangling modifier. A dangler is most often at the beginning of a sentence.

Do not place a participial phrase at the beginning of a main clause unless it modifies the subject of the main clause. Test the correctness of a phrase so placed by reading it after the subject.

Faulty: Having recovered from his illness, his mother took him abroad.
Use a clause: When he had recovered from his illness, his mother . . .
Faulty: Destroying the vegetable cover by cultivation, the wind picks up the fine, loose soil and piles it in great heaps.
Recast: The vegetable cover having been destroyed by cultivation, the wind . . .
Faulty: Knowing this and hoping to find an easy route to the deposits by way of the Parana and Paraguay rivers, a Spanish settlement was founded on the site of Asuncion.
Change the subject: Knowing this and hoping to find an easy route to the deposits by way of the Parana and Paraguay rivers, the Spaniards founded a settlement on the site of Asuncion.

Do not begin a sentence with an *if* or *when* clause unless the clause modifies the main verb.

Faulty: If the atmosphere is very moist, explain why killing frosts are not likely. (If the day is dry, don't bother to explain!)
Transpose the clause: Explain why killing frosts are not likely if the atmosphere is moist.
Faulty: When men had a desire to draw pictures, we can understand that they had made a great advance beyond the fist-hatchet stage.
Transpose the clause: We can understand that when men had a desire to draw pictures they had made a great advance.

Do not begin a sentence with an elliptical clause unless the omitted subject of the clause is the same as the subject of the main clause.

Faulty: Though rather cold, I expected he would take his daily swim.
Better: Though it was rather cold, I expected . . .
Faulty: When running, the wings hang down like those of a wounded bird.
Better: When he is running, the wings hang down like those of a wounded bird.
Faulty: Though summer, I knew he would like to see a cheerful hearth.
Better: Though it was summer, I knew he would like to see a cheerful hearth.
Faulty: Many crops cannot profitably be shipped to market because they are bulky and transportation rates high; but *if fed* to growing animals, the farmer can sell the livestock products for more money than he would receive for hay and grains.
Better: . . . but if they are fed to growing animals, . . .

Awkwardness. Do not place sentence elements in an order unnecessarily awkward.

Faulty: Assembly Bill No. 241 allows with the consent of the refunding commission the district to issue additional bonds.
Better: Assembly Bill No. 241 allows the district, with the consent of the refunding commission, to issue additional bonds.
Faulty: The people in the same way are wiser politically by far than the most of our politicians.
Better: In the same way, the people are far wiser politically than most of our politicians.
Faulty: It called the purpose it had been created for to the attention of sculptors.
Better: It called to the attention of sculptors the purpose for which it had been created.
Faulty: It is not practical or wise to leave the decision of entering any war to the people by vote.
Better: It is not practical or wise to leave to a vote of the people the decision of entering any war.
Faulty: The most interesting part, from the navigational point of view, of this inland water trip, is Seymour Narrows.
Better: From the navigational point of view the most interesting part of this inland water trip is Seymour Narrows.

OMISSIONS

Do not omit a word, phrase, or clause essential to a clear understanding of the structure and meaning of the sentence.

Verb omitted: After what seemed a long time, *but probably* only a couple of minutes, she resumed her normal keel. (. . . but was probably . . .)
Verb omitted: To make the coating a little heavier *or hold* its shape a little better, beat in a few drops of glycerine. (. . . or to make it hold . . .)

Part of verb omitted: Question arose as to whom the property should *belong.* (. . . belong to.)

Noun omitted: One level premium governs from *age 18 to 50.* (. . . age 18 to age 50.)

Noun omitted: Note the liberal charters given by Charles I *and II.* (. . . Charles I and Charles II.)

Pronouns omitted: Cook about eight minutes. In the gas oven *turn once.* Over bright coals *turn each* ten seconds. (. . . Cook it . . . turn it.)

Pronoun omitted: The description of this fellow *and the man* wanted in Chicago tally exactly. (. . . and that of the man . . .)

Expletive omitted: The total military forces numbered 644,540. In *addition were* thousands of civilian employees. (. . . there were thousands.)

Preposition omitted: Most protozoa divide much more rapidly at warm *than cold* temperatures. (. . . at cold . . .)

Preposition omitted: John always maintained that he was more grateful for that escape *than those* from dynamite and rifle fire. (. . . than for those . . .)

Participle omitted: Besides scholarship, a student in the University must have been active politically. (Besides possessing scholarship . . .)

Series. Series of words, phrases, or clauses may be defective because of the omission of prepositions or conjunctions. (See also p. 392.)

Faulty: It permits the use of different sizes and styles of type, spaces out the lines to an even right-hand margin, gives uniform impression and unusual legibility.

Better: . . . margin, and gives . . . [It does three things. Omission of *and* would indicate that it does several things, but only three are mentioned.]

Faulty: The discovery of the causes of tuberculosis by Koch, of diphtheria by Klebs and Loeffler, the invention of antitoxins by von Behring and Roux, control and prevention of diseases by Laveran, Ross, . . .

Better: The discovery of the causes of tuberculosis by Koch, and of diphtheria by Klebs and Loeffler, the invention of antitoxins by von Behring and Roux, control and prevention of diseases by Laveran, Ross, . . .

Faulty: Others involve safety as well—speed regulations, safety devices in factories, theaters, regulation of sale and use of firearms, explosives, and poisons.

Better: Others involve safety as well—speed regulations, safety devices in factories and theaters, and regulation of sale and use of firearms, explosives, and poisons.

Series are tricky forms to correct, and the editor and proofreader need to guard against haste. The following example at first reading seems to be faulty because of the omission of prepositions. On the contrary, a preposition should be omitted, because all four items of the series constitute one method of control. (The sentence is also faulty because the items of the series are not parallel in form.)

Faulty: Damping-off may be controlled by treating the seed before planting, proper thinning of seedlings, allowing the necessary ventilation, and by judicious watering.

Better: Damping-off may be controlled by treating the seed before planting, thinning the seedlings properly, allowing the necessary ventilation, and watering judiciously.

The omission of conjunctions sometimes makes a series of phrases out of two coördinate expressions.

Faulty: These laws require employers to install safety devices, maintain healthful working conditions and reasonable hours of labor.
Better: . . . to install safety devices and to maintain . . .
Faulty: They mark a beginning of, or effort at, self-regulation, elimination of child labor, long hours, and so on.
Better: . . . self-regulation and the elimination . . .

Words used in a double capacity. The omission of a word may result in some other word being used in a double capacity, one of which is ungrammatical.

Faulty: This dedication will serve for almost any book that *has, is,* or shall be published.
Better: . . . that has been, is being, or shall be published.
Faulty: Thus he did what many a man *has* and is *doing.*
Better: . . . has done and is doing.
Faulty: Nickel steel came into use for the *French,* and afterwards for all other European *navies.*
Better: . . . for the French navy, and afterwards for all other European navies.

One word used for two phrases may be ungrammatical in one of them. Correction often requires a transposition of phrases.

Faulty: He was either forbidden or *discouraged to* play with other children.
Better: He was either forbidden to play with other children or discouraged from doing so.
Faulty: I must add that it is as *interesting* if not more so *than* any other part of the magazine.
Better: I must add that it is as interesting as any other part of the magazine, if not more so.
Faulty: It is one of the finest, if not *the finest,* moving picture *productions* of the year.
Better: It is one of the finest moving picture productions of the year, if not the finest.
Faulty: The fishing is as good, if not *better,* at this season *as* it is in the summer.
Better: The fishing is as good at this season as it is in the summer, if not better.

PART VI—USE OF WORDS

MAIN DIVISIONS

Precision, freshness, appropriateness, conformity to idiom and usage—these are qualities that a writer must patiently attain if his work is to capture educated readers and hold their attention. If he fails to attain these qualities, if he blunders into wordiness, triteness, imperfect idiom, the fault is his own. The primary responsibility for good diction is his. But the editor also can be charged with slipshod work if he neglects obvious violations of good usage, and the proofreader should query any lapse from good diction that appears to be an error in typing or transcription.

WORDINESS

Redundancy, pleonasm, tautology, verbosity, and *circumlocution* are terms commonly applied to the use of superfluous words. Redundancy involves repetition of meaning, whereas circumlocution is merely a roundabout way of expressing an idea. Proofreaders may be allowed to query redundant expressions but not circumlocutions. Editors, however, should be watchful to correct both faults.

Redundant expressions. An adjective duplicating part of the meaning of the noun it modifies is redundant. The italicized words in the following, for example, are redundant.

complete master	as a *general* rule	*new* beginners
close proximity	*good* benefits	*present* incumbent
fellow playmates	*habitual* custom	*seeming* paradox
final climax	*important* essentials	*self*-confessed
final outcome	*invited* guest	*true* facts
first priority	*necessary* requisite	*successful* achievements
funeral obsequies		

402

Sometimes the noun is the redundant part of the phrase.

anthracite *coal*	connective *word*	undergraduate *student*
barracks *buildings*	Halloween *evening*	widow *lady*

A preposition or adverb used as part of a verb may be redundant.

ascend *up*	connect *up*	meet *up* with	termed *as*
assemble *together*	continue *on*	recoil *back*	think *for*
attach *together*	feel *of*	repeat *again*	unite *together*
christened *as*	fuse *together*	return *back*	

The italicized words in the following phrases are redundant.

adequate *enough*	over *with*	total effect of *all* this
totally annihilated	*but* nevertheless	mutual advantage *of both*
quite unique	*and* moreover	biography *of his life*
entirely completed	this *same* program	*surrounding* circumstances
still persists	*as to* whether	smattering *of knowledge*
may or might *possibly*	equally *as* well	endorse *on the back*
all *of*	throughout *the whole of*	2 p.m. *in the afternoon*
atop *of*	bisect *into two parts*	Rio Grande *River*
inside *of*	audible *to the ear*	Yangtze Kiang *River*
later *on*	universally *by all*	Sierra Nevada *Mountains*
as yet	*every* now and then	my *own* autobiography

Both is often used redundantly; it should be omitted in sentences like the following:

They are both alike.
They both go hand in hand.
Both the sons attend different universities.
Both of the other two are in the Marines.

Prepositional phrases in expressions like the following are redundant because they express ideas implied by the preceding words.

square in shape	blue in color	lenticular in character
few in number	graceful in appearance	day dawned in the east
big in size	contemporaneous in age	exchanged hats with each other

Tautology. Another fault to be avoided is tautology, which is defined by the *New Century Dictionary* as "the saying of a thing over again, especially in other words, in the immediate context, without imparting additional force or clearness; a needless repetition in the expression of ideas, as in 'an empty barrel with nothing in it.'"

cause of . . . is on account of

and so as a result

pair of twins

each and every

the modern business man of today

environment of rough surroundings

an entire monopoly of the whole shoe trade

lighter side of the aspect of events

the many resources of which she is possessed

Circumlocution. Circumlocutions are not ungrammatical or repetitious, merely open to criticism as wordy.

destroyed by fire = burned

during the time that = while

made a statement saying = stated

I had occasion to be = I was

in this day and age = today

the house in question = this house

from the commercial standpoint = commercially

are present in greater abundance = are more abundant

in the majority of instances they do not = the majority do not

innumerable number of faint stars = innumerable faint stars

in the neighborhood or vicinity of = nearly or about

I am in possession of = I have

Words and Phrases Often Used Superfluously

in the case of: In the case of employees who are late to work, a reduction of wages will be made = The wages of employees who are late to work will be reduced.

in some instances: These books in some instances were = Some of these books were.

character: The handwriting is of a distinctive character = The handwriting is distinctive.

nature: This project is of the same nature as the preceding one = This project is like the preceding one.

found or *known to be:* These mountains are known to be rich in tin = These mountains are rich in tin.

of such: The task is of such magnitude that = The task is so great that.

purposes: The building could be remodeled for manufacturing purposes = The building could be remodeled for manufacturing.

conditions: Production was retarded by strike conditions = Production was retarded by strikes.

is located or *situated:* The house is situated on a slight elevation = The house is on a slight elevation.

the fact that: She seldom loses any, owing to the fact that she sterilizes the jars = She seldom loses any because she sterilizes the jars.

along the line of: His work along the line of increasing plant production has been outstanding = His work in increasing plant production has been outstanding.

a number of: There is a large number of commercial varieties $=$ There are many commercial varieties.

as far as: As far as I am concerned, foreign languages might as well not exist $=$ As for me, foreign . . .

as long as: As long as we have to go anyway, we may as well go cheerfully $=$ Since we have to go, . . .

Sentences beginning with introductory *there* or *it* are often wordy.

It is the belief of many workers that . . . $=$ Many workers believe.

There are many who like the change $=$ Many like the change.

There are some places where . . . $=$ At some places . . .

There were the same number of molecules present in each case $=$ The same number of molecules were present in each case.

TRITE EXPRESSIONS [1]

Trite expressions flourish because they come easily to the tongue and are easily remembered. Some were at one time clever, or pat, or witty. Since they save time and effort needed for inventing fresh expressions, they still dot the pages (is that a cliché?) of unpracticed writers; but to an experienced reader they sound tiresome, or misfit, or insincere.

Clichés include hackneyed quotations, overworked proverbs, and stereotyped phrases which are memorable because of some rhythm, alliteration, or other characteristic of sound or form. The list below omits most proverbs and complete quotations, concentrating on phrases which have become inane through overuse. These are sometimes referred to as bromides. Overworked single words are noted in the section entitled Appropriateness (pp. 411–450).

A proofreader seldom challenges trite expressions unless they are conspicuously bad, but an editor who finds too many in a manuscript will suggest to the author that he rejuvenate his style.

For longer lists of trite expressions, consult Eric Partridge, *Usage and Abusage,* under "Clichés," and Logan Pearsall Smith, *Words and Idioms.*

abject apology	age before beauty
abreast of the times	a good time was had by all
accidents will happen	agree to disagree
aching void	all and sundry
acid test	all in a day's work
add insult to injury	all nature seemed
adds a note of	all that in me lies
affront to national honor	all that was mortal
after all has been said and done	all the world and his wife

[1] Also called clichés or hackneyed phrases.

all things considered
all things to all men
all too soon
all work and no play
almighty dollar
along the line of least resistance
along these lines
amiable qualities
among those present
ample opportunity
ancestral acres
and oblige
animated scene
apostle of culture
appear on the scene
apple of the eye
ardent admirers
arms of Morpheus
arrive on the scene
as far as in me lies
a shriek rent the air
as it were
as luck would have it
assuming this will meet your satisfaction
assuring you of our best intentions
at a loss for words
at a tender age
at his own sweet will
at long last
atmosphere of doubt
at one fell swoop
at the first blush
auspicious event
auspicious moment
awaiting further orders

bag and baggage
battered specimen of humanity
beat a hasty retreat
beautiful but dumb
beggars description
beginning of the end
beg to advise
beg to remain
beneath contempt
benefit of the doubt
best-laid plans of mice and men

better half
better late than never
better left unsaid
bitter end
blank amazement
blanket of snow
blissfully ignorant
bloated plutocrat
bloody but unbowed
bloom of youth
blushing bride
bolt from the blue
bone of contention
boon companion
borrowed plumes
bounteous repast
brave as a lion
breakneck speed
breathless silence
breathless suspense
bright and shining faces
briny deep
brutal atrocity
budding genius
bulwark of the state
burning question
burning the midnight oil
busy as a bee
by leaps and bounds
by the same token
by the sweat of one's brow

call a spade a spade
calm (or lull) before the storm
came in for their share of
captain of industry
casual encounter
caught like rats in a trap
checkered career
cheered to the echo
cherished belief
circumstances over which I have no control
claimed him for its own
clear as crystal
cloistered virtue
clothed and in his right mind
coign of vantage

colorful display
commercial world
common or garden
completed the scene
connubial bliss
conservative estimate
considered opinion
consigned to earth
consigned to oblivion
conspicuous by its absence
consummation devoutly to be wished
contents duly noted
controlling factor
could be seen
counsel of perfection
course of true love
coverlet of snow
cradle of the deep
cradled in luxury
crass stupidity
cup that cheers
curses not loud but deep
cut a long story short
cut down in his prime

daintily gloved hand
damask cheek
Dame Fortune
dashed madly about
dazed condition
dead as a doornail
deadly earnest
dear departed
deem it advisable
deliberate falsehood
demon rum
depths of despair
deserving poor
devotee of Terpsichore
devouring element
diamond in the rough
did ample justice to the meal
dim and distant
dim religious light
discreet silence
distinction with a difference
doom is sealed
doomed to disappointment

doting parent
double-dyed villain
downy couch
drastic action
drown your sorrows
due consideration
dull, sickening thud
durance vile
dynamic personality

each and every
easier said than done
eat, drink, and be merry
eloquent silence
eminently successful
enclosed herewith
endowed with this world's goods
enemy in our midst
engage in conversation
enjoyable occasion
entertaining high hopes of
epic struggle
equal to the occasion
ere long
errand of mercy
esteemed favor
eternal feminine
eternal verities
even tenor
everything went along nicely (or
    smoothly)
existing conditions
express one's appreciation

fair sex
far as in me lies
far be it from me
fatal (or fateful) day
fatal deed
fateful scene
fate worse than death
favor with a selection
feast of reason and flow of soul
feel a different person
feel well repaid for our efforts
festive board
festive occasion
few and far between

few well-chosen words
filthy lucre
finer side of life
finer things of life
finger of destiny
finishing touch
floral tribute
flourish like a green bay tree
flowing bowl
fond parents
food for thought
fools rush in where angels fear to tread
force of circumstances
foregone conclusion
foul play
fragile form
fragrant weed
from the sublime to the ridiculous
furrowed brow

gala occasion
generous to a fault
genuine impression
girlish glee
glass of fashion and mold of form
glowing cheeks
God made the country
goes without saying
goodly number
grateful acknowledgment
grave concern
great minds run in the same channel
great open spaces
green-eyed monster
green with envy
greet the eye
grim reaper
guide, philosopher, and friend

hale and hearty
hand of Justice
hands across the sea
happy pair
harbinger of spring
has the defects of its qualities
hastily summoned
have the privilege
heartless wretch

heart of the matter
heart's content
heart's desire
heated argument
heave a sigh of relief
height of absurdity
herculean efforts
hive of industry
Homeric laughter
hope springs eternal
hoping you are the same
horny-handed sons of toil
hurriedly retraced his steps

ignominious retreat
ignorance is bliss
ill-fated car
illustrious dead
imagination runs riot
immaculate attire
immeasurably superior
immortal bard
impenetrable mystery
in a pleasing manner
in close proximity to
infinite capacity
initial endeavor
in no uncertain manner (*or* terms)
in our midst
instructive and entertaining
in the limelight
in this day and age
in touch with
irony of fate
irreducible minimum
irreparable loss
it dawned upon me
it goes without saying
it isn't the heat, it's the humidity

labor of love
last analysis
last but not least
last sad rites
launched into eternity
leave no stone unturned
leave severely alone
leaves much to be desired

led her to the altar
lend me your ears
lent a cheerful aspect
light fantastic toe
like a bolt from the blue
like fairyland
logic of events
long arm of coincidence
long arm of the law
long-drawn sigh
long-felt want
love's young dream

made a pretty picture
malignant fate
mantle of snow
many and various
martial tread
material interests
matrimonial alliance
meets the eye
men were deceivers ever
merry as a marriage bell
metal more attractive
method in his madness
milk of human kindness
milling mass of humanity
miraculous escape
mirrored in her eyes
momentous decision
monarch of all I survey
more easily imagined than described
more in sorrow than anger
more sinned against than sinning
more than ordinarily impressive
Mother Nature
motley crew (or crowd)
music hath charms
my prophetic soul

name is Legion
needs no introduction
never in the history of
nipped in the bud
none but the brave deserve the fair
none the worse for his experience
no place like home
no sooner said than done

obvious even to the meanest intelligence
one of life's little ironies
one touch of nature
on more than one occasion
on unimpeachable authority
order out of chaos
other things being equal
out of the mouths of babes
overwhelming odds
own worst enemy

pageant of history
pageantry of nature
paid the debt to nature
palatial abode
pales into insignificance
paralyzed with fright
paramount issue
parlous state
partake of refreshments
patience on a monument
pet aversion
picturesque scene
pleasing scene
point with pride
poor but honest
poor but proud
powers that be
presided at the piano
primrose path
progressive and enlightened
pronounced success
proud father
proud possessor
psychological moment

quivered with excitement

ravishing beauty
reached our destination
refresh the inner man
regrettable incident
reigns supreme
reliable source
relieve the situation
render a selection
replete with interest
resplendent uniform

retort courteous
rich as Croesus
riot of color
riotous living
ripe old age
ripple of girlish laughter
rippling laughter
river like a silver ribbon
round of applause
rude habitation
ruling passion

sadder but wiser
sallied forth
saluted our ears
sanctity of the home
satisfy the inner man
saw the light of day
scathing sarcasm
seamy side of life
sea of faces
sea of matrimony
seat of learning
second to none
seething mass of humanity
select few
sequestered nook
seriously incline
shadow of the goal posts
shattering effect
sickening thud
sight that met my gaze
silence broken only by
silence reigned supreme
silhouetted against the sky
simple life
single blessedness
skeleton in the closet
sleep the sleep of the just
snare and delusion
social amenities
soft impeachment
soul of honor
speak volumes
specimen of humanity
spectacular event
speculation was rife
speed the parting guest

staff of life
strait and narrow path
straitened circumstances
strong, silent man
sturdy independence
such is life
suffer a sea-change
sum and substance
sumptuous repast
sunny south
superhuman effort
supreme moment
supreme sacrifice
sweat of his brow
sweet girl graduate
sweet sixteen
sweets to the sweet
swift as thought

table groaned
teach the young idea how to shoot
telling effect
tempting viands
tender mercies
tender one's thanks
thanking you in advance
thereby hangs a tale
there's the rub
this mortal coil
those present
threw caution to the winds
thunderous applause
tide in the affairs of men
tie that binds
tie the nuptial bond (or knot)
time immemorial
time of my life
tiny tots
tired but happy
too full for utterance
too numerous to mention
toothsome viands
trees like sentinels
trials and tribulations
tumultuous applause
'twas ever thus

unalloyed pleasure
unprecedented situation

untimely end
untiring efforts
untoward incident

vale of tears
variety the spice of life
vast concourse
venture the suggestion
view with alarm
viselike grip
voice the sentiments

walk of life
watery grave
wax poetic
wax sentimental
weaker sex
wealth of hair
wee small hours

weighty reasons
where ignorance is bliss
white blanket of snow
with bated breath
wondrous fair
words fail me
words fail to express
word to the wise
working like Trojans
work of supererogation
worm in the bud
worse for wear
wrapped in mystery
wreathed in smiles
wrought havoc

young hopeful
your valued favor

APPROPRIATENESS

The word *appropriateness* has been adopted as a title, instead of the usual terms *propriety* or *correctness,* because the terms the list consists of are not improper or incorrect except when used in the wrong context. Only a few dubious usages and still fewer illiteracies have been included, and these may of course be improper in any context; but most of the fifteen hundred or so terms listed would be used by a careful writer if his purpose or the context called for them.

The descriptive labels—*colloquial, local, provincial, slang,* etc.—appended to the definitions or illustrations are those used in dictionaries. The primary distinction implied by them is that between *conventional* and *unconventional, formal* and *informal, literary* and *popular,* or *written* and *spoken.* Occasionally, therefore, terms about which no question of appropriateness arises are labeled *literary, standard, accepted,* or *in good use.*

Colloquialisms are informal terms more likely to be used in conversation than in dignified, formal, or conventional writing. They are not, however, in equally good repute, some being dubious, some low, and some definitely slangy.

Slang is a class of colloquialism of low literary repute. It originates usually as the cant or jargon of a particular calling or class of society and finds its way into general use because of some forced, fantastic, humorous, imaginative, or grotesque appeal. Many terms now ranked as colloquialisms were once slang, but many slang terms have a long history without attaining the comparative dignity of colloquialisms. Most slang is, nevertheless, ephemeral; and in the list only those slang terms are included that have been recorded in histories for ten years or more.

Provincialisms are expressions peculiar to a major section of the country but not current nationally. They are, however, often expressive enough to be taken into general use and become recognized colloquialisms. Localisms are expressions peculiar to a limited locality. A special feature of the list is the noting of many words as American or English, national usage being a larger aspect of provincialism. (This section is followed by another on English and American Usage.)

Since usage is in a process of incessant change, the task of deciding whether a word is literary or colloquial, colloquial or slang, colloquial or provincial, is sometimes so difficult that even authorities disagree. In compiling the list, the great dictionaries have been consulted. When they have disagreed, the compiler has used his judgment.

accused It is sometimes maintained that *accused* is not a noun, and that *accused person* should be used instead. As a noun it is old—"The accused stood forth"—Pope, *Dunciad.*

act up For *assert oneself, misbehave*—colloquial.

addict As a noun—"a drug addict"—accepted, though objected to by some authorities.

advise For *inform* suggests commercial jargon, though the usage is fairly old. "Beg to advise" is both trite and stilted. Say "Beg to inform" or, better, "I have to inform" or "I am sorry to inform."

afeared Once in good use and occasionally still used poetically, but now local or colloquial.

after In the sense of *trying to get*—"Germany was after a place in the sun"—in good use, though sometimes labeled colloquial.

afterwards For *afterward*—in good use.

aggravate For *irritate, vex*—"That kind of music always aggravates me"—now established, though avoided by careful writers. *Aggravate,* in its older meaning, signifies *increase, add weight to or intensity to* (in an unpleasant sense). "The painfulness of the burn was aggravated by exposure." "The enormity of the offense was aggravated by the helplessness of the victim."

aim For *intend*—"I aim to do it tomorrow"—colloquial, U. S.

ain't The colloquial use of *ain't* in questions, when it stands for *am not*—"I'm a little incoherent, ain't I?" is sometimes defended, but condemned when it stands for *is not*—"Ain't that your hat?" "Ain't I?" is an old expression, often printed in old books as "An't I?" or "A'nt I?" giving place, especially in England, to "Aren't I?" *Amn't* has never gained wide currency and "Am I not?" seems stilted. We really need a contraction of *Am I not?* but none has been accepted in literary usage.

aired The literal use for *took out of doors, exposed to air, admitted air*—aired a dog, bedclothes, a room—is old. The metaphorical use for *exposed to view, made public*—"He aired his theories"—is also established, though sometimes challenged. In the latter sense it is often used carelessly for *divulge*—"No man is likely to air his secret vices."

alibi For *excuse*—"The pitcher had all sorts of alibis for losing the game"—dubious colloquialism or slang.

all hollow For *entirely, completely*—"They beat us all hollow"—colloquial.

all in For *tired out*—"After the long run I was all in"—slang, U. S.

all-out For *entire, complete*—"An all-out effort"—established.

all over For *finished, past*—"The storm is all over"—in good use. For *everywhere*—"I searched for him all over"—colloquial. For *completely*—"She is her mother all over"—colloquial. *All-overish, all-overishness*—colloquial.

allow For *assert, affirm, intend, propose*—"He allowed that we were richer than we admitted," "I came here allowing to ask him to pay up"—provincial.

all right An old colloquialism, often labeled an Americanism—"He's all right" (*i.e.*, dependable, a good fellow); "I'll do it all right" (*i.e.*, surely, dependably, or well); "That measurement is all right" (*i.e.*, correct); "Please come soon." "All right" (*i.e.*, Agreed. Don't worry). *Alright* (or *alrite*)—illiterate.

all-round For *general, not specialized, complete*—"He is an all-round athlete"—in good use. *All-around* for *all-round*—incorrect.

all the further For *as far as*—"This is all the further I go"—illiterate.

alone For *only*—"I affirm this, not alone because I believe it, but because others think as I do"—an old and permissible usage, often objectionable because not clear, as: "If he depended alone on his strength, he would . . ." If *alone* means *only* here, *only* should be used.

among other reasons or **things** Often illogical—"This, among other things, is the situation." The sentence probably means "This, along with other things," or, possibly, "This, aside from other things." The expression is accepted as idiomatic, however, and is usually clear.

and For *to*—"I'll try and find it"—now considered colloquial, though it has a long and honorable history.

anent In most homely contexts, pretentious.

angel For *backer* (of a play)—slang.

ante For *pay*, noun and verb, slang. Also *ante up*.

anxious For *desirous, eager*—"Write soon, for I'm anxious to hear from you"—condemned by some authorities, who would limit the word to the meaning *disquieted, ill at ease about*. But "anxious to succeed," "anxious to avoid quarrels," and similar expressions are common among good writers.

anywheres For *anywhere*—"I can't find it anywheres"—erroneous. So *everywheres, somewheres*.

aren't I "I'm very ignorant, aren't I?" *See* ain't.

around For *about*. "He catalogued about [*not* around] three hundred species." For *in this vicinity*—"He'll be around here, you'll see"—colloquial. For *about the time of*—"I'll see you around Christmas"—colloquial.

arty A convenient colloquialism to designate the affectedly aesthetic.

as how For *that*—"Why tell me this, seeing as how you won't believe me?"—provincial or illiterate. (*Note.* "Why tell me this, seeing you don't like me?" is idiomatic, and this use of *seeing* is very old. "Wherefore come ye to me, seeing ye hate me?"—Genesis 26:27.)

asset Much overworked for "something useful or desirable." Since the word retains a commercial connotation, careful writers prefer, in noncommercial contexts, to use one of its many synonyms: *property, advantage, benefit, help, service, interest, gain, utility, characteristic, attribute.* Examples of loose popular use: "A sense of humor is an asset to a teacher," "My freshly shined shoes proved an asset in getting the job," "Her lovely eyes were an asset in captivating men," "Mary the scrubwoman turned out to be an asset."

award Purists object to "He was awarded a prize," insisting upon "A prize was awarded to him." The form they object to is, however, in good use.

a while, awhile *While* is a noun meaning a short time—"I will go after a while." *Awhile* has been objected to as an incorrect formation; but it is established in the sense of *for a brief time*—"Angel faces smile, which I have loved long since and lost awhile."—Newman. (*Note. While* is also a verb, seen most often in the phrase "while away time." Unaware of this fact, some persons insist that the phrase should be "wile away time.")

awoken, woken For *awakened, waked*—though often called illiterate, are better described as obsolescent. The confusion about the principal parts of these verbs is very old and still persists. The correct forms are as follows:

PRESENT	PAST	PAST PARTICIPLE
awake	awoke *or less commonly* awaked	awaked *or less commonly* awoke
wake	woke *or less commonly* waked	waked *or rarely* woke *or* woken
awaken	awakened	awakened
waken	wakened	wakened

Attempts to distinguish between the forms, as to their use in a transitive or intransitive sense and in active and passive constructions, are so indefinite as to be hardly useful.

back of, in back of "Back of the house" is colloquial; "in back of the house" is objected to because the *in* is considered redundant.

bad egg For *person disapproved of*—colloquial. This is the older form, now varied slangily as *good egg, tough egg,* etc.

balance For *rest, remainder*—dubious colloquialism. "The rest [*rather than* balance] of the party left for home." Strictly, *balance* suggests two amounts and their difference; *remainder* or *rest,* parts of one amount.

ballyhoo For *noisy demonstration* or, simply, *noise*—slang.

bamboozle For *trick, hoax, baffle*—colloquial.

ban As verb and noun—overworked.

bang-up For *first-rate*—"That was a bang-up party"—colloquial.

bank on or **upon** For *rely on, count on*—"Don't bank on his coming"—colloquial.

barkeep For *barkeeper, bartender*—slang, U. S.

barn In England a barn is only a place for storage of hay, grain, etc. In America it is thought of as also a house for cattle.

bash For *blow*—"A bash on the head"—or for *strike a blow*—"He bashed him with a club"—colloquial or provincial.

baste For *beat with a stick* or *lash with the tongue*—colloquial.

batty For *crazy*—slang.

beam *On the beam* for *in line with success or pleasure*—"Your suggestion is right on the beam"—slang or colloquial.

beat For *defeat*—"The Dutch, in spite of their small numbers, beat the Spanish" —in good use. *Beat* has many colloquial uses, such as "That beats me" for "That baffles me"; "beat all hollow," "beat the Dutch," "beat the band." Slang uses are *beat it!* for *run away!; beat*, or, more usually, *dead beat*, for *a person who lives by borrowing or cheating. Beat* for *priority of publication*—"Jim's story was definitely a beat"—newspaper slang. *Compare* scoop.

belittle In good use, though often called an Americanism.

better than For *more than*—"Better than two hours ago"—colloquial.

bigwig Colloquial or literary, as are *bigwigism, bigwiggery.*

bit For *a short time*—"I'll come along after a bit"—colloquial, U. S. For *twelve and a half cents*—colloquial, U. S. Two bits is a quarter of a dollar; a short bit is ten cents and a long bit, fifteen cents. *Doing one's bit*—colloquial.

blame on Say "Don't blame me for it," not "Don't blame it on me."

blat For *talk loosely or loudly*—colloquial or slang. A form of *beat*, which is also used in the same way.

blimp For *a small dirigible balloon*—colloquial.

blind date Slang.

blow For *brag, bluster*—colloquial. *Blow in* for *appear unexpectedly* and *blow up* for *scold*—colloquial. *Blow* for *spend recklessly* and the noun *blow* for *a merry and extravagant meal*—slang.

blue For *despondent*—in good use. Also *blues* for *despondency* and as the name of a type of Negro music.

bluff For *deceive* or *intimidate*—"I bluffed him out of his anger"—probably established. Also as a noun—"His anger was only a bluff."

blurb For *laudatory advertisement*—colloquial. A coinage of Gelett Burgess.

boggle For *bungle, botch, fumble*—in good use.

bogus For *spurious, sham*—in good use.

bone For *study hard*—college slang.

bonehead For *ignoramus* or *fool*—slang.

boner For *stupid or ignorant mistake*—slang.

boo In good use as noun, verb, and interjection.

booby For *stupid fellow, dunce*—in good use.

booby-hatch For *jail* or, occasionally, *insane asylum*—slang.

booby-trap For *pitfall, buried bomb*—colloquial or slang.

boodle For *money, spoils* (specifically, money used for bribery)—"He's in politics for the boodle"—colloquial. Also used as an adjective—"boodle politics." Also *boodler* and *caboodle.*

boom For *prosperity, rapid development*—colloquial.

boost For *push upward*—"We boosted him over the fence"—colloquial, U. S. Also for *support enthusiastically*—"They're boosting him for governor." Also *booster.*

bosh For *empty talk, trash*—colloquial.

boss For *superintend, superintendent*—colloquial, U. S. For *dictator* (of a political organization)—"Boss Tweed"—in good use, U. S.

bottleneck For *partial stoppage, obstruction*—"The absence of chromium threatens to cause a bottleneck"—colloquial.

bounce For *peremptorily discharge*—"The bookkeeper was bounced today"—slang, U. S. As a noun for *vivacity, resilience*—"He is a man of great bounce"—colloquial.

bouncer For *ejector of disorderly persons*—slang, U. S.

bound For *resolved*—"I'm bound to do it"—colloquial, U. S.

brace For *ask*—"He braced me for a dollar"—slang.

brainy Colloquial.

bran new, brand new *Bran new* is usually considered a colloquial form; *brand new*, literary. The original metaphor was "new as a brand," *i.e.*, as fire.

brash In the sense of *impetuous, hasty*—colloquial, perhaps in literary use; in that of *pert, impudent*—colloquial.

brass For *impudence, unpleasant assurance*—colloquial.

brat For *child*—in good use.

break For *social error*—"That was a bad break"—colloquial, U. S. *Make a break* for *leave, depart*—"Let's make a break"—slang. *Break* for *cause bankruptcy*—"Such an act would break half the merchants in the state"—in good use. (See also *broke*.) *Break* for *deprive of standing or rank*—"Any officer doing that will be broken"—in good use. *Break with* for *break off relations with*—"Let's break with him"—in good use.

breather For *breathing space, short rest*—colloquial.

breezy For *cheerful, active*—"a breezy person"—often labeled colloquial, but in good use.

broadcast, broadcasted As preterit and past participle (in radio usage), both forms accepted.

broke For *bankrupt*—colloquial; for *broken*—illiterate.

bromide For *platitude, platitudinous person*—colloquial. The antonym, much less often used, is *sulphite*. (Inventions of Gelett Burgess.)

brunch Slang (of English origin) for a light repast between breakfast and lunch

buck For *contend, resist stubbornly*—"There's no use bucking against such odds"—colloquial. *Buck up* for *cheer up, brace up*—colloquial. As a noun, for *dollar*—"The price is one buck"—slang. *Pass the buck* for *decline, let another do* (something)—slang (from poker).

bucket-shop For *an office for gambling in stocks or shares*—in good use.

buddy For *mate, pal*—colloquial.

bug For *beetle, insect*—colloquial, U. S. In England *bug* means, usually, *bedbug*. In strict usage a bug is a hemipterous insect, not a beetle.

bulge For *slight advantage*—"to get or have the bulge on"—slang.

bulk For *greater part, majority*—"The bulk of the voters are independent"—though often challenged, in good use.

bull For *policeman* or *detective*—slang, U. S. For *go blindly or stupidly*—"You can't just bull in on them"—colloquial or slang. *Throw the bull* for *grossly exaggerate, boast, lie*—slang. Also *bull-thrower*.

bulldoze Colloquial, U. S. Also *bulldozer*.

bum For *bad, no good, useless*—"This is a bum fountain pen"—slang, U. S. As a noun, for *tramp, worthless person, loafer*—slang or colloquial. As a verb, for *loaf, dissipate, beg a ride*—colloquial or slang, U. S.

bumper For *unusually large, good, or successful*—"a bumper crop"—colloquial.

bumptious For *offensively conceited* or *self-assertive*—in good use.

bunch For *group or set of people*—slang.

bunco *See* bunko.

buncombe, bunkum For *inflated or specious talk*—"The good senator's oration is all buncombe"—colloquial; slangily abbreviated to *bunk* (though *bunk* may be an abbreviation of *bunko*).

bung For *bruise*—"all bunged up"—slang.

bungle For *botch, work inexpertly, execute faultily*—"He bungled the assignment"—in good use. Also as a noun—"I say, 'tis a poor cheat, a wretched bungle"—Browning.

bunk *See* buncombe.

bunko, bunco For *swindle, cheat*—in good use. Abbreviated as *bunk*—slang.

burble For *prattle, chatter*—colloquial.

burglarize Colloquial.

burgle Humorous.

bust For *break, tame*—"bust a bronco"—slang, U. S. For *fail* (in business)—slang or colloquial, U. S. For *burst*—dialectal or illiterate. As a noun for *spree* or for *flat failure*—slang. *Busted* for *burst* or *broken*—"The bag's busted," "My leg's busted"—low colloquial or dialectal.

buster For *something huge*—"That ox is a buster"—slang. For *spree*—slang. For *a breaker of horses*—"bronco buster"—U. S.; hence *trust-buster*—colloquial, U. S.

busy For *in use*—"The line is busy"—U. S.

butt in For *intrude, interrupt*—slang or colloquial.

buy As a noun, for *thing bought or to be bought*—"That's a good buy"—colloquial.

caboodle *See* boodle. (The word may be a fusion of *kit* and *boodle*.)

cagey For *shrewd, sly, cautious*—colloquial or slang.

cahoot or **cahoots** For *partnership, collusion*—"I think the two are in cahoots"—slang. *Go cahoots* for *share*—slang.

calculate For *intend, mean, think*—"I calculate to go tomorrow," "I calculate you are right"—colloquial or provincial, U. S.

caliber Used figuratively—"He is a man of low [*or* small] caliber"—established, but often used inappropriately.

canine For *dog*—pretentious or humorous. So *equine, feline*, etc.

cannot help but The form is in dispute, some authorities holding that it is a confusion of idioms, while others hold that it is in good colloquial use, is grammatically formed, and is found in many good authors. Webster and Century accept it. Most manuals, however, advise using either the gerund without *but* or *but* without *help*—"We could not help liking him," "We could not but like him." It is to be doubted, however, if "We could not help but like him" is to be rejected as wrong.

cantankerous A very old colloquialism.

can't seem Colloquial, but condemned by purists as illogical. "I seem unable" is a better form.

card For *odd, original person*—old colloquialism, used by Dickens, Arnold Bennett, and others, revived in this country.

case *In case, in case of, in that case* are all correct idioms. But the word *case* and the phrases just mentioned are much abused. The objection to them is mainly on the ground of verbosity; *e.g.,* "In the case of employees who are late to work, a reduction of wages will be made."

casket For *coffin*—usually pseudo-refined.

cat For *ill-natured woman*—colloquial. Also *catty, cattishness. Cat* is used as an abbreviated form of *cat-o'-nine-tails, i.e.,* a whip composed of nine thongs or cords.

catch on For *apprehend, perceive*—colloquial. For *catch*—"The house will catch on fire"—colloquial.

catch up with For *overtake*—"We'll catch up with him"—in good use. In England the form is "We'll catch him up."

catchy For *catching attention*—in good use.

category Often used where *class* or *kind* would do; a big word for a simple thing. Strictly, a category is a class especially formed or designated for purposes of discussion or classification.

caution For *something uncommon or alarming*—"That child is certainly a caution"—colloquial, U. S.

cave in For *yield, give up*—"He finally caved in under their questioning"—colloquial or slang.

cavort For *prance about*—colloquial, U. S.

cease, stop *Cease* is rapidly being supplanted by *stop* and is now used mostly in dignified or elevated contexts, though it remains in old phrases, such as "Cease firing!"

charwoman Usually labeled a Briticism, but the word is now common in the eastern U. S.

chatty In good use. Also *chattily, chattiness.*

cheek For *effrontery*—colloquial. Also *cheeky.*

chesty For *conceited, bumptious*—slang, U. S.

chipper For *lively, alert*—colloquial, U. S.

chisel For *cheat, obtain by flattery or influence*—colloquial. Also *chiseler.*

chore For *small job, routine duty*—colloquial, U. S., or provincial Eng. A form of *char*, as in *charwoman.*

chortle For *chuckle loudly*—colloquial. An invention of Lewis Carroll (*Jabberwocky*). Other words of his coinage are *bemish, uffish, whiffling.*

chump For *foolish person*—colloquial.

chunky For *thickset, short and thick*—colloquial, U. S.

cinch As noun and verb, formerly slang, now colloquial.

clam For *close-mouthed person*—colloquial, U. S. (The word *clam* used in the U. S., does not refer to the same mollusk as in England, where *clam* usually refers to a scallop or mussel.)

clapboard As a verb—"We have clapboarded the house"—U. S.

class The use of *class* of students of the same year is American, the English (and some schools in America) using *form* or *year. Class* in the sense of *superiority*—"That girl has class!"—is apparently in good use. *Classy*, however, in the sense of *stylish, high-class*, is colloquial.

clever For *good-natured, obliging*—"a clever horse"—homely colloquialism, U. S.

clip For *rate of speed*—"at a fast clip"—colloquial. For *smart, pert, daring person*—"That child's a perfect clip"—homely colloquialism. For *quick punch*— "I'll deal you a clip on the head"—colloquial.

close For *stingy*—in good use.

close call For *narrow escape*—colloquial.

clout For *blow*—"to hit one a clout"—colloquial or dialectal.

cobbler For a drink—"a sherry cobbler"—U. S.

cocky For *pert, conceited*—slang.

coed or **co-ed** U. S.

colored man *Negro* (capitalized) is preferred.

colorful Recently made popular by advertisers and now greatly overworked.

combine For *combination*—colloquial, U. S.

come *Come* has a number of colloquial uses: *come after* for *come to get*—"I have come after the book"; *come to mark, come to scratch; come to* for *become conscious. Come across* for *pay*—"Come across with ten dollars"—slang.

comeback For *return to former power*—"The pugilist says he can make a comeback"—colloquial. For *adequate reply*—"That was a snappy comeback"—slang.

comedown For *humiliating experience, change for the worse*—colloquial.

company For *guest, companion*—homely colloquialism. *See also* keep.

complected For *complexioned*—provincial. "A dark-complexioned person." *Complected* is a rare word meaning *interwoven, intertwined*.

conniption Usually *conniption fit*—local or humorous.

consensus There has been a great ado about the expression *consensus of opinion*, and many writers are painfully careful to avoid it. It appears, however, to be well established and in some contexts is clearer than *consensus* alone. The *Standard Dictionary* gives *consensus of opinion* without comment, and the phrase is used by the editors of *Facts About Current English Usage* but nowhere discussed by them.

considerable As a noun—a dubious colloquialism. "We lost much [rather than *considerable*] in the hurricane."

consummated For *performed, done, finished*—pretentious, sometimes illiterate. A consideration of the meaning of *consummated* will suggest that the word should be reserved for use in the sense of *completed to the highest degree, triumphantly accomplished*.

contact As a verb—"He contacted me by telephone"—business jargon taken over into general use. Not established as literary.

contraption For *doubtful contrivance*—colloquial, U. S.

coolth For *coolness*—humorous or dialectal. Coined by analogy with *warmth*.

coverage A business term, recently extended, as in "coverage of the news."

crack For *superior*—"a crack shot"—colloquial. As a verb, for *open, break into*— "crack a safe"—slang.

cracked For *eccentric, insane*—slang.

crackerjack For *first-class*—slang, U. S.

cracksman For *burglar*—slang.

crack up For *praise*—colloquial.

crack-up For *breakdown*—colloquial.

cram For *study intensively*—colloquial.

crank For *eccentric person*—colloquial.

crawfish For *crawl out of* (a position), *back down* or *back out of*—"I should call the governor's statement of alleged principles crawfishing"—colloquial.

crawl For *back down, sneak out of*—"Now, don't crawl. Say what you really mean"—colloquial or slang.

crawly For *eerie, creepy*—colloquial.

crook For *rogue, thief, sharper*—colloquial.

crooked For *not honest, fraudulent, not straightforward*—in good use.

crummy For *not in good condition, threadbare*—"That's a crummy suit he has on"—provincial or colloquial.

crush For *infatuation*—"She has a crush on her teacher"—slang.

cuckoo For *crazy, idiotic*—slang.

cunning For *pretty, piquant* (in looks or manners)—colloquial, U. S.

cups For *cupfuls*—"Take two cups of sugar," etc.—colloquial. So *baskets, tablespoons, teaspoons.*

cuss For *curse, mild swearing*—colloquial, U. S. Also *cussed* (adj.), *cussedness.* Also *cuss* as a humorous term of affectionate depreciation—"He's a cute little cuss."

cut For *absent oneself from*—"He cut too many classes"—college colloquialism. Also as a noun—"He took too many cuts." *Cut* for *snub, break off acquaintance with*—in good use. *Cut in half* for *cut in halves*—established. *Cut up* for *play pranks*—colloquial. *Cut in* (at a dance)—colloquial. *Cut that out, that doesn't cut any ice, cut a melon*—slang.

cute For *acute, shrewd*—colloquial or provincial: for *pretty, dainty*, etc.,—colloquial.

cut-up For *one who plays pranks*—colloquial.

dab For *skillful person*—"I am no dab at that sort of work"—old colloquialism.

dabster For *an expert, adept*—dialectal; for *dabbler, unskilled person*—colloquial.

daft For *foolish, flighty, idiotic, insane*—in good use.

daisy For *fine, charming*—"That's a daisy pair of skates"—colloquial. Also as a noun—"My aunt is a daisy."

damage For *cost, charge, bill*—"Waiter, what's the damage?"—slang.

dander For *anger, temper*—"He gets my dander up"—colloquial.

dandy For *fine, pretty*, etc.—"That's a dandy trout rod"—colloquial. Also as a noun—"That coat's a dandy"—colloquial.

dare As a noun—"I won't take a dare"—colloquial.

date As a verb, in the sense of *proclaims its date*—"Nothing dates so quickly as slang," "The trouble with modernistic music is that it so soon dates"—or as an adjective—"His style is dated"—condemned by some as neologistic. Though the usage is at present overworked, it is apparently accepted. In the sense of *record or note the date*—"Be sure to date the letter," "This letter is undated"—in good use. *Date* for *appointment*—"I've got a date for tomorrow night"—colloquial. *Blind date*—slang.

dead *Dead right, dead sure, dead beat, dead tired*, etc.—colloquial. *Dead game*—slang.

dead beat For *a sponger, parasite*—slang.

deadhead For *person attending a theater or riding on a train without having to pay*—colloquial.

deal "A deal of good literature fails to attract attention." This use of *deal* is old, as in Shakespeare's "an infinite deal of nothing," but is now usually qualified, "a good deal," "a great deal." *Deal* for *underhand agreement*—"The politicians have made a deal"—colloquial, U. S.

debunk For *divest of bunk*—slang, U. S. *See* bunk.

dele For *delete, take out*—in good use in printing and editing.

demean For *lower, degrade*—"I wouldn't demean myself by doing such a thing" —in good use (found in old authors, Fielding, for instance). The word is not the same as *demean* in the sense of *behave, comport*—"Be careful so to demean yourself that you will not give offense." (*Compare* demeanor.)

demise Used for the death of an ordinary person, pretentious. Traditionally, *demise* is used of a monarch or of a person transmitting great wealth.

demote Established as an antonym of *promote*.

depot For *railroad station*—colloquial or provincial, U. S. In British usage *depot* is restricted to the meaning *place of deposit, storehouse*.

dick For *person*—"He's a queer dick"—colloquial. For *detective*—slang.

dicker For *barter, haggle*—in good use, U. S.

diehard For *irreconcilable opponent*—in good use.

diggings For *lodgings, neighborhood*—colloquial.

diner For *dining car*—colloquial. So *sleeper, smoker*.

dinky For *small, pretty, neat*—"That's a dinky car"—slang.

dippy For *foolish, crazy, drunk*—slang.

directly For *as soon as*—"Directly we arrived, we sat down to dinner"—a Briticism, seldom heard in this country. Considered colloquial by some authorities and incorrect by others. *Immediately* is used in the same way.

dish For *cheat*—"He dished me out of all my money"—slang.

disremember For *forget*—humorous or provincial.

dive For *resort of criminals*—slang. By extension, usually humorously, *any resort* or even *residence*.

do *Do* has many idiomatic and colloquial uses that are well established: *To do away with, to do for the moment, to do one's job; "Do as you are done by," "She did up the parcel," "Up and doing," "What is doing?" "I have nobody to do for me" (help, care for me), "The women did out (cleaned out) the office," "Thirty cents will do (be sufficient) till I get home," "That did his business" (ruined him). All these are accepted as idiomatic or as established colloquialisms. The following are usually labeled as colloquial: *done brown, to do one out of property, to do a term in jail*. The following are low colloquial or slang: *to do one proud, to do one up* (beat him), *to do a person* (trick or harm him). The last is equivalent to the English slang *do in*—"If he tries that scheme we'll do him" (English, *do him in*).

dock For *shorten* or *make less*—"dock a horse's tail," "dock a man's pay"—in good use.

dog *Put on dog*, for *act or dress ostentatiously*—colloquial.

doggo For *in hiding*—"to lie doggo"—slang.

doggy For *attractive, fashionable*—slang (originally Navy slang).

doll For (pretty) *girl*—slang. As a verb, *doll up* for *dress up*—slang, U. S.

domine, dominie Both forms are used in the U. S. colloquially or provincially of a clergyman or a schoolmaster. *Dominie* is the Scottish form for *schoolmaster*.

donate By some authorities called an Americanism.

done for For *ruined*—in good use.

done up For *tired out*—in good use.

don't think Purists object to the familiar form "I don't think I'll go" on the ground that it is illogical, the proper form being "I think I'll not go"; but good usage is against them. There are, of course, contexts in which *don't think* is clearly wrong; for example, "He's not coming, I don't think" is a double negative and illiterate.

dope *Dope* as a noun signifying a thick liquid, such as opium paste, is apparently established and is colloquially extended to include any opiate or narcotic. *Dope, dope fiend* for *user of dope*—slang. Also *dope* in this sense as a verb, and the adjective *dopey*. *Dope* for *advance information*—slang, as noun and verb. Also *dopesheet*. *Dope* for *stupid person*—"You dope, why did you ever do that!"—slang.

dough For *money*—slang, U. S.

doughboy For *infantryman*—colloquial, U. S.

dove For *dived*—colloquial, becoming literary.

downwards In good use, as are *afterwards, heavenwards, homewards, towards*.

drag For *influence*—"I have a drag with the governor"—slang.

draggletail For *slattern, slut*—in literary use, though often classified as colloquial.

dream "Dream girl," "dream garden," though formed on the model of *dream-land, dream world, dream analysis*, suggests a cheap style of writing.

dress suit *Evening clothes* or *full dress* now preferred.

drunk As a noun meaning spree—"He is on a drunk"—or *drunken person*—"He is a drunk"—slang.

dry As a noun, for *prohibitionist*—"The wets and drys will both vote for him"—colloquial, U. S. *Dry town*—colloquial.

dub For *awkward or inexperienced player*—slang.

duck For *pet, darling*—"She's a perfect duck"—colloquial. Also *ducky*. For *person*—"a queer duck"—slang. *Lame duck* for *unreliable or insolvent person*—slang. As a verb, for *dodge out of sight*—"He ducked into the house"—colloquial.

dud For *shell that fails to explode, counterfeit check*—colloquial. Hence for anything that falls short of expectations.

duds For *articles of clothing* or *trivial belongings*—colloquial.

dumb For *stupid*—colloquial or vulgar.

dump For *dumping-ground*—in good use, U. S. For *uncomfortable or dirty living quarters*—"This room is a dump"—slang.

easy mark For *credulous person*—colloquial or slang.

eat (pronounced *ĕt*) For *ate*—"I eat two hours ago"—has historical defense and is labeled by some authorities as still debatable. It is now provincial or illiterate. For *eaten*—"I have eat my dinner"—provincial or illiterate.

eats For *food*—slang or humorous.

edgeways, edgewise Both forms in good use.

egg For *incite*—"His conscience egged him on to apologize"—in good use. For *pelt with eggs*—colloquial.

elective As a noun for *elective course*—college colloquialism, U. S.

elegant For *excellent, enjoyable, praiseworthy,* etc.—"We had an elegant time," "Isn't this elegant weather?"—dubious colloquialism. *Elegant* means *refined, finished, pleasing because of care and taste.*

eliminate Often pretentiously used where a simpler word would serve and be appropriate. Compare: "Mice are the pest we must try to eliminate" and "Mice are the pest we must try to get rid of."

else For *or, otherwise*—"He must do it, else we shall suffer"—accepted. It is, however, so often a poeticism that it seems pseudo-refined in simple prose. The colloquial form is *or else*—"You must attend or else be fined."

emulse For *emulsify*—illiterate.

end up For *end, conclude*—"We'll end up by losing our train"—colloquial.

endways, endwise Both forms are accepted.

enthuse Colloquial, U. S. Despite hostility the word has made its way, because of its brevity compared with "become enthusiastic." Several instances of its use by careful writers have been noted.

equine For *horse*—pretentious or humorous.

eventuate Though condemned by some, the word is in good use. It is, however, often used pretentiously, where a simpler word would serve.

every so often Colloquial.

evince For *show, exhibit*—pretentious in informal writing.

evolute A popular coinage for *evolve,* not in serious use.

ex For *former*—"his ex-wife"—poor form. Say, rather, "his former wife." The expression is, however, in general and perhaps good use when it refers to former officials: *ex-president, ex-chairman.*

expose For *exposé, exposure*—not now in good use.

extend For *offer, send*—"Please extend my greetings to him"—overformal or pretentious.

extra For *unusually*—colloquial. "It is an unusually fine day."

factor An overworked word, often used where another would be more accurate. Taken over from mathematics, it retains the meaning of *active element, cause, or agent;* but is often used where there is no suggestion of activity or work.

fake, faker Colloquial. So *nature faker. Faker* is not etymologically connected with *fakir* and therefore should not be spelled (as it sometimes is) *fakir;* although, as Sir J. Arthur Thompson says, "A fakir is sometimes a faker."

fall For *autumn.* Though it has had a long use in English, it is considered an Americanism or an English provincialism. As an adjective—"fall apples," "fall overcoat"—also American.

fall (*v.*) *Fall* has a few colloquial or slang uses; *fall down* for *fail*—"He fell down on the job"—colloquial; *fall for* for *be deceived or attracted by* (a person)—"I fell for him"—colloquial, U. S.; *take a fall out of* for *get the better of*—colloquial, U. S.

famed For *famous*—"The famed soprano of the Metropolitan"—a usage given vogue by the magazine *Time* and spreading rapidly but not yet accepted.

fan For *fanatic*—slang or colloquial, U. S.

fancy For *think, believe*—"It's going to rain, I fancy"—colloquial, Eng. Also as an exclamatory word—"Just fancy!"

fantods For *fidgets*—"She gives me the fantods"—localism or slang, given currency by Mark Twain.

faze For *disconcert, worry*—colloquial. *Faze* is a variant of *feeze*, which is now seldom heard.

feel For (physical) *feeling*—"The soft feel of worsted"—in good use. For *a mental sensation*—"The deadly feel of solitude" (Keats)—obsolescent.

feel like For *feel inclined*—"I don't feel like going"—colloquial.

feel of For *feel*—"Feel of this fur"—often objected to on the ground that the *of* is redundant; but in good use.

feline For *cat*—pretentious or humorous.

fiend For *one addicted to*—"camera fiend," "a fiend for accuracy"—colloquial, humorous.

filibuster For *buccaneer*, or *engage in military adventure*—in general standard use; for *obstruct legislation*—an Americanism.

filler For *a short item used to fill out a page*—colloquial or cant.

film As a verb, for *photograph on a film*—established.

fine For *well, much*—"I like it fine"—dubious colloquialism.

fire For *discharge*—"He fired the bookkeeper"—colloquial.

fix The standard meaning is *fasten, attach or secure firmly*. *Fix* for *procure the favor of*—"fix a policeman," "fix a jury"—colloquial, U. S.; for *adjust, repair*—"I'll fix the lock"—colloquial; for *arrange, make orderly*—"Let's fix up this room"—colloquial. *To be in a fix, i.e.,* predicament—colloquial, U. S.

fizzle For *fail* or *failure*—colloquial. Also *fizzle out*. The literary meaning of the word is *a hissing sound* or *make a hissing sound*.

flabbergast Colloquial and humorous.

flame For *beloved, sweetheart*—colloquial.

flip For *flippant*—"She's altogether too flip"—colloquial or slang.

flivver Slang.

flunk For *fail* (in a course or examination)—college slang, U. S.

flush For *supplied with money*—"Since Mr. James was flush, he could afford to be generous"—old colloquialism.

flustrate For *fluster, befuddle*—colloquial.

flyer For *venture*—"take a flyer in the stock market"—colloquial, U. S.

focus As a verb—overworked.

fogy For *old-fashioned fellow*—old colloquialism.

forecast, forecasted Both forms accepted for the preterit and past participle.

for keeps For *for good*—"It's mine for keeps"—colloquial.

fork out or **over** For *hand out, hand over*—slang.

fourflusher Colloquial or slang.

foxy For *shrewd*—in good use.

fracas For *brawl, uproar*—in good use.

frazzled For *distraught, worn out*—colloquial. The established meaning is *frayed, unraveled*.

freeze As a noun—"We'll have a freeze before morning"—in good use (Webster), colloquial (Standard). As a verb for *neutralize* funds or bank deposits—colloquial. *Freeze out* for *exclude, snub*—colloquial. *Freeze to* or *on to* for *keep close to, cling fast to* (persons), *take fast possession of*—"The little boy froze on to the gang of older boys and declined to be snubbed"—colloquial.

frisk For *pick pockets* or *search a person*—slang.

from whence The phrase is condemned by purists on the ground that, since *whence* means *from what place, from whence* is pleonastic. The judges quoted in *Facts About Current English Usage* disagreed, however, about its reputableness, the teachers condemning it and the linguists approving it. The editors accepted it as "among established usages," and it certainly is common in good writers. Of course, in spoken English one is likely to say "Where do you come from?" and this expression has generally displaced "Whence do you come?" even in literary usage, the latter seeming stilted. Similarly, *from there* is much more often used than *from thence*.

function For *social occasion*—best reserved for public or ecclesiastical reference. Of private, unimportant events, use *reception, wedding, funeral, dance, birthday party*, and the like.

funk For *fright*—colloquial. Also *blue funk* for *extreme fright*. (The word is a Scotticism.)

funnies For *comic pictures* ("comic strip")—colloquial, U. S.

funny The older meaning is *providing fun, comical, facetious*—a funny fellow, picture, story. Colloquially it has come to mean *odd, disturbing, unaccountable*— "That's a funny thing to say."

fuss, fussy In good use.

fussbudget For *fussy person*—provincial or colloquial.

gab For *talk too much, be loquacious*—colloquial. As a noun, for *idle talk, gabble*—colloquial. *Gift of gab* for *conversational fluency*—colloquial.

gadabout As an adjective, accepted; as a noun, colloquial.

gadget For *mechanical contrivance*—humorous colloquial.

gaff *Stand the gaff* for *endure pain or discomfort*—slang.

gag For *joke, humorous allusion*—slang (stage and radio). Also as a verb. *Gag man* for *one who manufactures gags*—slang.

game For *plucky*—in good use. For *lame*—"a game leg"—colloquial. For *competition* that is not a game—*e.g.*, "the advertising game"—slang.

gangling For *spindling, awkward*—colloquial.

gangster Colloquial, U. S.

gent For *gentleman*—vulgar.

gentleman Like *lady*, should be used with attention to its appropriateness and not used where *man* will serve.

gesture For *simulation of action, mere pretense*—"His captor's offer of food was a mere gesture"—a vogue word. The word is recent in this sense and in the other of *speech or behavior suggesting action*, good or bad—"The Senate is considering gestures of good will towards Chile."

get The following phrases are colloquial: *get through* (finish, complete), *get along* (manage somehow), *get there* (arrive), *get to* (arrive at), *get the idea, get the hang of, get together*. The following are colloquial, but often slangy: *get a gait on, get religion, get away with, get left, get going*. The following is local: "We shall not get to see (*or* get to go to) the play before it is closed." *See got*.

ginger For *mettle, energy*—colloquial.

glamour, glamorous Old words now cheapened and slangy.

glum For *moody*—in good use.

go The following are colloquial uses of *go*, as noun or verb, all in good standing: "He would succeed if he had more go," "I'll have another go at it," "I've tried, but it's no go," "Felt hats are all the go," "We've been on the go until we're tired," "The dog went for him viciously," "I simply can't go that." Dubious colloquialism or slang: "I go for it in a big way" (*i.e.*, "am attracted by it").

goat For *scapegoat, victim*—"They made him the goat"—slang.

gob For *sailor* of the United States Navy—slang, U. S.

go-by For *avoidance*—"Let's give them the go-by"—slang.

going places For *gadding about*—"Tonight we're going places"—slang. For *succeeding*—"That man is going places"—slang.

gone on For *in love, infatuated*—"They're simply gone on each other"—colloquial.

goner For *a person or thing lost or ruined*—colloquial or slang.

good For *well*—"Things are not going good with him"—illiterate. *Good and* for *very*—"It's good and wet this morning"—established idiom, though considered by some a homely colloquialism. *A good deal*—well-established idiom. *See* deal.

goof For *stupid or silly person*—slang. Also *goofy*.

goon For *a solemn, owlish person*—colloquial. Also *goonish*. The opposite of a goon is a *jigger*.

got *Get* has two forms for the past participle, *got* and *gotten*, but the latter, though common in the United States, is obsolescent. Strictly, the past participle *has got, have got*, should not be used in the sense of *possesses*, "The cat has got a long tail," because here the *got* is redundant. *Got* is correctly used in the sense of *acquired, procured*—"The cat has got a mouse."

gouge For *defraud, overcharge*—colloquial, U. S.

grab As a noun—"The taking of the land by eminent domain was just a grab"—colloquial.

grade crossing Correct in U. S. The English *level crossing* is, however, becoming general in parts of this country.

graft For *unjust gain*—in good use. Also *to graft, grafter*.

green For *inexperienced*—"a green hand"—in good use. Also *greenhorn* for *an inexperienced person.*

grifter For *trickster*—slang, U. S.

grind For *study hard*—colloquial. Also as a noun, for *a hard-working student.*

grip For *handbag*—colloquial, U. S.

gripe For *complain*—slang.

grit For *courage*—in good use. Also *gritty*.

groggy For *tipsy, dazed*—colloquial.

groom For *bridegroom*—colloquial, inelegant.

grouch For *complain, sulk*—colloquial, U. S. Also as a noun—"He has [*or* is] an awful grouch." In England (and occasionally in this country) *grouse* is used as a verb in the sense of *grouch*.

grow smaller Often condemned as illogical, but it is an old idiom, used by many great writers. So *grow less*.

grumpy For *glum, gloomy, moody*—in good use.

guess For *think*—"I guess I've had enough to eat"—colloquial, U. S., though the usage is as old as Chaucer. Compare the English use of *fancy*.

gump For *foolish person*—colloquial, U. S.

gumption For *discernment, common sense, acuteness*—colloquial. (The word is technical in the art of painting.)

gumshoe For *go stealthily*—slang, U. S. Also *gumshoer*.

gunman For *armed thug*—U. S.

gurry For *offal, refuse, oil waste*—in good use and, by extension, colloquially for damp and offensive stuff of any sort. As a verb *gurry* is local New England.

gush For *effusiveness*—colloquial.

guts For *stamina, grit*—slang.

guttersnipe For *street Arab*—colloquial or slang.

guy For *man* or *person*—"He's a good guy"—slang. The word is derived from Guy Fawkes and in the sense of *grotesque person* or *effigy* is in good use.

gyp For *swindle*—slang. The word has other cant or slang meanings in England.

had better, would better Both in literary use. Also *had rather, would rather*.

had ought, hadn't ought Illiterate. The correct forms are "He ought to go," "He ought not to go."

half *Half a* for *half of a* is idiomatic—"Half a league onward." *A half an hour* —incorrect: say *half an hour* or *a half hour*. *Not half bad* for *fairly good*— colloquial. *See also* cut.

half baked For *simple, moronic*—colloquial.

half cock For *without premeditation*—"He's always going off at half cock"— colloquial.

ham For *incompetent actor*—slang, U. S. (Short for *hamfatter*—slang.)

handy For *close by*—"The post office is very handy"—colloquial. Also *handy to*—"Our house is very handy to the post office." Both expressions are frowned upon by those who insist that *handy* should be used only of objects that are close to or convenient to the hand.

hang *Get the hang of* for *perceive, understand*—colloquial.

happen in For *make a chance call*—"I just happened in"—colloquial.

hard-boiled For *impervious, unemotional, cynical*—colloquial.

hard-shell For *unyielding, uncompromising*—colloquial, U. S.

harum-scarum In good use.

has-been For *antiquated person, failure*—colloquial.

haven't but For *have but*—"I haven't but ten hens"—dubious, if not incorrect. So *haven't only*.

heap, heaps For *a good deal, a good many*—"We had heaps [*or* a heap] of chances, but still failed"—colloquial.

hear of, hear to "I won't hear of your going"—colloquial. "He wouldn't hear to the proposal!"—provincial or illiterate.

hectic For *excited, restless*—"We had a hectic time," "She wore a hectic expression"—colloquial. Strictly, *hectic* denotes fever or the flush attending a feverish condition. So Shelley has "Yellow and white and pale and hectic red."

heel, heeler For *disreputable hanger-on or tool* (as of a political boss)—colloquial. So *ward-heeler*. By extension *heel* has come to mean any utterly unprincipled or immoral or disreputable man—"The hero of *What Makes Sammy Run?* is a heel" (from a review of the novel).

help "Don't move any more than you can help"—condemned by some authorities as illogical, logic requiring "Don't move any more than you cannot help," but the form is established. *Help* for *hired person, servant*—local, U. S.

helping For *portion* (of food)—colloquial.

helter-skelter In literary use.

hereabout, hereabouts Both in good use.

het up For *excited, angry*—provincial or humorous.

hex For *bewitch*—local or slang, U. S. Also *hexer*.

highbrow Colloquial. Also *lowbrow*.

highfalutin, highfaluting For *high-flown, bombastic*—colloquial.

hike The word appears to be colloquial, provincial, or dialectal in all its uses. *Hike* for *pull*—"He hiked up his trousers"—colloquial. *Hike* for *walk, tramp*—colloquial. Also *hike* as a noun, and *hiker* and *hitchhike*.

hindsight Humorous colloquial.

hit For *success*—"The play was a hit"—in good use. *Made a hit* for *won approval*—colloquial. *Hit it off* for *agree*—"The pair do not seem to hit it off"—colloquial. *Hit it up* for *increase speed*—slang.

hitchhike See *hike*.

hobbledehoy For *awkward, gawky fellow*—in good use.

hobo For *migratory worker, professional tramp*—in good use, U. S.

hocus For *cheat* or *adulterate*—long in good use. Also *hocus-pocus* for *trick or nonsense intended to cloak deception*.

hog For *take more than one's share*—slang.

holdup For *robbery*—colloquial, U. S.

hole *Be in a hole* for *be in a predicament*—colloquial.

hollow *Beat all hollow*—colloquial.

homely For *ill-favored, not good looking*—often labeled an Americanism, but is in good use. In England, *ugly* is commonly used, *homely* retaining its old meaning of *fond of home* or *domestic*.

homey For *homelike, cosy*—colloquial and perhaps, rarely, literary.

hooch For *illicit liquor*—slang, U. S.

hoodlum For *young rowdy*—colloquial.

hoodoo For *one who brings hard luck*—colloquial. Also as a verb.

hooky *To play hooky* for *play truant from school*—boy's slang.

hooligan For *rowdy, ruffian*—slang.

hoosegow or **hoosgow** For *jail*—slang, U. S.

hoot *Not care a hoot* for *not care at all*—colloquial or slang.

hope chest Colloquial.

horn in For *intrude*—slang.

hornswoggle For *hoax*—slang.

hubby, hubbly For *full of bumps or unevennesses*—provincial, U. S.

human For *human being*. Although the usage can be found in older writers of repute, it is not accepted generally today. Perhaps by analogy with *animal,* it is, apparently, becoming established, especially in the plural—"We poor humans." It is best avoided.

hunch For *premonition*—colloquial.

hunky or **hunkydory** For *satisfactory*—"Everything's hunky [*or* hunkydory]"—slang. *Hunky* for *foreign-born laborer* (especially a Hungarian or Slav)—slang, U. S.

hurt For *pain*—"My leg hurts"—colloquial.

hush money For *bribe paid to obtain silence*—slang.

hustle For *move energetically, hurry*—"I'll have to hustle or I'll be late"—colloquial. Also *hustler*. The literary meaning is *push, shove, cause* (people) *to move*—"The police hustled the crowd."

ice water English authorities insist that ice water is melted ice and iced water is water chilled by ice. In America, however, *ice water* is practically universal for the latter.

immediately For *as soon as*—see directly.

implement As a verb (a Scotticism) for (1) *furnish with implements or means;* (2) *carry into effect, accomplish*—a vogue word during the past decade. "This bill must be implemented," "Congress implemented the bill by adding an amendment."

in regards to For *in regard to*—illiterate.

inside of For *within, in less time or shorter distance*—"We'll be back inside of a week"—colloquial, U. S.

inter, interment For *bury, burial*—in familiar contexts, pretentious.

intrigue For *excite interest or curiosity*—"We were intrigued by her original costume," "Her unusual costume intrigued us"—a Gallicism, probably established, but still having some flavor of affectation.

invite For *invitation*—vulgar, humorous, or slang.

irregardless For *regardless*—illiterate.

jag For *enough liquor to intoxicate*—slang. *Jag* (local, U. S.) in this sense means *small load*, and *load* is also used slangily in the sense of *jag* for *liquor*.

jail As a verb—"There was nothing left to do but to jail him"—in good use, though sometimes objected to.

jam For *predicament, difficulty*—"I'm in a jam"—colloquial or slang.

jamboree For *noisy frolic*—slang.

jaywalker For *one recklessly crossing a street*—colloquial. Also *jaywalk*.

jazz As noun and adjective, in good use. As a verb, colloquial. *Jazzer, jazzy*—slang.

jell For *jelly* (verb)—provincial or colloquial. Also as a noun.

jibe For *be in harmony*—"His stories don't jibe"—colloquial.

jiffy For *instant*—"We'll be ready in a jiffy"—colloquial.

jig "The jig is up" for "It's all over"—colloquial.

jigamaree Like *contraption, jigumbob, thingumbob, gadget*—for *thing* (usually mechanical) *unnamable*—humorous colloquial.

jigger For *mechanical contrivance, gadget*—colloquial. *See also* goon.

job By derivation the word means *a piece of work, a special assignment*, as suggested by the phrases *odd jobs, job printer*. Colloquially it is extended to mean *an engagement to work, employment*—"He has found a good job," "His job is administering estates"—and it is often inappropriately used where the context demands a more dignified word—"A minister's job is saving souls." Colloquially *job* sometimes means *situation, circumstance*—"You have cut your hand! That's a bad job." *Job* in the sense of *unfair scheme, dishonorable transaction*, has long been in literary use.

job lot For *miscellany, inferior goods*—in good use, colloquially applied to a second-rate person.

jobber For *middleman*—in good use.

jollification Colloquial. Also *jollify*.

jolly For *keep in good humor, flatter*—"Let's jolly him along"—slang. For *uncommon, remarkable*—"a jolly nuisance"; for *really, certainly*—"You'll jolly well do it!"; for *pleasant, agreeable*—"You'll go? How jolly!"—all English colloquialisms.

josh For *banter, tease*—slang, U. S. Also as a noun.

jug For *jail*—slang. Also *jugged* for *jailed*.

just For *completely, perfectly*—"That's just fine!"—colloquial. So also *just about* for *almost*—"I'm just about tired out!"

keel over In all senses—colloquial.

keep *Keep from* for *refrain*—"I can't keep from teasing her"—in good use. *Keep up* for *not fall behind*—"It's hard to keep up with him"—in good use. *Keep company* for *associate with* (especially before marriage)—provincial. *See* for keeps.

kibitzer For *look on at cards, be officious or meddlesome as a spectator*—colloquial. The word is from the German through the Yiddish.

kibosh *To put the kibosh on* for *to get rid of, to defeat*—slang, U. S. In English slang, *kibosh* means *nonsense, stuff, humbug*—"That's all kibosh!"

kick For *enjoyment, stimulation*—slang. *Kick, kick about* for *object to*—colloquial or slang.

kick-up For *disturbance*—slang.

kid For *child*—colloquial. Also *kiddie*. *Kid* for *tease, deceive, fool*—"Don't kid yourself," "Stop kidding"—slang.

killing For *captivating*—"a killing glance"—old colloquialism. For *successful deal, large profits*—"He made a killing in the stock market"—slang. *Kill* for *overcome, fascinate* (by charm of person or dress)—"She was dressed to kill"—colloquial.

kindly requested "You are kindly requested to attend." Say, rather: "Will you be kind enough to attend?"

kite As a verb—"Stocks kited today"—colloquial or slang. For *raise a check, get money illegally*—commercial slang.

knickers Colloquial.

knife For *try to defeat* (by underhand means)—slang, U. S.

knock For *criticize, complain*—slang.

knockout For *stunningly attractive*—"She's a knockout!"—slang, U. S. *Knockout drops* for *opiate*—slang.

kudos For *fame, glory*—humorous. (Greek: *kydos*, glory.)

lady Often used, through false refinement, where *woman* is meant.

lag For *jailbird*—slang.

lam For *beat, strike*—"He lammed him on the head"—slang. *Take it on the lam* for *abscond, run away*—slang.

lame duck For *unreliable or insolvent person*—slang.

land-office business For *heavy, thriving trade*—colloquial.

landscaper, landscapist *Landscaper* is colloquial for *landscape gardener; landscapist* is in good use for *landscape painter.*

lark For *jolly time, frolic*—colloquial. Also *larky.*

larrup For *flog, beat*—colloquial. Also *larruping,* as a noun.

later on "We'll go to see him later on"—the *on* is superfluous, but accepted colloquially.

lather For *flog, whip*—colloquial.

layout For *planning, arrangement*—"The layout of the camp was obvious from his sketch"—in good use. Specifically, for *outline with directions* or for *make-up* (as of a book, newspaper, etc.)—technical, becoming colloquial. For *display, show, spread*—"That meal was a fine layout"—slang.

learn For *teach*—"I'll learn you not to disobey me"—now illiterate.

leatherneck For *U. S. Marine*—slang.

leave For *let*—"leave me be"—not accepted. *Leave me alone* for *let me alone*—colloquial. *Leave him come*—illiterate. *Leave hold, leave go*—provincial or dubious colloquial. *See lief.*

leery For *suspicious*—slang.

lend, loan Although *loan* is widely used in America as a verb—"Please loan me your pencil"—the usage is avoided by many careful writers, who prefer "Please *lend* me your pencil."

lengthy Though objected to by purists, *lengthy* for *long* is in good use—"a lengthy sermon." Applied to animals or persons it is, however, colloquial.

let *Let* has many colloquial uses: *let in for* (cheat, defraud)—"I was let in for a bad check"; *let off* (excuse from an obligation); *let on* (divulge, tell)—"Don't let on that you know"; *let oneself go; let slide; let up* (lessen, stop). *Let on* (pretend)—"He let on that he was afraid"—provincial or colloquial. *Let her go, let her rip*—slang, U. S.

let-down For *check to one's self-esteem*—colloquial.

level *On the level* for *truly, honestly*—colloquial.

level head Colloquial.

lick For *whip, defeat*—"Do you think Harvard can lick Yale?"—colloquial. Also *licking* for *beating.*

lief "I would [*or* had] as lief not do it" is a correct usage for "I would [*or* had] rather not do it. (*Lief* is sometimes ignorantly spelled *leave.*)

lie low For *hide*—colloquial.

lift For *steal*—"The thieves lifted a herd of cattle"—old colloquialism. *Shoplifter* is, however, in good use.

like For *as, as if*—"It looks like it's going to rain," "I feel like I have a fever," "I trimmed my hat like you did"—a locution much in dispute. No authority accepts it as literary, but some accept it as colloquial. How it sounds really depends on where one lives. To one person it will seem illiterate, to another provincial, and to a third a natural colloquialism. *Like to have died* for *came near dying*—dubious colloquialism. *Like* for *feel inclined*—"I don't feel like going"—in good use. *As like as not*—colloquial or, perhaps, established.

line Overworked in the senses of *business, occupation, direction, tenor*—"What is your line?" "He talked along that line."

lingo Old colloquialism.

lip For *vulgar talk, impudence, cheek*—slang. Also *lippy.*

liquidate For *clear up, dispose of*—overworked. For *annihilate, kill*—"There's nothing to do about rats except to liquidate them"—slang.

load See *jag.*

loan See *lend.*

lobby For *group seeking to exert concerted influence*—U. S. Also as a verb. Also *lobbyist, lobbyer.*

loco For *crazy*—colloquial or slang, U. S.

locomote Humorous colloquial.

log-rolling For *working together* (politically)—U. S. and Can.

looking up For *improving*—"Things are looking up"—colloquial.

look it For *look so*—"He's fifty, but doesn't look it"—colloquial.

loony For *crazy*—slang.

lopsided In good use.

lose out For *lose*—colloquial. Also *miss out, win out.* The *out* may be felt to have intensive force.

lot, lots For *much, many, a great deal*—colloquial. Also of a person, *kind*—"He's a bad lot"—colloquial.

loud For *showy, flashy*—in good use, though sometimes labeled colloquial.

louse For *contemptible person*—slang. *Lousy* for *infected with lice*—in good use; for *disgusting* or *mean*—slang.

love For *like*—"I love ice cream," "I'd love to go!"—colloquial. *Love* is usually emphatic in this sense. *Love* as a noun—"She has bought a love of a hat"—colloquial.

lowbrow Colloquial.

mad For *angry*—though used by some good writers in the past, now colloquial, U. S., or provincial, Eng.

make *On the make* for *avaricious, too enterprising*—slang. *Make up* for *become reconciled*—in good use. *Make up to* for *seek acquaintance or friendship* (perhaps hypocritically)—colloquial.

makings For *materials of a cigarette*—colloquial, U. S.

materialize For *appear*—except of ghosts, usually inaccurate and pretentious. "The guests failed to appear [*not* materialize]."

matter Too often used where a less vague word would be better, some such word as *affair, question, subject, request, trouble, delay.*

mean For *ill-natured, disobliging*—"I think you're mean"—colloquial. For *unwell, low-spirited*—"I'm feeling mean"—colloquial. *Mean* means, strictly, *ignoble*—"A person of mean instincts."

melon "To cut a melon"—commercial slang.

mess For *confusion, disorder*—colloquial. Also *messy.*

meticulous Recently a vogue word, so much used that careful writers avoid it. In Latin *meticulosus* means *cautious, timid*, but this meaning is obsolescent in English. The word now is used in the sense of *over-particular about details. Scrupulous, punctilious, fastidious* will often serve as well.

mind For *obey*—"Mind your mother"—often listed as colloquial, but in good use. For *look out for, be wary of*—"Mind your step"—colloquial. For *remember, call to mind, recall*—"I mind me of the days when I was young"—provincial or archaic.

miss Used without a following name, generally to be avoided. For *young girl*—chiefly colloquial or in trade use.

mixer For *sociable person*—colloquial.

mix-up For *confusion*—colloquial.

monkeyshine Colloquial, U. S.

monstrous For *excessively large, gigantic*—though often challenged, in good use. *Monstrous big*—"I saw a monstrous big bear"—colloquial.

mooch For *sulk, loiter*—now dialectic or slang. Also *moocher.*

moonshine For *illicit liquor*—colloquial or slang. Also *moonshiner.*

moony For *given to mooning, dreamy*—colloquial.

mosey For *move, walk* (without energy)—provincial or slang, U. S.

most For *almost*—"I'm most famished," "I'm most done"—dubious colloquialism.

mostly For *most*—"The man mostly desirous of being rich"—dubious.

movie, movies Colloquial.

muchly Obsolete, except as humorous. *Muchness*—humorous.

muddle For *confusion*—in good use. Also *muddle* as a verb, *muddler, muddle-headed.*

muff For *handle awkwardly* or *miss* (a catch)—colloquial. Also for *inexpert person, duffer.*

muss For *confusion, mess*—colloquial or dialectal, U. S. Also as a verb for *disarrange, wrinkle* (as a dress). Also *mussy.*

mutt or **mut** For *commonplace, stupid person*—slang; for *a cur, mongrel dog*—slang.

muzzy For *muddled, befuddled*—old slang, Eng.

name *By the name of* for *named*—established but wordy. "A man named John" rather than "a man by the name of John." *Named for* or *after*—"The baby is named for [or after] his uncle"—both in good use, though often labeled colloquial

nasty For *unpleasant*—"a nasty day"; *mean*—"a nasty trick"; *ill-natured*—"a nasty disposition"—colloquial. *Nasty* in strict usage means *disgusting, nauseous, filthy*—"a nasty person"; *morally unclean*—"a nasty story."

natty For *dainty, spruce*—colloquial.

near *Near* has some homely colloquial uses: for *stingy*—"Mr. Barkis was an excellent husband, she said, though still a little near"—Dickens; for *close* or *by a close margin*—"That was a near escape," "The disturbance developed into a near-riot."

near by, near-by "The church is near by," "He became drunk at a near-by saloon"—in good use, though sometimes called an American colloquialism.

née Say "Mrs. Roe née Doe" not "Mrs. Roe née Mary Doe," because a woman is not born with her Christian name.

nerve For *courage* or *effrontery*—colloquial or slang. So *nervy.*

nice For *pleasant, attractive, agreeable,* etc.—"a nice man," "a nice day," "a nice pudding," "a nice coffeepot"—in universal colloquial use, and some phrases, such as "nice people," in literary contexts. In older and stricter usage, *nice* means *acute, fine, delicate, exactly fitted or adjusted*—"In the nice ear of Nature which song is the best?"—Lowell.

nicely For *well, pleasantly, agreeably,* etc.—"This room will do very nicely,"

"Speak to your mother nicely"—colloquial. In stricter usage, *nicely* means *accurately, subtly*—"One cylinder must be nicely fitted inside the other."

nifty For *very good, stylish*—"That's a nifty hat of yours"—colloquial, U. S.

nobby For *stylish, aristocratic*—slang.

no good, no account, no use For *worthless, good for nothing*—colloquial.

normalcy Though President Harding was ridiculed for using it, *normalcy* is an accepted variant for *normality*.

nothing like For *not nearly*—"These shoes are nothing like as well made"—colloquial.

notions For *small goods, knickknacks*—colloquial, U. S.

nowhere near For *not nearly*—"This is nowhere near as good a saw as that"—colloquial.

nut For *eccentric or crazy person*—slang. Also *nutty*.

oats For *feel sprightly* or the opposite—"feel one's oats," "be off one's oats"—colloquial.

objective In the sense of *aim* or *end of action*—"His only objective in life is to make money"—a vogue word or jargon, often used when *aim, purpose, object,* or *end* would serve.

off "I bought these off [*or* off of] Mrs. Kendall"—illiterate. *Off* has a number of colloquial uses: "That child is a little off" (lacking in wits); "The stocks are a little off this morning" (below former prices); "This meat is a trifle off" (tainted); *off color* for *not quite respectable*, as "an off-color story"; *off horse* or *off ox*, the right-hand member of a team. *Off of* for *off*—"I jumped off of the roof"—colloquial, dialectal, or incorrect, according to various authorities. *Off* for *abstaining from*—"I'm off liquor for a month"—slang.

O. K., okay Used colloquially or slangily as noun, adjective, and verb for *right, agreed, correct,* or simply *yes*. (The spelling *okeh*, which is sometimes seen, is that of a Choctaw word meaning "It is so.") All sorts of derivations of *O.K.* have been offered.

old For *big, great* (an intensive)—"a great old time," "a mean old thing"—colloquial. As a term of favor or familiarity—"old girl," "old chap"—colloquial.

oldster For *elderly person*—colloquial.

omnium gatherum For *medley, catch-all*—old humorous coinage, colloquial.

on "I'm on" for "I see, understand"—slang. "I'm on to you" for "I detect your purpose"—slang. "The joke is on me" for "The joke is to my disadvantage"—colloquial.

on the beam *See* beam.

on the level *See* level.

on the side *See* side.

oodles For *a great many, a great deal*—colloquial or slang. (Originally southern U. S.)

open For *having no restrictions* regarding drink, gambling, etc.—colloquial, U. S. Also *wide open*.

orate For *wax oratorical*—colloquial, humorous.

or else *See* else.

ornery A corruption of *ordinary*, for *ill-natured, unprepossessing*—"Look out for that mule, he's ornery"—provincial or humorous.

ought *See* had ought.

out As a verb—"out the light"—dialectal or obsolete. For *over, dismissed*—"School is out"—colloquial, U. S. *Out loud* for *aloud*—colloquial. *Out* for *out of*—"in and out the window"—colloquial. *Out of sight* for *preëminent, of superior quality*—"He's simply out of sight as a billiard player," "This pie is just out of sight"—slang, U. S.

out-and-out For *thoroughgoing, unqualified*—"an out-and-out rascal"—in good use. *Out-and-outer*—colloquial or slang.

outs *At outs* for *at odds, estranged*—colloquial or literary. *On the outs*, with same meaning—colloquial.

outside For *besides, except*—dubious colloquialism. "Except him and me [*not* outside him and me] nobody knows." *Outside of* for *outside*—colloquial, though the *of* is superfluous. *Outside* for *reaching the extreme*, as to extent or quantity —"an outside estimate"—colloquial.

parlous For *risky, perilous*—in good use, but trite.

partial to For *fond of*—"I'm partial to cheese"—colloquial.

party For *person*—a legal usage. In ordinary contexts use *person*.

paw over For *handle heavily*—"Why do you keep pawing my things over?"— colloquial.

peach For *thing or person admired*—"That left fielder is a peach; he made a peach of a play"—slang.

peaked (dissyllable) For *sickly-looking*—colloquial or provincial.

peckish For *somewhat hungry*—colloquial.

peek For *peep*—"The boy peeked through the hole in the fence"—colloquial.

peeved For *peevish*—colloquial or slang. Also *peeve*, verb and noun.

peg *Peg at* for *work absorbedly*—in good use. Also *peg away, peg away at*. *Peg* for *render stationary*—"to peg prices"—in good use. Also *peg down*.

people As a general rule *people* is used as a collective noun, *persons* as a distributive one—"Let all the people sing," "How many persons are in the church?" *People* for *family, kindred*—"I'm going home to my people"—colloquial.

pep For *energy, ambition*—slang. Also *peppy*.

per For *a*—"What is the price of eggs a dozen?"—colloquial. *Per* is sometimes restricted to commercial and scientific contexts. However, *per annum, per cent,* and *per se* are established phrases.

per cent For *percentage*—"He paid me a percent of the profits"—not accepted.

percentage For *part, proportion*—dubious colloquialism. "A large proportion [*rather than* percentage] of the fish were cod."

perfect For *extreme, appalling*, etc.—"That woman's a perfect fright"—colloquial. *Perfect*, in conservative use, is an absolute term and should **not** be grammatically compared—*more perfect, most perfect*. It is better to say *more nearly perfect*.

perform For *play* (on a musical instrument, for example)—often pretentious. *Player* is often to be preferred to *performer*.

persuasion Correctly used of *settled belief*—"religious persuasion"—but slang and trite when it means *kind, sort*—"feminine persuasion."

pesky For *vexatious*—colloquial, U. S. Also *pessicating*.

peter out For *fail, become exhausted*—colloquial,

phone For *telephone*—colloquial.

phony For *counterfeit*—slang.

photo For *photograph*—colloquial.

piazza For *porch, veranda*—Americanism. In Europe a piazza is usually an open square in a city.

picturize Useful but objectionable. So *movieize, novelize,* etc. Since many words similarly formed are in good use, these will probably establish themselves.

piece For *distance, way*—"He lives quite a piece up the road"—provincial.

piffle For *gabble, nonsense, twaddle*—slang.

piker For *timid gambler* or *person who does things in a small or mean way*—slang.

pinch For *steal*—slang. For *arrest* (a person)—slang. *At or in a pinch* for *in an emergency*—in good use.

pinch hit For *act as substitute in a pinch*—slang.

pip, pippin For *person or thing greatly liked*—slang.

pipe down Nautical for *dismiss.* For *be still, stop talking*—slang.

pitch *Pitch in* for *go to work earnestly*—colloquial. *Pitch into* for *attack*—colloquial.

plug For *work hard*—colloquial or slang. Also *plugger* for *hard worker.* For *hit with a bullet*—"If you come nearer I'll plug you"—slang. For *interpolate* (in a program)—stage cant or colloquial. As a noun, for (disguised) *advertisement*—"I'll give you a plug during my talk"—slang; for *spiritless horse*—colloquial, U. S.

plum For *completely*—"I'm plum tired out," "The barrel is plum full"—provincial or colloquial. (The word is really *plumb,* but is now spelled *plum.*)

plunge For *gamble* or *spend recklessly*—colloquial or slang. Also *plunger.*

plunk In all meanings colloquial or slang.

poorly For *not well*—"I'm feeling poorly today"—provincial.

possible "It is not possible of accomplishment"—a dubious form. "It isn't possible to be done"—wordy or worse. Say, rather, "It can't be done."

possum For *opossum*—colloquial.

posted For *informed*—"I'll keep you posted"—colloquial.

powwow Referring to an Indian council—in good use; to a general talk or discussion—colloquial.

pretty For *fairly, moderately*—"How are you? Pretty well"—in good use. *Pretty much*—colloquial.

previous For *premature, hasty, untimely*—"He's too previous"—colloquial.

primp For *prink*—colloquial.

prissy For *overfastidious*—colloquial.

proceed For *go*—"After breakfast we proceeded to Haleyville"—in many such simple contexts, pretentious.

proposition In America, a vogue word or jargon, often used for *task, job, problem, objective, enterprise, undertaking, occupation, trade, opponent, project, area, field, method, experiment.*

prospect For *prospective customer*—business, U. S.

proud *To do one proud*—slang.

proven For *proved*—in dispute. *Proven* is rapidly spreading in the U. S., though rejected by most careful writers and speakers. (It was originally a Scotticism.)

providing "I will go providing he insists"—some rhetoricians insist upon *provided* in such sentences, but *providing* is found in excellent writers of the past two centuries.

psychological moment The phrase properly means *decisive moment, the precisely favorable time,* but it is a vogue phrase and very trite.

psychology Much overworked, as is *psychologize,* and often used trivially where a simpler word would serve: as when a shrewd man is called a profound psychologist and ordinary insight is called psychologizing.

pull For *influence*—"I have a pull with the police"—colloquial or slang. As a verb, for *produce unexpectedly*—"He pulled a fast answer"—slang.

pump For *extract information*—"We'll pump him to find out"—colloquial.

punish For *deal harshly or greedily, make an inroad on*—"The party certainly punished my provisions"—colloquial.

punk *See* spunk.

push For *energy, enterprise*—colloquial.

pusley A corruption of *purslane,* a common weed—"I feel mean as pusley"—provincial but widely colloquial or humorous.

put *Put in* for *enter* (a harbor)—nautical. *Put across* for *succeed against opposition*—slang. *Put in a hole* for *place at a disadvantage*—colloquial. *Stay put* for *not move*—slang or colloquial. *Put over on* for *deceive, take advantage of*—"They put one over on me"—slang. *Put over* for *succeed against opposition*—"Well, we put it over in spite of them"—colloquial. *Put it up to* for *leave the decision to*—"If they put it up to me I'll refuse"—colloquial. *Put upon* for *taken advantage of*—"I feel put upon"—provincial or colloquial.

queer As a verb—"If you don't look out, you'll queer the whole plan"—slang. As an adjective, for *suspicious*—"The plan looks queer to me"—colloquial.

quick As an adverb—"Do it quick"—established.

quite For *very, fairly, rather, to a great extent or degree*—"It's quite warm, isn't it?" "We live quite a way up the road"—an established colloquialism and often found in good writers (U. S.). *Quite a good deal, quite a lot, quite a little,* etc. —colloquial. In strict usage *quite* means *fully, totally, to the fullest extent or degree*—"Are you quite certain?" "He was quite in order in putting the question."

quiz For *examination, examine*—colloquial, U. S.

quote For *quotation*—in good use. For *quotation mark*—colloquial.

racket For *business* (usually dishonest)—colloquial, U. S. So *racketeer.*

raddled For *looking worn, fatigued*—colloquial.

radio As a verb, for *transmit by radio*—in good use, though often challenged.

rag For *taunt, irritate*—"They ragged him about the girl"—slang. Also *ragging* (as a noun).

rage For *object of popularity or acclaim*—"Mahjong was all the rage"—colloquial.

raid For *enter by legal force*—"The police raided the night club"—colloquial. Also used trivially—"We raided the icebox"—colloquial, humorous.

railroad As a verb, for *force or hurry through*—"The bill was railroaded through Congress"—colloquial, U. S.

raise For *increase* (of wages)—colloquial, U. S. So also for *secure, obtain*—"I can't raise the cost."

rake-off For *commission* or *share* (often illegitimate)—slang, U. S.

rally For *mass meeting*—"a football rally"—Americanism.

rambunctious Colloquial and humorous.

rarely ever For *hardly ever*—colloquial though illogical. *Rarely if ever* is logical. So *seldom ever*, which really should be *seldom or never*.

rat For *vile sneak, betrayer, deserter*—slang. Also *ratty* for *shabby*.

rate For *meet approval*—"He doesn't rate with me" or, merely, "He doesn't rate" —slang.

rather *See* had rather.

rattle For *embarrass, discompose*—"The noise rattled the speaker," "We were rattled by the noise"—slang or colloquial.

raving "A raving beauty"—colloquial.

raw For *unprincipled*—"a raw deal"—colloquial.

re For *concerning*—commercial. The word is in Latin the ablative of *res,* thing. It was taken over from law into business and to use it in any other context is vulgar, sometimes illiterate. In business it is most often found at the beginning of a letter or order; for example: *Re:* Order for 400 feet iron pipe." Here it is correctly used and means that the information to follow concerns this matter of iron pipe. *Re* is here used for *in re.*

reaction For *opinion, attitude*—a word taken over from psychology, physics, or chemistry, where it has specific meanings. It is sadly overworked and when loosely used is often jargon.

reactionary Use as a noun sometimes challenged on the ground that it is properly an adjective, the noun being *reactionist* or *reactor;* but it is established.

real For *really*—"I feel real good this morning"—incorrect or provincial. *Real* and *really* are often used where not needed.

realist A word to be used with caution. As popularly employed its meaning is often problematic or it is used in place of some other less vague word, such as *opportunist, cynic, egotist,* or *rationalist.*

reason why For *reason that*—"She would not tell the reason why she did it"— established. *The reason why . . . is because*—"The reason why I cannot go is because my mother is ill"—illogical. The correct form is: "The reason why . . . is that . . ."

receipt, recipe For *cooking directions*—both in good use, but *receipt* (in this sense) seems old-fashioned.

reckon For *think, suppose*—provincial or local.

recommend For *recommendation*—illiterate.

recountal For *account, recital*—accepted by Webster and Standard, though some-times objected to as an unneeded form. (See Fowler's *Modern English Usage,* under *-al nouns.*)

red For *radical*—colloquial or in good use. *To see red* for *to be furiously angry* —colloquial.

regular For *real*—"He's a regular fool"—colloquial. For *normal, right*—"He's a regular fellow"—colloquial.

relieved of For *robbed*—"I was relieved of my purse"—humorous or pretentious.

remains For *body*—old-fashioned and to be avoided. *Remains* refers more prop-erly to a dead author's works or to ruins of architecture.

reminisce Colloquial, humorous, though useful.

render For *sing, recite, play*—usually stilted. *Render,* if used in this sense at all, perhaps refers to interpretation, rather than to mere performance.

rendition Pronounced objectionable by the *Century Dictionary*, but given without comment by Webster's *New International Dictionary*. Some English authorities call it an Americanism.

renege (*properly* renig) For *go back on a promise*—colloquial.

repeat For *vote more than once in an election*—Americanism. Also *repeater*.

retire For *leave, go to bed*—usually pseudo-refined, affected.

riffle For *ripple, tiny rapids*—local, U. S.

rig For *carriage, outfit*—colloquial.

right (adv.) Few words have more idiomatic and colloquial uses. *Right* for *very*—"I'm right glad to see you"—colloquial or provincial. *Right smart* for *considerable, large*—"You've come a right smart journey"—provincial. *Right ahead* for *without turning*—idiomatic. *Right along* for *without stopping*—colloquial, U. S. *Right away* for *at once*—colloquial, U. S. *Right* for *directly, immediately*—"He walked right up to me," "We went right to bed"—idiomatic. *Right out* for *without delay* or *evasion*—"Speak right out"—idiomatic. *See also* all right.

rile For *vex*—colloquial or provincial. *Rile* is a folk pronunciation of *roil* (to muddy water), and country folk speak of "riling a spring."

rise up Often condemned as illogical, because one cannot rise down; but it is an old idiom. The Bible has: "If Satan rise up himself," "Rise up and walk," "I saw a beast rise up." Similar objection has been made to *fall down*, with as little justification. The Bible has "All kings shall fall down before him." Objection has also been made to *sit down* and *stand up*. In all of these expressions the adverb intensifies the sense of motion.

rodent For *rat*—stilted. So *canine, feline*, as nouns.

rookie For *raw recruit*—colloquial.

roomer For *lodger*—colloquial, U. S.

root For *cheer, incite*—slang. Also *rooter*.

rope in For *draw into an enterprise, inveigle*—colloquial or slang, U. S.

rot For *bosh, twaddle*—"Don't talk rot"—colloquial.

rotten For *bad, of poor quality*—"We had a rotten time"—slang.

rotter For *an undesirable or undependable person*—slang (formerly Eng.).

rough For *roughly*—"Treat him rough"—low colloquial.

roughneck Slang.

roustabout U. S. and Australian.

rout out For *arouse and drive forth*—colloquial.

row For *tumult, confusion, fight*—colloquial or literary. *Raise a row*—colloquial.

rowdy In good use.

rowdydow For *uproar*—colloquial.

rubber For *look about inquisitively*—slang.

rub in For *reiterate* (something offensive)—"Why do you keep rubbing it in?"—colloquial.

rumpus Colloquial.

run For *conduct, manage*—"He runs the Hotel Splendid"—U. S.

run-in For *argument, quarrel*—"I had a run-in with the boss today"—slang.

runt In good use for an animal especially small of its kind. *Runty*—colloquial or provincial.

rusty For *out of practice*—"He was rusty in his Latin"—in good use.

sack *To get the sack* for *to be dismissed, to give the sack* for *dismiss* (from employment)—slang.

sagatiate Colloquial and humorous.

said As an adjective—"Said person is no longer resident at this address"—to be avoided except in legal style.

sail in For *undertake with energy*—"Let's all sail in now and do it!"—colloquial.

saloon For *barroom, drinking place*—U. S. Other meanings that are British as well as American are: *a large hall or drawing-room, a hall for exhibiting works of art, a sumptuous railroad car or ship's cabin.*

salt "Worth his salt"—colloquial.

salutatorian, salutatory For *opening speaker* and for *speech in a commencement program*—U. S.

same As a pronoun—"I have written the person you mentioned and have sent a package to same"—suggests business jargon.

sand For *courage*—colloquial or slang. Compare *grit.*

sap For *fool, simple fellow*—slang.

saphead For *weak-minded or foolish person*—colloquial.

sashay For *move back and forth*—provincial or slang. A corruption of the French word *chassé.*

sauce For *speak impudently*—colloquial. Also as a noun—"Don't give me any of your sauce." *Saucy*—in good use. *Sassy*—colloquial.

save For *excepting, unless*—"All shall go, save one," "You care nothing for the plan, save you inaugurate it"—archaic or poetic.

scab For *strikebreaker*—slang or cant.

scads For *a great many*—slang or colloquial. (Originally western U. S. Compare *oodles.*)

scalawag For *rogue, worthless fellow*—colloquial.

scalper For *ticket broker*—colloquial, U. S.

scarce As an adverb, for *scarcely*—"Scarce had he disappeared when the message came"—in good use, but archaic or poetic.

scarehead For *sensational headline*—newspaper slang.

schoolma'am, schoolmarm Colloquial, U. S.

scoop For *priority of publication, obtaining news first*—newspaper slang. Compare *beat.*

scoot For *move very fast, dart*—colloquial. Also *scooter* for small sailboat and for child's vehicle.

scorch For *go at high speed*—slang.

scorcher For *one who goes at high speed* and for *a very hot day*—slang.

scout For *fellow, person*—"He's a good scout"—slang. For *an undergraduate's manservant*—college slang (at Oxford, Cambridge, Harvard, and Yale).

scram For *go* (fast), *get out*—slang.

scrap For *fight, quarrel*—slang. *Scrappy*, in all senses—colloquial or slang.

scrawny For *emaciated*—in literary use, though sometimes labeled an Americanism.

scrouge For *squeeze, grind down, press, crowd*—provincial or colloquial. (The word is pronounced in two ways, with the *ou* rhyming with *how* and with *who*.)

sculp For *carve, sculpture*—once literary, now colloquial or humorous.

secure For *get*—often stilted: "I was unable to secure any butter!"

seedy For *not in good health*—"I'm feeling rather seedy"—colloquial. For *worn, poor*—"His clothes looked seedy"—colloquial.

seldom ever Colloquial. The literary form is *seldom or never*. *See* rarely ever.

selection For *piece, composition*—usually stilted.

sense As a verb, for *feel, become aware of*—given as colloquial, U. S., by some authorities, but Fowler's *Modern English Usage*, while objecting to the usage as "precious," quotes English examples. "He sensed her nearness" is a favorite with the cheaper sort of writers.

set, sit While *set* for *sit* is in most cases provincial or illiterate, the old question of whether a hen sets or sits (on eggs) is still discussed. One may say that since a setting hen is not always merely a sitting hen, the former phrase is convenient. It is established as idiomatic. "Your coat sets well"—idiomatic.

settle For *pay*—"We settled the accounts"—in good use. "We settled for the meal"—colloquial.

set-to For *contest, bout*—colloquial.

shack For *crude cabin*—colloquial, U. S. and Can.

shake For *get rid of*—"We tried to shake him, but in vain"—colloquial, U. S. *Shake down* for *compel to contribute*—slang. Also as a noun.

shake-up For *reorganization* (as of a police department)—slang.

shape For *condition*—"My car is in good shape at last"—colloquial.

shark For *expert*—"She's a shark at French"—slang or colloquial. For *unprincipled dealer*—"loan shark"—slang.

shave For *escape*—"a close shave," "a narrow shave"—colloquial.

shaver For *small boy*—colloquial.

shebang For *establishment, outfit, contrivance, organization*—"I'd like to burn down the whole shebang"—slang. (A variant of the Irish *she-been*, a pothouse, low drinking place.)

shell out For *pay, hand over*—slang.

shine For *liking*—"I've taken quite a shine to him"—slang. *Shine up to* for *cultivate acquaintance*—"I think I'll shine up to him"—slang.

ship As a verb, best restricted to conveyance by ships, not by mail, express, or wheeled conveyance. A human body, by the way, is not shipped but sent.

shoestring For *the smallest means or margin*—"He runs his business on a shoestring"—colloquial, U. S.

shoplifter In good use.

show For *chance*—"He hasn't a show to win"—colloquial. *Show up* for *come, arrive*—"When do you suppose he'll show up?"—colloquial. *Show off* for *act theatrically, dramatize oneself*—colloquial. Also the noun *show-off*.

showdown For *revelation of intention*—colloquial.

shy For *short* (*e.g.*, of money)—"Your payment is shy ten cents"—colloquial.

shyster For *dishonest lawyer*—colloquial, U. S.

side For *airs, superior manner*—"put on side"—slang. *On the side* for *confidentially, secretly*—"He told me on the side that he was to be married"—colloquial.

sideway, sideways, sidewise All have the same meaning and are in good use.

sight For *many, much*—"a sight of people," "I'd a sight rather stay at home"—provincial or colloquial.

sign up For *register*—"Have you signed up for the tournament?"—colloquial.

simp For *simpleton*—slang.

simply For *really, truly*—"That is simply too bad," "That is simply ridiculous"—idiomatic.

since For *ago*—in good use, but properly of time recently past. "Two hours since," "a thousand years ago."

sissy For *effeminate man*—colloquial, U. S. Also *sissify*.

sit down *See* rise.

skate For *decrepit horse*—slang, U. S. For *person*—"a cheap skate," "a good skate"—slang.

skedaddle For *run away, get out*—humorous colloquial.

skimp For *act stingily, save meanly*—colloquial. Also *skimpy* for *meager*.

skin For *cheat*—slang. Also *skin game*.

skinflint Literary.

skitter To skitter a stone on water is to make it skip over the surface. *Skitter* is colloquially used of any motion, as of a small animal, suggesting skittering.

slabsided In good use, though sometimes labeled slang, U. S.

slack, slake In the sense of *mix with water*—"to slack or slake lime"—both established.

slam For *criticize, condemn*—slang. Also as a noun.

slant For *angle of observation or comprehension*—"a new slant on the subject," "take a slant on this"—slang.

slapdash Colloquial.

slapstick Colloquial or slang.

sleeper For *sleeping-car*—colloquial, U. S.

sleuth For *detective*—colloquial, U. S. Also as a verb.

slick A variant of *sleek*. In the sense of *dexterous, smooth, hard to catch*—"a slick performance," "a slick person"—colloquial. *To slick up* for *to make neat or clean*—colloquial.

slicker For *raincoat*—U. S. For *smooth rascal*—provincial.

slim For *slight*—"a slim chance"—in good use.

slimy For *very objectionable, treacherous*—"a slimy trick"—slang.

slippy For *slippery*—provincial or colloquial.

slither For *slide*—provincal.

sloppy For *slovenly*—"Why should she be so sloppy in her dress?"—colloquial. For *overeffusive in manner*—"He was positively sloppy to me"—colloquial.

slowdown For *gradual lessening of activity or speed*—colloquial, U. S.

slow up Colloquial.

slug For *strike heavily, punch*—slang. Also *slugger*.

slump For *decline, collapse*—colloquial.

slush For *gushing talk, sentimentality*—slang.

slush fund In the Navy a slush fund is a fund derived from the sale of useless materials. The popular use of the term for a fund to be used for bribery is slang.

smart For *shrewd*—"a smart Yankee"—colloquial, U. S. *See* right (smart).

smog For *mixture of smoke and fog*—a portmanteau or blended word, in good use in certain localities.

smoker For *smoking-car*—colloquial, U. S. For *a men's gathering*—colloquial.

smudge For *heavy smoke*—in good use, U. S. and Can.

snack For *light lunch*—colloquial.

snap For *something easily done or obtained*—slang. Also *soft snap*.

snicker, snigger Both in good use.

sniffy For *disdainful, haughty*—"His manner was very sniffy"—colloquial.

snifter For *drink of spirits*—slang.

snippity, snippy For *supercilious, airy in manner*—colloquial.

snoop For *pry, spy about*—colloquial, U. S. Also *snoopy, snooper*.

snoot For *face, nose, grimace*—colloquial, U. S. *Snooty* for *haughty, contemptuous*—colloquial, U. S.

snooze For *nap, short sleep*—colloquial.

snuff *Up to snuff* for *all right, sufficient*—colloquial.

soak For *toper, hard drinker*—colloquial.

soap *Soft soap* for *flattery*—slang. Also *soapy* for *unctuous* (in manner).

sociable For *social gathering*—"a church sociable"—U. S.

socialite For *social notability*—smart slang (*Time* magazine).

sock For *strike, drive, beat*—slang.

soft For *amorous, foolish, simple*—colloquial; for *nonalcoholic*—colloquial, U. S.

softy For *cowardly or sentimental person*—colloquial.

soldier, sojer For *make a mere pretense of working*—colloquial.

solon For *lawmaker, wise man*—objectionable as hackneyed.

so long For *good-by*—colloquial or slang.

some For *somewhat*—"His condition is some improved"—colloquial, U. S. *Some* as an intensive—"I'll say that's some fish"—slang.

something For *somewhat*—"The room is something under twenty feet long"—idiomatic. *Something* as an intensive—"This food is something terrible"—colloquial.

someways For *some way*—colloquial or provincial.

somewheres For *somewhere*—colloquial or provincial.

soon "I would as soon do it," "I would sooner do it"—established.

sooner For *one who does a thing prematurely,* in order to get an unfair advantage —slang, U. S.

soppy For *foolishly sentimental*—British slang.

so-so For *neither good nor bad*—colloquial.

sound out For *seek to know an attitude or opinion*—colloquial.

soupy For *softly sentimental*—slang.

souse For *make or become drunk*—slang, U. S.

southpaw For *left-handed*—baseball slang.

spark For *lover, beau, wooer*—established. As a verb for *court, woo, flirt*—colloquial.

spat For *slap, petty quarrel*—colloquial.

spell For *supply the place of for a time, relieve*—"I'll spell you when you are tired"—slang or cant; for *a short time*—"He will stay a spell," "a spell of bad weather"—colloquial or provincial; for *a fit* or *seizure,* as of illness—colloquial.

spit For *exact likeness*—"He's the very spit and image of his father"—dialectal or humorous colloquial.

spleeny For *changeable in mood, capricious*—provincial or colloquial.

split For *a share of booty*—slang; for *a half portion, half pint, half glass*—slang.

splurge Colloquial.

spoiling for For *having an eager desire for*—"spoiling for a fight"—colloquial.

sponge For *be parasitical*—colloquial. Also *sponge on, sponger. Throw, chuck,* or *toss up* (or *in*) *the sponge*—for *give up, admit defeat*—colloquial.

spoof For *deceive, humbug*—slang, Eng.

spread For *meal*—colloquial.

spring it on For *propose suddenly, surprise*—slang or colloquial.

spook For *ghost*—humorous colloquial.

spoon For *act amorously*—slang. Also as a noun and *spoony.*

sport For *sporting person*—"He's a good sport"—colloquial, U. S. *Dead sport, dead game sport*—slang. For *wear ostentatiously*—"I see he's sporting a new coat"—colloquial. Also *sporty.*

spot For *recognize, identify*—"We spotted her in the crowd"—colloquial.

spout For *speak in a grandiloquent manner*—colloquial.

spread-eagle For *pretentious in style*—colloquial, U. S.

spring it on For *proclaim or inform too suddenly*—"Let's not spring the news on his mother"—colloquial.

spruce (verb) For *dress smartly, improve one's appearance* (usually *spruce up*) —colloquial. As an adjective—in good use.

spud For *potato*—dialectal or colloquial.

spunk For *will power, daring*—colloquial. In literary usage, *spunk* is *tinder, touchwood,* popularly called *punk,* and this has become slang for *no good, worthless.* (*Punk* is old slang for *prostitute.*)

square For *honest*—in good use. Also *square deal.* Also *square* as a verb for *make even, balance*—"to square accounts." *Square* for *full, satisfying*—"a square meal"—colloquial. *Square shooter* for *fair dealer, honest man*—slang.

squash For *make pulp of*—in literary use, though often given as colloquial.

squeal For *be an informer or traitor*—slang.

squelch For *suppress*—in literary use.

stacks For *great amount*—colloquial.

stag For *male, man*—"stag dinner"—colloquial.

stage For *stagecoach, omnibus*—U. S.

stall For *avoid committing oneself*—"When I asked him what he thought, he stalled [*or* stalled along]"—slang.

stand, stand for For *endure, put up with*—"I can't stand it," "I won't stand for it"—colloquial. *Stand pat*—colloquial.

stand up *See* rise.

start in For *begin*—"It started in to rain"—colloquial. Also *start up* for *start*— "The truck started up."

stew For *fret, worry*—colloquial.

stick For *puzzle*—"That question sticks me"—colloquial. For *cheat*—"He was stuck with a bad bill"—slang. *Stick at* for *persist*—colloquial. *Stick up* for *hold up, rob*—slang. Also *stick-up* for *armed robbery.*

sticker For *paster*—U. S.

sting For *overcharge, cheat*—slang.

stodgy For *dull, unexciting*—colloquial.

stooge For *foil, confidant*—"Horatio might be called Hamlet's stooge"—stage slang, now becoming colloquial.

stoop For *veranda, porch*—"To sit on the back stoop"—colloquial or local, U. S. (Dutch *stoep.*)

stop For *stay*—"We stopped at the Ritz for three weeks"—colloquial, Eng. *Stop off, stop over*—colloquial. *See also* cease.

strafe For *shell, bomb, punish*—slang.

strapped For *hard up, short of money*—slang.

straw vote U. S.

stuck For *cheated*—slang.

stuck on For *enamored of*—colloquial, U. S.

stuck up For *conceited*—colloquial.

stunt For *feat*—colloquial. As a verb—"I stunt you to do it"—colloquial or slang.

sub As short for *submarine, subordinate, subaltern, substitute, sublieutenant,* etc. —colloquial. Also as a verb, short for *substitute*—"I'll sub for him."

subsequent For *subsequently*—"Subsequent to the earthquake the town became less and less prosperous"—incorrect, though common colloquially.

such As an intensive—"He's such a fine man"—not objectionable except when used too often.

sucker For *credulous person, easy victim*—slang; for *lollipop*—colloquial. *Sucker list*—business slang.

suicide As a verb—colloquial (Webster).

suit For *suite*—becoming archaic.

sulphite *See* bromide.

summers *See* days.

summons For *summon*—"The jury were summoned" (*rather than* summonsed)— dubious colloquialism.

super Short for *supernumerary*—stage slang; for *superfine* or *superior*—slang.

sure For *surely*—the usage is very old. "Sure he that made us of such large discourse"—*Hamlet*. *Sure* as equivalent to *yes*—"Will you do it?" "Sure"—colloquial. For *certainly*—"Are you hungry?" "I sure am."—slang.

suspicion As a verb, for *suspect*—dialectal.

swab For *lout, dull or useless person*—slang.

swag For *booty, plunder, spoils*—slang.

swank For *ostentatiously stylish*—slang. Also as a noun and *swanky*.

swap or **swop** For *exchange, barter*—colloquial.

swat For *hit hard*—chiefly U. S. *Swot* for *labor at*—slang (English).

swear off For *renounce, quit*—colloquial.

sweat For *work hard, drudge*—colloquial.

sweetening For *molasses* (long sweetening) or *sugar* (short sweetening)—local, U. S.

swell For *tiptop, first rate*—slang; as a noun for *fashionable person*—colloquial. Also as an adjective for *stylish, fashionable*—colloquial.

swingeing For *very large* or for *very good*—now colloquial.

swipe For *steal, pilfer*—slang, U. S.; for *strike with a swinging motion*—slang. U. S. Also as a noun. *Swipes* for *low-grade beer*—slang, U. S.

tab or **tabs** For *account, reckoning, check*—"to keep tabs on"—colloquial.

tablespoons For *tablespoonfuls*—colloquial.

tacky For *sticky*—"The varnish is still tacky"—in good use; for *dowdy, shabby, unkempt*—colloquial, U. S.

taffy For *cajolery, blarney*—colloquial.

tag For *follow closely*—"The little boy has tagged us round all day long"—colloquial.

tail For *follow closely and spy upon*—slang.

take *Take* has many colloquial uses: *take* for *study*—"I'm taking Latin"; for *assume*—"I take it you don't agree"; for *direct or aim a motion*—"I'll take a shot at it" (used both literally and figuratively); for *win popular favor*—"I hope my book takes well"; for *become*—"to take sick"; for *admit of being photographed*—"He takes well." *Take back* for *retract; take off* for *mimic; burlesque; take in* for *attend, visit*—"I think I'll take in the reception tonight"; *take it out of* for *punish*—"Why take it out of me?"; *take on* for *show one's feelings demonstratively; take to* for *be drawn to*—"Somehow I don't take to him"; *take up with* for *begin to associate with. Take-down* for *a humiliating talk or action. Take-off* for *an imitation, caricature. Take-in* for *cheat.*

taking For *contagious, infectious, catching* (of a disease)—colloquial.

talkie, talkies Of motion-pictures—colloquial.

tall For *large*—"a tall order"—slang; for *grandiloquent*—"tall talk"—colloquial; for *exaggerated, incredible*—"tall stories"—colloquial.

tan For *flog, thrash*—colloquial.

tattletale For *telltale*—colloquial.

tax For *price, charge*—"Waiter, what's the tax?"—slang.

teaspoons For *teaspoonfuls*—colloquial.

tell on For *tattle about, be an informer*—colloquial.

tender As a verb, more properly used of money or service than of a reception or party.

tenterhooks *To be on tenterhooks* for *to be very uneasy or anxious*—colloquial.

that As an adverb—"He isn't that bad"—colloquial. *That there*—"He lives on that there mountain"—illiterate; though "He lives on that mountain there" is defensible, *there* being intensive.

then As an adjective—"the then King of France"—a questionable use.

thence *See* from whence.

they As an indefinite pronoun—"In England they call a water-heater a geyser"—in good use. Also *they say* for *it is said.*

thick For *intimate*—"as thick as thieves"—colloquial; for *going too far*—"His saying that is a bit too thick"—colloquial; for *dull, stupid, obtuse*—in good use.

thingumbob, thingumagig, thingummy Colloquial.

thriller For *exciting story or play*—colloquial or slang.

through For *finished*—"When he was through, he turned away"—approved. Also "I'll come when I'm through reading."

thusly For *in this manner*—humorous colloquial.

tick For *credit, trust*—"to buy goods on tick"—colloquial.

ticket For *ballot*—U. S.

ticket chopper Colloquial or slang, U. S.

tickly For *ticklish*—colloquial.

tidy, tidy up For *arrange, make neat and orderly*—colloquial. For *gratifying, sufficient*—"a tidy sum of money"—colloquial.

tight For *stingy*—colloquial. For *drunk*—colloquial. For *snug, trim*—"a tight little craft"—colloquial.

tightwad Slang or colloquial.

till, until Both forms are in good use and are generally interchangeable. The popular notion that *till* is a contraction of *until* is erroneous. It is the older form. "Tarry thou till I come"—Bible. Therefore *'til* is incorrect.

time *To be on time* for *to be punctual*—U. S. *To have a good time*—colloquial, U. S.

tip For *hint, suggestion*—"stock market or racing tips"—in good use. *Tip off* for *tip* (verb) and *tip-off* for *tip* (noun)—colloquial.

to-do For *ado, excitement*—colloquial.

togs Colloquial. Also *toggery*.

too As an intensive—"You can't do it." "I can too!"—colloquial. *Too-too* for *excessive, extreme*—colloquial.

top of the morning Colloquial.

tops For *best*—"Sonja Henie is simply tops at skating"—slang.

tot, tot up For *add, calculate*—colloquial.

tote For *carry*—provincial (southern U. S.).

touch For *attempt to borrow* (money)—slang, U. S.

touched For *not quite sane*—"touched in his wits"—slang.

tough For *vicious*—"a tough customer," "a tough neighborhood"—colloquial. Also as a noun—"a gang of toughs." For *difficult*—"a tough job," "a tough time," "a tough question"—colloquial.

tousle For *disarrange, rumple*—colloquial.

tout For *racing spy or tipster*—marked as cant or slang by most authorities, but probably in good use. Also *touter*.

toward, towards Interchangeable.

traipse For *gad about*—colloquial or provincial.

tramp For *idle wanderer*—U. S.

transient For *temporary lodger*—colloquial, U. S.

transpire For *happen, occur*—though objected to by most authorities, used at times by writers of good standing. Classically the word means *leak out, become generally known*—"It transpired that Russia had had a treaty with France." The popular usage is shown in "Among the events which transpired last week, the explosion stands first."

traps For *personal belongings*—colloquial.

trolley car U. S.

truck For *vegetables*—U. S. Also *truck garden*.

try As a noun—"After three tries, he succeeded"—in good use. "Give (it) a try" for "Give it a trial"—colloquial.

tubby For *fat, squat, big-bellied*—in good use.

tunnel For *funnel*—the words are interchangeable, though *tunnel* in this sense is rare or local.

turn *Turn in* for *go to bed*—colloquial. *Turn in* for *help unitedly*—"Let's turn in and give him a lift"—colloquial. *Turn down* for *refuse, ignore*—colloquial. *Turn up* for *appear, arrive*—colloquial.

twaddle For *silly talk*—in good use. Also as a verb.

unbeknown, unbeknownst *Unbeknownst* is provincial. *Unbeknown* is labeled dialectal or obsolescent by most American authorities, but is accepted by the Oxford English Dictionary as a variant of *unknown* or *unknown to*.

up *Up in* for *conversant with*—"He's well up in American history"—colloquial. *Up to* for *intending, planning*—"What's he up to?"—colloquial. *Up to* for *rests with*—"It's up to you"—slang. *Up-to-date*, in spite of much hostility—established. *Up-and-coming*—colloquial. *Up till, up until* for *up to*—say "I was out of work up to [*not* up until] yesterday" or "I was out of work until yesterday." *Up* is used, after the verb, in many idiomatic phrases: *eat up, drink up, burn up, sit up*, etc., in the sense of *completely* or as an intensive. Colloquially it is used with many verbs when such sense is not needed: *open up, finish up, settle up, write up*, etc., though it is usually felt.

up As a verb, for *cause to rise*—"to up production or prices"—colloquial. As an adjective, for *in progress, doing*—"What was up?"—colloquial; for *confronted by*—"We were up against stiff opposition"—colloquial; for *before a court*—"He was up for trial"—colloquial. "It's up to you" for "It's your turn or responsibility"—colloquial or slang.

uppish For *conceited, superior in manner*—colloquial. Also *uppity*.

uptake For *apprehension* or *retort*—"He's quick on the uptake"—slang.

use "I have no use for him" for "I dislike him"—colloquial.

used up For *exhausted, tired out*—"I've worked so hard I am all used up"—colloquial.

vacate For *leave, go away*—slang. Its correct use is (1) *annul;* (2) *leave vacant*.

value A vogue word, much abused by those who have not maturely considered its meanings. It means *desirability* or *worth* of a thing. A value is an attribute, not a substance or ingredient; therefore, to speak, for example, of extracting values from coal tar is nonsense.

vamp For *designing woman*—slang. Also *to vamp*. The word is the first syllable of *vampire*.

verse For *stanza*—"We shall sing the first two verses"—established. In strict use a verse is a line of poetry.

vicious For *spiteful, malicious*—"a vicious remark"—colloquial. Strictly, *vicious* refers to vice.

victuals "Common in dialect, but in the standard language now seldom used, except depreciatively or jocosely."—Webster.

viewy For *visionary, unpractical*—colloquial.

vim In good use.

vintage Applied to works of art or manufacture—"I have an early vintage typewriter"—humorous.

walk-out For *strike* (of laborers)—colloquial, U. S.

wallop For *thrash, beat*—slang. Also as a noun.

walloping For *very large*—dialectal or colloquial; for *a beating, thrashing*—colloquial or slang. In standard usage, *wallop* means *move in a rolling manner, waddle, flounder*.

wangle Colloquial in all uses.

want For *wish*—"I want to go," "I want a drink of water"—in good use.

ward-heeler *See* heel.

washout For *complete failure*—slang. *Washed out* for *played out*—colloquial.

washed up *Played out, depleted*—colloquial.

washwoman, washerwoman Both forms accepted.

watch out For *beware, look out*—colloquial, U. S.

way The following are colloquial: for physical condition—"He's in a bad way"; for district or region—"He lives out my way."

weed For *tobacco*—colloquial. As a verb, for *rid of less desirable parts or things*——"To weed a stock of goods"—colloquial. *Weedy* for *gangling, scraggly*—colloquial.

welsh For *cheat* by avoiding payment of debts—slang.

wet For *one favoring free sale of liquor*—colloquial, chiefly U. S. Also as an adjective—"a wet town."

whack For *turn, spell*—"I'll take a whack at the job now"—slang.

whacking For *very large, whopping*—colloquial.

whale For *lash, strike* as if to produce wales—colloquial. A form of *wale* or *weal*. *Whale* as a noun, for something very large—"a whale of a good joke"—colloquial.

whence *See* from whence.

where For *the place at or in which*—"That is where he made his mistake"—colloquial. *Where . . . at* for *where*—"I couldn't tell where he was at"—humorous or illiterate.

wherever, where ever Exclamatory, expressing astonishment or curiosity—"Wherever [*or* where ever] did you get that!"—colloquial.

whether or no Both *whether or no* and *whether or not*—accepted. *Whether*, without the alternative—"I don't know whether it is going to rain"—accepted, the *or no, or not* being implied.

whichness Humorous.

whip For *defeat*—colloquial.

whip cream For *whipped cream*—incorrect.

white For *fair, honorable*—"He's certainly white in all his transactions"—slang or colloquial.

whitewash For *exonerate officially* (but falsely)—in good use. For *win a game* without allowing one's opponent to score at all—colloquial, U. S.

wig For *censure, rebuke, scold*—colloquial. Also the noun *wigging* for *scolding*.

wild For *licentious, dissolute*—colloquial. Also for *eager, keen*—"I'm wild to go, but can't"; for *angry, vexed*—"When I told him he was simply wild."

wildcat For *unsound business scheme*—in good use; for *runaway railroad engine*—local, U. S.

wile away For *while away*—a confusion of words. The form is *while away*—"I'll manage to while away the time before the train comes."

windjammer For *very talkative person*—slang.

wing For *wound without killing*—"to wing an adversary"—colloquial.

winker For *eyelash*—colloquial.

win out For *win at last, succeed fully*—colloquial.

winters For *during the winter*—"Winters we go south"—colloquial.

wire For *telegraph*—colloquial. Also for *telegram*.

wirepuller For *schemer, intriguer*—colloquial. Also *wirepulling*.

wise *Get wise to* for *become aware of*—slang, U. S. *Wise up* for *inform*—slang, U. S. *Put wise* for *put right, advise*—slang.

wisecrack For *smart remark*—slang, U. S.

wishy-washy For *insipid*—in good use. Also *wish-wash*.

without For *unless*—dialectal or illiterate. "I can't open the gate unless [*not without*] you help me."

wobble, wabble For *hesitate*—in good use. For *cause to vibrate*—"Don't wobble the boat"—colloquial.

woods *Out of the woods* for *escaped from perplexity or difficulty*—colloquial.

work For *make use of, make a convenience of*—"to work one's friends to obtain a benefit or privilege"—colloquial.

worser A redundant comparative, formerly used but now archaic.

Yank For *Yankee*—slang.

yank For *jerk, twitch*—colloquial. Also as a noun.

yap For *talk, gab;* for *hoodlum;* for *bumpkin*—all slang. Also as a verb, for *talk noisily or foolishly.* Also *yappy.*

yarn For *story*—colloquial. Also as a verb.

yawp, yaup For *yelp, bawl, scream*—dialectal. For *talk noisily*—slang.

yegg For *burglar*—slang. Also *yeggman,* with same meaning.

yell For *rhythmic cheer*—U. S. and Canada.

yellow For *sensational* and for *unfair, dishonorable, cowardly*—accepted.

yen For *desire, longing*—slang. Also as a verb.

yes-man For *toady, sycophant*—slang.

yokel An English provincialism, contemptuous for *rustic, countrified fellow.*

you For *one, a person*—"In Elizabethan times you wrote poetry as naturally as today you play bridge"—long established as colloquial.

you was For *you were*—now illiterate or provincial, though found in old authors, when *you* refers to one person.

AMERICAN AND BRITISH USAGE

The following terms are a selection of the most common words showing differences of usage in the British Isles and the United States, dialectal terms being excluded. Many other distinctions are given in the list entitled Appropriateness (pp. 411–450). A few of the terms given as British are also used, at least locally, in the United States. These are marked "U. S." [1]

AMERICAN	BRITISH
baby carriage	pram (perambulator)
baggage	luggage (U. S.)
baggage car	luggage van

[1] For more complete lists and for discussion the following books are recommended:

H. W. Fowler, *A Dictionary of Modern English Usage* (London, Oxford University Press, 1926).

H. W. Horwill, *A Dictionary of American English on Historical Principles,* 1936.

G. P. Krapp, *The English Language in America* (New York, The Century Co., 1925).

G. H. McKnight, *English Words and Their Background* (New York, D. Appleton and Company, 1933).

H. L. Mencken, *The American Language,* 4th ed. (New York, Alfred A. Knopf, 1936).

AMERICAN	BRITISH
bedbug	bug
beet	beet-root
billboard	hoarding
boarder	paying guest (U. S.)
bobsled	sledge
brakeman	brakesman
bumper (car)	buffer
bureau	chest of drawers (U. S.)
can (container)	tin
candy	sweets
canned goods	tinned goods
car (railroad)	carriage (U. S.), van, waggon
chicken yard	fowl-run
clipping (newspaper)	cutting, press cutting
coal-oil, kerosene	paraffin
coal scuttle	coal hod (U. S.)
conductor (train)	guard
corn	maize, Indian corn
corner (street)	crossing
cowcatcher	plough
cracker	biscuit (U. S.)
department store	stores
derby (hat)	bowler
dime novel	shilling shocker
druggist	chemist
drug store	chemist's shop
drummer	bagman
drygoods store	draper's shop
editorial	leader, leading article
elevator	lift (U. S.)
elevator boy	lift-man
excursionist	tripper
fish dealer	fishmonger
freight	goods
freight car	goods waggon
gasoline	petrol
grade (school)	form (U. S.)
grade crossing	level crossing (U. S.)
grain	corn, grain
grain broker	corn factor
grip (bag)	hold-all

AMERICAN	BRITISH
hardware dealer	ironmonger
haystack	haycock
headliner	topliner
hogpen, pigpen	piggery
huckster, peddler	coster, costermonger
installment plan	hire-purchase plan
legal holiday	bank holiday
letter box	pillar-box
locomotive engineer	engine driver (U. S.)
molasses	treacle
newspaper man	pressman
orchestra (theater)	stalls
overcoat	greatcoat
package	parcel (U. S.), packet
parlor car	saloon carriage
patrolman (policeman)	constable
payday	wage-day
peanut	monkey-nut
pitcher	jug
postpaid	post free
public school	board school
rails (railroad)	line
roast (meat)	joint
saleswoman	shop assistant
saloon (barroom)	public house
sewer	drain
shoe	boot
shoemaker	bootmaker
shoestring	bootlace
sick	ill (sick *usually means* nauseated)
silver (household)	plate
spool (thread)	reel
stockholder	shareholder
store	shop (U. S.)
street cleaner	crossing sweeper
street railway	tramway
subway	tube (U. S.), underground (U. S.)
suspenders	braces

American	British
switch (railroad)	points
switch (*verb*, railroad)	shunt
taxes (city)	rates
taxpayer (local)	ratepayer
ticket office	booking office
tin roof	leads
track (railroad)	line
trolley car	tram car
truck (vehicle)	lorry
trunk	box
warehouse	stores
washstand	wash-hand stand
water heater	geyser
wringer	mangle

THE RIGHT PREPOSITION

The prepositional idiom—that is, the use of certain prepositions before a noun or after a verb or an adjective—is the source of countless errors, especially among foreigners. The use of *at* or *in* before names of places; the differences of meaning in *angry with, at,* or *about* something; whether one should say *abhorrence of* or *to, acquit of* or *from, in accordance with* or *to:* these are examples of the part idiom plays in such locutions. As is true of idiom in general, these idioms have simply to be learned by heart, for no rule can cover their use.

abashed: *at, before, in.* He felt abashed *at* the other's actions. Pilate was abashed *before* Jesus. The culprit was abashed *in* the presence of the judge.
abate: *in, by.* The storm abated *in* fury. The nuisance was abated *by* law. No preposition: The law abated the nuisance.
aberration: *from, of.* The action was an aberration *from* his usual course. It seems like an aberration *of* mind.
abhorrence: *of.* He expressed abhorrence *of* the action.
abhorrent: *to.* The suggestion was abhorrent *to* us.
abound: *in, with.* The Bible abounds *in* metaphors. The field abounds *with* crickets. (The difference is between inherent or essential qualities and unessential or accidental things or properties.)
abridge: *from.* This version is abridged *from* the original book.
abridgment: *of.* It is an abridgment *of* the book.
absolve: *from* (rarely *of*). He is absolved *from* blame.
abstain: *from.*
abstinence: *from.*

abstract: *from, in, into.* The dye is abstracted *from* the seed. The correspondence was abstracted *in* (or *into*) a précis.

abut: *against, on.* The cottage abuts *against* the cliff. The house abuts *on* the line he surveyed.

accede: *to.*

accessories: *in, of.* In a picture; *of* dress; *of* the theater or stage.

accessory: *after, before, to.* *After* or *before* the fact; *to* a crime.

accident: *of, to.* By accident *of* birth. An accident *to* a person.

accommodate: *to, with.* We accommodated ourselves *to* the inconvenience. I accommodated him *with* a loan.

accompany: *by, with.* They were accompanied *by* their dog. His gesture was accompanied *with* a smile.

accord (*n.*): *between, of, with.* The accord *between* the two was obvious. An accord *of* interests would be advantageous. This passage is in accord *with* the rest.

accord (*v.*): *in, to.* They accorded *in* their opinions. We must accord *to* him what he deserves.

accordance: *with.*

accordant: *with, to.* (*With* preferred.)

according: *as.* According *as* you may decide.

accountable: *for, to.* For a trust; *to* an employer.

acquaintance: *among, between, of, with.* Many acquaintances *among* those present. Acquaintance *between* two. *Of* one *with* another; *with* a language.

acquiesce: *in.* (Formerly *to* or *with.*)

acquit: *of* (formerly *from*), *with.* One is acquitted *of* a crime. One acquits oneself *with* credit.

actuated: *by, to.* By anger; *to* revenge.

adapt: *for, from, to.* The seats in the boat are adapted *for* ten persons. The model of the boat is adapted *from* that of a ketch. The boat is adapted *to* heavy sailing.

addicted: *to.*

adept: *at* or *in.*

adequate: *for, to.* For the purpose; *to* the need.

adhere: *to.*

adherent (*n.*): *of, to.* *Of* a party; *to* a principle.

adhesion: *between, of, to.* Between the two; *of* one *to* the other.

adhesive: *to.*

adjacent: *to.*

adjust: *for, to.* I'll adjust your pillow *for* comfort. The dog will adjust itself *to* its new home.

admit: *of, into,* or *to.* The quarrel admits *of* no compromise. I shall never admit her *to* my confidence.

admittance: *to.*

admonished: *by.* (Biblical: *of.* Moses was admonished *of* God.)

adsorb: *by.*

advantage: *of, over.* You have the advantage *of* me. You tried to gain an advantage *over* me.

adverse: *to.*

advert: *to.*

advise: *of* or *concerning.* They advised us *of* his coming.

affiliate: *with* or *to.*

affinity: *between, with.* There was a strong affinity *between* them. They felt a strong affinity *with* their surroundings. Affinity *to* or *for* is also common, but is perhaps not established: Water shows a strong affinity *to* (or *for*) salt.

aggression: *on* or *upon.* (*Upon* preferred.)

alien: *to* or *from.* (*To* preferred.)

alienation: *from, of.* He felt alienation *from* such ideas. She sued for alienation *of* affection.

allegiance: *from, of.* A government exacts allegiance *from* the people. The people show allegiance *to* the government.

ally: *to, with.* This species is allied *to* that. England has allied herself *to* Greece.

alongside: no preposition. The boat lay alongside the wharf.

aloof: *from.*

alternate (*v.*): *with.*

amalgamate: *with.*

amateur: *in, of.* An amateur *in* acting; an amateur *of* the arts. (*Amateur* in the first sentence means *nonprofessional;* in the second, *lover* or *appreciator.*)

amazement: *at.*

ambitious: *of* (formerly *for* or *after*).

amity: *between* or *with.* *Between* nations; of one nation *with* another.

amorous: *of, by.* *By* nature; *of* a desired person or thing.

amplify: *by, on,* or *upon.* *By* illustrative remarks; *on* or *upon* a statement (or without the preposition: amplify a statement).

amused: *at* or *by, with.* I was amused *at* (or *by*) his antics. He amused us *with* his antics.

analogous: *in, to.* Oak and beech are analogous *in* qualities. This rite is analogous *to* the other.

analogy: *between, of, to, with.* The analogy *between* (or *of*) religion and the course of nature; *of* light *to* electricity; *of* crystallization *with* (or *to*) cellular growth.

anesthetize: *by.*

anger: *at, toward.* *At* an insult or injustice; *toward* the insulter or offender.

angry: *at, with.* *At* an action; *with* a person.

animadversion: *on* or *upon.*

animadvert: *on* or *upon.*

annoyed: *by, with.* *By* actions or things; *with* a person.

antipathetic: *to* or *toward.*

antipathy: *against* or *to, between, for* or *to.* *Against* or *to* a person; *for* or *to* a thing. Antipathy may exist *between* persons.

anxiety: *about* or *concerning, in regard to, for.* *About* (or *concerning* or *in regard to*) the future; *for* another's safety.

anxious: *about, for.* *About* a problem; *about* or *for* a person.

apart: *from.*

apathy: *of, toward.* *Of* feeling; *toward* action.

append: *to.*

appetite: *for.*

apply: *for, to.* We apply *for* a position *to* a person; and apply color *to* something.

apportion: *among, between, to. Among* several; *between* two; *to* one.

appreciation: *of.* The authors desire to express their appreciation *of* the assistance of their colleagues.

apprehensive: *of, for. Of* danger; *for* another's safety.

approximation: *of, to. Of* one type *to* another.

apropos: *of, to. Of* the subject; *to* the occasion.

arrive: *at, in, upon.* We arrive *in* a country or city; *at* or *in* a town. (*At* when we do not intend to stay; *in* when we do.) We arrive *in* port; *upon* the scene.

arrogate: *to, for. To* oneself; *for* another.

aside: *from.*

aspiration: *after, to, toward. After* righteousness; *to* deserve praise; *toward* heaven.

assimilate: *to* (or no preposition). Time is often assimilated (*i.e.,* compared) *to* a river. Food is assimilated (*i.e.,* converted, appropriated).

associate: *with.*

assuage: *by, with.* Assuage pain *with* hot cloths. Pain is assuaged *by* hot cloths.

assumption: *of.*

astonished: *at, by. At* that which is remarkable but deserving condemnation; *by* that which is remarkable, and worthy of praise.

attainable: *by* or *to.*

attend: *on, to. On* a person (but *on* is often omitted); *to* a duty.

attest: *to* (or no preposition). Your remark attests your acumen (or *to* your acumen).

attribute (*v.*)**:** *to.*

attribute (*n.*)**:** *of.*

augment: *by.* Our ranks were augmented *by* the arrival of fresh troops.

augmentation: *by, of.* The augmentation *of* our numbers by enlistment.

augur: *from, of, for. From* signs; *of* success; *for* a cause.

authority: *of, on.* The right is invested in him by authority *of.* He is an authority *on.*

auxiliary: *of, in, to. Of* the army; *in* a good cause; *to* success.

avaricious: *of.*

avenge: *on* or *upon.*

averse: *to.* (Formerly, and by some still preferred, *from.*)

aversion: *to* or *toward, for* or *toward. To* (or *toward*) a person; *for* (or *toward*) his acts.

babble: *about* or *of.*

basis: *for, of. For* an argument; *of* facts.

becoming: *to, in.* Dress becoming *to* wearer; conduct becoming *in* him.

begin: *by, in, with.* He began *by* opening the book. The legislation began *with* (*by* or *in*) the creation of . . .

beguile: *by, of, with. By* a sham; *of* our rights; *with* a dance or entertaining book.

benefactor: *of.*

bereaved, bereft: *of.*

blame: *for.*

borne: *by, upon.* The truth was borne *in upon* me. His statement was borne *out by* the facts. We were borne *up by* our hopes. (In these sentences, *in, out,* and *up* are not strictly prepositions, but parts of the verbs preceding them.)

break (*v.*): *with.* Break *with* precedents. (But break away *from.*)

break (*n.*): *in.* A break *in* relations.

calculate: *on* or *upon.*

candid: *about* or *in regard to.*

capable: *of.*

capacity: *of, for, to.* *Of* a hundred gallons; *for* work; *to* sign a document.

capitalize: *at.* The business was capitalized *at* $25,000.

careless: *about, in, of.* *About* dress; *in* one's work; *of* the feeling of others.

catastrophe: *of* (rarely *to*). The catastrophe *of* a play.

cause: *of, for.* *Of* trouble; *for* warning.

center: *in.* Rome centers *in* the Colosseum. (Not centers *about.*)

chagrin: *at* or *because of* or *on account of.*

characteristic: *of.*

characterized: *by.*

chastened: *by, with.* *By* sorrow; *with* (physical) pain.

choose: *among, between.* *Among* many; *between* two.

circumstances: "Mere situation is expressed by '*in* the circumstances'; action is performed '*under* the circumstances.'"—*Oxford Dictionary.*

clear (*v.*): *from* or *of.* Clear *from* or *of* blame.

coalesce: *in* or *into, with.* *In* or *into* one; *with* one another.

coincident: *with.*

collide: *with.*

common: *to.*

comparable: *to* or *with.*

compare: *to, with.* We compared him *to* a bear. He compared Disraeli *with* Talleyrand. (*Compare to* notes general or metaphorical resemblance; *compare with,* specific similarities and differences.)

compatible: *with.*

compete: *for, with.* *For* a prize; *with* others.

complacent: *towards.*

complaint: *against.*

complaisant: *towards.*

complement: *of.*

complementary: *to.*

compliance: *with.*

compliment: *on.* I wrote to compliment my friend *on* his promotion.

complimentary: *about* or *concerning.*

comply: *with.*

concentration: *of, on.* *Of* attention; *on* a problem.

concerned: *about, in, to, with.* *About* the welfare of a friend; *in* an affair; *to* be rightly understood; *with* business.

concur: *in, with.* *In* a decision; *with* other persons.

conducive: *to.*

confide: *in, to.* He confided *in* our discretion. He confided his savings *to* me.

conform: *to* or *with*.

conformable: *to* or *with*.

conformity: *to* or *with*.

congratulate: *on* or *upon*.

connect: *by, with.* Johnstown connects *by* good roads *with* Hicksville.

connive: *at, in, with.* I shall not connive *at* any such deception. They connived *with* one another *in* the deception.

conscious: *of*.

consist: *in, of.* Tolerance consists *in* respecting the opinions of others. Water consists *of* oxygen and hydrogen.

consistent: *in, with.* He is not consistent *in* his statements. The statements are not consistent *with* her former ones.

consonant: *with* or *to*. (*With* preferred.)

contact: *among, between, of, with.* *Among* many; *between* two; *of* the mind *with* literature.

contemporaneous: *with*.

contemporary: *with*.

contiguous: *to*.

contingent: *on* or *upon*. (*Upon* preferred.)

contrast (*v.*): *with*.

contrast (*n.*): *between, of, to.* *Between* this and that. This presents a contrast *to* that. This is *in* contrast *with* that.

convenient: *for, to.* *For* a purpose or use; *to* a place.

conversant: *with*.

convert (*v.*): *from, to.* *From* one purpose *to* another.

copyright (*n.*): *in* or *on*.

correlation: *between* or *of*.

correlative: *with*.

counterpart: *of*.

custody: *in, into.* He was *in* custody. He was taken *into* custody.

defect: *in, of.* *In* a machine; *of* judgment or character.

deficiency: *in, of.* *In* intelligence; *of* food.

defile (*v.*): *by, with.* *By* an act; *with* a substance.

definition: *of*.

derive: *from*.

desirous: *of.* Desirous *of* learning.

desist: *from*.

despair: *of*.

destructive: *of, to.* Poor food is destructive *of* health. Rabbits are destructive *to* young trees.

devoid: *of*.

devolve: *from, on, to, upon.* The word means *pass or cause to pass from one to another*. Authority devolves *from* the emperor *on* (or *upon* or *to*) the subjects. *On* or *upon* has better authority than *to*.

different: *from*.

differentiate: *among, between, from.* *Among* many; *between* two; this *from* that.

diminution: *of.*

disappointed: *in, with.* *In* a person, plan, hope, result; *with* a thing.

disapprobation: *of.*

disdain: *for.*

disgusted: *at, by, with.* *At* an action; *by* a quality or habit of a person or animal; *with* a person, because of his general attitude or point of view.

dislike: *of.*

displace: *by.*

displeased: *at, with.* *At* a thing; *with* a person.

dissension: *among, between, with.* *Among* friends; *between* friends. He was in dissension *with* the world.

dissent (*v.*): *from.*

dissociate: *from.*

dissuade: *from.*

distaste: *for.*

distill: *from.*

distinguished: *by, for, from.* *By* talent; *for* honesty; *from* another person or thing.

divert: *by, from, to.* He diverted funds *from* the treasury *to* his own use. We were diverted *by* the child's playfulness.

divide: *by, into.* *By* cutting; *into* parts.

divorce: *from.*

dominant: *over, in.* *Over* others; *in* power or manner.

dominate: *over.*

drench: *with.*

eager: *for, to.* *For* success; *to* succeed.

educated: *about* or *concerning, for, in.* *Concerning* (or *about*) the needs of life; *for* living; *in* liberal arts.

effect: *of.*

eligible: *to* or *for.*

embark: *on.*

emerge: *from.*

emigrate: *from.*

employ: *at, in.* *At* a suitable wage; *in* a gainful pursuit.

empty (*adj.*): *of.* The house is empty *of* furniture.

enamored: *of, with.* *Of* a person; *with* a scene.

encouraged: *by, in.* Encouraged *by* success; encouraged another *in* his work.

endue: *with.*

engage: *in.*

enjoin: *on* or *upon* (in law: *from*).

enraged: *against* or *with, at.* *Against* or *with* a person; *at* an action.

enter: *by, into, in.* *By* the window; *into* the specification of details; items *in* a daybook.

entertained: *by, with.* *By* persons; *with* their doings.

entrust: *to, with.* The money was entrusted *to* me; I was entrusted *with* the money.

enveloped: *in.*

envious: *of.*

equal (*adj.*): *in, to. In* qualities; *to* a task.

equivalent: *in, to.* These two vessels are equivalent *in* volume. That remark is equivalent *to* saying No.

essential: *in, of, to.* The first essential *in* study is concentration. He was well grounded in the essentials *of* mathematics. These things are essential *to* (or *for*) success.

estrange: *from.*

estrangement: *of.*

evidence: *of.* He furnished evidence *of* the fact.

example: *of, from, to.* This is an example *of* the split infinitive. These examples *from* history are instructive. Let this be an example *to* you.

excuse: *for, from. For* an action; *from* an obligation.

exonerate: *from.*

expect: *from, of.* One expects profit *from* investment; honesty *of* a person.

experience: *for, in* or *of.* Experience *for* oneself, *in* or *of* travel.

expert: *at, with. At* tennis; *with* a tennis racket.

exude: *from.*

faced: *by.* We are faced *by* a difficult problem.

fail: *in, of* (not *at*). Fail *in* an examination. Fail *of* success.

familiar: *to, with.* A scene is familiar *to* us; one person is familiar *with* another person.

favorable: *for, to.* Weather favorable *for* skating; I was favorable *to* his proposal.

flinch: *at* or *from.*

foreign: *to.*

free: *from, of* or *in. From* disease; *of* (or *in*) manner.

frightened: *at, by. At* something sudden and threatening, as a gesture; *by* something alarming or inexplicable, as a lion or a ghost.

frugal: *of.*

fugitive: *from.*

guard: *against, from. Against* peril; *from* a person.

habitual: *with.*

hanker: *after.*

hew: *in* or *out of.* Hew *in* (or *out of*) granite.

hint: *at.*

honor: *by, for, with.* I am honored *by* your invitation. We honored him *for* his honesty. He was honored *with* an invitation.

identical: *with.*

identify: *by, to, with. By* credentials; *to* the police; *with* the man known to be innocent.

immanence: *of, in. Of* divine power *in* human life.

immerse: *in.*

immigrate: *to.*

impatient: *at, with. At* action; *with* persons.

impeach: *of* or *for*, or no preposition. Impeach *of* (or *for*) disloyalty; impeach one's motives.

implicit: *in*.

impress (*n.*): *of*, *upon*. *Of* the design *upon* the coin.

impress (*v.*): *into*, *upon*, *with*. A man *into* service; a duty *upon* a child; wax *with* a die.

improve: *by*, *in*, *upon*. Trees may be improved *in* hardiness *by* grafting. I can improve *upon* that plan.

improvement: *in*, *of*, *upon*. *In* health *of* a patient. This machine is an improvement *upon* that.

incarnate: *in*. God incarnate *in* man.

incarnation: *in*, *of*. Incarnation *in* man *of* God.

incongruous: *with*.

incorporate: *in* or *into* or *with*. Incorporate laws *in* a constitution; incorporate this thing *in* (or *into* or *with*) the mass of others.

independent: *of*.

index: *of*. It is a rough index *of* the increase in knowledge.

infer: *from*.

infested: *with*.

infiltration: *by*, *of*. *By* coloring matter *of* a substance.

influence (*v.*): *by*, *for*. *By* actions *for* good.

influence (*n.*): *of*, *over*, *upon*. *Of* a good man *over* others. One may exercise influence *upon* others.

infuse: *with*.

inimical: *to* or *toward*.

initiate: *into*.

innate: *in*.

inquire: *into*, *of*. *Into* causes; *of* a person.

inquiry: *about* or *concerning*, *of*. *About* any destination; *of* a bystander.

inseparable: *from*.

insight: *into*.

inspire: *by*, *with*. *By* example; *with* courage.

instigate: *to*.

instill: *in* or *into*.

instinct: *with*. *With* life.

intention: *of*.

intercede: *for*, *with*. *For* a culprit; *with* a judge.

interest: *in*.

interfere: *in*, *with*. *In* an affair; *with* a person.

intermediary: *between*, *in*. *Between* persons; *in* a quarrel.

interpose: *between*, *in*. The referee interposed *between* the fighters. I refuse to interpose *in* the matter.

intervene: *between*.

intimacy: *of*, *with*. *Of* association; *with* persons.

inundate: *with*.

invest: *in*, *with*. We invest *in* stocks and bonds. We have invested the President *with* great power.

investigation: *of*.

involve: *in.*
isolate: *from.*

jealous: *of, for.* *Of* a person; *of* one's good name; *for* another.
jeer: *at.*
join: *to, with.* Join this *to* that. Join *with* me in this venture.

label: *with.*
labor: *at, for, in, under, with.* *At* a task; *for* or *in* a cause; *under* a taskmaster; *with* tools.
lag: *behind.*
lament: *for* or *over.*
laugh: *at* or *over.*
lend: *to.*
level: *at, to, with.* Level a gun *at.* This book is leveled *to* popular comprehension. The line is level *with* the horizon.
liable: *for, to.* *For* illegal acts; *to* have accidents.
liken: *to.*
live: *at, by, in, on.* *At* a place; *in* a town; *by* peddling; *on* a street.

make: *of, from.* Make the boat *of* pine. My dress is made *from* an old one.
martyr (*v.*): *for.* Martyred *for* his beliefs.
martyr (*n.*): *to.* A martyr *to* rheumatism.
mastery: *of, over.* Mastery *of* a craft; *of* one man *over* another.
meddle: *in, with.* I refuse to meddle *in* his affairs. Don't meddle *with* my things.
mistrustful: *of.*
mock: *at, with.* We may mock *at* a person; be mocked *with* vain desires.
monopoly: *of.*
mortified: *at.*
mortify: *by* or *with.*
motive: *for.*
muse: *on* or *upon.*

necessary: *for, to.* A strong will is necessary *for* success. Rhythm is necessary *to* verse.
necessity: *for, of, to.* He saw the necessity *for* quick action. I realize the necessity *of* consenting. A warm climate was a necessity *to* her.
need: *for, of.* *For* improving conditions; *of* a new coat of paint.
negligent: *of.*

obedient: *to.*
oblivious: *of.*
observant: *of.*
occasion: *for, of.* *For* thanksgiving; *of* distress.
offend: *against.*
offended: *at, with.* *At* an action; *with* a person.
opportunity: *of, to, for.* *Of* enlisting; *to* enlist; *for* enlistment.

opposite: *of*, or no preposition. Good is the opposite *of* bad. This house is opposite that.

originate: *from, in, with.* Baseball originated *from* the old game of rounders. The idea originated *in* his own mind. This plan originated *with* the Brain Trust.

overlaid: *by* or *with.*

parallel: *to* or *with.*

part: *from, with. From* a person; *with* a thing.

partake: *of.*

partial: *to.*

peculiar: *to.*

permit: *of, to.* The passage permits *of* different translations. I will not permit you *to* do it.

persevere: *against, in. Against* opposition; *in* a pursuit.

persist: *against, in. Against* objection; *in* an action.

persuaded: *by, of. By* a person; *of* the necessity.

pervert: *from.*

piqued: *at, by. At* something done to us; *by* ridicule.

place (*v.*): *in.* (Not *into*.)

plan (*v.*): *to.*

pleased: *at* or *by, with.* He was pleased *at* (or *by*) the suggestion. The child was pleased *with* a rattle.

plunge: *in, into. In* grief; *into* water.

possessed: *by* or *with, of. By* or *with* a desire for money; *of* much property.

practice: *of, in. Of* a profession; *in* an art.

precedence: *of.*

precedent (*n.*): *of* or *for.*

precedent (*adj.*): *to.*

precluded: *from.*

predestined: *to.*

preface: *of* or *to.*

prefer: *to.*

prejudice: *against.*

preparatory: *to.*

prerequisite (*adj.*): *to.*

prerequisite (*n.*): *of.*

prescient: *of.*

present (*v.*): *to, with. To* a person; *with* a gift.

present (*adj.*): *to. To* the senses.

preside: *at, over.*

prevail: *against, upon, with.* Patience will often prevail *against* force. We prevailed *upon* him to accompany us. David prevailed *over* Goliath.

prevent: *from.*

preventive: *of.*

preview: *of.*

prior: *to.*

privilege: *of.*

prodigal: *of.*

proficient: *in.*
profit: *by.*
prohibit: *by, from.* By law; *from* doing.
prone: *to.*
property: *of.*
propitious: *to.*
protest: *against.*
provide: *against, for. Against* future needs; *for* one's necessities.
punishable: *by.*
purchase: *of.*
put: *in* (or *into*), *on, to. In* (or *into*) *use; in* (or *into*) water; *on* the table; *to* work.

qualification: *of, for. Of* voters; *for* voting.
qualify: *for, to. For* a competition; *to* act.

ranging: *between, from . . . to, within. Between* boundaries; *from* 32 *to* 60 degrees; *within* a territory.
reason (*v.*): *about* or *on, with. On* (or *about*) a subject; *with* a person.
reason (*n.*): *for, of.* I told him my reason *for* doing it. I told him the reason *of* my action.
rebellious: *against* or *to.*
recognition: *of.*
reconcile: *to, with. To* a condition; *with* a person.
regard: *for, to. For* a person; *in* (or *with*) regard *to* a proposal.
regret (*v.*): no preposition. We regret having done it.
regret (*n.*): *for, over* or *about* or *concerning. For* one's misdoings; *over* or *about* or *concerning* misfortune.
relation: *of, to, with. Of* this *to* that; *with* persons.
removal: *from, of, to. From* a place; *from* normal; *of* snow; *of* difficulties; *to* another place.
repent: *of.*
repugnance: *against, between, for, of, to. Between* versions of testimony; *of* a person *against* (or *for* or *of*) another; *to* a deed or duty.
repugnant: *to.*
requirement: *for, of. For* admission to college; *of* a tax.
requite: *with.*
resemblance: *among, between, of, to. Among* members of a family; *between* two persons or things; *of* one thing *to* another.
resentment: *against, at* or *for. Against* a person; *at* or *for* a wrong.
respect: *With* respect *to.*
revel: *in.*
revenge: *for, upon. For* a hurt; *upon* a person.
reward: *by, for, with. By* conferring a prize; *for* heroism; *with* knighthood.
role: *of.*

sanction: *of, for. Of* the law; *for* an act.
satisfaction: *of, in, with. Of* desire; *of* honor; *in* well-doing; *with* another's deeds.

scared: *at, by.*

search: *for.* In search *of.*

seclusion: *from.*

secure (*adj.*): *in, of.* He felt secure *in* his position. We felt secure *of* their loyalty.

secure (*v.*): *by.*

sensible: *about, of.* Be sensible *about* this affair. We were not sensible *of* the cold.

sensitive: *to.*

separate: *from.*

serve: *for, on, with.* This will serve *for* (*i.e.*, in lieu of) that. He will serve *on* the committee. He will serve *with* the army.

significant: *of.*

similar: *to.*

similarity: *to, of.* He shows some similarity *to* his brother. The similarity *of* the brothers was marked.

skillful: *at* or *in, with.* At (or *in*) art; *with* the hand.

spy: *upon.*

stock: *in, of.* I do not take much stock *in* his plea. He took stock *of* his opportunities.

struck: *by.*

subscribe: *for, to.* For a purpose; *to* an occasion or action.

substitute (*n.* and *v.*): *for.*

suitable: *for, to.* For a purpose; *to* an occasion.

superior: *to.*

supplant: *by.*

supplement: *by* or *with.*

surprised: *at, by.* At actions; *by* unexpected arrival or appearance.

surround: *by.*

suspect: *of.*

sympathize: *in, with.* In another's mood; *with* another person.

sympathy: *for, with, in.* For another; *in* his sorrow; *with* his desires.

synchronous: *to.*

tally: *up, with.* Tally *up* means "check up, reckon"; tally *with* means "agree."

tamper: *with.*

tantamount: *to.*

taste: *for, in, of.* A taste *for* simplicity. Good taste *in* house furnishings. A taste *of* onion.

taunt: *with.*

temporize: *with.*

theorize: *about.*

thoughtful: *of.*

thrill (*v.*): *at* or *to, with.* At or *to* the song of a thrush; *with* pleasure.

thrilled: *by.*

thronged: *with.* The square was thronged *with* people.

tinker: *at* or *with.*

tired: *of, from, with.* From boredom; *of* noise; *with* exercise.

tormented: *by* or *with.* Tormented *by* or *with* headaches.
transmute: *into* or *to.*
treat: *for, of, to, with.* For peace; *of* a subject; *to* a soda; *with* care.
true: *to, with. To* thine own self be true. This cog is not true *with* the other.
trust: *in, to, with.* I trust *in* you; *to* your judgment. I trust you *with* my life.

umbrage: *at, to.* Take umbrage *at;* give umbrage *to.*
unconscious: *of.*
unequal: *in, to. In* qualities; *to* a task.
unfavorable: *for, to. For* action; *to* an attitude or person.
unite: *by* or *in, with. By* or *in* common motives; *with* another.
unmindful: *of.*
unpalatable: *to.*
unpopular: *with.*
use: *in* or *of.*
useful: *in, to. In* or *to* a group; *in* an activity; *to* a person or cause.

variance: *with.*
vary: *from, with.* This varies *from* that; each varied *with* the other.
vest: *in, with.* Power is vested *in* a man; a man is vested *with* power.
vexed: *at, with. At* a thing; *with* a person.
vie: *with.*
view: *of, to. In* view *of; with* a view *to.*
void: *of.*
vulnerable: *to.*

wait: *for, on. For* something to happen or a person to come; *on* people at a table; *on* another's convenience.
weary: *of.*
willing: *to.*
worthy: *of, to. Of* note; *to* be called.
write: *on, off, out. On* paper; *on* a subject; *off* a debt; *out* in full.

yearn: *after, for, over, toward, with. After* solitude; *for* a loved one; *over* a child; *toward* a nearby person; *with* compassion.
yield: *of, to.*

zeal: *for, in. For* a cause; *in* work.

WORDS LIKELY TO BE MISUSED OR CONFUSED

The following list is not primarily one of synonyms, though many appear in it. When synonyms are given, they are as a rule those that also show some resemblance of form or origin (*complacent, complaisant; expedient, expeditious*). A few others are included, though they show no such resemblance, because they are commonly confused (*empty, vacant; damage, injury; deserv-*

ing, worthy of) Many pairs or groups, however, are not synonymous at all, but because of some resemblance of look or sound are liable to be mistaken one for the other (*accept, except; adapt, adopt; imbrue, imbue*). And some isolated terms are given because of a general misconception of their exact meaning (*livid, lurid, beau ideal, cognomen, patronymic, blatant, temerarious*), or because they are trite, overworked, stilted, or pretentious (*mystic*). And, finally, an occasional pair appears merely because of the difficulty of remembering which is which (*diastole, systole; marten, martin; ferrule, ferule*).

Space did not permit an exhaustive discrimination of synonyms, but only a statement of the main ground of confusion. As a rule, therefore, the definitions indicate only meanings in which the members of a pair or group are not interchangeable, and ignore other meanings and other possible synonyms.

abjure, adjure *Abjure:* to renounce (an oath, for example); *adjure:* to beg or request earnestly; to charge (a person under oath).

abolishment, abolition It is doubtful if there is any distinction, though some authorities prefer to use *abolishment* for the specific act and *abolition* for the general principle. Lincoln used both words with reference to slavery.

about, approximately *About* is more vague than *approximately,* the latter suggesting an attempt at calculation or accuracy. "There are about twenty persons in the room." "There are approximately twenty-five pupils in each class."

absorb, adsorb *Absorb:* to take up or drink in; *adsorb:* to condense and hold (a gas) in a thin layer on the surface of a solid.

abysmal, abyssal The words mean the same, one being formed from *abysm* and the other from *abyss;* but *abyssal* is learned, used mostly in biology and geology, and is literal, while *abysmal* may be figurative. "Abyssal depths of the ocean." "Abysmal depths of the ocean or of ignorance."

Acadia, Arcadia *Acadia:* Nova Scotia; *Arcadia:* a region in Greece, an imaginary abode of peace.

accept, except (*v.*) The words have no connection but are often confused by those who do not enunciate clearly. We accept that which we desire; we except that which we exclude or object to. "From the list of vegetables I intend to raise I except parsnips."

acceptance, acceptation The words are often interchangeable, but in prevailing usage *acceptance* has reference to invitation or gift; *acceptation,* to meaning or interpretation. "She wrote a graceful letter of acceptance." "The different acceptations of the word *knowledge.*"

access, accession *Access:* (1) opportunity for entrance: "We did not have access to the fort because we did not know the password"; (2) a way of approach: "Access to the fort was barred by a gate"; (3) a sudden seizure or its approach: "She felt an access of enthusiasm." *Accession:* arrival, a coming to (something), a being joined with or by (something), an increase. "Accession to the throne is possible to a prince; access to it is possible to a petitioner." "There has been no accession to (*i.e.,* increase in) our army."

acclivity, declivity One goes up an acclivity, down a declivity.

act, action When the two words are not interchangeable, *act* is simple and specific; *action* complex and general. "The Acts of the Apostles." "The action of an acid." The difference between "His actions are deplorable" and "His acts are deplorable" is that the first sentence refers to his habitual behavior and the second to certain doings.

adapt, adopt *Adapt:* to adjust, make suitable, remodel; *adopt:* to accept, receive as one's own.

addicted to, subject to A person is addicted to some act or thing through his own inclination, habit, or weakness; he is subject, by reason of his condition or position, to certain effects whose cause is outside himself and without his volition.

adhere, cohere Two or more separate things may adhere (stick together). Parts of the same thing cohere (hold together).

adherence, adhesion The words are often interchangeable, though *adhesion* is more likely to refer to the physical; *adherence* to the mental or social. "The adhesion of lime and brick." "A man's adherence to a cause." In such a sentence as "France's adhesion (adherence) to the pact is certain," either word is acceptable, though *adhesion* perhaps suggests a more definite and active sticking to than the other term.

adjure *See* abjure.

admission, admittance *Admission* is now the generally used word, *admittance* being familiar only in the literal sense of *letting in*—"No admittance to beggars or solicitors."

admonishment, admonition The distinction, if any, is that *admonishment* is specific gentle reproof, and *admonition,* gentle reproof in general.

adsorb *See* absorb.

advance, advancement The words are distinct in meaning, *advance* having reference to forward motion, *advancement* to the action or means taken. "The advance of the troops was rapid." "Bacon's phrase 'the advancement of learning' assumed science as the means." *Advancement,* not *advance,* should be used of promotion: "His advancement in his profession was notable."

adversary, antagonist, enemy, foe, opponent All imply opposition, and *adversary, enemy,* and *foe* imply hostile opposition. In these three the idea of active hostility increases from the first to the third. An antagonist or an opponent may not be hostile at all. Lawyers who are antagonists in court may be good friends outside, and the same is true of opponents in politics or a game. Milton uses *adversary, antagonist, enemy,* and *foe* according as the idea of opposition to God or hostility to man is dominant.

adverse, averse *Adverse* (L. *advertare,* turn to): turned to or towards in opposition; *averse* (L. *avertare,* turn from): turned from in dislike or repugnance. We speak of adverse winds or circumstances and of a person's being averse to study. *Averse* implies feeling; *adverse* seldom does. "The statesman expressed himself as adverse to the bill."

advertising, propaganda, publicity Publicity is matter spoken, written, or printed in the interests of persons, organizations, parties, etc. It may include advertising and propaganda. Advertising is any kind of public notice, though most often of something for sale. Propaganda is ideas, views, or beliefs systematically spread to influence masses of people quickly, often hastily, commonly by emotional appeal, and usually without due regard to the fair appraisal of the issues involved.

aerie, eerie *Aerie:* the nest, on a crag, of a bird of prey; *eerie:* uncanny, weird or frightened, timid. (Also spelled *eery.*)

affect, effect *Affect:* to influence, to pretend; *effect:* to accomplish, complete.

affective, effective *Affective:* emotional or (of language) fitted for transmitting emotion; *effective:* (1) producing an effect; (2) impressive, striking; (3) operative, in effect; (4) ready for service or action.

aggregate, total An aggregate is a collection of particulars in a mass or whole; a total is a whole or entirety without special reference to parts.

alibi, excuse Strictly, *alibi* refers to the plea or fact of having been elsewhere, though colloquially it is used of any excuse.

aliquant, aliquot *Aliquant:* contained in another number, but with remainder; *aliquot:* contained in another number, without remainder. Five is an aliquant part of 16, and an aliquot part of 15.

allege, assert *Allege:* to say or affirm on insufficient grounds; *assert:* to say or affirm emphatically or with conviction.

all ready, already *All ready* is an adjective meaning *completely prepared; already* is an adverb meaning *before now.* "I am all ready to go." "He has gone already."

all together, altogether *Altogether,* meaning *entirely, completely,* is often misused for *all together,* meaning *collectively.* "Our state governments spend all together about two billion dollars a year." "All together, the purges left hardly a single leader of the 1917 Revolution alive." "They were all together in the room." "They were altogether in accord." "Apical growth is retarded or ceases altogether."

allude, elude, illude These verbs are confused only because of similarity of sound or spelling. *Allude:* to refer vaguely; *elude:* to dodge, slip away from; *illude* (a rare word): to cheat, mock, play tricks upon (in the manner of a magician or prestidigitator). The nouns *allusion, elusion, illusion* are similiarly distinguished.

allude, refer We refer to a thing by a clear and direct statement; we allude by a passing, indirect, sometimes obscure remark or hint.

alternate, alternative *Alternate:* first one and then the other; *alternative:* one without the other. "The flag has alternate red and white stripes." "Alternative plans."

altitude, elevation Altitude is absolute, elevation may be relative. The altitude of an object is its elevation above a norm, as sea level: "The altitude of the mountain top is 6,000 feet." Elevation is any distance above something else: "We reached an elevation on the mountain, halfway to the top." *Elevation* has metaphorical uses that *altitude* has lost, as "elevation of soul or mind"; in astronomy, topography, and art it has technical uses.

amateur, novice, tyro *Tyro* (L. *tyro,* a recruit) or *novice* (L. *novus,* new, through the French) signifies a beginner, both words suggesting inexperience. *Amateur* (F. *amateur,* lover) refers to one who is a beginner only in the sense that he is not a professional: he may have been an amateur for years. We distinguish "an amateur of the arts" from "an amateur in the arts," the former being a lover or appreciator, the latter a beginner or nonprofessional.

ambiguous, equivocal Both words mean *susceptible of more than one interpre-*

tation. Equivocal describes a statement intentionally so worded that two or more meanings can be inferred; but the wording which makes a statement ambiguous may or may not be intentional. Actions, as well as words, may be described as equivocal, but not as ambiguous. Since the apparent meaning of an equivocal statement may not be the actual meaning, *equivocate* and *equivocator* have come to be euphemisms for *lie* and *liar.*

amoral, immoral, nonmoral, unmoral *Immoral:* in violation of morals; *amoral, nonmoral,* and *unmoral:* neither moral nor immoral. *Amoral* is a learned word growing steadily in popularity, perhaps because *nonmoral* and *unmoral* might be interpreted *immoral.*

amusedly, amusingly "He told the story amusingly." "We listened amusedly."

anarchism, anarchy *Anarchism* is a philosophical or political term for the theory that all governments are wrong or unnecessary. Until 1872 the believers in anarchism were peaceful in their methods, but after that date they adopted terrorism as a means of promoting the doctrine and it was then called nihilism. *Anarchy* is the name of a state or condition of disorder during which government is absent or helpless. By extension it means disorder or lawlessness of any sort.

ancient, antiquated, antique *Ancient:* very old; *antiquated:* out of date or out of use or out of vogue. *Antique* refers to style rather than to age, or to the old that is valued or prized. The antiquated is not valued or prized.

anhydrous, hygroscopic Words often confused even by scientists. *Anhydrous:* destitute of water, dried; *hygroscopic:* capable of absorbing moisture. (*Hygroscopic* is seen ignorantly spelled *hydroscopic*. *Hydroscopic* refers to a device for looking at the bed of a body of water.)

anile, senile *Anile:* like an old woman, feeble-minded; *senile:* like an old person of either sex. *Anile* is a rare word, except in crossword puzzles. (The pronunciation of both words is in dispute.)

animal, beast, brute *Animal* is the mild and general word. There is not necessarily offense in saying that a man is an animal. *Beast* and *brute* we hesitate to use of any creature we are fond of. The beast is a creature of instinct and appetite; the brute, one that is dull of comprehension or of unreasoning strength and cruelty.

antagonist *See* adversary.

antique *See* ancient.

apperception, perception *Apperception:* self-consciousness, the act of mind by which it is conscious of perceiving; *perception:* knowledge derived from the senses, recognition of fact or truth.

apparently, seemingly, obviously *Apparently* and *seemingly* suggest that the senses or perception may be at fault and some doubt present, while *obviously* expresses certainty or complete clarity or recognition. Loose speakers and writers, however, constantly use *obviously* where *apparently* or *seemingly* would be more exact.

appear, seem It is probably vain to try to differentiate the meanings of these words. *Appear,* however, by etymology refers to an effect upon the senses; *seem,* to one upon the mind. The latter suggests more reflection than the former. "He appeared to be happy." "He seemed to love her."

appreciation, enjoyment Enjoyment is mainly emotional; appreciation, largely rational. We enjoy a picnic; appreciate a favor, music, a picture. In the arts enjoyment is necessary to appreciation, but appreciation not to enjoyment. By etymology *appreciate* suggests increase or enrichment of quality or value, a meaning it still has—"The stocks appreciated in value."

apprehend, comprehend To comprehend is to grasp completely; to apprehend is to perceive the main drift or to look forward to with foreboding. *Apprehend* has also a specific use in the sense of *arrest, make a prisoner of.* This is very near the original Latin meaning of *seize.*

apprise, apprize Both spellings are used for the meanings: (1) inform, notify and (2) appraise, though *apprise* is the preferred spelling for the former and *apprize* for the latter.

approximately *See* about.

apt, likely *Apt* has meanings which are not synonymous with those of *likely.* *Apt* suggests habitual tendency; *likely* emphasizes probability; but they are often interchanged. "He is apt to forget to wind his watch." "We are likely to postpone the trip if it rains."

Arcadia *See* Acadia.

art, artifice *Art* refers to the product of imagination or creation; *artifice* to that of skill or cunning. The latter word often suggests imitation or fraud.

> Suppose you say your worst of Pope, declare
> His jewels paste, his nature a parterre,
> His art but artifice.—Austin Dobson.

ascension, ascent The words are as a rule interchangeable, but *ascension* is used mainly in dignified contexts—the ascension of Elijah or Christ—though the "ascension" of an aeronaut or a balloon is a stock phrase. We speak of the "ascent of man" and of the ascent, rather than ascension, of a mountain.

assay, essay As verbs, *assay:* analyze, test; *essay:* attempt. We assay a metal, essay a task. The words are etymologically the same, and *assay* was formerly used as *essay* is now.

assemblage, assembly An assemblage is promiscuous and unorganized; an assembly is organized and united.

assert, say, state *Say* is the least formal and most general of the three. *State* is more formal than *say* and means *set forth in detail or completely.* To assert is to claim or state positively, sometimes aggressively. *See also* allege.

Attic, Greek, Hellenic, Hellenistic The first three words are often interchangeable. *Attic,* however, refers not to Hellas or Greece but to Athens or the dialect of Attica. It is therefore used of the highly civilized center of Greek culture— "Attic wit," "Attic purity." *Hellenic* is sometimes used to distinguish Hellas or Greece of the great period, before 300 B.C., from the Hellenistic (or decadent), 300–150 B.C. Compare *classic, classicist.*

audience, spectators An audience hears, spectators see.

aught, ought The distinction given in most handbooks is that *aught* means *anything whatever;* and *ought* means *should.* But *aught* or *ought* is in good use in the sense of *a cipher, nothing, naught,* and the symbol 0 is called *aught, ought, naught, nought.* Nevertheless the distinction given is observed by most educated persons. "You ought to pay me." "I do not owe you aught."

aura An aura is an emanation or exhalation from a body and should as a rule be distinguished from a halo or other glow or flood of light surrounding a body but proceeding from an outside source.

avenge, revenge Both mean *punish as a payment for wrong done,* but *revenge* is egotistical and *avenge* not. We may speak of an avenging God, but hardly of a revenging God. In avenging, the punishment is righteous; in revenging, the question of right and wrong may not enter at all. The nouns *avenging* and *vengeance,* as distinguished from *revenge,* share the distinction. The Bible speaks of the "God of vengeance," not "God of revenge."

averse *See* adverse.

avocation, vocation Although the words may be used in the same signification, careful writers use *vocation* of a person's calling by which he makes a living, and *avocation* of his way of occupying his leisure or of amusing himself.

bacchanal, bacchant As nouns the two words are interchangeable and may be used of both males and females, the feminine of *bacchant* being *bacchante.* As adjectives *bacchant* means *worshiping Bacchus, reveling; bacchanal* or *bacchanalian* also means this, but is more likely than *bacchant* to mean *drunken, licentious.*

baleful, baneful *Baleful:* malign, pernicious, or wretched, miserable; *baneful:* noxious, poisonous, dangerous. The little-used nouns *bale* and *bane* suggest the difference. *Bale:* evil or woe; *bane:* poison, or as dangerous as poison. (Cf. *wolfbane, dogbane, henbane,* etc.) We speak of a baleful glance and baneful circumstances.

barbarian, barbaric, barbarous A barbarian is not a civilized being, and therefore the adjective *barbarian* refers to a stage in human progress between the savage and the civilized. *Barbaric* is used of certain qualities of barbarians, especially their extravagance; as "barbaric splendor," "barbaric song." *Barbarous* may be used in the sense of *barbarian,* as "barbarous tribes," without implying anything except lack of civilization, but it usually denotes the cruelty which such tribes are likely to display: "barbarous treatment," "a barbarous crime."

bathos, pathos *Bathos:* a ludicrous descent from the lofty to the commonplace, anticlimax; *pathos:* tender, sorrowful feeling or that which rouses it.

beast *See* animal.

beau ideal The phrase means *ideal beauty,* not *beautiful ideal.*

before, ere In Anglo-Saxon *aer* means *before,* and the only distinction between *ere* and *before* is that *ere* is likely to be reserved for elevated or poetic contexts.

begin, commence, start If any distinction exists between *begin* and *commence,* it is that the latter is more formal and bookish. *Start* is more definite than the other words. We speak of starting a race, a watch, a quarrel, but beginning the school year, a friendship, travel.

behalf, behoof Compared with *behalf, behoof* is rare. "On my behalf" meant, in Middle English, *on my side; behoof* is in Anglo-Saxon *behof,* advantage. "He spoke on my behalf" or "in my behalf" (*not* in my behoof). A correct use of *behoof* would be: "This school was founded for the behoof of poor students." The verb *behoove,* because it is in the Bible, is better known: "It behooves every man to love his neighbor"; that is, is to his advantage, or is fitting.

being, entity The words are nearly synonymous. *Entity* is, however, used of inanimate objects and *being* is not—at least in popular usage.

below, under A sailor says: "I'm going below," "Davy Jones's locker is under [*not* below] the ship," and "The keel is under the ship." These are correct uses of the words. *Below* is in contrast with *above; under,* with *over.* *Above* and *below* refer to differences of level; *over* and *under,* to levels with reference to something else which is between them.

bemean, demean *Bemean:* to render or become mean, abase (oneself); *demean:* (1) to behave or conduct (oneself), (2) to render or become mean, abase (oneself). Although *demean* in the second sense is often challenged, it is accepted. In fact, *bemean* is seldom found, while *demean* (in the same sense as *bemean*) is common.

beside, besides *Beside:* at the side of; *besides:* in addition to, moreover. Although *beside* in the sense of *besides* is not incorrect, the distinction given is convenient and is generally observed by the careful.

bimonthly, semimonthly *Bimonthly:* every two months; *semimonthly:* twice a month. Compare *biennial, semiannual; biweekly, semiweekly.*

binnacle, binocle *Binnacle:* a case for a ship's compass; *binocle:* a double eyeglass or opera glass.

blanch, blench *Blanch:* to whiten; *blench:* to shrink back, flinch.

blatant Sometimes misused for *flagrant. Blatant:* offensively noisy, resounding, echoing; *flagrant:* scandalous, notorious, heinous.

bogey, bogie, bogy *Bogey:* a score in golf; *bogie:* a truck or carriage; *bogy:* a goblin. (*Note.* These spellings are only suggested. Each of the words is accepted in all three spellings.)

both, each, either *Either* for *each* or *both* is becoming archaic. The current idiom is to say *on each side* or *on both sides* of the street rather than *on either side.*

brute *See* animal.

cacao, coca, cocoa, coco *Cacao:* the tree providing *cocoa* or chocolate; *coca:* a shrub providing a stimulant drug; *coco:* the tree bearing coconuts.

can, may *Can:* is able; *may:* is permitted. In spite of the efforts of generations of teachers, the two are popularly confused, especially in questions—"May [*not* can] I leave the room?"

canvas, canvass *Canvas:* a heavy cloth; *canvass:* to solicit.

capital, capitol *Capital:* the city that is the seat of government; *capitol:* the building in which a legislative body sits.

careen, career *Careen:* to lean; *career:* to rush headlong. "The ship careened to the wind." "The ship careered before the wind."

censure, criticize To censure is to express disapproval or blame; to criticize may be this, but in a nobler sense it is to weigh the merits as well as the demerits of a person or work. Such phrases as *to criticize adversely, to criticize negatively,* suggest that the original meaning of *critic,* a judge, is still felt.

ceremonial, ceremonious *Ceremonial:* connected with, consisting of, or suitable for a ceremony; *ceremonious:* having an air of or resulting from ceremony, formal. We speak of a ceremonious person as of one who is elaborately polite, formal (probably too formal).

certainty, certitude *Certitude* signifies absolute conviction held as a habit of mind. *Certainty* may mean this, but often does not, having reference to some special or immediate assurance or conviction. We speak of the certainty of facts or truths; the certitude of belief of a pious person.

cheerful, cheery The words are usually interchangeable, though *cheery* suggests a more demonstrative gaiety of manner than does *cheerful*.

childish, childlike *Childish* refers as a rule to the less pleasant qualities of a child; *childlike*, to the more pleasant. "Don't be childish." "Childish old age." "Hans Andersen was a childlike person."

chute, shoot The words have become confused because of identity of sound. In America *chute* is applied to a fall of water, an inclined channel for water, or to the sort of toboggan slide seen at public playgrounds. The word is both noun and verb, and *shoot the chutes* was originally *chute the chutes*.

cicada, cicala Two names for the same insect.

cite, quote To quote is to repeat the words of the original; to cite is to refer to or to give the substance of the original.

classic, classical, classicist *Classic* and *classical* are interchangeable in most contexts. They are contrasted with *classicist*, in that they refer to the qualities, styles, productions of the ancients, while *classicist* refers to later imitations of these or to works inspired by Renaissance theory or practice derived from the ancients. The adjective *classicist* is giving way to *neo-classic*. As nouns, *classicist* may refer to either a follower of classicism or one devoted to the classics; while *classic* may refer to a work of art or literature of the highest rank or, colloquially, by extension, to any object or accomplishment adjudged to be first class. In the plural *the classics* refers to the works of the ancient Greeks and Romans or the greatest works of modern literature.

clench, clinch Two forms of the same word. *Clinch* is used in more meanings than *clench*, but we usually clench our teeth or hands.

clergy, clergymen *Clergy* refers to the profession; *clergymen*, to individuals. "Since I had seen him so often with clergymen, I assumed that he was of the clergy."

clew, clue Two spellings of the same word, *clew* now being used mostly as a nautical term for *a corner of a sail, one of the small cords at the end of a hammock*, etc.

climactic, climatic *Climactic* refers to climax; *climatic*, to climate.

climate, clime *Climate* refers to weather; *clime*, to a region, with or without regard to weather. The latter is mainly used in elevated contexts.

cocoa See cacao.

codger The usual American form of *cadger*, but somewhat differently used. In England a cadger is one who goes about peddling. In America a codger is an odd, queer character or a crotchety (usually old) fellow.

cognomen Often misused. Originally, in ancient Rome, a cognomen was a name added to a man's name to indicate the family or gens to which he belonged, as *Caesar* in *Caius Julius Caesar*. Colloquially the word is now used of any name or nickname. Compare *patronymic, q.v.*

cohere See adhere.

coincidence A coincidence requires at least two concurrent incidents. It is hardly accurate, therefore, to speak, for example, of good weather as a happy coincidence when one merely means a fortunate occurrence.

comic, comical The comical is droll, laughable, funny; the comic is that which aims at or has its origin in comedy. The comic may not cause physical laughter at all—as in "serious comedy"—but only laughter of the mind. To call, let us say, an opera singer a great comic actor would be high praise, but to call him a comical actor might not be. As a noun *comic* has been debased in some meanings, though it still retains its original sense of *that which excites mirth* or *one who can cause laughter.*

commence *See* begin.

commonplace, platitude, truism All three words are used derogatively of ideas or observations not worth making. The derogatory is strongest, however, in *platitude,* which by derivation suggests a flatness. Commonplaces and truisms, though trite, may still be valuable. We may say that poetry deals with the great commonplaces or truisms of life, but we should hardly say that it deals with platitudes.

complacent, complaisant *Complacent:* pleased with oneself; *complaisant:* desirous of pleasing, obliging. *Complaisant* is being supplanted by *complacent,* but the distinction is worth preserving. "His complacent manner was vaguely irritating." "The king appeared complaisant towards his council."

complementary, complimentary *Complementary:* completing, serving to make a whole; *complimentary:* expressive of admiration, commendation, congratulation; mildly flattering.

compose, comprise Parts compose a whole; a whole comprises parts.

comprehend *See* apprehend.

comprehensible, comprehensive *Comprehensible:* capable of being understood; *comprehensive:* large in scope or content or of large mental power.

conclude, decide *Conclude* implies previous consideration or exercise of judgment. One may decide on the spur of the moment, but concludes after reflection.

condign The word means *deserved, adequate,* or *fit,* not, as many writers seem to think, *severe.* Condign punishment is merited punishment.

condole, condone *Condole:* to grieve with, sympathize with; *condone:* to set aside an offense as if it had not been committed. The nouns are *condolence* and *condonation.*

conducive, conductive *Conducive:* helping, promoting a result; *conductive:* having the power to transmit or conduct. *Conductive* is used mainly in connection with electricity or other fluids. The verbs *conduce* and *conduct* show a similar differentiation.

confidant, confident In current usage *confidant* (fem., *confidante*) is a noun; *confident,* an adjective. A confidant is a person in whom one confides.

conjurer, conjuror Both spellings are used in the sense of *magician. Conjur'er* or *conjur'or* is obsolete in the sense of *one bound by oath to others. Con'jurater* or *con'jurator* is used in both senses.

connotation, denotation The connotation of a word is what it suggests apart from its explicit and recognized meaning, its explicit and recognized meaning being its denotation. The connotation of a word may differ with every hearer or reader, because it is due mainly to associations of idea or feeling; the denotation—the meaning given in dictionaries—is relatively stable and fixed. Poetry is concerned largely with connotation, while science carefully avoids it.

consequent, consequential *Consequent* (adj.): following as a natural result; *consequential* (in its popular use): self-important. "Sin and consequent remorse." "A consequential manner." *Consequential* also means *following as a sequel or logical consequence* but *consequent* has nearly monopolized this acceptation.

considerateness, consideration *Consideration* is taking thought for the comfort or feelings of others; *considerateness* is the general attitude or habit which shows consideration on particular occasions. "His temperamental considerateness made it natural for him to show consideration on this occasion."

contagion, infection There is much confusion concerning the medical use of the words. Perhaps the best usage is to call the transmission of disease directly or indirectly from person to person *contagion* and the communication of disease in any manner (by air, water, insects, etc., as well as contact) *infection*.

contemptible, contemptuous *Contemptible:* deserving contempt; *contemptuous:* exhibiting contempt.

contend, contest *Contend:* (1) to maintain by argument; (2) to strive in opposition or rivalry. In the first sense it is followed by *that;* in the second usually by *with.* "I contend that he had no right to do it." "On the voyage the ship had to contend with a strong head wind." *Contest:* to contend about earnestly, perhaps with physical force, or to strive to take, keep, or control; also, to challenge. *Contend* is used transitively with *that* and *contest* is not. "I contended that the method proposed was impracticable." "The Italians contested the Austrians' passage of the Alps." "The mayor contested the validity of the election returns." The intransitive use of *contest* is becoming rare, *contend* being used: "All night long the hermit contended [*rather than* contested] with temptation."

continual, continuous The continual lasts but with pauses or breaks; the continuous lasts without pauses or breaks. "He continually annoyed her." "The noise of the waterfall was continuous."

continuance, continuation, continuity *Continuance* refers primarily to lastingness; *continuation,* to prolongation. We speak, therefore, of the continuation (*not* continuance) of a story; but of the continuance of kindness. Continuity is the state or quality of being extended or prolonged or of being uninterrupted. The phrase "continuity of history" suggests unbrokenness primarily and lastingness only secondarily.

contradictious, contradictory *Contradictious:* inclined to contradict; *contradictory:* opposed, inconsistent with itself. *Contradictious* is applied only to persons.

contumacy, contumely The words have no connection but are sometimes confused. *Contumacy:* stubbornness, perverse obstinacy; *contumely:* haughtiness, scorn, insolence. "The judge pronounced the prisoner's behavior mere contumacy." "The proud man's contumely."—*Hamlet.*

corespondent, correspondent *Corespondent:* the person charged as the respondent's paramour in a suit for divorce; or a defendant in a suit in chancery or in an admiralty cause; *correspondent:* one party to an exchange of letters.

corporal, corporeal *Corporal:* of the body itself; *corporeal:* like or of the nature of a body, material, tangible. "Corporal punishment." "The specter appeared in corporeal form."

cost, price, value, worth The cost of a thing is whatever is paid for it; its price, what the seller asks for it; its value, the ratio it bears to a recognized standard; its worth, the ratio it bears to the buyer's desire or need.

councilor, counselor *Councilor:* a member of a council; *counselor:* one who gives advice.

couple, two Popularly, *couple* is used in the sense of *two*—"I'm going away for a couple of days." Strictly, it refers to two joined in some way: "hounds leashed in couples," "a married couple."

covetous, envious, jealous A covetous person desires what another has; an envious one feels ill-will towards another because the latter has more than he; a jealous one resents another's intrusion upon what he possesses. Covetousness may involve envy and jealousy. Covetousness and envy are always bad; but jealousy may be good or bad, according to the occasion and the object. One may, for example, be rightly jealous of one's good name; that is, resentful of slander. The Bible speaks of God as jealous—"I thy God am a jealous God."

credence, credit *Credence* means *belief* or *trust.* "I did not know whether to give credence to his declaration." *Credit* means this and many other things. It would no doubt be used by most persons instead of *credence* in the sentence just given, and not incorrectly.

credible, creditable *Credible* is used of things heard or read and means *believable.* *Creditable*, though often used interchangeably with *credible,* may mean *deserving of credit, worthy.* "Some of his alleged facts are hardly credible." "This action which you deplore I should call creditable."

crenelated, crenulated *Crenelated:* provided with battlements; *crenulated:* finely notched.

criticize *See* censure.

cryptic, gnomic *Cryptic:* secret, hidden, occult; *gnomic:* having the qualities of a proverb, maxim, or apothegm; pertaining to gnomes. The Book of Proverbs could be called gnomic. By extension *gnomic* is used as if it meant *mysterious, occult.* A short wise saying is sometimes called a gnome. (*Gnomic* is also a variant form of *gnomonic.*)

culture, Kultur—*Kultur* gained currency during 1914 to 1918 and was widely misunderstood. It refers, not to culture in the general sense, but to German culture—that is, the expression of German national and political ideals.

cynical The word is so often used trivially that its traditional meaning should be kept in mind. It early meant *exhibiting an ignorant and insolent self-righteousness,* and, later, *a skeptical attitude towards virtue and idealism and towards lofty or noble motives.* Historically, then, it suggests *pessimistic* or *misanthropic.* Nowadays it is often used where only *ill-natured* or *sarcastic* is meant.

daemon An old spelling of *demon,* but sometimes used in the Greek sense of *a supernatural being,* either good or bad.

daemonic, demonic, demoniacal *Demonic:* of or like a demon, as "demonic possession." *Demonic* and *demoniacal* are not clearly differentiated, though phrases like "demonic power" and "demoniacal leer" suggest that *demoniacal* connotes *wicked, devilish;* and *demonic, intense* (as a demon). *Daemonic* is sometimes used with a return to the Greek meaning of *possessing fascination* or *exercising hypnotic influence.* (*See* daemon.)

damage, injury *Injury* originally meant *that which is not right or just; damage* meant *loss.* As a rule we think of persons, feelings, rights, or reputation as being injured, our possessions, things, damaged. However, the distinction is not clearly drawn, for we also speak of injury to property. Damage involves loss; injury, hurt. Damage is impairment of value; injury, impairment of beauty, utility, integrity, dignity.

deadly, deathly Both are used in the sense of *having the aspect of death*—"deadly or deathly pale." But *deathly* is more often used in this sense than *deadly* and has no other, while *deadly* also means *capable of causing death, murderous*—"a deadly weapon," "a deadly serpent."

decide *See* conclude.

decimate *Decimate* means, strictly, *kill one in ten* or, rarely, *kill all but one in ten*. Popularly, it is used loosely to mean *kill any appreciable number* or *exterminate*.

declivity *See* acclivity.

deduce, deduct *Deduce:* to derive by reasoning; *deduct:* to take away or subtract. "We deduced his meaning by his manner rather than by his words." "You may deduct ten per cent for cash."

deduct, subtract *Deduct* applies to amounts or quantities; *subtract,* to numbers.

defective, deficient *Defective:* having defects; *deficient:* lacking completeness. Think of *defect* and *deficit*.

definite, definitive Very commonly confused. *Definite:* clear, precise, unmistakable; *definitive:* conclusive, permanent, unalterable, final. A definite offer is not necessarily a definitive one: the first is one that is clear; the second, one that is final.

deism, theism In ordinary usage, *deism* is a historical term for a form of religious belief that flourished in the eighteenth century; *theism,* a general term for belief in God or gods. Theologians and historians of religion make more elaborate or subtle distinctions than this.

delightedly, delightfully *Delightedly:* manifesting delight; *delightfully:* affording delight.

demean *See* bemean.

demonic, demoniacal *See* daemonic.

denotation *See* connotation.

depositary, depository Both forms are used of a place where anything is deposited, but *depositary* is also used of a person entrusted with anything for safekeeping.

depot Etymologically *depot* is connected with *deposit,* and refers to a place for deposit or storage, such as a warehouse. Its use for *railroad station* is American.

depravation, deprivation *Depravation:* the act of depraving or the state of being depraved; *deprivation:* the act of depriving or the state of being deprived. "The entire age suffered from a depravation of morals." "The destruction of works of art is a more severe deprivation than the vulgar realize."

deprecate, depreciate *Deprecate:* to express disapproval or regret; *depreciate:* to lessen in value, to cry down.

deserving, worthy of *Deserving* and *worthy of* are synonymous and may be followed by a substantive expressing either praise or blame, reward or punishment. Present usage, however, tends to restrict *worthy of* to expressions of reward, though it does not hesitate to speak of "deserving punishment." To many minds there seems to be a contradiction in using *worthy,* meaning *meritorious, excellent, estimable,* in an expression of blame or punishment.

determinism, fatalism Popularly fatalism is the attitude of mind of those who believe that events, especially death, will come when they will and that it is useless to try to avoid them. *Determinism* is not a popular term. Philosophically, fatalism is the theory that some external force controls our lives inexorably in every detail; determinism, the theory that the action of cause and effect makes our freedom of will only apparent or a delusion.

deterrent, detriment *Deterrent:* that which hinders, slows down; *detriment:* that which causes damage, injury, loss. "Severe penalties may not act as deterrents to crime." "Thoughtless gossip may cause detriment to our plans."

detract, distract *Detract:* to reduce or take away from; *distract:* to divert or perplex. "His unpleasant manner detracted from the credit his actions deserved." "A loud noise distracted our attention from the proceedings."

dialectal, dialectic A tendency is perceptible to limit *dialectal* to reference to dialect and *dialectic* to reference to dialectics; but the distinction, though useful, is not generally observed except among scholars.

diastole, systole The words refer to opposite movements of heart muscle. The diastole draws the blood inward from the veins; the systole forces the blood outward to the arteries.

discomfit, discomfort (*v.*) *Discomfit:* to frustrate, to vanquish; *discomfort:* to make uneasy.

discover, invent We discover what is already in existence; invent something new.

discreet, discrete *Discreet:* wise, prudent, judicious; *discrete:* disconnected, separate, discontinuous.

disinterested Endlessly misused for *uninterested.* A person may be disinterested without being uninterested. A disinterested person is impartial; an uninterested one is indifferent. "A judge should always be disinterested, but should never be uninterested in the action before him."

distract *See* detract.

dominance, domination Though the words are often interchangeable, *dominance* suggests, more than *domination,* a condition or fact of authority, and *domination,* more than *dominance,* an act or exercise of power, often arbitrary or insolent. "We rebelled against his domination." "The dominance of Rome in the first century does not suggest that its decline was to come so soon."

dower, dowry Originally these meant the same, but now they are differentiated A dower is a wife's life share in her husband's property; a dowry is the property brought by a bride to her husband. A dowager is a widow living upon her dower. A dower house is a house assigned to a widow to live in when the manor house passes to the heir. Poetically, *dower* is used in the sense of *dowry,* and both are used in the sense of *gifts* or *talents.*

durance, duress *Durance* is a term little used except in hackneyed phrases, such as "durance vile." It means *confinement. Duress* means *restraint,* not necessarily in confinement, and is used mostly in legal contexts.

each *See* both.

eerie *See* aerie.

effect *See* affect.

egoism, egotism The distinction is generally ignored, but is useful. *Egoism* suggests self-supremacy rather than self-conceit, and philosophically may be free from connotation of selfishness or vanity. *Egotism* is not philosophical but instinctive and usually expresses itself outwardly in speech and action.

either *See* both.

elemental, elementary *Elemental* refers to the great forces of nature or of feeling: elemental fire, cold, passion, power, hate; though it may be used in the sense of *elementary*. *Elementary* refers to the basic or rudimentary parts of a whole: elementary grades in a school, an elementary textbook, elementary knowledge.

elevation *See* altitude.

elude *See* allude.

emerge, immerge *Emerge:* to come forth or out; *immerge:* to plunge into or under. *Immerge* is rare, *immerse* being more often used.

emergence, emergency *Emergence:* a coming out or into notice; *emergency:* an occasion needing care or prompt action. "The emergence of the whale produced a commotion in the water." "Such extreme measures were justified by the emergency."

empty, vacant *Empty* is opposed to *full; vacant,* to *occupied.* "An empty bucket." "A vacant room."

endemic, endermic *Endemic:* peculiar to one place, as a disease; *endermic:* acting by absorption in or through the skin.

enemy *See* adversary.

enjoyment *See* appreciation.

enormity, enormousness *Enormousness* refers only to size; *enormity,* to morals. "The enormousness of the elephant." "The enormity of a cruel act."

enough, sufficient Despite much discussion no perceptible difference in meaning has been established. *Enough* is the homelier and blunter word.

entity *See* being.

envious *See* covetous.

epic, epopee, epos All refer to a long narrative poem, *epic* being the popular term, *epopee* (French) an old and now learned term, and *epos* a learned term. *Epic* is, however, used—often abused—in other senses, as an adjective.

equable, equitable *Equable:* of even or balanced range or uniform condition, not varying: "an equable disposition." *Equitable:* fair, just, impartial: "an equitable decision." *Equable* in the sense of *equitable* is obsolete.

equivocal *See* ambiguous.

ere *See* before.

eruption, irruption *Eruption:* a bursting out; *irruption:* a bursting in.

esoteric, exoteric *Esoteric:* secret, abstruse, known only to the initiated; *exoteric:* not secret, public.

especial, special The longer form is rapidly giving place to the shorter, and there are few if any uses in which *special* is not now employed; though among careful writers *especial* still connotes preëminent or exceptional, and *special,* particular or specific. "My especial friend." "He decided to enter a special class."

essay *See* assay.

eventful, eventual *Eventful:* abounding in events; *eventual:* final, ultimate, depending on events. "We spent an eventful evening." "The eventual result of our conference was exactly nothing."

evidence *See* proof.

exceedingly, excessively *Excessively* is stronger than *exceedingly. Exceedingly* means *much; excessively, too much.*

except *See* accept.

exceptionable, exceptional *Exceptionable:* objectionable; *exceptional:* out of the ordinary. Exceptional measures would be more than were expected; exceptionable measures, those that roused opposition. *Unexceptionable* means *not open to criticism or objection.*

excitation, excitement Excitation is the rousing of feeling; *excitement* is interchangeable with *excitation,* but also refers to feeling itself. "Excitation [*or* excitement] of the nerve centers by means of electricity." "In the excitement of the moment, he forgot to look."

excuse *See* alibi.

exit The fact that *exit* is a singular form of the verb, the plural being *exeunt,* is popularly ignored. Newspapers often use such incorrect headlines as "Exit the Fascists," "Exit straw hats."

exordium, peroration These parts of an oration are sometimes confused. The exordium is the beginning or introduction; the peroration is the conclusion, especially that part in which the speaker applies what he has said to the occasion or the audience.

exoteric *See* esoteric.

expedient, expeditious *Expedient:* advisable or advantageous; *expeditious:* quick, speedy. Expeditious action is fast action; expedient action is prudent action. The two words are often confused, perhaps because an obsolete meaning of *expedient* is *expeditious.*

extenuate Sometimes misused in the sense of *excuse. Extenuate* means, by derivation, *make thin;* now it means *represent as less blameworthy, mitigate, palliate.* When Hamlet says "Nothing extenuate . . ." he means that his deeds are to be told as they were, not softened for the sake of his reputation.

farther, further A useful distinction is made by the careful writer and editor. *Farther* refers to physical distance; *further,* to extent or degree. "We will proceed no further in this unpleasant business." "We can go no farther on this road."

fatal, fateful *Fatal* has to do with death, destruction, failure. *Fateful* may suggest the fatal, but is not needed in that sense. Originally *fateful* might be used of a happy fate, but now it usually signifies *fraught with malign fate, big with dangerous possibility.*

fatalism *See* determinism.

feasible, possible *Feasible* means *capable of being done or carried out.* In most contexts *feasible* and *possible* are interchangeable: "Transportation of troops by air is feasible" or "is possible." But often they are not. "A revolt is possible" and "a revolt is feasible" do not mean the same. *Feasible* should not be followed by *that,* as *possible* often is. Do not say "It is feasible that I should" but "It is feasible for me to."

ferrule, ferule *Ferrule:* a ring or cap (on a cane, for example); *ferule:* a flat stick or ruler for punishing children.

festal, festive *Festal:* having to do with feasts or merrymakings; *festive:* jolly, happy, exhilarated.

feverish, feverous The differentiation is not complete, but is widely observed. *Feverish:* having fever or its symptoms, excited, eager, flushed; *feverous:* likely to cause fever or excitement. "Feverish haste," "feverous exhalations."

fewer, less *Fewer* is used of numbers; *less*, of quantity—"Fewer men require less food."

flagrant *See* blatant.

flair, flare *Flair:* instinctive power of discriminating or taste combined with aptitude; *flare:* sudden or unsteady light or flame.

flaunt, flout Sometimes confused. *Flaunt:* make ostentatious display or vulgar show; *flout:* reject contemptuously, sneer at, jeer.

flee, fly *Fly* may take the place of *flee*, but *flew* cannot take the place of *fled* entirely—"The wicked flee when no man pursueth" might read "The wicked fly . . ." but "We fled (*not* flew) the country." It is pedantic to insist as some do that *fly* can be used only of motion upward or above the earth.

fleshly, fleshy *Fleshly:* having the qualities of flesh as compared with spirit; *fleshy:* having flesh or like flesh. "The fleshly school of poetry." "A fleshy person or face or fruit."

flotsam, jetsam, ligan *Flotsam* is goods found afloat; *jetsam*, goods found after they have been cast ashore. *Jetsam* is a corruption of *jettison*. *Ligan* or *lagan:* goods purposely set adrift with a marker attached.

foe *See* adversary.

folk, folks *Folk* refers to people generally, especially those of the lower as distinguished from the upper classes. Learnedly it means any or all of the people of a race or place who cannot read and write, the peasantry: as in *folklore, folkways, folk poetry, folk song, folk ballad*. *Folks* may mean more than one folk or, with an adjective, people belonging to the folk—"poor folks." *Folk, folks* are used colloquially for *family, kindred*, folk being preferred.

forceful, forcible *Forcible* implies the presence or use of force; *forceful*, the predominance or domination of force. Compare "forcible feeding" and "forceful personality."

forego, forgo In the sense of *refrain from, go without, deny oneself, quit, forgo* is the older and more correct form, but the words are now interchangeable in this signification. But *forego* also means *go before*, used now only in the forms *foregoing, foregone*, meaning *preceding, past*. Compare: "The foregoing sections should be revised" and "His forgoing [*or* foregoing] his claim deserves credit."

formally, formerly *Formally:* in a formal manner; *formerly:* before now.

fortuitous Sometimes confused with *fortunate*. *Fortuitous* means *accidental, chance, undesigned*. It does not mean *lucky*. Fortuitous circumstances are unanticipated, unplanned for, unaccountable.

further *See* farther.

gantlet, gauntlet *Gantlet:* a narrowing of two railroad tracks into one by overlapping; *to run the gantlet:* a punishment in which the victim is compelled to run between rows of men who strike him. *Gauntlet:* a kind of glove with a long wrist, formerly of mail or plate.

gibe, jibe *Gibe:* a sneer, to sneer; *jibe:* (naut.) to swing from side to side; (colloq.) to agree.

glairy, glary *Glairy:* sticky, viscous; *glary:* of dazzling brilliance.

glean *Glean* means *gather leavings*, or *gather laboriously*, little by little. It is incorrectly used to mean *acquire, get*.

gnomic *See* cryptic.

graceful, gracious *graceful:* elegant, charming, or appropriate in carriage, movement, or manner; *gracious:* exhibiting or inclined to show favor, mercy, kindness, condescension. A graceful lady is not always a gracious lady.

Granada, Grenada *Granada:* a city and a province in Spain; *Grenada:* one of the Windward Islands.

Greek *See* Attic.

grill, grille *Grill:* a gridiron; something broiled; *grille:* a grating or screen, usually of wrought iron.

grisly, grizzly *Grisly:* horrifying, ghastly; *grizzly:* grayish.

hardly, scarcely These words are interchangeable in popular use, but in strict use *scarcely* refers to quantity and *hardly* to degree: "It is scarcely a mile to town." "He will hardly reach town by noon."

hayrack, hayrick *Hayrack:* a frame mounted on a flat wagon for hauling hay; *hayrick:* a haystack or haycock.

healthful, healthy *Healthful:* promoting health; *healthy:* having health. "A healthful climate makes healthy people."

Hellenic, Hellenistic *See* Attic.

historic, historical *Historic:* memorable; *historical:* having to do with history. "Historic shrines." "A historical novel."

hoar, hore *Hoar:* white or whitish gray; *hore:* frost, frosty.

homogeneous, homogenous *Homogeneous:* of the same nature or constitution throughout; *homogenous:* of the same origin.

horrible, horrid Both terms are used colloquially in the sense of *very disagreeable* or, vaguely, *to the highest degree.* (So also *awful, terrible, ghastly,* etc.) *Horrid* originally meant *shaggy* or *bristling* and still occasionally has that meaning in poetry. By extension it means *obnoxious* or *abominable, dreadful, terrible.* It is giving place to *horrible,* which means *exciting horror or shuddering fear.* "A horrid monster." "A horrible incident."

humane, humanitarian, humanistic *Humane:* kind or merciful; *humanitarian:* broadly humane, benevolent, philanthropic; *humanistic:* pertaining to or characteristic of humanism, the system of thinking which makes man (rather than God or nature) central and dominant.

hydroscope, hygroscope *Hydroscope:* an apparatus for observing objects in the sea, or one for measuring time by the dropping of water; *hygroscope:* a device for measuring humidity.

hygroscopic *See* anhydrous.

hyperbola, hyperbole *Hyperbola:* a geometrical figure; *hyperbole:* an artistic exaggeration.

hypercritical, hypocritical *Hypercritical:* overcritical; *hypocritical:* pretending to be what one is not.

hypothecate, hypothesize Sometimes confused. *Hypothecate* is a legal or financial term meaning *to pledge, pawn, or mortgage. Hypothesize* means *to make hypotheses.*

ileum, ilium *Ileum:* the lower part of the intestine; *ilium:* a part of the hip bone. *Ilium* (cap.), ancient Troy.

ilk The Scottish word *ilk* is often used incorrectly, as if it meant *name, family* or *kind.* It means *same* in Scottish as it did in Anglo-Saxon. The phrase *of* *that ilk* means *of the same;* that is to say, the person's surname is the same as that of the estate; for example, Alexander Burnieside of that ilk, *i.e.,* of Burnieside.

illegible, unreadable That is illegible which cannot be read because of bad writing or printing; that is unreadable which is dull, dry, or irritating.

illude *See* allude.

imbrue, imbue *Imbrue:* moisten, especially with blood; *imbue:* permeate, pervade, color deeply. Macbeth's hands were imbrued with the blood of Duncan. A mind may be imbued with reverence, a fabric with color.

immanent, imminent *Immanent:* indwelling; *imminent:* impending. "God is immanent in nature." "The beginning of the battle was imminent."

immerge *See* emerge.

immoral *See* amoral.

immovable, irremovable The words are interchangeable in most uses, yet an irremovable judge is not necessarily an immovable judge. *Irremovable* here means *permanent, not to be removed* (from office).

impassable, unpassable, impassible, impassive *Impassable:* closed, offering complete obstruction to; *unpassable:* not to be passed (in speed); *impassible:* unfeeling; *impassive:* unemotional, stoical, apathetic, calm, serene. *Impassible* and *impassive* are often interchangeable, but *impassible* is likely to be used in a nobler sense than *impassive,* the former suggesting the restraint or government of feeling, while the latter suggests the absence of it.

imply, infer To use *infer* in the sense of *imply* or *suggest*—"I heard him infer that we had not told the truth"—is a dubious colloquialism. Strictly *infer* means *surmise, conclude*—"I inferred from his manner that he was disturbed in his mind." "From these data we infer an inevitable conclusion."

impress, impression *Impress* is mainly used to mean (1) *a mark made by pressure, an imprint,* or (2) *a characteristic trait, mark of distinction.* The first meaning it shares with *impression*—"the impress (or impression) made by a die." —but not the second—"The work bore the clear impress of genius." On the other hand, *impression* often means *a vague or indefinite remembrance or recognition*—"I have an impression that he is not entirely honest." This meaning is not shared by *impress.*

inartistic, unartistic *Inartistic:* not in accordance with the canons of art; *unartistic:* not gifted in or interested in art. A picture may be inartistic; a person unartistic.

incipient, insipient *Incipient:* beginning to exist; *insipient:* unwise.

incubus, succubus Originally an incubus was a male demon fabled to have intercourse with women in their sleep; hence it has come to mean *weight, load,* or anything harassing or oppressing. A succubus (or succuba) was a female demon that had intercourse with men in their sleep.

individual, person Individual should be confined to contexts in which individuality or particularity is indicated; *person,* used when it is not. "A poll-tax is levied on individuals." "I should say there were thirty persons [*not individuals*] in the car."

infection *See* contagion.

infer *See* imply.

inflammable, inflammatory *Inflammable:* readily set on fire; *inflammatory:* tending to produce heat or excitement; also, showing inflammation. Dry shavings, a susceptible heart, are inflammable; a seditious speech, a mustard plaster, inflammatory.

ingenious, ingenuous *Ingenious:* skillful in contriving, inventive; *ingenuous:* artless, open, naïve, magnanimous, sincere, innocent in a good sense.

injury *See* damage.

insoluble, unsolvable or **insolvable** All three words are used in the sense of *not to be solved or explained,* but *unsolvable* or *insolvable* means only that, while *insoluble* may mean *not to be dissolved.*

interpellate, interpolate *Interpellate:* to question peremptorily; *interpolate:* to insert or interpose.

invent *See* discover.

irremovable *See* immovable.

irruption *See* eruption.

jealous *See* covetous.

jetsam *See* flotsam.

join issue, take issue Both are correct forms and are used interchangeably in the sense of *disagree. Join issue* may, however, mean—and perhaps more properly—*to agree* on the grounds of a dispute. *Take issue* always means *disagree.*

judicial, judicious *Judicial:* of or pertaining to judges or law courts; *judicious:* having to do with judgment, well-calculated, wise, prudent.

junction, juncture The words are interchangeable in the sense of *the act of joining or union,* but *juncture* is used in the special sense of *a point of time, a crisis or exigency,* while *junction* is used in the sense of *crossroads.*

knot A knot is the measure of speed in an hour. *Knots per hour* is therefore incorrect.

Kultur *See* culture.

last, latest *Last:* that which comes after all others, the end; *latest:* last in time. Idiomatically, however, *last* may mean *the next before the present*—"last Tuesday" —and *the furthest from likelihood*—"the last person one would expect it of." "The last news" means that there will be no more; "the latest news," that there may be.

less *See* fewer.

liable, likely *Liable* suggests a penalty: "We are liable to lose our license if we drive so fast." *Likely* expresses mere probability: "We are likely to arrive on time."

libel, slander In law, a libel is written or printed; a slander, spoken, but the distinction is ignored in popular usage.

ligan *See* flotsam.

likely *See* apt.

liquid *See* fluid.

literal, oral, verbal, vocal *Literal:* pertaining to the letter; *oral,* to the mouth or to speech; *verbal,* to the word; *vocal,* to the voice. "A literal translation." "An oral recitation." "A verbal interpretation." "A vocal message."

livid The word does not mean *red,* as some think, but *black and blue, greenish,* or *ashy gray.* A person who is livid with rage is pale with rage.

lurid The word means *ghastly yellow* (flame with smoke) and by extension *pale, unearthly, gloomy.* Figuratively it means *sensational.*

luxuriant, luxurious *Luxuriant:* abounding, teeming; *luxurious:* given to indulgence of the senses, promoting bodily ease. A luxurious imagination dwells on images of luxury; a luxuriant imagination runs riot in invention.

mandrel, mandrill *Mandrel:* a shaft or spindle; *mandrill:* an African baboon.

marine, maritime *Marine:* of the ocean; *maritime:* bordering on or connected with the ocean. "Marine animals." "The Merchant Marine." "The Maritime Provinces." "The Maritime Commission."

marten, martin *Marten:* a fur-bearing animal; *martin:* a swallow.

masterful, masterly *Masterful:* strong, able to control; *masterly:* exhibiting great skill or ability. *Masterful* is occasionally used in the sense of *masterly,* but *masterly* in the sense of *masterful* is obsolete.

may *See* can.

meat cattle, neat cattle *Meat cattle:* cattle fed for the food market; *neat cattle:* bovine cattle generally.

momentarily, momently *Momentarily:* for or during a moment, transitorily; *momently:* from moment to moment, moment by moment, intermittently. News commentators and radio announcers constantly use *momentarily* as if it meant *in a moment, immediately,* or *momently.* "The news can be expected momently" (*i.e.* at any time now, very soon, immediately). It is a usage not yet recognized by dictionaries.

mooted, moot The form of the adjective is *moot,* meaning *still under discussion* —"a moot question." The verb *mooted* means *discussed, argued, pleaded*— "When the question was first mooted"; that is, "When the question was first brought under discussion," not, as is sometimes mistakenly supposed, "first proposed or mentioned."

morbid *Morbid* means *diseased, unhealthy,* in body or mind. We speak correctly of a morbid condition, mind, imagination. But popularly the word is often debased to mean merely *sad, unpleasant.*

mulatto, octoroon, quadroon A mulatto is, strictly, the offspring of a white person and a black person, especially when his color is intermediate. A quadroon is a person having one fourth Negro and three fourths white blood. An octoroon is one having one eighth Negro and seven eighths white blood, the offspring of a white person and a quadroon.

mutual, reciprocal *Mutual* relates to both parties at the same time; *reciprocal,* to one with relation to the other, though there are contexts in which either is correct. A mutual agreement is, for example, the same as a reciprocal one. We cannot, however, speak of Jones's mutual dislike of Smith; here *reciprocal* would be correct. *Mutual friend,* so often objected to, is now established by usage.

mystic, mystical Words much abused, being used where *mysterious, strange, enigmatic* would be better. *Mysticism* is also misused in the sense of *mystery.*

nausea, nauseation *Nauseation:* the act of nauseating or the condition of being nauseated. "A feeling of nauseation", though not incorrect, might better read "a feeling of nausea", as less stilted.

nautical, naval *Nautical:* pertaining to seamen or ships; *naval:* pertaining to the armed force of seamen and ships of a nation.

neat cattle *See* meat cattle.

Negro, Negrillo, Negrito *Negrillo* and *Negrito* are diminutive forms of *Negro* and refer to certain tribes of dwarfish African natives.

nocturn, nocturne *Nocturn:* a midnight prayer or service; *nocturne:* a kind of musical composition.

nonmoral *See* amoral.

novice *See* amateur.

observance, observation *Observance:* attending to or carrying out a duty, rule, or custom; *observation:* consciously seeing or taking notice. *Observance* is used of laws, rules, anniversaries; *observation,* of persons, things, events. "Reinforce imagination with observation." "The observance of Sunday was strictly enforced."

obverse The obverse of a coin is its face. The other side is the reverse.

obviously *See* apparently.

octoroon *See* mulatto.

official, officious *Official:* authoritative; *officious:* meddling.

Olympian, Olympic *Olympian* has reference to Mount Olympus, where the Greek gods lived; *Olympic,* to Olympia, where athletic games were held. *Olympian* therefore often means *divine, august, Jovian.*

ontogeny, ontology *Ontogeny:* a biological term for the history of the evolution of the individual; *ontology:* a philosophical term for the science of real being, the theory of reality.

opponent *See* adversary.

oral *See* literal.

orchid, orchis Botanically *orchis* is the name of a genus of the orchid family (Orchidaceae). Popularly *orchid* is used of any of the family, but especially of the showy or curious tropical kinds. Poets sometimes use *orchis* for *orchid,* perhaps because it is a less worn term. Popularly, *orchis* is used of American orchids, most often of the showy or purple orchis.

ought *See* aught.

paean, paeon, peon *Paean:* a song of joy; *paeon:* a type of metrical foot; *peon:* a peasant.

parol, parole *Parol:* by word of mouth (law); *parole:* to release on promise to return.

partially, partly The words are interchangeable in the sense of *in part, in some measure, not totally,* but only *partially* is used in the sense of *inclining to take one part or party, showing predilection or fondness.*

passable, possible *Passable:* capable of being passed; *possible:* capable of being felt.

pathos *See* bathos.

patronymic Often misused. A patronymic is a name that indicates relationship of child to father or other ancestor, a family name. Specifically, a patronymic is a family name formed by adding a prefix or suffix: *-son, Mc, Mac, M', O', Fitz, ap,* etc.

pendant, pendent *Pendant* is a noun, *pendent,* an adjective. *Pendant:* something that hangs; *pendent:* hanging. "Pendent nest and procreant cradle"—*Macbeth.* "She wore a jeweled pendant."

pennant, pennon Both words refer to small flags, but the former is the modern term, used in boating and the navy. *Pennon* is mainly associated with chivalry.

perception *See* apperception.

peroration *See* exordium.

person *See* individual.

phase Commonly misused as if it meant *phenomenon* or *general appearance.* "Stage people are popularly accepted as strange beings. Emphasis is laid on this phase in *Curtain Going Up!" Phase* means *limited or fleeting aspect, temporary state or appearance.*

piteous, pitiable, pitiful *Piteous:* feeling or exciting pity; *pitiable:* exciting pity or contempt; *pitiful:* feeling or exciting pity or contempt. The words cannot be strictly differentiated.

place, put *Put* is the more general term. *Place* denotes greater care and exactness. We put on our hat but place a crown on a king. Note that *put* may take *in* or *into*, but *place* takes only *in.* "I placed my model boat in the water." "I put my hand in [*or* into] the water."

platitude *See* commonplace.

point of view, standpoint, viewpoint All are in good use, despite objections to *standpoint* and *viewpoint. Point of view* or *viewpoint* does not always mean the same as *standpoint.* As the *Standard Dictionary* says, Lincoln and Douglas spoke from standpoints of their principles, but occasionally, for the sake of argument, adopted each other's point of view. Moreover, *point of view* or *viewpoint* has two meanings, geographical and metaphorical, while *standpoint* has only the metaphorical. The idea sometimes advanced that *standpoint* is not formed according to English idiom and should be *standing-point,* though perhaps originally sound, has little validity since *standpoint* has been established by usage. (The word was formed by analogy with the German *Standpunkt.) Standpoint* is overused and often causes wordiness. As for *viewpoint,* to writers who remember when it was a neologism or vogue word, it still faintly suggests affectation.

policy, polity Though the words are constantly used as interchangeable, they do not mean the same. Polity is the permanent system of government of a state, society, or church; for example, the national polity of Great Britain is that of a limited monarchy, of the United States, that of a republic. The ecclesiastical polity of a church is its administration and organization, as distinguished from its religion. Each British or American cabinet has its own policy; that is, a course or plan of action. "The newspaper, because of its unfortunate policy [*not* polity], suffered a serious decrease in circulation."

possible *See* feasible.

post card, postal card In the United States the official name for a card issued by the post office and bearing a printed postage stamp is *postal card;* in Great Britain, it is *post-card.* In the United States *post card* is the official name for a privately printed card for which postage must be separately purchased. *Postal* for *postal card* is colloquial.

practicable, practical *Practicable:* feasible; *practical:* suited to or fitted for use or action.

precedence, precedents *Preced'ence:* the condition of preceding or the act of going before; *prec'edents:* established usage or authority.

preceding, previous Dictionaries make the distinction that *preceding* refers to that which precedes without an interval and *previous* to that which precedes at any time. If, for instance, one were to refer on page 58 to something on page 57, the reference should be to "the preceding page," not to "the previous page." A reference to any other page should preferably be to "a previous page." Concerning acts or events occurring before a certain time or another act, the distinction is little observed. The use of *previous* in the sense of *premature, acting too soon* —"He was too previous in assuming that"—is colloquial.

precipitant, precipitate, precipitous *Precipitate:* hasty, premature; *precipitous:* steep (as a precipice). These are the more common usages, though each word may be used in the sense of the other. *Precipitant,* less often seen, is used in the sense of *precipitate* and in the sense of *falling or rushing headlong.* In chemistry, it signifies *falling* as a precipitate.

precisian, precision *Precisian:* a precise person; *precision:* accuracy.

predicate (*v.*) Does not mean *predict,* but *affirm, state.* "One cannot predicate virtue or vice of a creature which has no moral nature." Since the word is still learned, its use in ordinary writing seems pedantic, except in such sentences as "A verb is a part of speech that affirms or predicates."

presentiment, presentment *Presentiment:* prophetic apprehension; *presentment:* thing presented, exhibited, or the act of exhibiting. "The old woman had a presentiment that her son would be killed in battle." "The artist's presentment of his sitter's features is very moving." (The word *presentiment* has nothing to do with the word *present,* but is related to the word *sentiment.*)

presume *See* assume.

previous *See* preceding.

price *See* cost.

prone, supine *Prone:* face downwards; *supine:* face upwards.

proof, evidence Evidence may constitute proof, but does not always do so, for evidence may be false. Strictly, proof is the effect or result of evidence and evidence is the medium of proof.

propaganda *See* advertising.

protagonist In ancient Greece the protagonist was the first actor in a drama. By extension the word has come to mean *a chief personage, a leader.* Colloquially it is too often used pretentiously, when the speaker thinks he is being literary. The one who takes the leading part in a novel or a play may be properly spoken of as the protagonist.

prototype A prototype is a primal or original type. "The *Iliad* is the prototype of all classical epics." The word is sometimes mistakenly used to mean the main or representative type or example.

publicity *See* advertising.

put *See* place.

quadroon *See* mulatto.

quahaug The name in New England for what is called a hard-shelled clam in New York and elsewhere. A soft-shelled clam (New York) is in New England called, simply, a clam. (*Quahaug, quahog* is in New England usually pronounced *kohawg* or *kohog.*)

quote *See* cite.

rabbit, rarebit The original form was apparently *rabbit, Welsh rabbit* being a humorous name, like *Cape Cod turkey* for *codfish; rarebit* having later been substituted under a misapprehension of the joke.

radical, radically Often abused. Derived from the Latin *radix*, root, they should be reserved for strong meanings and not softened to mean *considerable, considerably*.

rapt, wrapt *Rapt:* in a condition of rapture, exalted in mood; *wrapt:* enfolded, covered.

rare, scarce A thing may be scarce without being rare. Blackbirds are not rare birds, but they may be scarce in a place or season.

realtor The word was originally applied to a real estate agent or realty broker affiliated with the National Association of Real Estate Boards.

reciprocal *See* mutual.

refer *See* allude.

replace There is no authority for the idea, often advanced, that *replace* must not be used in the sense of *substitute*. One meaning of *replace* is *put back in the same place*, but other meanings are *take the place of, supersede, find a substitute for*.

replica Strictly, a replica is a duplicate (of a work of art) made by the same person as made the original. Loosely, it is a duplicate or copy in general.

residue, residuum Both words mean *that which is left over*, but *residuum* is a learned word or technical term in mathematics, physics, and chemistry. For popular use, *residue* serves.

respective The word should be used with care and not used where not needed. It is really seldom needed and is often dragged into a sentence without necessity or logic. Such a sentence as the following is common: "Harvard and Yale men know far too little of their respective universities." This means that Yale men know far too little about Yale, and Harvard men about Harvard; but the author meant "Yale and Harvard men know far too little about each other's university."

responsible for Should not be used where the meaning would be better expressed by *produced, caused, resulted in*.

restrain, restrict *Restrain:* to curb, check, repress; *restrict:* to restrain within bounds, limit, confine. *Restrain* is used in the sense of *restrict* in speaking of trade, power, or a title and in the sense of *confine, deprive of liberty* in speaking of insane or criminal persons.

restricted Should not be used where the meaning would be better conveyed by *scant, scanty,* or *small.* Say "a man of scanty or small means," rather than "of restricted means." *Restricted* denotes *kept within limits or bounds, withheld from going too far.*

result, resultant *Resultant* as a noun is a learned or technical term and should be reserved for scientific contexts—mechanics or algebra.

revenge *See* avenge.

reversal, reversion *Reversal* should be thought of in connection with *reverse; reversion,* with *revert. Reversal* means *a turning round; reversion,* used mainly in science and law, means *a turning back.* "His reply showed a complete reversal of his former opinion." "The actions of the maddened man suggested a reversion to savagery."

rightfully, rightly The two words share the meaning of *justly, uprightly*—"The referee administered the claims rightly [*or* rightfully]." *Rightly* may also mean *exactly, correctly*—"You answered rightly." *Rightfully* commonly means *properly* —"You rightfully should have received a share."

rout, route Colloquially the words are commonly interchanged, at least as regards pronunciation. One constantly hears *rout* for *route,* even in radio broadcasts. *Rout* means, strictly, *an overwhelming defeat* or *a noisy or unruly rabble.* As a verb *rout* means *throw into confusion, defeat disastrously. Route* (pronounced *root*) means *a line or direction of travel; a road.*

rowan, rowen *Rowan:* the mountain ash; *rowen:* a second cutting of hay; aftermath.

sadism Often misused for *persecution* or *cruelty.* Its strict meaning is *sexual perversity exhibiting itself in cruelty to others.*

say *See* assert.

scarce *See* rare.

scarcely *See* hardly.

Scotch, Scots, Scottish In Scotland there is a tendency to reject *Scotch* as an adjective and use *Scots* or *Scottish.*

scrip, script *Scrip:* a provisional document, a scrap of paper; a wallet or knapsack; *script:* a type of engraved matter imitating handwriting; handwriting; colloquial abbreviation of *manuscript.*

seem *See* appear.

seemingly *See* apparently.

senile *See* anile.

sensual, sensuous *Sensual* suggests the indulgence of the senses; *sensuous,* appeal to the senses. The former usually refers to the sexual, the latter seldom does. In older uses this distinction did not prevail. Keats speaks of music addressed to "the sensual ear," but perhaps because "the sensuous ear" is a phrase less pleasing in sound. Milton describes poetry as "simple, sensuous, and passionate." (It is thought, in fact, that he invented the word.)

sewage, sewerage The best usage confines *sewage* to the waste matter run off in sewers; *sewerage,* to systematic drainage or a system of drains. "The sewage is disposed of in septic tanks." "The sewerage of the city was planned by Dakin."

shamefacedly, shamefully The adverb *shamefully,* characterizing an act as indecent or disgraceful, should not be used for *shamefacedly.* "He later shamefacedly confessed that he had been stage-struck." "He shamefully confessed his connection with the trade in narcotics." Note that *shamefacedly* may not indicate real shame, but only embarrassment or modesty. In the first sentence, *ashamedly* would suggest real shame. In the second sentence *shamefully* is not entirely clear, for it may mean *with shame* or *disgracefully, indecently.* The group of words should be used with care.

shoot *See* chute.

signal, single The phrase is "single out" not "signal out," as one sometimes sees it printed. "Why he singled me out for rebuke I couldn't understand."

slander *See* libel.

sleave, sleeve *Sleave:* a tangle; *sleeve:* a part of a garment covering the arm or a tubular part fitting over another part. *Sleave silk* is sleaved silk, that is, floss or untwisted silk that tangles easily.

sleek, slick Two spellings of the same word, though pronounced differently. The adjectival uses of *slick* are dialectal or slang.

special *See* especial.

speciality, specialty *Speciality:* the state or quality of being special; a peculiarity or distinguishing characteristic; *specialty:* an employment limited to one kind of work or an article or subject dealt in or with exclusively. "A speciality of function, by calling for a speciality of structure, produces . . ."

specie, species *Specie:* coin or coins; *species:* kind or kinds. "Specie payments." "One species, *Larix laricina,* is the common tamarack."

spectators Spectators see; an audience hears.

Spencerian, Spenserian *Spencerian:* of Herbert Spencer—"Spencerian philosophy;" *Spenserian:* of Edmund Spenser—"Spenserian stanza."

spiritism, spiritualism *Spiritualism* is the old word for the philosophy of Berkeley, for psychical research, and for a religious sect, but *spiritism* is preferred by some modern philosophers to distinguish their theory from older ones and by some scientific investigators of psychic phenomena.

stalactite, stalagmite Stalactites grow downward; stalagmites, upward.

standpoint *See* point of view.

stanza, verse The use of *verse* for *stanza* is popular but inaccurate. Strictly, a verse is a line of poetry or one of the numbered groups of lines in the Bible.

start *See* begin.

state *See* assert.

stimulant, stimulus *Stimulant* refers to the physical (alcohol, coffee); *stimulus,* to the mental (happiness, defiance, patriotism). In physiology and psychology, *stimulus* is, however, used of the physical as well as the mental.

stratagem, strategy *Strategy* is the general term for the art of planning and carrying out with skill and shrewdness; *stratagem,* the term for any particular device or trick for outwitting.

stultify To be used with regard to its derivation from *stultus,* foolish. Its older meaning was *to make a fool of,* though it has been broadened to signify *to render untrustworthy* or *to disgrace, dishonor.*

subject to *See* addicted to.

subtile, subtle Constantly used interchangeably by good writers, though a tendency to distinguish them is observable. *Subtile* (sub-tile), the older spelling, is used mainly of physical matters, with the meaning *delicately or daintily made, rarefied, penetrating,* or *finely drawn.* A spider's web is subtile. *Subtle* (suttle) is mainly used of mental or spiritual matters, meaning *crafty, acute, refined, ingenious.* Iago is a subtle villain.

subtract *See* deduct.

succubus *See* incubus.

sufficient *See* enough.

swingeing Liable to be confused with *swinging. Swingeing:* (1) welding together; (2) whipping, chastising; (3) lashing to and fro. "The swingeing horror of its folded tail."—Milton. Colloquially or provincially it means *very large, immense.*

synonymity, synonymousness, synonymy The first two words refer to a similarity of meaning; the third, to the general subject of synonyms.

systole *See* diastole.

tactile, tactual, tangible Little or no difference is recognized between *tactile* and *tactual*. The art critic, however, speaks of "tactile values"—meaning the effect in a painting of tangibility or solidity. A biologist would speak of the horns of a snail as tactual organs. *Tangible* is the literary term and, unlike *tactual* and *tactile*, is used of things of the mind. It is closely synonymous with *palpable*.

take issue *See* join issue.

tasteful, tasty *Tasteful:* conforming to the principles of taste; displaying harmony, beauty, or other esthetic qualities; or able to appreciate these qualities: "a tasteful person," "a tasteful arrangement." *Tasty:* pleasing to physical taste, savory.

technics, techniques *Technics:* technical rules, methods, etc., or the doctrine of an art or a technology; *techniques:* manners of performance.

temerarious Often misused in the sense of *timid*. It means *rash, unreasonably adventurous.*

tend, trend *Tend* and *trend* are both used in the sense of *have a drift or tendency*, but *tend* is used of both persons and things and *trend* of things. "Man tends generally to optimism." "The road tends to be rough." "The path trends to the right." *Trend* is sometimes confused with *trench* (in the sense of *encroach*)—"This idea trenches [*not* trends] closely upon that of *laissez faire.*"

terminal, terminus Both words are used in the sense of *end,* as of a railroad, but *terminus* is also used for *boundary, limit, final goal.*

terrain, terrane *Terrain:* a district; *terrane:* a series of rocks or geologic formations.

theism *See* deism.

therefor, therefore *Therefor':* for that, for it, for them, etc.—"The punishment therefor is death." *There'fore:* for that or this reason—"The message has not come: therefore I will not go."

topee, toupee *Topee:* a sun-helmet, a hat made of pith; *toupee:* a small wig.

tortuous, torturous *Tortuous:* winding, twisting; *torturous:* having the quality of torture.

total *See* aggregate.

transcendent, transcendental *Transcendent:* surpassing, of extreme excellence or greatness; *transcendental:* idealistic, beyond or above experience, visionary.

troche, trochee *Troche:* a medicated lozenge; *trochee:* a type of metrical foot.

troop, troupe *Troop:* an organized company, specifically of soldiers; *troupe:* a company, especially of actors.

troublesome, troublous *Troublesome:* vexatious, causing worry; *troublous:* (1) agitated, turbulent, (2) causing disturbance or disquiet. *Troublous* is a word of greater dignity than *troublesome* and is applied to more important troubles.

truism *See* commonplace.

two *See* couple.

tyro *See* amateur.

unartistic *See* inartistic.

under *See* below.

under way, under weigh Whether one should say "We have important projects under way" or "under weigh" has been much discussed. In nautical language *under weigh* means *in progress, going ahead,* though sometimes written (perhaps incorrectly) *under way*—"The ship was under way." It is doubtful if the general reader feels the nautical flavor of the phrase, except in nautical contexts. To write *under weigh* in any other contexts is somewhat pedantic.

unmoral *See* amoral.

unpassable *See* impassable.

unquestioned, unquestionable That which is unquestioned is not or has not been questioned; that which is unquestionable cannot be decently or sensibly questioned. "His veracity is unquestioned" and "His veracity is unquestionable" have not precisely the same meaning.

unreadable *See* illegible.

unsolvable *See* insoluble.

vacant *See* empty.

value *See* cost.

venal, venial *Venal* (L. *venalis,* sale): ready to sell that which should not be sold, as one's vote or influence; *venial* (L. *venia,* pardon): worthy of pardon, excusable. "A venal judge." "A venial offense."

verbal *See* literal.

vernacular Often misused in the sense of *dialect, patois.* The vernacular is the indigenous speech of a country. During the Middle Ages, for example, Latin was the literary or learned language of countries of which the vernacular was Italian, French, Spanish.

verse *See* stanza.

vice versa Strictly, denotes *a reversal of terms*—"High wages mean high prices, and vice versa"; *i.e.,* "High prices mean high wages." It is often misused as if it meant *the opposite* or *the contrary*—"A small egg does not necessarily have a correspondingly small yolk, or vice versa." The real vice versa of this statement would be "A small yolk does not necessarily have a correspondingly small egg," though the author meant, of course, that a large egg does not necessarily have a large yolk.

viewpoint *See* point of view.

virtu, virtue Both are from the Latin *virtus,* courage or virtue, but *virtu* is from the Italian and *virtue* from the French. *Virtu:* (1) a love of or taste for objets d'art, (2) the objects themselves—curios, antiques, etc.

virtually In popular usage commonly means *very nearly* or *almost*—"I'm virtually famished," "It was virtually midnight before we got home." More strictly the word means *in essence or effect, but not in fact*—"The bankers were virtually the rulers of the country."

vocal *See* literal.

vocation *See* avocation.

womanish, womanly *Womanish:* having the less admirable qualities of a woman, effeminate; *womanly:* having the more admirable qualities of women, feminine.

worth *See* cost.

worthy of *See* deserving.

wrapt *See* rapt.

ye *Ye* for *the*—"Ye olde book-shoppe"—is a popular would-be archaism, and not objectionable if pronounced *the.* The *y* in *ye* represents the old letter thorn (th).

WORD LIST FOR CHECKING ONE'S VOCABULARY

The following list is interesting to the student of words and useful to the editorial worker as a check-up of knowledge of word forms and meanings. It consists mostly of doublets—words of similar form or sound—among which are many that are treacherous to both the writer and the proofreader, fooling the ear of the one and the eye of the other. Mistakes in using such words are as often due to inadvertence as to ignorance, and the recognition of the presence of the wrong member of a doublet by the reader demands incessant watchfulness. The ease with which one writes *their* when he means *there* or *born* when he means *borne* hardly needs to be emphasized nor does the ease with which the reader fails to note the mistake.

The list has a further value in testing one's spelling and pronunciation, because some of these words are among those most often misspelled, and misspelling is commonly due to faulty pronunciation. It is suggested, therefore, that the list is a good one to read with attention and to read aloud with clear enunciation.

Finally, there are many words in the list that will be unfamiliar to some readers but that are likely to occur in manuscript or proof.

abbé	adherence	alizari	animalcula
abbey	adherents	alizarin	animalcular
abductor	advert	alley	animalist
adductor	avert	ally	animalculist
abetter	advice	allusion	annunciate
abettor	advise	elusion	enunciate
aboard	affective	illusion	ante
abroad	effective	altar	anti
abscess	afferent	alter	antecedence
absciss	efferent	alteration	antecedents
accede	affluence	alternation	anthropoid
exceed	effluence	alterative	arthropod
accept	aid	alternative	antimony
except	aide	alumina	antinomy
access	ailment	aluminum	apatite
excess	aliment	amend	appetite
accidence	albumen	emend	apiary
accidents	albumin	amide	aviary
acetic	alder	imide	apostil
ascetic	elder	analyst	apostle
Achaean	Algonquian	annalist	apposite
Archaean	Algonquin	anil	opposite
acme	alimentary	anile	appraise
acne	elementary		apprise

arc	balsa	bother	but
ark	balsam	pother	butt
area	baron	bouillon	buy
aria	barren	bullion	by
areola	bask	bourgeois	bye
areole	basque	bourgeoise	buyer
Arian	bass	bourgeoisie	byre
Orion	base	braise	calendar
arraign	bath	brays	calender
arrange	bathe	braze	colander
arrant	baton	braid	calix
errant	batten	brayed	calyx
ascent	battels	brake	call
assent	battles	break	caul
assay	bazaar	breach	callous
essay	bizarre	breech	callus
assigner	beatify	bread	calories
assignor	beautify	bred	collieries
assistance	begonia	breath	canaster
assistants	bignonia	breathe	canister
astray	benzene	brede	canon
estray	benzine	breed	cannon
Atalanta	benzil	Breton	cañon
Atlanta	benzol	Briton	capital
atypical	benzine	Britain	capitol
typical	benzoin	Brittany	carat
auger	bight	brews	caret
augur	bite	bruise	carrot
auricle	bit	bridal	carbolated
oracle	bitt	bridle	carbonated
avigation	black-letter	broach	carom
navigation	block-letter	brooch	carron (oil)
axial	bleach	broom	carrion
axil	pleach	brume	carousal
awful	bloc	brows	carrousel
offal	block	browse	carton
bad	bolder	bruit	cartoon
bade	boulder	brute	casemate
bail	bole	bur	casement
bale	boll	burr	cashmere
baited	bowl	bursa	cassimere
bated	born	bursar	cask
baize	borne	bus	casque
bays	bourne	buss	cassation
beys	borough	business	cessation
ballad	burro	busyness	cast
ballade	burrow		caste

caster
castor
cataclasm
cataclysm
cataplasm
catalectic
cataleptic
caul
col
Cecilian
Sicilian
celebration
cerebration
censer
censor
cerated
serrated
cereus
serious
cessation
secession
cession
session
chafer
chaffer
chagrin
shagreen
chamise
chemise
champagne
champaign
chasable
chasuble
Chihli
Chile
chili
chilly
chime
chyme
chrism
chrisom
crissum
cipher
sypher
cite
sight
site

clack
claque
claimant
clamant
clef
cleft
coak
coke
coal
cole
kohl
coamings
combings
coddling
codling
coign
coin
quoin
collision
collusion
coma
comma
committee
comity
complacent
complaisant
complement
compliment
condemn
contemn
confidant
confident
congenial
congenital
consequence
consequents
consigner
consignor
consol
council
consul
counsel
copse
corpse
coquet
coquette

coral
corral
corm
corn
corporal
corporeal
corset
cosset
cot
cote
courtesy
curtsy
cousin
cozen
coward
cowered
crape
crepe
crawl
kraal
creak
creek
crease
creese
cremation
crenation
crevasse
crevice
crewel
cruel
crews
cruise
cruse
croquet
croquette
crumble
crumple
cryptogam
cryptogram
cue
queue
curate
curette
currant
current
cygnet
signet

cymbal
symbol
Dairen
Darien
debauch
debouch
decadent
decedent
decare
deciare
defeasible
defensible
defy
deify
dental
dentil
descendant
descendent
devest
divest
device
devise
dextrorse
dextrose
diagram
diaphragm
dine
dyne
Dionysius
Dionysus
disapprove
disprove
disburse
disperse
discreet
discrete
discuss
discus
divers
diverse
doggies
dogies
Dom
Don
dragon
dragoon

draught
drought
droop
drupe
dual
duel
dyeing
dying
earn
erne
urn
elude
illude
Elysian
Elysium
emerge
immerge
emerse
immerse
emollient
emolument
endemic
endermic
enervate
innervate
entomology
etymology
entrance
entrants
envelop
envelope
equivalence
equivalents
erotic
erratic
eruption
irruption
escapement
escarpment
ethic
ethics
eugenics
euthenics
euphemism
euphuism
evert
overt

exercise
exorcise
expansive
expensive
expose
exposé
extant
extent
facet
faucet
facial
facile
facilitate
felicitate
factitious
fictitious
facundity
fecundity
faërie
fairy
fain
fane
feign
faint
feint
faker
fakir
falchion
falcon
farrier
furrier
fascial
faucial
faun
fawn
fays
faze
phase
felloe
fellow
ferment
foment
fiend
friend
filet
fillet

filling
fulling
filter
philter
fineness
finesse
fistula
fistular
flacon
flagon
flagrant
fragrant
fleck
flick
flounder
founder
fondu
fondue
foregone
forgone
fort
forte
fossa
fosse
freeze
frieze
funeral
funereal
fungous
fungus
fuse
fusee
gage
gauge
gallop
galop
gamble
gambol
gamin
gammon
gang
gangue
Garamond
Garamont
Gaspé
Gaspee

genie
genii
gest
jest
gimp
guimpe
glacier
glazier
glare
glair
gluten
glutton
gored
gourd
gorilla
guerrilla
gout
goût
grama
grammar
grip
grippe
grisly
gristly
grizzly
grocer
grosser
handsome
hansom
help
kelp
heroin
heroine
heron
Hesperis
Hesperus
hoard
horde
holey
holly
holy
wholly
holm
home
hoop
whoop

humerus	lac	loose	milk
humorous	lakh	lose	milt
human	lack	lumbar	millenary
humane	lath	lumber	millinery
idle	lathe	macrocosm	minister
idol	lickerish	microcosm	minster
idyl	licorice	magnate	missal
impatience	lade	magnet	missel
impatiens	laid	maize	missile
important	lama	maze	mistletoe
impotent	llama	mandatary	moat
impostor	lea	mandatory	mote
imposture	lee	mandrel	modal
inane	leaf	mandrill	model
insane	lief	manikin	moire
incidence	leak	mannequin	moiré
incidents	leek	mantel	monetary
incite	lean	mantle	monitory
insight	lien	marital	Monseigneur
indentation	lessen	marshal	Monsignor
indention	lesson	martial	moral
indict	lesser	mark	morale
indite	lessor	mart	motif
indigent	levee	marten	motive
indignant	levy	martin	much
inequities	lightening	Martin	mutch
iniquities	lightning	mask	mucous
ingenious	limb	masque	mucus
ingenuous	limn	massif	muscle
insidious	linage	massive	mussel
invidious	lineage	matrass	musical
insolation	lineament	mattress	musicale
insulation	liniment	medlar	nail
intension	liqueur	meddler	noil
intention	liquor	meat	nap
jactation	literal	meet	nappe
jactitation	littoral	mete	naval
jam	loath	mementos	navel
jamb	loathe	momentous	nicotian
joust	local	metal	nicotine
just	locale	mettle	nol-pros
judicial	load	mho	non-pros
judicious	lode	ohm	odeum
labile	loch	mews	odium
labial	lock	muse	ordinance
liable	lough	midges	ordnance
		midgets	

outre
outré
pacifist
passivist
paid
payed
palate
pallet
palette
pan
panne
panda
pander
paraclete
parakeet
parameter
perimeter
pardoner
partner
participial
participle
passable
passible
pastel
pastil
paten
patten
pattern
patience
patients
patios
patois
peak
pique
pearl
purl
peculation
speculation
pedal
peddle
pedicel
pedicle
peduncle
pencil
pensile
pendant
pendent

peninsula
peninsular
penitence
penitents
peremptory
preemptory
pericope
periscope
perpetrate
perpetuate
perquisite
prerequisite
persecute
prosecute
personal
personnel
personality
personalty
perspective
prospective
pervious
previous
petrify
putrify
phosphene
phosphine
phosphorous
phosphorus
physic
physique
physics
physical
psychical
pi
pie
pica
piker
picks
pix, pyx
piquant
poignant
pique
piqué
piquet
pistil
pistol

plaintiff
plaintive
plash
splash
pleural
plural
plum
plumb
Pluto
Plutus
poem
proem
pogrom
program
pole
poll
policy
polity
politeness
politesse
polygamy
polygyny
poppet
puppet
populace
populous
port
Porte
portion
potion
praise
prase
precession
procession
preposition
proposition
prescribe
proscribe
presence
prescience
preview
prevue
purvue
presentiment
presentment
princess
princesse

principal
principle
prophecy
prophesy
protean
protein
pubic
public
puling
pulling
quadrant
quadrat
quadrate
quash
squash
rabbet
rabbit
rack
wrack
radical
radicle
rail
râle
ran
rann
rancor
ranker
rapt
wrapt
rath
wrath
reality
realty
rebound
redound
recourse
resource
red
redd
rede
read
reed
reck
wreck
refection
reflection

relic	savant	spacious	Tatar
relict	servant	specious	Tartar
renaissance	scape	speculum	team
renascence	scarp	spiculum	teem
reported	scapula	staid	tear
reputed	scapular	stayed	tare
respectable	scorch	stationary	tears
respectful	scotch	stationery	tierce
respective	scull	statuary	taught
retch	skull	statutory	taut
wretch	scurfy	statue	tenor
reverend	scurvy	stature	tenure
reverent	sear	statute	tern
rheum	sere	steal	turn
room	seer	steel	terrain
rhyme	cere	stich	terrane
rhythm	senate	stitch	thrash
right	sennit	sticker	thresh
rite	sensual	stickler	thyme
wright	sensuous	stile	time
write	seraph	style	tic
ring	serif	stolen	tick
wring	serious	stolon	timbal
risqué	serous	stoop	timbale
risky	sheath	stoup	timber
roc	sheathe	stoep	timbre
rock	shimmed	straight	title
role	skimmed	strait	tittle
roll	shive	succor	titular
rood	skive	sucker	tutelar
rude	sign	surplice	tocsin
rued	sine	surplus	toxin
rota	syne	swath	ton
rotor	sleight	swathe	tun
sac	slight	swelter	travail
sack	slew	welter	travel
sacque	slue	tabular	tray
sailer	sloe	tubular	trey
sailor	slow	talesman	treatise
salutary	solid	talisman	treaties
salutatory	stolid	taper	trepan
salvage	souffle	tapir	trepang
selvage	soufflé	tarantelle	troche
sanitarium	sough	tarantula	trochee
sanatorium	sow	tarrier	troop
sanatory	spiritual	terrier	troupe
sanitary	spirituelle		

tule	verses	viscous	wean
tulle	versus	viscose	ween
turban	vertu	volt	weather
turbine	virtue	volte	wether
turbit	vertex	voltameter	whether
turbot	vortex	voltammeter	whirl
undersigned	vial	wain	whorl
undesigned	vile	wane	whither
valance	viol	waiver	wither
valence	vicious	waver	whosoever
venal	viscous	wangle	whosesoever
venial	villain	wrangle	wrack
vender	villein	ward	wreck
vendor	vindicative	warred	yaw
veracity	vindictive	weald	yore
voracity		wield	yoke
			yolk

SPELLING

The writer who is a poor speller can lean heavily on the editor and the proofreader, who correct misspellings as a matter of course. The poor speller who sets out to become an editorial worker or a proofreader is handicapped at the start, for accuracy in spelling is basic to acceptable work in these professions. Although it is not possible to anticipate the ingenuity of the poor speller and arm him against mistakes, the normally good speller can insure himself against error by a little study. Words often misspelled can be memorized; the *ei* and *ie* difficulty, for example, can be surmounted by a little effort. Many spelling difficulties arise in connection with suffixes, in changing a word from singular to plural, and in forming the possessive. The person who is never confused or uncertain about the correct form is exceptional; the following rules may, therefore, be found useful. They show American, not British, practice.

THE "EI" OR "IE" DIFFICULTY

The spelling difficulty of *ei* or *ie* is mainly with those words in which the vowel sound is *ee*. "Write *i* before *e* when sounded as *ee*, except after *c*."

niece   believe   siege   grievous

EXCEPTIONS: *either, neither, seize, weir, weird; sheik, leisure, inveigle; plebeian.*[1]

"When the letter *c* you spy, place the *e* before the *i*."

ceiling   conceit   receipt

EXCEPTIONS: *financier, specie.*

[1] Note also *obeisance*, pronounced by some ō-bē'sance.

In many words *ie* and *ei* have the sound of *ā*, *ĕ*, *ĭ*, or *ī*. Excepting *friend*, *sieve*, *mischief*, and *handkerchief*, these are spelled with *ei*.

neighbor   sovereign   surfeit   height

There should be no spelling difficulty with words like *science, piety, deity, soldier, view*, in which the two letters have two vowel sounds, not a single sound as in the words noted above.

FORMING DERIVATIVES BY ADDING SUFFIXES

Words ending in "e." Words ending in silent *e* generally drop the *e* before a suffix beginning with a vowel.

age	aging	line	linage [3]
blue	bluing, bluish	route	routing
cringe	cringing	sale	salable
force	forcible [2]	true	truism

EXCEPTIONS: *mileage; hoeing, shoeing,* and *toeing.*

The *e* is retained also in *dyeing, singeing, swingeing,* and *tingeing* (from *dye, singe, swinge,* and *tinge*) to distinguish them from *dying, singing, swinging,* and *tinging.*

Derivatives from proper names of persons retain the *e*, as *daguerreotype, morseograph.*

Words ending in silent *e* generally retain the *e* before a suffix beginning with a consonant.

awe	awesome	move	movement
hate	hateful	polite	politeness

EXCEPTIONS: Many words ending in silent *e* immediately preceded by another vowel (except *e*) drop the *e* in forming derivatives, as *due, duly; argue, argument.*

Other exceptions are the words *awful, wholly, nursling, wisdom, abridgment, acknowledgment, judgment, lodgment.* [4]

Words ending in "ce" or "ge." Words ending in *ce* or *ge* retain the *e* before suffixes beginning with *a*, *o*, or *u*, so that the *c* and *g* will not be pronounced with the hard sound.

advantage	advantageous	change	changeable
enforce	enforceable	peace	peaceable

EXCEPTIONS: *mortgagor* and *pledgor.*

---

[2] But note *enforceable.*
[3] Do not confuse with *lin'e-age.*
[4] The last four are in some British dictionaries written *abridgement, acknowledgement, judgement, lodgement.*

Words ending in "ie." Words ending in *ie* generally drop the *e* and change the *i* to *y* when adding *ing*.

die   dying   hie   hying   vie   vying

Words ending in "y." Words ending in *y* preceded by a vowel generally retain the *y* before any suffix.

annoy   annoyance   buy   buyer   enjoy   enjoyable

EXCEPTIONS: *daily, gaily, gaiety; laid, paid, said, saith, slain.*

Words ending in *y* preceded by a consonant usually change the *y* to *i* before any suffix except one beginning with *i*.

busy	business [5]	fly	flier [6]
country	countrified	body	bodiless

EXCEPTIONS: *fryer.*

Derivatives of adjectives of one syllable ending in *y* generally retain the *y;* as, *shy, shyness; wry, wryness.* The words *drier* and *driest,* from *dry,* are, however, commonly written with the *i*.

Before *-ship* and *-like*, as in *ladyship, citylike,* and in derivatives from *baby* and *lady* the *y* is retained.

Words ending in a consonant. Monosyllables and words of more than one syllable with the accent on the last syllable, ending in a single consonant preceded by a single vowel, double the final consonant before a suffix beginning with a vowel.

bag	baggage	corral	corralled
bus	busses [7]	forget	forgettable
allot	allotted	occur	occurrence
control	controller	prefer	preferred

EXCEPTIONS: Derivatives of the word *gas* (except *gassing* and *gassy*), *gaseous,* etc.; *chagrin, chagrined; inferable* and *transferable;* some derivatives in which the accent of the root word is thrown back upon another syllable, as *cabal', cab'alism; defer', def'erence; prefer', pref'erence; refer', ref'erence.*

Words accented on any syllable except the last, words ending in more than one consonant, and words ending in a single consonant preceded by more than one vowel, do not double the final consonant before an ending beginning with a vowel.[8]

[5] The form *busyness* is used to denote the state of being busy.

[6] Webster spelling *flyer* or *flier*.

[7] Omnibus, omnibuses.

[8] British dictionaries, including the Oxford, do not follow this rule but use a double consonant in many such derivatives. Note *biassed, focussed, marvellous, traveller, kidnapped, worshipped.* and many others.

benefit	benefited	marvel	marvelous
bias	biased	tranquil	tranquilize [10]
cancel	canceled [9]	transfer	transferee
combat	combated	persist	persistence
kidnap	kidnaper	repeal	repealed

EXCEPTIONS: *outfitted, outfitter; cobweb, cobwebbed; handicap, handicapped; diagram, diagrammatic; monogram, monogrammed* (but note *diagramed*); *humbug* and a few other words ending in *g* in which the *g* is doubled so that it will not be pronounced like *j; humbugged, zigzagged.*

Words ending in "c." Words ending in *c* usually have a *k* inserted when adding a termination beginning with *e, i,* or *y,* so that *c* will not be pronounced like *s.*

arc	arcing or arcking	panic	panicky
bivouac	bivouacked	physic	physicking
colic	colicky	rollic	rollicking
frolic	frolicked	shellac	shellacked
havoc	havocking	talc	talcky
mimic	mimicking	traffic	trafficker
picnic	picnicker	zinc	zincked

TROUBLESOME SUFFIXES

The terminations "-ceed," "-sede," and "-cede." Only three words of our language end in *-ceed;* one in *-sede.* Others with the same pronunciation end in *-cede.*

exceed	supersede	accede
proceed		antecede
succeed		concede, etc.

The terminations "-ise" and "-ize." Formerly the ending *-ize* was used if a word came from the Greek or Latin, and *-ise* if it came from the French; but in present-day American usage this rule is not followed. The following, together with their compounds and derivatives, use the *-ise.* All others preferably take *-ize* except in British spelling.[11]

9 Webster's Dictionary does not follow the rule in *cancellation.*

10 Note, however, *tranquillity. Tranquilize* is derived from *tranquil,* but *tranquillity* goes back to the Latin origin *tranquillus.* Similarly *chancellor* and derivatives of *crystal* and *metal,* like *crystallize* and *metallurgy,* get their double consonants from the Greek and Latin words from which they originated.

11 The *Oxford English Dictionary* uses the *-ize* ending as in American usage, but other English dictionaries use *-ise.*

advertise	compromise	exercise	premise
advise	demise	exorcise [13]	reprise
apprise [12]	despise	franchise	revise
arise	devise	improvise	supervise
chastise	disguise	incise	surmise
circumcise	enterprise	merchandise	surprise
comprise	excise		

Words ending in "-able" or "-ible." The correct spelling of words with the terminations *-able* or *-ible* is often puzzling. The student of orthography can find rules for the use of these endings, but the average proofreader will find it more practical to learn the spelling of each word and refer to the dictionary if memory fails for the moment.

Words ending in "-ance" or "-ence," etc. In all words in which the termination is preceded by *c* having the sound of *s*, or *g* having the sound of *j*, *-ence*, *-ency*, and *-ent* are used; where *c* sounds like k or *g* has its hard sound, the termination is *-ance*, *-ancy*, or *-ant*.

| beneficence | negligence | significance |
| coalescence | indigent | extravagant |

If the suffix is preceded by a letter other than *c* or *g* and the spelling is in doubt, the dictionary should be consulted.

FORMATION OF PLURALS

General rule. The plural of most nouns is formed by adding *s* or *es* to the singular, *es* being added if the word ends in *ch* soft, *s*, *sh*, *j*, *x*, or *z*, which when pronounced would not unite with *s* alone.

| desks | chiefs | traces | churches | rushes |

Nouns ending in "f," "ff," or "fe." Most nouns ending in *f*, *ff*, or *fe* form their plurals regularly, but a few change the *f*, *ff*, or *fe* to *ves*. *Staff*, *scarf*, and *wharf* have two forms.

beeves	knives	selves	wharves
calves	leaves	sheaves	wives
elves	lives	shelves	wolves
halves	loaves	thieves	

Nouns ending in "i." Nouns ending in *i* usually form their plurals by adding *s*.

| alibis | alkalis [14] | rabbis |

[12] The *Standard Dictionary* has *apprize* (to inform) and *surprize*.
[13] British spelling *exorcize*.
[14] Webster prefers *alkalies*.

Nouns ending in "o." Nouns ending in *o* preceded by a vowel form their plurals by adding *s* to the singular.

cameos   carabaos   taboos   ratios

No rule without numerous exceptions can be given for the formation of the plural of nouns ending in *o* preceded by a consonant. The more familiar words add *es* to the singular, generally speaking, while words rather recently borrowed from other languages usually add *s* only.

heroes   potatoes   banjos   octavos
mottoes   infernos   halos   zeros

Nouns ending in "y." The plural of nouns ending in *y* preceded by a consonant is formed by changing the *y* to *i* and adding *es*.

city, cities   fly, flies [15]   colloquy, colloquies [16]

A term like *henry,* derived from a proper name, usually retains the *y*.

henry, henrys   millihenry, millihenrys

Change of vowel. In the following nouns the singular and the plural differ in their vowels.

foot, feet   louse, lice   mouse, mice
goose, geese [17] man, men   tooth, teeth

Compounds ending with these words form their plurals in the same way.

workman, workmen   dormouse, dormice   clubfoot, clubfeet

Note also *manservant, menservants.*

Words that end in *-man* but are not compounds form their plurals regularly, by adding *s* only.

caymans   dragomans   Germans   Ottomans
desmans   humans   Mussulmans   Turkomans
dolmans   talismans   Normans

Similarly *mongoose,* ending in *-goose* but not a compound of *goose,* has the plural *mongooses.*

---

[15] *Fly* signifying a kind of carriage has the plural *flys.*
[16] Here the *y* is preceded by a vowel, but this vowel is pronounced like the consonant *w.*
[17] In the sense of tailors' irons, *gooses.*

Nouns with two plurals. Some nouns have two plurals, with different meanings.

brothers (of the same parents)	brethren (of the same society)
dies (for coining)	dice (for gaming)
geniuses (men of genius)	genii (imaginary spirits)
indexes (tables of contents)	indices (signs in algebra)
staves (poles, supports)	staffs (bodies of assistants)

Many nouns from foreign languages retain their original plurals, as, for instance:

agendum, agenda [18]	marchesa, marchese
crisis, crises	matrix, matrices
datum, data	monsieur, messieurs
differentia, differentiae	os, ossa (*bone*)
genus, genera	os, ora (*mouth*)
haggada, haggadoth	paries, parietes
indicium, indicia	phenomenon, phenomena
insigne, insignia	planetarium, planetaria
larva, larvae	phylum, phyla

Some nouns of this class, however, have also a second plural formed after English analogy, like the following:

adieu—adieux, adieus	femur—femora, femurs
animalculum—animalcula, animalcules	formula—formulae, formulas
appendix—appendices, appendixes	fungus—fungi, funguses
automaton—automata, automatons	gladiolus—gladioli, gladioluses
bandit—banditti, bandits	imago—imagines, imagoes
beau—beaux, beaus	medium—media, mediums
cherub—cherubim, cherubs	memorandum—memoranda, memo-
criterion—criteria, criterions	randums
curriculum—curricula, curriculums	virtuoso—virtuosi, virtuosos
dogma—dogmata, dogmas	vortex—vortices, vortexes

The following Latin words have a plural formed by adding *es*:

apparatus, apparatuses	impetus, impetuses
census, censuses	nexus, nexuses
consensus, consensuses	prospectus, prospectuses
hiatus, hiatuses	sinus, sinuses

Singular forms used as plurals. Some nouns, mostly names of animals, use the singular form of spelling to denote more than one individual, as:

deer	swine	moose	fish

[18] *Webster's New International Dictionary,* second edition, states that *agenda* is now sometimes construed as singular.

But these words, and some others which ordinarily have no plural, as *wheat, flour, coffee,* have a plural regularly formed which is used to denote more than one species or kind, or in some cases to emphasize the presence of the several component individuals.

| fishes | trouts | wheats | coffees |

NOTE. Names of shellfishes commonly use the regular plural forms.

| crabs | lobsters | scallops | shrimps |

Some nouns which have a regularly formed plural also use the singular form as a plural.

dozen [19]	head	score	youth
pair	couple	shot	heathen
brace	yoke		

... herded into concentration camps like so many head of cattle.

The word *people* is usually a plural, but it may be a singular, with a regularly formed plural, *peoples.*

Another people deserves brief mention.
... the benefits which a people derives from foreign trade.
What peoples have had a part in the making of our civilization?

Nouns with only one form. Many names of tribes and races have the same form in the plural as in the singular.

| Chinese | Portuguese | Norse |

Such words as *assured, beloved, educated,* and so forth, used as nouns (instead of *assured person* or *persons,* etc.) are construed as singular or plural according to the context.

Forms in *-ics* are construed as singular when they denote a scientific treatise or its subject matter, as *mathematics, physics;* those denoting matters of practice, as *gymnastics, tactics,* are often construed as plurals.

Politics has been studied as a science since the days of Aristotle.
Politics in school affairs are always detrimental to educational progress.

Other nouns which have only one form and may be construed as singular or plural are the following:

[19] Two dozen, a few dozens, many dozens.

aircraft	forceps	rendezvous
alms	goods	remains
amends	headquarters	samurai
bellows	mankind	series
bourgeoisie	means	shambles
cantharides	offspring	species
chassis	pains (*care, effort*)	sperm
corps	précis	sweepstakes
counsel (*a person*)	proceeds	United States
congeries	progeny	

Every means has been tried. All means have been tried.
It was a shambles.
The United States is; these United States are.

Plural in form, construed as singular:

aloes	measles	rickets
checkers (*a game*)	mews (*stables*)	shingles (*a disease*)
dominoes (*a game*)	mumps	whereabouts
heaves	news	works (*factory*)
hollands		

There is a works of the Hempill Manufacturing Company in our town.

NOTE. The words *biceps, Cyclops, gallows,* and *summons* are not of this group;
they have plural forms: *bicepses, Cyclopes, gallowses, summonses.*

Compound nouns. Compounds written as a single word form their plurals
regularly, adding the sign of the plural at the end. Mistakes are infrequent
except in the spelling of compounds ending in *-ful.*

| cupfuls | handfuls | teaspoonfuls |

Compound nouns written with a hyphen form their plurals by adding the
sign of the plural to the word that essentially constitutes the noun.

| sons-in-law | knights-errant | aides-de-camp |
| step-children | hangers-on | autos-da-fé |

If the compound noun consists of two words, the sign of the plural may
be used with both or with the noun portion.

| knights bachelors | chargés d'affaires | coups d'état |
| knights templar | tables d'hôte | |

A substantive phrase containing a possessive—*master's degree,* for example—
is changed to the plural by adding *s* to the second word.

| master's degrees | doctor's dissertations |

"The plurals of military titles are usually formed by adding *s* at the end, as *major generals, lieutenant colonels, surgeon generals,* but *sergeants major.* Civil titles usually add *s* to the first part, as *attorneys general, postmasters general.*[20]

Proper names. The plural of proper names is formed regularly, by adding *s* or *es* to the singular.

George, Georges	Adonis, Adonises
Charles, Charleses	Hughes, Hugheses
the Kallikaks and the Edwardses	Ruckers, Ruckerses

NOTE. Many persons seem to have difficulty with the plurals of proper names ending in *s,* and the proofreader often comes upon errors like the following:

Wrong: It can boast of fourteen Rubens and two Van Dycks.
Right: It can boast of fourteen Rubenses and two Van Dycks.
Wrong: There were several families of the name of Hanks. . . . The Hanks had come from Virginia.
Right: The Hankses had come from Virginia.

Proper names ending in *y* form their plurals regularly, and do not change the *y* to *i* as common nouns do.

The Raffertys
The three Marys (*Three Maries* would mean three women named Marie.)
The two Kansas Citys (*Cities* would be misleading.)
EXCEPTIONS: Alleghenies, Rockies, Sicilies; Ptolemies.

If the plural of a proper name cannot be formed without making a word ambiguous or awkward to pronounce, an apostrophe may be used:

of the other Louis'	honored by the Agassiz'
the Voorhees' of New York	the Euripides' of drama

Letters, figures, etc. The plural of a letter, figure, character, or sign is expressed by adding to it an apostrophe and *s.*

Mind your *p*'s and *q*'s.	ABC's
There are two *m*'s in *accommodate.*	three R's
2300 r.p.m.'s	I.W.W.'s
five D. H.'s [21]	Co.'s
during the 1850's [22]	6's, +'s

EXCEPTIONS: In stock and bond quotations, Govt. 4s, Bergen 8s, Treas. 3¾s. In golf scores, 3s, 4s.

[20] U. S. Government Printing Office style book.
[21] In British usage, M.A.s, M.P.s.
[22] The form 1850s is also used.

In expressions like "twos and threes," "pros and cons," "ins and outs," "yeas and nays," a regularly formed plural is used.

Count by twos to 20; by fives to 50; by fours to 40.
He wanted to know the whys and wherefores.
The Number Twos become guards.
He voted with the Noes.
It is usually instigated by the desire of the "have nots" to obtain some of the economic advantages possessed by the "haves."
Don'ts for Library Users.
There can be no ifs or ands or buts. (Meaning: There can be no conditions or objections.)

If the "ifs," "ands," and "buts" in the preceding example referred to the words as words, however, the correct form would be:

There can be no *if*'s or *and*'s or *but*'s.

That is, the plural of a word referred to as a word, without regard to its meaning, is indicated by apostrophe and *s*.

I used too many *and*'s.

FORMATION OF THE POSSESSIVE CASE

Common nouns. The possessive case of most singular nouns and of plural nouns not ending in *s* is formed by adding an apostrophe and *s*.

lady's	son's	children's

NOTE. Some persons prefer *witness'*, *countess'*, and the like, but spoken English is more accurately reflected by a regularly formed possessive, as *countess's*.

The possessive case of plural nouns ending in *s* is formed by adding apostrophe alone.

ladies'	sons'	brothers'

Various expressions ending in *s* or the sound of *s* form a possessive by adding apostrophe alone.

for old times' sake   for appearance' sake
for goodness' sake   for convenience' sake

Proper names. The possessive form of most proper names is formed by adding apostrophe and *s* to a singular or apostrophe alone to a plural.

Jack's	James's	the Davises' [23]

[23] Either is correct: *the Misses Smith's* or *the Miss Smiths'*.

Usage varies, however, in forming the possessive of proper names ending in *s* or the sound of *s*. If the name is monosyllabic, apostrophe and *s* is usually preferred.[24]

Burns's   Marx's   Schmitz's

If the name has two or more syllables, a possessive formed with the apostrophe and *s* is still good form, but many prefer to use the apostrophe alone. So we find:

Dickens's and Dickens'   Adams's and Adams'   Williams's and Williams'

NOTE. *Dickens's* is more common than *Dickens'*. Webster's Dictionary has *St. Vitus's dance, Amfortas's wound.*

Wherever the apostrophe and *s* would make a word difficult to pronounce, as when a sibilant occurs before the last syllable, only the apostrophe is used.

Moses' Well   Xerxes' army   Berzelius' symbols

Ancient classical names ending in *s*, by convention add only the apostrophe to form the possessive.

Mars' wrath   Achilles' heel   Hercules' labors

In forming the possessive of foreign names ending in a silent sibilant, as *Dumas, Vaux,* the usual practice is to use apostrophe and *s* whether the word is monosyllabic or not. Webster's Dictionary has the form *Rabelais's.*

Descartes's invention   Arkansas's problem   Des Moines's schools

Spanish names ending in *z* pronounced like *th* usually take an apostrophe and *s*.

Gomez's house   Lopertez's knife

Compound nouns. There are many compound nouns the first portion of which is a possessive. In most cases a singular possessive form is preferred.

cow's milk   fool's gold   confectioner's sugar

The spelling *oneself* is displacing *one's self*, the form which used to be the more common.

In modern usage the possessive of *somebody else* and similar expressions is formed by adding apostrophe and *s* to *else*.

someone else's   anyone else's   everybody else's

[24] The proofreader should be careful to follow the exact form of book titles containing a possessive form.

Phrases. The possessive case of a phrase or a combination of names is formed by adding the sign of the possessive to the last word only.

the governor of Maine's   Simon the Pharisee's

Joint ownership. If possession is common to two or more individuals, only the last name takes the possessive sign.

Teddy, Peggy, and Nancy's home
Lena and Bill's trip to the Fair
Tocqueville and Beaumont's Report
Burrows & Sanborn's store
Painters, Paper Hangers, and Decorators' Union
Drs. Sansum and Nuzum's theory

If possession is not joint, however, each modifying substantive should carry the apostrophe.

Teddy's, Peggy's, and Nancy's homes
Men's, women's, and children's shoes

A distinction should be made between true possessives like the examples above and expressions denoting something *for* two or more persons or groups.

Authors' and Printers' Dictionary
Editors' and Readers' Handbook
Boys' and Girls' Newspaper
Mothers' and Daughters' Banquet
Soldiers' and Sailors' Home

WORDS OFTEN MISSPELLED OR WITH VARIANT SPELLINGS

Editors and proofreaders must surmount a spelling difficulty not faced by the nonprofessional, that of remembering which words differ in spelling in the various dictionaries, and just what the differences are. They should of course know thoroughly the spellings of the dictionary preferred by their employers, but should also be prepared for the manuscript whose author prefers a different authority. Since the number of words varying in recognized spelling runs into the thousands, it is manifestly impossible to give here a comprehensive list of such words, but those most commonly used are included. Some words frequently misspelled are combined with this list because often one may be in doubt, at least momentarily, whether a spelling is incorrect or a variation from a more familiar form.

Generally speaking, words covered by the spelling rules given on previous pages are not included in the following list. Spellings of four dictionaries are given: Webster,[1] Century,[2] Standard,[3] and Concise Oxford.[4] The Webster spelling is given first—thus determining the alphabetical order—because Webster's Dictionary is the one most widely used in this country. A word appearing only once is spelled the same by all four. The following symbols for the dictionaries are used: W, Webster; C, Century; S, Standard; O, Concise Oxford; OED, Oxford English Dictionary.

abattoir	acknowledgment	align (W, O)
aberration	adviser	aline (C, S)
abridgment [5]	advisory	alkalies (W)
abscess	adz (W, C, S)	alkalis (C, S, O)
absorption	adze (O)	amide (W, C)
absinthe (W)	aegis (W, O) [7]	amid (S) [8]
absinth (C, S, O)	ægis (C)	amine (W, C, O)
abysmal	egis (S)	amin (S)
accommodate	aeon (W, O)	amoeba (W, O)
accompanist	æon (C)	amœba (C)
accordion	eon (S)	ameba (S)
accouter (W, S) [6]	aerate (W, S, O)	anesthesia (W, S)
accoutre (C, O)	aërate (C)	anæsthesia (C)
accoutering (W, S)	aerie (W, S, O)	anaesthesia (O)
accoutring (C, O)	aery (C)	analogous
accumulate	aide-de-camp	analyze (W, C, S)

[1] *Webster's New International Dictionary*, Second Edition. Springfield, Mass., G. & C. Merriam Co., 1934. This edition shows several changes from the previous one. The following should be observed:
Ligatures are no longer used for diphthongs except in French personal and place names: *aesthetic, hors d'oeuvres.*
Words previously spelled with a dieresis are now spelled with a hyphen: *co-operate, re-enter,* and the like. Exceptions are *microorganism, zoology, reinforce.*
The prefix *in-* has been changed to *en-* in several words: *enclose, endorse, ensnare, entrust.*
Several words from the French, and some others which originally had accented letters, are now written without the accent; as, *regime, role, phaeton, aerie.* But note *naïve, résumé.*
[2] *The New Century Dictionary of the English Language.* New York, D. Appleton-Century Company, 1946.
[3] *The New Standard Dictionary of the English Language.* New York, Funk & Wagnalls Company.
[4] *The Concise Oxford Dictionary of Current English.* Adapted by H. W. Fowler and F. G. Fowler from the *Oxford Dictionary.* Oxford, Clarendon Press, 1911. The spellings of this dictionary are not invariably those of the *Oxford English Dictionary.* Some variations are specifically noted in footnotes on the pages following.
[5] OED: abridgement, acknowledgement, judgement, lodgement.
[6] Many words ending in *-er* in American dictionaries are spelled *-re* in the Oxford and other English dictionaries: *centre, metre, sceptre, sombre, spectre, theatre,* and many others. The *e* of such words is dropped before a suffix beginning with a vowel: *accoutred, centring.*
All dictionaries use the ending *-re* in *acre, chancre, eagre* (tidal flood), *euchre, lucre, mediocre, nacre, ogre.*
[7] The Webster and Concise Oxford dictionaries print the diphthongs *ae* and *oe* as separate letters; Century and OED prefer the ligatures *æ, œ;* Standard usually substitutes *e.*
[8] In the Standard Dictionary the endings *-ide* and *-ine* are regularly shortened to *-id* and *-in.*

analyse (O) [9]
anemia (W, C, S)
  anaemia (O)
aneurysm (W, C, O)
  aneurism (S)
anoint
antediluvian
antitoxin
anyone (W)
  any one (C, S, O)
apollinaris
appall (W)
  appal (C, S, O)
appareled (W, C, S) [10]
  apparelled (O)
apprise (to inform) (W, C, O)
  apprize (S)
apropos
arbor (W, C, S) [11]

arbour (O)
argument
artisan (W, C, O)
  artizan (S)
ascendancy (W, C, O)
  ascendency (S)
assassinate
athenaeum (W, O)
  athenæum (C)
  atheneum (S)
atropine (W, C, O)
  atropin (S)
ax (W, C, S)
  axe (O)
aye (always) (W, O)
  ay (C, S)

bandanna (W, S, C)
  bandana (C)
banister

banyan (W, C)
  banian (C, S)
barcarole
bark (a boat)
bassinet
battalion
behoove (W, C, S)
  behove (O)
beneficent
benefited
biased [12]
bimetallism
bissextile
bizarre
blamable [13]
blond (adj.)
  blonde (fem. n.)
bonny
boulder
brevetted

[9] Words ending in *-yze* in American dictionaries are spelled by the Concise Oxford Dictionary *-yse*. This dictionary follows American usage for words ending in *-ize*, as *baptize, civilize.* OED and other British dictionaries use *-ise.*

[10] Other words varying in the same way are:

barreled	disheveled	imperiled	penciled	tinseled
beveled	doweled	kenneled	pistoled	totaled
boweled	driveled	laureled	quarreled	trammeled
canceled	dueled	leveled	raveled	traveled
caroled	enameled	libeled	reveled	tunneled
caviled	equaled	marshaled	rivaled	vialed
channeled	funneled	marveled	roweled	victualed
chiseled	gamboled	metaled	shoveled	yodeled
counseled	graveled	modeled	shriveled	
cudgeled	jeweled	paneled	sniveled	
dialed	impaneled	parceled	tasseled	

Note that *paralleled* is so spelled by all.

[11] Other words varying in the same way are:

ardour	demeanour	harbour	parlour	succour
armour	dolour	honour	rancour	tabour
behaviour	enamour	humour	rigour	tumour
candour	endeavour	labour	rumour	valour
clamour	favour	neighbour	savour	vapour
clangour	fervour	odour	splendour	vigour
colour	flavour			

Horror, mirror, pallor, stupor, tenor, terror, and *tremor* do not take the *u.* When an adjective is formed from any of the above *-our* words by adding *-ous,* the ending of the original word becomes simply *-or* as in American dictionaries, as *clamorous, dolorous, humorous, laborious.* Likewise, *discoloration, honorary, humorist, invigorate.*

[12] OED: biassed.

[13] In OED and other British dictionaries the final silent *e* of the root word is retained in some words, as *likeable, liveable. nameable, saleable.*

brier
bronco
brusque (W, C, O)
   brusk (S)
buccaneer
bulrushes
bur (*seed vessel*)
busses (W)
   buses (C, S, O)
bylaw (W)
   by-law (C, S, O)

calcareous
calcimine
caldron (W, C, S)
   cauldron (O)
calibration
caliph (W, O)
   calif (C, S)
callisthenics (W, C, S)
   calisthenics (O)
calk (W, C, S)
   caulk (O)
calligraphy
callus
calorie (W, S)
   calory (C)
camellia
cancellation (W, C, O)
   cancelation (S)
canister
cantilever
cantaloupe (W)
   cantaloup (C, S, O)
canyon (W, O)
   cañon (C, S)
carburetor (W)
   carbureter (C, S)
   carburettor (O)
carcass
caribou
carom
cartilage

casualty
catalogue (W, C, O)
   catalog (S) [14]
catastrophes
centigram (W, C, S)
   centigramme (O)
centipede (W, C, O)
   centiped (S)
chaperon
chautauqua
check (*bank*) (W, C, S)
   cheque (O)
chlorophyll (W, O)
   chlorophyl (C, S)
cigarette (W, C, O)
   cigaret (S)
clue (W, C, O)
   clew (S)
coconut (W, S)
   cocoanut (C)
   coco-nut (O)
coerce
colander
collectible (W, O)
   collectable (C, S)
collector
colonnade
colossal
combated [15]
confectionery
confidant (*m.*)
confidante (*fem.*)
connection (W, C, S)
   connexion (O) [16]
connivance
connoisseur
consensus
controlled
co-operate (W, O)
   coöperate (C)
   cooperate (S)
co-ordinate (W, O)
   coördinate (C)

coordinate (S)
corollary
corralled
cotillion
councilor (W, C, S)
   councillor (O)
courtesan (W, O)
   courtezan (C, S)
cozy (W, C, S)
   cosy (O)
crenelated (W, C, S)
   crenellated (O)
crenulated
criticize
crosier (W, O)
   crozier (C, S)
crystalline
cutlass (W, C, O)
   cutlas (S)
cyclopedia (W, C, S)
   cyclopaedia (O)

debacle (W, C, S)
   débâcle (O)
debarkation
debris (W, C, O)
   débris (S)
décolleté
defense (W, C, S)
   defence (O)
demarcation
dependent (*n.*) (W, C, S)
   dependant (O)
descendant (*n.*)
descendent (*adj.*)
desiccate
despicable
develop
dexterous (W, C, S)
   dextrous (O)
diaeresis (W, O)
   dieresis (C, S)

[14] Similar words spelled by the Standard Dictionary without the final *ue* are *analog, apolog, dialog, prolog*. Note: *United States Catalog*.

[15] Webster recognizes *combatted*, with the accent on the second syllable, as a variant.

[16] Note the British use of *x* in place of *ct* in *connexion, deflexion, genuflexion, inflexion, reflexion*, etc.

diarrhea (W, C, S)
  diarrhoea (O)
dictaphone
dictograph
dietitian (W, S)
  dietician (C)
dike
dilapidated
dilettante
disk
dispatch (W, S, O)
  despatch (C)
dissatisfied
dissyllable (W, C, S)
  disyllable (O)
distention (W, C, S)
  distension (O)
distill (W)
  distil (C, S, O)
domicile (W, C, O)
  domicil (S)
draft (W, C, S)
  draught (O)
dreadnought
dreamed (W, C, S)
  dreamt (O) [17]
drought
dryly (W, C, S)
  drily (O)
duffel (W, S, O)
  duffle (C)
dullness (W, C)
  dulness (S, O)
dumfound (W, C, S)
  dumbfound (O)

ecstasy
eerie (W, C, O)
  eery (S)
ellipse
embarkation
embarrass
embed
employee (W, C, S)
  employé (O)
encage

enclasp
enclose (W, S, O)
  inclose (C)
encumbrance
endorse (W, O)
  indorse (C, S)
enforce
enforceable
engulf
enmesh
enroll (W, C, S)
  enrol (O)
enrollment (W, C)
  enrolment (S, O)
ensnare (W, S, O)
  insnare (C)
enthrall (W, C, S)
  enthral (O)
enthrallment (W)
  enthralment (C, S, O)
entreat
entrench (W, O)
  intrench (C, S)
entrust (W, S, O)
  intrust (C)
entwine
envelop (*v.*)
envelope (*n.*) (W, C, O)
  envelop (S)
epaulet (W, C, S)
  epaulette (O)
erysipelas
esophagus (W, C, S)
  oesophagus (O)
ethereal
etiquette
excel
exemplification
exhilarate
expansible
extension
eying
façade
fagot (W, C, S)
  faggot (O)

feldspar
fetal (W, C, S)
  foetal (O)
fetish
filigree
fiord
fledgling (W, C, S)
  fledgeling (O)
flotage (W, S)
  floatage (C, O)
flunky (W, C, S)
  flunkey (O)
focused
font (*of type*) (W, C, S)
  fount (O)
fontanel (W, S, O)
  fontanelle (C)
forgather
forgettable (W, O)
  forgetable (C, S)
forgo
forswear
fricassee
frustum
fuchsia
fulfill (W)
  fulfil (C, S, O)
fulfillment (W)
  fulfilment (C, S, O)
fullness (W, C, S)
  fulness (O)
fusillade

gaiety
gaily
gantlet (run the) (W, C, S)
  gauntlet (O)
gasoline (W, C, S)
  gasolene (O)
gauge (W, O)
  gage (C, S)
gelatin
gender
gibe (sneer)
glamour [18]

[17] Note British spellings *dreamt, leapt, learnt, spelt*, etc.
[18] *Glamour* is of Scots derivation and not to be classed with *arbor, ardor,* and the like.

glamorous
glycerin (W, C, S)
  glycerine (O)
good-by (W, C, S)
  good-bye (O)
gram (W, C, S)
  gramme (O)
gray (W, C, S)
  grey (O)
grievous
gruesome
guerrilla
guild (*a society*) (W, O)
  gild (C, S)
guttural
gypsy (W)
  gipsy, (C, S, O)

handicapped
harass
hearken (W, O)
  harken (C, S)
hemorrhage (W, C, S)
  haemorrhage (O)
hindrance
hypocrisy
hypotenuse

idiosyncrasy
idyl (W, C, S)
  idyll (O)
impale (W, C, O)
  empale (S)
impel
impinging
impostor
impugn
incase (W, C, S)
  encase (O)
incrust (W, C, S)
  encrust (O)
indispensable
indiscriminately
inferable
infold (W, C, S)
  enfold (O)
ingrain (W, C, S)
  engrain (O)

innocuous
innovation
innuendo
inoculate
inquire
insanitary
insistence
install
installment (W, C, S)
  instalment (O)
instill (W)
  instil (C, S, O)
insure
intern
interpretative
intransigent
inure
iodine (W, C, O)
  iodin (S)
iridescent
irresistible
isosceles

jail (W, C, S)
  gaol (O)
jeweler (W, C, S)
  jeweller (O)
judgment

kidnaped (W, S)
  kidnapped (C, O)
kilt (*sing.*)

lachrymal (W, O)
  lacrymal (C)
  lacrimal (S)
lavender
license (*n.*) (W, C, S)
  licence (O)
license (*v.*)
licentiate
licorice (W, C, S)
  liquorice (O)
likable
lilliputian
liquefy
loadstone (W, O)
  lodestone (C, S)
loath (*adj.*)

lodestar
lodgment
lower (*frown*) (W, C, S)
  lour (O)

mamma (W, C, O)
  mama (S)
maneuver (W, C, S)
  manœuvre (O)
marvelous (W, C, S)
  marvellous (O)
medieval (W, C, S)
  mediaeval (O)
melee (W, S)
  mêlée (C, O)
metallurgy
metonymy
mileage (W, C, S)
  milage (O)
millenary
millennium
millionaire
mineralogy
mischievous
moccasin
mold (W, C, S)
  mould (O)
mollusk (W, C, S)
  mollusc (O)
molt (W, C, S)
  moult (O)
monogrammed
movable
mustache (W, C, S)
  moustache (O)

naphtha
nerve-racked
nickel
nonplused (W, S)
  nonplussed (C, O)
novitiate
numskull

obbligato
offense (W, C, S)
  offence (O)
omelet (W, C, S)
  omelette (O)

ordnance
organdy (W, S)
  organdie (C, O)

pajamas (W, C, S)
  pyjamas (O)
papoose
paraffin
paralleled
paralyze (W, C, S)
  paralyse (O)
partisan (W, O)
  partizan (C, S)
peddler (W, C)
  pedler (S)
  pedlar (O)
petrify
phaeton (W, S, O)
  phaëton (C)
pharaoh
phoenix (W, O)
  phenix (C, S)
phosphorus
piccalilli
plow (W, C, S)
  plough (O)
pollination
poniard
practice (*n.*)
practice (*v.*) (W)
  practise (C, S, O)
predominantly
pre-eminent (W, O)
  preëminent (C)
  preeminent (S)
pre-exist (W, O)
  preëxist (C)
  preexist (S)
pretense (W, C, S)
  pretence (O)
preterit (W, C, S)
  preterite (O)
preventive
primeval
procedure

program (W, C, S)
  programme (O)
promissory
propel
pusillanimity
putrefy
pygmy (W, C, O)
  pigmy (S)

quartet (W, C, S)
  quartette (O)
quaternary
questionnaire
quinsy

raccoon (W, S, O)
  racoon (C)
racket (*tennis*)
rarefy
reconnaissance
redoubt (W, C, O)
  redout (S)
reinforce (W, C, O)
  reenforce (S)
referable
repellent
reverie
rhyme (*verse*) (W, O)
  rime (C, S)
ruble (W, C, S)
  rouble (O)

saccharin (*n.*)
saccharine (*adj.*)
salable
saviour (W, O) [19]
  savior (C, S)
saxophone
scimitar (W)
  simitar (C, S)
  scimetar (O)
Shakespearean (W)
  Shakespearian (C, S, O)
shote
sibyl
sibylline

silvan (W, O)
  sylvan (C, S)
sirup (W, S)
  syrup (C, O)
skeptic (W, C, S)
  sceptic (O)
skillful (W)
  skilful (C, S, O)
spoliation
stanch (*v.*)
stanch (*adj.*) (W. C, S)
  staunch (O)
steadfast (W, C, O)
  stedfast (S)
stereopticon
story (*of a house*) (W, C, S)
  storey (O)
strait-jacket
strait-laced
stratagem
stupefy
subpoena (W, C, O)
  subpena (S)
sulphur (W, C, O) [20]
  sulfur (S)
supersede
supposititious
surprise (W, C, O)
  surprize (S)

taboo (W, C, O)
  tabu (S)
tarlatan
thralldom (W)
  thraldom (C, S, O)
today (W, O)
  to-day (C, S)
tonsillitis
toxin
tranquilize (W, C, S)
  tranquillize (O)
tranquillity
transatlantic
transcendent

[19] Commonly spelled *Saviour* when it refers to Christ.
[20] In chemical and other scientific work ordinarily *sulfur*.

traveler (W, C, S)   vilify   whirr (O)
traveller (O)   villainous   whisky
turmeric   vise (*a tool*) (W, C, S)   willful (W)
typify   vice (O)   wilful, (C, S, O)
tyro (W, C, S)   vizor (W, S)   wizened
tiro (O)   visor (C, O)   woeful (W, C, O)
    vitamin (W, S)   woful (S)
unwieldy   vitamine (C)   wolverine (W)
    vitreous   wolverene (C, S, O)
vacillate   vitrify   woolen (W, C, S)
velours (*sing.*)   vocal cords   woollen (O)
veranda (W, C, S)
verandah (O)   wagon (W, C, S)   zoölogy (W, S, O)
verdigris   waggon (O)   zoölogy (C)
vermilion   whir (W, C, S)   zwieback

BIBLIOGRAPHY FOR PARTS V AND VI

CRAIGIE, SIR WILLIAM, and others, *A Dictionary of American English on Historical Principles.* Chicago, University of Chicago Press, 1936.

CURME, GEORGE OLIVER, *Syntax.* Boston, D. C. Heath & Co., 1931.

FOWLER, HENRY WATSON, *A Dictionary of Modern English Usage.* Oxford, Clarendon Press, 1926.

FOWLER, HENRY WATSON, and FRANCIS GEORGE, *Concise Oxford Dictionary of Current English,* 3d ed. New York, Oxford University Press, 1934.

GREEVER, GARLAND, and JONES, EASLEY, S., *The Century Collegiate Handbook.* New York, D. Appleton-Century Company, 1939.

HORWILL, HERBERT WILLIAM, *A Dictionary of Modern American Usage.* New York, Oxford University Press, 1935.

KRAPP, GEORGE PHILIP, *A Comprehensive Guide to Good English,* 4th ed. Chicago Rand, McNally & Co., 1927.

—— *The English Language in America.* New York, The Century Company, 1925.

LEONARD, STERLING ANDRUS, *Current English Usage.* Chicago, National Council of Teachers of English, 1932.

MARCKWARDT, ALBERT H., and WALCOTT, FRED G., *Facts About Current English Usage.* New York, D. Appleton-Century, 1938.

MENCKEN, HENRY LOUIS, *The American Language,* 4th ed. New York, Alfred A. Knopf, 1936.

PARTRIDGE, ERIC, *A Dictionary of Clichés.* New York, The Macmillan Company, 1940.

—— *Usage and Abusage.* New York, Harper & Bros., 1942.

PERRIN, PORTER G., *An Index to English.* Chicago, Scott, Foresman and Company, 1939.

SMITH, LOGAN PEARSALL, *Words and Idioms.* Boston, Houghton Mifflin Company, 1925.

WESEEN, MAURICE HARLEY, *Words Confused and Misused.* New York, Thomas Y. Crowell Company, 1932.

WOOD, GEORGE McLANE, *Suggestions to Authors of Papers Submitted for Publication by the United States Geological Survey,* 4th ed., revised and enlarged by Bernard H. Lane. Washington, U. S. Government Printing Office, 1935.

WOOLLEY, EDWIN C., and SCOTT, FRANKLIN W., *College Handbook of Composition.* Boston, D. C. Heath and Company, 1928.

WYLD, HENRY CECIL KENNEDY, *History of Modern Colloquial English.* New York, E. P. Dutton Co., 1920.

APPENDIX

MAIN DIVISIONS

Glossary of Grammatical Terms   Book Publishers
Glossary of Printing Terms   Foreign Words and Phrases

GLOSSARY OF GRAMMATICAL TERMS

(In many definitions the word *substantive* is used, for the sake of brevity, to denote a noun or pronoun or any other part of speech or group of words used as a noun.)

ablative In Latin and some other languages, the case which expresses chiefly separation, source, or instrumentality. Its place is taken in English by the prepositions *at, by, from, in, with.*

absolute construction *See* nominative absolute.

abstract noun *See* noun.

accusative In inflected languages (*e.g.,* Latin), the case corresponding to the objective case in English.

active verb *See* verb.

adjective A word that modifies a substantive; *e.g., white* horse, *natural* piety, *young* child, *vegetable* matter, House *Beautiful.* Adjectives are classified syntactically as attributive and predicate. The former usually stand before the substantive; the latter, after the verb. The predicate adjective is a form of complement, *q.v.*

Attributive: the *angry* man, the *yellow* leaf, me *miserable.*

Predicate (or predicative): The man is *angry.* The leaf is *yellow.* I am *miserable.*

Adjectives are classified by kind as follows:

Demonstrative or definitive: *this* (*e.g.,* this man), *that, these, those.*

Descriptive: (1) common: *white, wise, heavy;* (2) proper: *French, Spencerian, April* (April showers).

Indefinite: *each, both, either, such, some,* etc., when these modify a substantive— *each* man, *such* nonsense.

Interrogative: *which* (*e.g.,* which man?), *whose, what.*

Limiting: *a, an, the.* (Also called articles.)

Numeral: *one, two, three, ten; first, tenth; quadruple, fourfold.*

Possessive: *John's, my.*

Pronominal: any possessive pronoun.

Relative: *whose, which, what,* when it both modifies a substantive and joins it to a qualifying clause (*e.g.,* We know what men are guilty).

523

Another part of speech or a phrase or a clause may be used as an adjective. The inflection of the adjective is called its *comparison, q.v.* See also pages 380 and 381 of the text.

adjective clause *See* clause.

adjective phrase A phrase that qualifies a noun or pronoun in the sentence. Adjective phrases are classified, from the words introducing them, as *prepositional, participial,* and *infinitive.*

Prepositional: the top *of the table;* the girl *with the green eyes;* a cure *for the grippe.*

Participial: a man *selling bonds;* a dog *stunned by a blow.*

Infinitive: work *to be done;* sights *to be seen.*

adverb A word that modifies a verb, adjective, or another adverb. The characteristic ending of adverbs is *-ly,* though some (*e.g., here, now, so*) do not have it. The inflection of the adverb, like that of the adjective, is called *comparison, q.v.* The classification of adverbs as those of time, place, degree, quality, number, and manner is not important to grammar. *See also* conjunctive adverb.

Modifying a verb: sleep *peacefully;* put it *there;* do it *now.*

Modifying an adjective: *too* loud for comfort; *very* glad; *severely* ill.

Modifying an adverb: *exceedingly* poorly; *so* excruciatingly painful.

adverb clause *See* clause.

adverb phrase A phrase used as an adverb. The most common form is one introduced by a preposition—"*After knocking at the door,* we listened a long while" (preposition and gerund); "*After breakfast,* let's go for a walk" (preposition and noun). Another form is that introduced by an infinitive—"I seek only *to be agreeable.*"

adverbial conjunction A name, now little used, for *conjunctive adverb, q.v.*

agreement The proper relations of words, especially in case, number, and person, in a sentence. The rule of agreement is that in a sentence every part should agree grammatically (and logically) with every other related part. Exceptions are the *absolute construction* and *parenthetical expressions.* Three types of agreement are often violated: of adjective and noun, of pronoun and antecedent, and of verb and noun.

antecedent A substantive to which a pronoun refers. *Examples:* Mine be a *cot* beside a hill. *To be or not to be,* that is the question. The *man* who hath no music in his soul.

apposition A relation of one substantive to another, when the second, called an *appositive,* repeats the meaning of or identifies the first. *Examples:* my sister *Cornelia;* Patsy, *a fox terrier.*

article The word *a, an,* or *the;* now usually called a *limiting adjective.*

attributive adjective *See* adjective.

attributive complement *See* complement.

auxiliary A verb used with another verb to indicate voice, mood, and tense. The auxiliaries are *be, can, do, have, may, must, shall, will,* and their conjugational forms.

case A form or position of a substantive indicating its relation to other words in the sentence. In English the cases are:

Nominative: that of the subject of a verb, of a predicate nominative (subjective complement), of a noun in apposition to another which is subject or complement, or of a substantive in certain absolute constructions.

Objective: that of the object of a verb, preposition, or verbal, and of the subject of an infinitive.

Possessive: that denoting possession.

(The classical names of cases, *genitive, dative, accusative,* are still widely used in English grammar. They are roughly equivalent to our *possessive* and *objective;* genitive for possessive, dative for objective of the indirect object, and accusative for objective of the direct object.)

The Athenians (*nominative*) defeated Darius's (*possessive*) fleet (*objective*).

He (*nominative*) gave him (*objective*) a letter (*objective*).

clause A group of words that contains a subject and a predicate and is part of a sentence. Clauses are classified as:

Main, principal, or independent. This is the sentence itself in its simple form; the clause on which the rest of the sentence depends. A *simple sentence* is nothing but a main clause. (*E.g.,* The son went into a far country.)

Subordinate or dependent. This is equivalent in office to a noun, an adjective, or an adverb, modifying a word in the main clause; *i.e.,* it is subordinate to or depends on the main clause. (The son went into a far country, where he did eat husks like swine.)

Co-ordinate. This is a clause of the same rank as another; main as that is main, subordinate as that is subordinate. (There had been a heavy rain, and John said it was too wet to go on.) Co-ordinate clauses are connected by co-ordinating conjunctions, *and, but, or.*

Adjective subordinate: The witness *who proved the guilt of the prisoner* is his best friend.

Adverb subordinate: He will be condemned *when all the evidence is in.*

Noun subordinate: *That he is guilty* is evident to both judge and jury.

cognate object An object which enforces a verb by repetition.

I dreamed *a dream.*

He sleeps *the sleep* of the just.

collective noun The name of a group or aggregate—*congress, congregation, mob.* Such a noun takes a singular verb unless the individuals of the group are to be emphasized.

The crowd shouts. (Singular verb)

The crowd run hither and thither. (Plural verb)

See also page 366 of text.

common noun *See* noun.

comparison Inflection of an adjective or an adverb to indicate degree. The degrees are called *positive, comparative,* and *superlative.* Monosyllables and some dissyllables are usually compared by adding *-r* or *-er* to form the comparative and *-st* or *-est* to form the superlative—*large, larger, largest; handsome, handsomer, handsomest; kindly, kindlier, kindliest.* The comparative and superlative are also formed by adding the adverbs *more* and *most* to the positive—*kind, more kind, most kind; dignified, more dignified, most dignified; pleasantly, more pleasantly, most pleasantly.* Descending comparison is formed by adding *less* and *least* in the same way. Some adverbs are not inflected. *See* adverb.

Some adjectives have an irregular comparison:

bad, evil, ill	worse	worst
far	farther	farthest
	further	furthest
good, well	better	best
late	later	last, latest
little	less	least
	smaller	smallest
much, many	more	most
old	elder, older	eldest, oldest

complement A substantive or an adjective that completes a predicate. A complement usually completes a verb of incomplete predication, such as *to be, to become, to appear, to look, to seem,* though it may complete a direct object or the object of an infinitive. Substantive complements of the first type are in the nominative case; those of the last two, in the objective case. All types of complement are illustrated in the following sentences:

He is in danger. *Danger* is a subjective complement (also called a predicate nominative), and is in the nominative case.

I call him a danger. *Danger* is an objective complement, in apposition with him, which it completes, and is in the objective case.

He is likely to be a danger. *Danger* is an objective complement, completing the infinitive *to be.* It is in the objective case.

He is dangerous. *Dangerous* is an attributive complement (also called a predicate adjective), modifying the subject *he.*

I call him dangerous. *Dangerous* is a predicate adjective, modifying the object *him.*

He is likely to become dangerous. *Dangerous* is a predicate adjective, completing the adjective infinitive phrase *to become dangerous.*

complex sentence A sentence consisting of a principal clause and one or more subordinate clauses. *See also* clause.

Who you are, I think I know.

When I remember that day, I shudder.

Do not forget that you are responsible.

compound preposition A preposition consisting of more than one word: *in place of, from under, with regard to, out of,* etc.

compound sentence A sentence consisting of co-ordinate clauses.

They look the same but they are different.

compound-complex sentence A sentence consisting of co-ordinate clauses, one or more of which contain subordinate clauses. Sometimes called *double* (or *multiple*) *complex.*

The children looked for birds' nests while they were going to Grandmother's, and they looked for tadpoles while they were coming back.

concrete noun *See* noun.

conditional sentence A sentence containing a clause expressing condition or limitation. Such a clause is introduced by a subordinating conjunction: *if, as if, if not, unless, except, without, whether,* etc.

conjugation Inflection of a verb to denote voice, mood, tense, person, and number. The complete conjugation or paradigm of such will include all the forms of the following: voice—active and passive; mood—imperative, indicative, infinitive, subjunctive (and interrogative forms, if significant); tense—present, present perfect, past, past perfect, future, future perfect; person—first, second, and third; and number—singular and plural. It might also include the tenses formed with *do, can, may, might, should, ought,* etc.

conjunction A connective used to join together sentences, clauses, phrases, or words. Conjunctions are classified as follows:

Co-ordinating: *and, but, or,* connecting elements of equal rank.

Correlative: *both . . . and, either . . . or, neither . . . nor,* co-ordinating conjunctions used in pairs.

Subordinating: *when, where, whither, whence, why, before, because, for, since, if, unless, though, although, than,* etc., connecting clauses of unequal rank. (Note that many of these are adverbs. They are often called *adverbial conjunctions.*)

See also conjunctive adverb.

conjunctive adverb An adverb used as a co-ordinating conjunction. It is not a true conjunction, but serves to carry the sense from one clause to another. The principal conjunctive adverbs are *however, so, then,* and *therefore;* others are *also, besides, consequently, furthermore, hence, nevertheless, otherwise, still, thus.* A conjunctive adverb is usually preceded by a semicolon and followed by a comma. I do not wish to go; besides, I am not ready.

We have little money; nevertheless, we shall try to send you some.

See also conjunction.

connective A connecting word or particle, such as a preposition, conjunction, or relative pronoun.

coordinate clause *See* clause.

copulative verb or **copula** A verb that links subject and complement. Sometimes factitive verbs (*q.v.*) are called copulative.

correlative *See* conjunction.

dangling modifier, unattached modifier, faulty reference A modifier the reference of which is not clear. It is commonly an adjective, a participle, or a participial phrase. The word "dangling" suggests that such a modifier hangs loose, unattached to any other member of the sentence.

Being about to close our books, will you kindly remit. (The phrase seems to modify *you* but really modifies an unexpressed *we.*)

dative In inflected languages, the case which expresses an indirect object. In English it is called *objective.*

declension The formation of the cases of nouns, pronouns, adjectives, by the addition of inflectional endings to the stem. In English the declension of nouns is very simple: *man, man's, man, men, men's, men;* that of the pronoun, more nearly complete: *I, my, me, we, our, us, mine, ours.*

defective verb A verb that lacks one or more of the usual parts or forms. For example, *must* has no inflection.

definite article The word *the.*

definitive adjective *See* adjective.

degree *See* comparison.

demonstrative adjective *This, that, these, those,* when used to modify a substantive—"*This* book belongs to *that* boy."

demonstrative pronoun *This, that, these, those,* and, idiomatically, *so* and *such.* Some grammarians call *he, she, it,* and *they* demonstrative. A demonstrative pronoun serves to indicate or point out the person or object referred to—"I don't believe that," "This is the package the postman brought," "Such is the difference between wishing and doing."

dependent clause The same as subordinate clause, *see* clause.

descriptive adjective *See* adjective.

direct address The use of a noun or pronoun to name the person or thing spoken to.

Fred, come here.

Roll on, thou deep and dark blue ocean. (When used rhetorically, as here, direct address becomes the figure of speech *apostrophe.*)

direct discourse or **direct quotation** The repetition without change of another's language. *Compare* indirect discourse.

"Have you finished?" she asked quietly.

direct object The substantive in a sentence that is the same of the person or thing acted upon. *See also* indirect object.

Chickadees eat *sunflower seeds.*

Right makes *might.*

Please let us know *your decision.*

distributive pronoun *See* pronoun.

double comparative and superlative Ways of forming the comparative and superlative—*more brighter, most unkindest.* It was once common in English, but is no longer correct.

double negative The use of two (or more) negative particles to express a single negation—"I don't know nothing about it." Once in good use, it is now a solecism. It appears in more subtle forms in such expressions as "I couldn't hardly do it."

double possessive The use of both an apostrophe and *of* to form the possessive case. It is an idiomatic usage.

That book of my father's is a great rarity.

ellipsis The omission of a word or words necessary to the complete grammatical construction of a sentence, but not necessary to the understanding of it. Faulty ellipsis, which is common, consists in omitting words needed for either comprehension or correctness.

The man I saw. (*Whom* elided.) Permissible.

I can and will see him. (*See him,* after *can,* elided.) Permissible.

It is my opinion he can do it. (*That* elided.) Faulty.

I am as old, if not older than you. (*As,* after *old,* elided.) Faulty.

expletive A word added, for smoothness or emphasis, to a sentence complete without it. The most familiar expletives are *it* and *there.* (In popular usage *expletive* may denote *interjection, exclamatory expression,* even *curse.*)

There are thirty days in September.

It will be best to go.

Now what shall we tell him?

factitive adjective One that denotes a quality or state produced by the action of the verb.

This medicine will make you *well*.

factitive object A substantive that both completes a predicate and describes or explains the object of the predicate. *See also* complement.

The manager appointed him *chief*.

factitive verb A verb which has both a normal object and an additional object or a complementary adjective. *Make, consider, call* are the most common of such verbs. *See* factitive adjective *and* factitive object.

We call him Penny.

I consider him guilty.

Shall we make a traitor senator?

finite verb One that with a subject can make a sentence; that is, one that does not require an object to make complete sense.

I run.

They rebel.

He philosophizes.

future tense *See* tense.

gender The form of a substantive denoting sex. The genders in English grammar are masculine, feminine, and neuter. Nouns which may be either masculine or feminine are sometimes called of common gender—*cousin, friend*. (There is no true gender in English, as there is, for example, in French and German; but only sex or sexlessness recognized in the meanings of the substantives and not by means of inflection (declension).

genitive The case usually called *possessive* in English.

gerund A nonfinite part of a verb having the form of the present participle (*i.e.*, ending in *-ing*) and used as a substantive. It is sometimes called "the infinitive in *-ing*." It may take an object and be modified by an adverb. It can be distinguished from the present participle by the fact that the former may be preceded by *the* and followed by *of*—"the making of hay."

Skating is a pleasant exercise.

We like skating.

Being a man he found to be a heavy responsibility.

She was surprised at its being I.

Being in love is not an entirely happy condition.

gerund phrase Either a phrase consisting of a gerund and its modifiers or a prepositional phrase in which a gerund is object of the preposition.

We enjoyed painting the house.

Doing the work hurriedly made me uncomfortable.

In leafing over the album, I came upon a ten-dollar bill.

After writing the essay, I went for a walk.

historical present The present tense used in speaking of past events.

While night hovers over the field of Waterloo, the Germans under Blucher are marching.

idiom A use of words peculiar to a particular language. An idiomatic phrase has a meaning as a whole that may not be suggested by its parts. For this reason one test of idiom is that it can be translated into another language not literally but only by an equivalent idiom. Examples of idiomatic phrases are: *to bring to pass, to come by, to go hard with, to put up with, to set about.* Such phrases should be distinguished from figurative expressions, in which the words have their customary meanings but are used metaphorically: *to break the ice, to stand in one's own light, to bring to light.*

imperative A mood of the verb expressing command.

incomplete predication A term used of certain verbs or forms of a verb that do not have a subject (nonfinite verbs) or that must be used with other verbs to affirm or deny (auxiliaries).

indefinite adjective *See* adjective.

indefinite article The word *a* or *an.*

indefinite pronoun *See* pronoun.

indicative *See* mood.

indirect discourse or **indirect quotation** The repetition without direct quotation of something said. It is expressed as a subordinate clause. *Compare* direct discourse.

They said that they saw it.

He reported that the troops had left for the front.

indirect object A substantive designating the person to whom or for whom an action is done.

He gave *us* a book.

We voted *James* a prize.

indirect question A question expressed as a subordinate clause.

She asked who sent it.

I asked whom he wanted.

infinite verb A participle, infinitive, or gerund.

infinitive The fundamental form of the verb, commonly preceded by *to: to go, to work, to be, to wish.* The *to* is not a preposition but is historically a kind of prefix, and is therefore called the "sign" of the infinitive. The infinitive has two tenses: present, both active and passive—*to see, to be seen;* and perfect, both active and passive—*to have seen, to have been seen.* It has also a progressive form—*to be seeing, to have been seeing.* Functionally it is a nonfinite verb or a verbal noun (verbal) and may have modifiers, may take an object or complement, and may have a logical, though not a grammatical, subject. It may be used as an adjective, adverb, or noun. Without the *to* it is used to make up compound tenses with the auxiliaries *do, may, shall, will—I shall go, he may do it.*

As a noun: *To name* him is *to praise.*

As an adverb: I come *to bury* Caesar, not *to praise* him.

As an adjective: This house is *to let.*

Compare gerund, *and see* split infinitive.

infinitive phrase A phrase introduced by an infinitive. It may be used as an adjective, an adverb, or a noun.

Do you dare to tell the truth?

To believe what you say, I should have to hear the evidence.

To hear her talk, one would think she was musical.

inflection Change in form of a word, especially in comparison, declension, or conjugation, to indicate voice, mood, tense, person, number, case, degree, etc. The part of a word that remains when inflections are removed is known as the *stem*. Since English is a synthetic language, not an inflected one, inflections play a much smaller part in its grammar than they do in Greek, Latin, or German.

intensive pronoun *Myself, thyself,* etc., when used in apposition to a noun or pronoun to increase its force: "I myself will do it." "I will do it myself." To be distinguished from the reflexive pronoun *myself, thyself,* etc.: "I burned myself."

interjection A word or words expressing sudden feeling: *O, oh, ah, pshaw, pooh, hurrah, amen.* The interjection is grammatically independent. Any part of speech may be used as an interjection—*Help! Well, well! What! The idea! Stuff! Bless me! Dear me!* Introducing words, such as *well, why,* may be parsed as interjections or expletives (*q.v.*), according to the amount of feeling they convey—"Well, look who's here!" "Well, after I had crossed the river . . ."

interrogative adjective An interrogative pronoun used to modify a substantive —Which man? Whose dog?

interrogative pronoun *Who, which, what* when used in questions: Who is that? What is it?

intransitive verb One that does not require an object, that is, one that denotes an action, state, or feeling that terminates in the doer.
The sun shines.
Father and mother walked, but Grandmother rode.
I shall lie down.
Let's sit down.
The kite rises.

irregular verb *See* verb.

limiting adjective *A, an, the.* (Also called *article.*)

locution A phrase; an idiom; an element in style; phraseology.

modifier A word, phrase, or clause that affects (changes, restricts, enlarges) the meaning of another word or group of words.

mood or **mode** A form of the verb indicating the manner of doing or being. The moods usually recognized in English grammar are the indicative, which includes interrogative and exclamatory forms, the subjunctive, and the imperative. The indicative indicates a fact; the subjunctive, a wish, condition, or concession; the imperative, a command.
Indicative: That is a starling. Is that a starling? That's a starling!
Subjunctive: If I were you, I'd wait. Far be it from me to suggest such a thing.
   Though he slay me, yet will I trust Him.
Imperative: Go! Come here! Let us start immediately.

nominative absolute A substantive modified by a participle and not grammatically connected with the sentence. (The word *absolute* is used in the old sense —of *absolve, absolution*—of *loose, untied,* because the absolute phrase does not modify.) The construction is to be used with caution.
The vote taken, the committee proceeded with other business.
The rain having washed out all traces, the clue proved useless.

nominative case *See* case.

nominative of direct address A substantive unrelated grammatically to any other word in a sentence and used as a salutation or form of address.
Boys, stop that noise.
Sir, may I speak with you?
How are you feeling, Fred?
See direct address.

nonfinite verb An infinite verb.

nonrestrictive element A word, phrase, or clause which, though it contributes to the general meaning of a sentence, does not limit or confine the meaning of the substantive it modifies. (The distinction between restrictive and nonrestrictive elements is important mainly in punctuation.)
See text pages 259, 260.

noun A word that is a name. A noun may be used as a subject, an object, a complement, an appositive, or a nominative absolute.
Nouns are classified as *common* and *proper*. A common noun is the name of one of a class or kind—*woman, deer, spade, wax;* a proper noun, the name of some particular person, place, or personified thing—*Italy, Chicago, Liberty, Mona Lisa, Mississippi, Vatican.*
Nouns are also classified as *abstract* and *concrete.* An abstract noun is the name of an idea, quality, action, or state, without regard to any person or thing. A concrete noun denotes a person or thing.
Abstract: *Ripeness* is all. *Beauty* is its own excuse for *being.*
Concrete: To hide a green *hill* in an April *shroud.* Fast-fading *violets* covered up in *leaves.*

noun clause A clause used as a substantive. Such a clause is usually introduced by a subordinate conjunction, an interrogative adjective or adverb, or a relative pronoun. It may be used as an appositive, an object, a predicate nominative, or a subject.
Subject: *When he would arrive* was a mystery.
Object: He asked me *when I should arrive.*
Object of preposition: Give the book to *whoever wants to read it.*
Complement: This map is *what you need.*
Appositive: The suggestion *that we should surrender* was greeted with jeers.

noun phrase A phrase used as a substantive.
Gerund: *Going to school* necessitated *walking five miles.*
Prepositional: *From here to there* is a long distance.
Infinitive: *To see the parade* was a problem of finding a handy tree.

number The singular or plural form of a noun, pronoun, or verb.

numeral adjective A cardinal or ordinal number used to modify a substantive—*twelve* apples, *second* base, etc.

object *Direct object:* a substantive which receives the action expressed by the verb and performed by the subject; *indirect object:* the person, animal, or thing to or for which the act is performed.
He sent me a message. (*Message* is the direct object and *me* the indirect. Note that the indirect object may be parsed as the object of a preposition—"He sent a message to me"—*to* being understood.)
See also cognate object.

parallelism The principle that parts of a sentence that are parallel in meaning should be made parallel in structure. In its simplest form it is seen in "Seeing is believing" or "To see is to believe" (not "Seeing is to believe"). Parallelism has more important rhetorical than grammatical applications.

parenthesis A word, phrase, or sentence inserted in a sentence by way of comment or explanation. The sentence is grammatically complete without it. It should always be set off by punctuation—commas, dashes, or parentheses.
I was thinking—this was yesterday evening—that Charles (he is my brother) will be forty-five tomorrow.

participial adjective A participle used to qualify a substantive—a *running* deer, a *defeated* candidate.

participial phrase A participle with its modifiers.
I saw the janitor *standing at the door.*
The vase, *broken by the fall,* disclosed the money.
Swinging his arms freely, he walked rapidly away.

participle A word that shares the properties of a verb and an adjective. It has, like a verb, tense and power to govern an object; and, like an adjective, power to qualify a substantive. The tenses of the participle are *present* and *past.* The present participle, ending in *-ing,* is used in forming the progressive conjugation. The past participle, ending in regular verbs in *-d* or *-ed,* is employed with aux·iliaries in the perfect, past perfect, and future perfect.
See also participial adjective, participial phrase, verb.

particle A term sometimes used to denote the minor parts of speech, *i.e.,* articles, conjunctions, interjections, and prepositions.

parts of speech Adjectives, adverbs, conjunctions, nouns, prepositions, pronouns, verbs. In older grammars the article was called a part of speech, but is now called a *limiting adjective.*

passive voice *See* voice.

past and **past perfect** *See* tense.

perfect *See* tense.

person Any one of the three relations in which a subject stands with respect to a verb, referring severally to the person speaking, the person spoken to, and the person spoken of. These forms are called the *first, second,* and *third* persons, singular or plural.

phrase A group of words not containing a finite verb. Phrases are classified by the type of word that introduces them as prepositional, participial, and infinitive. They are further classified by their office as adjective, adverb, and noun. *See these headings.*

positive *See* comparison.

possessive adjective A noun or pronoun in the possessive case used to modify a substantive—*my* hat, *Susan's* brother.

possessive case *See* case.

predicate The verb in a sentence, with or without its modifiers, as it relates to the subject. The verb alone is called the *simple* or *grammatical predicate;* with its modifiers and object or complement (if any), the *complete* or *logical predicate.* The term *predicate* is used correctly of the verb with relation to its office in the sentence, as affirming or denying something about the subject.
Simple predicate: I *have tried* to do it several times.

Complete predicate: I *have tried to do it several times.*

The predicate may be double or multiple.

We *shall run* and not *be* weary, *walk* and not *faint.*

We laboriously *climbed, slipped, slithered, found* precarious toe-holds and hand-holds, *saved* ourselves by clutching a bush, and at last *pulled* ourselves over the edge of the cliff.

predicate adjective *See* adjective *and* complement.

predicate noun, predicate nominative *See* complement.

predication The complete affirming or denying of something in a sentence. The center of predication in a sentence is the verb. *See* incomplete predication.

preposition A word governing a noun or pronoun or its equivalent, the preposition and the word it governs forming a *prepositional phrase.* The preposition may be simple (*e.g., at, in, from, on*), compound (*e.g., in place of, from under, with regard to, out of*), or verbal (*e.g., respecting, considering, notwithstanding*). One or two adjectives have prepositional force, *like* and *near* being the most important.

prepositional idiom A term applied to the use of prepositions (before a substantive or after a verb, adjective, or noun) natural to English. Since such use often differs from that natural to other languages, it presents great difficulty to foreigners whose English is imperfect. The use of proper prepositions following verbs, adjectives, or nouns has been made the subject of a separate section of this book.

Examples of idiomatic use of prepositions before nouns are: *in Boston, at the seaside, out of season,* the girl *with the green eyes, above stairs.*

prepositional phrase A phrase consisting of a preposition and the substantive it governs. It may be used as an adjective, an adverb, or a noun.

Over the hill is the long way to go. (Noun)

The animal *in the picture* is a panda. (Adjective)

We went *to the theater* last night. (Adverb)

present *See* tense *and* historical present.

present perfect *See* tense.

principal parts The present, past, and past participle of a verb, as *sing, sang, sung; herd, herded, herded; try, tried, tried.* The present participle—*singing, herding, trying*—is also often called a principal part.

pronominal adjective Any possessive pronoun used to modify a substantive—*his* car, the car is *his.*

pronoun A word used in place of a noun, to avoid repeating the noun. Pronouns are classified as follows:

Demonstrative: *this, that, these, those,* when used to point out, designate—*That* is a marten and *these* are weasels.

Distributive: *each, every, everyone, either, neither,* etc.

Indefinite: *any, few, many, none, one, some, such,* etc.

Intensive: *myself, himself, ourselves,* etc. "I myself will do it."

Interrogative: *who, which, what,* in questions. "Who is that?"

Personal: *I, thou, he, she, it, we, you, they,* and their declensional forms—*my, mine, me,* for example.

Reflexive: *myself, himself, ourselves,* etc., "I have burned myself."

Relative: *who, which, what, that,* when introducing a subordinate clause.

The personal pronouns are declined in case, number, and person—*I, my* or *mine, me; we, our* or *ours, us,* for example.

The indefinite pronouns are indeclinable, though some have a possessive case; *e.g., one's, everybody's.*

The relative pronoun *who* is declined—*who, whose, whom.*

proper noun The name of a particular person, place, or personified thing—John, Pittsburgh, Democracy.

reflexive pronoun See pronoun.

reflexive verb A verb whose object, expressed or implied, refers to the same person or thing as the subject—*He dressed; He dressed himself.*

relative adjective *Whose, which,* or *what,* when it combines the offices of adjective and relative pronoun. Also *whichever, whatever, whosoever.*

He did not see which way to go.

Take whichever book you please.

relative clause A clause introduced by a relative pronoun or a subordinating conjunction. In office it is an adjective, qualifying a substantive in the main clause; or an adverb, modifying the verb in the main clause; or a substantive, used as subject, object, or complement of the main clause.

That he is a good man is evident. (Subject)

The trouble is *that I do not know him.* (Complement)

They killed *whatever was alive.* (Object)

Call me *whenever you are ready.* (Adverb)

The reason *why he did it* is mysterious. (Adjective)

This is the place *where sandpipers love to come.* (Adverb)

It is a time *when great courage is needed.* (Adverb)

relative pronoun A pronoun introducing a subordinate clause. *See* pronoun.

restrictive modifier One not merely descriptive or parenthetic. The test of whether a modifier is restrictive or not is to read the sentence without it and note whether the omission destroys the exact meaning of the sentence.

I shall send it *if you write me.* (Restrictive)

The man *I saw* is said to be a spy. (Restrictive)

The man, *so open and plausible,* is said to be a spy. (Nonrestrictive)

The little girl dancing and singing is named Diana. (Restrictive if *dancing and singing* distinguishes Diana from others who are not dancing and singing; nonrestrictive, if it is merely a descriptive detail. If it is the latter, it should be set off by commas.)

See also nonrestrictive element.

sentence "A group of words so related as to convey a completed thought with the force of asserting something or of asking, commanding, exclaiming, or wishing, and marked at the close, in writing, by a period, question mark, or exclamation point."—*Webster's Collegiate Dictionary.* "A set of words complete in itself, containing subject and predicate and conveying a statement, question, or command."—*Concise Oxford Dictionary.*

Sentences are classified by type of predication as *declarative, interrogative, exclamatory,* and *imperative;* by grammatical structure as *simple, compound,* and *complex;* and by rhetorical structure as *loose, periodic,* and *balanced.*

sequence of tenses A phrase designating the idiomatic or logical order of tenses of verbs in a sentence.

singular and **plural** Names of the grammatical *number* of substantives.

split, or cleft, infinitive One in which the *to* and the infinitive proper are separated. "Its use, decried by purists, has been common among standard authors since the 17th century."—*Standard Dictionary*. In general, nevertheless, it is to be avoided, and always if the splitting leads to awkwardness.

stem *See* inflection.

strong verb One forming its preterit by vowel change—*grow, grew*—and its past participle by *-n* or *-en*—*bite, bitten; give, given.*

subject The substantive which in a sentence tells what the sentence is about; that which has a predicate. A distinction is made between the *simple subject* and the *complete subject,* the latter being the simple subject together with its modifiers. A subject may be compound or multiple. It may be a word, a phrase, or a clause. It is in the nominative case.

All *birds* but a very few can fly. Simple subject.

All birds but a very few can fly. Complete subject.

Certain birds, such as the auk, penguin, ostrich, and emu, which have lost the power of flight, are always in danger of extinction. Complete subject.

The auk, penguin, ostrich, and emu have lost the power of flight. Multiple subject.

subjunctive mood *See* mood.

subordinate clause *See* clause.

substantive A word, phrase, or clause used as a noun.

superlative *See* comparison.

syntax The section of grammar that deals with the relations of words in the sentence, their uses, agreements, and construction. More specifically, the syntax of a sentence-element is the part it plays in the sentence.

tense The time of the action expressed by a verb. There are three times: past, present, and future—I loved, I love, I shall love; and three types: simple, progressive, and perfect—I love (*simple*), I am loving (*progressive*), I have loved (*perfect*).

ACTIVE	PASSIVE
Simple present: I see	I am seen
Present progressive: I am seeing	I am being seen
Present perfect: I have seen	I have been seen
Simple past: I saw	I was seen
Progressive past: I was seeing	I was being seen
Past perfect: I had seen	I had been seen
Simple future: I shall see	I shall be seen
Progressive future: I shall be seeing	I shall be seeing
Future perfect: I shall have seen	I shall have been seen

verb A word or group of words that affirms (or denies) something about a subject. It expresses action, being, or state of being. In a sentence or a clause the verb is called the predicate when it is considered in relation to the subject.

The inflection of a verb is called its *conjugation* (*q.v.*)

Verbs are classified as follows:

Finite: those that with a subject can make a sentence and that agree with the subject in person and number: *I go, he goes, they go; Jack swims; Fish swim.*

Nonfinite or infinite: those that are employed as other parts of speech (though retaining some verbal force) and have no person or number: *to go, going.* Also called *verbal nouns, verbal adjectives,* or *verbals.*

Regular or weak: those that form their past tense and past participle in *-d, -ed,* or *-t: walk, walked, walked; bare, bared, bared; build, built, built.*

Irregular or strong: those that form their past tense by change of vowel and past participle in *-n* or *-en: be, was, been; throw, threw, thrown.* Some verbs are called irregular but not strong; those that form their past tense and past participle without change of vowel but show other irregularities: *e.g., cast, cast, cast; wet, wet* or *wetted, wet* or *wetted; have, had, had.*

Transitive: in ordinary usage, those that have a direct object. There is disagreement concerning whether a verb that may have an object but has none is transitive. Compare *She bakes. She bakes bread. The bread bakes.* (The first is potentially transitive; the second, transitive; the third, intransitive.) Many verbs are both transitive and intransitive but with a difference of meaning: *Birds fly. The boy flies a kite.*

Intransitive: those that (1) do not take an object or (2) in a given sentence do not have an object. *See* transitive. An intransitive verb may take a *cognate object, q.v.*

Copulative or linking: those that take a complement; *e.g., be*—"I am he"; *feel*—"I feel tired"; *become*—"The child will become a man"; etc.

Auxiliary: those used with other verbs to form mood and tense; *e.g., be, can, may, might*—"I was sleeping"; "He can skate"; etc. Auxiliaries may be used as *notional verbs;* that is, have a sense of their own; *e.g.,* "When Duty whispers low Thou *must,* the youth replies I *can."*

Defective: those whose conjugation is not complete, such as *shall, may, can, ought.* Defective and irregular verbs are sometimes called *anomalous.*

verbal A word derived from a verb, combining something of the meaning and use of a verb with the use of a noun or adjective. Specifically, *infinitive, gerund, participle, q.v.*

vocative The case of a noun of direct address or the noun itself.

voice The relation of a subject to its verb; that is, whether acting, acting upon or for itself, or acted upon. The voices are the active and passive; and these have two forms, the simple and the progressive.

Active: The soldiers put up a tent.

Passive: A tent was put up by the soldiers.

GLOSSARY OF PRINTING AND ALLIED TERMS

The following are commonly used terms that have been only briefly defined or mentioned in the text.[1]

accents In the printing office *accent* means the mark indicating stress: ´, heavy accent; `, light accent. In most fonts of type they differ from primes. The marks used over letters to indicate the quality of sound are named: é, acute; è, grave; ê, circumflex; ñ, tilde; ç, cedilla. These are usually cast on the letters, but are sometimes separate pieces, called *piece accents*.

agate An old name for a size of type slightly smaller than five and one-half point, measuring fourteen lines to the inch; for years the standard for measuring advertisements. Called *ruby* in England.

algorism The sign of division:)

alphabet length The number of picas occupied by the 26 letters of the alphabet in lower case. The relative condensation or expansion of linotype faces is determined by comparison of alphabet lengths.

aspects Signs used to denote certain positions of planets, such as ☌, ✳, □.

assemble To bring together. The workman in the printing office who assembles a job inserts in the galleys of text type all matter set in another size, such as extracts and footnotes, headings and side notes set by hand, initials, and the like.

backbone, backstrip The back of a book, connecting the front and back covers. Type set lengthwise of the backstrip commonly reads from the top down, but sometimes vice versa. Also called *shelfback* and *spine*.

bank A high table with a sloping top for holding pages or galleys of composed type matter.

bankman The worker at the bank. He usually measures the type as it comes to the bank from the machines, inserts in the galley the furniture needed to keep the type upright for proving, pulls the first proofs, and stores the galley of type in a rack.

batter Marred or flattened type that prints imperfectly.

bearers Strips of metal, type high, placed around pages of type when they are locked in a form from which electrotype plates are to be cast. These show as a black border on foundry proofs and proofs of molder plates.

bibliographical note British term for copyright page.

bleed Illustrations which extend to the edges of the page when printed are called bleed cuts. Printing is said to bleed when the margins are overcut in trimming and the printing mutilated.

blind-blocking, blind-tooling Impressing a design on a book cover by hot tools only, using no ink or gold leaf.

---

[1] Three good dictionaries of printers' terms are:
Technical Terms Used in Bibliographies and by the Printing Trades, by A. F. C. M. Moth (Boston: F. W. Faxon Company, 1915).
Bookman's Glossary, by John A. Holden (New York: R. R. Bowker Company, 1931).
Manual of Information, compiled by John H. Chambers.
For British usage a suitable reference is Collins's *Authors' and Printers' Dictionary* (London, Humphrey Milford, 7th ed. 1933).

blind stamp In the proofroom and the electrotype room to blind stamp is to mark proofs and plates in some way to distinguish them from other plates like or similar to them that are to be used in another book. On the foundry proof a distinguishing letter is inserted in the running head or at the bottom of the page. These letters are removed from worker plates and marked on the back; molder plates retain the letter on the face of the plate.

block quotations Excerpts in reduced type.

blocks Bases of wood or metal to which printing plates are attached to make them type high.

boards Stiff cardboards used for the sides of books, which may be covered with paper, cloth, leather, or other material. If the covering is paper only, the book is said to be "bound in boards."

bolt The uncut fold at the edge of an untrimmed book. Also called *edge-bolt*.

book card *See* card page.

book chase *See* chase.

bourgeois (bur-joice) An old name for 9-point type.

brayer A hand-roller for inking type.

breakline The last line of a paragraph.

break up (1) To separate solid matter into shorter paragraphs; (2) to dispose of pages of type that are of no further use, removing leads and foundry type, dumping machine metal to be remelted.

brevier An old name for 8-point type.

broadside (1) A large sheet of paper printed on one side only, like a poster, or printed on both sides and folded in a special way. (2) A broadside table or illustration is one printed with the top at the left side of the page, requiring a quarter turn of the book to the right to be in position for reading.

broken line A line shorter than the width of the page; a breakline.

bulk The thickness of a book, not including the cover.

butted Rules or lines of type placed end to end to form a longer line are said to be "butted."

© A copyright notice used for maps, works of art, models or designs for works of art, reproductions of a work of art, drawings or plastic works of a scientific or technical character, photographs, prints, and pictorial illustrations. It must be accompanied by the name, initials, monogram, mark, or symbol of the copyright owner.

calender A machine used to give smoothness and finish to the surface of paper. Paper so treated is commonly called "Super," or "S. & S. C.," for "sized and super calendered."

calometry Division of the text into short clauses or sense-lines, a device much used in modern display composition to facilitate easy reading. Early scribes often followed this practice in manuscripts intended for oral reading.

cancel A leaf reprinted to correct an error in a printed book, and inserted by the binder in place of the incorrect pages.

canceled figures Figures with a line across the face from lower left to upper right: 6, 11. Both monotype and linotype machines have matrices for the simple figures canceled, but if two or more figures are to be canceled with one line, a cut must be made.

caption   The heading above a chapter, article, table, etc.; much used, though inaccurately, for *legend*.

card page   An advertising page, usually a list of books by the same author, or on similar subjects, printed to face the title of a book. Often called *book card, facer,* or *face-title.*

case   (1) A tray in which type is kept (*see* type cases); (2) a cloth book cover before it is placed on the book.

cast   To electrotype or stereotype.

cast off   To estimate the number of pages a given manuscript will make.

cast proof   *See* foundry proof.

cast up   To measure the amount of type set, in order to find the cost of composition.

casting machine   The second machine required in the monotype system of typesetting. (*See also* keyboard *below*.) The perforated ribbon from the keyboard is placed in the machine, and compressed air passing through perforations directs a casting mechanism by which the metal types are manufactured.

catchline   A temporary headline on proofs; in display, short, unimportant words in small type between the main lines in larger type.

catchword   The word at the head of a page or column, as in a dictionary.

center point   A period cast higher than the base line of the face. Used to show syllabication, to indicate multiplication, to separate words set in roman capitals composed in the classic style of tablet inscriptions. Sometimes called a *space dot.*

chase   A rectangular iron or steel frame in which pages of type, slugs, or plates are locked up to be printed or cast. Pages for casting are usually locked in chases holding one to four pages; chases for letterpress printing may hold eight, sixteen, or more pages. Large chases are divided by solid strips of metal crossing in the center. The bar that divides the chase the longer way is called the *long cross;* the thick and short crossbar is called the *short cross.* A chase is sometimes called a *form.*

clean proofs   Proofs containing few errors.

cliché   An electrotype or stereotype plate.

close up   To push together, to remove spacing-out leads.

cold metal   Lead in the melting pot of a typesetting machine which has dropped below a certain temperature; types made of it are imperfect, having a pitted appearance, and must be reset.

collate   To examine the folded sheets, or signatures, of a book to see that they are in correct order.

collating marks   To make easier the accurate assembling of the signatures of a book for binding, it used to be customary to number each signature on the first page. This practice has been largely superseded by the use of collating marks. A short rule is inserted in the form in position to print midway between the first and last pages of a signature. The mark on the first signature is placed near the top, that on the second somewhat lower, the third lower still, and so on. When the signatures are assembled, the marks show in a regular series, which would be broken if a signature were missing or duplicated.

colophon   (1) A trade emblem used by a publisher on title pages of books, on his stationery, and stamped on book covers; (2) a bibliographical note at the end of a book (see p. 152).

compose To set up type for printing. Therefore a *compositor* is one who sets type, and *composition* denotes the act of setting or the matter set; a *composing room* is the room in which type is set, a *composing frame* is a stand or frame for holding the cases of type for the use of the compositor; a *composing rule* is a thin strip of brass or steel, type high, of length to correspond with the measure of the matter to be set, used in setting and handling type; and a *composing stick* is the small metal frame in which the compositor sets the type.

crop To trim off a portion of foreground, background, or sides of an illustration to secure desired proportions.

cursive Running, flowing; applied to certain faces of type similar to italic but more decorative.

cut The printers' term for a halftone engraving or a zinc etching.

cut edges All edges trimmed smooth, applied to the finish of a book.

cut-line *See* legend.

dead reprint An absolute facsimile.

delete Take out.

dies Brass or steel stamps used for impressing letters or designs on covers of books. Also called *brasses*.

digraph A combination of two letters to express a sound. *See* diphthongs.

dingbats Any small types such as ♥, used in job work to separate paragraphs or headings from following text, etc.

diphthongs Vowel digraphs, as ae, oe. The word *diphthong* is often used to designate *ae* and *oe* set as ligatures, *æ, œ*.

direct-typing offset The making of typescript books from plates prepared by inserting in the typewriter the metal sheets used in the small offset presses—rotaprint and multilith—to receive typescript directly. A special carbon paper or ribbon is required.

display type Heavy-face or large type used for headings, advertisements, etc., in contradistinction to ordinary reading or "body" type.

distribute To return types to their proper location in the cases after they have been used.

double, doublet Incorrect repetition of a word or words.

edge-bolt *See* bolt.

electrotyping A galvanic process of making a metal replica of a page of type or engravings. An impression is taken in a thin layer of softened wax. This wax matrix is coated with plumbago and then immersed in a bath of sulphate of copper in which plates of copper are suspended. By electrical action a shell of copper is deposited on the mold, which is removed when it is of proper thickness and backed up with metal to a thickness of .152 inch. If a nickel shell is made instead of copper, a "steel-faced" electro is produced.

end mark Any mark placed at the end of an article or story to indicate that it is completed—usually #, or 30 in a circle.

end papers The leaves used by a binder at the front and back of books, one of them pasted down on the inside of the covers. Also called *endleaves, lining papers, pastedowns,* or *waste papers*.

even pages The left-hand pages of a book, numbered 2, 4, 6, etc.; often called *verso pages*.

facer *See* card page.

face-title *See* card page.

figures The Arabic numerals 0, 1, 2, . . .   Type foundries supply scored figures —$\bar{1}$, $\bar{2}$, etc.—pointed figures—$\dot{1}$, $\dot{2}$, etc.—and canceled figures—$\cancel{1}$, $\cancel{2}$, etc.

flag *See* masthead.

fluent The sign of integration, $\int$.

flush With no indention.

fly leaves Blank leaves at front or back of books.

footline The bottom line of a page. Only a page number or a signature may properly be set in this line.

form Type matter, engravings, or electrotypes locked up in a chase for casting or printing.

foundry proofs Proofs taken of a form in chase immediately before casting. Sometimes called *cast proofs, guardline proofs,* or *final proofs.* Corrections marked by publisher or author on these proofs require correction of plates.

furniture Blocks or strips of wood or metal made in multiples of picas, used to blank out large areas of white space, but especially to hold type in position in a form for printing or casting.

galley A long and narrow metal pan, about half an inch deep and open at one end, in which lines of type are placed when they are first set, whether by hand or by machine. The first proof of composed type is, hence, a "galley" proof.

Greek ratio The law of proportion that "a line or measure is pleasingly divided when one part is more than a half and less than two-thirds the length of the other."

guard *See* bearers.

gutter The inner, or binding, margin of a page.

headband A reinforcing band used at the head and tail of a book in binding.

headpiece A small ornament or illustration at the head of a page or chapter.

high quads In monotype composition spacing types only slightly lower than the type face, called *high quads,* or *high spaces,* are used if plates are to be made. If printing is to be from type, shorter spaces, called *low quads,* are used because they are much less likely to work up and print.

imposition Arranging pages of type in a form in proper order for printing. The work is done on an *imposing stone,* a large, smooth slab of stone or marble, or a steel table. Printers who do this kind of work are called *stonemen.*

Because of the various sizes and shapes of paper, the different kinds of presses and of folding machines, many different arrangements of pages are in use. The workman must have exact instructions about margins, trim, the kind of stitching, and the folding machine to be used; and he must also know whether the form is to go through the press as a sheetwise, work-and-turn, or work-and-twist form.

In the *sheetwise* method, the two sides of the sheet of paper are printed with different forms. Sometimes called the *work-and-back* method.

For the *work-and-turn* method the pages for both sides of a sheet are imposed in one form. When one side has been printed and the ink is dry, the sheets are turned over end for end and printed on the other side. The sheets are then cut in two; each half is exactly like the other half. This method is sometimes termed the *flop-sheet* or *half-sheet* method.

The *work-and-tumble* method is like the work-and-turn except that after one side is printed the sheets are turned from side to side instead of end to end.

The *work-and-twist* or *work-and-whirl* method is used when two different pages of type or plates are required for one page, one to print over the other; for instance, a page with many rules, for which two printing pages are prepared, one with the rules and one with accompanying reading matter. After the sheets have been printed once from a form containing the two pages, they are "twisted" or "whirled" end for end and printed the second time. When the sheets are cut in half, the sections are alike.

imprint   The name and address of a publisher, printed on the lower part of the title page of a book; the name and address of the printer of a book, usually placed at the bottom of the copyright page.

inferior letters or figures.   Letters or figures smaller than the body type, so cast on the type body that they print below the alignment of normal letters. Often called *subscripts*.

insert   To put in.

insert   Illustrations, maps, or other material printed on different quality paper from the text and inserted in proper position before binding.

inset   A sheet or folded section of printed pages set within another in binding.

job work   Miscellaneous printing—all except newspaper, magazine, or book work.

juggled slugs   Misplaced lines. Specifically, corrected lines of linotype inserted in the galley or page in the wrong position.

justify   To make a line of composed type equal in length to all accompanying lines by inserting spaces between words; to make different sizes of type used in one line all of the same height by inserting leads or spaces above or below the smaller types.

keep standing   To hold composed type after printing or casting.

keyboard   The perforating machine which is the first of two machines required in the monotype system of typesetting. As the operator strikes one of the 276 keys which constitute the keyboard, a perforation is made in a paper ribbon about 4 inches wide. This ribbon unwinds from one spool on to another as the keys are struck. *See also* casting machine.

kill   To delete copy or printed matter; to indicate that composed type is not to be used.

leaders   Periods or dashes used to lead the eye across what would otherwise be open space. Open leaders run one dot to an em and close leaders one dot to an en; dash leaders run two to an em.

leader work   Simple tabulation, without rules.

legend   The title or short description printed below an illustration; frequently called a *caption*, occasionally a *cut-line*.

letterpress   Printing from type rather than plates.

lightface   Any type face with lines sufficiently fine to give a light effect when printed.

line gauge A printer's measuring rule, marked off in nonpareils and picas, sometimes showing other type measurements also.

lining papers *See* end papers.

lining series *See* standard line.

literals Alphabetic characters. In proofreading, to "read for literals" is to read for wrongfonts, defective letters, transpositions, spelling, and the like.

live matter Composed type, plates, or cuts which have yet to be printed or which are being kept for future use.

lock up To fasten pages of type in a chase so that they can be printed from or plated.

logotype Two or more letters cast on a single body. Distinguished from a ligature, in which the letters are joined to form a single character, as fi, ff, and diphthongs æ, œ.

long primer (primer) An old name for 10-point type.

low quads *See* high quads.

low to line A type that ranges lower than the rest of a line is called "low to line."

low to paper Types, slugs, or engravings that are lower than the rest of the form are "low to paper."

Ludlow Typograph A line-casting machine, used particularly for advertising display lines, large-type headlines, and similar matter. Brass matrices are set by hand in a special stick. The assembled mats are then placed over a slot in a steel table and molten metal forced up from beneath.

magazine On a linotype machine the case in which the brass matrices of letters are stored. By fingering the keyboard, a linotype operator sets lines of matrices from which the machine casts solid lines of type, afterward returning each matrix to its proper channel in the magazine.

majuscule A capital letter.

makeready The process of preparing a locked-up form for printing. A proof is taken of the form on the press. This is examined for evenness of impression. Light areas are outlined with lead pencil and patches of paper pasted on—called spotting up. The patched sheet is placed under the type—an underlay—or on the tympan—an overlay. Another proof is taken and examined, and the process repeated until an even impression of the whole form is obtained.

make up To arrange composed type in pages, inserting folios, running heads, cuts, etc.

masthead A statement of name, terms, ownership, platform, policies, and the like. In newspapers it is usually at the head of the editorial page. In magazines it is usually at the foot of the editorial page or table of contents. Sometimes called the *flag*.

matrix (*pl.* matrices) The mold from which the face of a type is cast. Often called a *mat*.

matrix case A metal frame used in a monotype casting machine; it contains the molds for the letters that are to be cast, of which there can be 225.

measure Of a page, the length of a full line.

M. F. Machine finish.

minion An old name for 7-point type.

minuscule A lower-case letter.

M's or **M paper**   Paper not up to the standard quality.

nonpareil (non-pa-rel)   An old name for 6-point type; still occasionally used to designate a 6-point slug.

odd pages   The right-hand, or recto, pages of a book, 1, 3, 5, etc.
oddments   The parts of a book separate from the body, such as title, contents.
off its feet   Type is off its feet when it does not stand square upon its base.
offcut   A portion of the printed sheet cut off and folded separately.
optical center   About one-eighth above the actual center of a page.   A line which is to appear to be in the center of a page must be in this position.
overlay   *See* makeready.

pastedowns   *See* end papers.
patent insides   The name for that part of country papers printed at a central office, usually the inside pages of the folded sheet.
peculiars   Infrequently used characters of a font of type.
pi   Type which has become disarranged or mixed up and must be sorted before it can be used.
pick for sorts   To take from standing matter types wanted for a job in hand, replacing them with types inserted feet up.
pick-up   Composed type matter which has been kept standing since its first use for printing or plating and which is being "picked up" for further use.
pigeonholes   *See* river.
plate   An electrotype or stereotype.
printing press   A machine in which plates or types are placed, inked, and brought into contact with paper which is to receive the impression.   There are three distinct methods of imparting the impression, exemplified by the platen press, the cylinder press, and the rotary press.   In a platen press the paper is pressed with a smooth, flat surface on to the face of the printing form.

In a flat-bed-and-cylinder-style press the flat bed containing the printing form moves backward and forward under a revolving cylinder.   The paper is printed as it passes between the cylinder and the type.

In a rotary press curved stereotypes or electrotypes are fastened to a cylinder.   The paper passes between this cylinder and another which presses it against the plates.

The rotary offset press has three cylinders.   The plate is fastened to one cylinder, the ink impression is offset on to a hard rubber blanket attached to a second cylinder, and again offset to a paper sheet on a third cylinder.   One great advantage of this press is the fact that the paper itself never touches the metal plate and there is less liability when printing halftones of the plates filling up.

A "perfecting press" prints both sides of a sheet before it leaves the press.

A "web press" prints a roll of paper instead of flat sheets.

A "web perfecting press" prints both sides of a roll of paper, cuts the fold, and delivers in folded signatures.

A "multicolor press" prints several colors before the paper leaves the press.   Also called a "chromatic press."
process printing   Printing in three or four colors.

recto pages Right-hand pages.

river A streak of white space in printed matter caused by the spaces between words in several lines happening to fall one almost below another. Also called *river of white, pigeonhole, staircase.*

S. & S. C. *See* calender.

saddle stitched Stitched through the back, the thread, silk, or wire showing on the back and in the middle fold.

scratch comma The diagonal stroke which was formerly used for a comma. It is still used in proofreading to separate corrections when several occur in one line. In this use called a *separatrix.*

series *See* type family.

sheetwise *See* imposition.

shelfback *See* backbone.

spine *See* backbone.

shell *See* electrotyping.

shoulder notes Words or numbers noting sections or chapters, year or topic or the like, placed at the upper outer corner of each page of a book. They are seldom used nowadays, because the same purpose can be achieved more easily and less expensively by placing the words or numbers in the running heading.

side sorts Letters not frequently used.

signature The pages of a book printed on one sheet of paper, usually sixteen pages. Also the letter or number set in the lower left corner of the first page of every signature to guide in collating. *See* collating marks.

sinkage White space left at the top of a page, as at the beginning of a new chapter. Sinkage throughout a book should be uniform.

small pica An old name for 11-point type.

sorts All the types in the boxes of a case. If few types remain in the boxes, the case is "low on sorts." When all the types in a box have been used, the box is "out of sorts."

spaceband The wedge-shaped device on a line-casting machine which automatically justifies a line of matrices.

space dot *See* center point.

staircase *See* river.

standard line Most American and English type founders now cut all types according to a standard line so that different faces on the same size body can be used together with an even alignment at the bottom. Before this standardization letters of different fonts varied in position on the type body and when two fonts were used together, they were rarely in exact alignment—one would be nearer the top or the bottom than the other. There are two standard lines, one for body type and the other for display type. All types cut on the display line are designated as *lining series* and they cannot be combined in the same line with types cast on the standard line for body type.

stereotype A metal printing plate cast from a paper matrix made from a page of type.

stet Let it stand.

stick *See* compose.

stone *See* imposition.

stonehand or **stoneman** *See* imposition.

stone proof A proof of type imposed in a form ready for letterpress printing. The proof is taken by inking the type with a roller, laying a sheet of damp paper over it, and forcing the paper onto the type with a planer and mallet.

sunk *See* sinkage.

super A strip of strong, thin cloth pasted over the back of the sections of a book and extending about an inch beyond the back at each side.

swash letters Ornamental italic letters much used for headings and initials.

sweat on To attach original halftones to electrotype plates.

tailpiece A small ornament or illustration at the end of a chapter.

take The amount of copy to be set that is taken by a compositor at one time.

teletypesetter A machine which sets telegraphic news on either Linotype or Intertype machines as it comes off the wire.

thirty or **30** A term used in newspaper offices, signifying "the end."

tip in To paste a leaf, or leaves, into printed sheets or bound books.

turned letters A type placed feet up in composed matter to show that no type of the right letter is available. It shows in the proof as two black marks.

type cases Shallow wooden trays divided into compartments of various sizes. There are about thirty styles of type cases, some holding a complete font, others only part of a font. The oldest, and the one most used before typesetting machines came into common use, requires two cases for each font. When in use they are placed on sloping racks, one beyond the other and more steeply slanting. In the lower case are all the small letters, figures, punctuation marks, and spaces and quads. In the upper are the capitals and small capitals and a few extra characters. It was from their position in the type cases that capitals acquired the name "upper-case letters," and small letters came to be called "lower case." Matter in capitals is said to be "up," and in small letters it is "down."

type family All the series of one general type design. Cheltenham, the largest type family, has twenty-three different series, each varying in some way from all others.

12 Point Cheltenham Extended No. 164—12 Set

12 Point Cheltenham Bold No. 86—12 Set

12 Point Cheltenham Bold Italic No. 86K—12 Set

12 Point Cheltenham Condensed No. 64—10½ Set

12 Point Cheltenham Bold Condensed No. 88—10½ Set

type high In the United States, .918 inch high.

underlay *See* makeready.

verso pages Left-hand pages.

waste papers *See* end papers.

widow A short line ending a paragraph at the top of a page; considered poor bookmaking.

work-and-turn *See* imposition.

wrong font A type of a face different from accompanying letters.

BOOK PUBLISHERS

The following list has been compiled as an aid in the writing and editing of bibliographies, reference or reading lists, bibliographical footnotes and the like, which require the names of publishers, together with their home office. For the correct form of the names of other publishers the best source is the *Publishers' Trade List Annual* (title page of each publisher's entry).

Current addresses of publishers may be found in the following volumes: *Publishers' Trade List Annual; Books in Print; Cumulative Book Index; Literary Market Place; Textbooks in Print; The Writers' and Artists' Yearbook* and *Cassell's Directory of Publishing* (chiefly British and Irish); *Whitaker's Cumulative Book List* (British); and *Publishers' International Year Book*.

Full Name	Home Office
Abelard-Schuman Limited	New York
Abingdon Press	Nashville, Tenn.
Academic Press, Inc.	New York
Addison-Wesley Publishing Company, Inc.	Reading, Mass.
Aldine Publishing Company	Chicago
Allyn and Bacon, Inc.	Boston
American Book Company	New York
American Elsevier Publishing Company, Inc.	New York
American Heritage Publishing Company, Inc.	New York
American Library Association	Chicago
Appleton-Century-Crofts	New York
Arco Publishing Company, Inc.	New York
Association Press	New York
Atheneum Publishers	New York
Baillière, Tindall & Cox, Ltd.	London
Walter H. Baker Company	Boston
Ballantine Books, Inc.	New York
Bantam Books, Inc.	New York
Arthur Barker, Ltd.	London
Barnes & Noble, Inc.	New York

Full Name	Home Office
G. Bell and Sons, Ltd.	London
Ernest Benn, Ltd.	London
William Blackwood & Sons, Ltd.	Edinburgh
The Bobbs-Merrill Company, Inc.	Indianapolis, Ind.
The Bodley Head, Ltd.	London
R. R. Bowker Company	New York
The Brookings Institution	Washington, D. C.
The Bruce Publishing Company	Milwaukee, Wisc.
Burns & Oates, Ltd.	London
Butterworth & Co. (Publishers), Ltd.	London
Cambridge University Press	New York
Jonathan Cape, Ltd.	London
Cassell and Company, Ltd.	London
Chandler Publishing Company	San Francisco
Chapman & Hall, Ltd.	London
Chatto & Windus Ltd.	London
Children's Press, Inc.	Chicago
William Collins Sons & Co., Ltd.	London
Columbia University Press	New York
Constable and Company, Ltd.	London
Coward-McCann, Inc.	New York
The Crowell-Collier Publishing Company	New York
Peter Davies, Ltd.	London
The John Day Company, Inc.	New York
Dell Books	New York
T. S. Denison & Co., Inc.	Minneapolis, Minn.
J. M. Dent & Sons, Ltd.	London
The Dial Press, Inc.	New York
Dodd, Mead & Company	New York
Doubleday & Company, Inc.	Garden City, N. Y.
Gerald Duckworth & Co., Ltd.	London
E. P. Dutton & Co., Inc.	New York
Elsevier, see American Elsevier	
Eyre & Spottiswoode, Ltd.	London
Faber and Faber, Ltd.	London
Farrar, Straus & Company	New York
Samuel French, Inc.	New York
Funk & Wagnalls Company, Inc.	New York
Ginn and Company	Boston
Victor Gollancz, Ltd.	London
Grolier Incorporated	New York
Grosset & Dunlap, Inc., Publishers	New York
Harcourt, Brace & World, Inc.	New York
Harper & Row, Publishers	New York
George G. Harrap & Company, Ltd.	London
Harvard University Press	Cambridge, Mass.

Full Name	Home Office
D. C. Heath and Company	Boston
William Heinemann, Ltd.	London
Her Majesty's Stationery Office	London
Hodder & Stoughton, Ltd.	London
Holt, Rinehart and Winston, Inc.	New York
Houghton Mifflin Company	Boston
Bruce Humphries, Publishers	Boston
Hurst & Blackett, Ltd.	London
Hutchinson & Co. (Publishers) Ltd.	London
Richard D. Irwin, Inc.	Homewood, Ill.
Jarrolds, Publishers, Ltd.	London
Herbert Jenkins, Ltd.	London
Orange Judd Publishing Co., Inc.	New York
P. J. Kenedy & Sons	New York
Alfred A. Knopf, Inc.	New York
John Lane, see The Bodley Head, Ltd.	London
T. Werner Laurie, Ltd.	London
Lea & Febiger	Philadelphia, Pa.
J. B. Lippincott Company	Philadelphia, Pa.
Little, Brown and Company	Boston
Liveright Publishing Corporation	New York
John Long, Ltd.	London
Longmans, Green and Co., Ltd.	London
Lothrop, Lee & Shepard Company, Inc.	New York
Sampson Low, Marston & Co., Ltd.	London
Lyons & Carnahan	Chicago
McGraw-Hill, Inc.	New York
The Macmillan Company	New York
Macmillan and Co., Ltd.	London
Macrae Smith Company	Philadelphia, Pa.
Meredith Publishing Company	Des Moines, Iowa
G. and C. Merriam Company	Springfield, Mass.
Charles E. Merrill Books, Inc.	Columbus, Ohio
Methuen & Co., Ltd.	London
Mills & Boon, Ltd.	London
The Modern Library, Inc.	New York
William Morrow and Company, Inc.	New York
John Murray (Publishers), Ltd.	London
Thomas Nelson & Sons	New York
George Newnes, Ltd.	London
Ivor Nicholson & Watson, Ltd.	Redhill, Surrey
Noble and Noble, Publishers, Inc.	New York
W. W. Norton & Company, Inc.	New York
The Odyssey Press, Inc.	New York
The Open Court Publishing Company	La Salle, Ill.

Full Name	*Home Office*
Oxford University Press, Inc.	New York
Stanley Paul & Co., Ltd.	London
Penguin Books, Inc.	Baltimore, Md.
Pergamon Press, Inc.	New York
Pitman Publishing Corporation	New York
Sir Isaac Pitman & Sons, Ltd.	London
Prentice-Hall, Inc.	Englewood Cliffs, N. J.
Princeton University Press	Princeton, N. J.
Putnam & Company, Ltd.	London
G. P. Putnam's Sons	New York
Rand McNally & Company	Chicago
Random House, Inc.	New York
Henry Regnery Company	Chicago
Reinhold Publishing Corporation	New York
Fleming H. Revell Company	Westwood, N. J.
Reynal & Company, Inc.	New York
Rinehart, *see* Holt, Rinehart and Winston	
The Ronald Press Company	New York
Routledge and Kegan Paul, Ltd.	London
Row, *see* Harper & Row	
St. Martin's Press, Inc.	New York
Howard W. Sams & Co., Inc.	Indianapolis, Ind.
W. B. Saunders Company	Philadelphia, Pa.
Scott, Foresman and Company	Chicago
Charles Scribner's Sons	New York
Silver Burdett Company	Morristown, N. J.
Simon and Schuster, Inc.	New York
Skeffington & Sons, Ltd.	London
Peter Smith, Publisher	Gloucester, Mass.
Sterling Publishing Co., Inc.	New York
Sweet & Maxwell, Ltd.	London
Charles C Thomas, Publisher	Springfield, Ill.
Time Inc. Book Division	New York
Tudor Publishing Company	New York
The University of Chicago Press	Chicago
University of Pennsylvania Press	Philadelphia, Pa.
The Vanguard Press, Inc.	New York
D. Van Nostrand Company, Inc.	Princeton, N. J.
The Viking Press, Inc.	New York
Ward, Lock & Co., Ltd.	London
Frederick Warne & Co., Ltd.	London
Western Publishing Co., Inc.	Racine, Wisc.
W. A. Wilde Company	Natick, Mass.

Full Name	*Home Office*
John Wiley & Sons, Inc.	New York
The Williams & Wilkins Company	Baltimore, Md.
The H. W. Wilson Company	New York
Winston, *see* Holt, Rinehart and Winston	
The World Publishing Company	Cleveland, Ohio
Wright & Brown, Ltd.	London
Yale University Press	New Haven, Conn.
Zondervan Publishing House	Grand Rapids, Mich.

FOREIGN WORDS AND PHRASES

We are constantly adopting words from other languages. The terminologies of art, literature, dress, cookery, diplomacy, law, medicine, politics, military science, sport, and so on, abound in words of foreign origin, appropriated as the standard words for the objects or ideas. These are ordinarily set roman. Many words and expressions are adopted because they are circumlocution savers; and these are italicized until usage accepts them as practically English. There are in addition many foreign phrases that are often used in an English text without any real excuse since there is an equally short English equivalent that would be more readily understood. Use of them is often affected and pretentious. Generally, these expressions are italicized.

It should be borne in mind that the number of words set roman is constantly increasing; that phrases are less quickly adopted than single words; that newspapers and magazines italicize less than books; that the setting in which a word is used often determines whether it should be italicized. The following list, therefore, can be only suggestive. The roman forms have been sanctioned by good usage.

abbé	ad interim	alfresco
ab extra	ad libitum	alias
ab origine	*ad nauseam*	alma mater
accouchement	ad valorem	alter ego
accoucheur	*affaire d'amour*	*âme damné*
a cappella	*affaire d'honneur*	amende honorable
acharnement	*à fond*	*à merveille*
à deux	a fortiori	amour
ad hoc	aiguille	*amour-propre*
à huis clos	*aîné*	*ancien régime*
adieu	à la carte	*Anglice*
ad infinitum	à la mode	anno Domini

Anschluss	beau ideal	café
ante bellum	beau monde	caïque
à outrance	*beaux-arts*	caisson
aparejo	*beaux-esprits*	*calembour*
apache	*béguinage*	camaraderie
aperçu	belles-lettres	camouflage
apéritif	*berceuse*	*campo santo*
à peu pres	bête noire	canaille
aplomb	*bêtise*	canapé
à point	bezique	canard
a posteriori	bibelot	cancan
appliqué	*bien entendu*	cangue
appui	*bienséance*	caoutchouc
a priori	bijou	capapie
apropos	billet-doux	capias
aqua	*bise*	caporal
aqua fortis	*blague*	capote
aqua regia	blasé	carcajou
aqua vitae	bloc	*carpe diem*
arête	Boche	carte blanche
argot	bona fide	*carte de visite*
armes blanches	*bona fides*	cartouche
arrière-pensée	bonhomie	casern
arrondissement	*bonjour*	*casus belli*
arroyo	bon mot	catafalque
artiste	*bonne*	causerie
assignat	bon soir	caveat
atelier	bon ton	caviar
attaché	*bon vivant*	certiorari
auberge	bon voyage	cestui que trust
au contraire	bouillabaisse	chaise longue
au courant	bourgeois	chalet
au fait	*bouleversement*	chamade
au grand sérieux	bourdon	chanson
au gratin	bourgeoisie	*chanson de geste*
au jus	boutonniere	chaparajos
au naturel	bourse	chapeau
au revoir	brassard	*chapeau-bras*
aurora australis	bric-a-brac	chaperon
aurora borealis	bricole	charabanc
baccarat	briquette	chargé d'affaires
baignoire	brochure	charivari
ballon(s) d'essai	burnoose	charlotte russe
barège	cabaret	chasse
baroque	cachalot	chassé
bas bleu	cachet	chasseur
bashi-bazouk	cachou	chassis
bateau	cadre	château

chatoyant
chaussure
chauvinist
chef-d'oeuvre
cheval-de-frise
chevelure
chez moi
chiaroscuro
chic
chignon
chose
ci-devant
cinquecento
claque
cliché
clientele
cloisonné
coiffure
col
colporteur
comedienne
comme il faut
communiqué
con amore
concierge
conciergerie
concordat
confrere
congé
connoisseur
conservatoire
consommé
contra
contretemps
convenance
cordon bleu
corrigendum
cortege
corvée
cosaque
costumier
coup de grâce
coup de main
coup d'état
coup d'œil
coupé
couvert
crèche

crepe de Chine
crépon
critique
cui bono
cuisine
cul-de-sac
daimio
danseuse
debacle
debris
debut
debutante
déclassé
décolleté
dedans
de facto
dégagé
déjeuner
de jure
delineavit
delirium tremens
de luxe
démarche
demitasse
démodé
denouement
de nouveau
de novo
Deo volente
de profundis
de quoi vivre
de règle
dernier
detente
de trop
deus ex machina
devoirs
diablerie
dilettante
dinero
dishabille
distingué
distrait
divorcee
doctrinaire
dolce far niente
dossier
double-entendre

doublure
doyen
dramatis personae
eau de cologne
eau de vie
écarté
ecce homo
echelon
éclair
éclat
ecru
edition de luxe
élan
elite
elenchus
embarras de choix
embarras de richesse
embonpoint
émeute
émigré
en arrière
en bloc
enceinte
en famille
enfant terrible
en masse
ennui
en passant
en rapport
en route
ensemble
entente
entente cordiale
entourage
entr'acte
entree
entrepôt
entrepreneur
entresol
entretien
eo nomine
épée
epergne
ergo
erratum
ersatz
esprit
esprit de corps

estaminet
et cetera
ex cathedra
exequatur
exempli gratia
ex libris
ex officio
ex parte
exposé
ex post facto
extempore
façade
faïence
facile princeps
fainéant
fait accompli
farceur
fauteuil
faux pas
felo-de-se
feme
feme covert
feme sole
femme de chambre
fete
feuilleton
fiancé
finale
fin de siècle
finis
flèche
flânerie
flâneur
fleur-de-lis
force majeure
fortissimo
foudroyant
foyer
fracas
frappé
frater
gauche
gaucherie
gendarme
genre
gentil
ghat
grand monde

gratis
gringo
grisaille
guilloche
guipure
gymkhana
Gymnasium
habeas corpus
habile
habitué
hachure
hacienda
hara-kiri
hauteur
haut monde
hegira
hors de combat
hors d'oeuvres
idée fixe
ignis fatuus
impasse
imprimatur
imprimis
infra dig
ingenue
innuendo
in propria persona
in re
in situ
insouciance
intelligentsia
in toto
in transitu
intrigant
ipse dixit
ipso facto
jalousie
jardiniere
je ne sais quoi
jeu d'esprit
jongleur
jujitsu
julienne
jupe
kepi
kraal
kudos
kulak

kumiss
Kulturkampf
Kyrie eleison
lacuna
laissez faire
lamé
lansquenet
lapis lazuli
lapsus calami
lapsus linguae
lares and penates
lazzarone
lei
leitmotiv
lese majesty
lettre de cachet
liaison
lingua franca
liqueur
literatim
littérateur
locum tenens
loggia
macabre
maestro
magnum
magnum opus
malaise
malapropos
mal de mer
malgré
mañana
mandamus
manège
mardi gras
matador
materia medica
matériel
matinee
mélange
melee
memorabilia
memoriter
ménage
mésalliance
métier
métis
meum and tuum

milieu
minestrone
mise en scène
mitrailleuse
modus agendi
modus operandi
modus vivendi
mondain
morale
mores
more suo
motif
mot juste
moyen âge
muezzin
multum in parvo
mutatis mutandis
naïve
naïveté
nee
negligee
nemine contradicente
ne plus ultra
névé
nil
nisi
nisi prius
noblesse
noblesse oblige
nolle prosequi
nolens volens
nolo contendere
nol-pros
nom de guerre
nom de plume
non compos mentis
nonego
non est
non-sequitur
nous
nouveau riche
nouveauté
nuance
nunc dimittis
obiter dictum
objets d'art
olla-podrida
omnium-gatherum

onus
opéra bouffe
opéra comique
opus
ordonnance
outré
padre
paletot
panache
papier-mâché
par excellence
pari mutuel
pari passu
parterre
parvenu
pas de tout
passé
pas seul
passim
pâté
paterfamilias
paternoster
patisserie
patois
peignoir
pelerine
penchant
pension
per annum
per capita
per cent
per centum
per contra
per diem
per se
persona grata
pièce de résistance
pied-à-terre
pince nez
pis aller
placebo
plafond
planchette
pleiu-air
point d'appui
point-device
porte-cochere
porte-monnaie

portiere
poseur
poste restante
postmeridian
post meridiem
post-mortem
post-obit
pourboire
pourparler
pousse-café
pratique
précis
première
prie-dieu
prima donna
prima facie
procès-verbal
prochein
pro forma
pro rata
protégé
pro tem
pro tempore
provenance
provocateurs
puisne
purdah
purée
qua
quasi
quenelle
quidnunc
quid pro quo
qui vive
quondam
quo warranto
raconteur
ragout
raison d'être
rapport
en rapport
rapprochement
rara avis
re
Realpolitik
réchauffé
recherché
regime

rencontre
rendezvous
repertoire
repoussé
résumé
retroussé
reveille
revenant
rigor mortis
riposte
risotto
risqué
rissole
ritardando
role
rotisserie
roué
roulade
rouleau
rumba
safari
sahib
salle à manger
salle d'attente
salmi
salon
samurai
sanctum sanctorum
sangfroid
sans-culotte
sans doute
sauté
sauve-qui-peut
savant

savoir-faire
savoir-vivre
séance
sec
seriatim
semé
sine
sine die
sine qua non
soi-disant
soiree
sotto voce
soubrette
soupçon
status quo
stemma
subpoena duces tecum
sub rosa
suede
sui generis
sui juris
summum bonum
svelte
table d'hôte
tabula rasa
tant mieux
tapis
terra firma
terra incognita
tertium quid
tête-à-tête
thé dansant
toilette
tour de force

tout court
tout ensemble
tuyère
ultimo
ultra vires
vade mecum
vale
variorum
verbatim
vers libre
versus
via
vice versa
vide ante
vide infra
vide post
vide supra
videlicet
virtu
visa
vis-à-vis
viva!
vivandière
viva voce
volte-face
vox populi
voyageur
vraisemblance
wanderlust
Weltanschauung
Zeitgeist
zenana
Zollverein

INDEX